OCEAN LINERS

A. M. CASSANDRE 1928
FOR REAL COMFORT
NEW STATENDAM
SPRING 1929

OCEAN LINERS

ROBERT WALL

NEW
BURLINGTON
BOOKS

A QUARTO BOOK

This edition published by
New Burlington Books,
London W1.

© Copyright 1977 Quarto Limited

ISBN 0 906286 20 4

This book was designed and produced by
Quarto Publishing Limited,
London W1.
Design and Picture Research: Roger Daniels.
Special ship profiles: Stephen Small.

Phototypeset in England by
Filmtype Services Limited, Scarborough.

Printed in Hong Kong by
Lee Fung Asco Printers Ltd

for Gabrielle

I wish to extend my especial thanks to
my wife Jean, without whose
encouragement and support this book
would not have been written.

The lines by Rudyard Kipling on page 92 from The Secret of the Machines *are quoted by kind permission of
the National Trust and the Macmillan Company of London and Basingstoke, and Doubleday and Company, New York.*

Frontispiece: a poster of 1929 by Cassandre advertising Holland America's new Statendam III.
Endpapers: the Lusitania *at Liverpool.*

Contents

THE LAST VOYAGES

*The funeral pyre of
the* Queen Elizabeth,
now renamed
Seawise University,
*in Hong Kong
harbor on
9 January 1972.*

THE GREAT SHIP sparkled as winter sunlight caught the white painted sides of her hull and danced off the waves that edged across the harbor from the Chinese shore. She looked magnificent, but a closer inspection would reveal the rust stains and seabird droppings that three years of neglect and disuse had brought to her superstructure. Her name stood out in bold black letters – *Seawise University* – an awkward pun on the initials of her Chinese millionaire owner, C. Y. Tung, and unsuited to her graceful, flowing lines.

In any case, her builders had welded her original name to her sides in metre-high letters of steel and these stood out clearly from under the white paint of her hull – *Queen Elizabeth*. For this ship was the giant Cunard passenger liner that had sailed the north Atlantic in a quarter-century of peace and war. One of man's largest mechanical creations, she now lay some 7,000 miles from her home waters in the harbor of the British Crown Colony of Hong Kong, while hundreds of Chinese workers labored to convert her for an imaginative but unlikely role – a seaborne, self-contained, floating university.

At 83,673 gross registered tons, the *Queen Elizabeth* was the largest vessel ever to come out of a shipyard, until her size was exceeded by a handful of supertankers in the late 1960s.

The Cunard Line's naval architects conceived her design as the logical successor and partner to the slightly smaller *Queen Mary*. The two ships were planned to dominate the passenger trade between Europe and the United States, providing a weekly service between Southampton and New York, something unheard of in the thirties.

Both ships were over 1,000 feet long and capable of more than 30 knots. Only the *Normandie*, pride of the French Line, ever rivalled them in size (she was measured at 83,423 tons and 1,029 feet, 250 tons less than the *Queen Elizabeth* and a few feet shorter!).

The Second World War interrupted

*The three greatest
liners ever built
brought together by
the fortunes of war:
the* Normandie, *the*
Queen Mary *and
the* Queen Elizabeth
*together at their
New York piers at
the outbreak of the
Second World War.*

plans for the maiden voyage of the *Queen Elizabeth* in 1940 and the ship spent five years as a trooper before her first peace-time crossing of the Atlantic in October 1946. Then she and the *Queen Mary* came into their own.

To an exhausted Europe, struggling to rebuild its economy from the ruins of six years of war, the *Queens* provided another taste of that luxury and elegance which had vanished on 3 September 1939. North Atlantic aviation was still in its infancy, and the two ships sailed with packed passenger lists on voyage after voyage: diplomats travelling out to the new United Nations headquarters (Molotov and Churchill were regular passengers), film stars travelling on promotion tours in Europe, monarchs and ex-monarchs, all rubbed shoulders with the businessmen and emigrants who made up the bulk of the passengers.

The *Normandie* was no longer there to provide a rival service and the big German and Italian liners had all been lost in the war. The great French liner had burnt out in an accidental fire in New York in February 1942, capsizing under the weight of water pumped aboard by the city's fire brigade.

So the *Queens* had the north Atlantic to themselves, if only for a while. In 1952, the United States Government sponsored a new American venture into big ships. The result was the spectacular *United States*, arguably the fastest ship ever built. Only two-thirds the size of the *Queens*, she was a good 7 knots faster (her true speed still remains a military secret) and she smashed the *Queen Mary's* fourteen-year-old record for the crossing. The *United States* initially creamed off some of the American passengers, but her interiors were somewhat 'super-cinema' in taste, and many soon drifted back to Cunard. Later still, the French Line at last produced a worthy successor to the *Normandie*, the elegant *France*, which went into service in February 1962, to maintain French traditions.

A fast ship (she achieved 35·2 knots on trial), the *France* embodied all the French

taste for an elegant, civilized life. But she had appeared too late. By the mid-fifties, substantial inroads had been made in the North Atlantic passenger figures by the rapidly expanding airlines, particularly the American airfleets. By 1958, 59 per cent of all passengers crossing the Atlantic travelled by air, and these figures were achieved using piston-engined aircraft. It was in October of that same year that the first American jet took off on the scheduled New York – Paris run and added new dimension to travel.

From that moment, it took the big jets just ten years to banish the super-liners from the world's oceans. By the end of the 1960s, only four people in every hundred who travelled the Atlantic went by sea. Yet it took several years for the hard reality to be recognized. In 1959, Cunard was still planning a replacement for the ageing *Queen Mary*, which was to be a conventional up-dating of the old ships. Tentatively known as *Q3*, the new ship got £18 millions of Government support before wiser counsels prevailed and the plans were abandoned. The reason for this was the experience of using the *Queens* for cruising in the winter season when North Atlantic seaborne passengers virtually disappeared. The big ships proved spectacular failures in the specialized cruising business, even when the Cunard Line spent over £1 million on a new lido for the *Queen Elizabeth* in 1965.

The cancellation of *Q3* led to the decision to build a smaller ship which could double on cruising haunts and the North Atlantic. The result was the popular *QE2* which entered service in 1969.

By the winter of 1965, the *Queens* were losing £8,000 each per day on the North Atlantic and not much less when cruising. Such economic nonsense could not continue forever and on 8 May 1967, Cunard announced the withdrawal of both the *Queens*. The news produced hardly a ripple in the world's press. Gone were those days when the superliners were never far from the headlines of newspapers in six or seven world capitals. Their size and speed had made them symbols of pride in an age when patriotism was a proven instrument of government policy. The passenger lists with their famous and infamous names, the rich man's suite, the poor man's 24-berth dormitory: all this fascinated the masses, most of whom would never even see a liner, let alone travel on one. The triumphant *Mauretania*, the tragic *Titanic*, the loved and majestic *Queen Mary*, all had 'fans' who sometimes totalled whole nations.

Now they were going – man's largest machines, destroyed by even more advanced products of his genius. The world hardly noticed the demise of liners, except for those middle-aged people who had nostalgic memories of their luxury in peace, or the sheer hell of their troop dormitories on war service.

But the old ships, unlike old lags, did not go quietly. Three of them, at least, had exits every bit as amazing as anything they had done in service.

One of the first large modern liners

to be taken out of service after the Second World War was the old French favorite *Ile de France*. In 1958 she was thirty-two years old and the French Line sold her to a firm of Japanese ship-breakers in Osaka. The *Ile* was popular with the French public, and when news leaked out that the Japanese had hired her out to a Hollywood producer, great indignation was expressed in the French press. The film company planned to blow up parts of the ship in order to make an epic that was 'for real', and to many Frenchmen they might just as well have proposed the demolition of the Eiffel Tower! The arguments raged for weeks and even the newly recalled President Charles de Gaulle joined the row. The Japanese, anxious to make amends (and no doubt worried about the possible loss of their double profit!), held a Shinto service on board 'to propitiate the spirit of the ship'!

All to no avail, the French protests eventually died away. The film was made, and was released as *The Last Voyage*, starring Robert Stack and George Sanders. Even a notable performance by Sanders as the liner's hesitant captain could not overshadow the film's main attraction. This was the *Ile de France* herself, and long after the scrapping of the old ship, the film still gets a regular re-screening on the television networks on both sides of the Atlantic.

The *Queen Mary* made her 1,000th and last Atlantic crossing in September 1967. Just before the final trip, Cunard had announced her sale to the City Council of Long Beach, California. The civic heads of Long Beach planned to use the ship as a hotel, conference centre and maritime museum and they paid Cunard £1,232,000 for the vessel. She was delivered to her new owners in December 1967 and a long rebuild followed. All three funnels came down, to be replaced with light alloy replicas, and an engine room was stripped to make room for the museum. When the ship reopened, she did steady business with thousands of visitors. Today the *Queen Mary* lives on

The eventual resting place for the Queen Mary detracted less from the dignity of the famous liner than had been the case with the final fate of some of her sister ships and competitors. Here she is seen anchored at Long Beach, where she is now used as a hotel, conference center and maritime museum.

QUEEN MARY TOUR

"81,000 tons of fun."

The final voyage of the France ended in a dramatic but fruitless strike by the crew in an effort to force the government to retain the liner in service.

at Long Beach, a permanent reminder of the days when she represented to the British people their recovery from the depression years and when the words 'Queen Mary' were a synonym for anything of gigantic size and strength.

The *United States* and the *France* sailed on in partnership, but the *Queen Elizabeth* was withdrawn in 1968. An attempt was made to repeat the Long Beach experience by preserving the Cunard flier as a hotel and museum at Fort Lauderdale in Florida. But the American businessmen who bought her did not have the substantial resources which Long Beach City Council draws from its oil revenues and the venture was not a success.

In September 1970, after two years as a lifeless hulk, the ship came under the hammer and was sold for $3,200,000, to Mr C. Y. Tung, the Hong Kong shipowner.

By this time, the end had also come for the *United States*. She had always received a United States Government subsidy, without which her owners could not afford to keep her at sea. President Nixon's economy axe fell in October 1969 and the world's fastest ship, of which its designer boasted 'the only wood on board is in the butcher's block and the piano', was laid up in mothballs in Virginia's Hampton Roads.

C. Y. Tung, having renamed the *Queen Elizabeth* as *Seawise University*, ordered her removal to Hong Kong, half a world away from Florida. Her last skipper, Commodore Geoffrey Marr, came out of retirement to act as adviser to the Chinese crew, who had the daunting task of coaxing the old and deteriorating Cunarder south round the Horn and across the wide Pacific to the Asian coast. The ship was plagued with boiler trouble during the voyage and at one time all of its 83,000 tons was adrift out of control in the Caribbean. Heroic efforts by the crew eventually got the giant under the helm again and she finally made it to Hong Kong by way of the Cape of Good Hope. There she was stripped of many of her fittings and work on conversion proceeded.

In this condition, with 200 people working on board, *Seawise University* lay at anchor in the unfamiliar scenery of Hong Kong harbor on 9 January

The France *was the last pure Atlantic liner to be built, entering service in 1962. Very much a prestige project for the French government, the* France *was in constant need of state subsidies, and when these were withdrawn in 1974, it was finally decided to take her out of service.*

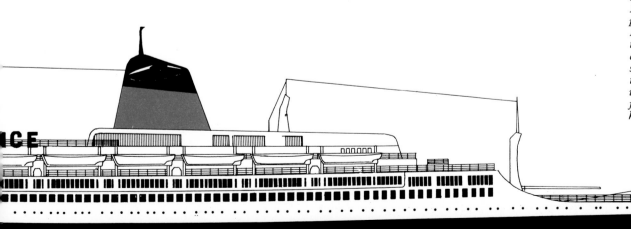

The Home Lines' Oceanic, the largest purpose-built cruise ship ever commissioned. The superstructure of the liner is notable for the large glass-covered lido amidships.

The events of 9 January 1972 have all the drama of a nautical *Götterdämerung*.

High drama was to intervene again. Just two years after the fire on the *Queen Elizabeth*, the French Government withdrew the operating subsidy they provided for the *France*. Her owners, the nationalized Compagnie Générale Transatlantique (known the world over as 'the French Line') therefore announced a programme of final cruises. After these, the *France* would be laid up indefinitely, although she was a modern ship with only twelve years service.

The *France* had replaced the *Ile de France* and the *Liberté* on the New York run from Le Havre via Southampton in 1962. The construction of the new ship coincided with that period of French history when French governments were seeking projects to boost flagging national prestige. The ship attracted a large government subsidy and President de Gaulle took a personal interest in the liner's progress. The *France* was built on the same slipway at Saint Nazaire that was used to build the *Normandie* and the President was at his wife's side on 11 May 1960 when Madame de Gaulle named the ship at her launching ceremony.

The accommodation provided for the 407 first-class and 1,637 tourist passengers was said by Atlantic veterans to be the best ever, and French cuisine did the rest. For the early years of her career, the *France* operated at 80 per cent of passenger capacity, which was an excellent result for the early sixties. Her huge red and black 'winged' funnels became a familiar sight on the Hudson and in Southampton Water, where she gained an early reputation for reliable machinery and good timekeeping. The *France* never made large profits for her owners, but under the benevolent guidance of de Gaulle, the French Treasury did not question too closely the economics of prestige projects.

When de Gaulle retired, President Pompidou continued the subsidy and it was only after his death in office in 1974, that his successor withdrew the finance

1972. Then, on this quiet winter's day, somewhere in her passenger accommodation, fire broke out and spread very quickly.

Hong Kong is one of the world's most overcrowded ports and fire a familiar hazard to the port authorities. They were able to direct over one hundred experienced harbor fire fighters to challenge the blaze. Service personnel from SEATO forces based at the port also joined in, but all efforts to save the ship failed completely.

The dilemma facing the ship firefighters was the old one of buoyancy. The more water is pumped aboard, the greater the danger of the ship capsizing. So it proved with the *Queen Elizabeth*. Her wide corridors and alleys fed the fire with all the forced draught of a thousand chimneys. The dense smoke of her pyre rose over Hong Kong and pictures of it

put the ship right back on the front pages of the world's newspapers. The fire raged through the upper decks almost unchecked until at last, after burning for twenty-four hours, the ship keeled over and the soothing waters of the harbor ended her agony.

Cunard's greatest ship had reached the end of the line. Designed as a Queen, named by a Queen, she had carried the famous and the wealthy in a style that was the apotheosis of elegant living, at a time when such style, although applauded by many, was also an affront to millions who would never be free of hunger. Now, at the end of her career, when the last reveller had long deserted her plush lounges to join the international jet set, she rested a crippled, burnt-out wreck in the mud of Hong Kong harbor. More than any other, this incident symbolized the passing of the superliner.

The last liner flying the flag of a famous line on the north Atlantic run: the graceful QE2 against the Manhattan backdrop.

that spelt life for France's last giant liner to sail the Atlantic.

The French Line planned the final cruises for the *France* to take place in the autumn of 1974, and, following the success of the *Queens'* final trips, which were sold out weeks ahead, ticket prices were substantially increased. But the owners never did get their profits on these overpriced rides into nostalgia.

It takes the efforts of a large crew to operate a superliner and the *France* carried 1,044 men and women to run the ship and attend the passengers. Unlike their British colleagues, many of whom transferred to the QE2 when the old *Queens* went, the French crew faced unemployment when their ship ended her

final voyage. In addition, many of them stoutly maintained that the *France* could still make profits, and they were determined to prove their point. On the evening of 11 September 1974, as the *France* approached the entrance to Le Havre at the end of an Atlantic crossing, the leadership of the French seamen's union ordered the crew to take over the ship. Crewmen immediately obeyed and the *France* came under the control of a strike committee headed by a dining room chef! The strikers (both sides avoided calling them mutineers) refused to let the ship enter port and the *France* dropped anchor square in the middle of the main entrance channel to Le Havre, where she disrupted traffic in and out of

harbor. After some delay, the crew allowed her stranded passengers to be taken off by one of the cross-Channel ferries that use Le Havre. Following protracted negotiations with the French Government, during which time the *France* was moved to the Bay of the Seine, the crew finally allowed her to enter Le Havre after several weeks at anchor. Once there, the strikers dispersed, their attempt to keep the ship in service eventually frustrated by stark economic reality. Indirectly, the airplane had triumphed again on the North Atlantic.

In the meantime, while world attention was focused on the climactic demise of the *France* and the *Queens*, all the big shipping companies gradually abandoned

passenger ships. The *QE2* was the last big liner to be built and today only passenger/car ferries and medium-size, purpose-built cruise ships are ordered by the companies. The Dutch Holland America Line sent their veteran *Nieuw Amsterdam* (36,287 tons) to a Taiwan shipbreaker in February 1974. The Americans had already sold the *America* to the Greek Chandris Line in 1965, four years before the *United States* was retired. Only the Italians carried on a while longer. The Italia Line had run a modern fleet on the Atlantic for all the post-war years and as late as 1966 had produced two splendid 46,000-ton sisters, the *Michelangelo* and the *Raffaello*. The entire Italia passenger fleet was phased out over three years from 1972 and the *Michelangelo* made her final voyage in June 1975. Only on the long runs from Europe to the Far East and Australia do a handful of liners survive, but all these depend in the seventies on cruising for a substantial part of their income. Typical of these are P. & O.'s *Canberra* and *Oriana*, and the Greek *Australis*, which began as the United States Lines' *America*.

The *QE2* still has a short season of scheduled runs on the north Atlantic each summer and so maintains the Cunard tradition. Paradoxically, in recent years she has been joined by smart, well-run liners from the Soviet Union with such exotic names as *Taras Schevchenko* and *Ivan Franco*. These operate with large subsidies as part of the Soviet strategy to become the world's major maritime power.

So passed the superliners. They were created – and destroyed – by the technology of twentieth-century man. Just as Parsons' invention of the steam turbine in the late 1890s realized at last Brunel's dream of vast passenger ships, so the application of these same turbine principles to aviation ensured the economic destruction of those ships before the 20th century was three-quarters over.

But in the years that intervened, when the liners were the largest transport machines on the planet, they caught the imagination of millions and made technological and social history.

CHAPTER ONE

PADDLE STEAMER TO SUPERLINER

A century of ship architecture

The Washington *of 1864, the first ship to be commissioned by the Compagnie Générale Trans-atlantique, the French Line.*

THE HISTORY OF OCEAN LINERS began with Brunel, the great British innovator and engineer. To claim that Brunel invented the steam engine, the screw propeller and the use of metal for ship construction would be untrue. But he did take all three techniques and used them in the design of a prototype ocean liner which first took to the water in 1843 as the *Great Britain*. The idea of mechanical propulsion for ships is almost as old as man himself. The paddle, and later the oar, were in use before the sail, and the Egyptians, Greeks and Romans all used mass manpower on banks of oars to take their wooden warships into battle. The Romans even used oxen-driven paddles on some of their galleys.

In the 15th century, Leonardo da Vinci produced many design sketches of paddle-driven ships. By the early 18th century, several experimental thinkers in Europe, particularly Papin (1647–1714) and Newcombe (1663–1729) had produced practical ideas for engines. Jouffroy in France (1783) and Fitch in America (1787) both operated small steamboats; in the late years of that century a number of engineers on both sides of the Atlantic had used steam engines in boats to drive paddle wheels with various degrees of success.

By 1807, techniques were far enough advanced for the American Robert Fulton to operate his *North River* steamboat on the Hudson between New York and Albany. Fulton used British engines supplied by Boulton and Watt, the company founded to exploit James Watt's practical steam engine of 1782, which used double-acting pistons for the first time.

Henry Bell, a Scots proprietor of steam baths, has the honor of having introduced steam navigation to Europe. His *Comet* started commercial sailings on the Clyde in 1812, and by the end of the second decade of the 19th century small steam vessels were operating on most of the estuaries of Europe and North America. The first steam crossing of the English Channel was in March 1816, and

soon men began to consider an Atlantic crossing. Before that event, however, the first German steamship, the *Prinzessin Charlotte*, commenced services on the Elbe on 6 November 1816. She too had a large single-cylinder engine by Boulton and Watt. The first European country to wholly build and engine a steamship was Sweden, although the engineer concerned was an expatriate Englishman, Samuel Owen. Italian engineers used the 247-ton, three-masted *Ferdinando Primo* on the run between Naples and Genoa in 1818, the first steamer in the Mediterranean. The first steam-powered ship to cross the Atlantic did so almost by accident, and was an early example of the New World exporting technology to the Old – a habit which has persisted.

In 1818, the Savannah Steamship Company of Savannah, South Carolina, decided to build a small ship for coastal trading along the east coast of the United States. Named *Savannah*, she was rigged as a ship and her small 90 i.h.p., single-cylinder engine, only intended as an auxiliary, was added as an afterthought. This was due to a visit made to her New York builders, Crocker and Fichett, by the colorful American pioneer steamboat captain, Moses Rogers. Rogers saw the possibilities of fitting an engine in the ship and persuaded her owners to do so.

*The first ship big
enough to carry
sufficient fuel for the
Atlantic crossing was
the* Royal William,
*which belonged to the
Quebec and Halifax
Steam Navigation
Company, whose
shareholders included
a certain Samuel
Cunard.
The* Comet *(inset)
heralded steam
navigation in Europe;
she started com-
mercial sailings on the
Clyde in 1812.*

This engine worked on a pressure of 2 p.s.i. and drove a pair of unprotected paddle wheels, 16 feet in diameter. The paddle wheels and cranked funnel gave the *Savannah* an odd appearance, and when completed, the paddles, which could be folded, drove the *Savannah* along at about four knots.

Due to bad trading conditions, *Savannah* proved too large for her owners' business and they decided to sell her in Europe! After a trial trip down from New York, she left her home port under Captain Rogers' command on 24 May 1819 at 1700 hours, outward bound for Liverpool. There were no passengers, although she could carry thirty-two, and the voyage had been well advertised in the Savannah papers, thus:

> 'For Liverpool, the steamship *Savannah*, Captain Rogers, will without fail, proceed direct tomorrow, 20 instant. Passengers, if any, can well be accommodated. Apply on board.'

But none did and *Savannah*, after an inspection by no less a dignitary than President Monroe, sailed empty of passengers and cargo. Twenty-seven days and eleven hours later, she turned up in Liverpool, the first ship to use steam power on an Atlantic crossing. But in all those four weeks at sea, *Savannah* had used her engines for only eighty-five hours. It had been an eventful voyage. Rogers soon discovered that paddles and sail were not a happy combination. Under sail, the ship keeled over and one paddle went too low in the water, while the other beat on nothing more tangible than air. Meanwhile the ship described an elegant circle. He therefore used sail whenever possible.

As the *Savannah* approached the Irish coast, a lookout on Cape Clear, observing the smoke from her boiler, reported the ship on fire and the Royal Navy despatched a sloop, H.M.S. *Kite*, to the rescue. The *Kite* discovered the *Savannah* rolling along at six knots and she had to fire a warning shot to halt the Americans. But Liverpool was reached at last and the *Savannah* had won her place in history.

Where *Savannah* had led the way,

GREAT BRITAIN
Bristol's prodigal ship

The first true ocean liner, the *Great Britain* was also the first large ship to be screw-driven, an idea which Brunel (below) took from Francis Smith's *Archimedes* (below center). Other novel features were her watertight bulkheads, double bottom and balanced rudder. She was launched at Bristol by Prince Albert on 19 July 1843.

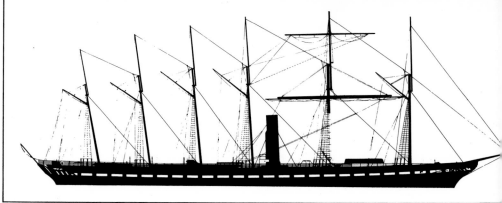

The return of the Great Britain to Bristol in 1970: divers prepare the hulk for her voyage. Below: the first great liner makes her final voyage to return to her original building dock.

Opposite page: workmen give the Great Britain a new propeller. Left: the Great Britain progresses up the Avon; the Clifton suspension bridge can be seen in the background. Above: the great bell of the Great Britain, used as a sheep bell by the Falkland Islanders, then returned to its original setting.

others soon followed. The *Rising Star*, built as a steam frigate for Chilean rebels, went out to Valparaiso in 1822, the first steamer in the Pacific. By 1825 a steamship, the *Enterprise*, had arrived in India by way of Cape Horn. In 1827, the Dutch *Curaçao* crossed to the Caribbean.

All these ships relied on sail more than steam for propulsion, but as naval architects and marine engineers gained experience, so hulls became more seaworthy and engines more reliable. The time had come for a ship to cross the Atlantic under sustained steam power, and unaided by sail. One of the problems was building a ship large enough to carry all the fuel required for the journey, and it is a curious fact that, once again, the pioneer ship came from the Western Hemisphere. She was the 800-ton *Royal William*, built at Three Rivers near Quebec in Canada. The *Royal William* was the property of the Quebec and Halifax Steam Navigation Company and among the major shareholders was a man from Halifax, Nova Scotia: Samuel Cunard.

Born in Halifax in 1787, Cunard al-

ready controlled a fleet of Canadian coasters, and he was chairman of the Quebec and Halifax company. Again, the object of the Atlantic voyage seems to have been to dispose of an uneconomic asset in Europe. The *Royal William*, all of 160 feet long and with a 200 i.h.p. Boulton and Watt designed engine, set off from Quebec 'direct for London' on 4 August 1833. She called at Picton, Nova Scotia, for coal and left on 17 August with eight passengers. She turned up in Cowes on the Isle of Wight twenty-one days later and made it to the Thames by 9 September.

The *Royal William* had steamed most of the way, apart from a four-hour period each day to clean salt from her boilers. Her performance was important in that it convinced Cunard that steam navigation of the Atlantic was practical, and he commenced planning a regular mail and passenger service between Britain, Canada and the United States.

Across the Atlantic, in London, another innovator had realized the potential of steam navigation. Isambard Kingdom

Brunel was born at Portsmouth, England, in 1806, the son of a prominent English engineer, Sir Marc Brunel. Young Brunel showed a precocious skill in mathematics as a child and at seventeen entered his father's office as an assistant engineer, working on the first Thames tunnel. Brunel had emerged as an engineer of importance by 1831 when his design for a bridge across the River Avon at Bristol was accepted; in 1833, at the age of twenty-seven, he was appointed engineer to the Great Western Railway Company. At that time, the company was planning its London to Bristol line and at a board meeting in October 1835, Brunel is alleged to have urged that the line 'be continued to New York' by transferring the passengers to an ocean steamship at the port of Bristol.

Brunel's ideas did not impress some of the Great Western directors who thought that Bristol was far enough, indeed too far, for the new line. But Thomas Guppy backed Brunel and in June 1836, the Great Western Steamship Company was formed. Brunel went to a local builder,

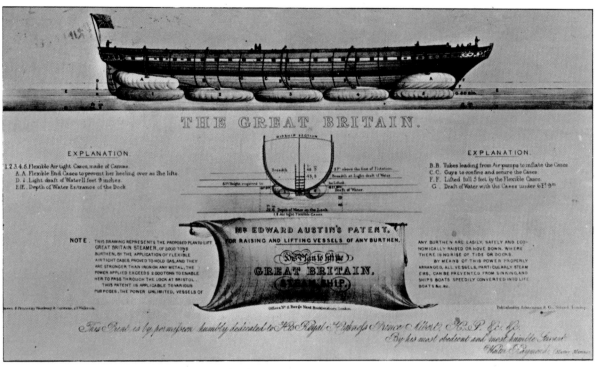

The Great Britain *aground in 1846 at Dundrum Bay in Ireland. Plan of a proposal to refloat the giant liner.*

William Patterson, who laid the keel of the new ship at his Bristol yard. Patterson designed the hull to Brunel's specifications and the specially strengthened wooden hull was ready for launching on 19 July 1837, when 50,000 people gathered to see her enter the water.

Safely afloat, the *Great Western* was sent round to the Thames to receive her engines. These were built by Maudsley Sons & Field to Brunel's design and under his personal supervision. As the *Great Western* approached completion, Brunel would soon test his theory that, while the usable space of a ship's hull increases as the cube of her dimensions, the resistance of the hull in the water only increases as the square of these dimensions. In other words, the larger the ship, the more economic she became. As it happened, Brunel was correct and on his simple discovery rests all the future development of giant liners.

But while the *Great Western* was being fitted out, a rival appeared on the scene. The British and American Steam Navigation Company had laid down the *British Queen,* but due to delays in the construction of her engines, she would not be complete for the autumn of 1837, when the *Great Western*'s maiden voyage to New York was due. Behind the venture was Junius Smith, an American lawyer turned businessman, whose lifetime ambition was a steamship line across the Atlantic, preferably American-operated. When it was obvious that their ship, which was equal in power and size to Brunel's, would not be ready in time, Smith and her partners chartered a small Irish coastal steamer, the *Sirius,* to take on the *Great Western.*

In the event, *Sirius* set out from Cork in Ireland on 5 April 1838, three days ahead of the *Great Western*'s departure from Bristol. The delay to the Bristol ship had been caused by a fire in her boiler room on the first day of her delivery voyage from the Thames to the Severn. With Brunel and his father on board, the big paddler was well down river when the lagging around the boiler ignited and filled the engine space with dangerous fumes. Brunel, going to in-

vestigate, fell headlong down a ladder, and lay unconscious in shallow water on the boiler room floor. Rescue was at hand in the form of another Great Western director, Captain Claxton, who dragged the stunned Brunel to the fresh air of the deck above, and thereby saved his life.

The accident cost the *Great Western* only forty-eight hours delay, so rapidly was the ship repaired, but it allowed the *Sirius* to leave ahead of her.

The voyage out to New York ended in triumph for Brunel's ship. The passage took fourteen and a half days and she steamed into New York only four hours behind the *Sirius.* The Great Western Steamship Company immediately announced a regular service and the *Great Western* put in several summer seasons on the route, sailing alone. At £31.10s. for a cabin and food, the fares were considered high, but there was no shortage of passengers. People were, as ever, prepared to pay for speed. The *Great Western*'s average eastbound crossing was 13·9 days while the crack sail skippers could not better 22·1 days. Cunard,

27

THE "QUEEN MARY" COMPARED WITH THE FIRST CUNARDER

The citizens of Boston regarded Cunard's first ship, the Britannia, as being so essential to the life of the town that they paid for a seven-mile channel to be cut through the ice in the winter of 1843–44, when she became stuck in the harbor. One of the most reliable of nineteenth-century Atlantic ships, the Britannia would have been completely dwarfed by the Queen Mary.

THE CUNARD ROYAL MAIL STEAMSHIP "BRITANNIA" (JOHN HEWITT, COMMANDER)
As she appeared leaving her Dock at East Boston February 3ᵈ 1844 bound from BOSTON TO LIVERPOOL. The original Print bore this inscription "Dedicated by the Publishers to the MERCHANTS OF BOSTON who projected and paid for a canal cut in the Ice 7 miles long 100 feet wide, much credit was due to the Committee and to the Contractors Messrs. Gage, Hittinger & Co and John Hill for their perseverance in accomplishing so arduous an undertaking.

Presented by the Cunard Steamship Company 99 State Street, Boston

meanwhile, still persisted in his efforts to found a transatlantic company, despite rejection of his ideas by the big financial houses in the City of London. Then in 1838, the British Government offered a lucrative contract to carry mails to North America. Cunard saw this as his opportunity, which it was. Turning his back on London, he formed a consortium with the engineer Robert Napier and two Scottish businessmen, George Burns and David McIver.

Cunard proposed to run a fortnightly service all the year round with three ships (later increased to four), each vessel identical in size and speed, and roughly equal to the *Great Western*.

It was now that the Bristol company made a historic decision which was technically brilliant, but proved an economic disaster. To win the mail contract from Cunard, they needed three ships equal to the *Great Western* to provide the required two-week service. Brunel's genius for innovation led them to build a single ship only. Twice the size of the *Great Western*, the new ship, named *Mammoth*, was to be built of iron, driven by paddles, and to sail only in summer.

Cunard's offer appeared the more acceptable to the British Government and he got the contract. To meet its terms he hired a small steamer, the *Unicorn*, to make his first mail run in May 1840 while the first of the new ships was being built. This was the famous *Britannia*, built at Port Glasgow by Robert Duncan and Company to Napier's

designs. Napier's own company supplied the engines.

The Cunard service was inaugurated on 4 July 1840, the sixty-fourth anniversary of the Declaration of American Independence. Under Captain Woodruff, with Sam Cunard on board, the *Britannia* crossed to Boston via Halifax in fifteen days and ten hours, and in doing so founded the great Cunard line. Joined by her sisters, *Acadia*, *Caledonia* and *Columbia*, *Britannia* was an instant success and Cunard's fortune was assured.

Meanwhile at Bristol, work continued on the *Mammoth*. So big was the ship that she was considered too heavy for a normal launch and a special dry dock was dug in which to build her. Patterson again built the hull and the Great

A saloon passenger list for the White Star Line of the 1870s.

GREAT EASTERN
Brunel's white elephant

After refusing to leave her slipway for three months, the mammoth *Great Eastern* finally advanced her massive bulk into the water in January 1858. At 18,915 tons, she remained the largest ship ever built for forty-one years. She never attracted sufficient trade, however, to sustain the huge costs required for her building and running, and the technical and economic problems of the launching hastened on an illness which was to kill Brunel only days after the ship sailed on her trials.

The Great Eastern
*laid up on the mud at
Birkenhead in 1888,
awaiting scrapping.
It took over three
years to dismantle
her.*

Below : the Great
Eastern *came into her
own as a cable ship;
between 1867 and
1874 she laid five
transatlantic cables
and one between
Suez and Bombay.*

Western Company set up its own foundry to build the engines to Brunel's design. Then, in May 1840, into Bristol steamed the small steamer *Archimedes* driven by a screw propeller to the design of one Francis Smith, a gentleman farmer of Hendon, London.

The principle of the Archimedean screw had already been applied to maritime propulsion by a number of engineers. Ressel, an Austrian, produced designs in 1812 and Ericsson, the Swede who later became an American citizen, patented a design in 1836. Ericsson's designs made no impression on a sceptical British Admiralty, who would be wedded to sail for a further half-century, but he

impressed an American, Robert Stockton, so much that he (Stockton) ordered a small iron-built screw-driven steamer to Ericsson's design. This contract led to Ericsson's domicile in the United States and his eventual design of the first ironclad warship to go into battle – the Civil War veteran *Monitor*.

Smith's *Archimedes* showed off her paces to Brunel, and the engineer was so impressed that the design of the *Mammoth* was promptly altered to include screw propulsion, although her paddle boxes were only half-built! Floated out of her dry dock on 19 July 1843, and now renamed *Great Britain*, she was the first large iron ship and the

first ocean-going vessel to be screw-driven. Other original features were her watertight bulkheads, double bottom and balanced rudder. Although she bankrupted her original owners, the *Great Britain* was the first true ocean liner. After her, ships could only get bigger, and the sole changes in the ship design, apart from the steam turbine, were refinements such as the use of steel for iron, and the abandoning of auxiliary sails. Ships are still designed today to principles first laid down by Brunel over 130 years ago.

By a remarkable quirk of destiny, the *Great Britain* survives to this day. Stripped of her second set of engines in 1882,

The Inman Line
City of Rome
(1881); Inman
ships were considered
outstandingly
beautiful examples of
ship architecture.

she traded under sail until 1886, when she was hulked in the Falkland Isles, and remained there until 1970 when a committee under Richard Goold-Adams organized her return to Bristol, where she rests in her original building dock as a preserved relic.

But it was Cunard who prospered and made money. Winter and summer, his red-funnelled ships ran in all weather with splendid reliability. So essential to Boston's prosperity did its citizens consider the service, that when *Britannia* was frozen in the harbor in the winter of 1843/44, the local merchants paid for a seven-mile channel to be cut to let her out. New ships, all larger in size, were added as the years went by. The *Arabia* of 1852 was the last wooden Cunarder, and the splendid sisters *Persia* (1856) and *Scotia* (1862), while being the first iron

ships in the fleet, were the last paddlers. From the late 1840s, the story of the liners is one of the race between the nations to put the largest and fastest ships onto the north Atlantic. Other seas would carry steamships, but nowhere was there the glamor and excitement to match the New York run from Europe.

In 1847 a company was founded in Hamburg to establish a line of sailing ships on the run from that port to New York. It took the title Hamburg American Packetship Co. The founder was Adolph Godeffroy and his company was to become world famous. Godeffroy bought his first steamship, the *Borussia* (2,349 tons), in 1856 and three other steamers were soon added. The sinking of the fourth steamer *Austria* by fire at sea in 1858 with the loss of 470 lives was a serious blow to the young company, but

it survived. In 1883, Hamburg-Amerika bought the Curr Line, also of Hamburg, and with it came a young man of destiny, Albert Ballin.

The Hamburg company's great rival, the North German Lloyd was founded at Bremen in 1857, two years after the French Compagnie Générale Transatlantique had been founded at Le Havre, although it did not commence running steamers until 1861.

From 1850 onwards, the steamship lines of Europe built ships which steadily grew in size and speed, as their owners gained experience of steamer operations and ever increasing profits met the cost of larger ships.

The sole exception was Brunel. Where ordinary men were content to allow development by experience and market forces, Brunel's vision led him forward

Our entire society rests upon—and is dependent upon—our water, our land, our forests, and our minerals. How we use these resources influences our health, security, economy and well being.

John F. Kennedy
February 23, 1961

CONTENTS

PREFACE

"There is a mine for silver
and a place where gold is refined.
Iron is taken from the earth,
and copper is smelted from ore.
Man puts an end to the darkness;
he searches the farthest recesses
for ore in the blackest darkness.
Far from where people dwell he cuts shafts
in places forgotten by the foot of man;
far from men he dangles and sways.
The earth, from which food comes,
is transformed below as by fire;
Sapphires come from its rocks,
and its dust contains nuggets of gold . . .
Man's hand assaults the flinty rock
and lays bare the roots of the mountains.
He tunnels through the rock;
his eyes see all its treasures.
He searches the sources of the rivers
and brings hidden things to light.
But where can wisdom be found?"

(Job 28:1–6, 9–12 RSV)

We live in a time of rapid changes in world population and technological innovation. The population is greater now than it has ever been and is increasing faster than at any time in world history. Technological changes are occurring at unprecedented rates and are projected to increase in the years ahead. These forces, combined with the desires of hundreds of millions of people in developing countries to raise their standards of living, are resulting in increasing demands for food, minerals, construction materials, and energy. At the same time, there is the increased recognition of human influence on the global environment and increased concerns about the long-term consequences of resource exploitation on nature and the ultimate habitability of the world.

Resources of the Earth: Origin, Use, and Environmental Impact has been written to present an objective view of the nature of Earth's resources, how and where they are generated, how they are extracted and used, and how these activities impact Earth's environment. These are complicated

issues that are made even more complex by the irregular distribution of resources and by political, social, and economic factors. This text has been prepared for use in first-year college courses that deal with the geology of resources, resources in general, and with human impacts on the environment. It is written in a manner to provide the geological background to understand the origin and occurrences of resources and thus does not require any prerequisite courses. In order to help students better understand the breadth and complexity of resource issues, this new edition incorporates numerous changes, including the following: (1) a new chapter on "The Origins of Mineral Resources;" (2) updated information on energy and other resource use; (3) increased emphasis on the environmental impact of resource extraction and use; (4) the addition of more than 30 topical discussions, each of which covers an area of general interest or emphasizes a specific important point; (5) "Focal Points" at the beginning of each chapter to summarize important issues to be presented in the text; (6) the addition of 50 new color plates; and (7) the addition of more than 100 new illustrations. A "Resources Calendar," presented as the appendix, demonstrates that every day is the anniversary of some event relevant to the issues surrounding Earth's resources; similar events continue to occur every day.

In this text, the term resources is used to mean those chiefly inorganic material resources that are traditionally part of the disciplines of geology, mineralogy, and soil science. Thus metals, industrial rocks and minerals, chemical minerals, water, and soil are discussed at length. Major sections are devoted to fossil fuels such as coal and oil (which are, of course, organic in origin) and to nuclear power and alternative energy sources (solar, wind, wave, geothermal, etc.). There are also chapters dealing with the sources, exploitation, and utilization of these particular resources and chapters dealing with more general questions concerning historical and environmental aspects of Earth's resources and with the question of resources for the future.

This edition, like the first, addresses the objective so well summarized by our friend Dr. Paul B. Barton, Jr. of the United States Geological Survey in his Presidential Address to the Society of Economic Geologists in 1979. He said, "It is as important for the future voter to appreciate the realities of our resource-environment situation as it is to be able to read the ballot. I believe that our principal hope is in education. . . ."

ACKNOWLEDGMENTS

The authors are indebted to a great many individuals whose various ideas, comments, questions, and criticisms have contributed to the final text of both editions. Countless former students and professional colleagues have stimulated us and either provoked us with questions or educated us with answers. We are especially grateful to those who critically reviewed the manuscripts at various stages—Dr. J. D. Rimstidt, Virginia Tech; Dr. Half Zantop, Dartmouth University; Dr. John E. Callahan, Appalachian State University; Dr. Barbara Dexter, SUNY at Purchase; Dr. George McCormick, University of Iowa; Dr. Lawrence D. Meinert, Washington State University at Pullman; and Dr. Udo Fehn, University of Rochester. For preparation of the manuscript, we wish to thank Peggy Keating, Christine Gee, and especially Margie Sentelle and Mary McMurray for the countless hours of typing and retyping. We are grateful to the many companies and individuals who contributed illustrations and to Llyn Sharp and Mark Fortney who helped in the preparation of the many photographs.

We dedicate this book to Lois, Nancie, and James Craig; Emlyn Vaughan; and Catherine, Adrienne, Stephanie, and Thalassa Skinner.

James R. Craig
David J. Vaughan
Brian J. Skinner

1 MINERALS: THE FOUNDATIONS OF SOCIETY

The world is constantly in a state of change. In order to meet the needs of a growing population, we must employ old and new techniques. The new technologies are more productive but require the use of greater amounts of resources. (Punjab, India; courtesy of the United Nations. Photograph by J. P. Laffonte.)

Resources are like air—of no great importance until you are not getting any.

Anonymous

FOCAL POINTS

- All materials needed for modern society are derived from the earth, directly or indirectly.

- World population grew slowly until about 1500 A.D.; increasingly rapid growth from around 1800 raised population to two billion by 1930 and to four billion by 1975; it will exceed six billion by 2000 A.D.

- Human population, presently approaching six billion, is projected to rise to at least 11 billion before stabilizing around 2100 A.D.

- The rates of population growth are much higher in less developed countries than in developed countries.

- Renewable resources consist of organic matter and their derivatives; nonrenewable resources consist of the mineral resources and their derivatives. (Some resources like coal, oil, and the tropical rain forest, while clearly organic, are not renewable with a viable timescale.)

- Earth's crust is a large *engine* with energy input from Earth's interior and from the sun; the energy fluxes result in movement of material, or *geochemical cycles.*

- *Resources* are naturally occurring concentrations of mineral substances from which economic extraction may occur.

- *Reserves* or *ores* are those concentrations of mineral substances for which extraction is presently economical.

THE COMPLEX NETWORK

All the materials needed for health and prosperity in our complex society come from the earth. Food and water, clothes and dwellings, automobiles, trains, radios, and even the paper on which these words are printed all contain one or more materials drawn from the earth. How straightforward it would be if we could consider uses and needs of each material irrespective of all the others. However, that is not possible because the way we use materials involves a network of complex dependencies by which use of each material contributes directly or indirectly to the use of every other material.

Consider bread, an everyday commodity most of us take for granted. Bread is made from the flour of cereal grains such as wheat and rye. The flour-making process employs grinding wheels made of steel alloys, and the grinder is driven by motors powered by electricity derived by burning oil, natural gas, or coal. The flour-making process, therefore, depends on supplies of fuel drawn from the earth and supplies of iron to make steel. When we take a step back in the bread-making process and consider the production of a grain such as wheat, a still wider pattern of dependency can be discerned. Wheat requires a fertile soil for growth and an adequate supply of water; both soil and water are important resources. The farmer who grows the grain uses a tractor to till the soil. The metals in the tractor and the fuel to power it all come from the earth. To reap the maximum harvest, the farmer must add fertilizer and any chemical constituents, such as nitrogen, phosphorus, and potassium, that the growing wheat may need but are not supplied in sufficient quantities by the soil. The source of these chemicals is once again the earth. Bread-making and modern bread-distributing processes are actually more complex than the picture just presented because they also involve baking ovens, storage systems for the grain, transportation systems for the bread, and chains of stores through which it is sold. The point to be appreciated is that material production and the use of natural resources are interdependent, whether the resources are renewable plants, trees, and cereal grains or nonrenewable mineral resources such as oil and steel. A less obvious point, but one that is equally important, is that supplies of food, metals, fertilizers, fuels, and innumerable other resources come from widespread geographic areas. No country is completely self-sufficient. Therefore, efficient and effective use of resources requires an efficient and effective trading system.

An impressive demonstration of the way that use-rates of resources are interrelated is shown in Figure 1.1. Agricultural production (a renewable resource) along with consumption of two kinds of nonrenewable resources, the tractors used by farmers and the fertilizer added to the soil, have increased in the second half of the twentieth century. Also shown is world population, which has more than doubled since 1950. Agricultural production has also more than doubled to keep pace (even though the amount of arable land has remained roughly constant), through a four-fold increase in the use of the resources needed to make and operate tractors and a nine-fold increase in the use of fertilizers. Food yields depend directly on the amounts of each of these nonrenewable resources. Whether the growth in agricultural production can continue to keep pace with increasing world population over the next half-century (when population is expected to double again) is an obvious cause for concern.

The interrelationships between our uses of Earth's materials grow ever more complex. As new technologies are developed and as larger and more complex social structures emerge, we tend to use materials in larger quantities and in ever more diverse ways. As a consequence, humans are building an increasing dependence on supplies of these materials. Just as the yield of crops depends on the use of fuel, fertilizer, and machinery, so does the size of another renewable crop. The human population also depends on supplies of food and water and supplies of fuels, metals, and other materials from the earth. The world's population has reached its present size of more than 5.5 billion because there is a complicated network that manages to supply us with the food we need. Terrible scenes of the famines in Africa, caused by disruptions in food supplies, are all too common in the newspapers and on television (Figure 1.2). Such local famines, whatever their cause, are small examples of what would happen on a much larger scale if the global food network were disrupted. Because adequate food production now requires adequate mineral and energy production, minerals and energy have also become parts of the foundation of all societies. If some of the important minerals and energy sources should run out or for some reason be denied us, social chaos could ensue; and the eventual but inevitable result would be a drastic reduction of the world's population.

POPULATION GROWTH: THE FORCE THAT DRIVES RESOURCE CONSUMPTION

Many millenia ago our ancestors were hunters and gatherers for whom nature's random production of grains, fruits, and animals provided a bountiful sufficiency. When local population needs began to exceed the natural yield of materials, farming was developed out of the necessity to control, and thereby to increase, the production of fruits, grains, and meats. Archeologists suggest that farming began in the Middle East about 10,000 years ago. From that time onward, the world's population has not only grown larger, it has grown ever more dependent on the controlled production of food and clothing and thereby on all the other materials we draw from the earth. Historians and archeologists believe that world population grew slowly but more or less steadily up to the end of the sixteenth century A.D. (Figure 1.3), interrupted only by occasional outbreaks of plagues, pestilences, and

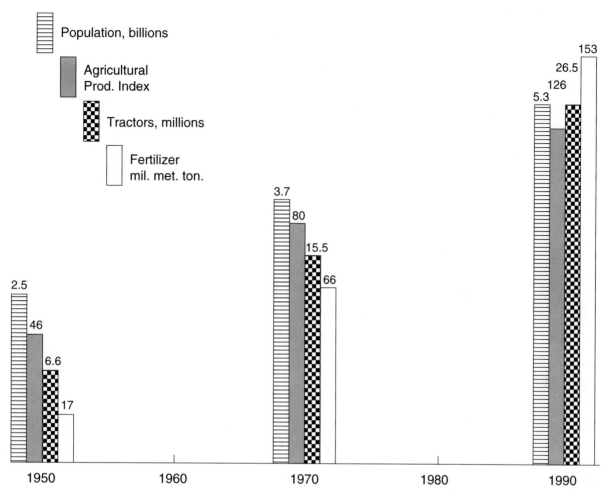

FIGURE 1.1. The relationship between world population, world agricultural production, and use of tractors and fertilizers in the second half of the Twentieth Century. As world population has more than doubled, agricultural production has been able to keep pace, but this has required a four-fold increase in the use of resources to produce and operate tractors and a nine-fold increase in the use of fertilizers to promote crop growth. (Data from FAO of the United Nations.)

famines. One of the worst epidemics started in Europe in 1348 when Crusaders inadvertently brought back rats bearing plague-carrying fleas from Asia Minor. Starting in Italy, bubonic plague swept through Europe over a period of two years. Between a third and a quarter of the entire population died, and the populations of some cities were reduced by half. This particular outbreak was known as the *Black Death.*

At about the end of the sixteenth century, the world population began to grow more rapidly. The initial causes for this increase seem to have been advances in medical care and in hygiene in the cities, but a marked improvement in the diets of Europeans also occurred when potatoes and maize were introduced from the Americas. World population reached one billion about 1800 A.D. One hundred and thirty years later (1930), the population reached two billion (Figure 1.3). A scant 45 years was all the time it took for the population to

double again to reach four billion in 1975. During the 1970s, the world population grew at a rate of about 2.2 percent a year. However, by 1983 the overall growth rate had declined to about 1.7 percent, and now it is about 1.5 percent. Nevertheless, in some regions, such as parts of Africa, populations are still growing at 2.5 to 3 percent per year. Despite a slowing of the overall growth rate, the world population will probably number more than six billion by 2000 A.D. This number, which almost defies imagination, means that mankind has a task of herculean proportions ahead if all of the new members of the human race are to be well fed and given the chance to enjoy a decent life. Many of the problems will be social and political in nature, but underlying everything will be the needed scientific and engineering expertise to exploit the earth's resources. Not only must the supplies be fairly divided but exploitation must be carried out in such a way that the

FIGURE 1.2. The dreadful evidence of starvation. This Ethiopian child of the Sahel region of Africa has suffered such severe malnutrition that he cannot recover to a normal life. (Photograph courtesy of the Catholic Relief Services.)

environment is not so fouled and irretrievably spoiled that we ruin the planet upon which we live.

Neither the density of population nor growth rates of populations are uniform around the world. The most populous countries today are China, with about 1.2 billion people, and India with more than 900 million; these two countries plus the United States, Russia, and Indonesia account for more than half of the present world population. But the situation is changing rapidly. The rates of population growth in different countries seem to vary inversely with the extent of industrial development and standard of living. As a result, the technologically advanced countries tend to have both low birth rates and populations that have reached or are now approaching a stable size. In such countries it is not necessary for people to have large families to support them in their old age. Less-developed countries, on the other hand, tend to have higher birth rates and populations that are still expanding rapidly. Such countries tend to have agriculturally based economies, and large families are a way to provide the needed manual labor in order to assure security in old age. The difference between the two kinds of society can be seen in the **age-sex pyramids** shown in Figure 1.4. The near stability of the more developed regions is reflected in the fact that the number of people below child-bearing years is nearly identical to the number of adults producing children. Hence, there is an approximate one-for-one replacement. By contrast, adults in less-developed regions of the world are bearing many more children than are needed to replace themselves. As long as such a trend continues, the pyramid will get broader and the population of such a region will grow ever larger. Even if the adults in these populous regions started today to have just enough children to ensure a one-for-one replacement, the populations of these regions would continue to grow for at least two generations because of the present ratio of children to adults.

What will the ultimate size of the world's population be? Obviously, the population cannot continue to grow unchecked forever. This is true if for no other reason than the fact that in a continually growing population a point must be reached when there is no longer enough room for everyone to stand up. Studies by the Population Council, the World Bank, and the United Nations have all drawn similar, but less than comforting, conclusions about the future of the world's population. Demeny's most encouraging conclusions, published in 1984 and shown in Figure 1.5, appear to be proving accurate and indicate a pattern of slowing growth rates. Some countries are further advanced in the pattern than others. Demeny suggests that the populations of today's less-developed countries will eventually level off despite the present high birth rates. The indication is that rates of population growth for all countries will decline and approach zero sometime during the next 120 years. Projecting demographic trends far into the future is an uncertain process at best. Nevertheless, present trends suggest that by about the year 2100 A.D. the world's population will have leveled off to between 11 and 12 billion people. The six most populous countries in the year 2100 A.D. are predicted to be, in decreasing order of size, India, China, Nigeria, Bangladesh, Pakistan, and Indonesia. These six countries will account for approximately 50 percent of the world's population. The times in the future when the populations of different countries level out will vary from country to country, but all will have reached a stable figure by about 2100 A.D.

Can the earth supply all the material needed for 11 billion people to enjoy a reasonable life? Some experts believe that 11 billion is far too large for a continuous and healthy balance to be attained in food and other material supplies. Others are convinced that economic and technological growth will help us find ways to meet the challenge, and that the world's population can safely grow to more than 11 bil-

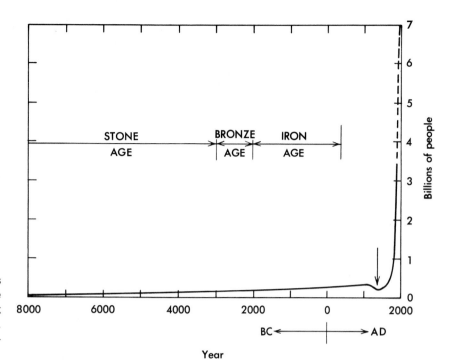

FIGURE 1.3. Growth of the world's population through history. Notice the sharp drop due to the Black Death that struck Europe in 1348. (Data from the Population Reference Bureau.)

lion. Possibly both sets of experts are too extreme in their conclusions, but the final answer lies in the future. Despite uncertainties, many of the problems that must be faced are already apparent—problems such as a disparity in living standards between regions that are industrially advanced but poor in mineral resources and regions that are rich in resources but little developed industrially. The forces that drive resource consumption are human needs and desires. However, the controls underlying resource availability and use are often geological and environmental. The interplay between availability and need is probably the most difficult problem the human race has to face, and it is one of the basic issues that must be confronted in trying to settle such a continuing scourge as war.

This book addresses the environmental and geological questions involved with resource use. However, we must remember that use and production of resources are inevitably intertwined with, and immensely complicated by, social, political, and strategic issues.

MATERIALS WE USE

No classification of natural resources is completely satisfactory, but one convenient way to start the classification is to separate resources into two broad groups—renewable resources and nonrenewable resources. **Renewable resources** are those materials that are replenished on short time scales of a few months or years. Examples are the growing plants and animals from which we get our food and the energy we draw from wind, flowing water, and the sun's heat. Use of re-

newable resources raises questions concerning rates of use rather than the ultimate total quantity of a given that shall ever be available. Given an infinite amount of time, it would be possible to grow infinitely large amounts of food and draw infinitely large amounts of water from a flowing stream. However, we cannot eat food faster than it can be grown, nor can we draw water from a flowing stream at a rate faster than a limit imposed by the volume of the water flowing in the stream.

Nonrenewable resources are those materials that are contained in the earth in fixed quantities and that are not replenished by natural processes operating on short time scales. Examples are oil, natural gas, coal, copper, and the myriad other mineral products we dig and pump from the earth. Notice that the definition includes a qualification concerning replenishment on short time scales. This is needed because new oil, gas, and certain other resources are continually being formed in the earth, but the formative processes are so slow that sizeable accumulations only develop over tens of millions of years—vastly slower than the rates at which we mine these materials. The substances we dig from Earth's crust today are the products that have accumulated over the past four billion years. The rates of replenishment of fuels derived from fossil organic matter and of metals distilled from Earth's mantle and core are so exceedingly slow that the crop we are mining today is the only crop we will ever have—hence, the term nonrenewable resources. Questions surrounding nonrenewable resources are therefore questions of total supply and of how fast we are consuming that total supply. The total amount ever to be available to us in the future is identical to that which is available today.

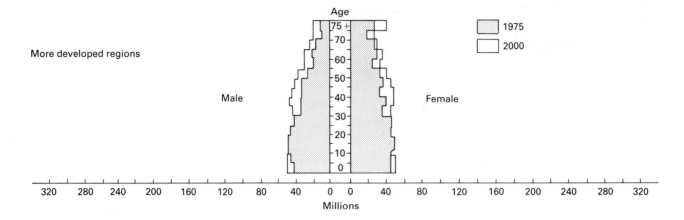

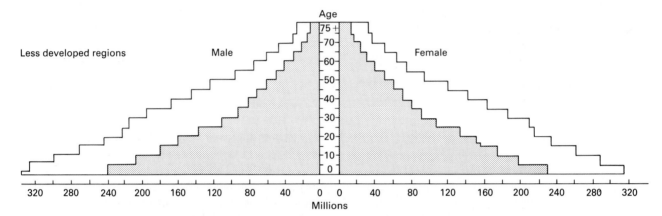

FIGURE 1.4.   The age and sex distributions in the populations of the more developed countries differ dramatically from those of the less developed countries. In the more developed countries, where sizes of populations are approaching stability, the number of young people below 25 years of age is approximately the same as the number older than 25 years. This means that adults producing children are doing so at a rate that is approaching the one-for-one replacement rate. By contrast, the child-bearing adults in less developed countries tend to produce many more children than are needed for replacement, so that populations grow larger and the age-pyramid grows broader. (From the Global 2000 Report for the President of the United States, 1980.)

Most nonrenewable resources are also **mineral resources**—all the nonliving, naturally occurring substances that are useful to us, both organic and inorganic in origin. We use this broad definition in order to include all natural solids, liquids such as petroleum and water, and gases such as natural gas and the gases of the atmosphere. A possible confusion in terminology becomes apparent when one considers a resource such as water. Water in a flowing stream is a renewable resource because it is replenished on a short time scale by rainfall. By contrast, water in a deep aquifer in a desert area, as in Israel, central Australia, or the High Plains of the western United States, is a nonrenewable resource be-

cause it is only replenished over time scales of thousands or tens of thousands of years.

To reduce the confusion arising from terminology, we have classified and discussed the mineral and energy resources covered in this book by the manner in which they are used. The general classification, as shown in Figure 1.6, divides resources into three major use groups. First, there are metals, which are a group of chemical elements that either singly or in combination have those special properties such as malleability, ductility, fusibility, high thermal conductivity, and electrical conductivity that allow them to be used in a wide range of technical applications. Metals have

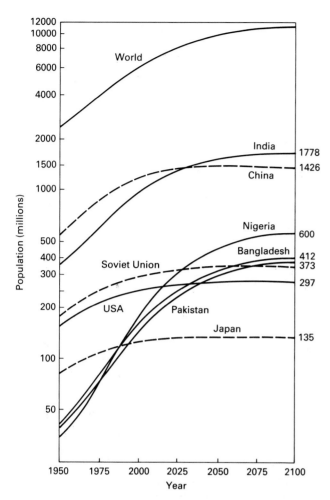

FIGURE 1.5. Projected growth of populations in several large countries and for the world as a whole to the year 2100. Demographers suggest that by 2100 A.D., the world will have attained a constant sized population. (From Demeny, *Population and Development Review*, vol. 10, no. 1 (1984) p. 103.)

been the key materials through which humans have developed the remarkably diversified society we now enjoy and by which we have managed to proceed from the primitive societies of antiquity to the present. It is not surprising that the metal-winning and metal-working skills of ancient communities have been used as a measure of societal development and that terms such as *Bronze Age* and *Iron Age* have become common.

Metals can be divided into two classes on the basis of their occurrence in Earth's crust. The geochemically **abundant metals** are those that individually constitute 0.1 percent or more of Earth's crust by weight. They are iron, aluminum, silicon, manganese, magnesium, and titanium. The term *abundant* is used for two reasons. First, because these metals

occur in so many diverse ways in the earth that reserves of rich mineable ores are truly enormous and even though rich deposits are not uniformly distributed around the world, the question of sufficiency for future generations is not in doubt. Second, because the geochemically abundant metals form most of the common minerals, they influence many of the geologic processes that shape the earth. Geochemically **scarce metals**, by contrast, are those that individually constitute less than 0.1 percent by weight of Earth's crust. They are metals such as copper, lead, zinc, molybdenum, mercury, silver, and gold. The scarce metals are present in such tiny concentrations in the earth that they play very minor roles in geological processes, and very special (even rare) circumstances are needed in order for local concentrations to form. Mineable deposits of scarce metals tend to be smaller and less common than mineable deposits of abundant metals. As a consequence, the question of sufficiency for future generations is a more important one where scarce metals are concerned.

The second major group in the resource classification in Figure 1.6 includes those substances and sources from which we now, or in the future might, draw energy. Some of the resources, such as the fossil fuels and uranium, are nonrenewable resources. Other energy resources, such as running water and solar heat, are renewable. The importance of the energy resources, which are now recognized as being vital to the operation of modern society, was first brought into focus by the so-called energy crisis of 1973 when Middle Eastern oil was withheld from Europe and the United States. Subsequently, worldwide attention has been focused on the cost and sufficiency of energy resources for the future.

The third group of resources includes all of those material substances used in one way or another for reasons other than their metallic properties or their energy content. Such resources include the minerals used as sources of chemicals—minerals such as halite (NaCl) and borax ($Na_2B_4O_7 \cdot 10H_2O$)—plus minerals used as the raw materials for fertilizers. The group also includes the water and soils vital to the production of foodstuffs. Also falling into this category are the wide range of industrial minerals that are used in everything from the smelting of metals to the drilling for oil and in such diverse products as paints, fillers, and abrasives. The construction and building industries use large volumes of resources such as crushed stone, sand, gravel, and the raw materials for cement and concrete.

CONSEQUENCES OF RESOURCE EXPLOITATION

Earth can be envisioned as a huge machine with two sources of energy. The first source is the sun's heat, which is responsible for the turbulence in the atmosphere that we call wind, for the temperature variations across the face of Earth that make equatorial regions warm and polar regions cold, for ocean currents, for evaporation of the water that forms clouds and leads to rain, and for most of the other phenomena, including growth of plants, that happen on Earth's surface. Flowing water, moving ice, blowing wind, and the downhill sliding of water-weakened rocks and mud are the main agents of erosion and transportation by which materials are moved as solids, liquids, and gases around the globe. If the sun were the only source of energy, Earth would by now be a nearly smooth globe devoid of mountains. Earth is not a smooth globe because the second major energy source, Earth's internal heat, causes slow horizontal and vertical movements in the seeming solid rocks of the mantle and crust. These slow movements produce the crumplings and bucklings of the surface that thrust up mountains and split continents apart to form new ocean basins and that cause continents to collide and destroy old ocean basins.

The two systems of forces—those driven by the sun's external heat energy and those driven by Earth's internal heat energy—maintain a dynamic balance. The balance involves myriad natural transfers of material through streams, oceans, atmosphere, soils, sediments, and rocks. As new mountains like the Alps are thrust up, erosion slowly wears them down. If a balance were not maintained, not only would the face of the earth be smooth, but the compositions of the ocean and atmosphere would be different. The movement of materials from rocks to soils to streams to oceans and back to rocks is called **geochemical cycling**, and the dynamic balance that results is called the **geochemical balance**. The formation of many of Earth's resources (including fossil fuels, metals, industrial minerals, and rocks) is a consequence of these geochemical cycling processes, which will be further described in Chapter 2.

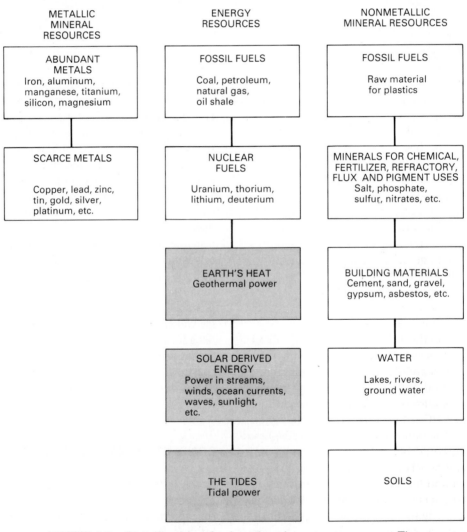

FIGURE 1.6. Classification of mineral and energy resources. The shaded boxes indicate those energy resources that are not mineral resources.

One of the major consequences of our exploitation of natural resources is that we humans are interfering with the balances of some of the natural geochemical cycles. An example is shown in Figure 1.7 where the major reservoirs and flow paths for carbon at Earth's surface are shown. There are five main reservoirs of carbon compounds: (1) the atmos- phere—carbon dioxide (CO_2); (2) the biosphere—carbon tied up in the cells of living plants and animals (the biomass); (3) buried organic matter including oil, natural gas, coal, and the small percentage of carbon compounds found in all sedi- ments and sedimentary rocks; (4) the hydrosphere—carbon dioxide dissolved in the oceans; and (5) buried calcium

CO_2 AND THE GREENHOUSE EFFECT

The greenhouse effect, its causes by the efforts of humans, and its potential effects on large scale climatological changes have been in the news for the past several years. The term, as applied by analogy to the way that the air in glass greenhouses becomes warmer than out- side air, refers to the heating of the atmosphere due to any increase in gases that absorb long wavelength (infrared) radiation from earth. Carbon dioxide is generally considered the greatest problem gas, but water vapor, methane (CH_4), nitrous oxide (N_2O), and chloro- fluorocarbons also contribute. These gases are transparent to solar radiation as it enters Earth's atmosphere from above, but they absorb and are heated by radiation given off by the earth below.

In 1896, the distinguished Swedish chemist S. Arrhenius recognized that Earth's at- mospheric temperature was related to the amount of CO_2 it contained and predicted that a tripling of CO_2 would lead to an average global increase of 9°C (16°F). Since that time, many warnings have been voiced, but there is much disagreement as to the magnitude of the impacts that could result from changes in atmospheric CO_2. It is clear that the CO_2 con- centration of Earth's atmosphere is increasing (see Figure 1.8) as a result of the combustion of massive quantities of fossil fuels (coal, gas, oil). Studies of atmospheric bubbles that were trapped in glacial ice before the Industrial Revolution, when large scale fossil fuel con- sumption began, indicate that CO_2 levels were only approximately 260 ppm by volume (0.026%) or about two-thirds of today's values. Detailed modern atmospheric analyses were begun in 1957 at stations on Mauna Loa, Hawaii, and at the South Pole. These data have revealed a steady increase in CO_2 from 316 ppm in 1959 to about 350 ppm in 1990. This is an average annual increase of 1.14 ppm, but the rate is increasing and is now ap- proaching 3 ppm per year.

The confusion and disagreements arise when trying to decipher where the added CO_2 will go and what the effects will be. The atmosphere actually holds relatively little of the total CO_2 involved in atmosphere-biosphere-hydrosphere circulation. The deep oceans contain 60 times more CO_2 than the atmosphere, but the rate of absorption is slow. The biosphere constantly removes CO_2 by photosynthesis, and many plants grow faster if given more CO_2. However, large-scale deforestation, especially in the tropics, is reducing the most effective natural CO_2 removal process. If most of the extra CO_2 from fossil fuel combustion remains in the atmosphere, the level of CO_2 is projected to in- crease to about 600 ppm by the year 2050. The exact effect this will have on temperature is debated, but several workers have modeled projections of an increase in average global temperature of 4°–5°C (7°–9°F). The changes would be less (2°C, 4°F) at the equator and more (7°C, 13°F) in polar regions.

The ultimate effects of the temperature rise are not clear, but most scientists agree that there could be significant shifts in growing seasons and rainfall patterns and that there would be a rise in sea level. That rise is likely because of melting of the West Antarctic ice sheet and the expansion of the surface layers of the oceans as they are warmed. A rise of 4–6 meters projected over a 500-year span could have devastating effects on coastal cities and low lying regions around the world, including the Netherlands in Europe and Florida, Louisiana, and Texas in the United States. Presently, there appear to be no realistic alter- natives to energy production by combustion of fossil fuels and no efficient methods of lim- iting the increases in the levels of CO_2 in Earth's atmosphere.

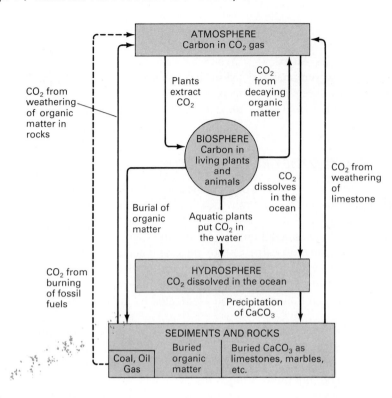

FIGURE 1.7. The carbon cycle provides an example of the way geochemical balances are maintained. There are five major carbon reservoirs—the atmosphere; the biosphere; the hydrosphere (which is principally the ocean); reduced carbon in sediments and rocks, including coal, oil, and natural gas; and oxidized carbon in sediments and rocks. Carbon moves between these reservoirs by processes such as photosynthesis, weathering of rocks, and burial of organic matter. The system has come to a balance so that the reservoir sizes remain constant. Humans are now changing the balance by burning fossil fuels and putting CO_2 into the atmosphere at a rate faster than the system can accommodate it.

carbonate ($CaCO_3$)—carbon tied up in shells, limestones, and marbles. The fluxes of carbon between the five major reservoirs are nicely controlled so that on time scales of thousands of years, the system remains in balance.

Human involvement with the geochemical cycling of carbon involves the rapid removal of organic carbon (in the form of fossil fuels) from sedimentary rocks and the conversion of that carbon to CO_2 through burning. Eventually, as burning is continued, the other reservoirs and fluxes must readjust, and the system will tend toward a new dynamic balance. But the rate of readjustment is slow when considered in terms of a human life span. Seen from our perspective, the CO_2 content of the atmosphere is slowly but steadily increasing (Figure 1.8). Because CO_2 plays a major role in the thermal properties of the atmosphere, a change in the CO_2 content of the atmosphere may cause slow changes in world temperatures and other geochemical cycles. For example, changes in climate could alter sea level and rainfall patterns that, in turn, could alter the availability of water. Changes in the water supply could, in turn, affect the use of soils and the growth of crops.

The production and use of every natural resource, from the clearing of forests and the tilling of fields, to the mining of copper and the burning of coal, causes changes in the natural geochemical cycles. The changes may be large or small, local or global, pleasant or unpleasant; and they may be given names, such as pollution and environmental degradation, or may even be called disasters; but they are all consequences of the exploitation of natural resources. Among the topics addresssed in this book, therefore, are some of the environmental consequences of the increasing exploitation of natural resources.

RESOURCES, RESERVES, AND ORES

Few things seem to cause more confusion than the words resource, reserve, and ore as they are applied to mineral deposits. It is not uncommon to find the words used interchangeably as if they all meant the same thing. The meanings are actually very different. In part, the confusion arises because resource and reserve are common words and each has a range of meanings depending on the materials being discussed. But, to a greater extent, the confusion arises for another reason. Even though mineral commodities are used in every aspect of our daily lives, few among us have actually seen a mineral deposit and thereby developed an understanding of how big they are, how they vary in richness, and what difficulties are involved in producing mineral raw materials. Further confusion results from the misuse of the words by those seeking to make financial investments in mineral resources. The terminology given below is that adopted by the United States Geological Survey, the United States Bureau of Mines, and most other geological organizations.

The use of standard and exact terms as shown in Figure 1.9 is necessary for valid estimates and comparisons of resources worldwide and for long-term public and commercial planning. In order to serve these purposes, the classification scheme is based on both geological characteristics, such as grade, tonnage, thickness, and depth of a deposit; and profitability assessments dependent on extraction costs and market values.

A mineral **resource**, according to the Geological Survey and the Bureau of Mines, is "a concentration of naturally occurring solid, liquid, or gaseous material, in or on the

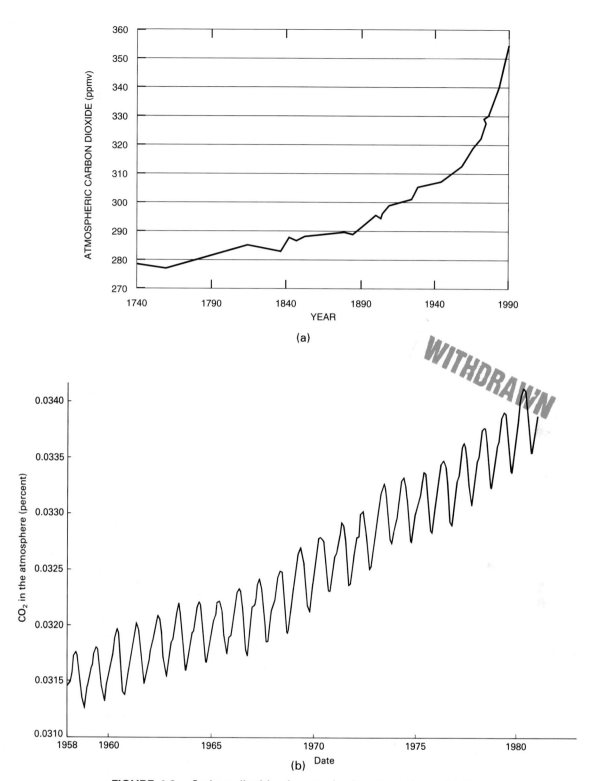

(a)

(b) Date

FIGURE 1.8. Carbon dioxide changes in the atmosphere. (a) The pre-industrial levels of carbon dioxide are estimated to have been below 280 parts per million by volume but have now risen to levels in excess of 350 parts per million. Note the rapid increases since 1940 as the rates of burning of fossil fuels have accelerated. (b) Since the late 1950s, detailed measurements have been taken at an observatory on Mauna Loa, an extinct volcano in Hawaii. These measurements show a yearly oscillation due to the control exerted by the seasonal growth of plants in the northern hemisphere. (a. From *The Climate System*, National Oceanic and Atmospheric Administration, 1991; b. From Carbon Dioxide Information Analysis Center, Oak Ridge National Laboratory, 1994.)

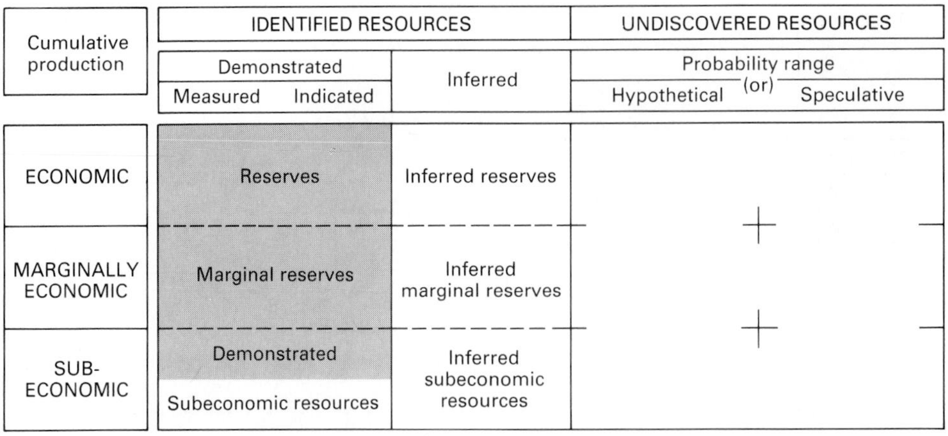

Cumulative production	IDENTIFIED RESOURCES			UNDISCOVERED RESOURCES	
	Demonstrated		Inferred	Probability range	
	Measured	Indicated		Hypothetical (or)	Speculative
ECONOMIC	Reserves		Inferred reserves	+	
MARGINALLY ECONOMIC	Marginal reserves		Inferred marginal reserves		
SUB-ECONOMIC	Demonstrated		Inferred subeconomic resources	+	
	Subeconomic resources				

FIGURE 1.9. Resources are classified according to geological understanding (increasing from right to left) and economic viability (increasing from bottom to top). The best known and most profitable of the resources fall into the category of reserves (commonly called ores when referring to metal-bearing deposits) and constitute our present source of mineral commodities. The shaded portion of the diagram illustrates which materials are included in reserve base, a term that is now being widely used. (Diagram from United States Bureau of Mines, Mineral Commodity Summaries, 1995.)

earth's crust, in such form and amount that economic extraction of a commodity from the concentration is currently or potentially feasible." In the geological sense, the resources are subdivided into those that have been identified and those as yet undiscovered. Depending upon the degree of certainty, the identified resources fall into the categories of measured (where volumes and tonnages are well established), indicated (where volume and tonnage estimates are based on less precise data), and inferred (where deposits are assumed to extend between or beyond known resources). In terms of profitability, resources are classed according to their current economic status as shown on the left side of Figure 1.9.

Reserve is a general term for "that part of the resources that can be economically and legally extracted at a given time." These are the materials that are mined or otherwise extracted and processed to meet the everyday needs of society. It is important to note that legal, environmental, and economic constraints must be considered because issues such as land ownership, the discharge of mining wastes, potential carcinogenic effects of products, or the incorporation of lands into National Parks or wilderness areas may exclude otherwise mineable resources from reserve status. In such cases, those materials would continue to be considered as resources. Their potential for extraction would be high, but they would not become reserves unless laws or other restrictions were changed. **Ore** is a commony used term when referring to metal-bearing reserves.

The quantities of reserves at any time are well defined but change constantly; they decrease as ores are mined out but increase as new discoveries are made or as technological advances occur. Also, they rise as the market value of mineral products rises, and they decrease when the market value falls.

There are many historical examples of resources becoming ores. A famous one occurred about the beginning of the present century when two young mining engineers, D. C. Jackling and R. C. Gemmell, discovered that copper deposits previously ignored because of their very low grades could be worked at a profit by using new bulk-mining processes. This greatly increased the supplies of copper available to the world for use. A second famous example occurred soon after the end of the second world war as the richest portions of the iron ores of the Great Lakes region were running out. New mining and processing technologies allowed the leaner and formerly unworkable low-grade deposits called taconites to be worked. Taconites are now highly desirable ores and supply most of the iron used in the United States.

There are many examples, too, of ores becoming too expensive to be mined and thereby slipping back again to resources. A very recent example of backward slipping concerns numerous gold mines around the world. When gold was selling for close to $800 an ounce in 1980, it was possible to work very low-grade ore—some grades were so low, in fact, that it cost about $700 per ounce to recover the gold. The reserves of all gold mines were expanded as a result of the high price. When the price of gold fell below $400 an ounce in the mid-1980s, reserves declined again as the previously low-grade ores once again became resources.

In recent years, the Geological Survey and Bureau of Mines have introduced a broad term called the **reserve base** to include the previous **reserves**, **marginal reserves**, and a portion of **subeconomic reserves**. It thus encompasses not only the reserves but also the "parts of the resources that have a reasonable potential for becoming economically available within planning horizons beyond those that assume proven technol-

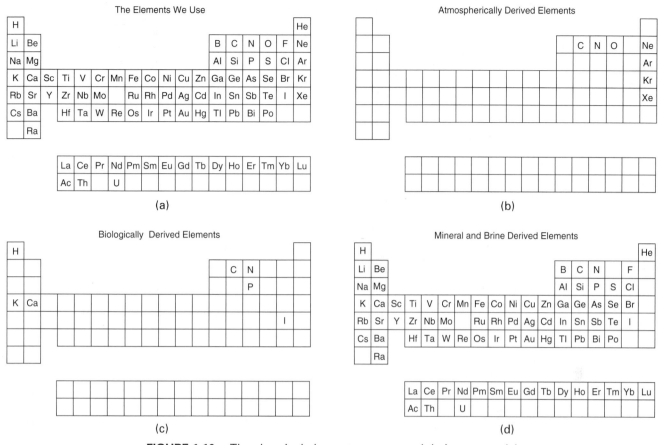

FIGURE 1.10. The chemical elements we use and their sources. (a) The elements that we use in modern society. Many are used in compounds in which their presence is not evident but is essential. (b) The elements that are extracted from the atmosphere. (c) The elements that are derived from biological materials. (d) The elements that are derived from the mineral resources and brines (ocean water and other salt-bearing waters). It is apparent that most of the chemical elements we use in modern society are derived only from the minerals and the brines.

ogy and current economics." Although this is a less well-defined quantity, it does take into account the resources that, although not now mineable, will likely be available for our use.

It is all too easy to overlook the fact that quite large concentrations of materials can, for one reason or another, be too expensive to exploit. We must always keep in mind that while mineral resources are the products of processes operating in the past, they become ores only if we are clever enough to discover the deposits and then find ways to exploit them profitably. As we shall see in Chapter 3, the history of our use of resources is a record of a steady increase in both the range of natural materials we have learned to use and the diverse ways in which we use them.

WHERE DO EARTH RESOURCES COME FROM?

Of the hundred or so known chemical elements, at least 86 are used in various ways by modern societies (Figure 1.10a).

In some cases, the use is obvious, such as the iron used to make steel for automobiles or refrigerators and the sodium and chlorine that combine in nature to give us common salt. In other cases, the use is not so clear, as when vanadium is alloyed with iron to make special steels or when rare earth elements (La, Ce, etc.) are used to make color phosphors for TV sets. Only seven of these elements are ever derived from the atmosphere (Figure 1.10b), and only seven are derived from biological systems (Figure 1.10c). The rest of the elements (and even some of those already mentioned) are derived from minerals dug from Earth or brines extracted within Earth (groundwaters) or the seas (Figure 1.10d). The answers to the questions "Do we really need all of the mines, quarries, and wells that we have?" and "Could we obtain the materials we want from other sources?" are clearly "Yes" in the first case and "No" in the second case if we wish to maintain our present standards of life.

2 THE ORIGINS OF MINERAL RESOURCES

Volcanic activity as expressed in the great explosion at Mt. St. Helens in Washington on May 18, 1980 is evidence of the heat within Earth and the movement of fluids in the crust. The physical and chemical processes within and on Earth are constantly generating and modifying the materials of Earth and locally creating the resources that humans use every day. (From the U.S. Geological Survey.)

The earth, from which food comes, is transformed below as by fire; Sapphires come from its rocks, and its dust contains nuggets of gold.

Job 28: 5–6

FOCAL POINTS

- If Earth were homogeneous, most of the mineral resources used to develop and maintain modern society would not be available.
- Mineral resources are natural concentrations that result from the physical and chemical processes active in Earth's crust.
- Nearly all geologic processes form, modify, or destroy some Earth resources.
- Igneous activity, generated by radioactive heating, may concentrate resources by means of circulating hydrothermal fluids or by means of selective precipitation of layers of metal oxides or sulfides in a magma.
- Regional metamorphism modifies the properties of preexisting rocks and converts some of them into construction materials such as slate and marble.
- Contact metamorphism, resulting from the heat and fluids released by igneous intrusions, may generate metal ores and even result in the formation of gems.
- The shallow subsurface zone contains valuable groundwater resources and is the site of the initial generation of fossil fuels when buried organic matter is altered by increasing temperature and pressure.
- Weathering generates soils and specific resources such as clays and bauxite (the primary ore of aluminum).
- Processes of weathering and erosion break down rocks and transport the residual materials; this may create large quantities of sand and gravel and may concentrate gold, tin, and titanium minerals as placer deposits.
- Evaporation in arid regions concentrates soluble salts that form deposits of halite (rock salt), potassium salts, gypsum, and, in rare instances, nitrates.
- Burial, and subsequent compaction and heating, may convert terrestrial organic debris into coal.
- The ocean basins are the ultimate site of deposition of the sediments that erode from the continents and thus contain vast quantities of sand and gravel as well as some placer ores.
- Evaporation of shallow seas and ocean margin lagoons over long periods of time formed the largest evaporate deposits.
- Burial of marine plankton, later subjected to compression and heating, forms petroleum and most natural gas.
- Manganese and iron-bearing nodules form slowly on the deep ocean floor.
- Modern submarine hydrothermal vents are generating iron-, copper-, and zinc-rich sulfide deposits analogous to the large ore bodies being mined in ancient rocks.

INTRODUCTION

If the crust of Earth were composed of only one type of rock with all of the chemical elements distributed uniformly and in proportion to their geochemical abundance, we would have very few of the resources that are needed to sustain modern society. Fortunately, Earth's crust is very inhomogeneous and there are numerous geologic processes that concentrate various elements and materials into the resources we use. There are many ways to classify these processes. A simple approach is as follows:

1. Subsurface igneous and metamorphic processes
   (a) Formation of granites and other relatively silica-rich rocks
   (b) Formation of basalt and other relatively silica-poor rocks
   (c) Regional metamorphism
   (d) Contact metamorphism
2. Surface processes
3. Shallow subsurface and diagenetic processes
4. Marine processes

These are somewhat arbitrary subdivisions, and the boundaries are not sharply defined. Furthermore, more than one process has commonly been involved in the generation of a particular resource (e.g., coal that originates as terrestrial plants undergoes metamorphism before reaching bituminous or anthracite rank; some gold that is concentrated and deposited by hydrothermal fluids is eroded and transported by streams and finally deposited in beach sands at the ocean margin as placer deposits). Nevertheless, the subdivisions help us recognize the relationships between processes and particular resources, and that recognition helps us understand where to search for additional resources as they become needed. Because the **rock cycle** (Figure 2.1) is more or less continuous, there is no obvious point at which to start this discussion. We shall begin with a discussion of igneous and metamorphic rocks followed by a discussion of surface processes and then by a discussion of marine processes.

This chapter provides a succinct overview of the processes involved in resource generation. The processes discussed are those that have generated the resources exploited today; however, the nature of the resources we use may well change in the future (e.g., today we use bauxite as the source of aluminum, but in the future we may be able to use feldspar). This discussion focuses only on the most important resource-forming processes presented in general terms. Additional details are provided in later chapters, along with discussions of the specific types of resources. It is not

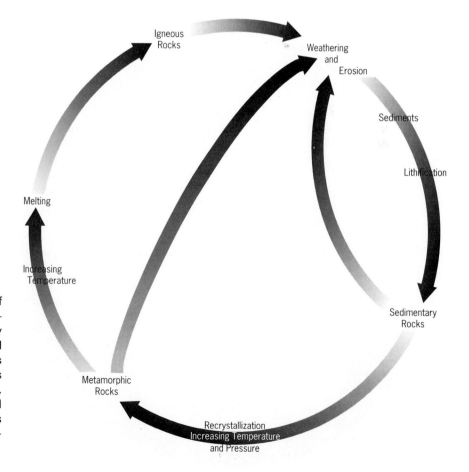

FIGURE 2.1. The outer circle of the rock cycle schematically illustrates the changes experienced by rock matter in an uninterrupted cycle. Crystallized igneous rocks may weather into sediments that, in turn, can be consolidated, buried and metamorphosed, and ultimately remelted. Interruptions in the cycle are indicated by the internal arrows.

intended to substitute for a thorough presentation of all the important processes active in physical geology.

There are two very important points to keep in mind while reading this book and discussing the exploitation of Earth's resources.

1. All earth resources have been generated by one or more geologic processes.
2. All geologic processes are forming, modifying, or destroying some earth resources.

SUBSURFACE IGNEOUS AND METAMORPHIC PROCESSES

The continents are composed primarily of granite, whereas the floor of the ocean is composed primarily of basalt. These *bedrocks* are usually covered with a veneer of sediments that are the products of the weathering and erosion of the granites and basalts. There are many specific types of igneous rocks, and a thorough discussion of their origins is far beyond the scope of this book. The discussion below focuses on two end-members of the range of igneous rocks—granite (and other silica-rich rocks) and basalt (or gabbro, the coarse-grained equivalent of silica-poor rocks)—and the processes of their

formation and that of their associated mineral resources. Since prehistoric times, these igneous rocks have been used as construction materials either as crushed stone (because of their strength and durability) or as dimension stone (because of their ease of shaping and polishing). Many other resources are directly generated during the formation of igneous rocks or by the movement of the significant amounts of fluids that are associated with their formation and that dissolve, transport, and precipitate metal-bearing ores. Similar fluids, even when devoid of metals, may prove important as sources of geothermal energy.

Formation of Granites and Other Relatively Silica-Rich Rocks

Granites, like all igneous rocks, form as a result of the melting of preexisting rocks as a result of heat buildup within the earth. The primary source of this heat is the radioactive decay of uranium, thorium, and potassium isotopes. Because the rocks are poor conductors and the isotopes are irregularly distributed, the heat generated by radioactive decay gradually builds up locally and may cause temperatures high enough to melt rocks and form magmas. It was this buildup of heat and the subsequent melting that produced the internally layered structure (Figure 2.2) of Earth, with the parti-

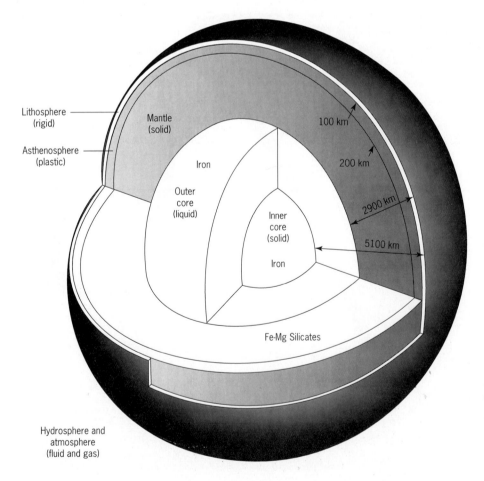

FIGURE 2.2. Earth is composed of a series of concentric shells with approximate thicknesses as shown. The interior, like the hydrosphere and atmosphere, is dynamic, but its movements are generally slower and episodic.

tioning of iron into the core, iron and magnesium silicates into the mantle, and the other lower density components into the crust. Despite this partitioning, many inhomogeneities persist and radioactive decay continues. The overall rate of decay is now less than during earlier periods of Earth history because the radioactive isotopes are now diminished in quantity. For example, the amount of U^{235} now contributing to this heat is only about 1.5 percent of that present at the time of Earth formation. U^{238} has been reduced to about 50 percent, Th^{232} to about 75 percent, and K^{40} to about 10 percent of the original amounts. Consequently, igneous processes are still active and Earth remains a dynamic planet as evidenced by volcanism, earthquakes, and hot springs, but the levels of activity are much lower than those of a few billion years ago.

In simple terms, granites form where there is a sufficient buildup of heat to melt the rocks of the crust. Different minerals and different groups of minerals together have very different melting points, and the presence of water and other dissolved substances can significantly affect the melting temperatures of rocks. The situation is further complicated because the increased pressure placed on the rocks by overlying strata generally raises the melting temperature. Hence, the more deeply a rock is buried, the greater the pressure and the more it must be heated before melting. The minimum temperature to form a granitic magma by the melting of rocks is about 675°C. When rocks begin to melt, they are able to move within the crust of Earth in response to pressure or density differences and may emerge at the surface. The most obvious example of this emerging is lava flowing from a volcano. Volcanic lavas, however, are nearly always basalts and are quite different chemically from granites. The basalts, because of low silica contents (that is, low amounts of silica as a part of their total chemical composition—not silica as quartz), are much less viscous (that is, they flow more easily) than are granite melts with high silica contents. Granite magmas move slowly but can move upward and laterally through Earth's crust for kilometers (Figure 2.3). They may be forced into regions of the crust where they physically push aside other rocks, or they may gradually melt their way upward incorporating other rocks (a process called *stoping*). When they reach their limit of movement because of heat loss, because of reaching isostatic equilibrium (that is, a balance based on their density), or because they encounter some physical barrier, they slowly crystallize. Subsequent erosion may remove up to several kilometers of overlying rocks and expose the granites. The removed material becomes the sediments transported by rivers and deposited on the continental shelves.

Sometimes the fluids generated by crystallizing magmas concentrate minor or unusual elements at the margins of the intrusions, forming very coarse grained masses called **pegmatites**. Pegmatites are composed primarily of feldspar, quartz, and mica but may contain large and significant quantities of crystals or minerals containing fluorine (e.g., apatite), beryllium (e.g., beryl), lithium (e.g., spodumene), or even rare earth elements. Consequently, pegmatites are major sources of minerals containing these elements as well as several types of gemstones (e.g., emerald and aquamarine).

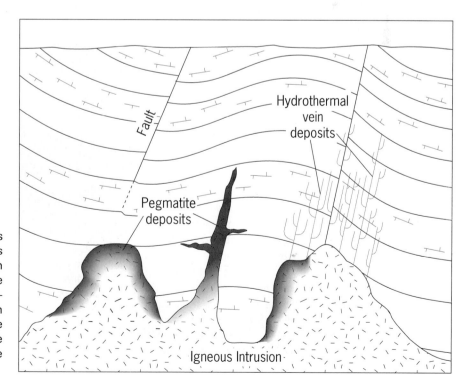

FIGURE 2.3. Hydrothermal veins commonly occur near igneous intrusions where fluids are given off from the intrusions or where ground water is heated by the intrusions. Pegmatites usually form at the margins of intrusions where fluids accumulate and where some minor and rare elements are enriched.

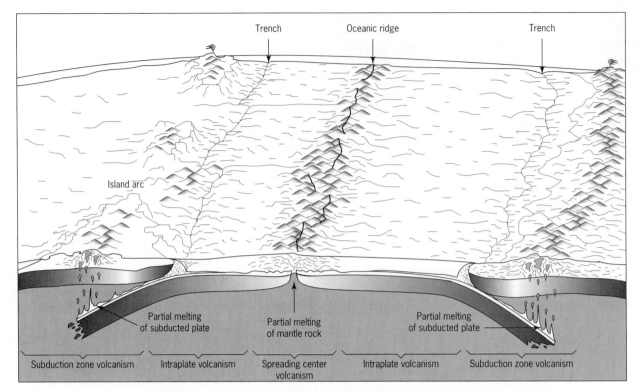

Trench   Oceanic ridge   Trench

Island arc

Partial melting of subducted plate   Partial melting of mantle rock   Partial melting of subducted plate

Subduction zone volcanism   Intraplate volcanism   Spreading center volcanism   Intraplate volcanism   Subduction zone volcanism

FIGURE 2.4. Basaltic oceanic crust is emplaced at spreading centers (mid-oceanic ridges). At subduction zones, oceanic crust slides beneath the granitic masses of the continents; these are active seismic zones and the sites of partial melting that appear on the surface as volcanoes and beneath the surface as porphyritic intrusions.

The development of plate tectonic theory since the 1960s and the recognition of the mechanisms of magma generation along subducting plate boundaries have significantly increased our understanding of the genesis of many types of resources. This is especially true for porphyry type deposits that contain the world's greatest quantities of copper and molybdenum ores as well as large amounts of gold and silver and significant amounts of zinc, lead, tin, and other base metals. The subduction of oceanic plates beneath the margins of continents (Figure 2.4) results in the melting of lower crustal rocks and the development of intrusions of relatively silica-rich rocks that are emplaced in the crust near the plate boundaries. During cooling, as described above, fluids containing dissolved metals are released along fractures where they precipitate the metals in large but low-grade deposits.

The silicate melts that crystallize to form granites and other igneous rocks all contain up to several percent dissolved water. When the rocks crystallize, most of the minerals that form (e.g., quartz—SiO_2, orthoclase feldspar—$KAlSi_3O_8$, and plagioclase feldspar—$CaAl_2Si_2O_8$ to $NaAlSi_3O_8$) do not contain any water. The smaller amounts of micas, such as muscovite, $KAl_2(AlSi_3)O_{10}(OH)_2$ or biotite, $K(Mg,Fe)_3(Al,Fe)Si_3O_{10}(OH,F)_2$, and amphiboles, such as actinolite, $Ca_2(Mg,Fe)_5Si_8O_{22}(OH)_2$), take up a lit-

FIGURE 2.5. Hydrothermal vein cutting across granite at Cligga Head, S.W. England. The vein is filled with white quartz and small amounts of tin, copper, and tungsten minerals. The dark zones on each side of the vein are where the hot vein-forming fluids have altered the surrounding rocks. (Photograph by J. R. Craig.)

tle of the water, but the remainder of the water escapes, commonly along faults and fractures that form during and after emplacement of the intrusion. This water often contains dissolved elements (Cu^{2+}, Pb^{2+}, Zn^{2+}, Ag^+, S^{2-}) and compounds (such as NaCl) that do not get incorporated into the principal granite minerals. As these water-rich solutions, generally termed hydrothermal fluids (*hydro* meaning water and *thermal* meaning hot), move outward from the crystallizing granite, they cool, undergo reduction in pressure, and may react with other rocks. Each of these changes can decrease the solubility of the dissolved species and cause precipitation of compounds in the faults or fracture to form *veins* (Figure 2.5). The veins range widely in complexity, richness, mineralogy, and size. The veins most valuable as resources may contain several percent of one or more sulfide minerals of copper, lead, zinc, and silver and, sometimes, traces of native gold. For lower-value metals such as lead and zinc, veins may need to be 0.5 meter or greater in thickness to be profitable to mine. In contrast, the much higher value of gold allows mineable gold-bearing veins to be only millimeters in thickness or to contain only tiny grains disseminated along the vein.

There is no clear boundary between the deeper subsurface zone and the shallower subsurface zone because veins and igneous intrusions that originally formed at considerable depths are commonly exposed at the present ground surface by erosion. Furthermore, igneous activity with veins, hot springs, and other associated phenomena may occur at Earth's surface in some areas, whereas other areas (e.g., the Mississippi Delta) contain thousands of meters of sediments with no evidence of igneous rocks except in the underlying *basement* at depths greater than 20,000 meters.

FLUID INCLUSIONS

The search for ore deposits to replace those being mined requires a detective-like approach to the examination and interpretation of clues, both large and small, in the rocks. On a large scale, geologists frequently use satellite images and high-level aerial photographs to look for structures or alteration zones in rocks that might indicate the presence of mineral resources. On a small scale are features that can often only be seen through a microscope. Among the most valuable of these tiny clues are *fluid inclusions*, small droplets of the fluids (Figure 2.6) that actually deposited the ores and that we now find trapped in the ore minerals and associated rocks. As such, they provide evidence of the processes by which an ore was formed, although that event may have occurred millions of years ago at high temperatures and deep within the earth.

Hot-water solutions, especially those containing dissolved chloride, sulfate, sodium, and potassium, can be extremely effective in dissolving and transporting the metals in ore deposits. In the exploration for new ore deposits, it is important to determine the conditions, causes, and locations where the valuable metals in these solutions precipitate to form mineable concentrations. Because fluid inclusions hold many of the clues to answer these questions, their examination and analysis has become an integral part of mineral exploration. Most ore minerals form as the metal-bearing solutions cool and give off dissolved gases or react with the rocks through which they are passing. Under ideal conditions, the ore and associated minerals could form as perfect, flawless crystals. However, under the real conditions of ore formation, there are many small imperfections that trap tiny droplets of the metal-bearing fluids. Once trapped, the fluids often remain unchanged except for some shrinkage as the mineralized area cools; this results in the development of a small vacuum bubble as seen in Figure 2.6.

Fluid inclusions are usually studied by cutting or breaking small pieces of rock and examining them with a microscope. By carefully heating and cooling the specimens while observing them, it is possible to determine the temperatures at which they were trapped and the salinities of the fluids. Further analysis using spectrometers sensitive to specific elements in solution may permit determination of the concentrations of metals and other compounds in the inclusions. (Note the small crystals in the inclusion shown in Figure 2.6.) Much can be learned about the types of fluids, the temperatures and pressures at the time of entrapment, and their sequence of introduction or evolution. These data, combined with field geologic observations, can give powerful insights into the mechanisms of ore formation and, hence, into the search for additional ores.

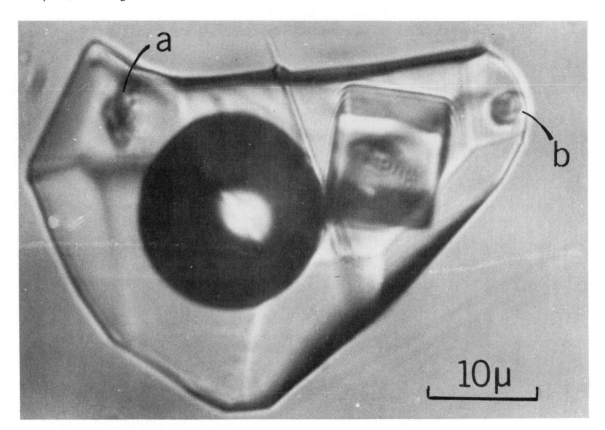

FIGURE 2.6.   Fluid inclusions are droplets of the ore-forming solutions that were trapped at the time the ores were deposited. This inclusion from the Laramesta tin and tungsten deposit in Bolivia contains a round vapor bubble that formed on cooling from its formation temperature of 430°C. The large white salt crystal and the smaller crystals, at *a* and *b*, crystallized from the saline solution as it cooled. (Reproduced from W. C. Kelly and F. C. Turneaure, *Economic Geology*, vol. 65 (1970) p. 651. Used with permission.)

Formation of Basalts and Other Relatively Silica-Poor Rocks

Basalts and other silica-poor igneous rocks are generated by partial melting of Earth's lower crust or mantle. Localized melting appears to result from a differential buildup of radioactive heat and may be followed by rapid upward flow of magma along faults or other zones of weakness with surficial expression in the form of volcanoes or basalt flows. Although these events may be spectacular and life threatening, their impact on resources is usually localized, such as the loss of cropland to volcanic ash fall. The rapid cooling of the lavas prevents the concentration of metallic ore minerals into economically recoverable resources. The minerals are dispersed throughout the lavas. In many areas, including beneath volcanoes, large masses of basaltic magmas are intruded and crystallize at depths of many kilometers. These magmas may *stope* their way upward into the crust by melting overlying rocks or move upward or laterally along major faults. Regardless of their mode of emplacement, these large bodies, which may be hundreds of kilometers across and thousands of meters thick, ultimately reach positions within the crust where they slowly crystallize (Figure 2.7).

Large masses of rock emplaced at 1000°C or more and surrounded by rocks that are poor conductors of heat may take millions of years to crystallize. The slow loss of heat, the incorporation of foreign matter as a result of melting surrounding rocks, and the sequential crystallization bring about major chemical changes in the magmas and may result in the formation of important resources. Crystallization proceeds, in general, following the principles of fractional crystallization. For example, the earliest minerals to crystallize are usu-

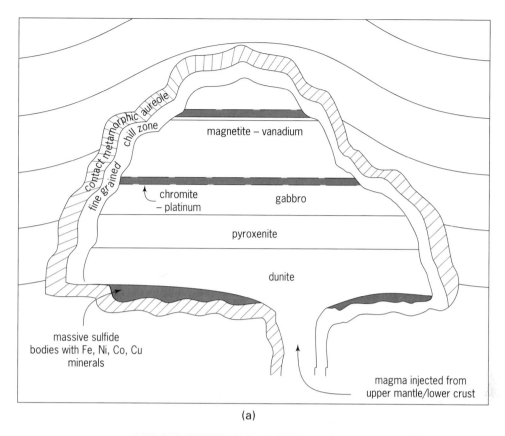

magnetite – vanadium

chromite – platinum

gabbro

pyroxenite

dunite

massive sulfide bodies with Fe, Ni, Co, Cu minerals

magma injected from upper mantle/lower crust

(a)

FIGURE 2.7. (a) After large masses of silica-poor magmas are emplaced or melt their way into Earth's crust, they may take tens of thousands to millions of years to crystallize. During crystallization, these intrusions acquire a distinctly layered structure with some zones being rich in minerals useful as mineral resources. (b) Chromite layers (black) crystallized in the large layered intrusion called the Bushveld Complex in South Africa. As the result of uplift and erosion, the chromite layers are now exposed along the Dwaal River. (Photograph by B. J. Skinner.)

(b)

ally olivines, $(Fe,Mg)_2SiO_4$, that settle to the bottom of the magma chamber and form layers of dunite, a rock composed primarily of olivine. The next minerals to form are the pyroxenes and calcic plagioclase feldspars that settle as layers of gabbro overlying the layers of olivines. As certain elements are extracted to form the early minerals, the composition of the remaining melt changes such that subsequent minerals are of a different composition. The final result is a layered, coarse-grained igneous rock. The layers are made up of minerals that are iron- and magnesium-rich and silica-poor at the base but grade into increasing iron- and magnesium-poor and silica-rich toward the top.

The layers of olivine-rich rocks are valuable resources because the olivine is widely used in refractory bricks and as casting sand. The layers rich in metal sulfide and oxide minerals that may form at particular stages during crystallization of the magma usually are much more valuable. For example, if the limit of sulfur solubility in the magma is exceeded as it cools, the sulfur expelled from the magma is very efficient in combining with iron, nickel, and copper, forming small droplets of a metal sulfide liquid. This liquid is more dense than the silicate melt, and, if there is sufficient time, the droplets settle in response to gravity and can form masses of millions of tons of metal sulfide ores. Such masses are found at the great nickel mining centers at Noril'sk in Russia or at Sudbury, Ontario, Canada.

Under other chemical conditions, the magma may become saturated in chromium so that the mineral chromite, $FeCr_2O_4$, begins to crystallize and settle, forming layers or *beds* (Figure 2.7b and Figure 8.6) up to several meters thick that may persist for tens to hundreds of kilometers. Such layers constitute the world's richest chromium ores. Either simultaneously with chromite precipitation or as a separate event, platinum metal minerals may begin to crystallize and settle out of the magma. The simultaneous precipitation of chromite and platinum minerals formed the UG-2 bed, a 1.3-meter thick layer in the Bushveld Igneous Complex in South Africa that is now mined for both metals. Separate precipitation of platinum minerals formed the *Merensky Reef*, a 30–45-centimeter thick layer that is traceable for at least 300 kilometers across the Bushveld complex.

The chromite layers generally form early in the crystallization of these large igneous bodies. In contrast, similar magnetite (Fe_3O_4) layers form somewhat later during crystallization. These layers, as shown in Figure 8.8, resemble the chromite layers in thickness and extent but may contain large quantities of vanadium that occurs bound up in solid solution in the magnetite.

Regional Metamorphism

Regional metamorphism is the modification of large masses of rocks in response to rising pressure and temperature when they have been buried to depths of 10 kilometers or more. As depths of burial increase, the pressure from overlying rocks increases at a rate of about 230 kilograms on each square centimeter for each kilometer of depth, and temperature increases at about 25°C for each kilometer of burial. Thus, at depths of 10 kilometers, the pressure is about 2300 kilograms per square centimeter (or about 16 tons per square inch), and the temperature is about 250°C (or 480°F). At burial depths of 20 kilometers, the

temperature and pressure are about twice these values. Under the elevated pressure and temperature conditions of regional metamorphism, the common minerals of sedimentary rocks recrystallize, and the rocks are transformed mineralogically and texturally as shown schematically in Figure 2.8.

Commonly observed effects of regional metamorphism include the conversion of shales into slates (and at higher grades into schists or gneisses), limestones into marbles, and sandstones into quartzites. All of these can be used as building materials, but the regionally metamorphosed rocks are harder and more durable. Furthermore, marble is much more prized than limestone for use in dimension stone and sculpture.

Different compositions of sedimentary rocks or compositional changes brought about by fluids squeezed out of the rocks during metamorphism can result in formation of some resources. Small amounts of garnet are common in high-grade metamorphic rocks, but where conditions have been ideal, the garnets may become very abundant or very large. Garnets as large as basketballs have been found at Gore Mountain, New York (see Figure 10.31). Similarly, kyanite (Al_2SiO_5) is common in small amounts in many high-grade regional metamorphic rocks, but locally (as at Willis Mountain, Virginia) it may become the dominant mineral. These deposits are rare but very valuable as sources of materials for the preparation of many kinds of ceramics. Some silica-poor but aluminum-rich zones of high-grade metamorphic rocks contain sufficient amounts of corundum to be mineable for use as abrasives.

Contact Metamorphism

Contact metamorphism is the transformation of minerals in response to the heat and fluids released by igneous intrusion. It occurs in zones adjacent to the intrusions and may vary in thickness from a few meters to several kilometers depending upon the size of the intrusion and the amount of fluid released. The baking effects on rocks adjacent to the intrusions are often similar to the thermal effects of regional metamorphism except that they are more localized. Shales adjacent to intrusions often resemble baked ceramic materials; limestones are locally recrystallized into marbles; and sandstones are converted into quartzites.

The most important resources formed by contact metamorphism are metalliferous ores, called skarns, that may occur at the margin of the intrusion or extend into the surrounding rocks (Figure 2.9). Skarns commonly contain iron oxides as well as sulfides of copper, lead, zinc, and iron; gold and silver are usually present and locally may be rich. The ores are deposited by fluids given off by the cooling igneous intrusion or by fluids in the adjacent rocks which are set into convective motion by the intrusion. Although skarn deposits may occur in many types of rocks,

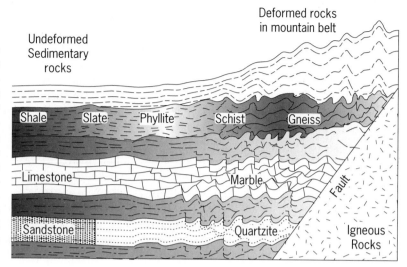

FIGURE 2.8. Idealized cross section through an area of regionally metamorphosed rocks. Progressing from left to right the rocks have been subjected to higher temperatures and pressures. Consequently shales are converted to slates, then to phyllites, then to schists, and ultimately to gneisses. Limestones are converted to marbles during the recrystallization that accompanies regional metamorphism, and sandstones are converted into quartzites.

they are generally most extensively developed adjacent to intrusion of silica-rich rocks because they usually contain more fluids that silica-poor intrusions. They are also usually better developed in limestones than in shales or sandstones because the limestone is more reactive and is relatively easily replaced by the sulfide or oxide ore minerals. A good example of limestone replacement by iron minerals is the Cornwall iron deposit in Pennsylvania, which is discussed in Chapter 7 and illustrated in Figures 7.2 and 7.3.

Contact metamorphic zones and the vein deposits that extend outward from them are, in some parts of the world, major sources of the most important gemstones. These are, however, usually very special environments where unusual elements concentrate (e.g., beryllium to form emerald, $Be_3Al_2Si_6O_{18}$) or where aluminum is more abundant that silica (e.g., to form the colored forms of corundum, Al_2O_3, that we call sapphire and ruby). These minerals are very resistant to weathering and are commonly extracted from weathered

zones or from sediments into which they have been transported during erosion.

SURFACE PROCESSES

The surface of Earth is a dynamic environment that is subjected to a wide variety of climatic and geologic processes. Some processes occur at very rapid rates, such as volcanic eruptions, floods, and tornadoes; others, such as glacial advances and continental drift, are so slow as to be imperceptible on the scale of human lifetime. Some of these processes are discussed in general here and in more detail in the relevant sections of this book. There are no sharp boundaries between the surface processes and those of the shallow subsurface or between surface processes and those of the marine environment. Processes that act directly on the continental surface transport materials into the marine environment and

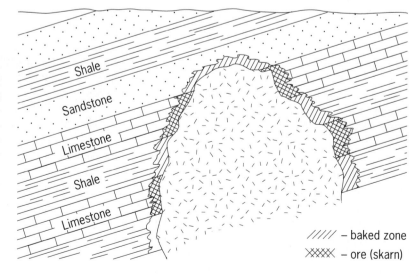

FIGURE 2.9. Idealized cross section through a zone of contact metamorphism formed adjacent to an igneous intrusion. Metal-bearing sulfide or oxide ore deposits most often form where the heat from the intrusion and hydrothermal fluids react with, and often replace, limestones. Adjacent to the intrusions, shales are baked to form hard ceramic-like rocks called hornfels, and sandstones usually become cemented to form quartzites.

result in burial and placement of materials into the shallow subsurface zone. Furthermore, the rain that falls on the continents becomes groundwater and the water of the sea. Hence, almost every geologic process links with other geologic processes in the dynamic evolution of Earth and the mineral resources it contains.

Weathering and Erosion

Earth's surface is characterized by constant changes and movement. The changes in rocks and minerals in response to agents such as rain, wind, frost, and biological activity are known as **weathering,** and the movements of materials downslope or down stream in response to gravity is **erosion.** Weathering may form or destroy the rocks or minerals that constitute resources, and erosion may concentrate or disperse these materials. A few examples are discussed below to demonstrate how these processes affect resources.

The weathering of igneous and metamorphic rocks is a continuous process on Earth's surface, but weathering rates vary widely and depend on factors such as moisture, temperature, and availability of organic matter. The common minerals that make up igneous rocks respond quite differently to weathering. Quartz grains are very resistant to chemical attack and merely weather out to accumulate in soil zones, in streams, and on beaches. The feldspar minerals are transformed by removal of some of their cations (K^+, Na^+, Ca^{2+}) and by their hydration (addition of water as OH^- into their structures) into clay minerals. The micas are already quite similar to clay minerals in structure and are also converted into clays. Ferromagnesian minerals such as olivine or pyroxene usually decompose relatively rapidly with the release of their metals (Fe^{2+}, Mg^{2+}) and silica, which may dissolve in water or be in a colloidal form. These transformations usually result in the formation of a very valuable, if not immediately obvious, resource, the soil. Whereas the minerals of igneous rocks, even if broken into very fine fragments, would serve only as a very poor base in which to grow crops, the minerals of the soils, especially the clays with their ability to store and release nutrients to the plants, provide the base for the world's agricultural production.

Weathering zones and soils vary widely in composition and texture, and some soils can be directly exploited to provide valuable resources. The weathering of some types of rocks under certain conditions can result in the development or accumulation of particular minerals. Probably the most widespread resource of this type is **clay.** Depending upon the type of clay and its color and purity, it may be extracted for use in making bricks, various ceramics, paint extenders, paper coatings, or even fine china. Another very important resource resulting from the weathering process is **bauxite** (see Figure 7.20), the world's major source of aluminum. Under conditions of subtropical to tropical weathering, rocks and soils may be subject to extreme leaching that extracts all but the most insoluble constituents. Leaching may gradually re-

move nearly all elements until the residual mass is highly enriched in aluminum hydroxides and can be mined for the aluminum. Under only slightly different conditions, it is not aluminum but iron hydroxides that accumulate as the other elements are removed; the result is a **laterite,** which may constitute a low-grade iron ore.

Weathering may also destroy potential resources. The deposits of metal sulfide minerals that form as a result of hydrothermal activity are rapidly attacked and decomposed by weathering processes if exposed by erosion. The iron sulfide pyrite, FeS_2, usually abundant in such deposits, rapidly decomposes, forming sulfuric acid that then dissolves away the valuable metals, leaving only a spongy mass of iron hydroxides of little or no value (Figure 2.10).

Once weathering has reduced the original rocks to fragments or individual mineral grains, the processes of erosion may transport these materials. Erosion may disperse previously concentrated minerals, may transport materials in roughly their same proportions, or may selectively concentrate minerals on the basis of their size durability, or density. The resources most commonly formed by weathering and erosion are sand and gravel. The processes that break down rocks allow them to be moved by flowing streams and rivers, and the abrasion during transport rounds the particles. As a result of the sorting of particles by size and weight, fragments ranging from cobbles or large pebbles down to fine sands and silt, depending upon the velocity of the water, may be accumulated. The finest and most resistant particles accumulate where rivers enter lakes or the sea and where wave action forms beaches (Figure 2.11). The accumulation of sediments

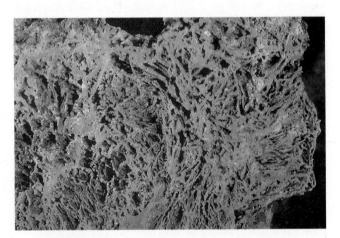

FIGURE 2.10.   Gossans are the weathered remains of many ores where they are exposed at the surface of the earth. The breakdown of iron sulfides, such as pyrite, generates acids that leach other metals from the ore masses and leave a characteristic spongy porous mass of iron hydroxides. Gossans have been used for iron ores but are usually only valuable as guides to the potential of ore-bearing zones below the weathered materials.

PLACER DEPOSITS: PANNING GOLD AND MINING GRAVEL

The processes of weathering and erosion are constantly at work decomposing the rocks of the continents and redepositing the material in rivers, lakes, and the oceans. These processes destroy many mineral resources by dispersing them. At the same time, however, new deposits may be created, such as *placer* deposits. The term placer is derived from the Spanish *plaza* meaning place.

During the transport of rock fragments by running water, there is a systematic sorting of the particles according to size and density. This process can be extremely efficient and can result in the concentration of some kinds of minerals into economically recoverable deposits. It was discoveries of placer gold that led to the establishment of all of the major gold mines before the development of sophisticated geochemical exploration methods in the past 30 years. The discovery of placer gold led to the opening of the first American mines in North Carolina in 1803, to the California gold rush in 1849, to the Black Hills mines in 1876, to the Australian rush in 1851, to the Klondike and Yukon in 1896, and to the world's largest gold deposits in South Africa in 1886. Placer mining has now been overshadowed by hard rock mining, but placer exploration techniques are still widely used in exploration, and gold panning for placer grains is a widespread hobby.

Placer gold deposits form because the specific gravity of gold (19.3 grams per cm^3 for pure gold) is so high relative to that of common minerals (about 2.6 grams per cm^3 for quartz, feldspar, etc.) that running water will constantly winnow out the lighter minerals while leaving concentrations of the heavier minerals. In essence, the gold panner tries to reproduce the action of a flowing stream by creating a water turbulence to separate minerals and a water flow to carry the unwanted minerals away (Figure 2.12). Gold pans vary in size and shape, but all are basically shallow conical dishes. Once gold-bearing sediment has been placed in the pan with water, the panner gently tips the pan and attempts to create a circular swirling motion that simulates stream flow. The movement of the water washes the lighter grains ahead and up the sides of the pan, while the gold and other heavier minerals remain behind at the lowest point in the pan. By careful swirling, the lighter minerals are selectively washed over the edges of the pan. The first to be separated are the lightest grains (quartz, feldspar, mica, clay, etc.), leaving the gold with the heavy minerals or "black sand" (minerals that are dark in color and have specific gravities of greater than 3.0 grams per cm^3). The most common minerals in the black sand are usually ilmenite ($FeTiO_3$, black, shiny, nonmagnetic), magnetite (Fe_3O_4, black, shiny, magnetic), and zircon (tan to pink, glossy, nonmagnetic); these are generally discarded but may be of economic value if quantities are sufficient. Continued careful swirling of the mixture of heavy minerals and gold in water will then push the black sands ahead leaving the gold grains at the rear where they can be seen and removed.

The same processes that form placer gold deposits form much larger placer sand and gravel deposits. The volume of sand and gravel in a deposit is generally at least one million times greater than the gold present, and, of course, many sand and gravel deposits contain no gold at all. In the United States in the mid-1990s, the total value of the sand and gravel mined was greater than the value of all of the gold mined from all types of gold mines (virtually all of it from hard rock mining). Furthermore, the country mined three million times more sand and gravel than gold per year. Thus, placer deposits, although generally thought of in terms of gold, are actually much more valuable for their sand and gravel contents.

as sand and gravel bars in rivers and as beaches along the shores of lakes and oceans constitutes one of the largest resources, in terms of volume, used by modern society. Our construction of roads and buildings depends on the very large quantities of sand and gravel that have been deposited in ancient rivers and oceans as well as those still forming today.

The erosional processes that sort sands and gravels are also very efficient in concentrating certain other valuable resources such as gold, tin, and titanium. The minerals that make up these concentrations, known as *placer* deposits, are all characterized by resistance to weathering and abrasion and by having a high density. Consequently, they may be transported long distances in streams and rivers after weathering out of their original rocks. Their high densities commonly result in their being segregated from quartz sand grains of the same size and also allow for the use of relatively

FIGURE 2.11. Beaches, such as the one shown above, constitute huge potential masses of sand for construction purposes. Many beaches are, however, highly valued as recreational areas and will never be used as sources of building material.

simple separation procedures to recover them (see page 25 and Figure 2.12). These minerals weather-out intact as the surrounding minerals of the original rocks dissolve or decompose. Once liberated, their downstream movement is usually very irregular, with long periods resting in sediments on the bottom of a river or stream, interspersed with brief episodic movement at times of heavy rains. If the rivers flow into the ocean, the valuable mineral grains may be deposited on beaches where wave action and longshore currents will gradually disperse them. The tin and titanium oxide minerals are gradually worn and chipped during erosion and thus get smaller as they proceed downstream. The malleable gold grains are rounded and flattened and are slowly reduced in size during transport. Although diamonds are formed within the mantle of the earth (see Chapter 10), many diamonds have been released by weathering and transported significant distances by rivers. Because of their extreme hardness, they

survive the erosional processes very well, and many are now recovered from placer deposits.

Evaporation

The evaporation of water at the surface of Earth (or from soils) concentrates dissolved salts and may leave them behind as crusts or beds (Figure 2.13). Evaporation occurs everywhere, but the effects become most significant and noticeable in arid regions where substantial deposits can be produced. The Dead Sea in Israel and Great Salt Lake in Utah are two well-known examples where the evaporation of initially *fresh* water has produced lakes that are now so concentrated in salts that the water is saturated and salt is precipitating out around the margins. However, smaller and less well-known saline lakes and deposits occur in the arid regions of all continents. In most places, the principal dissolved constituent to precipitate is sodium chloride (NaCl, the mineral halite, or common salt) along with lesser amounts of gypsum ($CaSO_4 \cdot 2H_2O$). In some places or under conditions where evaporation is even more intense, there may also be the precipitation of potassium, magnesium, or calcium salts.

Along the margins of some enclosed seas (e.g., the Persian Gulf), evaporation can form broad salt flats. Here, episodic flooding with seawater can result in significant thicknesses of salt and gypsum. The geologic record contains many very thick sequences of salt that apparently formed, not as a result of repeated periods of total evaporation of water, but in slowly subsiding basins that episodically received an influx of seawater. Continuous evaporation resulted in the waters becoming saturated, with consequent precipitation of salts on the floor of the basin. Rates of salt precipitation apparently corresponded roughly with rates of subsidence and resulted in the development of salt beds more than 1000 meters thick. In a somewhat similar way, the evaporation of water in lakes with unusual chemistries, commonly influenced by local volcanic exhalations, has episodically formed thick

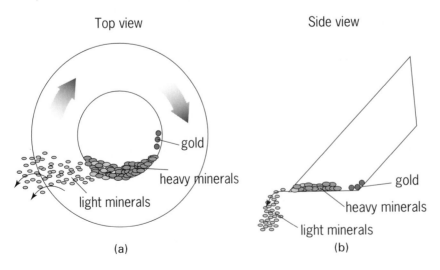

Top view   Side view

(a)   (b)

FIGURE 2.12. The gold pan has long been used to separate nuggets of placer gold from other sediments. (a) Top view of the gold pan showing the circular motion of water in the pan and how it is used to push the light minerals ahead of the *heavy minerals* and the gold grains. (b) Side view of the pan showing how the light minerals are pushed outward and over the edge of the pan leaving the *heavy minerals* and gold behind.

FIGURE 2.13. The evaporation of water from lakes and marginal basins along oceans results in the concentration of dissolved substances and may result in the precipitation of salts such as the halite (NaCl) as shown here at Don Juan Pond in Antarctica. Such salt deposits occur in the arid regions of all continents and are commonly exploited. This same process has occurred throughout geologic time and has resulted in the formation of some salt sequences up to nearly 2 kilometers (5000 feet) thick. (Photograph by J.R. Craig)

sequences of sodium sulfate. Such lakes, while not common in the geologic record, have left us with valuable resources.

Nitrates are rare in the geologic record because they are very soluble and are easily dissolved away by even modest amounts of rain. However, because of the extreme dryness of the Atacama desert of Chile, nitrate-rich sea spray formed outcrops of nitrates along the shoreline that once served as the world's most valuable fertilizer resources. These are discussed in Chapter 9.

SHALLOW SUBSURFACE AND DIAGENETIC PROCESSES

The shallow subsurface region is a zone in which rocks and minerals are influenced from above by downward percolating **meteoric** water, from adjacent areas by migrating fluids (Figure 2.14), and locally from below by rising thermal waters. It is a complex zone that may be composed of freshly deposited sediments or of previously deeply buried igneous,

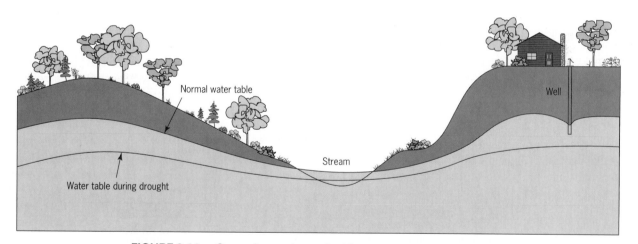

FIGURE 2.14. Groundwater is a valuable resource and provides the water supplies for much of the population of Earth. Depending upon the types of rock and soil, the vegetation cover, and the slope of the land surface, some portion of rainfall percolates into the subsurface. The boundary between the overlying unsaturated soil zones and the underlying saturated zone is the water table. The shape of the water table generally is similar to the shape of the ground surface, and the water table intersects the ground surface, at permanently flowing streams and lakes.

metamorphic, or sedimentary rocks that are being exposed by erosion. Where it consists of young sediments, it is a zone in which there is often significant **diagenesis**—the low-temperature modification, recrystallization, and cementation of sediments—because original trapped fluids are being squeezed out of the sediments as they become buried. In contrast, where it consists of metamorphic or igneous rocks, it is commonly a zone in which the preexisting minerals are breaking down to form new minerals, especially clays.

In many parts of the world, the most valuable resource in the shallow subsurface zone is fresh water. This zone contains most of the accessible fresh water for human use, much of it in water-bearing beds called aquifers. The water moves between particles (e.g., in sands and gravels), along fractures (e.g., in igneous and metamorphic rocks), or in open solution tunnels (e.g., in some limestones). The movement is in response to gravity, hence the water flows from higher elevation (recharge areas) to lower elevation (discharge zones). The flow is usually slow because the openings through which the water passes are small. Thus, the aquifers act as strainers to remove any large particulate matter, while bacterial action decomposes suspended organic or other contaminant material. At the same time, there may be dissolution or precipitation of other materials, such that the waters have a changing chemistry and they, in turn, slowly alter the rocks.

Among the most important processes active in the shallow subsurface zone are those that begin the transformation of buried terrestrial and marine organic matter into fossil fuels (Figure 2.15) as discussed in detail in Chapter 5. Most organic material that falls to the surface of the land or to the floor of the sea is rapidly decomposed by the action of a variety of organisms including bacteria and leaves no record of its former existence. Under some conditions, there is either a long-term buildup of organic debris (e.g., a peat swamp that is slowly subsiding with continuous overgrowth of new plants) or a rapid burial of organic matter so that it is protected.

If organic matter is buried in a slowly subsiding package of sediments, as in the delta of a large river (e.g., the Mississippi), it becomes subjected to a slow increase in pressure due to the overlying sediments and a slow increase in temperature due to the heat escaping from the interior of Earth. This burial process may continue for millions of years, and the overall effects of the rising temperature and pressure are the breakdown of the original organic structure and an increase in the ratio of carbon to hydrogen in the material. Land plant material, rich in cellulose, is transformed slowly through stages we recognize as **ranks** of coal (lignite, bituminous, anthracite). In contrast, marine planktonic debris that is poor in cellulose is transformed first into a waxy material called **kerogen** and then, gradually, into the viscous liquid called petroleum.

Natural gas is actually generated at two stages as a result of two very different processes. Immediately after burial, organic matter is usually subjected to attack by methanogenic bacteria. These bacteria consume organic debris and release *biogenic* methane, CH_4, the principal component of natural gas. The gas may slowly escape, as in some of the bubbles seen coming to the surface in swamps and bogs, or it may remain trapped in sufficiently large quantities to be extracted. The bacteria, although ubiquitous in near-surface environments, do not survive the rising temperatures encountered during deeper burial. On the other hand, the rising burial temperatures, which often more or less conform with the average geothermal gradient of 25°C/km, result in some breakdown of large organic molecules into smaller ones, releasing methane. This *thermogenic* methane, so-called because it forms as a result of temperature increase, can become a major resource in petroleum-bearing strata or in coal beds where it may also be a resource or a danger to underground mining.

MARINE PROCESSES

It is not surprising that the geologic processes active in the marine environment play a major role in the development of Earth's resources (Figure 2.16). After all, oceans presently cover about 70 percent of Earth's surface, and more than half of the exposed continental land area is covered by sediments originally deposited within ocean basins. It is not possible here to review all known marine processes, but some of the most important are outlined below. Furthermore, many marine processes are similar in principle to those active on land, or they represent the final stages of processes that were initiated on land.

The formation of evaporites, already described above, applies equally well to marine evaporites. Indeed, the largest evaporite deposits clearly formed in marginal marine basins that episodically received an inflow of large quantities of seawater. A well-known and important example is the Jurassic age salt that underlies the United States Gulf Coastal region. A thousand-kilometer-long region from Florida to Texas is underlain by beds that are nearly 2000 meters thick and contain billions of tons of salt.

Usually, the sediments eroded from the continents are washed downstream into the oceans and spread along the continental margins. Thus, beaches constitute the largest sand deposits in the world. Numerous placer deposits of gold, tin, and titanium (and a few with diamonds) have been exploited from beaches and near-shore sediments around the world. These are the seaward extensions of the placer deposits described in the discussion of weathering and erosion. The one marine process that has significantly altered the resource potential of some of these is the hurricane. It is now recognized that brief but violent storms, probably hurricanes, are responsible for concentrating marine placer titanium deposits by wave-driven winnowing processes. The results have been large accumulations of titanium minerals at concentrations of six percent (or more) in sediments that may originally have averaged only one percent or less of titanium minerals.

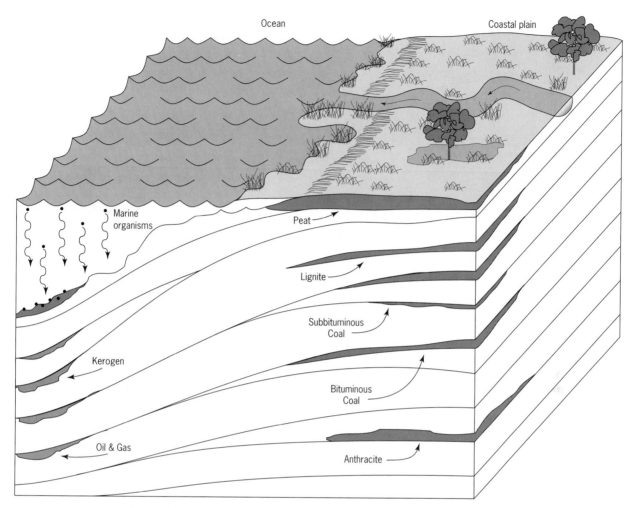

Ocean

Coastal plain

Marine
organisms

Peat

Lignite

Subbituminous
Coal

Kerogen

Bituminous
Coal

Oil & Gas

Anthracite

FIGURE 2.15. Schematic diagram illustrating how the burial of terrestrial organic matter can lead to the formation of coal, and the burial of marine organic matter can lead to the formation of oil and gas. The increasing temperature and pressure at greater depths of burial compact and modify the terrestrial matter as it progresses through the various ranks of coal. Marine organic debris is converted into a waxy material call kerogen, which upon additional heating is converted into petroleum.

The warm, shallow seas along the margins of subtropical and tropic continental areas are today the sites of great coral reefs and limestone beaches (Figure 2.17). The organic and inorganic processes active today in forming these limestones are essentially the same as those that have precipitated the great thickness of carbonate rocks over the past 600 million years. These limestone beds, which are abundant on nearly all continents, constitute a great resource for construction materials (crushed stone, dimension stone, and cement). They were formed as a result of carbonate precipitation by marine plants and animals in a variety of forms, from coral reefs to limestone sands.

Rich phosphate deposits are more localized than the limestones and currently serve as the world's major source of fertilizers. The processes involved in their formation are not thoroughly understood, but it is clear that upwelling phosphate-rich ocean waters may wash across relatively shallow continental shelves for significant spans of geologic time. During these times, there is vast accumulation of phosphatic debris, such as fish teeth and bones, and precipitation of phosphate minerals as nodules, grains, and crusts in beds up to tens of meters thick. It is likely that organic activity influences much of the precipitation of the fine-grained crusts and small rounded grains.

The deep ocean floor is the site of **manganese nodule** formation. These nodules, which usually contain more iron than manganese, occur in vast quantities over tens of thousands of square kilometers of the deep ocean floor. The

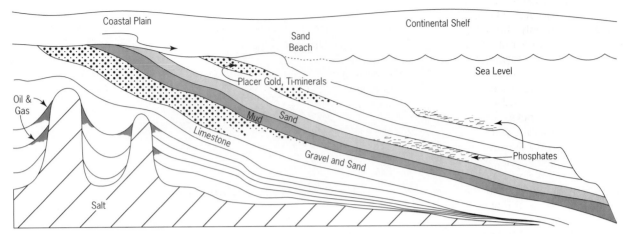

FIGURE 2.16. Highly idealized cross section of a composite continental shelf showing the presence of sands, gravels, limestones, phosphates, placer minerals, and salt beds. The sands and gravels are washed down rivers and deposited as deltas and spread along the coasts to form beaches. Phosphates precipitate by inorganic and organic processes on the outer portions of the shelves. Salt domes may develop locally where previously deposited salt beds are deeply buried. The upturning of sedimentary beds resulting from the upward movement of the salt provides good sites for the migration of oil and gas that form in the sediments from organic matter.

nodules range from about the size of peas up to the size of grapefruit, are roughly spherical, and internally consist of fine but irregular concentric layers of iron and manganese hydroxides. The rates of growth appear to be very slow (~1 millimeter/1000 years), and the precise mechanisms of growth remain unknown. However, it is believed that microbial activity causes much of the precipitation of the metal-bearing minerals.

FIGURE 2.17. Shallow, warm water marine environments such as that at Lee Stocking Island in the Bahamas are the sites for the deposition of limestone reefs and muds. The thick beds of limestone found throughout the world are evidence of former marine conditions similar to those shown here. (Photograph courtesy of the Caribbean Marine Sciences Institute.)

FIGURE 2.18. Ocean spreading zones where crustal plates diverge are commonly the sites of volcanic activity and may be the sites of sulfide ore formation at *black smokers.* Hydrothermal fluids, generated as seawater circulates through the cracks in the oceanic crustal rocks, dissolve and transport metals and sulfur. When the hot fluids reemerge along faults at the spreading centers on the ocean floor, the clear fluids are cooled rapidly, and very fine grained sulfide minerals are formed and appear as a black smoke (see Figure 8.26). The deep ocean floor is also the site of deposition of manganese nodules as the result of organic and inorganic processes; these are potential resources of several metals.

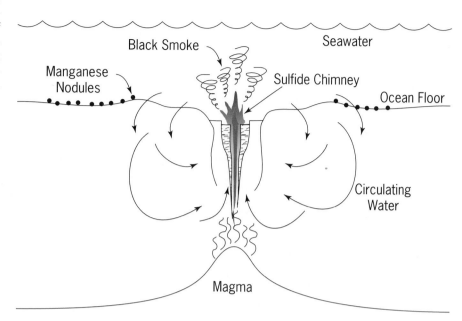

The mid-ocean ridges have long been known as the sites of volcanic activity, such as the extrusion of basaltic lavas, and of associated geothermal activity (as is seen in Iceland). In recent years, these ridges have been found to be the sites of active metalliferous mineral deposit formation (Figure 2.18 and Figure 8.26). Examination of the ridges using submersible exploration vessels led to the discovery of *black smokers,* which are vents on the seafloor from which hot (up to 350°C) hydrothermal fluids are issuing. Upon entering into the cold ocean waters, these fluids rapidly mix, cool, and precipitate very fine iron sulfides that appear as *black smoke.* The hydrothermal fluids issuing from many of these vents have formed large mounds and "chimneys" that consist of ore minerals of zinc, copper, and iron in textures very similar to those found in large ore deposits of much greater age. These active processes are the marine equivalent of hydrothermal activity discussed above under *deep crustal* processes, and they are similar to the processes that have formed many of the world's largest metalliferous deposits.

CONCLUSIONS

Earth's resources are formed by a wide range of geologic processes. Particular resources may be formed by one or more processes, and virtually all of these processes are active in the generation, modification, or destruction of resources. The most important processes are those that concentrate valuable minerals to levels far greater than their normal levels of occurrence in average crustal rocks.

FURTHER READINGS

GUILBERT, J. M., and PARK, C. F., *The Geology of Ore Deposits.* New York: W. H. Freeman and Co., 1986.

HEDENQUIST, J. W. and LOWENSTERN, J. B., "The role of magmas in the formation of hydrothermal ore deposits." *Nature* 370 (1994) pp. 519–527.

SAWKINS, F. J., *Mineral Deposits in Relation to Plate Tectonics,* 2nd ed. Berlin: Springer-Verlag, 1990.

TARBUCK, E. J. and LUTGENS, F. K., *The Earth: An Introduction to Physical Geology,* 4th ed. New York: Macmillan Publishing Co., 1992.

3 EARTH'S RESOURCES THROUGH HISTORY

Hadrian's wall, built between 122 and 136 A.D., was a Roman defensive barrier guarding the northern frontier of the Province of Britain until the end of the fourth century. It extended 118 kilometers (73 miles) across the narrowest portion of Britain and was 6 meters (20 feet) high for most of its length and 3.3 meters thick. (Photograph courtesy of the British Tourist Authority.)

When man rose above the brutish individualism of his primordial state, he turned to the soil, to win food for his family; he paused in his migration; the soil held him; it gave root to the primitive community. . . . But the nomadic habit lingered. . . . The hills beckoned, the sea called, the more venturesome left . . . in search of material wherewith to fashion their implements. They sought gold for ornament, copper for tools, iron for weapons and . . . they became miners. . . . Civilization developed on . . . a basis of . . . metals. The need of them . . . induced enterprising men to probe the hills and scour the deserts in search of the mineral deposits that are distributed with such perplexing diversity in the outer crust of the earth. . . . The miner . . . advanced far across the world, ever pioneering the advance. . . . He was not only the pioneer, but he left marks to show the way; he blazed the trail for civilization. He has done it with geographic exuberance and equatorial amplitude. . . . Trade follows the flag, but the flag follows the pick.

T. A. Rickard, *Epilogue of Man and Metals, 1932*

FOCAL POINTS

- Earth's resources have been used by all cultures throughout history.
- The earliest uses of Earth's resources involved water, salt, and simple tools made from rocks.
- The first metals used by humans, which happened before 15,000 B.C., were probably gold and copper, both of which occur as *native* metals.
- A steady increase in the use of resources reached a peak at the time of the Greek and Roman Empires. This was followed by a prolonged period from about 400 A.D. until the late 1400s, during which there were few new developments.
- The voyage of Columbus and others to the New World opened a period of global exploration and colonialism by several major European countries that lasted almost 400 years. This brought great wealth to the European countries (e.g., gold and silver to Spain) and imposed their cultural influences on the rest of the world.
- The Industrial Revolution during the 1700s and 1800s transformed countries from agrarian and rural to industrial and urban; it greatly expanded the use of mineral resources, especially iron and coal.
- Beginning in the late 18th century, the development of modern chemistry led to the discovery of many new metals and their subsequent utilization.
- Today, every country depends on other countries for supplies of needed mineral resources, and much of the world's production is controlled by large multinational groups or companies.
- The two most well-known organizations involved in the production and control of resources are OPEC (Organization of Petroleum Exporting Countries) and DeBeers (which controls most of the world's gem diamonds).
- The control of strategic world resources continues to play a major role in world politics.

INTRODUCTION

Earth's natural resources are the raw materials from which all products used in our society have been directly or indirectly made. The utilization of Earth's resources either in their natural or processed form dates from our early ancestors' dependence on water and salt in their diets, their need for stone tools, and their use of natural pigments for decorations and illustrations. From such simple and individual needs, mineral resources have acquired national and international importance as they have become the materials of trade and the basis for profit and power. This is perhaps best demonstrated by petroleum, which is the world's most valuable and vital international mineral commodity.

The quantities of various mineral resources used by particular societies vary widely but generally correspond per capita to a nation's degree of development and standard of living. Figure 3.1 illustrates the annual per capita consumption of a variety of mineral resources in the United States. The quantities would be similar for other highly industrialized countries, such as Canada, Britain, Germany, France, Sweden, or Australia. Of course, very few of us, if any, individually use 4700 kilograms (10,300 pounds) of stone or 165 kilograms (360 pounds) of salt in a year, but for our society to provide the vast array of products and services we enjoy, various industries use these quantities on behalf of each of us.

The international importance of mineral resources is evidenced by the fact that the annual value of world crude mineral production exceeds $200,000,000,000 (£150,000,000,000). Processing raises the annual value of these commodities to more than $500,000,000,000 (£360,000,000,000). Minerals account for about 30 percent of all traded materials. This chapter summarizes the changing and growing uses of mineral resources through history as well as some of the influences these resources now have on the politics and economies of modern societies.

RESOURCES OF ANTIQUITY

The beginnings of our uses of Earth's resources are lost in antiquity, but it seems likely that our ancestors' earliest concerns were obtaining water and salt for their diets and suitably shaping rocks for hunting. The constant need for water was a dominant factor in choices of dwelling sites, and it determined early migration routes. Some things never seem to change; in spite of our technological advances, water remains a key factor in the location of major population centers. Meat-rich diets originally provided salt, but the development of societies with cereal-based diets required the use of salt as a food additive. Beyond being a necessary dietary component, salt was also the cheapest and easiest way to preserve food and enhance its taste. Consequently, salt became a commodity of exchange before recorded history, and salt routes crisscrossed the globe long before the birth of Christ. Salt (in Latin, *sal*) was a good antiseptic, hence the Roman goddess of health was named Salus. A Roman soldier's pay, which included a certain amount of salt, was known as *salarium*, which gave us the word *salary*. From this, and the use of salt as payment for slaves, came the expression of a worthless individual being "not worth his or her salt."

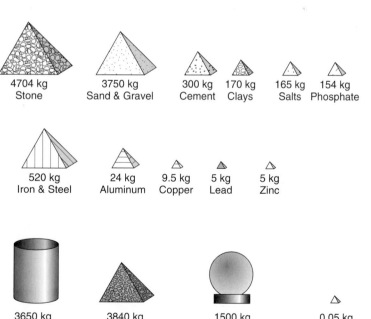

FIGURE 3.1. The per capita consumption of mineral resources is both varied and large. (Data from the United States Bureau of Mines.)

4704 kg
Stone

3750 kg
Sand & Gravel

300 kg
Cement

170 kg
Clays

165 kg
Salts

154 kg
Phosphate

520 kg
Iron & Steel

24 kg
Aluminum

9.5 kg
Copper

5 kg
Lead

5 kg
Zinc

3650 kg
Petroleum

3840 kg
Coal

1500 kg
Natural Gas

0.05 kg
Uranium

United States Total is 5000 million metric tons

The use of rocks as tools extends back at least one million years. At first, stones were crudely chipped into useful shapes, but subsequently, numerous prehistoric peoples developed techniques to shape **flint, obsidian,** and other tough rocks with uniform properties into delicate implements and tools (Figure 3.2). A major advance in tool-making occurred prior to 9000 B.C. when our ancestors began to fire clay to make pottery. The pottery, which represented the first synthesis of materials from minerals, provided an excellent means for the storage and transport of food and water. This led to the development of the ceramic arts, which included brick-making, glazing, the making of mineral pigmented paints, and even glass-making, by about 3500 B.C.

Before 15,000 B.C., gold and copper were the first metals utilized by man because they commonly occur in their metallic, or *native,* states. The first finds were most likely treated as curiosities because the metals felt, looked, and behaved differently than the other brittle rocks; however, the ability to shape these metals into useful and desirable forms

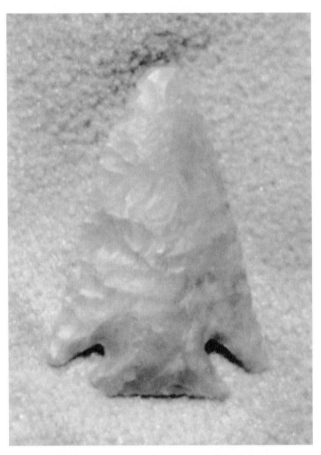

FIGURE 3.2. Tools shaped by the chipping of flint and obsidian were among humans' earliest uses of mineral resources. The arrow point shown here was prepared by the Native Americans in West Texas. (Photograph by J. R. Craig)

developed rapidly (Figure 3.3). Before 4000 B.C., our ancestors had learned that copper could also be extracted from certain kinds of rocks by using primitive smelting techniques in which charcoal supplied the heat to reduce copper ores to free copper metal. Within about a thousand years, silver, tin, lead, zinc, and other metals were also being extracted and ultimately combined to form alloys such as brass (copper and zinc), bronze (copper and tin), and pewter (tin and other metals such as lead, copper, or antimony).

Iron, though much more abundant in Earth's crust than most other metals, is more difficult to extract than gold or copper. Hence, its use occurred somewhat later. It is believed that the first utilized iron metal came from meteorites. It is easy to imagine that if a meteorite were seen to fall to Earth by primitive people, its contents must have evoked much wonder. The strength and hardness of the iron made it superior for weapons. This led to its widespread use and apparently generated numerous myths concerning its magical powers when it was shaped into weapons. Pliny described iron as the "most useful and most fatal instrument in the hand of man." Perhaps its usefulness is best summarized by the lines of Rudyard Kipling's "Cold Iron":

"Gold is for the mistress—silver for the maid—
Copper for the craftsman cunning at his trade.
Good! said the Baron, sitting in his hall,
But iron—Cold Iron—is master of them all."

Although we commonly center our attention upon particular metals by using terms such as **Bronze Age** or **Iron Age,** our ancestors used an increasingly broad range of mineral resources as the ages passed. Simple crudely shaped rock fragments were replaced by carefully shaped knives, arrow points, and spear points. The use of animal hides for storage gradually gave way to pottery and ceramics. Shelters of plant materials and animal skins gave way to more permanent and protective bricks and mortars.

The development of first the Greek and then the Roman Empires saw the extensive development of mining and stone-working industries to provide the building materials for their great palaces, stadiums, theaters, temples, roads, and aqueducts. These cultures not only used much greater volumes of mineral resources, but they also vastly expanded the varieties of such resources. They began to use large quantities of processed resources, such as cements and plaster, to supplement and bond cut stone (Figure 3.4). The Greeks developed domestic metal mines and used silver mined near Athens to finance the fleet that defeated the Persians at Salamis in 480 B.C. They also used gold from northern Greece to support the conquests of Alexander the Great around 330 B.C. As the Romans expanded their control throughout the Mediterranean and beyond, they extracted metals first by plunder, then by tribute, and finally by mining. Examples of such extractions include mercury from Spain, copper from Cyprus, and tin from the British Isles.

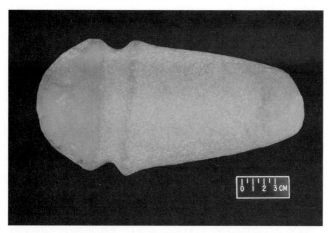

FIGURE 3.3. This stone ax head, prepared by carefully shaping and polishing a piece of fine-grained quartzite, is an example of the tools made by cultures before metals became available. This specimen is from the Tye River area of Nelson County, Virginia. (Photograph by J. R. Craig)

FROM ROME TO THE RENAISSANCE

The gradual collapse of the Roman Empire resulted in a breakdown of its organized society, including the production, transportation, and marketing of mineral resources. The onset of the Dark Ages in Europe saw trade decline, mines close, and most people turning to subsistence through agriculture. Mineral resource needs were met primarily by reusing the materials at hand, and mining was confined to salt needed for food, some alluvial gold recovery, and other metals at a few centers such as Cornwall, Devonshire, and Derbyshire, in England, and Saxony in the Erzegebirge in what is now Germany.

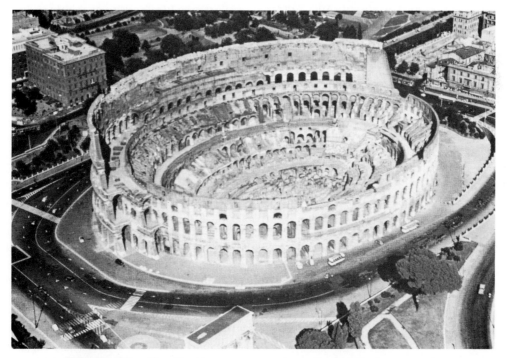

FIGURE 3.4. The Romans were masters of construction as evidenced by the carefully cut and fitted limestone blocks of the Colosseum in Rome. (Photograph courtesy of Istituto Italiano di Cultura, New York.)

Europe's emergence from the Dark Ages began after 800 A.D. and coincided with the discovery and development of mineral deposits in what is now southern Germany. These and other reopened deposits provided metals, especially silver and gold, to use in trade for spices, gems, and silks from China and India. The ancient overland trade routes through Assyria and Persia were replaced by new routes through Egypt, down the Red Sea, and across the Indian Ocean. The flow of metals from northern and central Europe southward changed Mediterranean ports, such as Venice, from small fishing villages to major trade centers.

Spain and Portugal rose to new prominence as Christopher Columbus opened the seas westward to the New World in 1492 and Vasco da Gama found the eastward sea route around the Cape of Good Hope to India. This shifted the trade centers from Venice to the Iberian Peninsula. Spain's fortune grew rapidly as significant quantities of gold and silver from the New World flowed into its coffers. Spanish treasury reports confirm that at least 181 metric tons (5,800,000 troy ounces) of gold and 16,887 metric tons (540,000,000 troy ounces) of silver were brought to Spain between 1500 and 1660. Although these quantities are only the equivalent of today's annual silver production and about one-tenth of today's annual gold production, they were of enormous value in the sixteenth and seventeenth centuries. This treasure helped finance the Renaissance developing in Europe as well as Spain's participation in several wars (Figure 3.5).

The revelation of new lands and precious metals stimulated other European countries—namely, England, France, and the Netherlands—to also look westward. After Pope Alexander VI's decree of the Treaty of Tordesilla—also known as the "Line of Demarkation," which divided South America—England, France, and the Netherlands searched the coastal areas of North America. Although the impacts of their explorations have greatly changed the world, their initial ventures were disappointing because the native peoples they encountered were hunters with no gold and generally no metals at all. The British and French did partially compensate themselves for this disparity of gold distribution through the use of pirates who were only too happy to relieve Spanish galleons of their cargo.

GLOBAL EXPLORATION AND COLONIALISM

Humankind's curiosity and sense of adventure combined with a desire for riches and a need for resources have made us explorers since before recorded history. The Phoenicians, who sailed throughout the then-known world of the Mediterranean, and the Romans, whose empire extended from Britain to the Orient, were among the first great explorers and colonizers to exploit resources from vast areas. It was, however, the explorations of the Europeans from the fifteenth until the nineteenth centuries (Figure 3.6) that left their mark

upon the ownership and exploitation of mineral resources in the twentieth century. Portugal and Spain became the first of the modern European countries to send explorers in search of sea routes to India and the Far East in the 1400s. This culminated in the discovery of America by Christopher Columbus in 1492 and the finding of the route around the Cape of Good Hope by Vasco da Gama in 1498. The new lands and trade routes were encouraging, and finding gold in the hands of natives of Africa and the West Indies provided a strong incentive to explore further. Upon his return Columbus reportedly said, "The gate to the gold and pearls is now open, and precious stones, spices, and a thousand other things may surely be expected."

Conflict over the rights to explore and claim the New World seemed inevitable for Spain and Portugal, the two major Catholic sea powers. The Pope intervened in 1494 to proclaim the Treaty of Tordesilla. This edict drew a north-south boundary 100 leagues (later moved to 360 leagues) west of the Cape Verde Islands. Portugal was granted the rights to lands east of this line, and Spain was granted the lands to the west. Portuguese is spoken east of this line, which is now Brazil. In contrast, Spanish is spoken in nearly all other countries of South and Central America, west of this line. The discovery of gold proved to be a powerful incentive to the Spanish whose conquistadors, under Pizarro and Cortez, rapidly subdued the large indigenous empires centered in Peru and Mexico, plundering their gold and silver. King Ferdinand, in a letter to Pizarro wrote, "Get gold, humanely if you can, but get gold," and Cortez once said, "I came to get gold, not to till the soil like a peasant." The King's and Cortez's desires were richly met as the Spanish galleons carried an estimated 181 metric tons of gold and 16,887 metric tons of silver back to Europe between 1500 and 1660.

The British, Dutch, and French carried out the exploration of eastern North America hoping to find gold and silver just as the Spanish had in South America. They, of course, encountered only forest-dwelling Indians who used little or no metals and who knew nothing of gold. As a result, the exploration and colonization of North America proceeded much more slowly than that of Central America and Western South America. As described in more detail on page 39, the search for gold also led to the great migration to California in 1849, consequently opening up the *American West*.

While the Spanish made great inroads in South America, other European countries explored and established colonies in the coastal regions of Africa. However, it was not until the 1800s, with the Industrial Revolution in full swing, that the great interior of Africa was opened to colonialism. Then, driven by the desire to take possession of all available lands that could provide raw materials and potential markets, the European countries divided the rights of exploitation of all of Africa and parts of Southeast Asia among themselves. Since the middle of the twentieth century, concerns for human rights, the decline of power by the European countries,

Clafsis Hispanica celeberrima, quæ anno celeberrimo. MIDLXXXVIII. inter Galliam Britaniamq̃ venit. & periit.

(a)

FIGURE 3.5. (a) Spain's recovery of large amounts of gold and silver from the lands claimed in the Americas resulted in growing animosity between Spain and England because the English desired a share of the wealth. In the hope of ending English raids on Spanish ships and ports, Philip II of Spain assembled the Spanish Armada, a fleet of 130 ships that sailed for England on May 20, 1588. The defeat by the English on July 29 was a great blow to the prestige of Spain and reduced its influence on the high seas. (Courtesy of the Beverly R. Robinson Collection of the United States Naval Academy.) (b) The silver eight real coin, commonly called a *pieces of eight,* was used throughout the Spanish-speaking world. These fragments show how the coins were commonly chiseled into smaller denominations called *bits.* The most popular bit was a quarter of a coin and led to the slang term *two bits* for the American quarter. (Courtesy of the Colonial Williamsburg Foundation.)

(b)

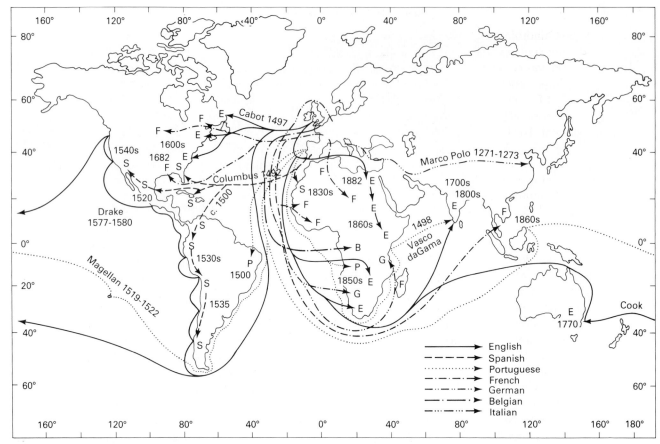

FIGURE 3.6.   Major colonial routes and the extension of the influences of the major European powers from the late 1400s through the late 1800s. There has been no attempt to include all European excursions nor to represent multiple, often successive, colonial influxes.

and the rise of nationalistic feelings have sparked these colonies to, one-by-one, gain their independence.

HUMANS AND METALS

The developing complexity of society linked to an increasing dependence upon a variety of resources is best illustrated by the increasing use of many different metals over time. Archeological records indicate that primitive, or **stone age,** man relied upon tools that were broken or shaped from stone. The earliest records of metal usage are lost in antiquity, but it certainly dates from before 15,000 B.C. Native copper and gold were the first metals used in virtually all cultures because they were the only metals available. These metals were used in the production of ornaments, amulets, tools, and weapons because they can be pounded, carved, melted, or cast into many shapes (Figure 3.3).

By 4000 B.C., copper was being smelted from sulfide ores in Egypt and Mesopotamia. The steps leading to the origins of smelting, the intentional extraction of a metal from its

ores, are unknown. However, they probably began before 4000 B.C. with the accidental melting of metallic copper from copper-bearing sulfide, oxide, or carbonate minerals in a hearth, camp fire, or pottery kiln. Many copper-bearing minerals, such as malachite and azurite, are brightly colored and were easily recognized. Thus, after some of these were reduced by charcoal in a fire and produced copper metal, the people noted the relationship of the minerals to the metals, and intentional smelting was carried out. Either through rapid communication of these techniques or through many separate discoveries, copper smelting was practiced throughout southwest Europe, the Middle East, and India by shortly after 3000 B.C. The earliest smelted coppers were often impure, containing small amounts of arsenic and antimony minerals that also occur in copper sulfides. Thus the smelting created unintentional, but nevertheless useful, alloys that were actually superior to pure copper in terms of hardness, especially when the work was hardened by pounding, a process that removes the brittleness associated with cast objects. As beneficial as the arsenic and antimony were, it was the impurity of tin, either from tin sulfide (**stannite**) or oxide

THE CALIFORNIA GOLD RUSH

The California Gold Rush, like many other important events in world history, resulted from an unexpected discovery in an unlikely place. In the late 1840s, the United States' population was concentrated along the eastern seaboard with only modest numbers of farmers, explorers, and hunters venturing to the Far West. The area known as California, which had its first European settlers (from Spain) land in 1542, was a neglected province of Mexico. The Russians had built a fort near San Francisco in 1812, and American settlers began to arrive in 1841. However, the area remained uneventful. An American revolt in 1846 led to the Mexican War and ultimately to the purchase of the provinces of California, Nevada, Utah, New Mexico, and Arizona by the United States for $15 million.

However, on January 24, 1848, nine days before the treaty was signed, and hence before California actually belonged to the United States, the discovery of gold occurred. James Marshall, foreman at John Sutter's sawmill, picked up two gold nuggets while examining a mill race under construction along the American River (Figure 3.7a). Finding the nuggets to be malleable and not brittle like *fool's gold,* he immediately realized what he had found and took the nuggets to Sutter. Despite Sutter's desire to keep the discovery secret, the workers talked of their findings, and local merchants spread the word. By July more than 4000 men, a quarter of California's total non-Indian population, were digging for gold along the tributaries of the American River. The word of gold reached the east coast by the fall of 1848. In the following spring the most extensive immigration the world had ever seen occurred as the "Forty-Niners" moved to California to become rich. Adventurers came from all parts of the world, with 90,000 arriving by January 1850. Tragically, disease killed one-fifth along the way or shortly after arrival. Wagon trains crossed North America, ships offloaded passengers who walked across Panama to other ships, and some ships braved the long and stormy route around the tip of South America. The population of California reached 269,000 by November 1852 and more than 500,000 by 1856. Many did not complete the trip to California but stopped along the way. Consequently, the Gold Rush did more to populate the American West than any other event.

Many people found no gold, but enough did so that the total production of gold in the United States increased from about 50,000 troy ounces per year in the late 1840s to more than 3,000,000 troy ounces per year in 1853. The value of the gold extracted in any one of the first 10 years of the American ownership of California was more than twice the amount the government paid to Mexico in 1848, quite a good deal! The *Mother Lode* country of California, as this land was known, and adjacent areas were scoured by prospectors trying to strike it rich. Mining towns sprang up with incredible speed, and the prices of food, lodging, and nearly everything else fluctuated wildly depending on the gold available and the whims of the miners. However, within a few years the shallow diggings containing the placer gold became exhausted, causing many once-busy towns to become ghost towns as the miners moved on.

By 1852 large scale hydraulic mining began and remained the major source of gold for about 30 years. These operations destroyed the rivers, caused much silting of navigable portions downstream, and even resulted in the infilling of parts of San Francisco Bay. Court actions were brought in 1884 to stop the devastation, but most of the damage had already been done.

Few names are remembered from the Gold Rush. Sutter never benefited and finally left; he died, heartbroken in Pennsylvania. James Marshall lived on odd jobs and handouts for a few years until his death. The one name that is most known is that of a man who probably never used a goldpan. His name is Levi Strauss, an Austrian tailor (Figure 3.7b), who capitalized on the miners' needs for rugged work clothes. After all, the miners needed good pants whether or not they found any gold. Gold fever gradually waned, with placer operations giving way to hard rock miners. Fewer people mined, and gold production declined, but the impacts of the great immigration have continued to the present day. Not only that, many of those reading this will own a pair of Levi's jeans.

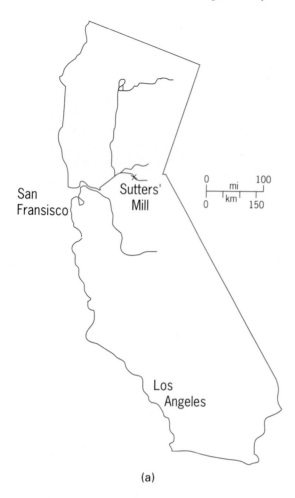

San
Fransisco

Sutters'
Mill

Los
Angeles

(a)

(b)

FIGURE 3.7 (a) Map of California showing the location of Sutter's Mill on the American River where James Marshall found the gold that led to the California Gold Rush of 1849. (b) Levi Strauss, the most famous name from the California Gold Rush, did not pan for gold but made his fortune selling clothes to miners. (Photograph courtesy of Levi Strauss & Co.)

(**cassiterite**), that effectively ended the Copper Age and ushered in the Bronze Age.

The addition of tin to cast copper objects adds considerable strength in its as-cast state, removing the need for **cold-working.** This discovery, first documented in Iran between 3900 and 2900 B.C., spread rapidly throughout southeast Europe, the Mediterranean area, and India, resulting in the development of the tin trade. The first significant sources of tin were probably in Italy, Bohemia, Saxony, and possibly even Nigeria and marked the first instances of foreign dependency on natural resources for many nations. The usefulness of bronze led to a large increase of metallurgical operations; ingots of bronze weighing more than 30 kilograms were being produced in the Mediterranean area by about 1600 B.C. The Bronze Age reached its zenith between 900 and 750 B.C.

Throughout the Copper and Bronze Ages, people in the Middle East gathered gold from placer deposits and extracted it from lode (vein-type) deposits. Because most naturally occurring gold is relatively pure (less than 20 percent of the impurity contents of silver and copper) and occurs as the native metal, the production of gold was more a question of manpower rather than smelting techniques. Silver also occurs in the native state, but it is probable that silver bars found with lead bars at Troy (from 2500 B.C.) were extracted from natural gold-silver alloys by a refining process known as **cupellation.** This process, which is still used today, employs lead, which is relatively easily smelted from the lead sulfide *galena,* to extract the silver from the gold alloy. This silver was formed into a variety of ornaments, but lead was not widely used until the Romans used it in making pipes to transport water.

The earliest archeological iron implements were from meteoritic iron that can be identified by its characteristic nickel contents; these items have been found from the Middle East, the Americas, and even Greenland. The rarity and uniqueness of iron led to its being highly prized; indeed, the knife that lay upon Tutankhamun's mummy within its sarcophagus was made of wrought iron.

The first working of terrestrial iron began about 1300 B.C. in Asia Minor. It may have resulted from the accidental building of a fire on iron-oxide rich rocks, or it was an unanticipated extraction from rocks while trying to refine copper. The early production of iron was made by heating the iron ore in a hot charcoal fire. The iron was slowly reduced when the carbon reacted with it by removing the oxygen impurities and releasing them as carbon dioxide. The fires were not hot enough to melt the iron, but they did soften it enough for it to be pounded or forged into wrought iron. The scale of iron production gradually increased from its initial production of small jewelry items to large-scale production of weapons by about 1200–1000 B.C. Knowledge of iron-working spread from Turkey and Iran to areas around the Mediterranean by about 900 B.C., to Coastal Africa and Great Britain by about 500 B.C., and to India and possibly China by 400 B.C. By the early days of the Roman Empire, iron was in use in nails, hinges, bolts, keys, chains, and weapons. The small foundries dotting the Empire persisted until the Romans withdrew from the land, after which time iron-making, like many other forms of industry, slowed down. In spite of iron's usefulness, the difficulty of producing large quantities kept the supply limited until about 1340 A.D. when the invention of the blast furnace permitted iron workers to obtain temperatures high enough to melt the iron. This technological breakthrough has had a profound and lasting effect on civilization because it made iron, and subsequently steel, cheap and available on the large scale, ushering in the Industrial Revolution.

Molten metal could be easily fabricated into useful cast iron objects using preformed molds. This practice became widespread, but the iron was relatively brittle and soft due to the impurities of carbon and other elements. Nevertheless, as noted earlier, there was a rapidly growing demand for the iron, which consequently fed seemingly insatiable appetites for the forests to provide charcoal fuel. The British Admiralty became alarmed about the supplies of timber for ships, and royal edicts were issued in the 1530s and 1550s forbidding the use of certain forests for manufacturing charcoal. The demand for hardwood to make charcoal devastated the forests in Europe, especially in England, and led to an *energy crisis.* The shortage of charcoal put some iron-makers out of work and led others to seek alternative energy sources, such as coal. After many failures and more than 100 years, iron was successfully smelted in England in the early 1700s using coke produced from coal. The use of coke opened up England's ample coal resources, led to the development of the mining industry, and placed England at the forefront of the Industrial Revolution.

However, there was one more major breakthrough to come—steel. Iron was strong and useful, but it had little flexibility and the castings were brittle. The desire to improve the properties of iron led to the discovery of steel. The first type of steel formed, and still the most widely used one today, is carbon steel. It is formed by blowing air through the molten iron; this lowers the carbon content to less than 1 percent. The result is a harder, stronger, more workable and flexible metal that has thousands of uses. The date of the first steel-making is not known because some was probably accidentally synthesized from time to time in normal melting and forging processes. The birth of the modern steel industry occurred in 1740 when a process was devised to produce a uniform quality of carbon steel.

Although there were many developments in mining and smelting techniques, it was not until the Industrial Revolution in the eighteenth and nineteenth centuries that scientists and metallurgists discovered large numbers of new metals

THE INDUSTRIAL REVOLUTION

The Industrial Revolution, which spread across Europe in the 1700s and 1800s, was made possible by the development of the coal and iron industries. In turn, it stimulated a vast increase in the consumption of these and other mineral resources. The Industrial Revolution converted the western world from a rural and agricultural society, in which people raised most of their own food and made their own material goods, into a largely urban and industrial society. Two events occurring near the beginning of the eighteenth century in Great Britain played major roles in the onset of the Industrial Revolution. The first was the manufacture of the commercial steam engine in 1698 by Thomas Savery. In 1712, Thomas Newcomen improved on Savery's engine and built a steam engine that provided a previously unimagined power to remove water from coal and copper mines. The Newcomen engines, although widely used for more than 50 years, were inefficient, especially in the loss of steam, because there was no way to bore the 40- to 100-inch diameter cylinders perfectly round. This problem was finally solved by James Watt and John Wilkinson who developed and sold a new, more efficient steam engine in 1776. The importance of the Newcomen and Watt engines to early British mining is demonstrated by the presence of more than a thousand abandoned engine houses (Figure 3.8) that still dot the Cornish landscape.

The building of massive steam engines for use in mines and factories required a second major development—the use of coal to make iron and fuel the steam engines. From earliest times through the 1600s, Great Britain's hardwood forests had provided the fuel (as charcoal) for the early iron-making as well as for manufacturing processes, construction, and home heating. By 1700, the British faced a fuel crisis because so much of the forest had been harvested. Although coal had been used locally as a fuel, its use had not become widespread. Not only was wood in short supply, but it also lacked sufficient heating capacity to drive some of the new steam engines. Coal proved to be an abundant substitute for wood, generating more heat than an equal volume of wood. Furthermore, iron-makers

FIGURE 3.8. Wheal (mine) houses that contained the steam engines used to drive machinery and to pump water from the tin mines in southwest England in the 1700s and 1800s still dot the Cornish countryside. This restored structure and beam engine is near Camborne. (Photography by J.R. Craig.)

discovered that coal could be converted to coke, which proved to be better than the charcoal that had once been used for the smelting of iron. The use of coke combined with new smelting and iron-rolling techniques vastly expanded the British capability to produce more iron to make more machines. This, in turn, required more coal as a fuel.

The onset of the Industrial Revolution necessitated the development of transportation systems to move the coal, iron ore, and other freight. Until the early 1800s, waterways were the only inexpensive and efficient means of moving large quantities of materials. The British widened rivers and streams and built an impressive system of canals (Figure 3.9) linking large cities with the coal fields and major rivers. In the early 1800s, the steam engine was modified to drive land vehicles and locomotives, ushering in the great era of railroad transportation.

Although it took some time for the products and the ideas of the Industrial Revolution to reach the Americas and other parts of the world, the ideas arrived with a powerful impact, producing major changes in lifestyle, such as migration of populations to the cities, vast expansion in the mining of coal and iron ore, and the development of much more effective transportation systems.

FIGURE 3.9. The English canal system, here shown at Paddington Junction where the Grand Union Canal joins the Regents Canal, was developed to transport coal, iron ore, and finished products in the early 1800s. (This reproduction was drawn by Thomas Shepherd between 1820 and 1830; courtesy of the British Waterways Museum.)

(Figure 3.10). Many of these metals were at first novelties with few practical uses. For example, nickel was discovered in 1751, and several grains were isolated in 1804, but it remained a scientific curiosity and was not commonly used until nickel-steels were developed in 1889. Similarly, aluminum was first discovered in 1827, but because of the difficulty of its extraction it was very expensive. Consequently, Napoleon III had aluminum forks and spoons for himself and honored guests while lesser guests ate with gold utensils. Only after the development of efficient electrical extraction techniques did the price of aluminum drop from more than $200 per kilogram to less than $1.00 per kilogram, opening a door to many significant uses.

The Industrial Revolution brought iron and carbon-steel into a new prominence both in terms of variety of uses and in the volume of metals consumed. They were used in industrial machines and many of their products. The first

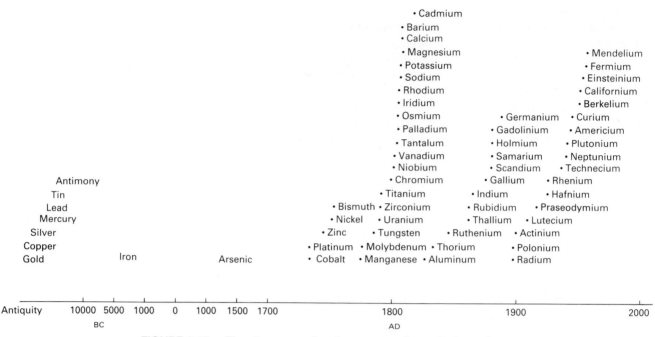

FIGURE 3.10.   The discovery of various types of metals throughout history. Note that the time scale is not linear but is expanded after 1700 when the growth of modern chemistry and the onset of the Industrial Revolution led to the discovery of a large number of metals.

iron-based alloys were carbon steels that resulted from the dissolution of carbon in the iron during smelting. Recognition of the superior properties of this steel relative to iron prompted, in the latter part of the nineteenth century, the search for other useful alloys based on the newly discovered metals. Consequently, metallurgists developed many new varieties of steels that incorporated nickel, cobalt, titanium, niobium, and molybdenum. Such work with alloys accelerated after the development of the internal combustion engine, aircraft, and weaponry during the twentieth century.

The advent of aircraft spurred the development of new lightweight metals, especially aluminum and titanium. When the jet engine replaced the piston engine, new high-temperature alloys were needed, placing more emphasis upon metals such as cobalt, vanadium, and titanium. With the dawn of the nuclear age in 1945, much of the world's attention turned toward two long-known but little-used metals, uranium and thorium. In recent years, there has been remarkable utilization of metals in fields such as medicine (e.g., barium dyes for X-ray diagnostic work and synthetic radioactive isotopes for cancer treatment), electronics (e.g., the use of gallium and germanium in transducers and the rare earth elements in color TV screens), and energy production (e.g., platinum group metals as catalysts in gasoline production and as catalytic converters in automobile exhaust systems). Our progression from the use of simple native metals to accidentally discovered alloys, to engineered compounds, to exotic rare metals, and even to artificial elements is a measure of our technological advancement. At the same time, it is necessary to recognize that our dependence on virtually all naturally occurring metals (and, indeed, all elements) results in a vast and complicated worldwide supply network. We also know that there are no new naturally occurring metals in the earth; thus, we must learn how to make the best use of those available now.

MODERN TRENDS IN RESOURCE USAGE

The modern era of resource extraction and usage began with the Industrial Revolution. In practical terms, the amount of nearly any resource used before that time is negligible in comparison to today's consumption. The onset of the Industrial Revolution brought about the need for more coal, iron, and other metals to build and fuel new machines, supply factories, and develop cities. The demands required larger and more efficient mining methods and transportation systems to move the products. The continued growth of industry, fed both by a growing world population and a rising standard of living, has resulted in ever increasing demands for Earth's resources to feed, warm, house, and accommodate humankind. W. C. J. van Rensberg, a noted resource analyst, pointed out that in the period from 1770 until 1900, when world population approximately doubled, mineral production grew tenfold. From 1900 until 1970, when world population increased about 2.3 times, mineral production increased twelvefold. From 1970 until 2000, when population will have about doubled, mineral production will probably have tripled.

This worldwide trend is especially pronounced in the more developed countries, such as the United States, and is illustrated by comparing the increases in population and increases in the production and usage of some important mineral commodities. Table 3.1 reveals two very important points about the production and use of mineral resources by industrialized nations such as the United States.

1. The rate of mineral resource usage has risen much more rapidly than has population growth.
2. The percentage of mineral resources being supplied domestically has decreased; conversely, the percentage of imported resources has increased.

The first point results from the rise in the standard of living and the expansion of industry that relies upon the mineral raw materials. To a lesser degree, it also reflects the increased size of the population. It is important to note that the United States, with approximately 5 percent of the world population, uses approximately 30 percent of the mineral resources. Also, the per capita use of nearly every commodity in America dwarfs that of developing countries. To bring all peoples up to the American level of mineral resource consumption would require a 700 percent annual increase in the production of each commodity. To do this by the year 2050, when world population is projected to have doubled, it would be necessary for annual production to increase by 1400 percent!

The second point illustrated by Table 3.1 is that the United States (and many other highly developed countries as well) was essentially self-sufficient in its production of most metals in 1875. Now it relies heavily upon imports and accumulated stocks. This lack of self-reliance is, in some cases, due to economics (i.e., United States mines cannot produce some materials as cheaply as foreign sources be-

cause the foreign labor is cheaper or because the foreign governments subsidize mining), but in many cases it is also the result of the depletion of the country's richest ores. Increasing foreign dependence creates a drain on capital, a loss of jobs, and a loss of security over the supply of strategic materials. The degree of the United States' dependence on foreign sources for nonfuel commodities is illustrated in Figure 3.11. This shows some of the broad range of imported materials and the highly variable degree of import dependence. The United States is not alone in its dependence on foreign suppliers; this is apparent from the comparison of the import reliance of Japan. Communist countries such as China have, in contrast, generally had very little dependence on foreign imports. This self-sufficiency has been a result of greater domestic availability of mineral resources associated with a heavily subsidized mining industry (a policy aimed at providing jobs and avoiding reliance on other countries) and a more limited demand associated with relatively smaller internal markets (much fewer consumer goods such as automobiles and domestic appliances).

The general trends in the changing number of working mines, amounts of domestically produced metals, and amounts of imported metals were outlined for industrialized nations as early as 1929 by Hewett (Figure 3.12). The curve defining the amount of metal produced annually starts at zero when mining first commences in a country. It ends again at zero when all ore deposits have been depleted. The area under the curve is a measure of the total amount of metal produced in the useful lifetime of the mines. The curve defining the number of mines is a measure of the rate of extraction of the metal. A small, easily extracted orebody is mined early in a country's development, but the bulk of the metal comes from larger, longer-lived mines. Ultimately, the mines become exhausted, and domestic metal production drops; as this occurs, the country becomes increasingly dependent upon imports from foreign sources. The relative positions of the United States, Britain, and China are shown in terms of

TABLE 3.1

Comparison of the United States production and usage of some important metals and of population in 1875 and 1995

	1875 (× 1000 mt) Produced and Used	1995 (× 1000 mt) Produced	Used	Increase in Production	Increase in Use
Aluminum*	not used	4000	6500	—	—
Copper	18.3	1800	2500	98.0×	137.0×
Lead	53.2	400	1300	7.5×	24.4×
Pig Iron**	2,057	80,000	90,000	38.9×	43.8×
Zinc	15.2	500	1400	32.9×	92.1×
Silver (million troy oz.)	24.5	54.7	129	2.2×	5.3×
Gold (million troy oz.)	1.6	11.3	9.6	7.1×	6.0×
Population (millions)	45.1	263		5.8×	

(Data from U.S. Bureau of Mines; 1995 estimated.)
*Approximately 90 percent of the bauxite from which the aluminum was produced was imported.
**Pig iron in 1875; steel in 1995

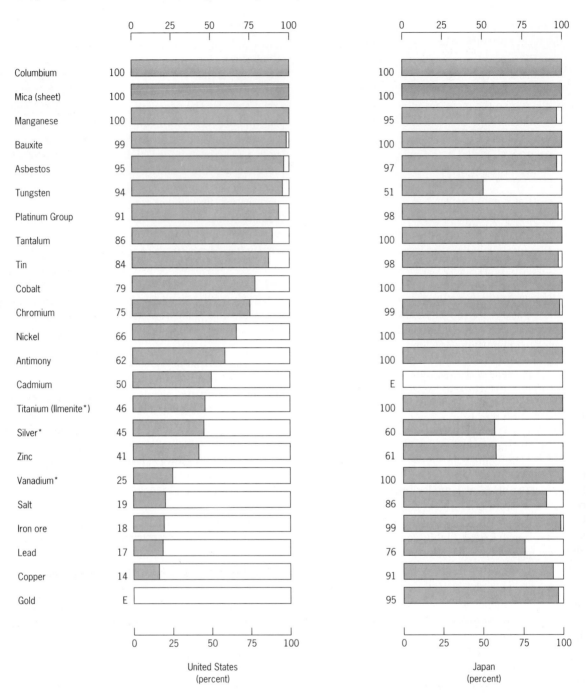

	United States (percent)	Japan (percent)
Columbium	100	100
Mica (sheet)	100	100
Manganese	100	95
Bauxite	99	100
Asbestos	95	97
Tungsten	94	51
Platinum Group	91	98
Tantalum	86	100
Tin	84	98
Cobalt	79	100
Chromium	75	99
Nickel	66	100
Antimony	62	100
Cadmium	50	E
Titanium (Ilmenite*)	46	100
Silver*	45	60
Zinc	41	61
Vanadium*	25	100
Salt	19	86
Iron ore	18	99
Lead	17	76
Copper	14	91
Gold	E	95

FIGURE 3.11. Comparison of the import reliance of the United States and Japan in the late 1980s and early 1990s for several types of mineral resources as shown by the shaded bars. Notice the variable but generally higher degree of import reliance of Japan. (*Very approximate as investor and government stocks are constantly changing. From the United States Bureau of Mines.)

the three curves. These curves are generalizations and do not fit all countries. Indeed, there are industrialized countries, like Japan, that have never had a strong mineral base and many less developed countries, like Bolivia, that have not developed major industrialization.

The aging and depletion of mines in the major developed countries, coupled with their high labor costs and the discovery and development of mines in other parts of the world, has resulted in a dramatic decrease in the developed countries' share of world metal production. This has already

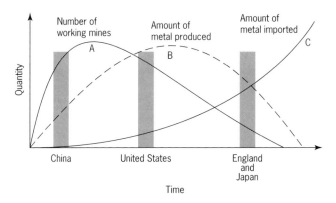

FIGURE 3.12. Traditional stages in mine development, metal production, and imports in industrial countries. Curve A, representing the number of working mines, rises rapidly as a new country is prospected, but it declines when the rate of mine exhaustion exceeds the discovery rate. Curve B, representing metals produced, also rises and falls as mines are worked and eventually exhausted. Curve C, representing metals imported, rises exponentially and expresses the increasing inability of a country to meet its own needs. The approximate present positions for four countries are indicated. With traditional development, each country moves along the time axis from left to right. For example, England was in about the position of the United States in the late nineteenth century, at which time the United States was at about the same stage of development as China is today. Consequently, China is self sufficient in most metals, the United States in a declining number, and England and Japan in very few.

TABLE 3.2

The changing proportion of the United States' production of some important metallic resources

Mineral Resource	United States' Share of World Production (%)				
	1955	*1965*	*1975*	*1985*	*1995**
Copper	37.3	25.4	18.4	13.5	19.0
Lead	14.0	10.1	16.4	11.9	12.5
Zinc	16.3	12.9	7.6	3.7	7.6
Silver	19.7	15.5	11.8	10.9	11.3
Iron ore	28.2	13.4	9.0	6.0	5.8

(Data from U.S. Bureau of Mines.)
*estimated

twentieth century. In the early 1900s, oil provided gasoline to power the growing number of automobiles, but coal continued to be the major energy source for industry. The Depression of the 1930s saw only a slow growth in oil demand due to difficult economic times, and the World War II years saw only controlled growth because of wartime restraints. However, after World War II, the rapid expansion of the world economy, the shift of industry from coal to oil as an energy source, the growth of the automotive industry, and the ready availability of cheap oil from the recently opened Middle-Eastern oil fields led to a rapid rise in the demand for oil. This has led to both an unprecedented dependence of much of the world upon a small geographic area for its major energy supplies and a heavy flow of money to the Middle Eastern countries.

GLOBAL DISTRIBUTION AND THE INTERNATIONAL FLOW OF RESOURCES

The Irregular Distribution of Resources

It is important to realize that mineral resources in general, and the scarce metals in particular, are not evenly distributed within Earth's crust. Furthermore, only 0.0001 to 0.01 percent of the total amount of any metal has been significantly concentrated into economic deposits and is ever likely to be extracted and utilized. Because the geological processes which have concentrated the minerals and metals have not been random, the distribution of the resources and the reserves is also not random. The geographic irregularity of resources, like the number and size of deposits (Figure 3.13) is, in general, a function of the abundance of the resources. The geographic distribution is also a function of the variety of processes by which a resource may be generated. Thus, iron ores, comprising the most abundant metal oxides and generated by a variety of sedimentary, igneous, and metamorphic processes, are widely distributed. Even though aluminum is more abundant than iron in Earth's crust, the most desirable ore of aluminum, bauxite, is only

happened for several metals in the United States (Table 3.2). The slight upturn in the proportion of many metals produced by the United States between 1985 and 1995 resulted mainly from increased efficiency of production for existing mines. This increase is unlikely to be sustained; in fact, mines in the United States are gradually becoming exhausted, and the development of new mines to replace existing ones is unlikely because of high development costs and environmental restrictions. As a result, most jobs in the mining industries and profits from the export of mineral commodities have shifted from the United States and the other major developed countries to developing countries. Another consequence, discussed in a later section, is the increasing dependence of the major developed countries upon foreign sources for strategic mineral commodities.

In terms of impact on lifestyles and revenues generated, the most important modern trend in resource usage has been the rapid rise in the use of petroleum throughout the

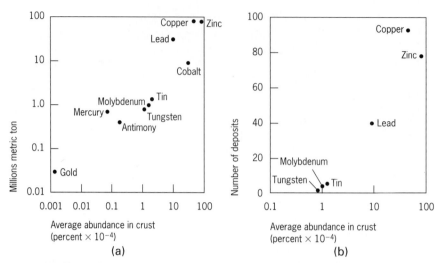

FIGURE 3.13. (a) Size and (b) number of ore deposits of many types of metals as a function of general crustal geochemical abundance. It is apparent that the number and size of the deposits of a metal are larger for metals of greater abundance. (From B. J. Skinner, *Earth Resources,* 3rd ed., Prentice-Hall.)

concentrated into potentially economic deposits by one process: tropical weathering. Bauxite aluminum ore is therefore less available than iron ores and is much more limited in its geologic and geographic distribution. The base metals (copper, lead, and zinc) are nearly three orders of magnitude less abundant than iron and aluminum (Figure 3.13a); however, their ores may form by several geological processes, causing them to be relatively widely spread out in terms of geology and geography. Metals such as platinum, gold, and mercury have very low crustal abundances (Figure 3.13a), are concentrated only by a limited number of geologic processes, and are distributed very irregularly.

Our estimation of the mineral resources available in any area depends on our understanding of the geology of that area and the degree to which exploration has occurred. Thus, it is not too surprising to discover that a few of the major industrial countries where there has been detailed geologic exploration are the sites of many mineral resources and reserves. Areas such as Antarctica, which have not been explored very much, have fewer known resources. It is reasonable to expect that intensive future exploration of poorly known remote areas will add to the number of known mineral resources and reserves.

Even taking the disparities in the degree of our geological knowledge of different areas of Earth's crust into account, it is apparent that the various mineral resources display great geographical irregularities in distribution and abundance. These irregularities result from the nonuniform distribution of the geological processes that formed them and give particular economic and political significance to many types of resources. Nowhere is this more vividly seen than in the Middle East where the large reserves of petroleum have

led to an enormous influx of the world's wealth and a constant vying between the world's powers for political favor.

The irregularity of geographic distribution of mineral resources is exemplified in Table 3.3. It is apparent that five of the major industrial nations (the United States, Canada, South Africa, Australia, and the former Soviet Union, composing 34 percent of the world's land area) possess a disproportionate amount of many of the world's important mineral resources. Other prime examples include the Middle East holding more than 50 percent of the world's known oil reserves, Brazil holding 95 percent of the world's columbium reserves, China holding 44 percent of the world's tungsten reserves, and Zaire holding 50 percent of the world's cobalt reserves.

The existence of mineral reserves within a country's borders has historically been a requirement for the country to have a minerals industry, although Japan has demonstrated an ability to develop such an industry on the basis of imported raw materials. However, the existence of mineral deposits alone is not sufficient to ensure a viable mineral industry. Other factors such as high labor costs or low productivity (tin in England), environmental restrictions (coal in the United States), absence of transport systems (Brazil), availability of cheap imports (oil in the United States in the 1960s), high transportation costs (fluorspar in the United States), and political instability (many developing countries) may deter development of this industry.

Even if resources were uniformly distributed and developed, the differences in population and, more importantly, the differences in demand would still result in the great political and economic significance of minerals. Unfortunately, political and economic aspects have commonly dominated

TABLE 3.3

Percentages of known world reserves of some important mineral commodities possessed by the five major industrial mining countries

	United States	Canada	South Africa	Australia	Soviet Union*	Total
Percent of world land area	6.4	6.7	0.8	5.2	15.0	34.1
Platinum	0.4	0.4	88.6	—	10.5	99.9
Gold	11.4	3.6	42.9	5.9	12.9	76.7
Vanadium	0.4	—	29.8	0.3	50.0	80.5
Molybdenum	49.5	8.2	—	—	8.2	65.9
Potash	0.9	46.8	—	—	29.8	77.5
Chromium	0.4	—	68.6	—	9.3	78.3
Manganese	—	—	46.3	3.3	37.5	87.1
Zinc	11.1	14.6	2.1	11.8	6.9	46.5

(Data from the U.S. Bureau of Mines.)
*as constituted prior to 1991

the other more utilitarian and humanitarian aspects of resources exploitation and probably will continue to do so in the future.

The International Trade of Resources

The irregular distribution of mineral resources and the tendency for industrialized nations to use much larger quantities of resources than they produce result in the massive movement of mineral commodities along world trade routes. In 1990 the annual value of mineral resources in world trade exceeded $500 billion. By far, the most valuable traded commodity was petroleum, exceeding $300 billion. The importance of mineral products to the economies of some developing countries is evidenced by the fact that they account for about 70 percent of Bolivia's foreign exchange earnings, about 70 percent of Chile's total exports, and about 60 percent of Zaire's foreign exchange. Even industrialized countries such as Australia and South Africa rely upon the export of mineral resources for about 40 and 50 percent of their total export values, respectively. Not surprisingly, several of the Middle Eastern oil-producing countries derive nearly all of their export earnings from oil. The United States, like many other industrialized nations, imports large quantities of many raw and processed mineral commodities, although much of this is subsequently exported as finished products.

Although most of us are aware that countries like the United States import many commodities, we tend to overlook the fact that the same commodities may also be exported. Thus, the United States imports and exports coal, oil, and numerous other mineral goods. This seems peculiar at first, but it often results from the differences between shipping rates and overland transportation rates. Thus, the city of Boston has sometimes found ship-transported coal from Europe cheaper than rail-transported coal from the nearer domestic Appalachian fields of Kentucky and West Virginia.

Another cause for the importing and exporting of the same commodities is the **spot market.** Most large corporations require a stable, long-term supply of raw materials and therefore often enter into multi-year contracts with suppliers at pre-agreed prices. When these companies, or smaller noncontract companies, need extra amounts of raw materials, they bid for them on an open, or spot, market in which prices may be higher or lower than long-term contact prices; these prices also may fluctuate rapidly whereas contract prices are stable. The materials available on the spot market vary in quantity, quality, and place of origin from one day to another.

The increasing dependence of the industrialized nations, such as the United States, upon other nations for resource materials clearly emphasizes the need for international cooperation and highlights the impossibility of a country becoming isolationist.

The Control of Resources: Corporations, Governments, and Cartels

Corporations. Private companies and corporations have long been the traditional owners of the mineral industries in capitalist societies. Most began either through single individuals or through small groups who put together *venture capital* to finance the extraction and processing of minerals. The more successful ones prospered, often expanding into large corporations; the less successful went out of business or were bought by the larger corporations. Today there remain many small mining, drilling, and processing operations, but the overwhelming bulk of mineral commodities are produced by a relatively small number of large corporations. Indeed, it is not uncommon to read about large corporations purchasing large mines and mining companies for billions of dollars. Most mineral companies began with a single product, but in recent years there has been a tendency to expand into multiple mineral commodities in order to have greater flexibility in changing markets. Typical examples are the large oil companies, many of which eventually expanded into coal and metal mining. However, as a result of the downturn in metal mining in the 1980s, many of these companies have closed their metal mining divisions.

Throughout the first half of the twentieth century, many American, European, Canadian, Australian, and South African corporations expanded into the developing countries in Africa, South America, and Southeast Asia. Subsequently, especially in the 1960s and 1970s, the desire for independence and control of their own resources led many of these former colonies to alter the original terms of their mineral exploitation agreements with their host country. Either through nationalization (acquiring more than 50 percent control of a company) or through expropriation, the ownership of the mines and oil fields of many of the developing countries has been assumed by the host countries. This has not only weakened the dominance of some of the large mineral companies but has also given greater political significance to their mineral commodities.

The first major act of nationalization to affect American companies and supplies occurred in 1938 when the Mexican government nationalized its oil industry and formed PEMEX, the state-run petroleum company. Nationalization of American oil interests also occurred in Peru during the early 1960s, but it was a more gradual process. More recently, a wave of nationalization has affected the world's copper industries. This began in 1967 when Chile announced plans to gradually nationalize the copper mines developed by major American companies; expropriation was finally announced in 1973. Between 1970 and 1975 the Zambian government assumed complete ownership of its major mines, and in 1973 and 1974 Peru nationalized its major copper producers.

Although nationalization and expropriation have commonly been justified by the host countries on the grounds that foreign companies have been improperly exploiting the local resources, the actions have often backfired because the threat of future repetition limits the willingness of foreign companies to participate further in the development of a country's resources. Without the expertise and venture capital of the major companies, developing countries commonly do not have the financial capability to discover and exploit their resources for themselves.

Governments.   The degree of control over mineral resources exercised by governments varies widely from one nation to another and within individual nations, depending upon the philosophy of the rulers of the country or ruling party. Traditionally, the governments of capitalist countries have regulated mining methods and imposed taxes on earnings or profits, but they have left the extraction of minerals and fuels to private corporations. In contrast, socialist and communist societies have tended to have state operated or quasi-governmental companies. In a capitalist society, a company must mine at a profit or go out of business. Reductions in demand for a domestically produced mineral commodity, resulting from economic recession, importation of lower-priced foreign materials, or other circumstances usually causes cutbacks in production and manpower; if these cuts are too severe, the operation may be forced to close. In socialist or communist societies, mining at a profit is desirable but not essential to survival. Thus, state-run mines often continue to produce large amounts of mineral commodities even at a loss because the government guarantees employment for the workers; also, the government needs the mineral commodities for foreign trade.

In countries such as Norway, unprofitable mines have frequently been subsidized by the government because such expenditure is cheaper than the welfare that would be required for the unemployed from the mines if they were closed. Also, many northern and interior parts of the country would depopulate if the mines did not provide jobs. Other governments, such as those of the Irish Republic and some Canadian provinces, have provided cash subsidies, tax relief, or low interest loans to companies in order to continue operation of unprofitable mines and to maintain jobs.

It is apparent that the governments of the developing countries now realize the importance of their mineral resources to the developed countries and to their own development. They need foreign capital to develop their resources but are no longer willing to give up control to foreign companies. Accordingly, as the United States and the countries of Western Europe become more dependent upon these countries for resources, the negotiation of mining rights, production quotas, taxes and royalties, and the prices of the minerals will become more delicate issues as time passes.

In recent years, the breakup of the former Soviet Union and changes in policy by communist countries such as China and Cuba have led them to ask major international oil and mining corporations to help in developing their resources. Hence, companies such as Texaco, Exxon, and Chevron have been invited to develop partnerships with these governments or newly created private companies in order to exploit the latest exploration and production technologies in producing resources to sell on world markets.

Cartels and Syndicates.   Cartels and syndicates are groups of companies or individuals that join together to control or finance the production of a commodity. Their primary aims are usually to control the availability of their commodity and to maximize the profits from its sale. Numerous cartels, syndicates, and trade organizations (less formal groups) exist in the mineral industries, but most remain relatively inconspicuous and little-known to the general public. The one obvious exception is OPEC (Organization of Petroleum Exporting Countries), which shocked the world by announcing an embargo on shipments to the United States and several European countries in 1973 after it achieved the dominant position in oil production. Ever since, most other cartels have wanted to control the prices of their commodities the way in which OPEC controlled world oil prices through the 1970s. A less conspicuous, much longer-lived, and even more successful organization is the DeBeers syndicate, which has controlled the distribution and pricing of the world's gem diamond supply for nearly a century.

Some of the major mineral commodity organizations are listed in Table 3.4. No other organization has had the success of OPEC and DeBeers because they have not controlled such an important commodity, nor have they controlled any commodity with such dominance. The increasing number of developing countries participating in cartels and other trade organizations suggests that such groups may play a more important role in the future availability of mineral resources. In order to better understand cartels and syndicates, we shall briefly examine the development of the two most important ones—OPEC and DeBeers.

OPEC and Middle Eastern Oil. OPEC became a familiar word worldwide when it achieved international importance. The birth and development of OPEC are rooted in the early discoveries and subsequent partitioning of oil rights in the Middle East. The control of the oil resources of the Middle East did not become an important concern of Western nations until World War I because the energy needs of industrial Europe had been met by coal, and the United States had sufficient resources of domestic oil. However, a far-sighted British engineer, William D'Arcy, was granted in 1901 by Shah Muzaffaral-Din the exclusive privilege to "search for, obtain, exploit, develop, render suitable for trade, carry away and sell natural gas, petroleum, [and] asphalt . . . throughout the whole extent of the Persian Empire" (modern Iran) for £20,000 ($30,000) cash, £20,000 ($30,000) stock, 16 percent of annual net profits, and a rent of £1800 ($2700) per year. Just as D'Arcy approached bankruptcy, oil was finally discovered in 1908. In 1911 the British Admiralty, under Winston Churchill, signed a 20-year supply contract. The coup by the Reza Shah in 1921 required new agreements that provided new income, but at the same time they extended D'Arcy's company exclusive rights until the year 1993.

American interests entered the scene in the 1920s when British and American companies merged; the United States believed that it had an *energy crisis* and sought more foreign oil to supply its growing needs. The American

TABLE 3.4

The major mineral cartels, syndicates, and trade groups

Name	Commodity	Membership
Organization of Petroleum Exporting Countries (OPEC)	Petroleum	Algeria, Gabon, Indonesia, Iran, Iraq, Kuwait, Libya, Nigeria, Qatar, Saudi Arabia, United Arab Emirates, Venezuela
DeBeers	Diamonds	Operates in several countries but does not have members
Intergovernmental Council of Copper Exporting Countries (CIPEC)	Copper	Chile, Peru, Zambia, Zaire
International Bauxite Association	Bauxite	Australia, Guinea, Guyana, Jamaica, Sierra Leone, Surinam, the former Yugoslavia
Tungsten Producing Nations	Tungsten	Australia, Brazil, Bolivia, Canada, China, France, Peru, Portugal, South Korea, Thailand, Zaire
Association of Tin Producing Countries (ATPC)	Tin	Australia, Bolivia, Indonesia, Malaysia, Nigeria, Thailand, Zaire
International Tin Committee	Tin	All major producers and consumers

involvement came through the purchase of oil rights throughout the Middle East, especially the Arabian peninsula, by the famed *seven sisters* Standard Oil of New Jersey (Exxon), Texaco, Gulf, Mobil, Standard Oil of California (SOCAL or Chevron), Anglo-Persian, and Royal Dutch/Shell. Gulf bought Saudi Arabian leases, which had originally been granted to a man named Major Holmes for £2000 ($3000) a year; Holmes had found no oil. SOCAL obtained concessions in Saudi Arabia in 1933 for 60 years for £5000 ($7500) per year, a £150,000 ($225,000) loan, and a royalty of 4 shillings ($0.30) per ton *for all time* and a promise of *no taxes*! Finally, in 1938, after much searching and drilling, the first of the large oil fields was discovered (Figure 3.14). The German threat to overrun North Africa and the Middle East in the early years of World War II ended with their defeat at El-Alamein in 1942. In spite of the consolidation of a patchwork of regional governments and some new negotiation of concessions, the seven sisters increased their control during and after World War II and began major oil exports to Japan and the nations that were rebuilding in Europe. By 1949 they controlled 65 percent of the world's oil reserves and 92 percent of reserves outside the United States, Mexico, and the Soviet Union.

The 1950s was a bonanza period for the international oil companies in the Middle East as production and profits rose to a total of nearly $15 billion. Production of this low-cost oil led to a surplus of crude oil and increased imports into United States markets. Import quotas, which protected those markets for higher priced United States domestic oil, increased the supply of crude oil in the Middle East, which was now forced to seek European markets. This led the international companies, without consultation with the producer governments, to reduce posted oil prices by about 7.5 percent to about $1.80 per barrel; actual oil prices dropped as low as $1.30 per barrel by the mid-1960s. This brought about a significant and unanticipated drop in the revenues to the Arab countries who were enraged by such unilateral action. In September, 1959, the oil ministers of Saudi Arabia, Kuwait, Iran, and Iraq were joined by the minister from Venezuela in Baghdad to form the Organization of Petroleum Exporting Countries. OPEC's main objective was to maintain the stable oil prices at a restored pre-1959 level. OPEC failed to restore prices, but it did succeed in preventing further cuts and gradually increased the proportions of the share of the profits that went to the countries from 50 percent to more than 85 percent. As shown in Table 3.5, three more major oil producing countries joined OPEC within 3 years and the membership ultimately grew to 13 nations. The only country to leave OPEC has been Ecuador, which did so in 1993.

During the 1960s, political and economic divisions within OPEC and the availability of excess production capacity worldwide prevented OPEC from increasing oil prices. The OPEC countries relied upon the increase in oil supplies (from 8.7 to 23.2 million barrels per day in 1960 and 1970, respectively) to provide more oil revenues ($2.5 billion in 1960 to $7.8 billion in 1970). By about 1970, the oil scene was changing as the crude oil output capacity of the world (and especially the United States) dropped. The Suez Canal remained closed as an aftermath of the 1967 Israel-Egypt war, the 500,000 barrel per day Trans-Arabian pipeline (Tapline), which transported Saudi Arabian crude oil to Syrian ports, was ruptured, and the Middle Eastern

FIGURE 3.14. The discovery well at Masjid-i-Sulaiman in Persia (present-day Iran) was a gusher and ushered in the major oil discoveries of the Middle East. (Photograph courtesy of BP America, Inc.)

TABLE 3.5

Membership of the Organization of Petroleum
Exporting Countries (OPEC)

Algeria	Saudi Arabia*
Ecuador**	United Arab Emirates
Gabon	Abu Dhabi
Indonesia	Fujairah
Iran*	Sharjah
Iraq*	Dubai
Kuwait*	Ras al Khaimah
Libya	Ajman
Nigeria	Umm al Qaiwain
Qatar	Venezuela*

*organizing members in 1960
**resigned in 1993

Arab world grew hostile toward the West in general and toward oil companies in particular. In 1971, OPEC began to form a united front and even threatened an embargo; consequently it won price concessions, which raised the price to about $3.00 per barrel. Arab frustration over the stalemated Arab-Israel conflict and the reluctance of oil companies to raise prices grew until late 1973.

On October 6, 1973, Egypt and Syria moved militarily to dislodge Israel from land it had held since 1967. As a result, the atmosphere at the OPEC meeting that began in Vienna two days later was electric. OPEC moved swiftly in rejecting company proposals to raise oil prices by 8 to 15 percent and countered with a staggering 100 percent increase proposal. On October 16, the price was finally pegged at a 70 percent increase ($5.12 per barrel), and on October 17, OPEC pronounced that oil-consuming countries were divided into four categories. The United States was among the *embargoed* nations. The communique said that the Arab oil cutback would let the United States know "the heavy price which the big industrial countries are having to pay as a result of America's blind and unlimited support for Israel."

Panic struck the oil industry and the Western world in general as the principal energy source of the industrialized nations, previously assumed to be always cheap and available, suddenly became scarce and expensive. By January 1979, OPEC raised oil prices to $11.65 per barrel, and the energy crisis caused lines of customers at gasoline stations. OPEC had become a household word.

Although there have been no more embargoes, OPEC was very effective in raising the price of world oil and did occasionally threaten to withhold oil (Figure 3.15). The rapid rise in the price of oil, especially between 1979 and 1981, stimulated the exploration for new oil fields, substitution of other fuels, and conservation.

The success of the new exploration was coupled with a price that was high enough to make previously known, but uneconomic, oil profitable and resulted in a significant increase in the world's oil supply. England, Norway, Mexico,

and many other countries became major exporters of oil, thus providing competition for OPEC. This resulted in a gradual slide in the price of oil after the peak of about $35 per barrel in 1980 and 1981. The culmination came at the end of 1985 when both OPEC and non-OPEC suppliers began undercutting prices in order to maintain or secure larger portions of the oil markets. Oil markets had a flood of excess oil, and prices tumbled for Arab Light crude (a premium grade from Saudi Arabia), selling for $6.08 per barrel in late July 1986. OPEC oil ministers had agreed since December 1985 that they should cut production in order to dry up the excess of oil on the market and drive prices higher, but they had been unable to agree on how much each country's production quota should be reduced. Economic considerations were constantly influenced by a long Iran-Iraq border war and the reluctance of either of these OPEC members to see the other benefit from added oil revenues. Furthermore, Saudi Arabia, the dominant OPEC producer, was upset by the failure of the other members to follow its lead or recommendations on quotas.

The situation in the Middle East rose to new heights of tension when Iraq invaded Kuwait in 1990; at this time the price of oil on world markets rose sharply as did the fear of widespread shortages (Figure 3.15). The military response by a coalition of United States, European, and other Arab countries quickly drove the Iraqi forces out of Kuwait. This reassured the world of continuing oil supplies from the Middle East and resulted in a return of oil prices to pre-Gulf War levels.

It is difficult to predict the future of OPEC oil production and the price of oil, but, as will be discussed in Chapter 5, OPEC controls the bulk of the world's known oil reserves. If they can again agree on policies and quotas, they will play a very significant role in world energy matters and politics in the decades to come. It is also apparent that future OPEC efforts to dramatically raise the price of oil will likely increase production from non-OPEC crude oil sources as it did in the early 1980s. This will result in increased conservation, and it will stimulate interest in alternate forms of energy. Consequently, many analysts believe that the world may see future tightening of oil availability, but they believe that crises like those in 1973 and 1979 are unlikely.

Diamonds and the DeBeers Syndicate. The earliest known accounts of **diamonds** are of Indian stones being transported to Greece in about 480 B.C. Throughout most of subsequent history, diamonds have been among the most valuable mineral commodities in proportion to unit weight or size. Diamonds were once mostly found in alluvial deposits in river beds in India and Brazil. Because they were rarely found in other parts of the world, they remained relatively scarce and valuable until late in the nineteenth century. This situation changed dramatically after a South African Boer farmer's children found a "pretty pebble" in the sandy bed of the Vaal River in 1866. By the 1870s, prospectors had located

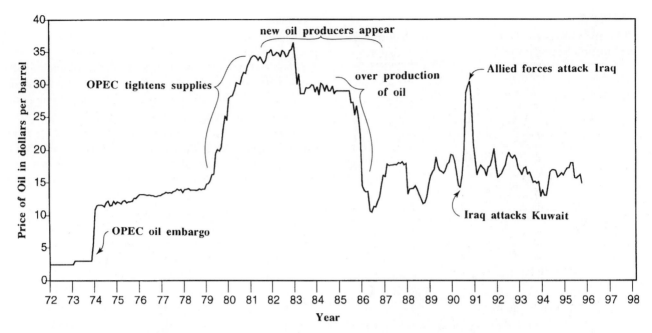

FIGURE 3.15. The cost of crude oil since the early 1970s. Arabian Light, used here as an example, is one of the premier petroleum crudes on the world market; there are many qualities of petroleum, but their prices all move more or less in the same pattern in response to world events. The sharp rise in 1973 was the time of the OPEC embargo; the rise from 1979 through 1980 resulted from OPEC limiting production; and the sharp fall in 1985 resulted from over production and price cutting. The effects of the 1990 Gulf War are evidenced by the brief increase in prices in 1990 and 1991.

rich alluvial deposits and diamond pipes in South Africa. The deep weathering allowed the rock to be easily removed by steam shovels as if they were loose gravel. The sudden influx of millions of **carats** of diamonds into a relatively small world market resulted in a price collapse, which saw diamond's value drop to less than one dollar for a carat and the abandonment of many no longer profitable mines.

Cecil John Rhodes, a famed British Colonial statesman, founder of Rhodesia (now Zimbabwe), and sponsor of the Rhodes Scholarships at Oxford University, moved to South Africa in 1870 at the age of seventeen and became a supervisor at his brother's diamond mine the following year. Over the next 15 years he gradually gained control of several additional mines and formed the DeBeers Consolidated Mines, Ltd. in 1888. He established a consortium to control the production and sale of the world's diamonds, nearly all of which now came from Rhodes' mines (Figure 3.16). The basic operation was simple and exceedingly successful; the mines would release only the number of gem diamonds needed to meet the demand—mostly stones for the rings of American brides.

By contracting to buy all gem quality stones from new operations, DeBeers continued to control the total world market even as new mines outside of South Africa opened. When the demand for diamonds dropped during the depression years of the 1930s, DeBeers merely cut back on production and stockpiled stones. Subsequently, the American and European markets grew and stabilized through the 1960s. DeBeers then turned its attention to the nearly untapped market in Japan, where diamonds were not traditionally prized. As a result of the trend toward Westernization and aggressive advertising, the Japanese market rapidly expanded. From 1967 to 1977, the percentage of Japanese brides receiving diamonds rose from 5 percent to more than 60 percent.

After saturating the United States' bridal market, DeBeers has aggressively promoted the importance of *anniversary rings* and other diamond jewelry since the mid-1980s. This has been quite successful and has resulted in the sale of more gem diamonds to the same individuals.

Over the years, numerous individuals have pointed out that the perceived value of diamonds, like that of gold, has been purely arbitrary and bears little relationship to their intrinsic value. It has generally been believed that DeBeers created and maintained an illusion through advertising that "diamonds are forever," that they are the best symbol of love,

FIGURE 3.16.   The *Big Hole* at Kimberley in South Africa was one of the early rich diamond mines brought into the DeBeers Syndicate by Cecil John Rhodes. The hole is 495 meters deep and is now partially filled with water. In its short life, it produced more than 14 million carats of diamonds. (Photograph courtesy of DeBeers Consolidated Mines Ltd.)

and that they have a market value far greater than almost any other substance. The major diamond producers have cooperated with DeBeers in maintaining a limited availability of diamonds because it is the only way that prices could be kept high. If an open market for diamonds developed, the price would probably plummet first and then fluctuate widely. Since the late 1970s, the world's diamond market has lacked some of the traditional stability that the DeBeers syndicate had provided. This has resulted in considerable uncertainty regarding the future value of diamonds.

The decline of the American dollar in the late 1970s led to much speculation in diamonds as investments and, consequently, a rapid rise in their value. This trend was reversed in the early 1980s when high interest rates drew investment money out of diamonds and resulted in the *dumping* of many diamonds onto the world market. The availability of these

stones and the flow of new diamonds from recently opened mines in Russia, Africa, and Australia reduced DeBeers' influence over the world market and stretched its financial resources as it tried to continue buying gem-quality stones. Over the past 15 years, there have been several reports of De-Beers becoming overextended or losing control of the gem diamond market, but these reports have always been incorrect. It is not clear whether or not DeBeers will be able to continue to maintain prices and its control of the world's diamond markets due to the increasing numbers of gem stones on the market. The future of the diamond market is further clouded by the potential production of synthetic diamonds of gem quality. Previously only industrial stones have been produced synthetically, but even DeBeers has been an active participant in the attempts to synthesize stones of sufficient size and quality to be used in the gem market.

Resources in World Politics

Strategic Resources.   The term *strategic* has been applied to a variety of mineral resources, especially metals, which have become important to key industries. There is no absolute definition of a strategic mineral, but the term is most often employed today in referring to metals used in military defense and energy programs—chromium, cobalt, niobium, nickel, platinum, and tantalum. Titanium, manganese, aluminum, and up to ten or more other mineral commodities are often added to this group depending upon who compiles the list. Furthermore, we have come to recognize the vital importance of chemical minerals, fuels to drive our industries, and fertilizers to grow our foods.

What constitutes a strategic resource has changed throughout time. For the earliest humans, the only strategic mineral materials were water and salt. In the Bronze Age, copper and tin assumed vital roles as the principal metals for tools and weapons. The Romans probably required three basic metals for their society: iron for weapons, gold to pay the soldiers, and lead to make pipes to transport water. The vast complexity of modern technology has expanded the list of important, if not vital, minerals upon which we depend for our lifestyles.

The primary concern of many governments now, as in the past, is that there should always be a reliable and adequate supply of the strategic materials. The United States, Great Britain, Japan, and most of the other major industrialized nations do not have adequate domestic supplies of most mineral commodities considered strategic. Figure 3.11 shows the high degree of American and Japanese dependence on foreign supplies for many important mineral commodities. The need to ensure the availability of strategic materials in times when political, economic, social, and military factors can disrupt the flow of foreign supplies affects governmental and industrial policies. Major mining and manufacturing companies in industrialized countries will often participate in joint ventures in foreign countries, especially in the developing areas of Africa, Latin America, and Southeast Asia, but they will cooperate only if they feel that their investments are safe. Consequently, American governmental policies in trade, assistance, and even military presence are directly affected by the nation's needs for mineral resources and, to some extent, by the foreign investment of American companies. This has been especially evident in dealings with the oil-rich countries of the Middle East because of the dependence of the United States and its allies on oil.

To prevent disruptions in supplies, especially from foreign sources, and halting necessary industries, many governments have developed *stockpiles.* The concept of the stockpile as applied to food stuffs and mineral commodities is as old as recorded history; the Biblical story in Genesis 41 relates how the stockpiling of grain during seven years of plenty permitted Egypt to survive the ensuing seven years of famine. Nations today have responded not so much to prophecy, as did Egypt, but to actual or imminent shortages, and now nearly all major industrialized countries have stores of important materials.

The modern American stockpile of strategic mineral commodities was conceived during World War I when the United States found itself cut off from supplies of several minerals that had been imported from Germany. The first substantive action, however, was taken in 1938 when Congress, fearing the likelihood of another war, appropriated funds to initiate the procurement of materials. This was followed by the passage of the Strategic Materials Act of 1939 and the purchases of materials such as tin, quartz crystals, and chromite. At the end of World War II, the surplus government stocks of minerals were transferred to the Strategic Stockpile, and Congress enacted the Strategic and Critical Materials Stock Piling Act of 1946. This act, which is the basis of the present Stockpile, reads in part "the purpose of this act . . . is to . . . decrease and prevent wherever possible a dangerous and costly dependence of the United States upon foreign nations for supplies of . . . materials in times of national emergency." The paramount importance of strategic minerals for economic prosperity and for waging war was recognized by both Germany and Japan during the 1930s, and both countries acquired stocks of the mineral commodities they deemed necessary for their aggressive plans (see page 57).

Although the United States' military establishment has maintained specific reserves of petroleum (such as the Naval Arctic Petroleum Reserve that covers vast areas southwest of the North Slope oil fields in Alaska), the oil embargo of 1973 raised great concern regarding the nation's petroleum reserve status. Accordingly, the government authorized the development of a strategic oil reserve of 1 billion barrels of oil (see page 147). It subsequently began to acquire oil and store it in large caverns carved into Louisiana and Texas salt domes. Despite episodic development and the opposition of OPEC, who feared such stores could be used to lessen their control of the world oil supply, the oil reserve had risen to more than 600 million barrels by 1994. Although the goal of 1 billion barrels is quite large, it could sustain American oil needs for only 60 days!

There is little doubt that the strategic importance of mineral resources will increase in the years ahead as the industrialized nations increasingly turn to the developing countries for more resources. At the same time, the increasing populations and needs of the developing countries will stretch their abilities to provide the resources. This will be tempered by developing countries' needs for foreign revenues, generated largely through the export of mineral resources. It is clear, however, that the international flow of strategic minerals and fuels will continue to play a major role in the world's political and economic activities in the future.

Resources and International Conflict.   Mineral resources are the raw materials and fuels modern industrialized societies need to function. To deprive a nation of them would rapidly lead to the collapse of its economy and industry. So vital are these resources that countries have before, and may again, go to war for them.

The primary mineral resource today is oil, and the world's principal reserves lie in the Middle East. Accordingly, there has been considerable speculation that the next worldwide conflict could begin over the control of the oil in the Middle East. Although the breakup of the former Soviet Union and the ending of the Cold War has eased many fears of an oil conflict between superpowers, the rise of nationalism and ethnic or religious tensions has led to new concerns. These concerns have been justified by events in recent years, notably the Gulf War. The importance of oil and other minerals has been apparent in earlier times of conflict as well. Prior to World War II, both Japan and Germany considered their needs for oil, steel, and other minerals before taking aggressive action.

In the 1920s and 1930s, Germany was rebuilding from its defeat in World War I and clearly recognized the need for resources to run any future war machine. In 1936, Hitler declared that Germany should be 100 percent self-sufficient in terms of the raw materials—oil, steel, iron ore, synthetic rubber, and aluminum—in the event of war. Because of the crude oil shortage, Germany constructed synthetic oil plants that produced petroleum from coal. Once World War II began, Germany found its iron ores to be insufficient, so ores were imported from Sweden and the occupied areas of Austria, Czechoslovakia, and the Alsace-Lorraine area of France. Metals used in alloys were in short supply, but the occupied countries often provided the sources: Norway, nickel; Ukraine, manganese; Balkans, chrome. Germany's copper, lead, and tin reserves were limited, but the seizure of stocks of these metals in occupied countries and energetic salvage drives provided what was needed.

Japan, which had been bogged down in a semi-colonial war over the control of the coal and oil in China, used the distraction of the German defeat of France and Holland to move into the rice fields of Indochina, the rubber plantations of Malaysia, and the oil fields of the Netherlands East Indies and obtain the resources needed for World War II. President Roosevelt reacted to this action in July 1940 by placing an embargo on the top grades of scrap iron and oil sales to Japan from the United States. Relations between the two countries deteriorated for a year until the United States broke off negotiations in July 1941, and Japan found itself in a total embargo of all strategic materials. Japan's greatest concern was for oil; the Navy had only an 18-months supply and the Army only had a 12-months supply. The military leaders argued vehemently for war as they saw their fuel supplies growing ever smaller. They believed that a swift attack to incapacitate the American Pacific fleet would leave Japan free to exploit and import the oil it needed from Southeast Asia. Hence, Japan attacked Pearl Harbor on December 7, 1941.

The wartime shortages emphasized the critical importance of many mineral resources, especially oil. Consequently, all of the major industrial nations have become very concerned with stockpiling strategic materials and maintaining access to the major supplies. Developing and future technologies may redefine which mineral resources are vital, but they will not lessen our future dependence upon resources in general.

FURTHER READINGS

AGRICOLA, *De Re Metallica*. Translated by H. C. Hoover and L. H. Hoover. New York: Dover Publication, Inc., 1950.

BUTOW, R. J. C., *Tojo and the Coming of the War.* Stanford, CA: Stanford University Press, 1969.

FLAWN, P. T., *Mineral Resources.* New York: John Wiley and Sons, 1966.

RICKARD, T. A., *Man and Metals.* New York: Arno Press, 1974.

SCHROEDER, P. W., *The Axis Alliance and Japanese American Relations 1941.* Ithaca, NY: Cornwall University Press, 1958.

SEYMOUR, I., *OPEC: Instrument of Change.* New York: St. Martin's Press, 1981.

SIMON, J. L., WEINRAUCH, G., and Moore, S., "The reserves of extracted resources: Historical data." *Nonrenewable Resources* 3 (1994) pp. 325–342.

TYLECOTE, R. F., *A History of Metallurgy.* London: The Metals Society, 1976.

WARREN, K., *Mineral Resources.* New York: John Wiley and Sons, 1973.

YERGIN, D., *The Prize.* New York: Simon and Schuster, 1991.

4 ENVIRONMENTAL IMPACTS OF RESOURCE EXPLOITATION AND USE

The collapse of the main street of Silver City, Nevada, into the Bonner Shaft of an old silver mine illustrates unexpected environmental impacts of resource extraction. The Comstock silver mines that made Silver City famous were discovered in 1859 and mined extensively through the 1880s, but this collapse, which swallowed a car and then filled with water, occurred in 1992. (Photograph by Craig Sailor; used with permission of the Reno Gazette-Journal.)

"During the period roughly up to 1975, governments were concerned primarily with setting up institutions and adopting new laws and regulations to abate and control environmental pollution. Today a second generation of environmental policies is emerging. In addition to the abatement of gross pollution there is a growing commitment to the wise husbandry of all natural resources and to the improvement of the quality of life."

(From a report on "The State of the Environment in OECD: The Organization for Economic Cooperation and Development" that includes the United States, Australia, Japan, United Kingdom, Canada, New Zealand, and 18 other, chiefly European, member countries.)

FOCAL POINTS

- Environmental impacts result from the extraction of resources, the use of resources, and the disposal of resource products.
- The two primary means of extracting solid mineral resources are underground mining and surface mining. Wells are used to extract fluids and gases such as oil, water, and natural gas.
- Underground mining is more dangerous and expensive than surface mining because of the potential for rock falls, water inflow, and gas buildup in the workings.
- Surface mining generally creates more obvious environmental impacts than underground mining because there is a larger volume of rock moved, and a large open pit with a large pile of waste rock is created.
- Underground mines usually have little impact at the surface unless there is a collapse into the mined-out areas or unless the mining requires lowering of the groundwater table to prevent mine flooding.
- The processing of metalliferous ores to extract the relatively small concentrations of metals within them creates large quantities of rock waste, and the smelting and refining of ores can release atmospheric pollutants.
- The use of some resources, especially the burning of fossil fuels, releases large amounts of pollution-causing gases (CO_2, NO_x, SO_x) into the atmosphere.
- Many believe that the increase of CO_2 concentration in the atmosphere is leading to an increase in Earth's atmospheric temperature and that the release of nitrogen and sulfur oxides generates acid rain.
- Nuclear power plants generate radioactive waste, requiring special disposal sites that must remain safe for many thousands of years.
- The resource cycle for many materials ends in disposal, reuse, or recycling. For example, the United States generates about 200 million tons of municipal solid waste per year, with paper and cardboard constituting the largest proportion.

INTRODUCTION

The second half of the twentieth century has seen a rapidly growing awareness by scientists, political leaders, and the public of the importance and complexity of environmental problems. In many instances, people suddenly recognized that activities we once viewed as beneficial—such as changing waterways, draining wetlands, clearing forests, and burning fossil fuels—can damage the environment. A well publicized photograph from the 1940s shows a row of smokestacks at a steel plant billowing clouds of smoke; it was titled "Progress." Today the same scene would bring outcries of *pollution* and incur the wrath of state and federal environmental agencies. Earlier in this century, we hailed the development of a practically indestructible material called plastic and viewed it as an example of living better through chemistry. Today we use plastics for innumerable purposes from automobiles to synthetic heart valves but complain about the materials forming nearly indestructible, omnipresent pollutants. Now the public is calling for new kinds of plastic that biodegrade and decompose.

Environmental pollution is not new, but the scale of pollution problems in the modern world is much greater than ever. The principal causes are a much larger human population (the 1890 world population was only one-quarter of what it is today, and the 1955 world population was only one-half of today's) and advances in technology. As our ancestors learned to harness energy—from fire to explosives to the steam engine to the internal combustion engine to nuclear power—the ability to modify the environment vastly increased. Until the twentieth century, the principal construction materials were rock and wood, neither of which created significant pollution problems. Rock buildings lasted but, except for the cities, were used only for small, isolated dwellings; wood structures, once unoccupied, rapidly decomposed and disappeared as vegetation restored areas to their previous conditions. Today, the widespread use of asphalt, concrete, plastics, and a host of other resistant synthetic materials ensures that natural vegetation will not recover the areas.

Our increasing concern about modern environmental problems and pollution has also increased our recognition of problems faced and created by our ancestors. Recent studies have shown that the Romans, in their exploitation of lead-rich silver ores, spread lead pollution over wide areas of Europe. In the seventeenth and eighteenth centuries, Great Britain simultaneously suffered two major environment impacts. Expanding population and the emerging Industrial Revolution called for a large reserve of energy, which was supplied by cutting down the forests of England, Scotland, Ireland, and Wales. Their energy crisis was alleviated by using coal as the fuel source, but the burning of the sulfur-rich coals led to massive air pollution throughout the

cities. To this day, most of the hillsides of Great Britain remain bare; only now are reforestation efforts of the twentieth century beginning to be visible. In the United States, the widespread use of mercury in the recovery of placer gold has left a legacy of mercury pollution in thousands of streams. Following the California Gold Rush of 1849, extensive hydraulic mining (Figure 4.1) destroyed the natural channels of many rivers and bays and flushed out fish and other aquatic life. Today, hydraulic mining is banned in most areas, and much effort has gone into the restoration of natural river environments. The recognition of detrimental human activities in the past and present and the need to maintain a healthy environment for our own survival has led to intensive research on environmental problems. It has also stimulated courses on environmental science at colleges and universities, the formation of campaigning groups and political parties united by environmentalist causes, and, ultimately, legislation aimed at helping prevent deterioration of the natural environment through human activities. This rising tide of activity results both from public awareness of our abused environment and the rapidly increasing levels of resource exploitation. Much of these causes are linked to population growth and growing rates of material consumption in many countries.

In this volume, the nature and utilization of Earth's resources (fuels and other energy sources, metals, industrial rocks and minerals, fertilizers, water, and soils) are discussed along with the environmental effects resulting from their exploitation and use. These are matters that concern every one of us and carry very serious implications for future generations. In this chapter, we first examine the ways in which exploitation of resources directly affects the environment—the effects of mining, quarrying, dredging, well drilling, and production and the effects of processing and smelting ores. Next, we examine ways in which using these resources affects the environment—the burning of fossil fuels, the use of nuclear fuels, the disposal of the hazardous wastes created from fuels, and the problems of **pollution** caused by other industrial processes. Finally, we examine the problems involved in the disposal (or, where possible, recycling) of wastes that are produced in vast amounts, not only by manufacturing industries, but by each one of us in our everyday lives.

The discussion of each type of resource, as well as its extraction and use, in the following chapters is accompanied with consideration of specific environmental impacts. It is important, as we examine the individual resources, to remember that all resource extraction and use is accompanied by some kind of environmental impact. Unfortunately, some of these impacts may be subtle, removed from the site of usage, or delayed in appearance. Hence, it is very important to carefully identify and assess impacts, minimize deleterious effects, and weigh them against the benefits received from the resources.

FIGURE 4.1 Hydraulic placer mining in California in the 1860s yielded large amounts of gold but dramatically altered the nature of the rivers and the bays into which they flow. (Photograph courtesy of Levi Strauss and Company.)

HOW EXPLOITING RESOURCES AFFECTS THE ENVIRONMENT

Many of the most obvious, and some of the most severe, disruptions of the environment come from the exploitation of resources. Mining, quarrying, dredging, drilling, and extracting from wells are all activities that have marked impacts on the landscape and environment. Directly linked to these activities are problems concerned with the disposal of their waste products. Further environmental problems may occur at the site of exploitation when various extraction or concentration processes are employed. For example, most metal mines remove ores that contain only small proportions (commonly less than one percent) of the metal being extracted. A range of physical and chemical processes, often culminating in smelting, are then needed to extract the metal from the ore. For metal extraction, at least three aspects of the process create potential environmental problems—the mining operation, the disposal of very large quantities of waste rock, and the smelting and refining of the ore.

Mining and Quarrying—The Methods

The method used to extract metallic, industrial, or chemical minerals, building materials, or solid fuels, such as coal or uranium, depends on the nature and location of the deposit. Depending on the deposit size, shape, depth beneath surface, and **grade** (percentage of valuable material or quality and

purity), a choice is made between surface mining or underground mining.

Surface mining, which accounts for about two-thirds of the world's solid mineral production—especially that involving sand and gravel, stone, phosphates, coal, copper, iron, and aluminum—generally involves **open pit mining** or a form of **strip mining.** Open pit mining is an economical method of extraction involving large tonnages of reserves and high rates of production. The waste material overlying the deposit (**overburden**) must be thin enough to be removed to make the operation lucrative. Surface mining is preferred over underground mining by mining companies when possible because it is less expensive, safer, and involves fewer complications with air, electricity, water, and rock handling. However, surface mining often results in a greater environmental impact than underground mining. Underground mines are usually much smaller in scale, typically producing less than 10,000 tons per day, and they involve much less surface disruption. The term **quarry** generally refers to an open pit mine from which building stone or gravel is extracted. Many of the largest open pit mines, such as the copper and gold mines in the southwestern United States (Figure 4.2, Plate 37), are developed as conical chasms with terraced benches that spiral downward to the bottom of the pit. These benches serve as haulage roads and working platforms on the steep, often at a 45° angle, sloping sides of the pit. Extraction proceeds by drilling, blasting, and loading material into large trucks to haul the rock and ore out of the pit. The depth and diameter of the pit increase as mining takes place, in some

FIGURE 4.2. The giant smelter at Morenci, Arizona, is one of the world's largest copper-producing complexes and demonstrates the impact of mining, smelting, and waste disposal on the environment. Ore from an open pit mine is brought by truck to the mill and smelter, which make up the complex of buildings surrounding the two smokestacks. There the valuable copper minerals are separated from the rock, and the copper-rich concentrate is smelted down to copper metal. (Photograph by B. J. Skinner.)

cases reaching diameters of more than 2 km and depths of several hundred meters.

The world's largest open pit mine at Bingham Canyon, Utah, involved cutting away an entire mountain to form a pit roughly 3.5 km by 2.5 km and 1 km deep (Plate 37). At the height of production, more than 100,000 metric tons of ore grading from about 0.3% copper were being produced per day. With a waste to ore stripping ratio of 3 to 1, this involved drilling, blasting, and removing an average of 400,000 tons of material per day. Power shovels of 5 to 20 cubic meter capacity, rail cars of up to 80 metric tons capacity, and diesel trucks capable of handling up to 140 metric tons were needed for this feat.

Strip mining is employed when the material to be extracted forms a flat-lying layer just beneath the surface. Many coal seams are exploited in this manner, but the method is also widely used in mining tar sands, phosphates, clays, and certain kinds of iron and uranium ores. These are all materials that can occur as thin, nearly horizontal layers, often underlying enormous areas of country. The mining method involves removing the overburden to expose the resource, which is then scooped up and loaded into trucks or trains. The waste rock is dumped to the rear (Figure 4.3), and the mining continues along a strip that extends as far as is practical. A new strip is then started parallel to the first, and waste from this strip is dumped on the preceding strip. Large mechanical shovels and drag lines remove overburden and the resource. Clearly, the ratio of overburden to resource is a crucial factor in this type of operation.

Underground mining, involving a system of subsurface workings, is used to extract solid mineral resource that

cannot be found near the surface. Most mines consist of one or more means of access via vertical **shafts,** horizontal **adits,** or inclined roadways (**inclines**) (Figure 4.4). These provide transportation for the men, machinery, materials, extracted ore, and wastes. They also form part of the systems for ventilation and the control of underground water that are essential to mining operations. In many underground mines, substantial amounts of energy are expended in pumping air and water to keep the working areas dry and well ventilated. This is particularly the case where mining takes place in an extremely hostile environment. For example, the zinc mine that operated for many years at Friedensville, Pennsylvania, was in a karst terrain where water had to be routinely pumped out at rates of close to 25,000 gallons (95,000 liters) per minute to prevent flooding the workings (Figure 4.5). When heavy rains fell on the mine area in February 1976, the pumping rate was raised to a peak of 60,000 gallons (227,000 liters) per minute to keep the mine from flooding. At the Konkola Mine in Zambia, possibly the wettest mine operating in the world today, the pumping rate is 73,000 gallons (280,000 liters) per minute. In the deep gold mines of the Witwatersrand, South Africa, mining levels are often more than 3000 meters below the surface, and the rock temperatures are over 32°C (90°F). Deeper mines in South Africa are planned with depths exceeding 3500 meters (11,500 feet) and rocks expected to reach temperatures of 43°C (100°F). At the Magma Mine in Superior, Arizona, and in the Toyoha Mine in Japan, mining is routinely conducted where rock temperatures reach 50°C (122°F) and the humidity is 100 percent. Humans cannot survive in such conditions, so it is necessary to refrigerate the air. This is extremely expensive

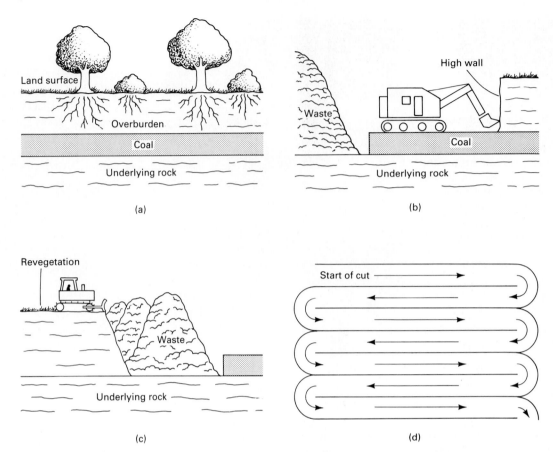

FIGURE 4.3. The sequence of steps involved in strip mining. (a) Profile before mining; (b) profile during mining; (c) profile as land surface restoration begins; (d) plan view of the mining sequence.

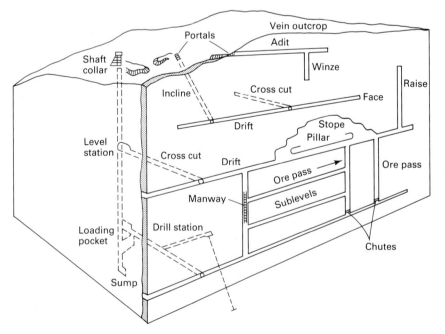

FIGURE 4.4. A schematic diagram of an underground mining operation. The roomlike areas where ore is removed are called stopes. The drifts and crosscuts are the tunnels leading to the mine entrance. Most deep mines have vertical entrances called shafts, but many near surface mines have inclined or horizontal entrances called inclines or adits. (From W. C. Peters, *Exploration and Mining Geology,* John Wiley & Sons, 1978.)

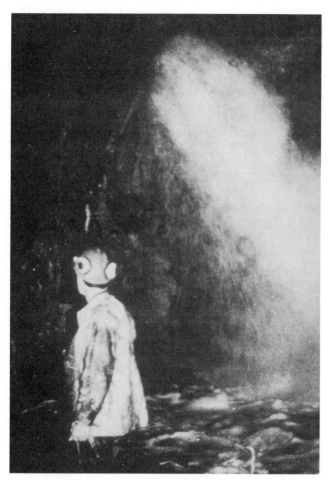

FIGURE 4.5. The high rate of water flow into mines can make mining difficult, dangerous, and expensive. The flow of 95,000 liters (25,000 gallons) per minute into the Friedensville Mine in Pennsylvania lowered the water table through the area and increased the cost of electricity to operate pumps. (Photograph by R. Metzger.)

and requires special technology to cool and handle the air. One might think that it is only necessary to blow large quantities of air into the mine, but mine ventilation systems are far more complicated. When air descends down shafts to depths of 3000 meters (10,000 feet), it is compressed by gravity and heated nearly 6°C (10°F).

Underground workings usually consist of intersecting horizontal tunnels (**drifts** and **crosscuts**) often on several **levels** and joined by further vertical openings (**raises** or **winzes**). The region where ore is extracted in a metalliferous mine is referred to as a **stope,** and the area that is actually drilled and removed is called a **face.** Examples of some of the many underground mining methods are shown in Figure 4.6. The method employed in any mine will depend on the shape,

size, and grade of the ore body, or seam, that is being worked. This, in turn, will determine the kinds of machinery needed to break up and carry away the ores and waste rocks. In most mines, ore extraction and mine development involve drilling and blasting, removal with mechanical diggers onto underground railway cars or dump trucks that reach the surface on a shaft, incline, or adit. Some coal mines today are only about 1 meter high, just high enough to allow the use of continuous mining machines (see Figure 5.18) that cut the coal with rotating teeth and feed it back to transport cars or conveyor belts. In contrast, some large stopes that have been excavated in the zinc mines of the Appalachians stand as open galleries more than 70 m high and 100 m long (Figure 4.7). Other factors that will affect the mining methods are related to *ground conditions,* such as the strength of rocks encountered underground, fracturing in these rocks, and the groundwater conditions. For example, drifts, crosscuts, and stopes in a tin mine found in granite may require little or no roof support, whereas in a coal mine in weaker, sedimentary rocks, extensive roof support with timbers or other props may be needed.

Underground mining is inherently dangerous because of the potential for rock falls and cave-ins, but probably the most feared problem is the build-up of poisonous or explosive gases. Mine systems are carefully designed so large volumes of air move from the surface to the workings to flush out natural gases and the fumes from blasting and operating equipment. All underground vehicles and equipment operate from electricity, compressed air, or diesel fuel; gasoline is forbidden because its higher volatility can potentially cause fires or explosions. Despite the best efforts to ventilate underground mines, methane gas is sometimes rapidly evolved by coal seams and can reach explosive levels (Plate 24). Miners once carried canaries into the mine workings to test for *bad air,* and some even sent workers wrapped in wet clothes to burn out methane accumulations (Figure 4.8). Gas-generated explosions have been the major cause of death in coal mines for hundreds of years and tragically, despite modern testing devices, still kill many miners every year. Metal mines rarely contain methane gas because there is no concentrated organic matter from which it can be derived, but carbon dioxide or carbon monoxide can build up. Underground uranium mines actually have very low levels of emitted radiation but are always monitored for levels of radon gas, which is released during the natural radioactive decay of uranium. Usually ventilation eliminates any problems, but the radiation and radon levels are so high at some mines, such as the Cigar Lake Uranium Mine in Canada, that mining must be done with remote control equipment and robots.

A number of more unusual methods are also used to extract particular resources. **Hydraulic mining** uses high-pressure water jets to wash soft sediments down an incline toward some form of concentration plant where dense mineral grains (such as gold) are separated. **Solution mining** involves dissolving the ore in water or other fluid introduced

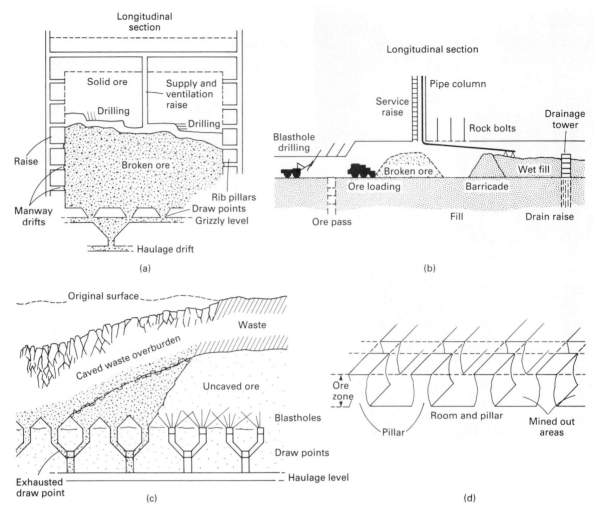

FIGURE 4.6. Schematic representation of the major mining methods. (a) Shrinkage stoping—ore is drilled and blasted from the ceiling (called the back) and allowed to fall; subsequent drilling and blasting is carried out by workings on top of the broken ore. (b) Cut and fill stoping—as ore is removed, the open space left is refilled with waste materials. This method has the advantage of filling the open mined-out stopes and disposing of the wastes below ground. However, it is very expensive. (c) Block caving— an entire mass of ore is blasted from below, allowing it to slowly flow through the draw points. (d) Room and pillar—ore is mined in a series of rooms, leaving pillars to support the overlying rocks. (a,b,c from W. C. Peters, *Exploration and Mining Geology,* John Wiley & Sons, 1978.)

into the ore body; this has been used mostly to extract salt or sulfur (Figure 4.9a and b). An extension of the principles involved in solution mining has been applied to the extraction of metals by *in situ* **leaching** (Figure 4.9c). This method is used to recover copper, gold, and uranium from low-grade ores. The value of *in situ* leaching is that it permits the economic open pit extraction of gold ore grades as low as 0.02 troy oz/m.t. (0.6 ppm), whereas conventional underground

mining requires a minimum grade of about 0.2 troy oz/m.t. (6 ppm). Some believe *in situ* leaching is likely to have much wider applications in the future. One proposal includes detonating nuclear blasts at the bottom of large ore bodies to cause extensive fracturing, drilling of wells into this mass for injection, and recovering leach liquors, such as sulfuric acid, that will dissolve the valuable metals. There are many problems still remaining with such futuristic mining methods.

FIGURE 4.7. A large hydraulic drill cuts blast holes in a zinc ore between the pillars that support the overlying rock more than 15 meters above. (Courtesy of ASARCO Inc.)

Environmental Impact of Mining and Quarrying

Much of the impact of mining and quarrying is obvious. The disruption of land otherwise suitable for agricultural, urban, or recreational use; the deterioration of the immediate environment through noise and airborne dust; the creation of one of the most dangerous environments for its workers and potentially hazardous for the public are all environmental problems associated with mining. However, mining is a relatively short-term activity, and much can be done both to limit environmental damage during mining and to restore the land when mining operations are complete. Today, in many countries, legislation has been enacted at nearly all levels to ensure that these steps are taken, but laws must also protect the environment while recognizing that extreme restrictions could make mining completely uneconomical. Unfortunately, the absence of adequate controls over some mining activities in the past has left numerous scars on the surface of Earth and a resistance among many members of the public toward new mining activities in their localities.

Fortunately, many underground mines leave little evidence of their presence even after the mining operations have ceased. They are usually filled by percolating groundwaters over time, but the rocks are usually strong enough to hold in spite of the abandoned mine openings and passageways. Sometimes the old mines can be put to very good use. Examples include an important archive of seeds of the world's major grains in an old coal mine on the island of Spitzbergen in the north Atlantic, the burial of nuclear wastes in abandoned German salt mines, and the development of an extensive office and shipping complex in an old limestone mine in Kansas City, Missouri (Figure 4.10). In all three of these examples, the old mines are watertight, and the air temperatures and humidities are nearly constant.

FIGURE 4.8. In 19th century coal mines, a miner called a "penitent" was wrapped in water-soaked rags and carried a long candle-tipped stick to try to burn off pockets of methane gas so the other miners could safely enter the work area. (Original wood engraving from Simonin 1869; from U.S. Geological Survey Circular 1115.)

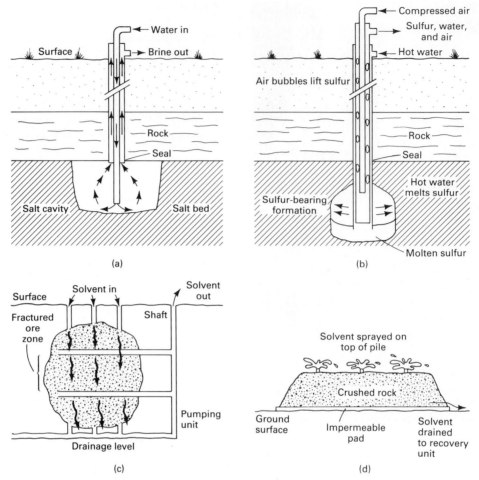

FIGURE 4.9. Solution mining techniques include: (a) bottom injection systems used to dissolve soluble materials such as salt; (b) the Frasch system in which superheated water is pumped down to melt sulfur; the molten sulfur is carried upward in the innermost pipe; (c) *in situ* ore leaching in which a solvent (commonly an acid) is drained downward through a previously broken ore zone; and (d) heap leaching in which broken rock is placed on an impermeable pad on the ground, and a solvent is sprayed over the rock; this is the method used today for most gold recovery.

When an open pit mine closes, a large hole remains without any readily available waste rocks to fill it. The pit slopes are often very steep and cannot be reclaimed by soil coverage and planting. If the water table is high enough, the bottom of the pit may flood, creating an artificial lake. Therefore, the very large open pit mines are difficult, if not impossible, to reclaim. Smaller open pit mines and quarries, on the other hand, can often be filled with waste rock or, if the geologic and groundwater conditions permit, can be used for the disposal of refuse or other waste materials (see page 91). Gravel pits or rock quarries can sometimes be filled with water and become recreational lakes.

Strip mining (Figure 4.11a) can leave mounds of waste material too steep for building or farming and groundwater poisoned by the effects of mining. Because the mounds are without vegetation and fertile soil, they are eas-

ily eroded. Many thousands of acres of land in coal mining areas of Kentucky, West Virginia, Illinois, and other parts of the United States have been devastated in this way. Nevertheless, reclamation as a part of strip mining can be straightforward, and nearly all modern operations are required to include this as a normal final stage of mining. Waste mounds can be smoothed out, topsoil can be stored and returned, and ground-covering plants, such as clover, can be planted until the soil is sufficiently restored to allow other crops to flourish (Figure 4.11b). In some of the most mountainous areas of West Virginia, the horizontal benches left after reclaiming strip mines prove useful because they provide the only flat land, with excellent meadows for cattle and wild deer. In many places, surface mines from sand, gravel, phosphates, and titanium oxides in unconsolidated rocks have been reclaimed to form small lakes

FIGURE 4.10. The underground openings left after a mining operation has ceased can sometimes be put to good use. This former limestone operation in Kansas City, Missouri, used a room and pillar method and has been converted into a large underground storage area. Other parts of the same mine contain a trucking operation, an office complex, and a post office. The addresses are appropriately known as Underground Drive. (Courtesy of Hunt Midwest Real Estate Development, Inc.)

and wetlands that support fish, birds, and other wildlife (Figure 4.12).

Underground mining does not lead to such drastic disruptions of the surface as open pit and strip mining, but a new hazard known as **subsidence** can be encountered. This problem occurs most often where underground mining has approached the land surface or where the rocks are naturally weak or highly fractured. This is commonly seen where mining has been undertaken in soft sedimentary rocks, as in many coal mines, and where the *room and pillar* method was used (Figure 4.6d). More than 8000 km² of land in the United States has subsided due to underground coal mining, and many more areas are threatened. Subsidence of farmland or rangeland into old coal mines (Figure 4.13b) is a problem but generally has little impact on people's lives. On the other hand, subsidence under towns and roads can leave homes uninhabitable and transportation severely disrupted (Chapter-Frontispiece, Plate 15, and Figure 4.13). In March 1995, a coal mine that was last mined in the 1930s collapsed under a 600 meter (1800 foot) stretch of Interstate Highway 70 in eastern Ohio, closing the road for more than three months. Thus, a severe impact of the coal mining appeared 60 years after the mining activity ceased. Solution mining and the pumping of brine or water into the ground can also cause local subsidence. Subsidence is usually gradual and causes cracks, surface troughs, depressions, or bulges (Figure 4.13), but sometimes it is sudden and results in the destruction of houses, other buildings, roads, and farm areas.

An extreme example of this occurred in 1968 at a zinc mine at Friedensville, Pennsylvania. Gradual subsidence with occasional minor episodic movement was noticed in 1964. Careful monitoring, including the installation of

acoustic **seismographs** (rock movements were often discernable to the unaided ear), allowed a geologist to define and isolate the problem area. At 10:41 A.M. on March 27, 1968, a block of rock 225 m long by 115 m wide and over 180 m thick dropped. The energy released by this 11,000,000 m.t. block was equivalent to an earthquake of magnitude 3 on the **Richter Scale** and was recorded on several area seismographs. A vacant house and a portion of state highway were destroyed, but fortunately there were no injuries or lost work time.

A similar event occurred in March 1994 at the United States' largest salt mine at Retsof, New York, when a collapse occurred 300 m (1000 ft) below the surface and was recorded as a 3.5 magnitude earthquake. No immediate damage occurred to buildings, and no one was injured. However, the fractures extended to the surface, and the mine began to fill with groundwater at a rate of 76,000 liters (20,000 gallons) per minute. There was immediate concern that local wells would drain as the water table dropped. Also, a long-term concern was that salt water from the salt beds could contaminate groundwater supplies.

In addition to the impact that mining activities may have on the landscape, the environment may be disrupted over a wider area by changes in the distribution and chemistry of surface waters or groundwater. An example of this is **acid mine drainage,** which is drainage produced when iron sulfide minerals, namely pyrite and marcasite (both forms of FeS_2) or pyrrhotite ($Fe_{1-x}S$), are exposed to oxidation by moist air to form sulfuric acid plus various other sulfate compounds and iron oxides. Pyrite and marcasite occur as minor minerals in many coals; they and pyrrhotite are important in many metallic mineral deposits. The generation of

(a)

(b)

FIGURE 4.11. (a) An operating coal strip mine in eastern West Virginia. In the foreground the overburden has been removed, exposing the coal bed (on which the front end loader is sitting). Once the coal has been removed (as in the background where the pickup trucks are parked), reclamation will begin. The cliff at the right, known as the "high wall," reveals how much overburden had to be removed to excavate the coal bed. (Photograph by J. R. Craig.) (b) Proper reclamation procedures can restore previously mined areas to productive and attractive landscapes. (Courtesy of Lee Daniels.)

FIGURE 4.12. Reclaimed wetlands in the area of a former phosphate mine in Florida are now a productive wildlife habitat. (Photograph courtesy of Florida Institute for Phosphate Research.)

sulfuric acid can occur when these minerals are exposed to air in underground mines, open pits, or the dumps of waste material left by mining operations. Water passing through the mines or dumps becomes acidified, later finding its way into rivers, streams, or the local groundwater system. It has been estimated that up to 10,000 miles of streams have been affected in this way in the U.S. alone, largely because of the impact of abandoned mine workings. The result is a major pollution problem, resulting in barren soils and rivers and streams devoid of living things.

Butte, Montana, has been called "the richest hill on Earth" because of deposits rich in copper, lead, zinc, silver, gold, and several other metals. It has been the site of intense mining since the mid-1800s. Mining these riches has left the scars of abandoned open pits, large waste piles, and contaminated streams. The Berkeley Pit (Plate 18) is now abandoned but is filling with groundwater. It will ultimately become one of Montana's largest lakes; unfortunately, the water contains 8000 ppm dissolved solids and has an extremely acidic pH of 2.7.

Although not so widespread as the problem of acid drainage, other undesirable compounds enter streams or groundwater from some mines and mineral processing plants. These include arsenic and various compounds of heavy metals, such as lead, cadmium, or mercury. The mining of uranium leads to particular problems that are discussed later in this chapter.

Disposal of Mining Wastes

Nearly all mining operations generate waste rocks, often in very large amounts. Strip mining waste can be used in reclamation, but an alternative method of disposal must be found for underground mining operations and most kinds of open pit mining. Usually, this simply involves dumping the wastes in piles at the surface next to the mine workings. Sometimes, the waste rock is put back into the openings created by the mining; this is called **back-filling.** However, the cost involved in doing this is often prohibitive, and back-filling may seriously restrict the development of the mine by making large areas no longer accessible.

Piles of waste rock are unsightly and may be dangerous. Often, these wastes have been crushed to separate them from the coal, metalliferous, or industrial minerals being exploited. This increases the volume of the rock by as much as 40 percent and produces material that may be unstable when placed in steep piles. A tragic illustration of this occurred in 1966 in the Welsh mining village of Aberfan. A 400-ft high pile of rock, which had accumulated on a mountainside during nearly a century of coal mining, slid down and engulfed many houses and a school, killing 144 people. This avalanche comprised an estimated two million tons of coal-mining waste.

Alternatives to the dumping of mining wastes, such as using them to fill land, are likely to be expensive and impractical in most cases. However, waste dumps can certainly be made safe and often reclaimed as recreational or agricultural land. Such reclamation may involve lowering the slopes on dumps and encouraging vegetation growth through **hydro-mulching** or **hydro-seeding.** These processes consist of spraying the dumps with a pulp or mulch from organic material such as bark or hay mixed with a binding substance and seeds. The organic substance provides some bed material for germination of the seeds. Once this happens, the roots hold the mulch in place and form a protective layer of vegetation to minimize water erosion. The lower the slope on the dump, the more likely that revegetation will be successful.

(a)

(b)

FIGURE 4.13. (a) The effects of subsidence in an old coal mining area are evident near Sheridan, Wyoming. Mining in the 1920s used only a room and pillar method. Subsequently, there has been collapse of the overlying rocks into many of the rooms. (From C. R. Dunrud, U. S. Geological Survey Professional Paper 1164, 1980.) (b) A sudden collapse in the Friedensville Mine in Pennsylvania resulted in a small earthquake and severely damaged the overlying state highway. (Photograph courtesy of R. W. Metzger.) (c) Subsidence of the land surface into an abandoned anthracite mine in Scranton, Pennsylvania, has resulted in damage to this house, which has tilted on its foundations. (Photograph courtesy of the Bureau of Mines, U.S. Department of the Interior.)

(c)

Numerous examples of successfully reclaiming mining waste materials range from planing down large piles of tailings outside Johannesburg, South Africa, to seeding white quartz sand waste tips surrounding the china clay pits of Cornwall, England (see Figure 9.18).

Dredging and Ocean Mining—Methods and Environmental Impacts

Dredging involves removing unconsolidated material from rivers, streams, lakes, and shallow seas with machines such

FIGURE 4.14. A small dredge operating in Alaska recovers placer gold from river gravels. The bucket line at the left side cuts into the sediments and carries them into the dredge. The coarse rocks are dumped off a conveyer belt projecting out on the right side. Gold particles are recovered by sluices and jigs within the dredge, and the fine sediments are pumped back into the river. The dredge moves slowly by digging on one end of its own small lake and dumping waste rock on the other end. (Photograph by Ernie Wolford and Joe Fisher, courtesy of Alaska Division of Mining and Geological Survey.)

as the bucket-ladder dredge, dragline dredge, or suction dredge (Figure 4.14). These methods are used extensively for the recovery of sand, gravel, and minerals such as tin oxide ore (cassiterite), gold, and diamonds. The largest and most advanced dredgers are those employed in the tin fields of Southeast Asia, handling up to five million cubic meters per year and recovering material as deep as 45 m (150 ft) below a pond's surface. In Sierra Leone and Ghana, large-scale diamond mining operations use draglines well suited to the swampy ground. There is no chemical pollution from dredging, but the process disperses large quantities of fine sand and silt, having severe effects on fish and other wildlife that require clean water to survive.

The oceans have long been a source of sodium, magnesium, and bromine salts from materials dissolved in seawater. However, with the depletion of more conventional sources of other minerals, increasing attention is being paid to the mineral potential of deeper seas and oceans. Metal-rich sediments are known to occur in the Red Sea and along certain of the ocean ridges, but the main interest centers on **manganese nodules** (see page 229). These pea- to cobble-sized, roughly spherical nodules cover large areas of the deep ocean floor. They contain substantial amounts of manganese, nickel, copper, and cobalt and lesser amounts of a wide range of other elements. In fact, the total quantities of such metals as copper, nickel, and cobalt in manganese nodules probably equals the total of these metals in all known land deposits. They are very attractive as a resource, but mining the nodules poses technical, legal, and potential environmental problems. Because most nodules lie beneath 4000 to 5000 m of water, various dredging or siphoning methods have been proposed for their recovery. Although the technical problems can probably be overcome—some systems have already been tested and proved feasible— rights to mine nodules and the distribution of profits is a matter of international disagreement. Because the nodules

largely lie in international waters, all nations can claim some right to their ownership.

Dredging and any form of ocean mining involves significant disruption of natural bodies of water and may result in the destruction of biological systems. There may also be long-term effects on river and ocean currents, sedimentation patterns, and patterns of erosion. The severity of the environmental impact of nodule mining is not known, but there are concerns that the disruption and dispersal of the sediment may harm delicate, little-known deep-sea fauna.

Well Drilling and Production— Environmental Impact

The drilling of wells is a method of exploiting liquid and gaseous resources that goes back many centuries; in 1500-year-old Chinese manuscripts it is mentioned as a means of tapping underground strata for brine. Modern drilling methods are used in the exploitation of water and geothermal energy and in the exploration and production stage for oil and natural gas. Apart from the relatively minor environmental disruption caused in the actual drilling of water or geothermal wells, there is little danger of damage from these activities. Drilling for oil and gas, on the other hand, involves certain risks, although the disruption to the environment is generally much less than that from major mining operations.

The technology involved in modern rotary drilling to locate and exploit oil and gas is discussed in detail in Chapter 5. The greatest hazard that may be encountered during drilling is the **blowout,** which occurs when a high-pressure oil or gas accumulation is unexpectedly encountered and the column of heavy drilling fluid in the hole fails to contain the oil or gas that erupts from the wellhead (Figure 4.15). The fire hazard is great, and severe pollution of the surrounding area can occur very rapidly. Today, blowouts are

FIGURE 4.15. A blowout such as that shown here is one of the greatest hazards that can be encountered while drilling for oil. Extremely high pressures have forced the drill rods out of the hole and destroyed the drill tower. (Courtesy of Shell International Petroleum Company Limited.)

comparatively rare due to improved equipment and monitoring of the drilling process. Thus, symptoms such as an increase in drilling rate accompanied by an increase in return flow of the drilling mud indicate that fluid from the hydrocarbon reservoir is entering the wellbore. Valves at the surface known as blowout preventers can then be closed, and corrective measures, such as increasing the density of the drilling mud, can be taken to enable drilling to continue. In spite of these safety measures, major problems still occur; a well blew out and caught fire in the Gulf of Mexico near the Yucatan Peninsula in 1979. It spewed oil for more than nine months with an oil loss estimated at more than 130 million gallons (3.1 million barrels).

Clearly, the dangers to human life and the environment are greater in the offshore oil fields that have been so extensively exploited over the last two decades. Nevertheless, major accidents have been relatively rare, although risks must increase as fields in deeper offshore waters and less hos-

pitable seas develop. Some spillage of oil into the seas seems inevitable at such sites, and, as at all operations, care must be taken to prevent oil and brine seepage at the well head.

Although there have been many significant oil spills from tankers, one of the largest and most publicized was that of the **Exxon** *Valdez,* which ran aground in Prince William Sound, Alaska, on March 24, 1989 (Figure 4.16). Over 56 days, more than 11 million gallons (260,000 barrels) of oil spread along nearly 800 km (500 miles) of coastline. Besides the waste of oil, an estimated 400,000 sea birds (including 900 bald eagles) and 4000 sea otters died as a result of oil on their feathers and fur. Large numbers of workers cleaned beaches and skimmed up oil for months; $100 million was spent on research; and more than $1 billion was paid in fines, but we shall not know the full effects of the spill for years to come. The National Oceanographic and Atmospheric Administration (NOAA) has estimated that 50 percent of the oil spilled biodegraded, 20 percent evaporated, 14 percent was recovered, 12 percent sank to the bottom of the Gulf of Alaska, and 1 percent still drifts in the seawater.

All wars cause environmental devastation, but the Gulf War of 1990–1991 (see page 143) had particular environmental impacts related to mineral resources. The retreating Iraqi army blew up more than 700 oil wells, resulting in as much as 1 billion barrels of crude oil spread over the Kuwait desert and into the Persian Gulf and another 1 billion barrels burned from pools and uncontrolled gushers for several months. The effects on the desert sands were relatively slight, but there are concerns about long-term groundwater contamination; the effects on the aquatic life of the Persian Gulf will not be fully known for many years. The plumes of smoke from the burning oil wells blackened the skies and extended for hundreds of kilometers, creating health and agricultural problems downwind.

Processing and Smelting of Ores

The ores of all metals (see Chapters 7 and 8) and most of the industrial minerals (see Chapter 10) require processing following their removal from the earth. Such processing is usually done at or near the sites of mining.

Metal in an *as mined* ore ranges from about 30 percent in many aluminum and iron ores down to as little as 0.000001 percent in the case of gold (Figure 4.17 and Table 4.1). Even in copper mines, metal in the as-mined ore (known as the **grade**) in many currently worked deposits averages only 0.1–0.5 percent. In most ores, the metal-bearing minerals (commonly oxides, sulfides, arsenides, or, more rarely, alloys of the metals) are intergrown on a microscopic scale with valueless minerals (termed **gangue**), such as silicates or carbonates of the rocks acting as *hosts* to the ores (Figure 4.18). In many operations, the first stage of processing is a size reduction (**comminution**) of blocks up to a meter across down to particles only a few tenths or hundredths of a millimeter in

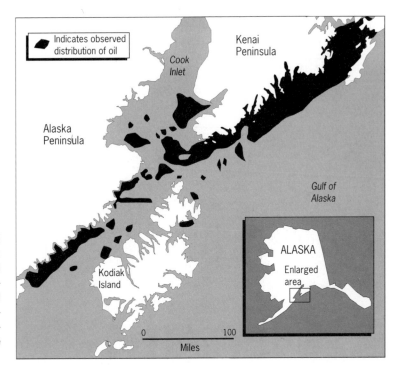

FIGURE 4.16. The oil spilled when the Exxon *Valdez* ran aground in Prince William Sound in Alaska exceeded 11 million gallons (260,000 barrels) and spread along nearly 500 miles (800 kilometers) of coastline. Litigation continued for years with an ultimate cost in the billions of dollars.

diameter. This is achieved by first **crushing** and then grinding (**milling**) the ores (Figure 4.19). Whereas crushing is commonly a dry process, milling involves the abrasion of particles suspended in a fluid (usually water) and is therefore a wet process; this makes handling easier and reduces dust problems. The object of comminution is to break down the ore so that the ore mineral particles are freed, or **liberated,** as much as possible from the gangue. The second stage in ore processing involves separation of the ore and gangue minerals, and this may involve one or more of several methods. These commonly make use of differences in density, magnetic, electrical, or surface properties between the ore and the gangue minerals (Table 4.2).

The end products of such mineral processing operations (often termed **beneficiation**) are a **concentrate** of the ore minerals and a much larger quantity of waste gangue material known as **tailings.** Commonly, the tailings that are in the form of a fine-grained slurry are dumped into an artificial pond or lake and allowed to settle. This water may be recirculated because the quantities used in many operations are very large, and laws commonly forbid its reuse for domestic purposes. In the past, tailings dumped in this way were often left as surface scars when mining ceased or were discharged directly into streams. Problems arose from potentially toxic concentrations of certain elements in tailings and the waters used in processing operations. This and the harmful effects of these fine-particle contaminants on aquatic organisms have led to laws prohibiting or controlling this type of dumping. Special problems associated with the disposal of uranium mill tailings are discussed later in this chapter.

The concentrate usually contains the metal in the form of oxides, sulfides, or related compounds, and the traditional method of recovery of the pure metal is by **smelting.** The most familiar smelting process is the recovery of iron from its oxide ores, discussed in detail in Chapter 7. Carbon monoxide resulting from the incomplete combustion of coke reacts with iron oxide at high temperatures to form metallic iron and carbon dioxide.

Many other metals are produced by reducing oxides sometimes present as such in the ore and sometimes formed by **roasting** the ore prior to smelting. The process of roasting heats the metal in the air without melting it to transform sulfide minerals (also metal arsenides, antimonides, etc.) into oxides by driving-off the sulfur as gaseous sulfur oxides. Lead, zinc, copper, and nickel are examples of metals usually found as sulfides that are roasted before reduction. Copper and nickel sulfide ores, instead of being roasted and smelted directly, are often smelted to a **matte** that is a mixture of copper or nickel and iron sulfides. Then, it is *converted*, a process in which air is blown into the molten matte to oxidize the sulfur to sulfur dioxide and change the iron to an oxide that combines with a silica flux to form a slag, leaving the copper or nickel as an impure metallic ore. For metals of a low boiling point, such as zinc, cadmium, and mercury, distillation may be employed in the later stages of extraction.

Smelting and other kinds of **pyrometallurgy** are very significant sources of air pollution because smelters may emit substantial amounts of gases, such as sulfur dioxide and carbon dioxide, and particulate matter. Small quantities of toxic metals, such as arsenic, lead, mercury, cadmium,

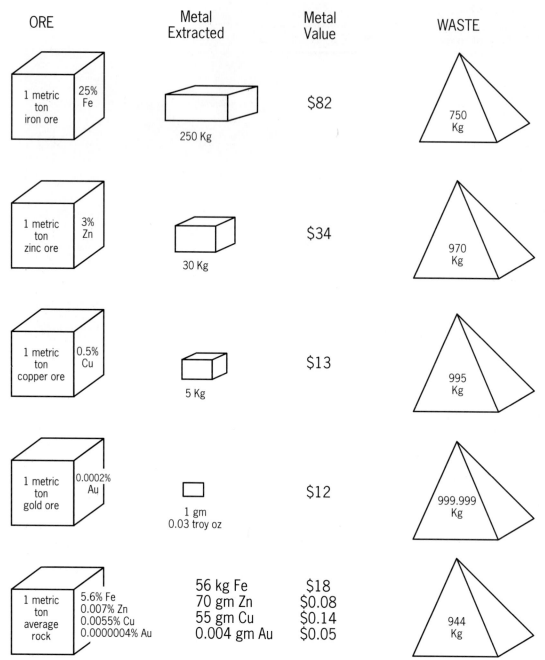

ORE	Metal Extracted	Metal Value	WASTE
1 metric ton iron ore — 25% Fe	250 Kg	$82	750 Kg
1 metric ton zinc ore — 3% Zn	30 Kg	$34	970 Kg
1 metric ton copper ore — 0.5% Cu	5 Kg	$13	995 Kg
1 metric ton gold ore — 0.0002% Au	1 gm 0.03 troy oz	$12	999.999 Kg
1 metric ton average rock — 5.6% Fe, 0.007% Zn, 0.0055% Cu, 0.0000004% Au	56 kg Fe, 70 gm Zn, 55 gm Cu, 0.004 gm Au	$18, $0.08, $0.14, $0.05	944 Kg

FIGURE 4.17. The amounts of metal extracted from one metric ton of typical ores range from as much as 250 kilograms for iron ores to as little as 1 gram for gold ores. The amounts of waste left for disposal are greater than the quantities of the metals extracted. The approximate amounts of the same metals that could be extracted from average crustal rocks are shown for comparison.

nickel, beryllium, and vanadium, may be released. Monitoring of the trace amounts of such metals in air and rainfall shows that they can travel long distances in considerable quantities, generally within fine particulates. The long-term effects of this pollution on human, animal, and plant life remain poorly understood.

Most gold recovery today is accomplished by dissolution of the gold using cyanide-bearing solutions in a method called **heap leaching;** this is an example of **hydrometallurgy** in which metals are dissolved from rocks (Figure 4.13 and Figure 8.45 and page 287). The ore is extracted by conventional mining techniques (usually in open pits), crushed so that

TABLE 4.1

Concentrations of metals in Earth's crust, their minimum grades to be mined, and the degree of natural concentration required for exploitation

Metal	Crustal Abundance (%)	Approximate Minimum Grade to Be Mined (%)	Approximate Degree of Concentration Needed to Be Mined
Aluminum	8.2	40	5 ×
Iron	5.6	25	5
Titanium	0.57	1.5	25
Manganese	0.095	25	260
Vanadium	0.0135	0.5	35
Chromium	0.010	40	4000
Nickel	0.0075	1.0	130
Zinc	0.0070	2.5	350
Copper	0.0055	0.5	90
Cobalt*	0.0025	0.2	80
Lead	0.00125	3	2400
Uranium	0.0027	0.01	40
Tin	0.00020	0.5	2500
Molybdenum*	0.00015	0.1	660
Tungsten	0.00015	0.3	2000
Mercury	0.000008	0.1	12,500
Silver*	0.000008	0.005	625
Platinum	0.0000005	0.0002	400
Gold*	0.0000004	0.0001	250

*Much of these metals is recovered as by-products of the mining for other metals.

fragments are 1–3 cm in diameter, and piled onto large sheets of impermeable plastic. Then, dilute solutions of sodium cyanide are allowed to slowly percolate down through the ore and dissolve the gold. The process may take several months but allows the commercial treatment of ores containing as little as 0.02 troy oz (0.6 ppm) of gold. When operated properly, gold dissolution using cyanide is very efficient and safe. However, cyanide solutions are highly toxic and their accidental release into the environment can kill many animals and plants. Responsible mining companies are very careful about cyanide use, but small releases have occasionally occurred. Probably the worst example, but one that made the mining industry even more careful, happened in Summitville, Colorado. In 1984, Summitville became the first mine in Colorado permitted to use cyanide heap leach techniques to recover gold. Unfortunately, the leach pads were poorly designed and were constructed in winter against the advice of professionals; leaks were detected within six days, and corrective actions were ordered. Nevertheless, mining and cyanide leaching continued until 1991. The company went bankrupt in 1991, abandoning the mine and allowing large amounts of cyanide to be released into the Alamosa River. The Environmental Protection Agency (EPA) intervened to take over the mine water recovery systems and stop pollution, but it has been spending millions of dollars on remediation. It will take years to totally stop the cyanide leakage. The problems at Summitville are being analyzed carefully by the mining industry to avoid any similar recurrences.

HOW USING RESOURCES AFFECTS THE ENVIRONMENT

Once resources have been extracted from Earth and processed, further disruption of the environment may be caused by their actual use. The principal example is the burning of fossil fuels in power stations, homes, and engines (particularly in automobiles) that results in gases, particles, and excess heat emitted into the environment. Using nuclear fuels for power generates extremely toxic radioactive waste products requiring special disposal. The utilization of oil to manufacture a wide range of petrochemicals and the use of metals and minerals to make industrial chemicals and products also generates wastes and pollutants.

Burning Fossil Fuels

The greatest problem caused by the burning of fossil fuels is air pollution. A good example of this is in urban areas in the United States and Europe (Figure 4.20) where the pollutants come mainly from motor vehicles, power plants, and heating systems. Industrial processes, such as smelting (see p. 221), can make significant contributions, and the burning of solid wastes also adds to air pollution.

The main pollutants from these sources are carbon monoxide, carbon dioxide, hydrocarbon compounds, nitrogen oxides, sulfur oxides, and particulate matter. Complete combustion of pure fossil fuels yields carbon dioxide (CO_2)

(a)

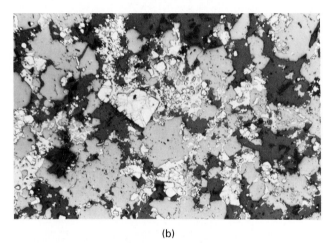

(b)

FIGURE 4.18. These photomicrographs of polished surfaces of ore samples from Japanese volcanogenic ores are only 0.6 mm across and illustrate the very fine-grained nature and intimately intergrown textures of ore minerals. In order to separate the various types of minerals, the ores must be crushed fine enough to free, or liberate, the individual grains. (a) Crystals of pyrite (FeS_2) in a matrix of chalcopyrite ($CuFeS_2$). (b) An intimate mixture of galena (PbS) and sphalerite (ZnS) with pyrite. (Photographs by J. R. Craig.)

(a)

(b)

FIGURE 4.19. (a) The fine grinding required to liberate the ore minerals is often accomplished by large ball mill, such as these, which are approximately 4 m in diameter. Coarse fragments of ore and steel balls 3–10 cm in diameter are fed into the mill, which revolves rapidly. The tumbling action of the balls and the ore grinds the ore to a fine powder. Water is added to prevent the generation of dust and to allow the powered ore to flow out in a slurry. (Photograph courtesy of Cleveland Cliffs, Inc.) (b) After grinding, a process of selective flotation is commonly used to separate the various types of ore minerals. The ore minerals attach themselves to small air bubbles pumped through the pulp. Addition of an organic substance to produce a stable froth enables the ore minerals to float off the tops of the cells at the right side of the photograph. Once separated, the ore minerals are taken to a smelter to extract the metals. (Photograph by J. R. Craig.)

and water vapor. These products are not really pollutants; they are already present in the atmosphere in significant amounts. Nevertheless, the burning of fossil fuels is leading to a steady increase in the CO_2 content of the atmosphere (see Figure 1.8) and consequent changes in other geochemical cycles and thermal properties of the atmosphere (see page 9). The most serious pollution arises from incomplete combustion and from the release of impurities. For example, carbon monoxide (CO) is a highly toxic gas given off in substantial amounts by incomplete combustion of gasoline. Such incomplete combustion also gives rise to fine particles of carbon (**soot**). Both oil and coal contain sulfur-bearing compounds as impurities; these give a mixture of sulfur oxides, mainly

TABLE 4.2
Mineral processing: methods of mineral separation

Mineral Property Exploited	Method	Applicable to
High density (S.G.)	Mineral jig	Coarser-grained ores of lead (galena), barytes, etc.
	Shaking tables	Finer-grained ores of tin (cassiterite), gold, etc.
	Heavy media (liquid) separation	Preliminary separation of many denser ore minerals
Magnetism (chiefly ferro- or ferrimagnetism)	Magnetic separator	A small number of ferro- or ferrimagnetic minerals (magnetite, pyrrhotite, etc.) Some more weakly magnetic minerals (wolfram, ilmenite, etc.)
Electrical properties	High tension separation	Dry particulate ores containing metallic conductors (e.g., ilmenite, cassiterite) and insulators (e.g., monazite)
Surface chemical properties	Froth flotation	A very wide range of metal sulfides and oxides as well as nonmetallic minerals

sulfur dioxide (SO_2) and trioxide (SO_3), when burned. Nitrogen compounds are also found in all fossil fuels, producing various oxides of nitrogen, mainly nitrogen monoxide (NO) and nitrogen dioxide (NO_2), when burned. Coal also contains incombustible fine particles of mineral matter emitted as **fly ash** from chimneys when it is burned. Various hydrocarbon compounds and more complex substances also result from burning fossil fuels. Some undergo reactions with the atmosphere, as in the **oxidants** produced by hydrocarbons and nitrogen oxides reacting in the presence of sunlight. These pollutants produce a **photochemical smog** found in the atmospheres of sunny urban areas with large volumes of automobile traffic (Figure 4.21). Other pollutants produced in far smaller quantities include various particulate lead compounds from leaded gasoline and a considerable range of often toxic metals, gases, and complex compounds given off during various industrial processes and the burning of waste.

How do these pollutants behave when they enter the atmosphere? This depends on the atmospheric conditions at the time, in particular on the temperature of the air at various heights. Under what could be called average conditions, air temperature drops steadily at a rate of about 1°C for every 1000 m increase in altitude. In this case, gains and losses of energy in the atmosphere (mainly as heat from the sun or

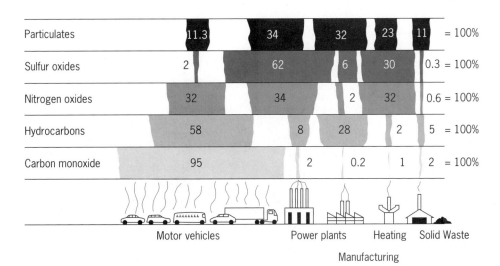

FIGURE 4.20. Schematic representation of the sources of air pollution. (From the New York State Department of Environmental Conservation.)

FIGURE 4.21. The effects of atmospheric inversions on atmospheric pollution. These three views of downtown Los Angeles show: (top) a clear day; (middle) pollution trapped beneath an inversion layer at about 75 meters; (bottom) pollution under an inversion layer at about 450 meters. (Photographs courtesy of South Coast Air Quality Management District, from J. N. Birakos, "Profile of Air Pollution Control," County of Los Angeles, 1974.)

radiated from Earth's surface) are in balance. At any particular time and place, the actual temperatures may be cooler than the equilibrium conditions (Figure 4.22). Smoke warmer than the atmosphere rises, gradually mixing with the air and being dispersed. It is also possible for the air at some given altitude to be warmer than the equilibrium conditions. Such a warm layer may rest stably over the cooler and denser air beneath and form a condition known as an **atmospheric inversion.** These conditions can develop at the end of a sunny day when the air near the ground starts to lose heat rapidly. This can continue through the night and the following early morning before heat from the sun causes turbulent mixing of the layers of air and a breakup of the inversion. Sometimes, weather conditions may allow the inversion to persist for several days. Exhaust gases from motor vehicles and smoke from chimneys that do not penetrate above the inversion layer are trapped and may blanket the affected area with a dense smog.

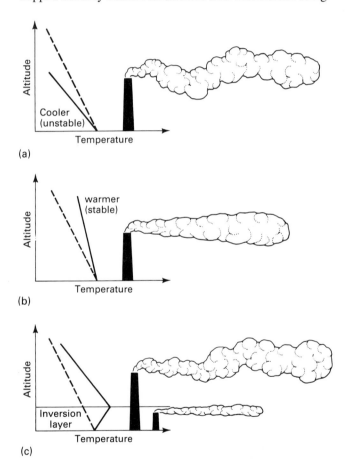

FIGURE 4.22. The effects of air temperature on pollution. The dashed line is the normal temperature gradient; the solid line is the actual gradient in each diagram. (a) Air is cooler than normal, creating unstable but smoke-dispersing conditions. (b) Air is warmer than normal, creating stable smoke-dispersing conditions. (c) An inversion traps the smoke from the lower stack.

Smoke that does penetrate this layer (which may extend from tens to hundreds of meters above the ground) will disperse in the much larger volume of air in the overlying atmosphere. This is a major reason for building tall chimneys, the tallest of which approach 400 m (about 1200 feet) (Figure 4.23) and rival the world's tallest buildings.

What are the harmful effects caused by air pollution, whether from burning fuels in vehicles and power plants or from other industrial processes? Some of the effects are obvious: reduction of visibility, soiling of buildings, and creation of an environment that is bad for human health. There have been notorious cases of deaths directly caused by air pollution. For example, in London in 1952, a severe smog lasting several days led to close to 4000 more deaths than would have been expected at that time of year. Many of those who died already suffered from respiratory and cardiac disease. Such episodes led to clean air laws that have restricted the burning of certain types of fuels and greatly reduced the problem in London.

The question of how the air pollution we create affects climate is more controversial. Dust particles can potentially reflect the sun's rays and cause lower temperatures, but major volcanic eruptions introduce far more dust into the upper atmosphere than human activities, and the effects of even the largest such eruptions have generally been local and short lived. Air pollution promotes fogginess, cloudiness, and possible rainfall on a local scale by providing nuclei for the condensation of drops of moisture. However, worldwide effects on precipitation are much more difficult to assess.

The burning of fossil fuels certainly changes the chemistry of the atmosphere. One such effect already mentioned is the worldwide increase in carbon dioxide (see Figure 1.8). Although CO_2 constitutes only about 0.03 percent of Earth's atmosphere (Figure 4.24), an increase in CO_2 is important because it, along with water and ozone, absorbs heat given off by Earth. This trapping of heat is called the **greenhouse effect.** Some scientists have estimated that Earth's CO_2 concentration will increase enough over the next half century to raise the average surface temperatures by 0.5°C. It is hard to assess the accuracy of such predictions, let alone the effects of such a change on world climate.

There are similar problems regarding the effects of pollution on the upper atmosphere, particularly the layer of ozone (O_3) that protects Earth from much of the sun's ultraviolet radiation. The exhaust from high-flying supersonic jets creates reactive nitrogen oxides that could damage the ozone layer and introduce particles, water, and CO_2. Compounds called chlorofluoromethanes (or freons), such as the $CFCl_3$ formerly used as propellants in aerosol cans, can also damage the ozone layer. If these compounds reach the upper atmosphere, they can react with and destroy the ozone. Such changes in the chemistry of the upper atmosphere may cause an increase in Earth's surface temperatures, and increases in ultraviolet radiation could affect human health. The formation and destruction of ozone are shown schematically in Figure 4.25.

FIGURE 4.23. Very tall stacks such as this one, 370 m (1216 ft) high, at the Homer City Electric Generating Station in Pennsylvania are constructed so that waste gases and particles that escape entrapment in filters are released high enough in the atmosphere to allow for dilution and dispersal to minimize pollution problems. (Photograph courtesy of the Pennsylvania Electric Company, a member of the General Public Utilities System, and New York State Electric and Gas.)

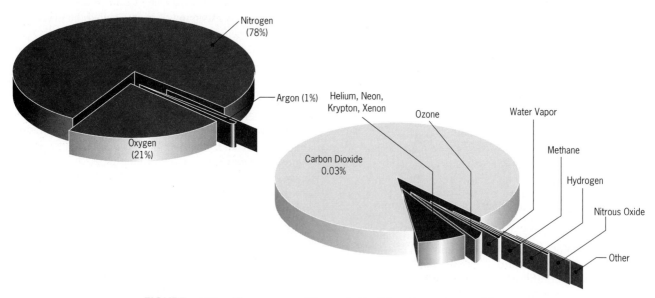

FIGURE 4.24. The composition of Earth's atmosphere. (From NOAA.)

ACID RAIN

Rainfall has generally been thought of as beneficial and pure, washing and watering Earth's surface. While this pristine image is still true in many places, it has been highly tarnished as we come to realize that the water is not always pure, and its effects are not always beneficial. As early as 1872, British chemist Robert Smith coined the term *acid rain* to describe the nature of precipitation containing significant sulfuric acid. He attributed this to burning coal during the Industrial Revolution. Little more was said about this phenomenon until the 1950s when European scientists reported abnormally low pH values in Scandinavian lakes with no source of acids except from rainfall. Subsequently, acidic precipitation has been recognized, debated, and sometimes addressed in many parts of the world.

What is acid rain? This term describes precipitation—including rain, sleet, hail, and snow—that is acidic. In general, this means precipitation with a pH lower than 5.0 (Figure 4.26a). The pH of a substance, the conventional measure of the hydrogen ion content of aqueous solutions, ranges from 0 to 14 with a neutral 7. This actually means that the concentration of hydrogen ions is 10^{-7} mol/L. Rain water naturally contains dissolved carbon dioxide from the atmosphere, forming weak carbonic acid (H_2CO_3). This acid decomposes slightly to release H^+ and HCO_3^- ions, resulting in rainfall that is normally slightly acidic. The pH is about 5.6. The increase of carbon dioxide due to the burning of fossil fuels may have some significant effects on atmospheric warming, but it probably does little to the pH.

In contrast, it is clear that the introduction of large amounts of sulfur oxides and nitrogen oxides into the atmosphere by fossil fuel combustion can have a significant impact on the acidity of rain. Sulfur oxides, which combine with water vapor to form sulfuric acid (H_2SO_4) are created when sulfur in the coal is burned. Nitrogen oxides, which react with the water vapor to form nitric acid (HNO_3), are created as an unintentional by-product of high-temperature combustion in an atmosphere containing 78 percent nitrogen. Small amounts of these two strong acids in rainfall can sharply lower the pH of rainwater.

On a worldwide basis, it appears that natural phenomena, such as volcanoes, forest fires, and the decay of vegetation, probably result in more sulfur and nitrogen oxides in the atmosphere than do human activities. These natural emissions are very widespread and appear to lower the pH of rainwater to the range of 5.0–5.6. Accordingly, most researchers now consider precipitation acidic if its pH is below 5.0. Using that threshold, it is apparent that considerable portions of North America and Europe are subject to acid rain. Local effects of smokestack emissions have long been evident. However, the first recognition of a large scale problem came from European scientists in the 1950s when they recognized abnormally low pH values in many Scandinavian lakes. Subsequently, large numbers of monitoring stations have been established in North America and Europe to define the scope of the situation. The map (Figure 4.26b) for a year in the 1990s shows that the pH of precipitation for most of the eastern United States is below 5.0, and for large areas of the upper Mississippi Valley and northeast it is below 4.5.

Most of the acid rain effect is attributed to power plant emissions where coal containing 1–2.5 percent sulfur is burned. Nitrogen oxides come from both power plants and motor vehicles. Acid rain damages vegetation, limits fish growth by acidifying streams and lakes, causes deterioration of human structures (especially metals, limestones, and paints) (Figure 4.27), and increases the leaching of nutrients from soils. This has resulted in the passage of the 1990 Clean Air Act. Implementation of the sulfur and nitrogen oxide emissions of this Act is estimated to cost $25–35 billion per year, but the effect is anticipated to cut U.S. power plant sulfur oxide emissions in half (10 million tons annually) and nitrogen oxides emission by one-third (4 million tons annually) by the year 2000. In addition, passenger car emissions of nitrogen oxides will be cut by 60 percent by 2003. There are still arguments that the detrimental effects of acid rain have been exaggerated and the costs of implementing these controls are too high. On the other hand, increasing public concern for environmental pollution continues to push for tighter controls on emission.

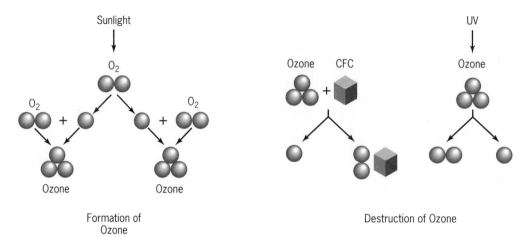

FIGURE 4.25. Ozone (O_3) is formed in Earth's atmosphere when sunlight breaks diatomic oxygen into single oxygen atoms. These then combine with other diatomic oxygen. Ozone may be destroyed by ultraviolet (UV) radiation and by reacting with CFCs produced by humans.

The sulfur dioxide (SO_2) emitted from burning coal (see Chapter 5) and many smelters is thought to be the cause of **acid rain** (see page 81). Sulfuric acid, produced on combination of the SO_2 with rain water, damages plants and soils and lowers the pH in many streams and lakes throughout the world. Normal rain water has a pH of about 5.6, but much of the rain in Europe and the eastern U.S. has an average pH of 4.0; readings as low as 2.1 have been reported. If the pH drops below 5.0, fish often die, and plant life is severely affected.

The effects of the sulfur and nitrogen oxides released by coal burning have been the subject of much debate, often from very biased viewpoints. In 1983, the United States National Academy of Sciences released a report noting that the burning of fossil fuels, especially coal in power plants, is the principal source of the oxides responsible for the acid rain in the northeastern United States. Furthermore, the report noted a direct correlation of sulfur oxide content in acid rain with the sulfur content in fuels. Reduction of the sulfur oxide emissions by half, the recommended target, can be achieved by only three methods: (1) a change to another type of fuel (oil, nuclear, etc.), (2) installation of expensive air cleaner systems, and (3) a switch to lower-sulfur coals. Critics of the National Academy's report point out, however, that the United States and Europe burned the same amount of coal in the 1950s and the 1980s, but there was much less acid rain in the 1950s. They suggest that either coal burning is not the culprit or that alkaline impurities in the coals previously used to neutralize the acid are now being cleaned up too thoroughly. Clearly, the problem of acid rain is far from being completely understood or solved. Regardless of the debates, more than 15,000 lakes in Scandinavia and Canada have been damaged by acid rain, much of which is possibly attributable to emissions from other countries. Acid rain also speeds up the decay of buildings, sculptures, and other structures, particularly those made of **limestone** or **marble** (Figure 4.27).

The control of air pollution involves both legislation limiting emissions and the use of various devices to remove as many of the noxious substances as possible from exhaust gases, power plant emissions, and smelter emissions. Because polluted air may travel hundreds of miles, affecting areas far away from the pollution source, the difficulties of introducing adequate legal controls are compounded by the need for international agreements.

A final, and rather ironic, form of pollution that results from burning fossil fuels and certain other kinds of power generation is **thermal pollution.** Most power plants take water from rivers, lakes, and sea coasts, use it for cooling, and then return it to its source at a higher temperature. This affects ecosystems and may kill fish and other aquatic life accustomed to the cooler water conditions. One alternative is to dissipate waste heat into the air with cooling towers, but this can affect the local climate and involves unsightly structures. A much better solution employed in some areas is to make use of such excess heat to warm nearby homes and factories, thereby also conserving energy.

Disposing of Nuclear Waste Products

The mining and processing of uranium ores, the fabrication of nuclear fuels from these ores, and the use of fuels in nuclear power stations all generate waste products requiring disposal. The safe disposal of these products of the "nuclear fuel cycle" (discussed in detail in Chapter 6) is a matter of great public concern, particularly because the small amounts of lethal radioactive poisons cannot be detected by human senses. Nuclear weapons manufacture and development also generate significant amounts of highly radioactive waste.

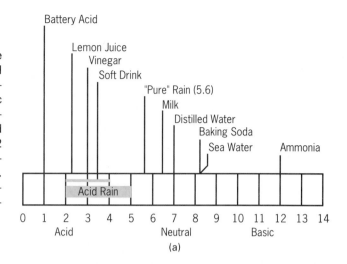

FIGURE 4.26. Acid rain. (a) The pH scale shows the pH of several common compounds. Rain is generally considered to be acidic when it lies below 5.0. (b) The average pH of rainfall in the United States measured throughout 1992 shows the lowest values are concentrated in the OhioValley area. (Map courtesy of National Atmospheric Deposition Program, Colorado State University.)

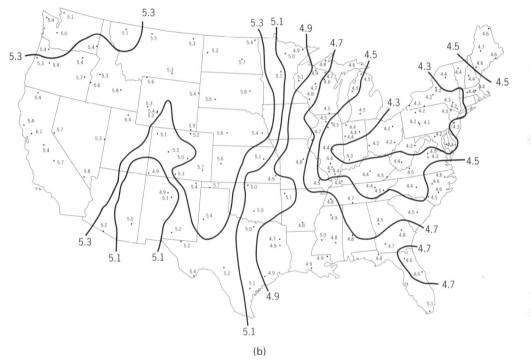

(b)

The long-term disposal of radioactive wastes is still an unresolved problem. Before considering the possible answers to this problem, we need to discuss the various kinds of radioactive wastes and the quantities in which they are produced.

Categories of Radioactive Waste. The nature of a radioactive waste material, in addition to whether it is in solid, liquid, or gaseous form, depends on the concentrations of radioactive **isotopes** present. Although such wastes emit rays or subatomic particles that can damage living tissue, the level of this emission decreases with time. The rate of this decay of radioactive isotopes varies widely and is measured in terms of **half-life,** the time taken for the level of radiation emitted by an isotope to be reduced to one-half of its initial value. For example, one gram of the radioactive iodine isotope ^{131}I, with a half-life of eight days, emits one-half of its original radiation after eight days, one-quarter after 16 days, one-eighth after 24 days, one-sixteenth after 32 days, and so on. Half-lives can range from only fractions of a second to millions of years; consequently, some materials remain lethal for hundreds or thousands of years while others become virtually harmless in a matter of seconds. Most radioactive wastes are mixtures of short- and longer-lived isotopes. These isotopes include species produced directly by the use of the fuel, and others are produced when the materials in close proximity to the fuel are irradiated. The principal radioisotopes involved, along with information on emitted radiation, half-life, and the units used to measure radioactivity, are given in Table 4.3.

FIGURE 4.27. The corrosive effects of acid rain and other atmospheric pollutants have eaten away the top of this limestone ornamental feature on the Organization of American States Building in Washington, D.C. (Photograph by E. McGee.)

The main subdivisions of these materials as far as disposal is concerned are **low-level, intermediate-level,** and **high-level** wastes. Low-level wastes are generally those in which the maximum level of radioactivity is up to 1000 times that considered acceptable in the environment. Intermediate-level wastes have 1000 to 1,000,000 times that considered acceptable. High-level wastes have even greater activities. The volume of high-level waste produced is a very small proportion of the total (Table 4.4); however, it does account for 95 percent of the total radioactivity of these wastes.

Low-Level Wastes and Their Disposal. Large quantities of waste are produced at uranium mines. Although the mined ores are processed by crushing, grinding, and separating concentrate rich in the uranium minerals, the residue (**tailings**) commonly contains much of the total radioactivity originally associated with the ore. This is because there is a far greater volume of material in this than the concentrate. This disposal of uranium mill tailings can give rise to human exposure at unacceptable levels of radiation because the material has been finely ground and can be transported by wind and water. Also, radon, a radioactive gas produced by the decay of uranium, can escape into the atmosphere more easily from this pulverized material. Furthermore, several of the radioisotopes present in the tailings are very long lived; for example, thorium-230 has a half-life of 77,000 years. This means that the containment of these wastes must be de-signed to take erosion and redistribution occurring over very long time periods into account. In practice, the wastes are usually dumped at or near the mine and subsequently stabilized by earth cover and vegetation. Water seeping through the wastes should not enter groundwater systems that provide water supplies for human or animal consumption. It is also important to keep the wastes far away from human activities other than the mining operation. Unfortunately, this has not always been so in the past. For example, at Grand Junction, Colorado, more than 300,000 tons of radioactive tailings were used as fill material for land on which many buildings were later constructed. Some of the waste was even used to make concrete blocks used in the foundations of some houses. The recognition of elevated levels of radioactivity in these buildings led to a cleanup program costing many millions of dollars.

One of the principal isotopes monitored is radon (Rn^{86}) because it is a gas and can be breathed into the human body, increasing risks of cancer. Concern about radon levels in homes resulting either from radioactive wastes or natural radioactivity in underlying rocks increased dramatically in the United States in 1985 when a worker at a nuclear power plant in Pennsylvania set off radiation alarms as he came to work in the morning. Surveys of his home in Colebrookdale, Pennsylvania, revealed that radon gas, seeping from the uranium-bearing rocks beneath his house, had built up because the house was very tightly insulated. Subsequent surveys in different parts of the United States have revealed that houses in many areas have radon gas levels higher than recommended safe levels. Most problems of this type can be remedied by installing ventilation systems, but some require the removal of the building materials that contain the radioactive elements.

Large volumes of low-level waste are also produced in nuclear power stations, research laboratories, hospitals, or various nuclear industries. Typical items include contaminated laboratory equipment, protective clothing, and even contaminated animal wastes. The lower-activity wastes are usually sealed in drums, commonly after being burned in special incinerators to reduce their volume, and buried in

RADON

Radon is a naturally occurring, odorless, colorless, and radioactive gas that forms from the normal radioactive decay schemes of uranium and thorium. Many believe that the higher rates of radon exposure experienced by uranium miners contribute to their higher-than-normal cancer rates. The potential for radon effects on other people was not even considered until December 1984 when an engineer from the Limerick nuclear plant in eastern Pennsylvania was found to have too high a level of a radiation exposure—not on his way home, but on his way to work! Investigators finally determined that his high levels of radiation resulted from exposure to high levels of radon gas in his home.

Subsequent studies have found that as many as one in fifteen homes in the United States have radon gas concentrations in excess of what the EPA considers safe. Furthermore, the EPA has suggested that the radon gas exposure causes between 7000 and 30,000 lung cancer deaths per year in the United States. The effects, however, are slow, cumulative, and often linked with the effects of smoking. Hence, it is difficult to isolate and document the impact of radon on human health. However, we can still discover where it comes from and what can be done.

Radon, atomic element 86, forms as a result of the decay of radium, which forms during the complex stepwise decay schemes of uranium-235, uranium-238, and thorium-232. All previous elements in the decay schemes are solids, but radon is a gas, which can exist as a vapor or dissolved in groundwater. When radon decays, it becomes radioactive bismuth or polonium, which readily attaches to fine dust particles. The radioactive breakdown of radon and its daughter products gives off high-energy gamma rays, which can harm body cells.

Radon is generated in the greatest amounts where underlying rocks contain high levels of uranium and thorium, for example, granites. As the uranium and thorium undergo natural radioactive decay, radon is released moving along fractures in the rocks. If houses are built in such areas, some of the radon may enter through cracks in the basement, through drains, and even in water pumped from wells for household use (Figure 4.28). Radon has always entered houses in these manners, and if levels are low and there is adequate ventilation, there is no problem. In recent years, however, many people have become more conscious of energy loss from houses that are poorly insulated. In the process of sealing cracks around doors and windows to conserve heat, the home owners have also sealed in any radon that is being released. Furthermore, before the radon incident in 1984, virtually no one tested houses for radon, so we really do not know if there were many problems.

Since 1984, people have become more aware of the radon problem, and many states require radon testing performed on all homes when they are sold. The general solutions are to either prevent the radon from entering the house by sealing cracks or other points of entry or to install a ventilation system that removes radon before it builds to harmful levels. Costs can range from a few hundred to a few thousand dollars. The cost is relatively small compared with that of a house, however. It is not possible to stop radon from being formed, but it is possible to prevent it from accumulating in a home.

shallow trenches beneath a meter of soil (Figure 4.29). The site should be carefully chosen for geological and geographical setting. Radioactivity in the area is monitored regularly to ensure that any contamination of plants, soils, and groundwater is within accepted limits. The upper limits of radiation exposure, or dosage, for workers in the nuclear industries and for the general public are commonly governed by legislation based on the recommendations of the International Commission on Radiological Protection (ICRP). The ICRP limit for public exposure is given in Table 4.5 along with doses arising from various sources for the population of England.

Low levels of wastes of somewhat higher activity have often been cast into concrete, enclosed in sealed drums, and dumped into the deep ocean. Tens of thousands of tons of such wastes have been dumped at an internationally agreed site in the Atlantic Ocean 800 kilometers from southwest England. The concrete enables proper handling and ensures it reaches the bottom of the sea intact, where it should remain for many years. The safety of this disposal method is based on the vast dilution of the activity as it slowly disperses in the ocean five kilometers below the surface.

Low-level liquid wastes arise at nuclear power stations and at plants where nuclear fuel is reprocessed. Such wastes are often treated and then discharged into rivers and into the sea. When this is done, the levels of radiation in waters and marine life are closely monitored and kept to acceptable

TABLE 4.3
Radioactive isotopes occurring in nuclear wastes

Principal Fission Products		Products of Irradiation of Nonfuel Materials	
Isotope	Half-life	Isotope (and Source)	Half-life
krypton-85	<9.4 yr	From air and water:	
strontium-89	54 d	tritium, H-3, (^{2}H)	12.3 yr
strontium-90	25 yr	carbon-14 (^{14}N)	5700 yr
zirconium-95	65 d	nitrogen-16 (^{16}O)	7.3 sec
niobium-95	<35 d	nitrogen-17 ^{17}O)	4.1 sec
technetium-99	$<5 \times 10^5$ yr	oxygen-19 (^{18}O)	30 sec
ruthenium-103	39.8 yr	argon-41 (^{40}A)	1.8 hr
rhodium-103	57 min	From sodium (coolant):	
ruthenium-106	1 yr	sodium-24 (^{23}Na)	15 yr
rhodium-106	30 sec	sodium-22 (^{23}Na)	2.6 yr
tellurium-129	<72 min	rubidium-86 (^{85}Rb)	19.5 hr
iodine-129	1.7×10^7 yr	From metals and alloys:	
iodine-131	8 d	aluminum-28 (^{27}Al)	2.3 min
xenon-133	<5.3 d	chromium-51 (^{50}Cr)	27 d
cesium-137	33 yr	manganese-56 (^{56}Fe)	2.6 hr
barium-140	12.8 yr	iron-55 (^{54}Fe)	2.9 yr
lanthanum-140	40 hr	iron-59 (^{59}Co)	45 d
cerium-141	32.5 d	copper-64 (^{63}Cu)	12.8 hr
cerium-144	590 d	zinc-65 (^{64}Zn)	250 d
praseodymium-143	13.8 d	tantalum-182 (^{181}Ta)	115 d
praseodymium-144	17 min	tungsten-187 (^{186}W)	24 hr
promethium-147	2.26 yr	cobalt-58 (^{58}Ni)	71 d
		cobalt-60 (^{59}Co)	5.3 yr

Units of Radioactivity
Unit of activity is the Curie (Ci); 1 Ci = 3.7×10^{10} disintegrations/sec
Unit of exposure dose for X-rays and γ-rays = Roentgen (R)
1 R = 87.8 erg/sec (5.49×10^7 MeV/g) in air
Unit of absorbed dose = Rad; 1 rad = 100 erg/g (6.25×10^7MeV/g) in any material
Unit of dose equivalent (for protection) = Rem (Si unit equivalent = Sievert; 1 rem = 10^{-2} sieverts)
Rems (roentgen equivalents for people) = rads $\times$ QF where QF (quality factor) depends, for example, on type of radiation
(γ-rays QF $\cong$ 1, thermal neutrons QF $\cong$ 3, α particles QF $\le$ 20)

levels. Radioactive gases are also given off from power plants in very small amounts. These procedures and emissions have given rise to public concern and pressure from environmental groups.

Intermediate-Level Wastes and Their Disposal. Materials, such as certain components from nuclear power plants, flasks used to transport fuel, and various liquids used in these plants, have intermediate levels of activity. At present,

TABLE 4.4
Estimated volumes of solid radioactive waste resulting from the generation of electricity from a 1 megawatt (10^6) nuclear power plant operation for 1 year (including wastes generated at fuel manufacturing and reprocessing plants)

Category of Waste	Volume (m^3)
Low-level wastes (untreated)	2000
Intermediate-level wastes (after treatment)	100
High-level wastes (after solidification)	2

(Data from United Kingdom Atomic Energy Authority, 1982.)

these are often stored in tanks or other containers at nuclear plants eventually to be disposed of by methods similar to those used for the low-level wastes. Another possibility involves treatment to remove long-lived active constituents so that the bulk of the material is discharged or buried as low-level waste.

High-Level Wastes and Their Disposal—A Great Debate? The high-level wastes from the nuclear power industry account for roughly 95 percent of the radioactivity, but only about 0.1 percent of the volume of waste generated. These consist of large quantities of liquid wastes and used fuel rods that give off extremely high levels of radioactivity and heat. The high levels of radioactivity produced by a variety of isotopes require that the high-level wastes be isolated from human exposure for approximately 10,000 years. After that time, the level of radioactivity will have decreased to about one ten-thousandth of its original level (Figure 4.30). At present, they are stored in stainless-steel tanks (Figure 4.31) at the fuel reprocessing plants or power plants where they are generated. The problem of their eventual disposal has been the subject of much research, and no agreeable

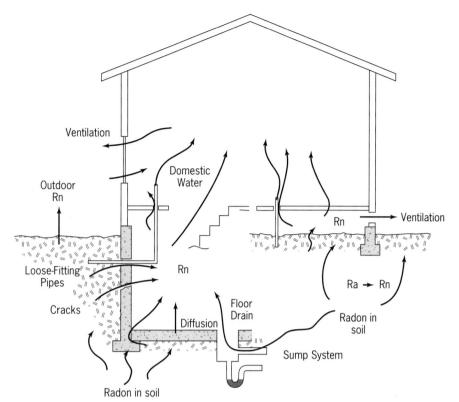

FIGURE 4.28. Radon gas is generated in the rocks and soils by the radioactive decay of uranium and thorium. Once generated, radon can move either as a free gas or dissolved in groundwater and enter a house. If the house is well ventilated, the radon disperses; but if a house is tightly sealed, the concentrations of radon can build up to hazardous levels.

FIGURE 4.29. Low-level nuclear waste is packed in drums and buried in shallow trenches where it is isolated from surface runoff and groundwater. (Courtesy of U. S. Geological Survey.)

TABLE 4.5

Radiation doses experienced by average citizens of Great Britain with their sources and the internationally accepted upper dosage limit

Radiation Source	Annual Dose in Microsieverts (μSv)*
ICRP limit (for public citizens)**	5000 (5 rem)
Natural background (average)	1860
Natural background (range)	1500–3000+
Medical diagnosis and treatment (average)	500
Air travel, television watching, nuclear weapons tests, etc.	18
Discharges from the nuclear industry (excluding Chernobyl)	3

*The sievert (Sv) is a unit of radiation that takes into account the biological effectiveness of different types of radiation. There is no evidence of harmful effects from radiation at levels below about 1/100 of a sievert (10,000 μSv).

**ICRP = International Commission for Radiation Protection
(From United Kingdom Atomic Energy Authority, 1982).

solution has yet been found. Meanwhile, these lethal substances continue to accumulate. One estimate of their toxicity suggests that less than four liters of the waste would be enough to bring every person in the world to the danger level for radiation exposure if it were evenly distributed; hundreds of millions of liters are now in storage. Although the safety record in the storage of these highly active wastes has been good over the nearly 40 years of their existence, some leakages from the storage tanks have occurred, resulting in nearby contamination.

Most long-term nuclear waste disposal strategies require that the waste first be solidified. One method of doing this is to incorporate the waste into glass, a process known as **vitrification.** The French have developed a method for doing this on an industrial scale using a glass containing boron and silicon. This process can be designed such that the glasses survive the effects of heating and radiation from the wastes, but there is concern about the ability of such glasses to survive attack by water or brine solutions at elevated temperatures. These are important considerations because the solid wastes are likely to be buried deep within the earth. The alternative to vitrification is to incorporate the wastes into ceramics or synthetic minerals. The radioactive elements would be more tightly and stably bound in these crystalline minerals much as they were before mining. An example of such a material is the mixture of titanium oxide minerals (titanates) called **SYNROC,** which was developed by an Australian group (Table 4.6). As the name suggests, it is actually a synthetic rock. Proponents of this method of waste processing point out that the radioactive elements are being returned to the sort of chemical environment in which they are most stable in the earth. Certainly, experiments show that SYNROC remains stable in contact with brine solutions to much higher temperatures (even in excess of 700°C) than glasses.

Solidification is only the first step in the ultimate disposal of nuclear wastes. After being sealed into concrete and stainless-steel canisters, solidified waste can be stored in vaults or reinforced, shielded buildings above ground. Such methods are used in France where canisters containing vitrified waste are placed in a vault and cooled in a stream of air. Perhaps wastes in such stores could be kept safely for the indefinite future with minimal surveillance and maintenance. However, there are inevitable concerns of the vulnerability of such stores during war, acts of terrorism, or major disasters.

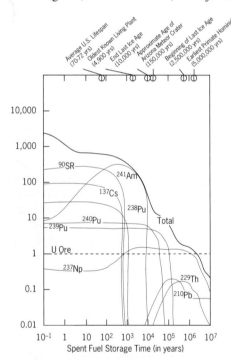

FIGURE 4.30. The relative amounts of total radiation released from high-level nuclear wastes (upper heavy curve) and the amounts from several major radioactive isotopes decrease with time. The storage time considered necessary for this high-level waste to drop to levels considered safe is about 10,000 years. (From U. S. Department of Energy.)

FIGURE 4.31. Temporary above ground storage of high-level nuclear waste in a mobile canister at the Surry Nuclear Power Plant in Virginia. (Courtesy of Virginia Power.)

Various options have been considered for the ultimate disposal of the solidified wastes. The more extreme proposals, such as removal from Earth by rocket or burial in the polar ice caps, have been rejected on technical or safety grounds. The remaining options include disposal in the ocean, burial beneath deep ocean sediments, or deep burial in land. It is possible that larger amounts of high-level wastes could be disposed of in the ocean bed or buried within deep ocean sediments. There are areas of the ocean floor where sediments have remained undisturbed for millions of years and are likely to remain very stable. Although technically these appear to be good possibilities for disposal sites, there are certain to be major legal problems in obtaining the necessary international agreements to use these sites. Also, despite several decades of research, more needs to be known about dispersal mechanisms of the wastes before further ocean-bed dumping could be considered acceptable. Considerable research has also been done on suitable deep-burial sites on land. Clearly, a very stable environment, and one relatively impervious to groundwater, is needed. Some have suggested burial in salt deposits because they deform plastically rather than fracture. Also, because they are water soluble, their presence is evidence of a dry environment. However, all salt beds contain a small percentage of water as small fluid inclusions, and some salt beds are known to contain *pods* of brine that could prove highly corrosive if brought in contact with solid wastes. Furthermore, some experiments have suggested that the 1–2 percent of water dispersed in salt beds may actually slowly migrate toward the hot area around the radioactive wastes. Other environments being considered include shales or crystalline rocks such as basalts or granites. Uranium minerals have originally occurred in nature in these types of rocks.

Ideally, the geological environment should form a natural barrier to fluids that could attack and disperse the waste. It should be an environment as free as possible from any risk of earthquake or volcanic activity. As well as natural barriers to the escape of the wastes, there should also be artificial, or engineered, barriers. These might include sealing the solid wastes in corrosion-resistant canisters, perhaps stainless steel, and surrounding them with absorbent materials, such as clays or zeolites. The waste might be deposited in the site simply by drilling deep holes. In the case of SYNROC, it is proposed that one-meter diameter holes be drilled down to a depth of four kilometers. The bottom three

TABLE 4.6

Mineralogical and chemical composition of SYNROC,* the titanate ceramic wasteform designed to incorporate radioactive wastes in a stable form for disposal by burial in Earth

Component (wt %)	Formula	Acts as Primary Host for
Hollandite (33)	$Ba(Al,Ti)Ti_6O_{16}$	Cs, Ba, Rb, K, Cr
Zirconolite (28)	$CaZrTi_2O_7$	Th, U, Pu and tetravalent actinides, Zr
Perovskite (19)	$CaTiO_3$	Sr, Na, trivalent actinides rare earths
Rutile (15)	TiO_2	
Alloy (5)		Tc, Mo, Ru, Pd, S, Te

(Data are from Ringwood, A.E., *Mineralogical Magazine*, vol. 49, p. 159–176, 1985).
*Actually the commonest of several forms of SYNROC known as SYNROC-C.

kilometers would be filled with waste in its stable form. Other sites would be more like mines with shafts allowing access for men and materials. Wastes would be stored in galleries (Figure 4.32). To save costs, old mine workings would be evaluated for this purpose.

Several countries have already made decisions on the geologic environment for long-term high-level waste disposal (e.g., Belgium—clay; Germany—salt; Sweden—granite; India—granite), but the United States remains without a functioning permanent repository. In the United States, experiments have been conducted at the Waste Isolation Pilot Project (WIPP) site in New Mexico salt beds, but it has been decided that the best site for a repository is in volcanic tuffs at Yucca Mountain, Nevada (Figure 4.33, Plates 26 and 27, and see page 168). Unfortunately, the site, originally expected to be completed in 1998, will not be ready to accept high-level wastes until at least 2010.

Since the construction of the first nuclear power plants, much effort has been put into the problems concerning the disposal of the dangerous wastes that they produce. There appear to be technical solutions to this problem that involve only small risks to humans and the rest of the living world. These risks would be less than the risks involved in current methods of storage. Many concerns about the secure long-term disposal of high-level nuclear wastes remain, and there are many people who feel that much of this mater-ial will ultimately be retrieved as recycled fuels. The principal driving force for the development of high-level nuclear waste storage facilities must come from the nuclear power industry.

Other Industrial Processes—Waste Products and Pollution

Many industrial processes based on mineral resources create substances that can have adverse effects on the environment. The releases of such substances may be accidental, as in the case of oil spills, or they may result from direct application, as in the use of fertilizers, pesticides, and herbicides. Such agricultural pollutants pose particular problems because they are widespread **non-point sources** of pollution; they are unlike dumps, power plants, or factories that emit pollutants from a **point source,** or a small and precisely defined area.

Although many of the substances deliberately released into the environment appear to enter various chemical and biological cycles without harmful effects, some cause widespread concern. Certainly, our knowledge of the paths followed by many of these substances after their release is inadequate. We know very little of the long-term effects that may result from prolonged buildup of many substances in particular environments. A well-known example of the problem comes from the chemical industry.

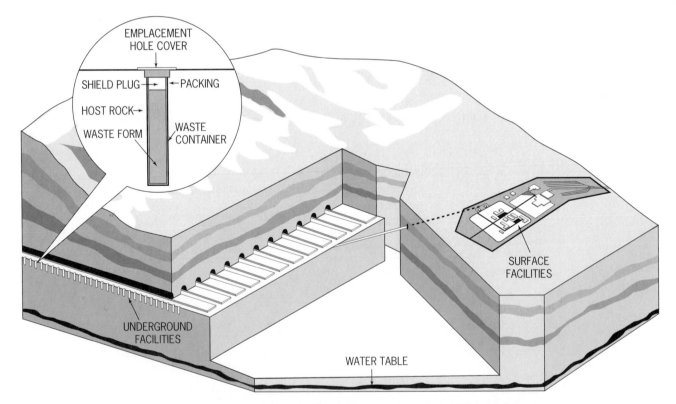

FIGURE 4.32. Schematic representation of a high-level radioactive waste burial site such as that planned for Yucca Mountain, Nevada. (From U. S. Department of Energy.)

(a)

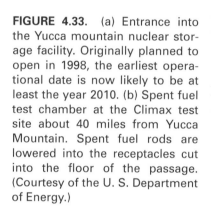

(b)

FIGURE 4.33. (a) Entrance into the Yucca mountain nuclear storage facility. Originally planned to open in 1998, the earliest operational date is now likely to be at least the year 2010. (b) Spent fuel test chamber at the Climax test site about 40 miles from Yucca Mountain. Spent fuel rods are lowered into the receptacles cut into the floor of the passage. (Courtesy of the U. S. Department of Energy.)

A Japanese chemical plant that started production in 1932 emitted mercury-containing waste into Minamata Bay. This waste included a highly poisonous compound, methyl mercuric chloride, which was not diluted to a harmless level. It accumulated in fish that constituted a major portion of the diet of the local inhabitants. As a result, more than 1500 people suffered mercury poisoning, which has been referred to as Minamata disease ever since; many others were seriously disabled. Unfortunately, the disease was not identified until 1956, and although the toxic discharges were stopped in 1960, their effects still linger.

DISPOSAL OR RECYCLING OF INDUSTRIAL AND DOMESTIC WASTE PRODUCTS

Archeologists have learned much about past civilizations from studying their waste products. The archeologists of the future will surely have a rich supply of material from our age because our advanced industrial societies produce vast quan-

tities of waste each year. These include agricultural wastes, domestic or municipal refuse, and the waste products of the manufacturing industry. Most of these materials are in the form of solid waste. Lesser amounts of liquid waste are generated by industry and by people in the form of sewage.

The disposal and treatment of many of these wastes are important in regard to Earth's resources because they are potential sources of energy. Also, through recycling, raw materials originally obtained from Earth can be reused. Their disposal involves disruption of the environment; their recycling reduces some of the need for mining and the problems associated with disposal.

Solid Waste Disposal

In the United States, over 5 billion tons of solid waste are generated every year, and this quantity continues to increase. The majority is agricultural waste, and a substantial amount is mineral waste previously discussed (waste rock, tailings, etc.). Domestic or municipal refuse accounts for less of the bulk, but it contains many valuable raw materials and potential pollutants. Manufacturing wastes may also contain valuable metals, fibers, chemicals, and toxic by-products. Typical domestic trash in the United States is made up of roughly 40 percent paper, 15 percent wastes, 9 percent plastics, 8 percent metals, and a variety of materials including garden wastes, wood, food wastes, cloth, and rubber (Figure 4.34a). The amount of municipal solid waste generated in the United States continues to increase, approaching 200 million metric tons per year (Figure 4.34b).

Prior to the 1960s, the majority of solid wastes was disposed of by open dumping; much less material was incinerated or disposed of in sanitary landfills. The open dump is the most primitive and was the most widely used means of solid waste disposal, accounting for more than half of the waste generated in the United States and the world. Today, in the United States, state and federal regulations prohibit open dumping and require that solid waste be disposed of in specially permitted and regulated landfills. Municipal waste is often compacted after collection, hauled to the dump, and spread on the ground by bulldozers (Figure 4.35). Although at one time this waste was set on fire to help reduce the total volume, such open burning is now prohibited because of local fire hazards and air pollution. The open dumps themselves, as well as being unsightly, are a potential breeding ground for diseases carried by flies and rats. They can also contaminate rivers and groundwaters with hazardous chemicals or organisms. Many coastal cities, including New York City, dump their municipal wastes in the ocean; barges carry the waste out to sea and discharge it into a natural trench or canyon on the ocean floor. This causes disruption of the marine environment with the destruction of communities of the bottom-dwelling organisms.

The sanitary landfill is now the principal means for disposal of solid domestic trash. In this case, the refuse is deposited at a carefully chosen site where contamination of surface water or groundwaters will not be a problem. After the waste is brought to a site, bulldozers or other heavy machinery compact it. Each day the waste is covered with a layer of soil 15 to 30 cm thick to exclude air and vermin. Three types of sanitary landfills are commonly used. In the *area method,* which is well suited to flat ground or broad depressions, wastes are spread on the surface and covered with soil to form a *cell* that usually represents one day's waste (Figure 4.36). Additional waste cells can be deposited on top of finished cells, and a thick layer of soil forms a cap. In the *trench method,* a broad trench is excavated and filled with compacted refuse. The excavated material provides a soil cover that is well suited to level terrain. The *ramp method* is well suited to sloping areas. Refuse is spread over the hillside, compacted, and covered with soil that is often excavated from a cut at the base of the slope. Present regulations in the United States require that the landfills have two impermeable layers of natural or synthetic (e.g., heavy plastic)

materials beneath them to prevent any **leachate** from leaking into the groundwater. There must also be a leachate removal system, some means of testing between the two underlying barriers, and wells adjacent to the landfill that can test for groundwater pollution. Upon closure, landfill sites must be covered by an impermeable layer and 0.5–1.0 m of soil. The surface slopes should also be low enough that erosion will not be a problem. Furthermore, modern regulations require post-closure monitoring of sites for 30 years and a posting of a bond or insurance to pay for any damages that might occur. Completed landfill sites are usually covered with a layer of soil that may then be seeded and used for park land or recreation areas. In some cases, hills have been constructed for ski slopes or other developments.

A good example of this use is Mount Trashmore (Figure 4.37) at the City of Virginia Beach, Virginia. The shallow depth to the water table would not permit excavation of a pit to use as a waste dump site. Thousands of tons of garbage per day were dumped, spread, compacted, and covered with soil to build a hill 100 m by 260 m, 22 m high and containing 580,000 metric tons of solid domestic waste. By the daily compaction of alternating layers of 45 cm of waste and 15 cm of soil, a structure free from problems of unpleasant odors, fires, vermin, and groundwater pollution was created. This has been used to site a recreational area with a playground, amphitheater, soap-box derby track, picnic areas, and a freshwater lake. The success of Mount Trashmore has led to the development of a second similar site in Virginia Beach.

Landfills are generally not suited as sites for buildings because of possible subsidence and escape of gases or contaminated waters. Although the advantages of sanitary landfills over open dumping are obvious, they still present problems in terms of available space. On average, a well managed landfill operation requires one hectare of land each year for 25,000 people. For a city like New York (population in excess of 12 million people) this could demand 480 hectares of land every year. Also, as the more obvious locations for landfill sites are used, more distant sites have to be employed, increasing transportation costs and disrupting the surrounding countryside. An additional concern is that the slow decay of organic matter in landfill sites generates methane gas that must be vented to prevent potential explosions or collected for use as a fuel.

Automobile tires have become a major problem in domestic solid waste disposal. In the United States alone, about 250 million tires are discarded every year (Figure 4.38, Plate 11). Landfill operations discovered that tires do not decompose in any reasonable length of time, and they gradually rise to the top of any landfill (probably as the result of air pockets and episodic changes in temperature) unless they have been cut into pieces. The rubber and petroleum compounds in tires burn very well and can serve as fuels, but they are difficult to handle and frequently create pollution problems when incinerated. Many landfills will no longer accept old

FIGURE 4.34. (a) The percentages of the various materials that composed municipal solid waste in the United States in 1994. (b) The generation and disposal of muni-cipal solid waste in the United States since 1960. The amount of landfill waste increased until about 1989. The amount of waste recycled and composted has been rising steadily. (From Franklin Associates Ltd, Prairie Village, KS., *Characterization of Municipal Solid Waste in the United States: 1992 Update.* Prepared for the U.S. Environmental Protection Agency.)

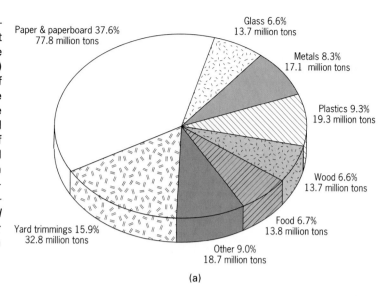

(a)

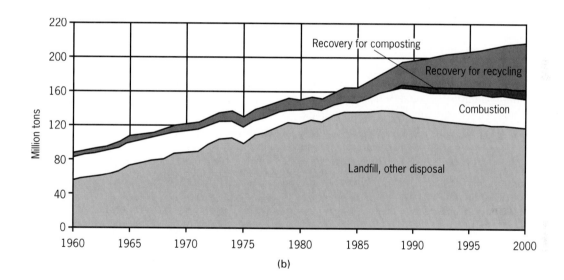

(b)

tires and there are no comprehensive recycling programs in most countries; consequently, many illegal tire dumps have been created.

Incineration has been used to generate power while reducing the volume of waste (up to 90 percent). Although there has been increasing interest in incineration as a way to reduce landfill needs, the ash, which concentrates most of the trace metals from the waste, has been ruled to be hazardous, requiring special landfills for disposal. The burning of materials as complex as municipal trash is not simple. Substances that release poisonous gases or particles when burned are often present; costly pollution controls are needed to meet modern standards of air cleanliness. The capital cost of building a modern incinerator and the costs of operation are often

much greater than those for landfill operation. In addition to air pollution, certain materials commonly found in refuse produce gases that corrode furnace interiors. For example, polyvinyl chloride (PVC), a plastic widely used in toys, containers, and records produces highly corrosive hydrogen chloride gas when burned.

One important factor that helps to compensate for these difficulties is the energy generated by waste incineration. The heat given off by the process of incineration is used for space heating of buildings or electrical power generation (Figure 4.39). The increasing problems of refuse disposal combined with increasing energy costs has led to the construction of many solid waste power plants throughout the world over the past decade.

FIGURE 4.35. Municipal solid waste being compacted after being dumped into a landfill before the end-of-the-day burial. Compaction reduced the volume of the waste, hence lengthening the life of the landfill. Some of the synthetic liner used to prevent groundwater contamination by leachate is visible in the foreground. (Photograph courtesy of Draper Aden Associates.)

The generation of energy in the form of heat by burning solid wastes leads to the general question of how energy may be extracted from solid wastes. A number of these alternative energy sources are discussed in Chapter 5 and, in particular, the ways in which organic wastes and plant materials (including manure, sewage, and wastes from crop cultivation) can be used to produce gas or liquid fuels. It has also been suggested that methane gas given off by the degradation of material in sanitary landfill sites could be tapped and used for energy generation. This would involve trapping methane below an impermeable (e.g., clay) cover and extracting it from wells drilled into the mass of decaying material. A more direct method of extracting potential fuel materials from wastes is pyrolysis, a process that involves heating the wastes in the absence of air to drive off and collect volatile substances; this is further discussed on page 205.

Recycling

Most of the refuse discarded by people in modern industrial societies contains large amounts of material that could be reused or processed to reclaim valuable raw materials. Such **recycling** (see page 98) often conserves not just material resources, but fuel as well. For example, nearly 20 times as much energy is required to produce aluminum from bauxite as is required to remelt aluminum scrap; over twice as much energy is needed to manufacture steel from primary raw materials as from scrap metal. Recycling operations also generally emit less pollutants than the original process because the recycling does not require roasting or smelting.

Recycling ranges from simple reuse or reclamation of an object (e.g., the reuse of bottles for beverages) to complex processes of recovery by physical or chemical means (e.g., revulcanization of rubber). Certain finished products, parts of products, or raw materials are clearly more easily recycled than others. For example, scrap paper and related materials made up of cellulose fiber can readily be pulped and used again to make paper and cardboard. A junk automobile, however, presents a formidable recycling problem. Many of its components are made of diverse materials ranging from rubber and plastic to glass and a whole range of metals and alloys.

It is possible to envisage a society in which most durable goods are used for much longer than at present and then broken into their component parts to reclaim their raw materials. Throughout the United States, the percentages of solid waste being recycled have been rising since the mid-1980s, and they are expected to be about 25 percent higher in the mid-1990s. However, before considering the social and economic aspects of recycling, we shall consider the technology of recycling.

Except for the larger items of machinery, such as automobiles, most of the rubbish of modern society finds its way into municipal trash. There are also more specialized forms of rubbish generated by agricultural and other industries. Most of this material cannot be reused and must be broken down into raw materials. Examples of the processes by which this is done include the following:

Melting metals, glass, and some plastics, which can then be purified, recast, and remolded;

Revulcanizing rubber, which cannot simply be heated and remolded. It must be shredded, broken down chemically, and then reacted with sulfur compounds;

Pulping to reclaim fiber from waste paper or other natural material containing cellulose fiber (e.g., wood, reeds, and sugar cane stalks). The material is stirred and beaten to form a slurry, inks are dissolved, and the pulp is put through the usual paper-making process;

Pyrolysis, which is heating materials in the absence of air to about 1650°C so that it decomposes to a range of chemical compounds.

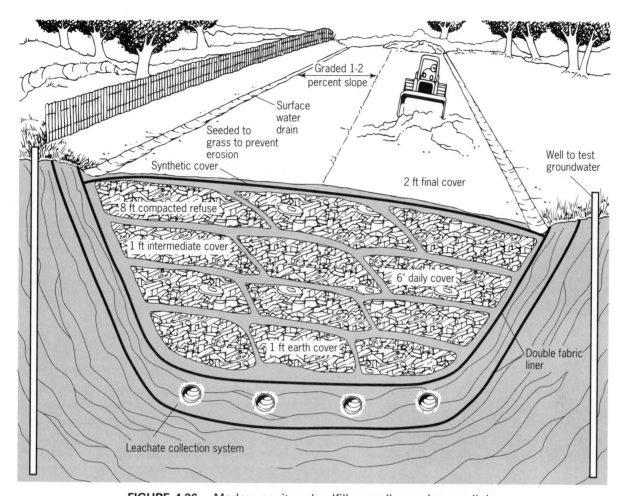

Graded 1-2 percent slope

Surface water drain

Seeded to grass to prevent erosion

Synthetic cover

8 ft compacted refuse

1 ft intermediate cover

1 ft earth cover

Leachate collection system

2 ft final cover

6" daily cover

Well to test groundwater

Double fabric liner

FIGURE 4.36. Modern sanitary landfills usually employ a cellular design such as the one shown here. After cutting a large trench or pit, one or two impermeable liners (sometimes compacted clay, but usually plastic sheets) are placed in the bottom and covered with a layer of sand. Refuse is dumped into cells, compacted as shown in Figure 4.35, and covered at the end of each day. Drainage pipes are placed between the liners and at the base of the refuse fill zone so leachate can be removed. In addition, test wells are drilled around the landfill to detect any contamination of groundwater. When a landfill is closed, a liner and a thicker layer of soil are placed over the refuse cells; vegetation is planted to prevent erosion. Monitoring of the closed landfill is usually mandated for at least 30 years. (After a diagram from the New York State Department of Environmental Conservation.)

There are also the processes by which organic wastes can be broken down, such as *composting* to make fertilizers, *rendering* of animal wastes to make such products as soaps and glues, and *fermentation* to make alcohols, gases, and a variety of other products (see Chapter 5).

Although agricultural and industrial wastes may be fairly homogeneous and simply recycled through one of the processes mentioned above, domestic trash is a mixture of many kinds of materials. Although the collection of bottles or cans was widely successful during World War II, such schemes generally ended in the 1950s and 1960s. Since the 1980s, many regions in the United States and western Europe

have reinstituted curbside recycling requiring separating metals, glass, plastics, and papers. Notable success has been achieved in certain other countries, particularly Japan, where very high percentages of municipal waste are recycled. In that highly organized industrial country, with very limited natural resources, the necessary incentives have been provided to develop alternatives to the *throw-away society*. In Hiroshima, for example, disposal of raw refuse has been reduced by 40 percent since 1976 because the government pays for separated wastes using monies saved from the landfill sites. Separation at the source is often undertaken by nonprofit groups, such as student clubs and parent-teacher

FIGURE 4.37. Subsurface burial of municipal waste may be impractical in coastal or other areas where the water table is very shallow. Virginia Beach, Virginia, solved the waste disposal problem by building 20-m high Mount Trashmore, incorporating 575,000 metric tons of solid waste. After final sealing and landscaping, it is now a city recreation area. Because of its success, the Virginia Beach area is now constructing even larger additional mounts. (Courtesy of the City of Virginia Beach.)

FIGURE 4.38. Approximately 250 million tires are discarded in the United States every year—probaly 500 million worldwide. Many billions line refuse piles (see Plate 11). Like many materials made from Earth's resources, the tires are extremely durable. Note the size of the tree that has grown through the tire while it lay in an unauthorized dump. (Photograph courtesy of the Virginia Department of Waste Management.)

associations. A program involving source separation and computerized processing is now enabling 90 percent of the garbage of Machida, Japan, to be recycled. Commonly, however, the problem has to be tackled by separation at the disposal facility. Various devices including screens, magnets to remove iron, or the use of compressed air to separate light from heavy items have been used. A series of devices are needed to bring about complete separation (Figure 4.39). In this system, large items are removed manually, and the remaining refuse is fed with water into a pulper. The fiber component is pulped, brittle material such as glass is pulverized, but stronger solid objects are not affected. The fiber slurry is drained through a screen (2-cm mesh size) and large objects are removed and washed. From this, iron is separated magnetically, and other metals manually, and sold as scrap. The fiber slurry is pumped to a cyclone that removes pulverized glass, metals, bone, sand particles, etc. The remaining slurry is made of paper, food wastes, cloth, and plastics. Via further pulping and screening operations, paper fiber is extracted. Organic materials are used as fuel.

Such schemes for the recycling of domestic waste are unfortunately rare; recycling of metals is much more widespread. Of course, in industries using metals, as in a metal fabricating shop, large quantities of uncontaminated scrap are generated, and this has a ready market. Consequently, in the United States, roughly 40 percent of copper and lead, 30 percent of stainless steel, 25 percent of aluminum, and 14 percent of zinc are recycled along with high percentages of the precious metals. Nevertheless, the quantities of such metals annually discarded in the United States are vast—over 11 million tons of iron and steel, 800,000 tons of aluminum, and 400,000 tons of other metals.

As already noted, recycling saves both the raw materials and energy. It has been suggested that recycling the more than 50 billion steel cans used annually in the United States would save the energy equal to the output of eight 500 MW power plants. Furthermore, discarding an aluminum beverage container wastes as much energy as pouring out such a

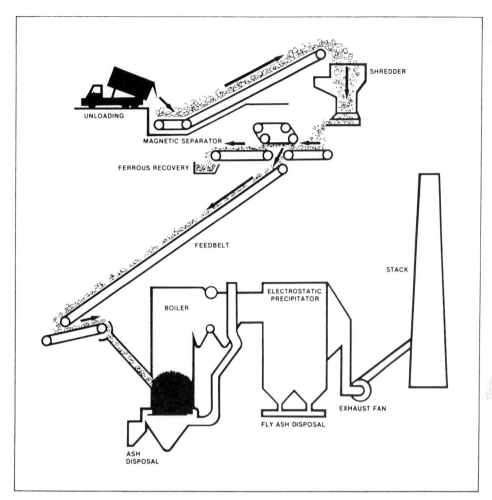

SHREDDER

UNLOADING

MAGNETIC SEPARATOR

FERROUS RECOVERY

FEEDBELT

STACK

ELECTROSTATIC
PRECIPITATOR

BOILER

EXHAUST FAN

FLY ASH DISPOSAL

ASH
DISPOSAL

FIGURE 4.39. Schematic diagram showing a modern waste treatment system in which ferrous scrap is recovered and useable heat is generated by burning most of the other waste. The amount of ash for disposal is only a small fraction of the initial mass of the waste. (From R. Davies and P. Ketchum, "Energy from Waste" GEOS, vol. 15, no. 2, p. 18, Energy, Mines and REsources Canada, 1986. Used with permission.)

can half-filled with gasoline. It is particularly the two metals, iron and aluminum, for which recycling offers the greatest benefits through savings not only in raw materials, but also in energy and environmental damage. For example, recycling aluminum reduces air emissions associated with its production by 95 percent. One other major recyclable material is wood as a fuel, building material, and raw material for chemical industries and paper manufacture. Paper products use about 35 percent of the world's commercial wood harvest, and recycling half of the paper used in the world today would meet nearly 75 percent of the demand for new paper, freeing 8 million hectares (20 million acres) of forest from paper production. In spite of the great advantages, however, only about one-quarter of the world's steel, aluminum, and paper is recovered for reuse.

Why is recycling not undertaken on a much larger scale? The factors that dictate this are not technical, but economic and social. In the field of metals, the ore mining and processing industries are established groups often operating on a large and highly organized scale. Scrap metal operations are often small and labor intensive and incur heavy transportation costs. A domestic refuse reclamation plant currently costs more than landfill disposal. This cost will have to be borne by local citizens in their rates and taxes. Some citizens may be prepared to pay extra to remove the need for unsightly landfill operations and save precious raw materials, but many, not being directly affected, will not make this sacrifice.

Two factors are likely to bring about more widespread recycling in the future. One will be the need to use land area

THE MOVE TO RECYCLE

Recycling is not new, but over the past several years it has received a new impetus. The long established reason for recycling has been that recycled resources (e.g., iron, aluminum, glass, and paper) could be provided to industry at a lower cost than through the use of virgin materials. Consequently, there has long been a viable market for scrap iron, lead, copper, and aluminum. Other materials were recycled locally and episodically with special efforts during national emergencies, such as World War II.

In the post-World War II era, the United States began to diverge from its European allies in terms of recycling. The rebuilding of Europe required enormous resources, and the post-war shortages made recycling very attractive. At the same time, the United States, buoyed by prosperity and the development of a suburban society, largely abandoned citizen recycling and rapidly became a *no-deposit-no-return* society. Despite the concerns of numerous individuals and environmental groups, recycling interest waned, and the volume of household and commercial waste generated in the United States grew (Figure 4.34).

During the 1980s, the dual impacts of a rising environmental consciousness and reports about the shortage of landfill capacity suddenly brought recycling back into focus. Landfill regulations had generally become more stringent, requiring some protection of groundwater from leachate, requiring the daily cover of solid waste, and preventing the open burning of waste. However, landfilling was still the least expensive way to dispose of the unwanted material. The threat of federally imposed mandates (which were finally issued by the EPA in 1991) forced many states to develop their own regulations for better operation and environmental monitoring of landfills and resulted in large and rapid increases in landfill tipping fees, the charges paid to dispose of wastes. This forced states and individual communities to reexamine the merits and costs of landfilling solid waste materials. Suddenly, it became clear that recycling not only saved resources, it usually saved energy. Less energy was required to recycle than to manufacture a material from the raw mineral resources. It usually reduced the potential for groundwater pollution, and it certainly reduced the volume of material going to landfills. Consequently, several state legislatures passed mandates for recycling 10, 25, or over 50 percent of their waste by dates in the 1990s.

Two major problems arose. First, it became apparent that the infrastructure to recycle on a broad basis in suburban areas was very expensive. Second, no adequate markets existed to absorb all of the recycled material. Tipping fees for dumping into landfills vary widely and are generally rising. However, in the mid-1990s tipping fees typically ran $20–50 per ton. In contrast, the cost to recycle frequently ran $100 or more per ton. Aluminum cans were of sufficient value to pay for the effort of collection, but glass and plastic markets were inconsistent and rarely did better than break even. Newsprint, the largest volume of American solid waste, usually cost more to collect than could be obtained from selling it. In the late 1980s, only relatively few companies reprocessed paper, and they had little market for the finished products. Some communities cut back or abandoned recycling efforts. By the mid-1990s, there had been a significant increase both in demand for recycled goods and in the industry capacity to process waste. Prices for recycled commodities rose and helped offset more of the high handling costs.

The amount and percentage of materials recycled remained constant through the 1960s, and it increased only slowly through the 1970s and early 1980s (Figure 4.34). About 1985, the rate of recycling increased and has grown steadily, reaching about 22 percent of all municipal solid waste by 1994. It is projected to reach about 25 percent by 2000. Many communities have taken a long-term view and recognized that, despite the high costs, there is great value. Future landfill costs could typically run from $50,000 to $250,000 per acre to purchase and prepare. Present tipping fees to operate existing landfills may only be $50 per ton, but future costs may raise the tipping fees in many places to over $100 per ton. Thus, looking ahead generally indicates that the extra costs of recycling now will save much cost and aggravation later. It is apparent that recycling has returned, but it has done so for different reasons than in the past.

for more valuable purposes than for landfills. The other will be the cost of the raw material produced from its primary source that will increase as supplies become more scarce or expensive to extract. The benefits of recycling, in saving both precious raw materials and energy and reducing problems of waste disposal and pollution, are very clear. Unfortunately, in most countries, the economic and social incentives needed to set up large-scale recycling operations do not exist at the present time.

Liquid Waste Disposal

The human race generates two main kinds of liquid waste. The first, common to primitive and advanced societies alike, is made up of sewage and domestic wastewater. The second is the wastes produced by industrial activity, particularly by such industries as pulp and paper production, food processing, and the manufacture of chemicals.

Sewage and domestic wastewater amounts to enormous volumes. On average, every man, woman, and child in a modern industrial city generates between 75 and 200 gallons of wastewater per day (700 liters per day). The most convenient place to discharge these wastes, whether treated or untreated, is nearby bodies of water. This has been the practice since the earliest times, leading to countless illnesses and deaths from water-bourne diseases when controls were inadequate. The reasoning behind this disposal is that small volumes of waste do little harm when diluted into the vast oceans. However, mixing is far from complete in coastal waters and estuaries, and the volumes discharged are quite substantial. For example, an estimated 3.5 billion gallons of wastewater are discharged into estuaries and coastal waters of the United States per day. The city and county of Los Angeles together discharge 700 million gallons per day. What is the nature of this wastewater, and how is it treated?

Municipal sewage is 99.8 percent water. The remaining 0.2 percent, however, may contain a variety of organic compounds in suspension or solution, some of which may be toxic. Many of these compounds biodegrade but still lead to consumption of oxygen in the environment. Others may serve as nutrients that can promote growth of algae. The greatest concerns are over toxic substances, such as heavy metal compounds and pathogenic organisms that can cause disease, such as typhoid, dysentery, diarrhea, and cholera.

A wide variety of mechanical, chemical, and biological methods can be used to clean up sewage water. Some treatment plans remove only the coarsest fraction of the pollution, whereas others may yield outgoing water (effluent) that is of drinkable (potable) quality. A typical full-scale treatment plant may involve two or three stages of processing (Figure 4.40). Primary treatment usually involves screening to remove large objects and a series of settling tanks to remove successively finer suspended solids. Secondary treatment often uses the action of bacteria in the presence of ample oxygen to decompose much of the remaining matter. The sewage may be sprayed over a bed of stones in a trickling filter or, in the activated sludge process, may be mixed in an aerated tank with a bacteria-laden sludge. The sludge residue is usually dried and may be incinerated or disposed of in a sanitary landfill. The bacteria remaining in the effluent are killed by a disinfection process, usually chlorination. In some cases, tertiary, or advanced, treatment is used to remove specific pollutants, such as synthetic chemicals and salts; this may involve the addition of certain chemicals or substances to adsorb these pollutants. The ultimate destination of most effluents that have undergone primary, secondary, or even no treatment are rivers, estuaries, seas, and oceans. Increasingly, cities concerned about adequate water supplies are reusing properly treated water rather than discharging it into rivers. Some beverage industries are

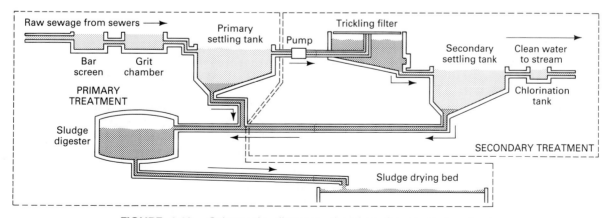

FIGURE 4.40. Schematic diagram showing the steps involved in the treatment of sewage wastes. (From *The Living Waters*, U. S. Public Health Service Publication No. 382.)

concerned, however, that news of the use of recycled treated water, regardless of purity, would not be good for business. Some sewage wastes are disposed of on land to utilize the nutrient materials as a fertilizer.

The range of liquid wastes that are generated by industrial processes is considerable. They include many oil-based materials, such as spent lubricants and fuel oil residues, along with various solvents, paints, and resins. Industry is also the source of much of the hazardous chemical wastes containing toxic heavy metals and dangerous organic chemicals. Some examples of the tragic problems caused by uncontrolled or poorly controlled discharge of such toxins into the seas have already been discussed. Aside from these severe cases, what are the likely consequences of pollution of rivers and seas by wastewaters, and what sort of safety standards should be applied?

Although slow filtration of groundwater through the earth and dilution of wastes by oxygen-rich surface waters can absorb and degrade varying amounts and types of waste, these natural systems of purification are easily overburdened. Introducing nontoxic organic substances into natural waters depletes or consumes the oxygen supply in these waters. This is because oxygen is used by microorganisms feeding on the organic pollutants, hence increasing the **biochemical oxygen demand** (BOD). Exhaustion of the oxygen supply kills all the natural organisms, and putrification begins. Another group of harmful, although nontoxic, pollutants are the phosphates and nitrates. These are often introduced onto the land as fertiliz-

ers, later finding their ways into rivers and lakes where they stimulate excessive algae growth. They are often not removed by standard treatment plants. Particularly in shallow bodies of standing water, this leads to a degrading process known as **eutrophication** in which the water becomes overburdened with dead and dying organisms. In addition to these pollutants, a whole range of toxic substances directly hazardous to man as well as other forms of life exists. The levels of all such pollutants can be controlled ultimately by appropriate legislation. The Environmental Protection Agency (EPA), for example, requires that most wastewater be treated to the equivalent of *secondary treatment,* involving the removal of over 85 percent of suspended solids and a five-day BOD. The consequence of inadequate control of pollution caused by liquid wastes can be seen today in areas such as the coastal waters around New York City and the coastal areas of the Mediterranean (Figure 4.41). In such areas, fish and shellfish harvests are contaminated or destroyed along with the ruin of tourist and recreational facilities.

On the other hand, unnecessary or overly strict regulation can be dangerous. An example is the Wisconsin lead-zinc district, a significant region for the production of these metals for the last 150 years. The EPA demanded there be no more than 0.5 ppm of zinc in water effluent from a mine in this district, one-tenth of the 5 ppm limit set by the Public Health Service as a maximum for this metal in drinking water. In fact, zinc is not toxic to humans even at much higher levels, and this limit was based on taste tests, not possible

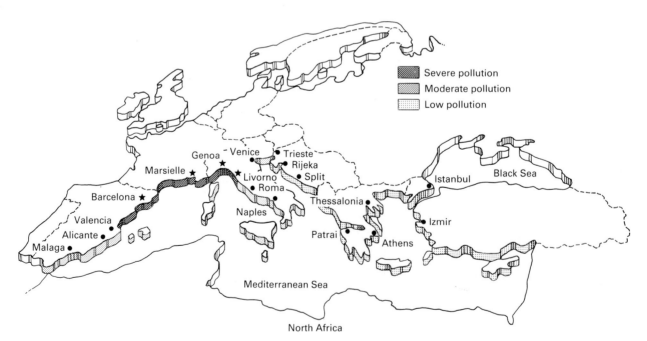

FIGURE 4.41. The problems of pollution along the Mediterranean coastline resulted from domestic sewage and industrial waste in the mid-1970s. This is illustrated by the shading along the coastline. The stars indicate the major sources of pollution.

health hazards. Zinc, in fact, is often considered beneficial. The operating mine's effluent actually contained 2.5 ppm, fine by Public Health Service standards, but five times that demanded by the EPA. Unable to comply, the mine had to close with the subsequent loss of metal production and jobs. The reason for setting the limit at 0.5 ppm was to permit more fish in the streams, but this has not happened since closing the mine because the natural local groundwater contains about as much zinc as the mine's effluent. An ironic footnote to this story is that the EPA offices in Washington were using drinking water containing 20 ppm zinc—40 times the level imposed as an acceptable maximum for the Wisconsin mine's effluent.

FURTHER READING

COATES, D. R., *Environmental Geology.* New York: John Wiley and Sons, 1981.

Council on Environmental Quality, *Environmental Trends.* Washington, DC: U.S. Government Printing Office, 1989.

DETWYLER, T. R., *Man's Impact on Environment.* New York: McGraw-Hill, 1971.

Environmental Protection Agency, *Reusable News.* Solid Waste and Emergency Response Office of the United States Environmental Protection Agency, published annually.

Environmental Protection Agency, *Characterization of Municipal Solid Waste in the United States: 1994 Update. Executive Summary.* Solid Waste and Emergency Response Office of the United States Environmental Protection Agency, 1994.

HOLDGATE, M. W., KASSAG, M., and WHITE, G. F., eds., *The World Environment 1972–1982. A Report by the United Nations Environment Programme, Natural Resources and Environmental Series,* Vol. 8. Dublin: Tycooly International Publishing Ltd., 1982.

HOLDREN, J. P., "Radioactive waste management in the United States." *Annual Reviews of Energy and Environment* 17 (1992) pp. 235–259.

International Geosphere-Biosphere Programme, *Global Change: Reducing Uncertainties* (1992).

KELLER, E. A., *Environmental Geology.,* 6th ed. New York: MacMillan Publishing Co., 1992.

KLEE, G. A., *Conservation of Natural Resources.* Englewood Cliffs, NJ: Prentice Hall Publishing Co., 1991.

LEHR, J. H., ed., *Rational Readings on Environmental Concerns.* New York: Van Nostrand Reinhold, 1992.

MACDONALD, E. H., *Alluvial Mining.* London: Chapman and Hall, 1983.

National Academy of Sciences, "Mineral Resources and the Environment." Committee on Minerals Resources and the Environment, February 1975.

Organization for Economic Cooperation and Development, OECD, *Environmental Data Compendium 1991,* Paris: OECD, 1991.

PETERS, W. C., *Exploration and Mining Geology.* New York: John Wiley and Sons, 1978.

TESTA, S. M., *Geological Aspects of Hazardous Waste.* London: Lewis Publishers, 1994.

University Corporation for Atmospheric Research, "Our Ozone Shield." *Reports to the Nation* (1992).

University Corporation for Atmospheric Research, "The Climate System." *Reports to the Nation* (1991).

WILLS, B. A., *Mineral Processing Technology,* 5th ed. New York: Pergamon Press, 1992.

5 ENERGY FROM FOSSIL FUELS

The rapid expansion of the oil industry in the early part of the twentieth century combined with the views of nearly limitless supplies of oil sometimes led to the intense clustering of oil swells as seen at Signal Hills, California, in the 1920s. (Courtesy of Shell Oil Company.)

It is difficult for people living now, who have become accustomed to the steady exponential growth in the consumption of energy from the fossil fuels, to realize how transitory the fossil-fuel epoch will eventually prove to be when it is viewed over a longer span of human history.

M. King Hubbert, in Scientific American (1971)

FOCAL POINTS

- The most familiar fossil fuels, which are major present-day energy sources, are coal, petroleum, and natural gas. Less known, but of local importance, are oil shales, tar sands, heavy oils, and peat.

- Coal, which forms from the accumulation, burial, and compaction of land plants, is part of a series of increasing compaction and heating that progresses to peat, lignite, bituminous coal, and anthracite.

- Petroleum formed when buried marine organic matter underwent a natural transformation under increasing temperature and pressure.

- Natural gas, composed primarily of methane (CH_4), forms biogenically when bacteria decompose shallowly buried organic matter or thermogenically when the temperature and pressure of deep burial cause decomposition of the organic matter.

- Petroleum, although known in ancient times, has a modern production history dating back to a well drilled by Edwin L. Drake in Titusville, Pennsylvania, in 1859.

- Accumulations of petroleum are valuable only where the petroleum has migrated from its source rocks into porous and permeable rocks that serve as structural or stratigraphic traps.

- Petroleum only rarely comes out of a well in the form of a gusher; oil is either forced out by pumps, or its extraction is assisted by the injection of chemicals or steam to release it from the rock pores. Even so, close to half of the original petroleum remains trapped in the rocks.

- World petroleum production rose sharply during the 1950s, 1960s, and 1970s, reaching about 60 million barrels per day and 22 billion barrels per year in the 1980s.

- United States' oil production peaked in 1970 and has been slowly declining since then. This trend, coupled with an increase in demand, has resulted in increased oil imports.

- OPEC (The Organization of Petroleum Exporting Countries) controls two-thirds to three-quarters of the world's total oil reserves of about 1000 billion barrels; Saudi Arabia, with 260 billion barrels, has the largest reserves.

- Natural gas use has increased more than four-fold since 1960, and much is now transported in pipelines and as liquified natural gas.

- Tar sands, heavy oils, and oil shales contain very large amounts of potentially extractable oil, but they remain uneconomic at the present time.

INTRODUCTION

Every action we take—even the process of reading these words and thinking about their meaning—requires **energy,** which is the actual or potential ability to do **work.** The primary function of machines is to convert energy into useful work. Our own bodies are machines that convert stored food energy into our activities. The human body is capable of doing enough work to keep a 100-watt lightbulb continuously burning. Far back in our history, we found it worthwhile to turn to other sources of energy to do things that we did not want to do or things we were not physically capable of doing. The first of these supplementary sources were probably other humans and animals. Because these sources proved inadequate to meet our needs, we turned to progressively more sophisticated means—sails for ships, windmills, water wheels, steam and internal combustion engines, electric motors, and eventually nuclear power plants.

The human appetite for energy in modern society has grown so large that the supplemental energy expenditures now greatly exceed our individual muscle energy. Whereas our earliest ancestors relied upon the energy from their own bodies as "one-manpower," we now augment our own body energy with that from a vast variety of supplemental sources. If we envision this supplemental energy as *energy slaves* working continuously to feed, clothe, and maintain each one of us, we find that the number of these energy slaves varies widely from one culture to another. The supplementary energy used per person is equivalent to 15 energy slaves in India, 30 in South America, 75 in Japan, 120 in Russia, 150 in Europe, and 300 in the United States and Canada. Each of the machines has an Earth-supplied energy source, such as petroleum, natural gas, coal, running water, or uranium. Just how dependent we have become on these energy slaves can be envisioned by considering the consequences of them going on strike (i.e., if all of Earth's energy supplies ran out or were not available). We would then be reduced to our own muscle power to supply all of our needs. Our technological society would come to an abrupt halt, and we would very soon find ourselves unable to feed and maintain the world's population. Muscle power alone could not hold back the inevitable starvation, famine, and pestilence that would strike. The survivors would be forced to live as our early ancestors did thousands of years ago.

ENERGY UNITS

There are many types of work—mechanical, electrical, and thermal—thus, there are many different types of units by which energy is measured. The **joule** is the electrical energy needed to maintain a flow of one ampere for one second at a potential of one volt. The **calorie** is the heat energy needed to raise the temperature of one gram of water one degree Celsius. The **British thermal unit** (BTU) is the heat energy needed to raise 1 pound of water 1 degree Fahrenheit. The variety and interchangeability of energy units is shown in Table 5.1. In order to compare the stored energy that we might be able to extract from various sources, the joule will be our standard unit of energy. Joules will be equated with common industrial energy units such as metric tons of coal, barrels of oil, and trillions of cubic feet of gas.

Although the total energy available from any source is important, so is the rate at which energy is used and the maximum rate at which it can be supplied. For example, a windmill cannot supply energy any faster than is supplied by the wind pushing the blades. We must, therefore, also consider a time-dependent function called **power**, which is the energy used per unit of time. **Horsepower** originated from the use of horse-drawn plows and wagons. It has persisted as a measure of the strength of engines, including those in automobiles, because James Watt measured the power of his 1766 steam engine against the power of a horse. For the sake of consistency, we shall use the **watt**, defined as one joule electrical energy per second, as our power unit. The watt is commonly used in the everyday use of household appliances and lightbulbs. It will become even more familiar with an increasing use of energy from renewable sources, such as heat and light from the sun. As with food and other renewable resources, the total amount of solar energy that has or will reach Earth is not as important as its rate.

THE CHANGING USE OF ENERGY

The progression from a simple hunter-gatherer society to modern technology is characterized by both vast increases in the amounts of supplemental energy consumed and marked changes in the sources of that energy. Supplemental energy use remained relatively low until the Industrial Revolution swept across Europe and North America in the eighteenth and nineteenth centuries. Prior to that time, our primary sources of supplemental energy were wood, wind, running water, and animals.

The onset of the Industrial Revolution required unprecedented amounts of fuel to drive the new machinery. It was soon obvious that wood could not supply the needs, because the entire British Isles were in danger of being deforested. Consequently, the British turned to coal, a heat source superior to wood. Coal soon became the fuel for the Industrial Revolution worldwide, leading to two significant changes in the energy-use pattern in the industrialized nations of the world. The total amount of energy used rose dramatically, and coal rapidly replaced wood as the major fuel. The scene was similar in all industrialized countries, especially for the United States (Figure 5.1). In 1850, wood constituted approximately 90 percent of the United States fuel sources. By 1880, this had dropped to 50 percent. By 1900,

TABLE 5.1

Energy equivalences

1 btu	= 252 gram-calories = 1055 joules = 2.93×10^{-4} kwh
1 joule	= 0.239 gram-calorie = 0.00095 btu = 2.78×10^{-7} kwh
1 gram, calorie	= 4.189 joules = 0.00397 btu
1 watt	= 1 joule/sec = 0.239 cal/sec = 0.0569 btu/min = 0.00134 horsepower
1 Quad (btu)	= 10^5 btu = 1.05×10^{18} joules = 2.93×10^{11} kwh

1 million (10^6) btu equals approximately:

90	pounds of bituminous coal and lignite production (1982)
125	pounds of oven-dried wood
8	gallons of motor gasoline or enough to move the average passenger car about 124 miles (1981 rate)
10	therms of natural gas (dry)
11	gallons of propane
1.2	days of per capita energy consumption in the United States (1982 rate)
2	months of dietary intake of a laborer
20	cases (240 bottles) of table wine

1 million btu of fossil fuels burned at electric utilities can generate about 100 kilowatt-hours of electricity, while about 300 kilowatt-hours of electricity generated at electric utilities can produce about 1 million btu of heat.

1 quadrillion (10^{15}) btu equals approximately:

44	million short tons of bituminous coal and lignite production
63	million short tons of oven-dried wood
1	trillion cubic feet of natural gas (dry)
170	million barrels of crude oil
500	thousand barrels per day of crude oil for 1 year
35	days of petroleum imports into the United States (1982 rate)
30	days of United States motor gasoline usage (1982 rate)

1 barrel of crude oil equals approximately:

5.7	thousand cubic feet of natural gas (dry)
0.26	short tons of bituminous coal and lignite production
1700	killowatt-hours of electricity consumed

1 short ton of bituminous coal and lignite production equals about:

3.9	barrels of crude oil
22	thousand cubic feet of natural gas (dry)
6600	kilowatt-hours of electricity consumed

1 thousand cubic feet of natural gas equals approximately:

0.18	barrels (or 7.5 gallons) of crude oil
0.045	short tons (or 90 pounds) of bituminous coal and lignite production
300	kilowatt-hours of electricity consumed

1 thousand kilowatt-hours of electricity equals approximately:

0.59	barrels of crude oil (although it takes about 1.7 barrels of oil to produce 1000 kWh)
0.15	short tons of bituminous coal and lignite production (although it takes about 0.5 short tons to produce 1000 kWh)
3300	cubic feet of natural gas (dry) (although it takes about 10,000 cubic feet to produce 1000 kWh)
27.2	gallons of gasoline

it was only about 10 percent. Coal remained the dominant energy source, providing nearly 75 percent of the nation's energy in 1920. The rapid expansion of oil and gas use finally surpassed coal in the 1940s and 1950s. Total energy production in the United States and the world rose dramatically from the 1940s until the 1970s and the 1973 OPEC oil embargo when rapid fossil fuel price increases shocked the world. These events led to a slower growth rate of world energy demand and a slight decrease in energy consumption of some major countries (Figure 5.1). Nevertheless, the total energy produced for use in the United States at the end of the twentieth century will be more than 10 times the total amount produced for use in 1900. In that same time span, the country's population will have increased about 3.5 times (from 76 million to about 265 millon).

Since about 1880, fossil fuels have served as the major sources of energy for the United States and other industrialized nations. It has now become clear that supplies of these fuels, though large, are limited; some day, other fuels will be needed to replace them. The period from about 1880 to about 2100 or 2200 A.D. will be known as the "fossil fuel era" to future historians. This leads to an important question: "What will be the energy sources beyond the fossil fuel era?" The relatively rapid rise in nuclear power in the 1960s and 1970s as well as the large number of nuclear power plants in the 1970s seemed to ensure that the use of nuclear power would ultimately surpass that of fossil fuels. The generation of electricity by nuclear power plants was originally projected to be safe, efficient, and so cheap that household electric meters would become unnecessary. The enthusiasm of the nuclear

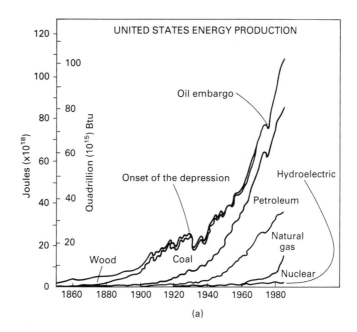

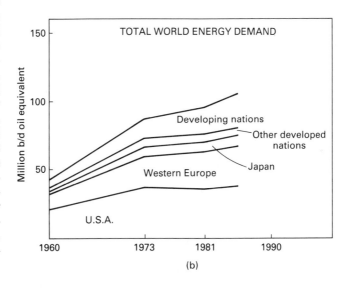

FIGURE 5.1. (a) The energy requirements for the United States have risen dramatically since the mid-nineteenth century. Note also the progression from wood to coal and then the rapid growth of oil and gas use since the middle of the twentieth century. (From United States Geological Survey, after D. L. Gibson, Energy Graphics, Prentice-Hall, Inc., 1983.) (b) World energy demand grew rapidly from 1960 until 1973 when the rates of growth were reduced. The United States proportion of total world energy demand has decreased as other economies, especially those in developing nations, have risen. (From International Petroleum Encyclopedia, 1984.)

power industry was severely dampened, however, when the reactor at Three Mile Island, Pennsylvania, partially melted down in May 1979. This event, along with huge cost overruns in the construction of power plants, reduced electricity demands, and the widespread realization that safe disposal of nuclear wastes is an enormous problem, led to the cancellation of many projected power plants, including many already partially constructed. The magnitude of the nuclear power industry problems in the United States is perhaps best exemplified by the default of the Washington Public Power Supply System (WPPSS) in the construction of power plants after the investment of $2.8 billion, much of which was in privately held bonds. The meltdown at Chernobyl in the Ukraine region of the then Soviet Union in April 1986 compounded these problems. The ultimate fate of the approximately 110 nuclear power plants operating in the United States is uncertain. Despite these problems, additional nuclear power plants are still being planned and constructed in other countries, such as France and Japan. These countries, with few fossil fuel resources of their own, see nuclear energy as preferable to the increasing cost and potential unreliability of imported fossil fuels.

In any discussion of energy, it is important to consider its use as well as its source (Figure 5.2). The nature of energy generation and the end distribution of energy in the transportation, industrial, residential, and commercial realms is

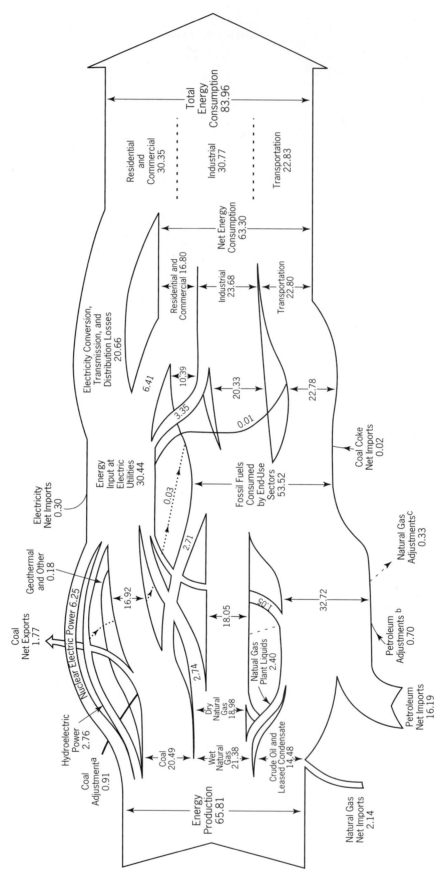

FIGURE 5.2. Energy flow diagram for the United States in 1993. (From *Annual Energy Review*, U.S. Energy Information Administration, 1993.)

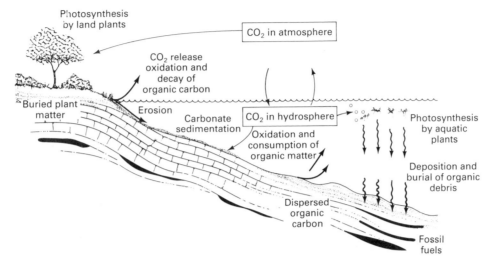

FIGURE 5.3. The main components of the carbon cycle. Fossil fuels are formed as a result of atmospheric carbon dioxide being converted by photosynthesis into organic matter. Subsequently, some of the organic matter has been trapped in the sediments; a small portion is preserved as fossil fuels.

complex. The laws of thermodynamics state that no machine can be 100 percent efficient. This results in the loss of approximately 25 percent of the energy in its conversion and transmission. The rapid rise of energy costs in the 1970s and early 1980s led to much energy conservation and significant improvements in efficiency, but the overall efficiency will probably never rise above 80 percent. Modern society is heavily dependent upon the fossil fuels.

FOSSIL FUELS

Almost all sedimentary rocks contain organic matter. The amount they contain ranges from trace amounts in some sandstones to the major constituents in coals and oil shales.

All of this organic matter, consisting of various hydrocarbons, is part of the **carbon cycle** (Figure 5.3), a complex series of chemical reactions by which carbon may pass amongst solid rock, air, dissolved gases, plants, and other organisms. Most of the organic matter formed in the biological realm has been consumed or destroyed, returning it to other parts of the carbon cycle. However, a small fraction of the organic matter, estimated to be no more than 1 percent of the total, has been preserved buried in various types of sediments. Of this preserved material, most occurs as minor disseminated components of fine-grained sediments (Figure 5.4). Lesser amounts are present in carbonate rocks, sandstones, and bituminous (hydrocarbon-containing) rocks. Only a very small percentage of the preserved organic material is present in a form concentrated enough to form a **fossil**

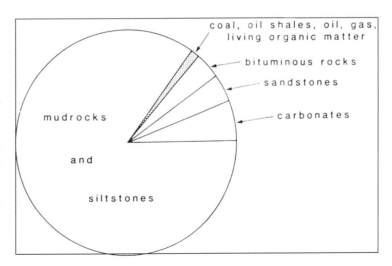

FIGURE 5.4. The distribution of organic matter in sediments in terms of the total mass of organic carbon. Fossil fuels constitute only a very small proportion of all organic carbon. (From M. A. Barnes, W. C. Barnes, and R. M. Bustin, "Diagenesis 8: Chemistry and evolution of organic matter," *Canada Geoscience* 11 (1984). Used with permission.)

fuel. This term, rather loosely defined, generally includes the organically derived sedimentary rocks and rock products that can be burned for fuel.

Fossil fuels occur in three forms that are familiar to most people—**coal, petroleum,** and **natural gas.** Less well known, because of only limited use, are **oil shales,** tar sands, heavy oils, and **peat.** Although the various fossil fuels are quite different in appearance and are processed and utilized in different ways, they all share a similar origin: trapped organic debris in sedimentary rocks (Figure 5.5). Their variety results from differences in the types of the original organic matter. For example, leaves and stems in a freshwater swamp create a different fossil fuel than phytoplanktonic organic matter in a marine basin. Also, the degree of alteration occurring after trapping as a result of bacterial decay, rising temperature, and rising pressure due to increasing depth of burial adds to this variety.

The changes that occur in buried organic matter tend to be both progressive and irreversible (Figure 5.5). In general, the earliest changes that take place at very shallow burial depths are biochemical, occurring as a result of the metabolism of bacteria, fungi, and other microorganisms. A primary product of this activity, regardless of the type or location of the organic matter, is **methane gas** (CH4), sometimes known as **swamp gas** or **marsh gas.** At greater sediment depths, the microbial activity is slower, but the increased temperature and pressure tend to result in driving off water and **cracking,** or breaking up, complex hydrocarbon molecules.

The original type of organic matter plays an important role in the generation of fossil fuels. Prior to the Devonian Period there were few land plants; hence, photosynthetic ma-

rine phytoplankton and bacteria were the principal sources of the organic matter in the sediments. These types of organisms, which still constitute most of the organic material in the modern marine sediments, contribute mainly proteins, lipids, and carbohydrates. In terrestrial environments, the higher plants contribute resins, waxes, lignins, and cellulose. Different types of living matter serve as precursors to fossil fuels, determining the carbon, hydrogen, sulfur, nitrogen, and oxygen contents of the fossil fuels (Table 5.2). In the conversion from organic debris to fossil fuel, there is the expulsion of water, a general reduction of oxygen and nitrogen, and a general increase in carbon and hydrogen content. These changes make the fossil fuels superior heat sources compared to fresh organic matter, such as wood and leaves. Those organics in the marine realm are usually altered into gas and petroleum, whereas those in the terrestrial rocks may form gas and coal. In some organic-rich shales (called oil shales), the burial temperatures have never been high enough to completely break down the original organic molecules but only sufficient to alter them to large waxy molecules known as **kerogen.** These can be converted to oil and gas by various refining processes.

All of the fossil fuels are similar chemically in that they consist primarily of hydrocarbon molecules. The differences in the physical properties—from an invisible gas, such as methane, to a yellow to brown syrupy liquid, such as petroleum, to a black solid, such as anthracite—reflect the vast differences in arrangements and sizes of the hydrocarbon molecules and the differing ratios of hydrogen to carbon contents. During burning, it is the combustion of carbon and hydrogen with atmospheric oxygen that produces nearly all of

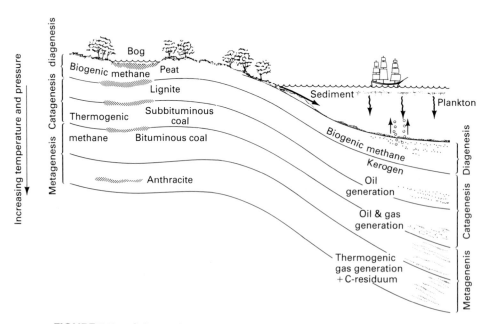

FIGURE 5.5.   Schematic diagram of the generation of various ranks of coal, petroleum, and gas from terrigeneous and marine organic matter.

TABLE 5.2

Representative compositions of living matter and fossil fuels

Part A: Living Matter

| | Major Constituents (wt%) | | |
Substances	Lipids	Proteins	Carbohydrates
Green plants	2	7	75
Humus	6	10	77
Phytoplankton	11	15	66
Zooplankton	15	53	5
Bacteria (veg.)	20	60	20
Spores	50	8	42

Part B: Petroleum

| | Elemental Composition (wt%) | | | | |
Substances	C	H	S	N	O
Lipids	80	10	—	—	10
Proteins	53	7	2	16	22
Carbohydrates	44	6	—	—	50
Lignin	63	5	0.1	0.3	31
Kerogen	79	6	5	2	8
Natural gas	75–80	20–25	trace–0.2	trace–minor	—
Asphalt	81–87	9–11	0.3–6	0.8–2.2	0–4
Petroleum	82–87	12–15	0.15	0.1–5	0.1–2

Part C: Coal

| | Elemental Composition (wt%) | | | | |
Substances	C	H	S	N	O
Peat	21.0	8.3	—	1.1	62.9*
Lignite	42.4	6.6	1.7	0.6	42.1*
Subbituminous	76.3	4.7	0.5	1.5	17.0
Bituminous	87.0	5.4	1.0	1.4	5.2
Semianthracite	92.2	3.8	0.6	1.2	2.2
Anthracite	94.4	1.8	1.0	0.7	2.1

*Remainder is ash and moisture.
(From Chilingarian and Yen. *Bitumens, Asphalts, and Tar Sands,* and from *Coal Development,* U.S. Bureau of Land Management, 1983.)

the heat; hence, the higher the contents of hydrogen and carbon, the better the fuel.

Coal

The fossil fuels bearing the greatest similarity to the original organic matter from which they were derived are peat and coal. Peat is the precursor of coal. Most forms of these substances contain abundant imprints of leaves, stems, seeds, and spores of the plants from which they were formed.

Coal was a very common household fuel in the United States and Europe in the second half of the nineteenth century and first half of the twentieth century. In the second half of the twentieth century, its use in homes was largely replaced with oil, gas, or electricity because these were more readily available and much cleaner to use. Although coal is no longer directly used in many homes, it has become the major heat source in the electrical power plants that supply the homes (Figure 5.6). The cheap and convenient petroleum replaced some coal usage in power plants in the 1950s and 1960s, but there has been a return to increased coal usage since the 1973 OPEC oil embargo caused concerns over supplies and brought sharp rises in the cost of petroleum. Today, much more fossil fuel energy worldwide is recoverable coal than recoverable oil; hence, society will probably rely upon coal as an energy source for many years to come.

Coal materials occur in four major classes: *peat, lignite, bituminous,* and *anthracite.*

History of Coal Use. The origins of coal use are not known, but evidence shows that 3000–4000 years ago Bronze Age tribes in Wales used coal in funeral pyres. Coal was probably also used by the Chinese as early as 1100 B.C. and by the Greeks in 200 to 300 B.C., but nearly

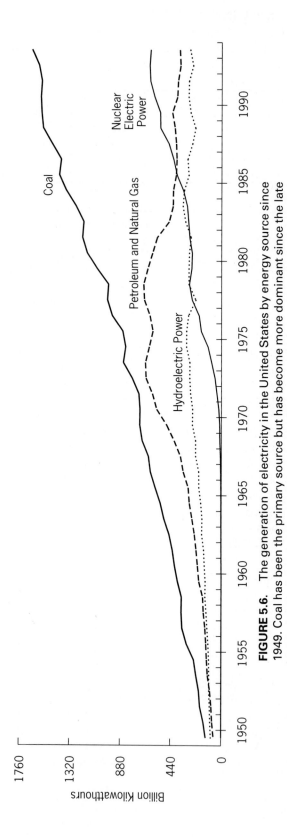

FIGURE 5.6. The generation of electricity in the United States by energy source since 1949. Coal has been the primary source but has become more dominant since the late 1970s; nuclear power has risen to the second most important source since 1985. (From the United States Energy Information Administration.)

a thousand years passed before coal had any lasting impact on civilization.

The widespread use of coal as a fuel began in the twelfth century A.D. when the inhabitants of the northeast coast of England found that black rocks weathering out of coastal cliffs would burn hotter than wood. The name, in fact, is derived from the Anglo-Saxon *col,* first used to refer to charcoal. This evolved to *cole,* a spelling used until about 300 years ago. Inefficient burning of impure coals released repugnant odors, causing Londoners to complain about air pollution in 1273; it ultimately led to an edict from King Edward I in 1306 that banned the use of coal. However, during the Industrial Revolution, England faced a crisis as its forests were depleted to make charcoal. The Admiralty feared for sufficient timber to maintain its fleets, and the value of coal as a substitute for fuel wood became apparent. Two other developments further brought coal into its own as a fuel. About 1710, Abraham Darby, a Shropshire ironsmith, developed a method of using coke, made by heating coal in the absence of air, to smelt iron. The first commercial steam engine, produced in 1698, burned wood or charcoal; however, as these engines were perfected and came into wide usage during the 1700s, coal became their fuel.

Although the Pueblo Indians of the southwestern United States used coal in pottery-making for many years, the first recorded discovery of coal in North America was by a French exploration party in 1679 along the Illinois River, about 130 kilometers southwest of Chicago. The first New World mining effort began in 1750 near Richmond, Virginia, where a Huguenot colony worked exposed seams. Coal mining began in western Pennsylvania in 1759 and soon spread throughout the Appalachian coal fields.

The developments of the Industrial Revolution rapidly increased the demand for coal both in Europe and in the United States. In England and in several parts of the eastern United States, the most efficient way to transport the coal was by canal systems. The development of railroads in the early 1800s supplanted, in part, the canal systems, but it also provided another major market for the coal. In the 1890s, with the development of the steam-driven electric generator, coal became the principal fuel for electric power plants, a position it continues to hold today.

It was this discovery and widespread use of coal that probably saved the great forests of the eastern areas of North America. If this coal had not been available when the Industrial Revolution reached North America in the late 1800s, the only fuel alternative was wood. The availability of coal and its superiority as a heat source (one ton of coal roughly equalling about 1.2 cords of dried hardwood) rapidly turned attention from the forests to the coal mines. The forests were spared and North America escaped the massive deforestation that had earlier occurred in Great Britain. Since major agriculture moved westward and southward, the eastern forests have actually increased in area relative to the 1880s.

Formation of Coal. Coals of all types comprise the compacted and variously preserved remains of land plants. Many plant remains, such as leaves, stems, and tree trunks, are visible to the naked eye, but many others, such as spores, are visible only under the microscope. Most of the plant matter today, as in the past, is not preserved but is decomposed where it falls or gets buried. Only where plant growth is abundant and the conditions for preservation are optimal can thick masses of coal-producing organic matter accumulate. The higher forms of plants with cellulose-rich stems and leaves that make coals did not evolve on the continents until the Devonian Period. Hence, Precambrian and early Paleozoic rocks contain no coal beds. The Paleozoic coal beds of the Carboniferous Period in Europe and North America were dominated by ferns and the scale-tree (Figure 5.7). In contrast, the Mesozoic and Tertiary swamps consisted of flowering plants much like those of today.

Most of the world's coals are known as **humic coals** and consist of organic debris that has passed through a peat stage. Their major components are lustrous black to dark brown materials known as **macerals,** the organic equivalents of the minerals that constitute a rock (Figure 5.8). Much less common, but locally important, is another type of coal known as **sapropelic coal.** The two varieties of sapropelic coals, **boghead** and **cannel coals,** consist primarily of fine-grained, featureless algal debris or spores that collected in oxygen-deficient ponds, lakes, and lagoons. These coals have compositions similar to the kerogen precursors to oil; indeed, when subject to higher temperatures and pressures, they yield oil and gas rather than the black vitreous macerals seen in humic coals.

The formation of the humic coals begins with the accumulation of organic debris in peat swamps where the stagnant waters prevent oxidation and decomposition. It has been estimated that only about 10 percent of the plant production is preserved under average peat-forming conditions. The highest rates of plant growth occur in tropical forest swamps, but these are also the sites of the greatest bacterial activity that destroy vegetable matter; hence, few peats develop in the tropics. Today, the major peat-forming areas occur in the temperate and cold regions such as Ireland, Scandinavia, Alaska, and Canada, where abundant rainfall promotes rapid plant growth but cooler temperatures retard bacterial decay. If the rates of peat accumulation in the past were similar to the 1 millimeter per year formation we see now, the major coal basins must represent swamps that persisted for tens of thousands of years.

The geologic study of coal-bearing sequences reveals that much coal formed in areas of successive transgression and regression of shore lines. This is seen in the interbedding of marine sediments with the coals, lacustrine beds, and terrestrial beds. A near-coastal swamp along the margin of a basin with the accumulation of thick masses of peat as the basin slowly subsided would have developed a common

(a)

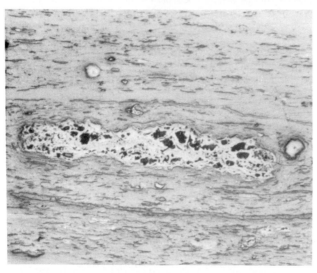

(b)

FIGURE 5.7. (a) Many coal beds contain imprints of the plants from which they were formed. Here the bark of a Cycad tree from a Mississippian (Carboniferous) age coal is visible. (Photograph courtesy of S. Scheckler.) (b) A microscopic view of a Mississippian-age coal in which layers of macerals, the organic constituents of coal, are visible.

FIGURE 5.8. The horizontal layering in the coal represents the layering of compacted organic matter. Differences in the reflectivity result from differences in the content of the macerals. Pyrite (FeS_2), although not visible in this sample, occurs locally in coal beds and is the principal contaminant resulting in environmental pollution. (Photograph by J. R. Craig.)

coal basins contain scores of individual coal beds separated by sandstones, shales, and limestones (Figure 5.9). The individual coal beds range in thickness from only a few centimeters to tens of meters. The individual coal seams often split into two or more, indicating that deposition in the peat swamp was continuous in some areas but interrupted in others. This situation is seen today in swamps that lie in major deltas where the distributaries keep changing direction and where many differences in the rates of subsidence and sediment accumulation exist.

Peat formation has taken place continuously since land plants developed in the Devonian Period, but the size of the swamps and their degree of preservation have not been uniform. By far, the greatest period of coal-swamp formation took place in the last 70 million years of the Paleozoic Era (Figure 5.10). During this time, the great coal beds of Britain and the eastern United States were laid down. The abundance of the coal in these British beds led to this span of geologic time being named the Carboniferous. Another great period of coal deposition extended from the beginning of the Jurassic until the mid-Tertiary; it was during this period that the major coals formed in the western United States. Deposition continues today in localized areas such as the Everglades of Florida, the Dismal Swamp of Virginia and North Carolina, and the coastal swamps of Canada, Scandinavia, and Ireland. Although these do not rival the peat swamps of the past, they do give us a first-hand opportunity to understand the conditions that must be present for peats and coals to form.

sequence. If the rate of subsidence exceeded the slow buildup of peat and sediment, the sea would have advanced, or transgressed, over the swamp, covering and preserving the peat with sands and muds. Lime muds often accumulated where the seawater was warm and clean. Frequently, a reemergence of the coastal area (with a retreat, or regression, of the ocean), a subsequent reestablishment of a swamp, and the deposition of another layer of peat followed subsidence. As a result of such cyclical deposition, many parts of the world's major

FIGURE 5.9. The cyclical development of coal-forming conditions resulted in the deposition of multiple coal beds in many areas such as this roadcut in western Virginia. (Photograph courtesy of Geological Consulting Services, Inc.)

Compaction occurs immediately after the accumulation of dead plant remains, and bacterial and fungal attacks begin. In the formation of peat, the cellulose and other original plant components decompose resulting in the production of biogenic methane gas (CH_4), carbon dioxide (CO_2), and some ammonia (NH_3). Only a mass of brown, hydrated gels, rich in large hydrocarbon molecules remains.

Coalification occurs when organic components that survived peat-formation undergo further physical and chemical changes as a result of biochemical action and rising temperature and pressure. As burial depth increases, temperature is the most important factor in coalification. The progressive increase in the **rank** of coal is peat, lignite (or brown coal), bituminous (or hard) coal, and anthracite (Figure 5.11). The precise assignment of rank is determined by the carbon content, the caloric value (heat given off when burned), the moisture content, and the volatile matter content. The most significant chemical changes are the progressive decrease in the oxygen and hydrogen contents, resulting in the increase of carbon content, as shown in what is known as a van Krevelen diagram (Figure 5.12). As this process proceeds, the number of distinguishable plant remains decreases and more of the shiny black macerals form. There is also a progressive decrease in moisture and an increase in density, caloric value, and the degree of polymerization (chemical bonds between carbon atoms).

The World's Coal Reserves and Coal Production.
The coal resources of Earth are large, but very irregularly distributed. Of the nearly one trillion tons of recoverable coal reserves, two-thirds can be found in the United States, the former Soviet Union, and China (Figures 5.13 and 5.14). Other countries with significant reserves include Germany, Poland, Australia, and South Africa. Coal reserves are virtually absent in the entire continent of South America. However, the United States, the former Soviet Union, and China account for nearly 55 percent of the world's total coal production.

Four major provinces accounting for most of the reserves are found within the United States' coal fields (Figure 5.15). In general, the Eastern and Interior provinces contain bituminous coal, whereas the Rocky Mountain and Northern Great Plains provinces are richest in subbituminous coal and lignite. Anthracite occurs locally in all provinces, but the country's major production and reserves lie in eastern Pennsylvania. Alaska contains significant amounts of subbituminous coal, but its remote location causes these deposits to be considered largely as resources rather than reserves.

The mining of coal, like that of metal ores, began as a labor-intensive industry. The coal beds were easy to follow and mine because many were nearly horizontal, and the rocks were much easier to break with a pick and shovel than those containing metal ores. On the other hand, conditions were difficult and dangerous because many coal seams were less than 1 meter thick and the mine openings only as high as the seam was thick. Furthermore, mine fires and explosions resulting from seepage of methane gas into the workings were common. In the 1800s, in Britain, the United States, and several other countries, children commonly worked in the coal mines because of their small size and because they could be paid so little.

Prior to 1898, the work week in the United States bituminous mines was 60 hours; it was then reduced to 52 hours, remaining such until 1917 when it was cut to 48 hours. It was

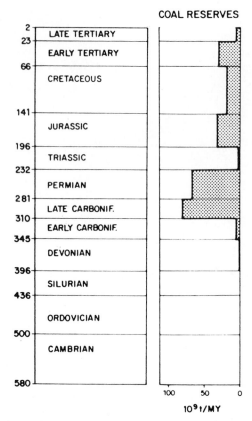

FIGURE 5.10. The graph on the right shows the worldwide distribution of coal reserves in terms of millions of tons of accumulations per million years during geologic time. The absence of land plants prior to the Devonian precludes earlier coals; the late Carboniferous (Mississippian) and Permian were the periods of most prolific deposition. (From Demaison (1977) and Bestougeff (1980) and from Bois, Bouch, and Pelet, *American Association of Petroleum Geologists Bulletin* 66 (1982) p. 1264. Used with permission.)

finally made 40 hours in 1933. The problems of low pay and long hours brought about the establishment of strong unions in the early years of the twentieth century. In spite of union efforts to maintain jobs, mechanization has markedly changed coal mining and resulted in a reduction in the number of United States miners from more than 700,000 in 1923 (producing 510 million metric tons of coal) to only about 120,000 in the mid-1990s (producing about 900 million metric tons of coal). Similar trends have been seen in all of the major coal-producing countries. For example, in Great Britain, where the coal mining industry was publicly owned for many years, a return to private ownership combined with mechanization has led to a drastic reduction in the size of the workforce. Increased competition from cheaper, imported coal led to the closure of many mines during the 1980s and 1990s. Similarly, the breakup of the former Soviet Union and

the shift away from a heavily subsidized state-owned mining industry has led to the closure of many mines because they could not compete economically with more efficient operations elsewhere. World coal production rose steadily but slowly during the nineteenth century, reaching 1 billion metric tons in 1907 (Figure 5.16). This slow increase continued with World War II disruptions until the 1950s when production rates markedly increased. After reaching 2 billion metric tons in 1953, it rose to 3 billion in 1970, 4 billion in 1982, and about 5 billion in the mid-1990s.

Modern coal mining is accomplished by either the underground or surface methods described in Chapter 3. In underground mining, the pick and shovel of the past has been replaced by drills and cutting machines which cut much more efficiently into the coal and dump it onto a conveyor belt for removal to a loading site on the surface. This most common type of mining removes only about 50 percent of the coal while leaving the rest as pillars to support the overlying rock (Figure 5.17). The spacing and size of the pillars depends upon the depth below the surface, the thickness of the coal, the stability of the roof rock, and the number of individual coal seams being mined. After the completion of initial mining, usually some of the coal in the pillars is also recovered in a process called *robbing the pillars*. This occurs during the "retreat" or final stages of mining.

A newer and more efficient mining method makes use of a *continuous mining* machine (Figure 5.18) that moves back and forth, removing nearly 100 percent of the coal by a rotary cutter. The machine and the conveyor belt that carries the coal are protected by a steel canopy. The machine, the belt, and the canopy advance together as coal is cut, and the overlying rock is allowed to subside in a continuous, controlled manner.

The thickness and quality of coal determine whether a given seam is economical to mine. Most beds greater than 61 centimeters (24 inches) in thickness are mineable. Underground mining is inherently dangerous, and, tragically, many miners are killed every year by roof falls. Many coals also yield large amounts of methane. Although methane is a great hazard, it can also prove a valuable resource (see page 150). Despite the former use of canaries and the modern use of air sensing equipment to test for methane, rapid gas buildups can still result in explosions (see Plate 24 and Figure 4.8). Since 1870, more than 120,000 coal miners have been killed in the United States (more than 20,000 in West Virginia mines alone) from such explosions. Even with all of today's precautions, more than 50 miners die in United States' coal mines every year (Figure 5.19).

Surface mining requires the removal of the overlying strata to expose the beds of coal. Once exposed, they are removed by bulldozers, front-end loaders, power shovels, and large drag lines. In order to rapidly and efficiently remove large tonnages of overburden, the equipment has constantly increased in size. The largest power shovel in the United

Rank stages			Characteristics	H₂O %	Heat content
		Peat	Large pores Details of original plant matter still recognizable Free cellulose	~ 75	3000 kcal/kg (5400 Btu/lb)
			No free cellulose		
Brown coal or lignite		Soft brown coal			
	Hard brown coal	Dull brown coal	Marked compaction of plant structures	~35	4000 kcal/kg (7200 Btu/lb)
			Plant structures partly recognizable	~25	5500 kcal/kg (9900 Btu/lb)
		Bright brown coal			
Hard coal		Bituminous		~10	7000 kcal/kg (12,000 Btu/lb)
		Anthracite	Plant structures no longer recognizable		8650 kcal/kg (15,500 Btu/lb)

Rank increasing (vertical label, arrow pointing down)

FIGURE 5.11. The ranks of coal, the caloric value, and some important physical characteristics. (From *The International Handbook of Coal Petrography*, 1963.)

States, the Gem, which operates in Ohio, weighs about 7000 metric tons. It is about 60 meters high, has a shovel capacity of 130 metric tons, and is said to be the largest mobile land piece of equipment in the world (Figure 5.20). Economics generally dictates which coal beds can be extracted through surface techniques. The *rule of thumb* has been that surface extraction is economical if the ratio of the depth of overburden to be removed to the coal thickness does not exceed 20:1. Where the overlying rock thickness is too great for surface removal, the mining may proceed as an underground mine, or coal may be removed by augering. Augers are drills, up to 1 meter or more in diameter, that can be driven into horizontal or gently-dipping coal beds. As the auger turns, it cuts the coal and feeds the broken pieces out just as a hand drill feeds out wood chips. Although the augers can remove only about 50 percent of the coal in a seam, the coal could not be economically recovered by any other means.

Most coal production in the first half of this century came from underground mines because coals exposed at the surface were too deeply weathered to be useful. Also, there were no practical means of removing the large quantities of overlying rock to expose deeper coal beds. Most of the beds that were amenable to surface mining, such as those in the western United States, were so far removed from the markets that transportation was either not available or not economical. The development of large power shovels and drag-lines made surface mining of 30-meter deep beds economical. The conversion of an area from underground to surface mining is visible in the Powder River Basin area of Wyoming (Figure 5.21) where subsidence of early 1900s underground workings occurs adjacent to a modern strip mine that removes the same coal bed. Over the past half-century, there have been a series of progressive changes in United States' coal mining practices (Figure 5.22). The most important changes include a rapid increase in mining west of the Mississippi River, a significant increase in the mining of subbituminous coal and lignite, a sharp decline in the mining of anthracite, and a rapid increase in surface mining at the expense of deep mining. The

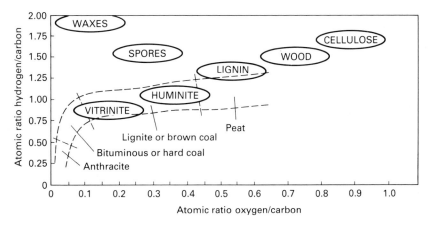

FIGURE 5.12. The van Krevelen diagram illustrating the evolution of the composition of organic matter as it is converted into coal. The carbon content and the caloric value rise as the organic matter progresses to lower hydrogen/carbon and oxygen/carbon ratios.

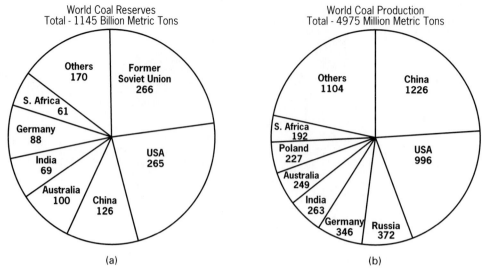

FIGURE 5.13.   (a) International recoverable reserves of coal in 1992. (b) International coal production in 1992 in millions of metric tons. (From *Annual Energy Review,* U.S. Energy Information Administration, 1993.)

main reasons for these changes include (1) greater demand for the lower-sulfur, near-surface coals found in the western states, (2) the development of power plants near the western coals, (3) concern for increased safety, (4) the greater per person productivity in surface mines, and (5) the absence of unions in many of the surface mines in the west.

Coal mining and coal use have been the subject of many environmental concerns, especially in recent years.

Most of these concerns have centered on the problems of acid mine drainage, acid rain (see page 81), increased carbon dioxide levels in the atmosphere, and surface mine reclamation. The first two concerns are related to the sulfur present in all coals in amounts of 0.2–7.0 percent. Generally, about one half of the sulfur present is bound within organic macerals; the remaining sulfur occurs principally as the two forms of iron disulfides, pyrite and marcasite (FeS_2). The sulfur was

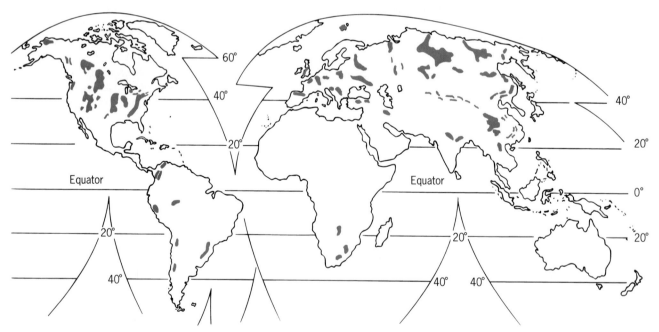

FIGURE 5.14.   The geographic distribution of coal fields throughout the world. (From Fettweis, *World Coal Resources,* Amsterdam: Elsevier, 1979.)

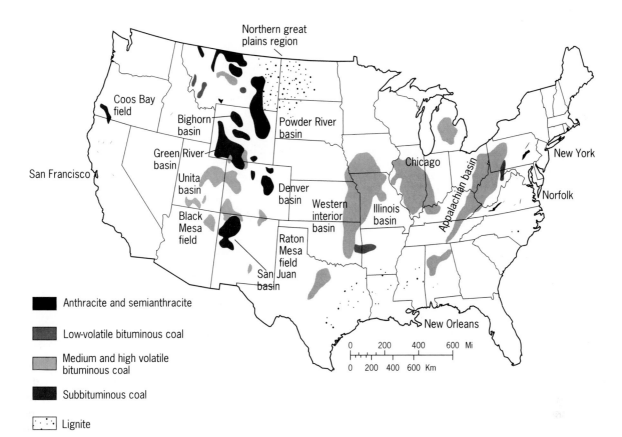

FIGURE 5.15. The major coal fields of the United States. Eastern Pennsylvania contains nearly all of the anthracite. The Eastern and Interior provinces are dominantly bituminous coal, whereas the Rocky Mountain province contains mostly subbituminous coal and lignite. (From the United States Department of Energy.)

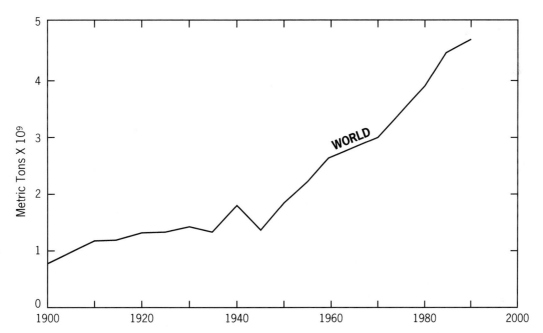

FIGURE 5.16. The world production of coal has risen from less than 1 billion metric tons in 1900 to nearly 5 billion metric tons today. Note the sharp rise in production after World War II.

FIGURE 5.17. Pillars of coal are often left on each side of the area where coal is removed to support the roof as mining progresses. These pillars, which may contain a large proportion of the coal, are commonly removed as miners retreat from a mine when its reserves are exhausted. (Photograph courtesy of Bethlehem Steel Company.)

originally derived from the organic matter and sulfate in groundwaters, which was reduced by bacterial action. Once coal is exposed to air and water by mining, the iron sulfide is converted to ferrous sulfate ($FeSO_4$) and sulfuric acid (H_2SO_4). The washing of these compounds by rainwater into rivers and streams has left thousands of kilometers of waterways devoid of fish and other aquatic organisms. The ferrous iron is readily soluble in the strongly acidic waters, washing off exposed coal beds or waste piles, but is oxidized to ferric iron as these waters are diluted by stream water. The result is the precipitation of iron hydroxides as gelatinous, reddish-brown coatings on the rocks and plants. Our understanding of the processes involved in stream pollution and the concern that no further abuses occur has led to much more stringent regulations regarding the discharge of mine waters and the dumping of iron sulfide-rich mining debris.

FIGURE 5.18. A continuous mining machine in operation. The coal is cut by the rotating cutting drum at the front and is carried by conveyor belt to the back where it is loaded into rail cars or placed on another belt for removal from the mine. (Photograph courtesy of The A. T. Massey Coal Co., Inc. and Heffner and Cook, Inc.)

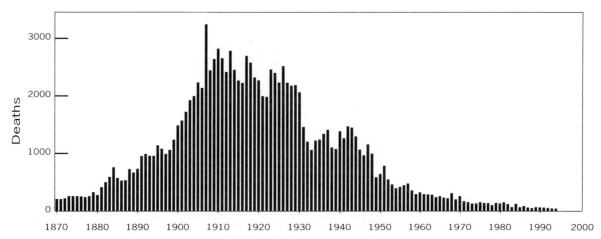

FIGURE 5.19. Since 1870, more than 120,000 miners have been killed in coal mine accidents in the United States. More than 3200 were killed in 1907 alone. Since the 1920s, union efforts and more stringent safety measures and codes have reduced the numbers of deaths, but even in the 1990s, more than 50 miners were killed each year.

In spite of cleaning efforts to remove the pyrite from coal before it is burned, some pyrite and the organic sulfur remain in the coal. Burning the coal releases some sulfur dioxide (SO_2), which has been considered a significant contributor to acid rain.

Regarding the third concern, there is no question that the burning of coal raises the CO_2 levels of the atmosphere. However, there is a very large question as to its ultimate effects. As we have progressed through the fossil fuel era, the atmospheric CO_2 levels have nearly doubled (see Figure 1.8). Because carbon dioxide keeps infrared radiation from escaping Earth's atmosphere, global warming could result. Presently, however, there is a great deal of uncertainty about how high the carbon dioxide levels are likely to rise and to what the magnitude of the warming is likely to be.

All types of underground mining can lead to problems of subsidence after the mining is finished (see Figure 4.13). An example may be seen in the foreground of Figure 5.21 and in Figure 5.23 that shows an area in Wyoming where many of the mine openings, only a few tens of meters below the surface, have caved in. Similar closed mines underlie many areas in England, India, and the eastern and central United

FIGURE 5.20. The GEM, or giant earth mover, the largest power shovel in the United States, is shown here mining in Ohio. The shovel, with a capacity of 300–500 metric tons per shovel load, is used to strip off the overburden to expose the underlying coal beds. (Courtesy of Consolidation Coal Company.)

FIGURE 5.21. In the Powder River Basin of Wyoming, a modern surface mine lies beyond an area where underground mining in the early 1900s removed coal from the same bed. The holes in the foreground are the result of surface collapse into the old workings. (From U.S. Geological Survey Professional Paper 1164, 1983.)

States. More spectacular than the subsidence of old coal mines are underground coal fires (Plate 16). In the United States, where there are an estimated 300 coal fires, and many other parts of the world, coal beds have been accidentally or spontaneously ignited. If there is an adequate oxygen supply, the underground fires can smolder for years and travel for considerable distances. The most famous mine fire has been at Centralia, Pennsylvania, where a burning waste dump ignited an exposed coal seam in 1961. The fire, despite the expenditure of millions of dollars trying to smother it by flooding the coal seam with water, continues to burn. The fire has progressed under much of the town, causing local subsidence and giving rise to the sudden appearance of cracks that issue hot, noxious gases. Many residents left the town, and those who remained had their households regularly monitored for deadly gases, such as carbon monoxide. Ultimately the decision was made to move the entire town because it was impractical, if not impossible, to put the fire out.

In eastern India, at least 65 major underground mine fires, some burning since 1916, have burned or made inaccessible at least 1 billion metric tons of coal. The area is pock marked by crevasses and holes that belch steam, smoke, and poisonous gases, and the rates of burning appear to be increasing. Even where there is no visible fire, the ground has been so heated that the land is unfit for farming.

Peat Resources

Peat has been used as a fuel in several European countries for centuries but is little known as an energy source in most of the rest of the world. In those other areas, including the United States, peat is widely used for agricultural purposes. Generally considered as a young coal, peat consists of plant matter that has been only slightly compacted and decomposed. Peats are classified into three general categories on the basis of biological origin and state of decomposition.

Those that are the least decomposed and richest in mosses are widely used for horticultural purposes as peat moss. Those that are more decomposed and compressed have heat values after air drying of only about 25 percent lower than lignite and have considerable potential as a fuel. This peat, when air-dried to about 35–40 weight percent moisture, contains more nitrogen and less sulfur than higher ranks of coal. Direct combustion is the simplest way to derive heat from peat, but there has been increasing research into the conversion of peat into methane gas by bacterial digestion or by thermal breakdown at 400–500°C.

The world's largest peat producers are the nations of the former Soviet Union, especially Russia, where 150–200 million metric tons were produced per year in the mid-1990s. As much as 80 million tons of peat are burned in scores of power plants, accounting for 2–3 percent of electricity production. Ireland is famous for its peat production and has a long history of hand cutting and drying peat for use in home heating (Figure 5.24a). Although Ireland's production is only about 8.5 million tons per year, it is the second largest in the world and accounts for about 25 percent of Ireland's total energy generation.

Little is known of the extent of the world's available peat resources; the values in Table 5.3 are among the more conservative values. Only a few countries, such as the former Soviet Union, Finland, and Ireland, actively exploit peat as a fuel source, but many other countries, such as the United States and Canada, are considering its potential. In fact, Minnesota has begun converting some heating plants in public buildings to peat-burning systems, and there was a trial peat-to-energy project in 1984 in which special sodding machines scooped up wet peat and extruded it as log-shaped blocks (Figure 5.24b). That particular project did not prove viable as a fuel, but large rectangular pits dug 1–2 meters deep to extract agricultural peat in North Carolina have become productive catfish farms. A peat-fired power plant in Maine

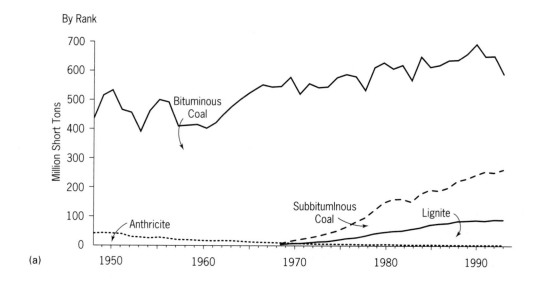

(a)

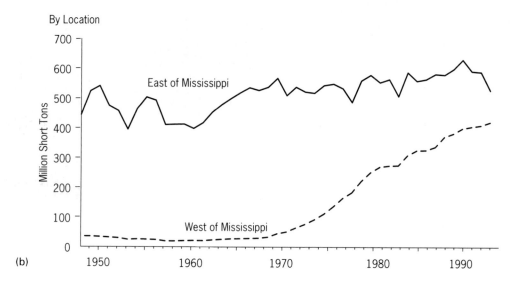

(b)

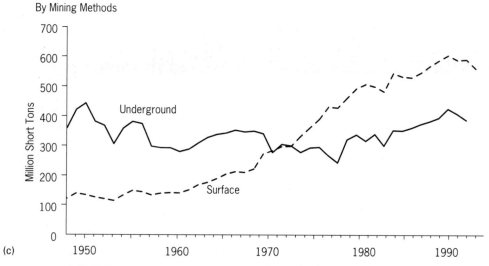

(c)

FIGURE 5.22. Changes in the United States coal industry since 1949. (a) Bituminous coal still dominates, but there has been a significant rise in subbituminous and lignite mining since 1970. (b) Mining west of the Mississippi River has risen since 1970. (c) Surface-mined coal has exceeded underground-mined coal since the early 1970s. (From the U. S. Energy Information Administration.)

FIGURE 5.23. Subsidence resulting from collapse into old coal mine workings in Wyoming is a threat to cattle grazing. (Photograph by Gary Glass.)

began supplying electricity in 1989 and has been successfully operated on a competitve and environmentally acceptable basis. Several additional plants were scheduled to be constructed in Florida for operation in the mid-1990s, but they were delayed because they would not have been cost competitive with plants using natural gas as a fuel. The peat occurrences of the United States are similar to those in many other parts of the world because they are concentrated in coastal areas and glacial terrains. Consequently, much of the United States peat lies in environmentally sensitive or restricted zones such as protected wetlands and game refuges. Canada's great peat resources commonly occur in remote, sometimes arctic, regions where their extraction would not be economical. Nevertheless, peat does constitute a considerable fossil fuel resource; however, its use will probably remain relatively limited in the near future.

(a)

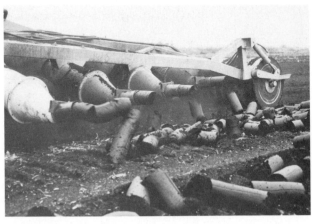

(b)

FIGURE 5.24.   (a) Mining peat in the traditional manner in Ireland. After digging, the peat is stacked and dried before burning. (Photograph courtesy of Irish Tourist Board.) (b) Logs of compressed peat being extruded as the sodding machine moves across a drained portion of a bog in North Carolina. (Photograph courtesy of First Colony Farms, Inc.)

TABLE 5.3

World peat resources and production

	10^6 Hectares With >30 cm Peat	Reserves ($\times 10^6$ m.t.)	Production, Mid-1990s (10^3 tons)		
			Fuel	Horticultural	Total
Canada	170	10,000	—	900	900
Former Soviet Union	150	20,000	20,000	150,000	170,000
United States	40	7,000	—	600	600
Finland	10.4	7,000	5,500	500	6,000
Germany	—	500	500	3000	3500
Ireland	1.2	200	7,000	—	7,000
Others	49.2	5,300	—	—	—
World total	420.8	50,000	33,000	155,000	188,000

(Data from U.S. Bureau of Mines, 1993.)

Petroleum

Petroleum, long scorned by most of society as a sticky, foul smelling material, has emerged as the principal fossil fuel of our times. In contrast to coal, the physical appearance of petroleum bears no evidence of its origin as marine planktonic materials because complete reconstitution occurred during its formation. The following discussion will consider the origin, occurrence, extraction, refining, and future potential of petroleum as a fuel.

History of Petroleum Usage. Petroleum, commonly thought of as the most important of the modern fuels, has actually been used in a variety of manners since before recorded history. In the petroleum-rich areas of the Middle East, near the Tigris and Euphrates Rivers, petroleum and **bitumen** occur in numerous natural seeps. The Akkadians, Babylonians, and Assyrians found numerous uses for the sticky bitumen such as a glue for arrowheads and for setting inlays in tile designs and as a mortar for holding bricks together. The famous Tower of Babel, a seven-stage pyramid that reached a height of 90 meters (295 feet) above the roofs of Babylon, consisted of bricks cemented with bitumen. Meanwhile, the people living along the rivers found that the tar waterproofed their boats. Biblical narratives note that Noah, after building an ark of gopher wood, was to "coat it with pitch [or tar] inside and out" and that Moses's mother got a "papyrus basket for him and coated it with tar and pitch." Natural floating masses of bitumen were harvested from the Dead Sea. In fact, Mark Anthony included the concession for the gathering of the material as one of his many love tokens to Cleopatra. The Egyptians also found bitumen to serve well as a preservative for mummies when they ran short of the resins they normally used. In the Americas, the Indians used tar and oil from natural seeps to caulk canoes and waterproof blankets. They had additional uses in medicines, the gluing of Toltec mosaic tile designs, and probably as a fuel.

The use of bitumen probably changed little from the days of early Babylonia until about 1000 A.D. when Arab scientists discovered distillation. By the twelfth century, the Arabs were producing tons of kerosene. Unfortunately, this technological advance was lost with the decline of scientific progress in the Middle East after the twelfth century and was not rediscovered until the nineteenth century.

Through the 1600s and early 1700s, most Europeans and early American settlers knew little, if anything, of petroleum. By 1750, numerous oil seeps had been found in New York, Pennsylvania, and West Virginia and wells drilled for water and salt often produced small amounts of oil. This oil was generally considered a nuisance because of its smell and stickiness. Some uses were discovered, but it wasn't until 1847 when Samuel M. Kier, who operated a salt business in Pittsburgh, began bottling oil to be sold as a sideline. Even the famed frontiersman Kit Carson collected oil and sold it as axle grease to pioneers moving west. Until the 1850s the major sources of lubricants and illuminants were vegetable and animal oils, especially whale oil. In 1852, a Canadian geologist named Abraham Gesner made the discovery that kerosene (then referred to as coal oil) used in lamps could be produced from oil by distillation. The usefulness of oil was rapidly realized in various parts of the world, and, in 1857, James M. Wilson dug an oil well and built a refinery to produce lamp oil near Oil Springs, Ontario. In the same year, oil production from hand-dug pits reached 2000 barrels in Romania.

In spite of these accomplishments, the modern oil industry generally traces its origins to the first American oil well, which was drilled by Edwin L. Drake along Oil Creek near Titusville, Pennsylvania, in 1859. Prompted by the potential of oil as a fuel, lubricant, and illuminant, New Haven, Connecticut, businessman George H. Bissel established the Pennsylvania Rock Oil Company in 1854. He planned to drill for oil near Titusville, Pennsylvania. The company's hopes were spurred when Professor Benjamin Silliman of Yale University analyzed a sample of crude oil skimmed from a

Pennsylvania spring and reported: "In conclusion, gentlemen, it appears to me that there is much ground for encouragement in the belief that your company have in their possession a raw material which, by simple and not expensive process, they may manufacture very valuable products."

Bissel's initial effort failed and ended in bankruptcy, but the investors regrouped under the new name Seneca Oil Company and hired Drake, an unemployed railroad conductor, to direct its operation. Drilling began in June 1859 using a wooden rig and a steam-operated drill (Figure 5.25a). Because water and cave-ins threatened the well, Drake drove an iron pipe 12 meters (39 feet) into the ground and proceeded to drill inside the pipe. Oil-bearing strata were encountered at a depth of 21.2 meters (69.5 feet) on August 27, 1859. The oil rose to just below the ground surface, Drake mounted a pump on the well, and the well began producing 10–35 barrels per day. The oil was initially sold for $20 a barrel, and the success resulted in the drilling of numerous other wells (Figure 5.25b). The price of oil dropped to 10 cents a barrel within 3 years. Boom towns of tents and shacks sprang up rapidly, and wagons and river barges carried the oil in wooden barrels to refineries built along the Atlantic Coast. Railroads soon built branch lines to the oil fields, and, by 1865, the first oil pipeline was constructed to carry oil 8 kilometers to a railroad loading area. In 1874, a 97-kilometer pipeline was constructed to transport 3500 barrels a day from the oil fields to Pittsburgh. After Drake's success, oil discoveries spread rapidly—West Virginia (1860), Colorado (1862), Texas (1866), California (1875). In many of these areas, the initial discoveries led to the drilling of numerous, very closely spaced wells (Figure 5.25B). The first of the giant fields in the Gulf Coast area was opened when a well known as Spindletop gushed nearly 60 meters into the air on January 10, 1901, yielding 100,000 barrels a day (Figure 5.26).

Meanwhile, commercial oil production also spread rapidly throughout the world. Italy became a small producer in 1860 and was rapidly followed by Canada, Russia, Poland, Japan, Germany, India, Indonesia, Peru, Mexico, Argentina, and Trinidad. The knowledge that oil and tar seeps had been worked in the Middle East for thousands of years stimulated considerable exploration interest in the region in the late 1800s and early 1900s. Small, encouraging discoveries were made in Iran in 1908 and Iraq in 1927. The true potential of the area finally became apparent when the first of the large fields was discovered in Saudi Arabia in 1938. Subsequent drilling since that time has shown that the Middle East contains more than half of the world's known reserves.

Petroleum exploration after World War II expanded throughout the world and led to discoveries on every continent from the tropics to the polar regions. Although numerous small fields have been found, the two discoveries that have received the greatest publicity in recent years have been those of the North Sea in 1965 and the Alaskan North Slope in 1968 (Figure 5.27, Plate 21).

(a)

(b)

FIGURE 5.25.   (a) Edwin Drake (right) in front of his oil well on the banks of Oil Creek in Titusville, Pennsylvania, in 1861. This well represents the beginning of the modern extraction of oil. (b) The success of Drake's first well resulted in the drilling of large numbers of closely-spaced wells in 1861 on the Benninghoff Farm along Oil Creek. (Photographs courtesy of American Petroleum Institute Photographic and Film Services.)

FIGURE 5.26. Spindletop, in southeast Texas, was one of the most famous gushers. It began flowing on January 10, 1901, at a rate of 100,000 barrels per day and reached a height of 60 meters (175 feet). (Photograph courtesy of the American Petroleum Institute.)

(a)

(b)

FIGURE 5.27. (a) Oil platforms such as these in the North Sea are used to drill for oil and then to pump it via submarine pipes to onshore facilities. The smoke results from the flaring or burning of excess natural gas. (Photograph courtesy of Shell U.K.) (b) The Alaskan Pipeline, which extends for 960 miles and cost $9.5 billion to build, transports 1.5 million barrels of oil per day from Prudhoe Bay on the North Slope of Alaska to Valdez where it is loaded onto tankers for transport to refineries. (Photograph courtesy of Sohio Petroleum Company.)

The Formation of Petroleum and Natural Gas.
The most important fossil fuel in the modern industrial world is **petroleum,** the base for most lubricants, fuels, and more than 7000 organic compounds. Early discoverers applied the Latin terms *petra* (rock) and *oleum* (oil) because they found it seeping out of the rocks. Petroleum, also called crude oil or *black gold,* has its origin, just as all fossil fuels, in organic matter trapped in sediments.

Natural gas, a mixture of light molecular weight hydrocarbons that are gaseous under Earth surface conditions, usually is found with petroleum. In contrast to the petroleum, which consists of scores of different hydrocarbon compounds, often 99 percent or more of natural gas is composed of methane (CH_4). Minor amounts of the other hydrocarbon gases—ethane (C_2H_6), propane (C_3H_8), and butane (C_4H_{10})—may also be present. In addition, variable amounts of carbon dioxide (CO_2), hydrogen sulfide (H_2S), helium (He), nitrogen (N_2), hydrogen (H_2), water vapor, and ammonia (NH_3) can also be found. Petroleum forms almost exclusively from the organic matter in marine sediments, whereas natural gas forms in both marine and terrestrial rocks. As early as 1781, the Abby S. Volta of northern Italy provided insight into the formation of oil and gas when he noted, "Fermentation of buried animals and plants generates oil, which is transformed into naptha [a term for volatile colorless gasoline-like fluids], by distillation due to the underground heat and in turn is elaborated into vapors."

The Abby's views were quite accurate, for we now know that the modification of buried organic matter leads to formation of oil and gas. Natural gas forms with both oil and coal and by at least two processes (Figure 5.5). Most organic matter, even when buried, is totally decomposed by organisms or by oxygen in circulating waters. The portion that survives is still subject to attack in the oxygen-free environment by anaerobic bacteria. The product of the bacterial action, which may occur any time from immediate burial to millions of years later, is **biogenic gas.** This gas is mostly methane (CH_4), although variable amounts of other gases may also be present. It constantly rises in small amounts from swamps, soils, and the sediments on the seafloor.

The principal types of organic matter trapped in the seafloor sediments are the remains of free-floating planktonic organisms which constantly rain onto the seafloor (Figure 5.28). The depth scale of oil and gas formation, which also corresponds to a general increase in time and temperature as well, is only approximate and may vary with the nature of the original organic matter (Figure 5.29). The depth of burial has been subdivided into three major zones in which the processes of diagenesis, catagenesis, and metagenesis are active. These processes constitute a continuum of increasing burial temperature and pressure in response to which minerals and organic matter change. **Diagenesis** occurs from the surface of the depositing sediment to depths of a few hundred meters where temperatures are generally less than 50°C. Minerals are dissolved and precipitated by groundwater, and much organic matter is oxidized or consumed by burrowing organisms or bacteria. Anaerobic methanogenic bacteria are commonly very active in the upper parts of this zone and are responsible for the generation of considerable amounts of biogenic gas. **Catagenesis,** which occurs in the temperature range of 50–150°C and pressures up to 1500 bars at depths to about 3.5–5 kilometers, brings about compaction of the rock and expulsion of water. The organic matter is progressively converted into kerogen and then into liquid petroleum. Biogenic gas-producing processes decrease in effectiveness, but thermogenic gas processes become important and result in the formation of gas by thermal cracking of some of the kerogen. As depth continues to increase, petroleum-forming processes give way to **thermogenic gas** production. This gas is commonly considered *wet* because the dominant constituent, methane, is accompanied by minor amounts of ethane, propane, and butane that are easily removed by condensation. Below depths of 3500–4000 meters, temperatures exceed 150°C and pressures rise above 1500 bars. The early stages of metamorphism occur here and are referred to as **metagenesis.** At this stage, the remaining organic matter is either converted to dry gas, nearly pure thermogenic methane,

or a carbon-rich residue. With deeper burial, metamorphic effects increase, and the residue is converted to graphite.

It is apparent that rocks containing different types of organic matter or similar organic matter that has been subjected to different burial depths could yield very different ratios of oil and gas. Marine sediments with lipid-rich organic matter tend to yield oil and wet gas when subjected to catagenesis; terrestrial, cellulose-rich matter yields coal and dry gas when subjected to the same conditions. Organic-rich marine sediments buried to depths of 2000–3000 meters usually yield considerable oil and gas, but the same sediments, if buried an additional 1000 meters deeper, usually yield much gas but little oil.

The formation of petroleum and natural gas depends on the availability and preservation of marine planktonic organisms. These creatures have been present in the world's oceans since the late Precambrian Era, and their abundance has generally increased with the progression of time. The known reserves of liquid and gaseous hydrocarbons reflect this plankton increase over time (Figure 5.30). The increased abundance of hydrocarbons in younger rocks probably indicates that some oil and gas in the older rocks escaped or was destroyed by weathering and erosion. Methane gas can form through some types of metamorphic and igneous reactions and is found trapped in tiny inclusions in some minerals. Most petroleum geologists believe, however, that only organically produced gas will ever be found in sufficient quantities to be economically recovered.

The initial amounts of organic matter in nearly all sediments are too low and dispersed to form commercial quantities of oil. Economical accumulations only occur where the petroleum has migrated from its **source rocks** into porous and permeable carrier or **reservoir rocks** (usually sandstones or porous limestones). The final requirements for commercial oil and gas accumulations are **traps** (Figure 5.31), zones in which the migrating hydrocarbons become confined and prevented from further movement by an impermeable seal or cap rock. There are two general types of traps: **structural traps,** formed by folding or faulting, and **stratigraphic traps,** created where layers of porous, permeable rocks are sealed off by overlying impermeable beds. In the Gulf Coast region of the United States and a few other geologically similar areas, considerable amounts of petroleum occur in structural traps that have developed adjacent to salt domes. They have bowed up and penetrated oil-bearing strata (Figure 5.31). The migration of water and natural gas along with the oil usually results in a layered configuration in the traps with the more dense water below and the less dense gas above.

Oil Recovery. The earliest oil recovery came from natural seeps where oil and natural gas migrated along faults or bedding planes either to the surface or into zones of moving groundwater that carried it to a spring. At the surface, the natural gas dissipated and the light fractions of the oil evaporated, leaving behind tar. This had been gathered from the

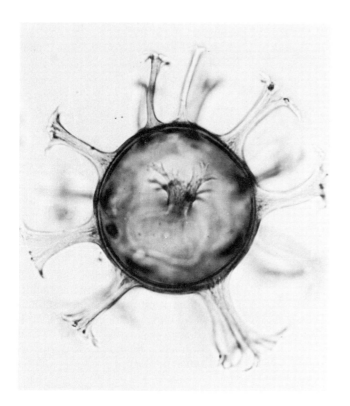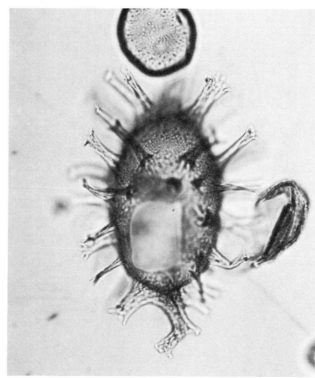
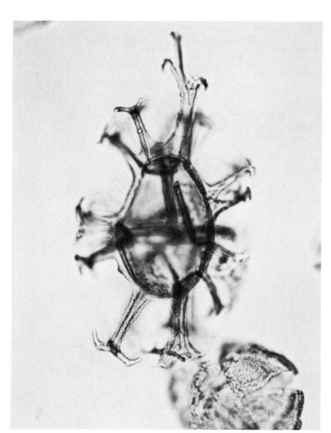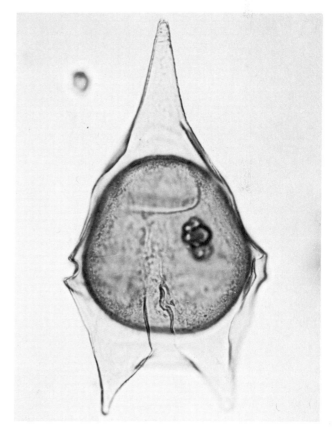

FIGURE 5.28. Petroleum forms from the accumulation of small floating plankton such as these modern dinoflagellates. The hydrocarbons of each of these organisms, which average 0.55 mm in diameter, are converted into kerogen and ultimately into oil and gas. (Photograph courtesy of D.M. McLean.)

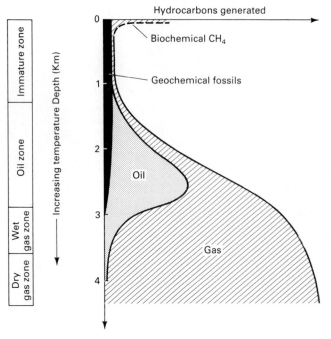

FIGURE 5.29. The conversion of organic matter to kerogen and to oil and gas is shown as a function of the depth of burial (with corresponding increases in temperature and pressure). Biogenic methane is generated by near-surface bacterial activity. The actual depths of the thermogenic generation of oil and gas vary slightly from one area to another depending on rock type, the geothermal gradient, and the nature of the organic matter.

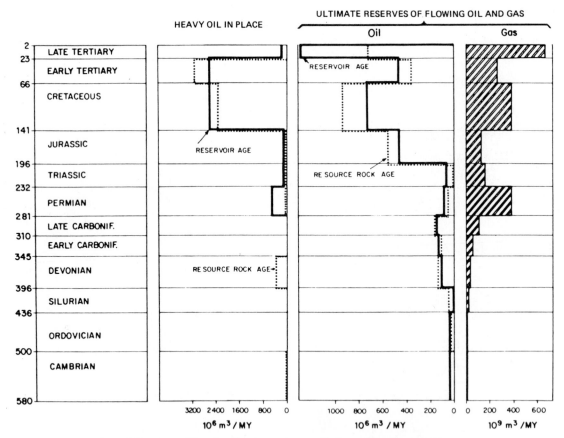

FIGURE 5.30. The distribution of the ultimate reserves of oil, gas, and heavy oil in terms of millions of cubic meters per million years as a function of geologic time. (From Demaison (1977) and Bestougeff (1980) and from Bois, Bouch and Pelet, *American Association of Petroleum Geologists Bulletin*, 66 (1982), p. 1264. Used with permission.)

Types of Oil and Gas Accumulations

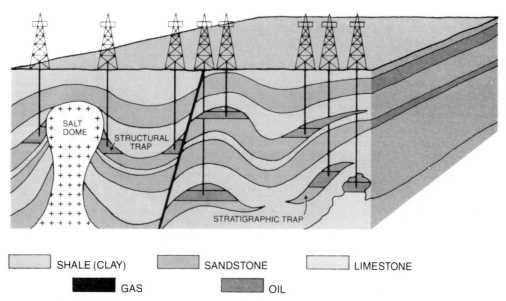

SHALE (CLAY)   SANDSTONE   LIMESTONE

GAS   OIL

FIGURE 5.31. Although caused by different natural phenomena, all types of hydrocarbon traps provide a site for the subsurface accumulation of oil and gas and, thereby, create the fields that are sought by the drill. This simplified sketch shows examples of major traps. (From *How Much Oil and Gas*, Exxon Background Series. Reprinted with permission of Exxon Corporation.)

shores or scooped off the surface for thousands of years in the Mideast and the Americas. Although oil still seeps to the surface, virtually all that is produced in the world today is recovered through wells employing primary or secondary methods of extraction.

The earliest oil wells were drilled by driving rotating pieces of pipe with cutting teeth into the soil and rock. These simple drills were replaced by **cable-tool drills,** which consist of heavy bits attached to long steel cables. The cable raises the bit and drops it in quick succession so that it cuts little by little into the rock. Periodically, the cable and bit are withdrawn from the hole, and the loose fragments of rock are flushed out. The cable-tool drills, which effectively reached depths of several thousand meters, have now been replaced by more efficient **rotary drills** that can operate at depths greater than 10,000 meters. These drills employ complex bits with a group of rotating teeth that cut into the rock as it rotates (Figure 5.32). The bit is attached to the base of a series of hollow steel pipes, and motors rotate them on the drill platform. Drilling fluids and muds are pumped down the center of the pipe to cool the bit and flush the rock chips out of the hole. In order to change drill bits, the drill crew must raise the entire stem of drill pipes and disconnect them in 10- to 20-meter lengths. Once the bit has been replaced, the entire stem must be reassembled pipe-by-pipe as it is lowered into the

hole. In recent years, much drilling has been carried out on the continental shelves and has employed either floating, stationary, or boat-mounted rotary drills (Figure 5.33; Plate 19).

Once a series of holes has been drilled, they are often linked together by a production manifold, allowing oil from the individual wells to be more efficiently and safely transported to loading sites. A good example is the Strathspey oil field in the North Sea where 15 wells—including water-injection wells, gas wells, and oil wells—are linked to a single manifold. Oil then flows to the loading platform through a 36-inch pipeline. Early oil well drillers assumed that their holes extended vertically beneath the drill rig to a depth equal to the length of the cable or drill pipe. This was often true, but in many instances the differences in the composition and hardness of rocks, especially when they are dipping or folded, cause the drills to veer off course, missing their original targets. As the technology for drilling has improved so drills can be kept on target, *directional drilling*—the capability to drill holes at a variety of angles—was developed (Figure 5.34). These techniques are now used to reach previously unattainable oil (under lakes, rivers, or bays). These can also more effectively probe for oil accumulations that occur in vertical fractures, more efficiently extracting it from broad horizonal zones, and they can also drill into several reservoirs from a single drill site. Drill motors lowered into

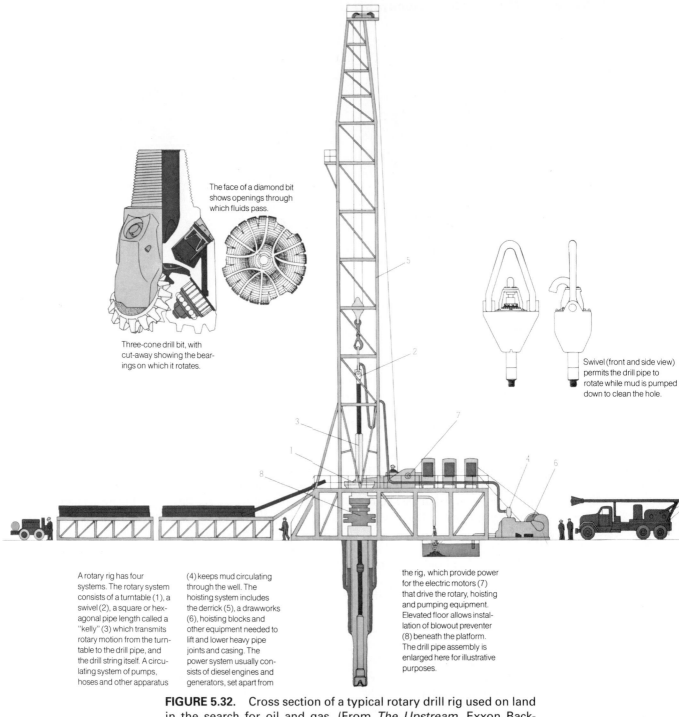

The face of a diamond bit shows openings through which fluids pass.

Three-cone drill bit, with cut-away showing the bearings on which it rotates.

Swivel (front and side view) permits the drill pipe to rotate while mud is pumped down to clean the hole.

A rotary rig has four systems. The rotary system consists of a turntable (1), a swivel (2), a square or hexagonal pipe length called a "kelly" (3) which transmits rotary motion from the turntable to the drill pipe, and the drill string itself. A circulating system of pumps, hoses and other apparatus (4) keeps mud circulating through the well. The hoisting system includes the derrick (5), a drawworks (6), hoisting blocks and other equipment needed to lift and lower heavy pipe joints and casing. The power system usually consists of diesel engines and generators, set apart from the rig, which provide power for the electric motors (7) that drive the rotary, hoisting and pumping equipment. Elevated floor allows installation of blowout preventer (8) beneath the platform. The drill pipe assembly is enlarged here for illustrative purposes.

FIGURE 5.32. Cross section of a typical rotary drill rig used on land in the search for oil and gas. (From *The Upstream*, Exxon Background Series. Reprinted with permission of Exxon Corporation.)

the holes and guided by complex navigational and survey systems accomplish this task. Directional drilling is especially important when drilling from a single stationary site, such as the large rigs in the North Sea or the Gulf of Mexico, and in areas where vertical drilling may be considered environmentally unacceptable, such as in Chesapeake Bay.

One good example of the effectiveness of horizontal drilling can be seen in the Captain Field, which holds 1.5 billion barrels of oil 130 kilometers (83 miles) off the north coast of Scotland. The use of horizontal drilling reduced the number of needed wells from 100 to 30 and drilling locations from 6 to 2. It also allows single wells to produce from a

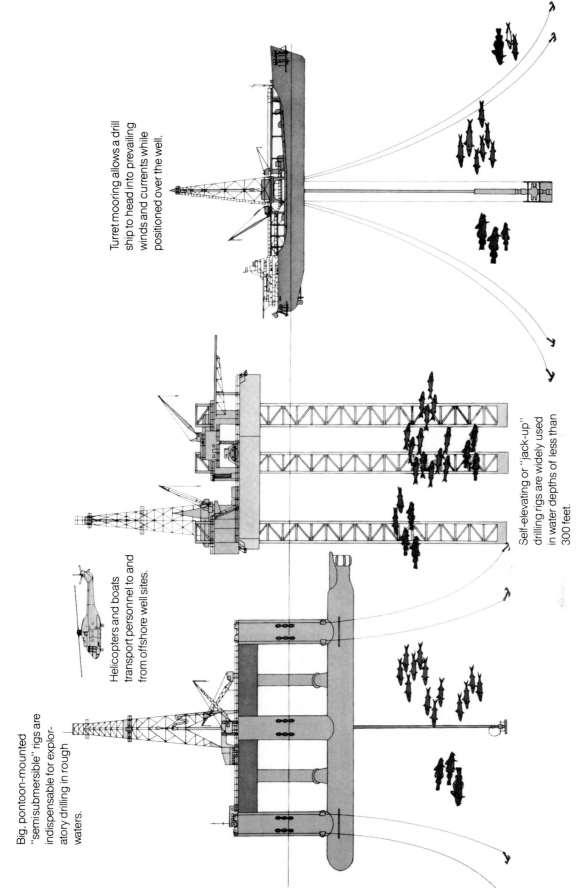

Big, pontoon-mounted "semisubmersible" rigs are indispensable for exploratory drilling in rough waters.

Helicopters and boats transport personnel to and from offshore well sites.

Self-elevating or "jack-up" drilling rigs are widely used in water depths of less than 300 feet.

Turret mooring allows a drill ship to head into prevailing winds and currents while positioned over the well.

FIGURE 5.33. Floating, stationary, or boat-mounted drilling rigs have become vital to the search for offshore oil and gas. (From *The Upstream*, Exxon Background Series. Reprinted with permission of Exxon Corporation.)

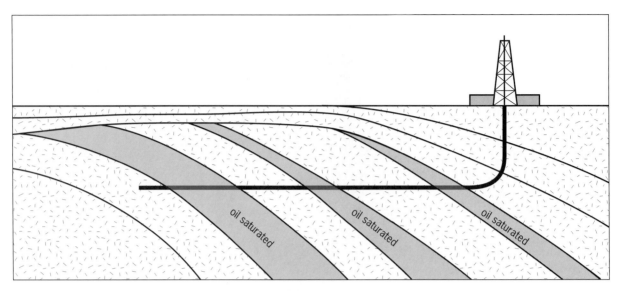

FIGURE 5.34. Directional drilling, including horizontal drilling, is now common in many oil fields. Inclined or horizontal holes can be useful in increasing recoverable oil or gas by cutting through wider producing zones or across multiple vertical or sloping fractures or sands.

2000-meter-wide zone across the oil field. A conventional vertical well could only have produced oil from a zone a few hundred meters in thickness.

Because petroleum within rocks occurs as small droplets, films between grains, and along small fractures, its movement is usually very slow (Figure 5.35). In order to allow the petroleum to flow more readily, it is often necessary

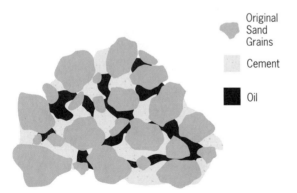

Original Sand Grains

Cement

Oil

FIGURE 5.35. Oil and gas occur in, and move through, the interstices of the grains in the reservoir rocks. The porosity rarely exceeds 30 percent of the total rock volume. Natural gas moves rapidly through interconnected pores, but oil sticks to the mineral surfaces and in cracks so that the primary recovery is usually only about 30–35 percent. Additional oil can often be recovered by use of the secondary recovery methods.

to either enlarge the natural channels in the rock or make new ones. One common method is to inject strong acid solutions to dissolve cementing agents that restrict the permeability between pore spaces. In another commonly employed method, water and coarse sand are pumped into the well under pressure high enough to fracture the oil-bearing rock; the sand grains permanently prop open the fractures to allow the oil to move. In other areas, high-caliber bullets or small explosive charges are used to fracture the rock near the well. All of these procedures also increase the amount of total oil recovery because they open new channels and break open tightly constricted pores.

Primary recovery is the simplest and least expensive method of recovering oil from wells because it takes advantage of natural pressures within the petroleum reservoir to push the oil to the well. If natural pressures are extreme, the initial drilling into a reservoir can produce a **gusher** (Figure 5.26), in which the oil is sent spouting out of the hole. Gushers were quite rare in the past, and they are nearly always prevented today with the use of special valves to stop or control the flow of oil. If the natural pressures are low, the oil must be lifted to the surface by pumps placed at the bottom of the oil well.

Natural pressures result from water drive, gas expansion, and the evolution of dissolved gas from the oil (Figure 5.36). Most petroleum contains dissolved gases held in solution by pressure, similar to how CO_2 is held in soda water. When petroleum removal begins, the confining pressure drops and some of the gas comes out of solution. Just as the evolution of CO_2 causes some of the soda to overflow

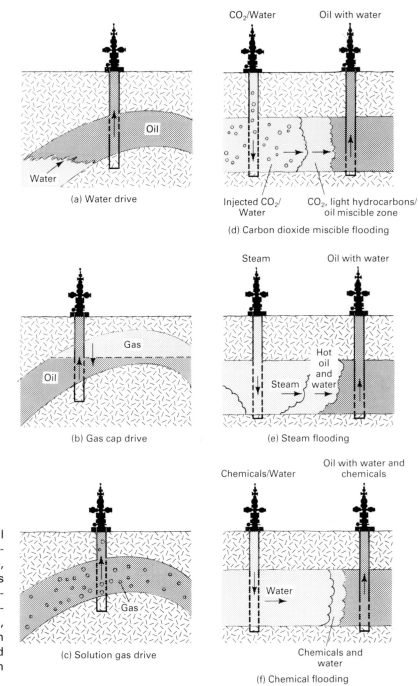

(a) Water drive

(d) Carbon dioxide miscible flooding

CO₂/Water — Oil with water

Injected CO₂/Water — CO₂, light hydrocarbons/oil miscible zone

(b) Gas cap drive

(e) Steam flooding

Steam — Oil with water

(c) Solution gas drive

(f) Chemical flooding

Chemicals/Water — Oil with water and chemicals

Chemicals and water

FIGURE 5.36. Recovery of oil and gas from traps may be by primary methods—(a) water drive, (b) gas drive, and (c) solution gas drive—or by secondary methods—(d) carbon dioxide miscibility flooding, (e) steam flooding, and (f) chemical flooding. (From *The Upstream,* Exxon Background Series; Reprinted with permission of Exxon Corporation.)

from the can or bottle, the evolution of the natural gases can force some of the oil from the rock, into the reservoir, and up the well.

In many traps, natural gas lies above the petroleum and exerts considerable pressure from above (Figure 5.36b). The gas cap expands as oil enters the well, and thus pushes more oil toward the well. Water drive (Fig. 5.36a), usually the most efficient of the natural processes, occurs when the pressure in the water underlying the reservoir pushes the oil into the well.

Although natural processes can help significantly in oil migration and recovery, primary oil recovery commonly reaches only 20–30 percent of the total oil in the reservoir. In order to increase the recovery of the oil, artificial, **secondary recovery** techniques are employed. These procedures often employ water, steam, or chemical flooding to displace or dissolve and mobilize the oil (Figure 5.36d, e, f). **Water flooding,** the most common and economical method, involves the injection of water into one or more wells at the periphery of the trap. The water displaces some of the oil and drives it toward production wells where it is pumped out. **Steam flooding** is a variant of water flooding in which super-heated steam is injected into a well (Figure 5.36e). The heat lowers the viscosity of the oil, permitting it to move more easily; the condensed steam then serves as water flooding. **Chemical flooding** is similar to water flooding except that it employs a chemical to either reduce the petroleum's viscosity or reduce the tendency for the petroleum to stick to mineral grains (Figure 5.36f). Generally, chemical solutions are injected into one well, and petroleum is extracted from another.

Sometimes natural gas recovered with oil is separated and reinjected into an expanding gas cap to help maintain reservoir pressure and improve oil recovery. This gas then also represents a potential future resource because much of it can be extracted later if needed. In spite of expensive secondary recovery procedures, 50 percent or more of the original oil often remains in the ground.

In recent years, especially after the rapid rise in oil prices from 1979 to 1981 (see Figure 3.15), there has been considerable speculation about **oil mining.** Interest in such procedures has been fueled by economics, the declining amounts of proven liquid petroleum reserves, and the observation of the American Petroleum Institute that the 10 largest oil fields in the United States will still contain 63 percent of their original oil in place after full production. This amounts to an estimated 300 billion barrels in the United States alone, ten times the country's known recoverable liquid petroleum reserves. Worldwide, the potentially recoverable original oil is most likely many times larger than 2 trillion barrels; this is in addition to oil shales and tar sands discussed later. Oil mining could be carried out (1) as surface mining, much as low grade copper ore is extracted in many parts of the world today; (2) as underground mining, using large tonnage extraction procedures as employed in many metal mines; or (3) as underground drainage systems, in which the oil drains into underground cavities in response to gravity. In the first two techniques, the rock—which may contain 0.1–0.5 barrels of oil per tonne—is extracted, crushed, and treated with either steam or chemical solvents to liberate the oil. The underground drainage systems would involve mining tunnels under the oil-bearing horizons and then drilling up into those horizons. The rock would be fractured and perhaps treated to lower the viscosity of the oil and its tendency to stick to the sediments. The oil would drain out through the holes into storage chambers from which it would be pumped to the surface for processing.

The digging of surface oil pits occurred in the Baku area of Persia as early as the sixth century B.C. In 1830, this area reportedly produced 30,000 barrels of oil per year from pits and springs. Hand-dug shafts and wells yielded oil that seeped into them in the sixteenth and seventeenth centuries in Sumatra, Germany, Cuba, Mexico, and Switzerland. The only serious twentieth century oil mining efforts came about during World War II when Germany and Japan, faced with wartime needs, carried out limited operations. In the United States, the need for a special grade of oil spurred an oil mining attempt in Pennsylvania. The reduction in price since the mid-1980s removed the major incentives for oil mining (as well as oil shale recovery), and all proposed operations have been postponed or cancelled. They will likely be revived when the price of oil once again rises significantly.

Petroleum Refining. Crude oil extracted from an oil well is a black, sticky fluid with a consistency that varies from watery to syrupy. It often bears little resemblance to the gasoline, kerosene, lubricating oils, chemicals, plastics, or other petroleum products we use every day. The crude oil actually consists of a mixture of thousands of hydrocarbon compounds that must be separated and isolated before they can be made into these products. This process is called **refining.** Arab scientists developed a primitive method of refining in about 1000 A.D. when they boiled bitumen and condensed it on a hide or in a water-cooled glass column. Although these technological innovations were lost with the decline of science through the Middle Ages, they were rediscovered and serve as the basis for modern refineries (Figure 5.37). The first step in refining is the **distillation** or **fractionation** of the crude oil based on the components' condensation temperatures. The crude oil is first heated to nearly 500°C and then separated into a large number of different products (Figure 5.38; Table 5.4). The lightest of the fractions, light gasoline, rises to the top of the tower; heavier fractions, diesel fuel and heating oil, condense at lower levels; the heaviest fraction, that used for asphalts, is taken out at the base of the tower.

In the early days of the oil industry, distillation was the primary means of separating products. The most useful fractions were kerosene, heating oils, and lubrication oils; gasoline was too explosive for household use and was commonly discarded. With the invention of the automobile, there was an increased demand for gasoline. This brought about the development of techniques that convert less useful heavier fractions into lighter ones.

Thermal cracking applies heat and pressure to heavy hydrocarbons to crack, or break, them into lighter ones. **Catalytic cracking** accomplishes the same result through the use of a catalyst, usually a synthetic zeolite mineral, that speeds and facilitates the process. Zeolites not only reduce the energy requirements for cracking, but they have also been proven useful in adding hydrogen through a process called **hydrogenation,** which increases the production of gasoline. Crude oils range widely in terms of the distillation products and the amounts of contaminants (mostly sulfur but occasionally nickel and vanadium), but modern refineries can produce nearly 50 percent gasoline, 30 percent fuel oil, and 7.5 percent kerosene from the original oil. Separation of the sulfur is necessary to make use of the fuel products environ-

FIGURE 5.37. Crude oil is converted into a wide variety of usable products in a series of complex physical and chemical steps in a refinery.

mentally acceptable. This has resulted in petroleum refineries producing large quantities of sulfur. In fact, United States petroleum refining now accounts for more than 55 percent of domestic sulfur production.

Where in the World Is Oil Found?   Two of the most important concerns regarding the sufficiency of oil are (1) where it is, and (2) how much there is. Neither can be answered with complete certainty, but exploration for more than 100 years and the drilling of millions of wells allow for some reasonable estimates.

The search for oil is confined to the approximately 600 sedimentary provinces known to exist around the world (Figure 5.39). By the mid-1990s nearly all of these basins had been tested by at least exploratory drilling. Virtually all of these provinces contain some hydrocarbons, and more than 240 have oil or gas that is economically producible. However, the widespread occurrence of hydrocarbons should not mislead us from recognizing that significant accumulations of oil or gas are very rare events, both geologically and statistically.

After more than 100 years of exploration in nearly all of the potential oil-bearing sedimentary areas—including all of the largest and most accessible ones, only seven provinces contained more oil than the world used in a single year in the peak-consumption years of the 1970s (Table 5.5). Seven provinces (each with at least 25 billion barrels of recoverable oil) contained more than two-thirds of known world reserves. There is only one megaprovince, the Arabian-Iranian, in the Middle East, and it contained 626 billion barrels, nearly one-half of the world's presently known resources. The 25 major provinces, those each with at least 7.5 billion barrels of known recovery, contained 1118 billion barrels, more than 88 percent of the total world oil reserves. This means that only 6 percent of the world's explored sedimentary provinces (10 percent of those with producible oil) contained almost 90 percent of the known recoverable oil.

We do not know where, when, or how much additional oil will be found. However, the largest and most accessible sedimentary areas have already been extensively explored; hence, future discoveries will most likely be made in smaller and more remote areas where production will be more difficult and costly. Furthermore, the rates of worldwide oil discovery have been decreasing, and some areas, such as the North American Atlantic continental shelf, once thought to possess significant oil potential, have failed to yield any recoverable oil. Prior to 1935, the worldwide rate of oil discovery (based on 5-year running analyses) was never greater than 12 billion barrels per year. From 1935 to 1970, it averaged 25–30 billion barrels per year; since 1970, it has averaged 15–18 billion barrels.

The geologic and climatic conditions necessary for oil occurrence and preservation have been present in many parts of the world at different times. Petroleum formation has been a continuous process since Precambrian time, but there were four periods that seem to have been most productive in terms of oil source sediment generation (Figure 5.30): (1) Devonian (396–345 million years ago), (2) late Carboniferous (310–281 million years ago), (3) late Triassic and Cretaceous (200–65 million years ago), and (4) Oligocene to middle Miocene (35–12 million years ago). Each of these intervals began with plate tectonic activity creating rapidly subsiding basins that filled with organic-rich sediment. Petroleum formation continues today and will do so in the future as the same types of geologic processes operate, but the rate of its development is so slow compared to the rates of consumption that it cannot be considered a renewable resource.

International Petroleum Production and Trade.
Petroleum has become not only the principal energy source in the world today, it has also become the most important and most valuable commodity of international trade. A complex web of trade routes crisscrosses the world's oceans and continents, linking the politics and economics of countries with otherwise little in common (Figure 5.40). Since the 1940s,

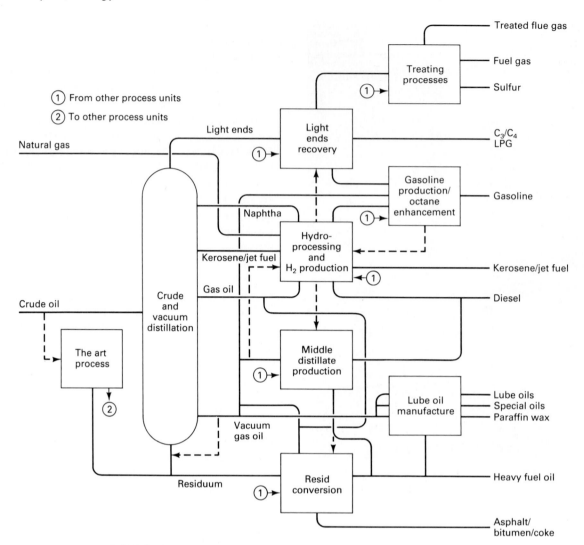

FIGURE 5.38. Within the refinery, crude oil is distilled by heating it to temperatures up to 500°C; some fractions are reacted with natural gas. The final products include gases, gasoline, kerosene, diesel fuel, and several types of oils, waxes, and tars. Contaminants, such as sulfur and metals, are removed. (Photograph courtesy of the M. W. Kellogg Company.)

international oil trade has more or less followed total world production. After peaking in 1980, when the international flow of oil exceeded 31 million barrels per day, it decreased to approximately 28 million barrels per day in 1984 and has remained at about this level. This represented only about 50 percent of total world production because some major producers use much of their own oil. As might be expected, the oil-rich Middle East is now the world's major oil exporter with supplies going mainly to Western Europe, Japan, and the United States. Western Europe also obtains oil from the North Sea fields and Africa, Japan from Indonesia, and the United States from Mexico, Venezuela, Africa, and the North Sea. In order to meet the large and constant demands and to minimize the transportation costs, modern oil tankers are the

biggest ships afloat, with the largest ones reaching lengths of more than 430 meters (1300 feet) and widths of more than 66 meters (206 feet) (Figure 5.41). Some can carry more than 3.5 million barrels of oil (500,000 metric tons). Prior to the closing of the Suez Canal in 1967, most tankers carrying Middle Eastern oil to Western Europe or the United States passed through the canal; now none of the largest tankers will fit and must sail around the Cape of Good Hope.

The United States was the world's principal petroleum producer from the days of the Drake well in 1859 until the mid-1970s when it was surpassed by Saudi Arabia and the former Soviet Union. The former Soviet Union kept most of its oil for domestic and satellite use. In contrast, Saudi Arabia and the other OPEC members (the history of this organi-

TABLE 5.4

Composition of typical crude oil

Components (molecular size)	Volume %
Gasoline (C_4 to C_{10})	27
Kerosene (C_{11} to C_{13})	13
Diesel fuel (C_{14} to C_{18})	12
Heavy gas oil (C_{19} to C_{25})	10
Lubricating oil (C_{26} to C_{40})	20
Residuum ($>C_{40}$)	18
TOTAL	100

(From Hunt, *Petroleum Geochemistry and Geology*, 1979.)

zation is discussed in Chapter 3) became the major suppliers for the noncommunist world. The share of world oil produced by OPEC rose from about 41.5 percent in 1960, to more than 55 percent in 1973 and 1975. The subsequent increased production in the former Soviet Union and other countries along with the reduction in OPEC production after 1979 had reduced the OPEC share to about 33 percent by 1983. Through the latter part of the 1980s and the first half of the 1990s, total world oil production gradually began to increase even as United States' and the former Soviet Union's production declined. By the mid-1990s, world production had again exceeded 60 million barrels per day, and the share produced by OPEC had grown to more than 40 percent of the total. Furthermore, the OPEC nations are estimated to retain 70–75 percent of the world reserves.

The total annual world production of petroleum rose from a few thousand barrels in 1859 to more than 20 billion barrels in 1979 (Figure 5.42). The rise was gradual and irregular through the first half of the twentieth century as wars promoted petroleum use and the depression in the 1930s lessened its demand. After World War II, production and demand both rose steadily until 1973 when the OPEC oil embargo spread fear of oil shortages. After a slight dip in 1975, world production rose again until 1979 when energy conservation, stimulated by a tripling of oil prices, reduced production by approximately 15 percent in 1983 (Figure 5.43). This reduction in oil consumption, and especially in dependence on

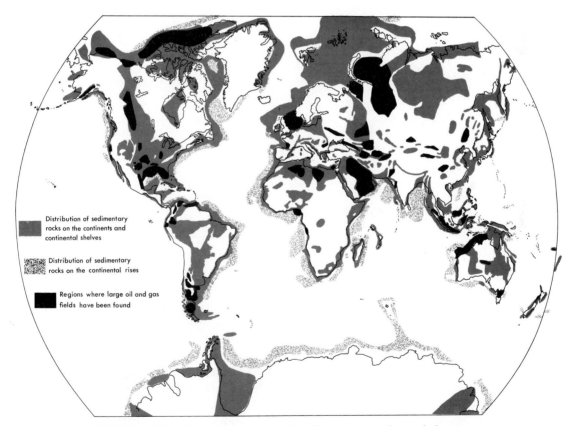

FIGURE 5.39. The major areas of sedimentary rocks and the regions where major occurrences of oil and gas have been found. The largest field occurs in the vicinity of the Persian Gulf (Table 5.7). Future discoveries will most likely be made on the deeper portions of continental margins and in areas that are little known, such as the continental shelves around Antarctica. (From B. J. Skinner, *Earth Resources*, 3rd ed. Englewood Cliffs, NJ: Prentice-Hall, 1986, p. 38.)

TABLE 5.5

The major oil provinces of the world

Province	Location	Known Recoverable as of 1/1/81 (billion barrels)	Age of Major Source Rock(s)
Megaprovinces (100 billion barrels plus)			
1. Arabian-Iranian	Arabian-Persian Gulf	626.3	Cretaceous, Jurassic
Superprovinces (25–100 billion barrels)			
2. Maracaibo	Venezuela-Colombia	49.0	Cretaceous
3. West Siberian	Former Soviet Union	45.0	Jurassic, Cretaceous
4. Reforma-Campeche	Mexico	42.2	Jurassic, Cretaceous
5. Volga-Ural	Former Soviet Union	41.0	Devonian
6. Permian	United States	32.6	Permian, Pennsylvanian
7. Sirte	Libya	28.0	Cretaceous, Paleocene
Superprovinces Subtotal		237.8	
Other Major Provinces (7.5–25 billion barrels)			
8. Mississippi Delta	United States	22.4	Miocene-Oligocene
9. Northern North Sea	UK-Norway-Denmark	22.4	Jurassic
10. Niger Delta	Nigeria-Cameroon	20.8	Oligocene-Miocene
11. Eastern Venezuela	Venezuela-Trinidad	19.5	Cretaceous
12. Texas Gulf Coast-Burgos	United States-Mexico	18.7	Oligocene-Miocene, Eocene
13. Alberta	Canada	17.0	Cretaceous, Devonian
14. East Texas-Arkla	United States	15.2	Cretaceous
15. Triassic	Algeria-Tunisia	13.5	Silurian
16. San Joaquin	United States	13.0	Miocene
17. North Caucasus-Mangyshlak	Former Soviet Union	12.0	Oligocene-Miocene, Jurassic
18. South Caspian	Former Soviet Union	12.0	Miocene
19. Anadarko-Amarillo-Ardmore	United States	10.8	Pennsylvanian
20. Tampico-Misantla	Mexico	10.7	Jurassic, Eocene
21. Arctic Slope	United States	10.3	Cretaceous
22. Central Sumatra	Indonesia	10.0	Miocene
23. Los Angeles	United States	8.9	Miocene
24. Chautauqua	United States	8.5	Pennsylvanian
25. Sung-liao	China	8.5	Cretaceous
Other Major Provinces Subtotal		254.2	
All Major Provinces Subtotal		1118.3	
All Other Provinces Subtotal		146.7	
WORLD TOTAL		1265.0	

(From R. Nehring, *Annual Reviews of Energy*, 1982.)

OPEC, is well demonstrated in the case of the United States (Figure 5.44). The total oil usage by the United States rose from 6.1 million barrels per day in 1949 to 19.2 million barrels per day in 1978, but it then dropped to less than 16 million barrels per day in 1983. However, by the mid-1990s, the rate of consumption had again moved back over 17 million barrels per day with the likelihood of continuing to slowly increase. The use of imported oil, especially from OPEC nations, followed similar trends. Total imports reached 8.5 million barrels per day (the OPEC portion was 6.2 million barrels) in 1977 but were reduced to 5.3 million barrels per day (the OPEC portion was only 1.8 million barrels) by 1983. By the early 1990s, United States petroleum imports had grown back to more than 7.5 million barrels per day with OPEC supplying more than 5.3 million of them.

The reduction in the rate of increase of world oil usage that began in about 1980 will extend the life of world oil supplies, reducing the political and economic impact of OPEC. Nevertheless, it is clear that the two-thirds to three-quarters of known world oil reserves held by OPEC nations will become increasingly important in meeting world needs as other reserves in the United States, the North Sea, and the former Soviet Union are depleted (Figure 5.45).

The political importance of oil is greater than that of any other commodity. Consequently, concern remains about the continuous flow of supplies to meet world needs. Any disruption or threat of disruption of oil supplies creates tension, rapidly raises prices, and can bring military responses. Never was this more apparent than at the time of the Gulf War in 1990–1991 as described in page 143 (see also Figure 5.46).

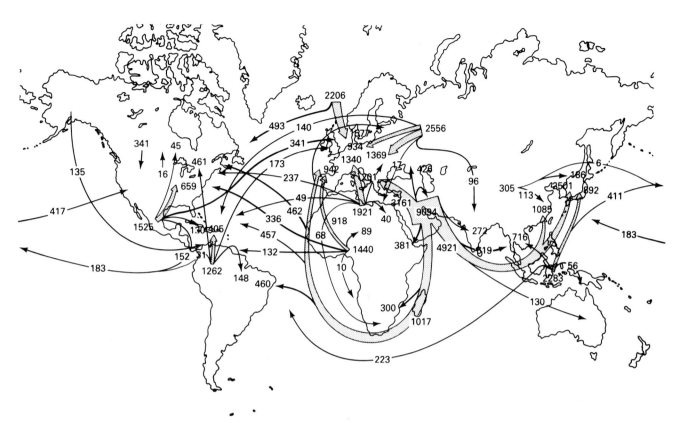

FIGURE 5.40. The complexity of international crude oil trade routes in 1984. All numbers are in thousands of barrels per day. Arrows indicate origins and destinations of the major shipments but not necessarily specific routes. (From *Annual Energy Review,* U.S. Energy Information Administration, 1986.)

FIGURE 5.41. The tanker *Batillus* (550,000 tons = 499,000 metric tons, 1350 feet = 430 meters long, 206 feet = 66 meters wide), shown here loading oil in the Persian Gulf, is representative of the modern large oil transport ships. (Photograph courtesy of Arabian American Oil Company and American Petroleum Institute, Photographic and Film Services.)

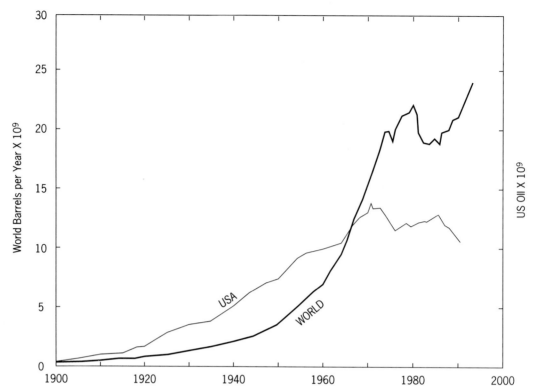

FIGURE 5.42. The United States and world production of oil since 1900. World production rose rapidly in the 1950s and 1960s and is rising again. United States production peaked in 1970 and is now declining.

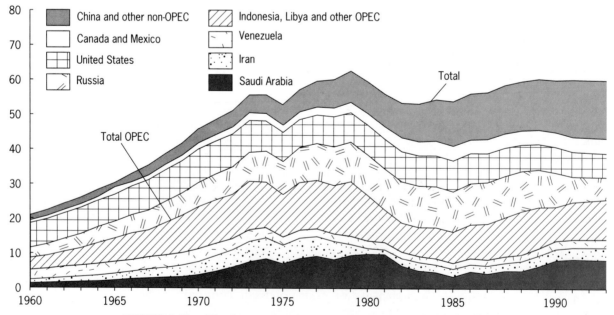

FIGURE 5.43. The international production of crude oil from 1960 to 1993. (From *Annual Energy Review*, U.S. Energy Information Administration, 1993.)

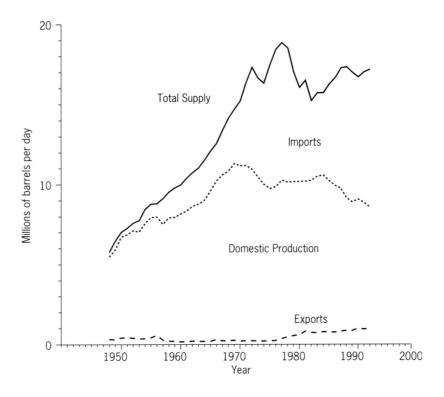

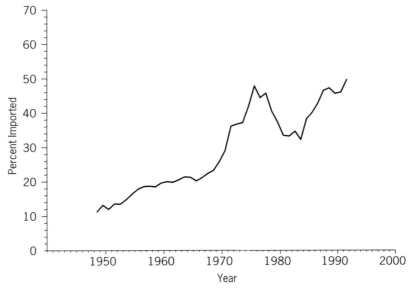

FIGURE 5.44. The United States oil supply is presently composed of approximately equal amounts of domestically produced and imported oil. The amount and percent of oil imported rose rapidly in the late 1960s and 1970s. Imports decreased in the late 1970s and early 1980s but have risen again since about 1985. (From U. S. Energy Information Administration Annual, 1994.)

How Much Oil Is There, and How Long Will It Last? Throughout the first 100 years of the modern petroleum industry, little thought was given to how much extractable oil could be found in Earth. The exploration of new sedimentary basins and the drilling of new wells on land and the continental shelves continuously led to the discovery of new fields, and world oil reserves rose faster than people could use them. The availability, relative cleanliness of use, and low price of oil-based products—especially gasoline—promoted ever-increasing usage. It was not until 1973, when the OPEC embargo cut off a significant proportion of petro-

leum supplies to Western Europe and the United States, that most of the general public began to realize that there are limits to the world's oil supplies. The shock of the embargo coupled with a subsequent increase in the price of oil (from $3 to $10 in 1973–1974 and from $10 to $35 in 1979–1981) led to the frequent reference to the terms *oil crisis* and shortage. These terms may have been overused, but they have helped focus attention on the very real fact that the world's oil supplies are indeed limited.

As early as 1948, Dr. M. King Hubbert of the United States Geological Survey presented a diagram that indicated

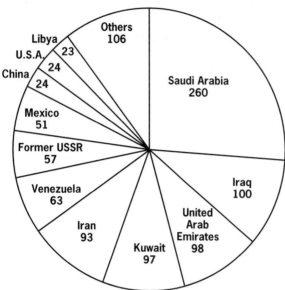

FIGURE 5.45. The world's proven oil reserves in the mid-1990s. Approximately three-quarters of the reserves are held by OPEC nations with the largest quantity held by Saudi Arabia. (From the U.S. Energy Information Administration Annual, 1994.)

a severe decline in the world's oil reserves before the year 2000 if oil production were left unrestricted (Figure 5.47). His prediction, made at a time when the expanding post-war economies of Europe, Japan, and the United States were being fueled by seemingly endless supplies of oil, was not noticed by the general public or the oil industry. However, the massive amounts of exploration, drilling, production, and computer modeling of world oil supplies in the intervening years have all served to confirm Dr. Hubbert's conclusions. His original curve assumed that unrestricted production would lead to a constant increase in world output until the mid-1990s, then an equally rapid decline. Since the late 1970s, world oil consumption has declined and now appears to have more or less leveled off (Figure 5.47). By curtailing consumption, yearly production will not reach the values originally anticipated, and the period over which production can remain near present values is extended by approximately 25 years. The important point to note is that regardless of the curve employed, the world production of oil will begin to decline rapidly sometime between 2015 and 2035.

An important aspect of the Hubbert-type curves concerns the total amount of petroleum in Earth's crust. No one knows how much petroleum exists, but the expanding knowledge of the world's sedimentary basins and the mechanisms of oil generation now permit reasonable estimates. There is always the hope that future technology will increase

oil discoveries or improve extraction techniques, but for the moment only the liquid petroleum extractable by conventional recovery procedures is considered. It is important to bear in mind that the oil recovered by simple pumping is usually only approximately one-third of the total amount present because most of the crude petroleum remains stuck on mineral surfaces and trapped in small pore spaces and fractures in the rock. The added procedures (water flooding, CO_2 injection, etc.) used to liberate more of the oil generally raise the total production to no more than 50 percent.

Accordingly, two meaningful questions remain: (1) How many oil reserves exist? and (2) How much liquid petroleum can we ultimately recover? The first question can be quite accurately answered, but the second one can only be estimated. The present oil reserves are irregularly dispersed geographically with more than 65 percent of the world total occurring in the Middle East (Table 5.6). Saudi Arabia's 25 percent of the world reserves (260 billion barrels) dwarfs all other nations; only Kuwait, the former Soviet Union, and Iran have more than 50 billion barrels. The United States, which consumes approximately 26.5 percent of world production, has only 25 billion barrels, 2.4 percent of world reserves. At current rates of production, world reserves would last about 45 years; United States reserves would last only about 9 years.

The shock of the 1973 oil embargo impressed upon the United States that disruptions of the international imports of oil could cripple the country. Therefore, following the general idea of a strategic materials stockpile of a variety of commodities, the United States has developed the Strategic Petroleum Reserve as discussed on page 147 (Figure 5.48).

The question of total oil recovery is subject to estimates of the volumes, ages, and types of sedimentary rocks and the percentages of recovery obtainable. Although all of these estimates are subject to potential inaccuracy, there has been a general consensus of opinion among university, oil company, and governmental workers (Figure 5.49). With the exception of two estimates, one at 4 trillion barrels and the other estimating 5.6 trillion barrels, all estimates since 1958 are between 1.2 trillion and 3.5 trillion barrels. The average post-1970 estimates of approximately 2.0–2.3 trillion barrels suggest that another 300–500 billion barrels remain to be discovered beyond the 750 billion barrels already consumed (through 1995) and the approximately 1000 billion barrels of proven reserves.

It is important to note that there is no proof that any of this additional 300–500 billion barrels exists. None of it is of any value or utility until it has been discovered and exploited. Furthermore, it is highly probable that most future oil discoveries will be small fields that will be harder to find, occur in deeper rocks or under deeper water, and reside in more remote and hostile areas of the world. The statistical distribution of known oil fields and the extensive degree to which the world's sedimentary basins have already been explored,

THE PERSIAN GULF WAR 1990–1991: OIL, POLITICS, AND THE ENVIRONMENT

The world focused its attention on the Middle East from the summer of 1990 through the fall of 1991 as a drama involving resources, politics, and the environment played out. This region, with more than two-thirds of the world's recoverable liquid petroleum reserves, has been a concern of major world countries since 1973 when OPEC, with many members in the area, imposed an oil embargo. Through the summer of 1990, tensions grew as Iraq threatened occupation of its small, but oil-rich, southern neighbor, Kuwait (Figure 5.46). On August 2, Iraq overran Kuwait, claiming it as a province of Iraq. The world gasped, western oil exports from Kuwait ceased, and oil prices soared. As the United Nations worked out a plan, Western nations feared for continuity of the oil supplies from the Middle East and worried about the effect a war in the region would have on their economies. Oil prices, which had been below $20 a barrel, peaked over $40 per barrel in late September and early October, but they began to slide and dropped below $30 per barrel by late October. Other OPEC nations, especially Saudi Arabia, increased production to meet world needs.

With negotiations deadlocked, the United Nations poured hundreds of thousands of troops into Saudi Arabia. Sensing that an allied strike was imminent, the Iraqi army began setting fire to 749 Kuwaiti oil wells on January 28, 1991 (Figure 5.46, Plates 22 and 23). Millions of barrels of oil burned every day and the smoke was so thick that it appeared to be nighttime in the middle of the day. The high gas pressure in the escaping oil resulted in roaring plumes of fire that rose scores of meters in the air and created trails of black soot and smoke that extended hundreds of kilometers downwind. Simultaneously, the Iraqi army began releasing crude oil into the Persian Gulf as a means of slowing any United Nations amphibious assault on the coast of Kuwait or Iraq. These actions constituted an enormous loss of crude oil and were widely viewed as ecological terrorism. The United Nations forces attacked on February 24, 1991, raced rapidly through western Kuwait and southern Iraq, and forced a surrender by Iraqi forces within 5 days.

The combatant side of the war was over, but the flames of 749 burning wells and the outflow of oil into the Persian Gulf continued. Initial estimates were that well fires might burn for as long as two years and that the oil spill into the Gulf was as large as 11 million barrels. Fortunately, both of these estimates were wrong. Close to 9000 workers from 37 countries completely extinguished the fires one by one by November 6, 1991.

The true volume of oil released into the Persian Gulf will probably never be known, but estimates ranged from 2 to 11 million barrels; this represents the largest spill in history. At the time of the war, individual oil slicks exceeded 130 km in length and killed countless birds, fish, turtles, and other types of aquatic life. One year after the war, as much as 600 km of Saudi Arabian beaches remained *paved* with slabs of sticky crude oil-sand mixtures. This devastated the marine life of the intertidal zone; the best estimates for complete recovery are 80 to 100 years.

strongly suggest that we shall not find any more large oil fields like those listed in Table 5.5.

Natural Gas

The History of Natural Gas Usage. The first recorded use of natural gas was in ancient China where the people had learned to pipe it through bamboo poles so that they could boil saline brines and obtain the residual salt. By about 600 A.D., temples in what is now the Baku area of Azerbaijan, on the west coast of the Caspian Sea, contained eternal flames fueled with gas piped from fractures in the rocks.

The use of gas as an illuminant in the modern world began with gas distilled, or manufactured, from coal, wood, and peat in Belgium and England in the early 1600s. Although several men experimented with gas lamps in homes, abbeys, and even university classrooms in the late 1700s, it was not until 1802–1804, when William Murdock, a Scottish engineer, installed coal gas lights in cotton mills that the gas industry became industrially important. This led to the establishment of the commercial gas light companies in London in 1812 and Baltimore in 1816. Within a few years, gas lighting had spread throughout Europe, the Americas, and the Orient. Manufactured gases are still important and are produced by a variety of methods involving heating coals and reacting water with calcium carbide, but their usage has been much overshadowed by that of natural gas.

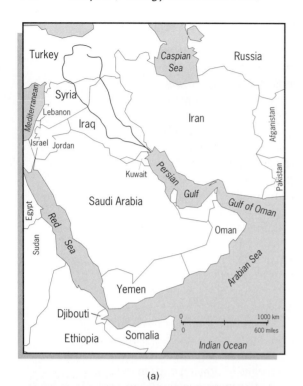

(a)

(b)

FIGURE 5.46. (a) The Gulf War developed in 1990 when Iraq invaded Kuwait. It ended in 1991 when the allied forces liberated Kuwait. (b) Damaged oil wells in Kuwait at the end of the Gulf War burned for up to six months, consuming large quantities of oil and creating extensive pollution. (Photograph by Jonas Jordan, U.S. Army Corps of Engineers.)

The modern natural gas industry traces its origins to the United States, where in 1775 French missionaries reported seeing "pillars of fire," seeping gas that had accidentally been set on fire. The same year George Washington saw "burning springs," flaming gas that rose from the water near Charleston, West Virginia. In 1821, mysterious bubbles were found rising from a water well drilled at Fredonia, New York. After the driller abandoned the well, small boys accidentally ignited the escaping natural gas, creating a spectacular sight. Shortly thereafter a gunsmith named William Hart recognized the commercial potential and drilled a gas well 8 meters (27 feet) deep at the same site. The initial wooden pipes (made from hollowed logs) were replaced with lead pipe, and the gas was piped to a local inn where it fueled 66 gas lights. More gas wells were completed, and a natural gas distribution company was formed at Fredonia in 1865.

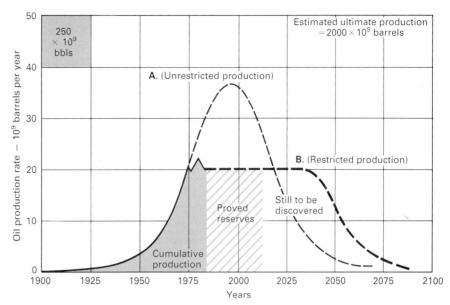

FIGURE 5.47. World oil production as a function of time. The original estimates projected unrestricted production along curve A, but the reductions in usage and the restricted production since 1979 now suggest that the curve will be more like B. (From L. F. Ivanhoe, *Oil and Gas Journal,* December 24, 1984. Used with permission.)

Natural gas was also found with oil at Titusville, Pennsylvania, in 1859 and other subsequent oil wells, but there was little market and no pipelines for its distribution. Its usage was much overshadowed by manufactured gas, which could be produced wherever needed. Long distance pipelines to transport natural gas finally appeared in 1872 when a 40 kilometer (25 mile) wooden pipeline was constructed to supply hundreds of customers in Rochester, New York, and a 9 kilometer (5.5 mile) metal pipeline carried gas to Titusville, Pennsylvania. The fledgling industry nearly died when Thomas Edison's electric lightbulb appeared in 1879, but it then grew slowly on the basis of its use as a heating fuel rather than as an illuminant. A major impetus came with the discovery of large gas fields in Texas, Oklahoma, and Louisiana. By 1925, there were 3.5 million gas consumers, but all were situated near the gas fields. The great expansion of the gas industry and its growth to the status of a major energy source came about in the late 1920s and 1930s with the introduction of much stronger seamless and electrically welded pipe that could carry much greater quantities of gas under high pressure. In 1947, two pipelines known as the *Big Inch* and the *Little Inch,* originally built during World War II to transport oil from east Texas to Pennsylvania, were converted to carry natural gas. This opened up the United States East Coast and brought about the dominance of natural gas over manufactured gas.

The Modern Natural Gas Industry. Prior to the 1940s, the growth of the gas industry was slow (Figure 5.50), and vast quantities were allowed to escape or were burned off or *flared* because there was no market for them. Seamless pipes that made possible the transmission of natural gas over long distances became available in the 1920s, but it was not until after World War II that the rebuilding of Europe and the growth of the American suburbs provided large new markets. The gas was found to be especially attractive as a fuel because it required no refining and only minor processing. It was also easily handled, burned cleanly, and provided more heat per unit weight than any other fossil fuel. Now it is piped to tens of millions of homes, businesses, institutions, and industries and provides approximately 25 percent of the total energy needs of the United States and Europe. In addition to its common use as a heating fuel, it is widely employed in the manufacture of thousands of chemicals with such diverse uses as plastics, detergents, and drugs and as a major component in fertilizers.

The gas industry is composed of three major sectors—production, transmission, and distribution. The production of the gas is very similar to that of petroleum, but the extraction of the gas is often easier because it moves through pores and cracks in the rock more readily and does not stick to the mineral grains. Generally, more than 99 percent of the useful gas consists of methane, but minor amounts of ethane, propane, butane, carbon dioxide, hydrogen sulfide, helium, hydrogen, nitrogen, and ammonia may also be present (Figure 5.51). Approximately 80 percent of the world's gas reserves are believed to be of thermogenic origin and are recovered from wells that range from a few hundred to about 10,000 meters in depth. The 20 percent of the natural gas that was biogenically produced usually is found at relatively shallow depths. More than 95 percent of the gas used today has been obtained in its present state. However, for special purposes, gas is manufactured by heating coal or by reacting steam or hydrogen with coal or heavy oils. Probably the most widely known synthetic gas is acetylene (C_2H_2), formed by reacting water with calcium carbide or by thermal cracking methane. Acetylene is used in welding because it produces a hotter flame than other gases.

TABLE 5.6
International recoverable crude oil reserves as of January 1, 1993

	Reserves (bbls × 10⁹)
North America:	
Mexico	51.3
United States	23.7
Canada	5.3
Total	80.3 (8.1%)
Central and South America:	
Venezuela*	62.7
Brazil	3.0
Others	6.8
Total	72.5 (7.3%)
Western Europe and former Soviet Union:	
Former Soviet Union	57.0
United Kingdom	4.1
Norway	8.8
Others	5.2
Total	75.1 (7.5%)
Middle East:	
Saudi Arabia*	260.3
Kuwait*	96.5
Iran*	92.9
Iraq*	100.0
United Arab Emirates*	98.1
Others	14.0
Total	661.8 (66.4%)
Africa:	
Libya*	22.8
Nigeria*	17.9
Algeria*	9.2
Egypt	6.2
Others	5.8
Total	61.9 (6.2%)
Far East and Oceania:	
China	24.0
Indonesia*	5.8
India	6.0
Others	8.8
Total	44.6 (4.5%)
WORLD TOTAL	996.1 (100%)
OPEC TOTAL	766.2 (76.9%)

*OPEC member
(From U.S. Energy Information Administration, 1994.)

After extraction from wells, the gas is piped to processing plants where impurities such as water, sulfur, and other gases are removed. At the same time, traces of the characteristic coal gas scent are added to enable human detection of the otherwise odorless gas. The gas is then sent through the transmission lines under high pressure (at velocities of about 24 kilometers per hour). Compression stations along the line restore the pressure that has dropped due to friction and tapping by communities. Within each community, the gas is sent via smaller distribution lines to individual homes and businesses. From the original 9-kilometer pipeline used to transport gas near Titusville, Pennsylvania, the pipeline system in the United States has grown to more than 1,800,000 kilometers. This does not even count the individual service lines to homes. Natural gas consumption for home heating is much greater in the winter months than in the summer months, and the long-range transmission system cannot handle sufficient gas to meet demands on the coldest days. Accordingly, much gas is pumped into underground storage facilities such as caverns and old gas fields along transmission lines during the summer months so that it may be extracted when needed during the winter.

Until recent years, it was impractical to bring natural gas from oil fields scattered around the world to the major industrial consumers because there was no way to economically transport it. Now, however, much natural gas from the fields of the Middle East, Africa, and South America that used to be burned off is liquified and transported in large, liquified natural gas (LNG) transport ships (Figure 5.52). The gas is cooled and held below $-162°C$ ($-259°F$) where it condenses and occupies only 1/600 of its original volume. The refrigerated tanks on the ships permit large quantities of the LNG to be economically transported worldwide. Upon arrival at its destination, the LNG is allowed to warm and return to the gaseous state and is fed into the normal gas transmission lines.

International Gas Production and Reserves. The increasing demand for natural gas and its irregular global distribution has led to it becoming a major commodity of international trade (Figure 5.53). Western Europe is the recipient of piped gas with major supplies coming from Russia and from the North Sea fields of England, Norway, and the Netherlands. Large amounts of gas are also piped from the fields of western Canada and from Mexico to the United States. Japan, now a major consumer of natural gas, receives gas from liquid natural gas carriers from Southeast Asia and the Middle East. The anomalous situation of the United States being a major gas importer but still sending the gas from Alaska to Japan has developed because the companies can sell that gas for more on the international market than on the regulated domestic market.

International gas reserves and production are given in Table 5.7. The former Soviet Union is the world's leader in reserves and has, since the mid-1970s, become a major exporter, having built large pipelines to transport the gas to western Europe. Most of the former Soviet Union's gas reserves lie in Russia, but other satellite states also have significant natural gas reserves and are trying to develop the fields in order to export gas to Europe. The other European countries with major reserves and production were gas importers until the North Sea oil and gas fields were developed in the 1960s and 1970s. England, Norway, and the Netherlands are now self-sufficient and able to supply part of the needs of the rest of western Europe. Iran is behind Russia in

THE UNITED STATES STRATEGIC PETROLEUM RESERVE

The oil embargo of 1973 made OPEC a household word, and it made many Americans and western Europeans realize the degree to which their societies had become dependent upon oil imports. The United States, recognizing that any future cutoffs of imported oil could create many problems in the American economy, decided to establish an oil reserve that could provide oil as needed. The Strategic Petroleum Reserve was created in 1975 for the express purpose of being a source of oil for the United States if there were any cutoff of imported oil. The goal was to place one billion barrels of oil into storage, enough to supply the country's import needs for more than 100 days.

Several alternatives were considered, but it was decided that the best storage sites would be cavities within salt domes in Louisiana and Texas. These domes formed over millions of years as salt slowly moved upward through the overlying sediments to create roughly cylindrical bodies up to 5 miles across and 10 miles in height. These salt domes have been the sites of much oil exploration because oil often migrates along upturned beds at the margins of the domes. Furthermore, tests in Germany showed that oil could be stored in salt for years with no deterioration in its quality. Ultimately five salt domes were selected as sites for the development of underground storage cavities; a sixth site was a converted salt mine (Figure 5.48). The Sulphur Mines site has subsequently been closed. The caverns, created by solution mining, are typically cylindrical in shape, about 200 feet (65 meters) in diameter and 2000 feet (650 meters) in height. Each would easily hold the Empire State Building, the New York World Trade Center, or three Washington Monuments on top of one other.

Solution mining began with the drilling of a standard well into the salt dome. Fresh water was pumped into the well to dissolve salt, and the resulting brine was pumped into deep injection wells or into the Gulf of Mexico. Once the cavity expanded to the desired width, a small amount of oil was injected into the cavity to float on the water and to protect the salt roof of the cavern from any additional solutions. Selective injection of the water was used to increase the size of the cavern and to control its shape (Figure 5.48B).

The individual cavities were designed to ultimately hold between 25 and 220 million barrels of petroleum. Filling of the Strategic Petroleum Reserve began in 1977. By late 1994, it contained approximately 600 million barrels of petroleum and had a total capacity of about 750 million barrels. America hopes that it shall never again be faced with an embargo of imported oil, but if it is, the Strategic Petroleum Reserve will be available to help fill the needs.

An unfortunate footnote to the development of the Strategic Petroleum Reserve has been the report, in October 1995, that one of the caverns has developed a serious leak. This forces costly repairs, extraction of some of the oil, and reconsideration of the entire concept.

gas reserves, but its internal and international political problems, especially its long war with neighboring Iraq in the 1980s, resulted in low gas sales through that period. If political stability can be maintained in the Middle East, it is likely that Iran and several of its neighbors will become major suppliers of gas on the world markets. The United States is well endowed with natural gas, but it is also a very large gas consumer and imports approximately one-third of its needs. From 1975–1995, the rate of discovery of new gas was slightly less than the rate of domestic gas consumption; hence, the reserves have declined about 10 percent in that time. This has left the United States with a reserve that can last about 9 years. In contrast, the world reserves could last 65 years.

The world's ultimate resource potential of natural gas is not known, but the heat potential for worldwide gas reserves is presently equal to that of petroleum reserves. As with petroleum, most of the major sedimentary basins have been tested, and most of the major gas fields have been found. Future discoveries will be smaller than the large fields found in the past, and their development will be more costly. The relatively recent development of coal bed methane recovery systems has significantly added to potential gas reserves. (See discussion on page 150 and Figure 5.54.) We are not in impending doom with regard to natural gas, but we must recognize that in the foreseeable future, reserves will decrease and costs will rise.

Heavy Oils and Tar Sands

The early history of petroleum centered on the use of bitumen, a black, viscous hydrocarbon material that is found

THE STRATEGIC PETROLEUM RESERVE
BARRELS OF OIL IN STORAGE BEFORE LIMITED SALE

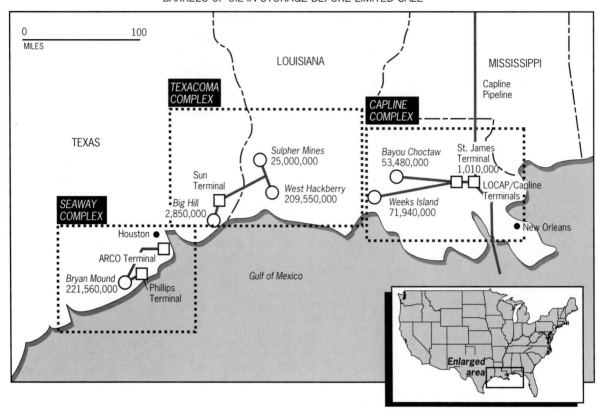

(a)

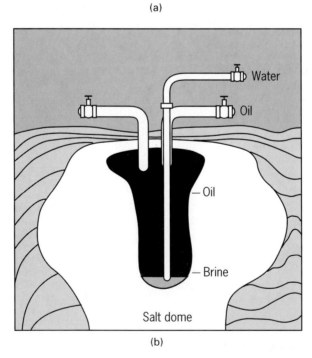

(b)

FIGURE 5.48. (a) Location map of the United States Strategic Petroleum Reserve. (b) Schematic cross-section showing the shape and location of the oil-containing chambers in the salt domes.

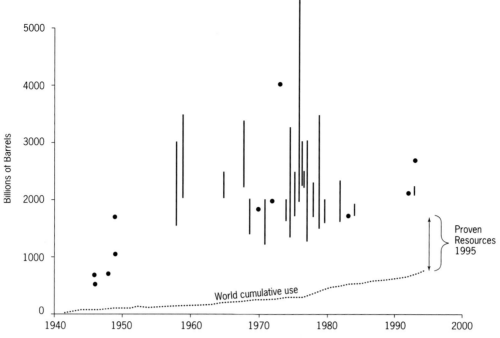

FIGURE 5.49. The estimates of the total conventionally recoverable reserves of liquid petroleum made by governmental, university, and industrial experts between 1946 and 1985 are plotted in terms of the date they were compiled. Dots represent estimates given as a single value; vertical lines represent the ranges of estimates that gave minimum and maximum values. The estimated quantities of ultimately recoverable oil rose from 1946 to the 1960s as worldwide exploration expanded, but they have generally come into agreement at about 2 trillion barrels since the late 1970s.

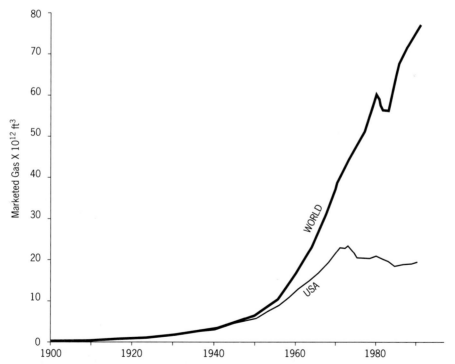

FIGURE 5.50. World production of natural gas has risen sharply since 1950 when pipelines and transport ships became available. The production in the United States peaked in the 1970s but remains at nearly the same level.

COAL BED METHANE

Methane gas in coal mines has long been feared because it has caused explosions that have killed tens of thousands of miners around the world. Most people think of methane, a colorless and odorless gas, as the natural gas widely used for cooking, home heating, and industrial processing. Most of what we use today is derived from oil and gas fields. After the gas has been cleaned to remove impurities, a special odorant is added so that it is easily detected by the human olfactory system.

Early coal miners carried canaries into the workings as their means of testing for the presence of methane. The canaries would pass out from the gas before the workers. Sometimes, brave individuals were sent ahead of the miners to try to burn out small pockets of the gas before it created explosions (Figure 4.8). At concentrations below 5 percent, methane is inert; at concentrations above 15 percent, it burns with a steady, easily controlled flame. But between 5 and 15 percent, methane mixed with air is violently explosive (Plate 24). Although methane explosions still occasionally occur, modern detection devices can usually provide sufficient warning to prevent the concentrations from becoming deadly.

Today, coal bed methane is being viewed in many places as an undeveloped, valuable resource. After all, the same gas that can explode when accidentally released can be used as an energy source when systematically extracted. The methane in coal forms as the result of biogenic or thermogenic action. Biogenic gas can be generated by anaerobic bacterial decay either early in the burial history or much later when groundwater flow introduces these bacteria into a coal bed. Thermogenic gas is generated during burial as hydrocarbons and other gases (such as water and nitrogen) are given off by the organic matter as it is heated and compressed.

Whereas the methane gas associated with petroleum occurs as a free or dissolved phase, nearly all of the methane in coal beds is present as monomolecular layers adsorbed on the internal surfaces of the coal. Coal appears solid, but it is actually a microporous material with a very large internal surface area (10s to 100s of square meters of surface per gram of coal). Hence, it can adsorb very large quantities of gas. The volumes of adsorbed gas can vary with many factors, but the high-volatile bituminous coals that dominate American coal production can readily contain 25–30 cubic centimeters of adsorbed gas per gram. Economical production of methane gas from coal beds is accomplished by drilling into the coal, lowering the pressure of water present (because that tends to prevent the release of methane from the coal), sometimes introducing extra fractures (called cleats in coal beds), and pumping out the gas. As pressure drops, the gas desorbs from micropores, diffuses through the coal, and escapes along the cleats (Figure 5.54).

The recoverable amounts of coal bed methane are not well known, but the U.S. Geological Survey made estimates in 1994 (Table 5.8). The world total of between 85 and 262×10^{12} cubic meters of methane could be greater than the known world reserves of conventional natural gas, estimated at 119×10^{12} cubic meters. The United States coal bed methane reserves of 11×10^{12} cubic meters is more than twice the volume of U.S. conventional gas reserves (4.7×10^{12} cubic meters).

Coal bed methane is a largely undeveloped resource that will likely see increased development in the years ahead. Some of the methane to be recovered will be extracted from coal beds that would not otherwise have yielded any energy product. However, some methane will be extracted from mineable seams so that a substance that could have caused a tragedy will instead serve as a valuable energy resource.

where oil has lost its lightweight volatile components through exposure to air. The modern oil industry concentrates on liquid petroleum, which is much more easily extracted and processed. Nevertheless, large quantities of natural bitumen-like hydrocarbons, which will likely serve as important sources of oil in the future, remain. There is no simple single definition for these materials, but all are characterized by being (1) dark in color; (2) so viscous that they will not flow naturally and respond poorly to primary or secondary recovery techniques; (3) high in sulfur (3–6 percent), nickel, and vanadium (up to 500 ppm); and (4) rich in **asphaltines** (a primary constituent of asphalt). Heavy oils and

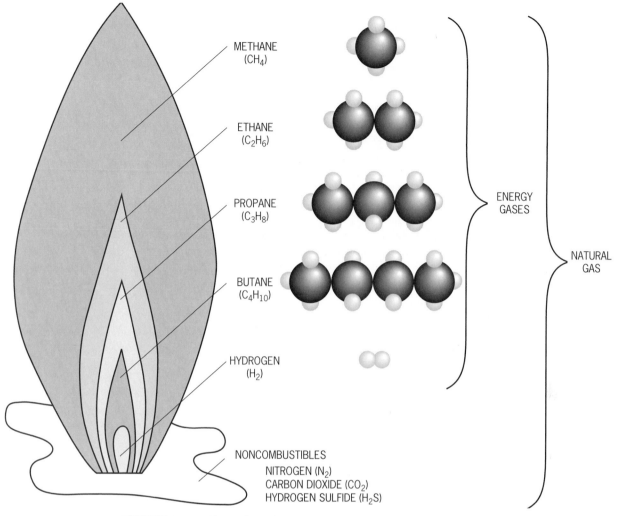

METHANE
(CH$_4$)

ETHANE
(C$_2$H$_6$)

PROPANE
(C$_3$H$_8$)

BUTANE
(C$_4$H$_{10}$)

HYDROGEN
(H$_2$)

NONCOMBUSTIBLES
NITROGEN (N$_2$)
CARBON DIOXIDE (CO$_2$)
HYDROGEN SULFIDE (H$_2$S)

ENERGY
GASES

NATURAL
GAS

FIGURE 5.51. Natural gas is composed of 80–100 percent methane, but small quantities of other gases may also be present. (From U. S. Geological Survey Circular 1115.)

tar sands occur alone or with liquid petroleum and owe their origin to at least three processes that may have operated singly or jointly on the petroleum. Some have formed, as did most early discovered bitumen, through **oxidation** and the loss of the lightweight volatile fractions. The two other modes of origin recognized are **thermal maturation,** in which the light fractions have been driven off or converted to gas due to natural heating, and **biodegradation,** in which bacteria consume the lighter fractions and leave their heavier components behind.

Heavy oils and tar sands are known from several parts of the world (Figure 5.55a), but they remain relatively unpublicized or exploited because their recovery and use is more difficult and expensive than liquid petroleum. They have received significant attention during times of high oil prices, but interest wanes rapidly when liquid petroleum prices drop. The largest deposits occur in Northern Alberta, Canada, and in the Orinoco district of Venezuela, but significant resources also exist in the United States, the Middle

FIGURE 5.52. Liquid natural gas transporting ship. The gas is liquified by cooling, transported, and then allowed to return to a gaseous state by warming so it can be transmitted through pipes for industrial, commercial, and domestic use. (Photograph courtesy of American Gas Association.)

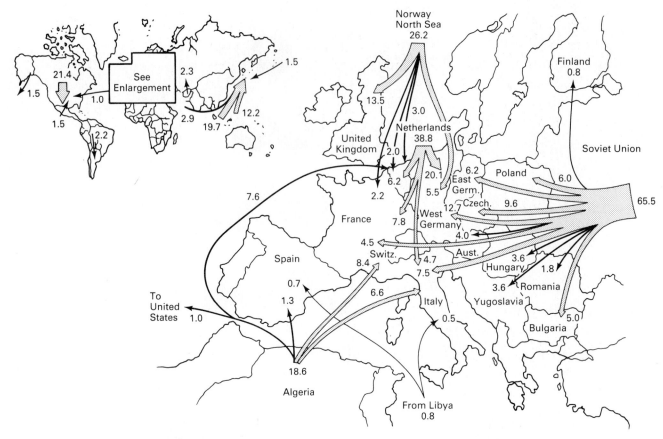

FIGURE 5.53. The international flow of natural gas in the mid-1980s. The numbers are in billions (10^9) cubic meters. Arrows indicate origins and destinations of the major shipments, but not necessarily specific routes. (From *Annual Energy Review,* U.S. Energy Information Administration, 1986.)

East oil fields, and the former Soviet Union. The estimates of the oil in place and recoverable often vary widely from one study to another (Table 5.9).

In Canada, two commercial plants have extracted tar sands in the Athabasca area (Figure 5.55b), but these two open pit operations will be able to extract only a few percent of the hundreds of billions of barrels of oil held there in their operating lifetimes of 25 years or so. The tar-rich sands are removed by large rotary bucket wheel excavators or drag lines and then processed with hot water and chemicals to separate the oil from the sand. Once separated, the oil is processed in special refineries to remove sulfur and produce a variety of useable petroleum products (Figure 5.56). Canadian pilot plants have also begun to experiment with a variety of *in situ* extraction techniques, including the so-called *huff-and-puff* procedure. This involves injecting superheated steam into an oil zone for about a month to heat and soften the oil; then more fluid oil is pumped out for at least a month before the cycle is repeated.

The physical and chemical properties of heavy oils have severely limited their recovery, and countless problems remain. Nevertheless, their ultimate exploitation is certain when reserves of liquid petroleum are reduced. Because the hydrocarbons in these deposits are too viscous to be pumped, the recovery methods needed will employ enhanced recovery techniques or conventional mining of the oil-bearing rock. The most commonly employed enhanced recovery techniques involve softening or liquifying the oil by heating it with injected high pressure steam or by some sort of electrical device lowered into drill holes. Another experimental technique involves igniting some of the oil underground and then letting the heat generated by the fire melt or fractionate the lighter components so that they can be recovered from wells. Other efforts utilize the injection of natural gas to dissolve some of the heavy oil and allow it to flow.

Oil Shales

Oil shales belong to a diverse group of fine-grained rocks that contain significant amounts of a waxy insoluble hydrocarbon known as kerogen. Kerogen is actually a mixture of complex, high-molecular-weight hydrocarbons, most of which can

Plate 1. Strip mining for coal can cause total destruction of arable farmland, but careful reclamation can restore the original productivity. The devastation of unreclaimed spoil piles is plainly visible at this coal mine in northern Texas, but when the spoil heaps are leveled and the topsoil is replaced, as in the foreground, a verdant pasture grows within 12 months. (Photograph by B.J. Skinner.)

Plate 2. Every scrap of arable land must be cultivated in order to feed the growing population of Nepal. When hill slopes are steep, terraces must be built to prevent topsoil from washing away, to reduce the possibility of landslides, and to increase the efficiency of irrigation systems. (Photograph by Howard Massey.)

Plate 4. Mabry Mill on the Blue Ridge Parkway in Virginia is an example of a nineteenth century mill that used water to power saws, to cut lumber, and to grind grain. Water power was a major source of energy before the development of modern fossil fuel energy systems and the wide availability of electricity. (Photograph by J.R. Craig.)

Plate 3. The growing human population and rapid advances in technology create changes in the patterns and types of resources used. This is especially apparent in many parts of the developing world, such as Tongling, Anhui Province, China, where human-powered carts are pushed past buildings with satellite dishes on their roofs. (Photograph by J.R. Craig.)

Plate 5. Many mines used water power to help grind and process ores before there were regulations about water pollution. The Crystal River Silver Mine in the White River National Forest of Colorado, once a thriving operation, would probably not have been permitted to operate today because of environmental laws. (Photograph courtesy of the U.S. Forest Service.)

Plate 6. Remains of engine-houses and shaft-towers of the Botallock Mine cling to the rugged cliffs of Cornwall, England. From such mines, some of which extended far out under the ocean, a rich stream of tin, copper, lead, and other metals flowed for over 2000 years. In the nineteenth century, the Cornish production was so great that England was a major world producer. (Photograph by J.R. Craig.)

Plate 7. Production of gold ore at the Bessi Mine, Japan, during the fourteenth century. When the miner had broken enough ore to fill a basket, his assistant would carry it to the surface for processing by climbing a system of ladders made by notching tree trunks. (Photograph by W. Sacco.)

Plate 8. Before miners had access to explosives or power equipment, tunnels were commonly cut by heating rock with fires to cause cracking. Cold water was thrown on the rock to cause more cracks and the broken rock was removed by hand. This nearly round fire cut tunnel was cut by this method at the famed silver deposits at Kongsberg, Norway. (Photograph by J.R. Craig.)

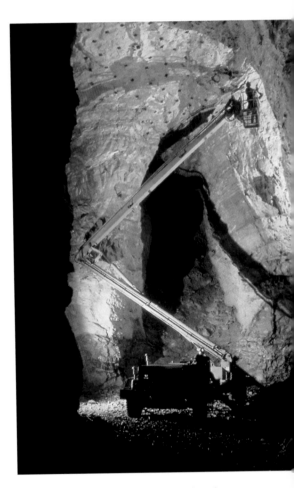

Plate 9. Room and pillar mining has commonly been used to remove areas of rich zinc and lead ore (the rooms) while leaving supporting columns (the pillars) of waste rock. In some areas, the rooms may reach heights of 60 meters and lengths up to 100 meters. (Photograph courtesy of ASARCO Inc.)

Plate 11. Approximately 250 million automobile and truck tires are discarded every year in the United States (and perhaps 500 million worldwide). This aerial view of a single illegal dump containing 5–8 million tires in King George County, Virginia, shows what has happened to too many tires despite efforts to find constructive uses for them. (Photograph by U.S. Army Corps of Engineers; courtesy of Virginia Department of Environmental Quality.)

Plate 10. This collapse of Interstate 70 in north-eastern Ohio occurred in March 1995, approximately 60 years after coal had been mined about 25 meters below. It exemplifies how some effects of resource exploitation may be long delayed in their appearance. (Photograph by Sandy Brandt; courtesy of Ohio Department of Transportation.)

Plate 12. Despite the efforts of many groups to prevent the pollution of waters and wetlands by solid waste and fluids, there are still many situations of indiscriminate dumping such as this one on Tangier Island, Virginia, in the Center of Chesapeake Bay. (Photograph by J.R. Craig.)

Plate 13. Municipal solid waste, here being dumped into a modern lined landfill, contains a vast variety of materials, but most of it could potentially be recycled or converted into energy. Nevertheless, land filling is commonly chosen because it is usually the cheapest method of disposal. (Photograph courtesy of Draper-Aden Associates.)

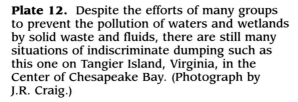

Plate 14. Acid waters seeping from the base of a pile of waste rock left after coal mining in southwest Pennsylvania. When iron sulfide minerals in the coal are exposed to the air as a consequence of mining, they become oxidized and produce soluble sulfates that cause the acidity. The yellow crust arises from sulfate compounds that precipitate from the seeping drainage water. (Photograph by J.R. Craig.)

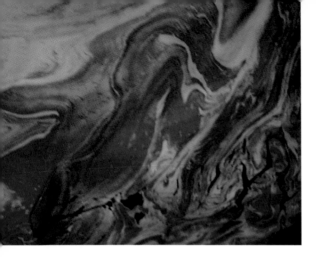

Plate 15. A colorful but dangerous oil slick on the surface of the sea off the coast of California. The oil leaked from a shallow reservoir during drilling operations in the Santa Barbara channel in 1973. Oil from such slicks can clog the wings of the sea birds and the fur, eyes, and noses of aquatic mammals. Prolonged exposure leads to death. The field of view is two meters across. (Photograph by B.J. Skinner.)

Plate 16. Underground coal mine fires, such as this one near Sheridan, Wyoming, represent waste of a potential resource and can create extreme local environmental hazards. Once ignited, underground coal fires have commonly proved to be very difficult to extinguish. (Photograph by C.R. Dunrud, U.S. Geological Survey.)

Plate 17. Surface collapse features above the old Hanna Number 3 Mine in Wyoming are environmental hazards; their presence suggests that the entire area underlain by the old mine is dangerous. (Photograph courtesy Gary B. Glass, Wyoming Geological Survey.)

Plate 18. The Berkeley Pit at Butte, Montana, represents an extreme case of water pollution at an old metal mine site. The lake is filling by groundwater inflow and will ultimately become one of the largest lakes in Montana. Unfortunately, it contains about 8000 parts per million dissolved solids and has a pH of 2.69. (Photograph by U.S. Department of Energy, Western Environmental Technology Office; courtesy of MSE Inc., Butte, Montana.)

Plate 19. An increasing amount of the world's oil production is coming from off shore fields and requires the construction of sophisticated drilling platforms. (Above) Oil drilling platform being towed from port toward the North Sea. (Left) Oil drilling platform in operation in the North Sea. (Photographs courtesy of Elf Enterprises and U.K. Texaco.)

Plate 20. The Clinch River power plant in south-western Virginia is a typical coal-fired electricity generation facility burning approximately 2000 tons of coal per day. (Photograph courtesy of Appalachian Power Company.)

Plate 21. The Alaskan pipeline transmits more than one million barrels of oil per day from Prudhoe Bay on the Arctic Ocean to the shipping port at Valdez. Fortunately, concerns that the pipeline would disturb migration of the caribou have not come true; they routinely walk over or under the pipeline. (Photographs courtesy of BP America.)

Plate 22. During the 1991 Gulf War, the retreating Iraqi army set fire to more than 700 oil wells, some of which burned for nearly six months. The loss of oil from wells, such as those seen behind a damage Iraqi tank, was more than a million barrels per day. (Photograph by Jonas Jordan, U.S. Army Corps of Engineers.)

Plate 23. As much as one billion barrels of oil were spilled into the Persian Gulf, spilled onto the desert, or burned as the result of Iraqi army sabotage during the Gulf War in 1991. The effects of the pollution are expected to be felt for the many years to come. (Photograph by Jonas Jordan, U.S. Army Corps of Engineers.)

Plate 24. Methane gas and coal dust explosions, such as this one at an experimental mine in Pittsburgh, have been a major cause of deaths and injuries in coal mines. Sparks generated during mining can ignite methane gas if it is suddenly released from the coal. Once the methane ignites, the air pressure generated may raise much coal dust which then also becomes explosive. (Photograph courtesy of U.S. Bureau of Mines.)

Plate 25. The Rossing Mine, Namibia (S.W. Africa), is one of the world's largest and most mechanized uranium mines. A truck load of ore has just passed under a radioactive scanning device that measures the richness of the ore and sends the information ahead to the processing mill in order to recover the uranium as efficiently as possible. (Photograph by B.J. Skinner.)

Plate 26. Yucca Mountain, in southern Nevada is the site chosen by the United States government for a permanent repository for the United States' high-level radioactive waste. (Photograph courtesy of U.S. Department of Energy.)

Plate 27. This entrance provides access into the Yucca Mountain nuclear waste storage facility in Nevada. Years of development, as well as many political decisions, remain before the facility is ready to accept nuclear waste (now scheduled as the year 2010). (Photograph courtesy of U.S. Department of Energy.)

Plate 29. Modern waste incinerators reduce the volume of municipal solid waste by about 90 percent and often produce commercially salable steam and electricity during their operation. Gas emissions are strictly controlled, but the disposal of the ash, which concentrates metals in the waste, remains the subject of considerable debate. (Photograph courtesy of Ogden-Martin Systems Inc.)

Plate 28. A forest of windmills at Altamont Pass Windmill Farm, California. The windmills convert the kinetic energy of flowing air (wind) into electrical energy. The amount of electricity produced by each mill is small, but the total from all mills on the farm is large. (Photograph courtesy of U.S. Department of Energy.)

Plate 30. Solar cells, such as the one attached here to an oil well, provide electrical power in remote locations. The 240 watts produced by these solar cells are used to protect the steel oil well casings from corrosion. (Photograph courtesy of Solarex Corporation.)

Plate 31. Molten steel is held in a huge ladle prior to being poured into useful forms. At this point impurities are removed and alloying metals added to provide the desired properties. (Photograph courtesy of Wheeling-Pittsburgh Steel Company.)

Plate 32. Nodular bauxite, the preferred ore of aluminum. This rich ore is the highest grade product mined at Weipa, in Queensland, Australia. Weipa contains one of the worlds largest resources of bauxite. (Photograph by H. Murray.)

Plate 33. Finely banded layers of cherty silica (white) and hematite (red) in a specimen of a banded iron formation known as the Negaunee Formation, Marquette District, Michigan. Banded iron formations are ancient chemical sediments. They are known on every continent, and they contain the largest resources of mineable iron in the world. (Photograph by H.L. James, *Economic Geology*.)

Plate 34. Titanium mineral-bearing sands are mined by the use of high-pressure water cannons at Eneabba, Australia. The titanium minerals, which make up less than 5 percent of the sands, are removed, and then the remainder of the sand is returned to the original sites. (Photograph courtesy of RGC, Inc.)

Plate 35. The weathering of iron sulfide-rich ores usually produces gossan, masses of porous iron oxides and hydroxides. Gossan have sometimes served as sources of iron but usually are of little value except for indicating the likely presence of ores beneath the surface. (Photograph of the Sulphur Mine, Louisa County, Virginia, by J.R. Craig.)

Plate 36. Rich ore from Almadén, Spain, one of the world's most famous mercury mines, is red because of the high content of the mineral cinnabar (HgS). Many parts of the ore body also contain free liquid mercury. thus, the ore is rich, but the fumes pose health hazards to the workers. (Photograph by J.R. Craig.)

TABLE 5.7

World natural gas reserves of January 1993

	Reserve	
	$(ft^3 \times 10^{12})$	$(m^3 \times 10^{12})$
North America:		
United States	165.0	4.68
Canada	95.7	2.71
Mexico	70.9	2.01
South America:		
Venezuela	126.5	3.58
Argentina	22.7	0.64
Others	39.4	1.12
Europe and former Soviet Union:		
Former Soviet Union	1942.3	55.04
Norway	70.6	2.00
Netherlands	68.9	1.95
United Kingdom	19.1	0.54
Others	54.2	1.54
Middle East:		
Iran	699.2	19.81
Qatar	227.0	6.43
Saudi Arabia	183.1	5.19
United Arab Emirates	204.6	5.80
Others	206.2	5.84
Africa:		
Algeria	128.0	3.63
Nigeria	120.0	3.40
Libya	46.2	1.31
Others	52.7	1.49
Far East and Oceania:		
Malaysia	67.8	1.92
Indonesia	64.4	1.82
China	49.4	1.40
Others	159.4	4.52
WORLD TOTAL	4,883.3	138.38

(From *Annual Energy Review,* Energy Information Administration, 1994.)

TABLE 5.8

Coal bed methane resources

Country	Trillion (10^{12}) meters^3
Russia	17–113
China	30–35
United States	11
Canada	6–76
Australia	8–14
Others	13
WORLD TOTAL	85–262

(From U.S. Geological Survey Professional Paper 1570.)

be converted to oil upon heating to a temperature of 500°C or more. The oil shales are part of the spectrum of organic-bearing, fine-grained sediments that include carbonaceous shales, oil shales, and sapropelic coals. The amount of organic matter ranges from as little as about 5 percent to more than 25 percent, and the yield of petroleum during processing can be as much as 100 gallons per ton of shale.

Although oil shales are generally considered fuels of the future, the history of their exploitation dates at least to 1694 when an English patent was granted for a process to make "oyle out of a kind of stone." Because the richest of oil shales burn much like coal, they were probably used as solid fuels long before the potential for oil extraction was discovered. During the nineteenth century, small scale oil shale industries developed in Europe, Africa, Asia, Australia, and North America, where petroleum was in short supply. A small oil shale industry flourished in France from 1838 to about 1900, and a few deposits continued to be mined through government subsidized operations until 1957. The largest and best known operations were those in central Scotland where oil shale processing began in 1850 and continued until 1963. The average yields from the earliest Scottish operations were at least 30 gallons per ton; yields gradually decreased to about 25 gallons per ton, but the total production was about 100 million barrels. Less documented, but equally large, production has been derived from both Estonia and the Fushun area of Manchuria. Production has also been reported from Spain, Sweden, Italy, Germany, Australia, and Switzerland.

Oil shales form where there is simultaneous deposition of fine-grained mineral debris and organic material in a nonoxidizing environment free of destructive organisms. The fine-grained nature of the sediments indicates that deposition must have occurred in quiet lakes, swamps, or marine basins that were rich in organic matter. Many types of organic debris have contributed to the formation of the kerogen, but the principal precursor appears to have been the lipid fraction of blue-green algae species that can thrive in both fresh and salt water. Relatively rapid accumulation of the clays and organic debris under stagnant, reducing conditions protected them from destruction. Continued sedimentation

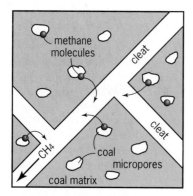

FIGURE 5.54. Coal bed methane (black spheres) desorbes from micropores in the coal matrix, diffuses through the coal, and flows along the cleats (fractures). It once only constituted a threat to mining, but now its recovery produces valuable resources and reduces dangers in some of the coal mines.

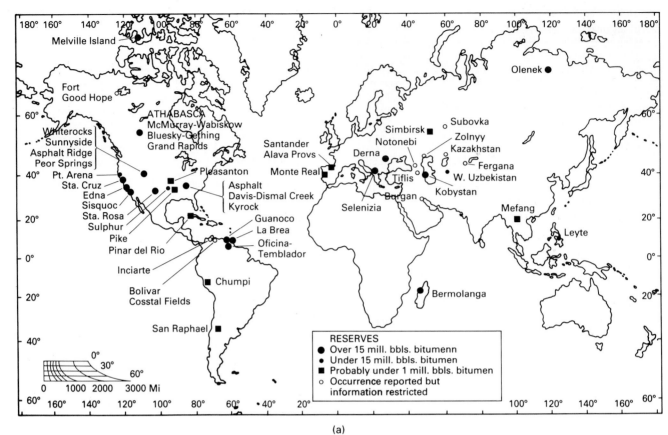

(a)

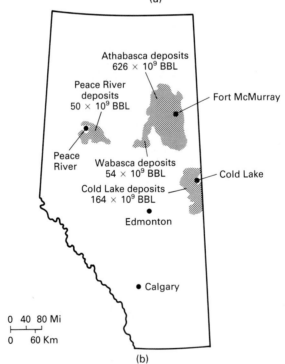

(b)

FIGURE 5.55. (a) The distribution of major tar-sand deposits in the world. (b) The location and size of the heavy oil deposits in Alberta, Canada. (From P. H. Phizackerley and L. O. Scott and from F. K. Spragins, respectively, in G. V. Chilingarian and T. F. Yen, *Bitumens, Asphalts and Tar Sands*. Amsterdam: Elsevier, 1978 p. 57 and p. 94. Used with permission.)

TABLE 5.9

Heavy oils and tar sands (in millions of barrels)

Country	Oil in Place	Recoverable
Canada	2,950,200	213,340
Venezuela	700,000–3,000,000	500,000
United States	77,160	30,065
Former Soviet Union	630	30
Middle East	50,000–90,000	4700
TOTAL	3,777,990–6,117,990	748,135

of overlying rocks provided the compaction and burial depth so that temperatures probably rose to 100–150°C. This mild heating resulted in the loss of much of the most volatile fractions and left the heavier, more refractory organic residue.

Although oil shales have been exploited on a small scale for many years, they began to receive a great deal of attention in the mid-1970s when the price of liquid petroleum rose sharply and the world's supply was uncertain. Oil shales are found in all of the continents in lower Paleozoic through the Tertiary age rocks (Table 5.10). In the United

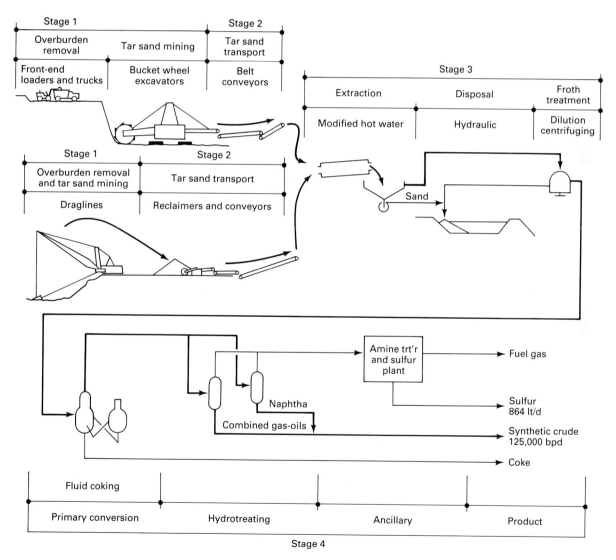

FIGURE 5.56. Diagrammatic outline of the mining and processing of a heavy oil deposit to extract crude oil, gas, sulfur, and coke. (After F. K. Spragins in G. V. Chilingarian and T. F. Yen, *Bitumens, Asphalts and Tar Sands*. Amsterdam: Elsevier, 1978, pp. 108–110. Used with permission.)

TABLE 5.10

Shale oil resources of the world, in 10^9 barrels in terms of oil content

Continent	Identified Resources		Hypothetical Resources		Speculative Resources	
Gallons of oil per tons of shale	25–100	10–25	25–100	10–25	25–100	10–25
North America:						
U.S.—Green River Shale	418	1400	50	600	—	—
U.S.—Chattanooga Shale	—	200	—	800	—	—
U.S.—Alaskan Marine Shale	Small	Small	250	200	—	—
U.S.—other shales		Small	—	—	600	23,000
Canada	Small	Small	50	100	1000	23,000
South America	Small	800	—	3200	2000	36,000
Africa	100	Small	—	—	4000	80,000
Asia	90	14	2	3700	5400	110,000
Europe	70	6	100	200	1200	26,000
Australia and New Zealand	Small	1	—	—	1000	20,000
TOTALS	678	2221	552	8800	15,200	318,000
GRAND TOTAL	345,451					

(From U.S. Geological Survey Professional Paper 820.)

(a)

FIGURE 5.57. (a) Oil shale deposits in the United States. (b) The major oil shale deposits in the Green River formation of Wyoming

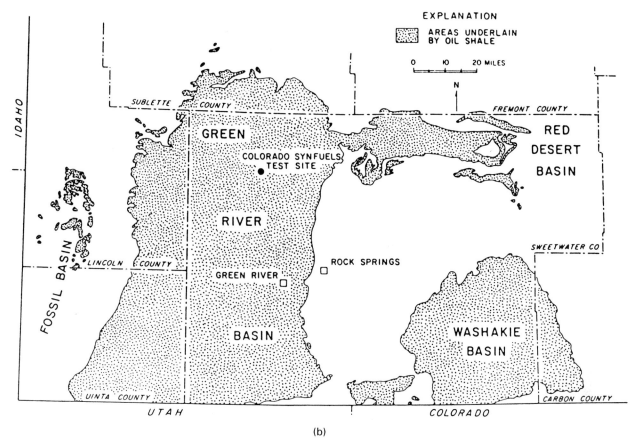

(b)

FIGURE 5.57. *(cont.)* are considered the most likely to be processed for oil. (From C. F. Knutson and G. F. Dana, "Developments in oil shale in 1981." *AAPG Bulletin*, vol. 66, no. 11, (1982).) (C) A closeup view of a sample of an oil-rich shale.

States, the greatest attention has been focused on the Piceance Creek basin in eastern Colorado and the Uinta basin in western Utah (Figure 5.57) in which the Eocene Green River formation contains perhaps as much as 2 trillion barrels of oil (Table 5.10). Very large quantities of the hydrocarbon-rich Devonian Chattanooga shale underlie at least ten states in the eastern United States (Figure 5.57). Unfortunately, most of this formation and its equivalents yield only 1–15 gallons of oil per metric ton by the conventional processing techniques discussed below; hence, their extraction for oil is not feasible in the foreseeable future. Several major projects were initiated in the western United States in the mid-1970s. However, a combination of rising production costs and declining liquid petroleum prices resulted in a suspension of all major operations in the early 1980s. They may yet produce oil, but only after a considerable rise in the price of oil or a severe shortage.

Several production methods have been proposed for the recovery of the hydrocarbons from oil shales. The two principal ones are surface mining and processing and *in situ* retorting (Figure 5.58). The first method involves open pit mining or bulk underground mining of the shale, grinding it into fine particles, and heating it to about 500°C in a large high-pressure kiln called a **retort.** The volatilized hydrocarbons condense and can then be processed in the same manner as conventionally recovered oil and gas. In order to be visible, the refining process must yield more fuel than it consumes. The mining and processing facilities are very expensive to construct and present environmental problems such as the generation of dust during mining, the need for very large quantities of water during processing, and the generation of very large quantities of waste rock. This last problem results from the expansion, or *popcorn effect,* of the shale when it is heated; there is a larger volume of rock waste than there was when mined.

The second technique, *in situ* retorting, is similar to processes used for enhanced oil and tar sand recovery. It involves the development of underground tunnels either above and below or on both sides of a block of oil shales. After the tunnels are completed, the rock is shattered by thousands of kilograms of explosives. The broken rock is then ignited, and the rate of combustion is controlled by a flow of air, diesel fuel, and steam. As the fire burns

(a)

FIGURE 5.58. (a) A close up view of a sample of rich oil shale. (b) Schematic diagram of the processing of oil shale after mining. The retort would be operated at 400–500°C to release the gas and oil from the crushed shale. (c) The *in situ* oil shale retorting process relies on the movement of a combustion zone through the shale by injecting air into one well and extracting oil and gas from another well ahead of the combustion zone. The shale is first broken to permit the movement of air and gases.

downward in a vertical retort or from one side to the other in a horizontal retort, the rock ahead of the combustion zone is heated to approximately 500°C, and much of the kerogen is vaporized and driven ahead to be drawn out as oil and gas through wells or drains. The remaining bitumen serves as a fuel for the advancing fire. This method lowers mining costs, greatly reduces the problem of disposal of processed rock, and requires much less water. The burned shale expands to fill the original chamber and leaves a relatively stable ground surface that reveals little evidence of the activity below. One potential problem, although less so in the arid, oil-shale-rich areas of the western United States, is possible contamination of groundwater supplies by waters that leach through the burned out retorts.

The ultimate commercialization of oil shales will depend upon the costs of producing the oil; however, there will also be useful by-products, such as ammonia and sulfur, produced in the processing of the gases. Furthermore, some oil-shale deposits, such as those in the Piceance Creek Basin of Colorado, are rich in the minerals halite (NaCl), dawsonite [NaAl(CO$_3$)(OH)$_2$], and nahcolite (NaHCO$_3$). These could be recovered and used as sources of their elements. Estimates have been made that a commercial, above-ground processing plant in the Piceance Creek Basin in Colorado producing

13,000 barrels of oil per day would also produce 220,000 tons of Al$_2$O$_3$, 550,000 tons of Na$_2$CO$_3$, and 1,600,000 tons of NaHCO$_3$ per year.

FUTURE FOSSIL FUEL RESOURCES

We now live at the height of the fossil fuel era, and many aspects of our lifestyles depend on a constant supply of fossil fuels. These fuels are not, however, evenly distributed geographically; hence, the fossil fuels have become important in the complex web of international economics and politics.

Table 5.11 lists the present known reserves of fossil fuels along with least order of magnitude estimates of potentially recoverable resources. The world's present dependence on oil for more than 50 percent of energy supplies cannot continue indefinitely. Far greater energy potential exists in coal and in oil shale, and it is to these fuels that we shall have to turn as the world's oil supplies dwindle. Massive, sudden changes in lifestyles are unlikely; however, as oil reserves decrease and oil prices rise in the years ahead, it is probable that alternative fuels, which are not now economical, will become cost competitive.

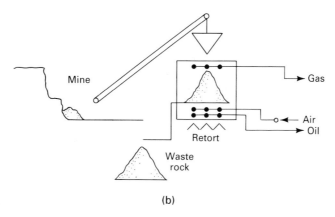

(b)

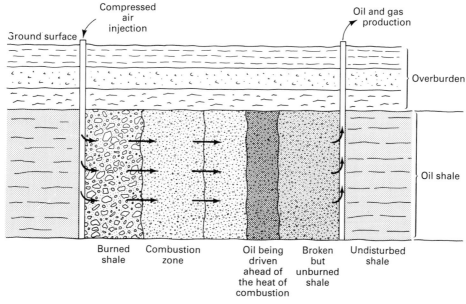

(c)

FIGURE 5.58.   (*cont.*)

TABLE 5.11

Energy potential of the world's fossil fuels

	Reserves*			Resources**		
Fuel	Conventional Units	kw hr (× 10¹²)	Joules (× 10¹⁹)	Conventional Units	kw hr (× 10¹²)	Joules (× 10¹⁵)
Petroleum	996.1 × 10⁹ bbls	1694	610	1420 × 10⁹ bbls	2414	869
Natural gas	3402 × 10¹²ft³	1021	367	16,000 × 10¹²ft³	4800	1728
Heavy oil and tar sands	748 × 10⁹ bbls	1272	458	4000 × 10⁹	6800	2448
Peat	50 × 10⁹ tons	269	97	240 × 10⁹ tons	1289	464
Coal	986.54 × 10⁹ tons	6511	2344	7800 × 10⁹ tons	51,480	18,533
Shale oil	—	—	—	345 × 10¹² bbls	586,500	211,000

U.S. power consumption in 1984 = 73.7 × 10¹⁵ btu = 21.6 × 10¹² kw hr = 77.7 × 10¹⁸ joules
World power consumption in 1983 = 280.1 × 10¹⁵ btu = 82.1 × 10¹² kw hr = 295.2 × 10¹⁸ joules

*Basis for calculations of wattage: 1 bbl oil = 1700 kw hr = 6120 × 10⁶ joules; 1000 ft³ gas = 300 kw hr = 1080 × 10⁶ joules; 1 mt peat = 5370 kw hr = 19,332 × 10⁶ joule; 1 ton coal = 0.9078 mt = 6600 kw hr = 23,760 × 10⁶ joules.
**Resource estimates vary widely. These values should only be taken as order of magnitude.

FURTHER READINGS

BOURRELIER, P. H. and DE LA TOUR, X B., "Fossil fuels and other energy resources in the 21st Century." *Nonrenewable Resources,* 2 (1993) pp. 207–225.

DEGOLYER, E. L. and MACNAUGHTON, L W., *Twentieth Century Petroleum Statistics, 1992.* Dallas: DeGolyer and MacNaughton, 1992.

Energy Information Administration, *Energy Annual Review,* Washington DC, published annually.

Energy Information Administration, *Monthly Energy Review,* Washington DC, published monthly.

International Energy Agency, *Energy Policies of IEA Countries: 1992 Review.* Organization for Economic Cooperation and Development, Paris, 1993.

International Petroleum Encyclopedia, Tulsa, Oklahoma: Pennwell Publishing Co., published annually.

McCABE, P. J., GAUTIER, D. L., LEWAN, M. D., AND TURNER, C.,"The future of energy gases." *U.S. Geological Survey Circular* 1115 (1993).

NEHRING, R., "Prospects for conventional world oil reserves." *Annual Review of Energy* 7 (1982) pp. 175–200.

PARENT, J. D., *A Survey of United States and Total World Production, Proved Resources and Remaining Recoverable Resources of Fossil Fuels and Uranium.* Chicago: Institute of Gas Technology, 1983.

RICE, D. D., LAW, B. E., and CLAYTON J. L., "Coalbed gas—An undeveloped resource", in HOWELL D. G. (ed), *The Future of Energy Gases.* U.S. Geological Survey Professional Paper 1570 (1993).

SINGER, S. F., "World demand for oil," in SIMON, J. L. and KAHN, H. (eds.) *The Resourceful Earth.* New York: B. Blackwell Publishers, 1984, pp. 339–386.

TISSOT, B. P. and WELTE, D. H., *Petroleum Formation and Occurrence,* 2nd. ed. Berlin: Springer-Verlag, 1984.

United States Geological Survey, HOWELL, D. G., (ed.), "The future of energy gases." U.S Geological Survey Professional Paper 1570, 1993.

YERGIN, D., *The Prize.* New York: Simon and Schuster, 1991.

6 ENERGY FOR THE FUTURE—NUCLEAR POWER AND OTHER POSSIBLE ALTERNATIVES

Nuclear power plants such as the North Anna Power Station in Virginia are supplying increasing amounts of electrical power in many nations. The reactors are housed in the large dome-shaped concrete buildings. (Courtesy of Virginia Power.)

Energy is the sine qua non of a modern society's ability to do the things it wants to do. Such goals as maintaining the standard of living for a growing population, national security, improved quality of life, increased affluence and increased assistance to less developed societies can only be attained with increasingly large amounts of energy. While lower energy costs allow a society more freedom of action in seeking its goals, the availability of energy is the first requirement of having any freedom of action at all.

Dixy Lee Ray in Report to the President of the United States, December 1973

FOCAL POINTS

- The radioactive isotopes of uranium and thorium that spontaneously decay slowly with the emission of heat may be artificially induced to break down rapidly in the process of *nuclear fission.*
- ^{238}U is the most naturally abundant isotope of uranium (99.3 percent), but ^{235}U (0.7 percent) is the primary fuel of most nuclear reactors.
- Uranium is extracted from ores commonly containing less than 1 percent U_3O_8, is concentrated into oxide masses called *yellowcake,* is processed to enrich it in the ^{235}U isotope, and is prepared into pellets that are loaded into fuel rods.
- Nuclear reactors contain large numbers of fuel rods. The radiation from these rods creates a chain reaction in which large but controlled amounts of heat energy are released to create steam and drive turbines to generate electricity.
- The first commercial nuclear reactor started operation in England in 1956; subsequently, hundreds of reactors were built in more than 40 countries.
- A partial meltdown at the Three Mile Island plant in the United States in 1979 resulted in many design changes, much higher costs, and the cancellation of a large number of nuclear power plants.
- An explosion and fire at the Chernobyl plant near Kiev in the Ukraine in April 1986 resulted in widespread radioactive fallout, particularly throughout eastern Europe and Scandinavia.

- Solar energy may be used to heat homes or water, or it may be used to generate electricity by means of photovoltaic cells.
- Hydroelectric power is generated by using flowing water to drive turbines. There is no resulting pollution but there may be significant environmental impact resulting from the disruption of free-flowing streams.
- Wind energy, used since the earliest time to power ships and windmills, is increasing in use to generate electricity on *wind farms;* wind energy is, however, only locally available.
- Wave power, making use of wind-generated wave action, and tidal power, making use of the regular rise and fall of tides in response to the gravitational pull of the moon on the oceans, can be used in certain areas to generate electricity.
- Geothermal energy comes from heat in the interior of Earth that is originally produced by the breakdown of naturally occurring radioactive elements. It is extracted from hot water and steam coming out of wells drilled in areas of unusually high geothermal gradients.
- Nuclear *fusion,* the process that occurs in the sun, stars, and the hydrogen bomb, is the fusing together of light atoms to form heavier atoms, releasing vast amounts of energy. The process requires temperatures of millions of degrees and creates very little radioactive waste but will not likely be commercially available until well into the twenty-first century because of the great technical problems associated with controlled fusion.

INTRODUCTION

Although we now live in the *fossil fuel era,* as evidenced by the fact that 95 percent of the energy used by modern humans is derived from fossil fuels, it is clear that this heavy dependence on coal, oil, and related fuels cannot continue indefinitely. Accordingly, it is important to consider the nuclear and alternative energy sources that can be used to meet our needs in the years to come.

Energy actually reaches Earth's surface from three sources (Figure 6.1). The most evident and most important source is the sun. As well as being a direct source of heat, the sun warms the atmosphere and oceans, producing wind, rain, and ocean currents. Eventually, most of the energy from the sun is radiated back into space so that Earth's surface remains in thermal balance. Humans have long made use of **solar energy** indirectly by harnessing the power of running water and the wind and by burning plant matter that represents energy stored by photosynthesis. Subsequently, we have built our modern society primarily on the fossil solar energy locked in oil, coal, and natural gas. Now we are beginning to harness solar energy more directly through solar collectors and photovoltaic devices. The second source of energy comes from Earth's interior and is derived from the disintegration of radioactive elements such as uranium and thorium. When this process is speeded up under artificial conditions, we have nuclear power plants. Such processes occur naturally within Earth and provide a source of heat that can be exploited as **geothermal energy.** The third source of energy comes from the gravitational interaction between Earth and the moon that produces the tides. **Tidal energy,** although very small compared to the other sources, is a renewable resource that is being exploited.

The natural disintegration (or **decay**) of radioactive elements takes place very slowly within the earth and involves a complex series of steps that ultimately result in the formation of various stable isotopes of lead. Each step in the decay produces heat energy that we see as geothermal energy, but the radioactive decay is so slow that we could not directly derive useful energy from it. However, the breakdown of uranium and thorium can be artificially induced in **nuclear fission,** a process discussed in detail in this chapter. In nuclear fission, the breakdown is very rapid, and it immediately releases very large amounts of energy. Today, the burning of nuclear fuels such as uranium and thorium takes place in nuclear power plants. Uranium and thorium are, therefore, nonrenewable nuclear fuels mined in much the same ways as other metals. Because nuclear power occupies a special place among the energy sources developed in our own age and has been regarded by many people as the most important energy source for the future, it is discussed first in this chapter. Later sections are devoted to discussing "alternative" sources such as solar, hydroelectric, wind, wave, ocean, tidal, and geothermal energy and also energy from biological materials and wastes. Finally, we return to a different and as yet undeveloped form of nuclear power—that derived from **nuclear fusion.**

The one thing that is already clear from Figure 6.1 and will be emphasized in this chapter is that *energy is not in short supply.* The questions are how to use it economically, safely, and responsibly.

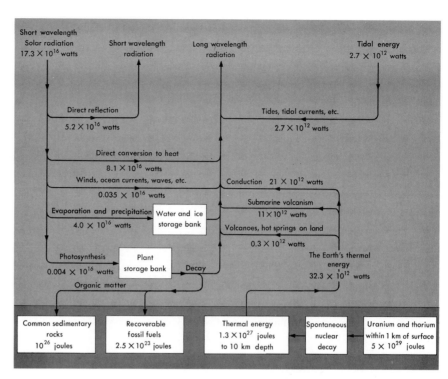

FIGURE 6.1. Energy flow diagram for the surface of Earth. The principal source of energy reaching the surface is short wavelength solar radiation; additional energy comes from tides and from heat flowing from Earth's interior. The nearly constant average temperature of Earth's surface indicates that the total energy radiated back into space must be just equal to the total energy reaching the surface. (From M.K. Hubbert, "Energy Resources." Publication 1000-D, Committee on Natural Resources, National Academy of Sciences—National Research Council, Washington, DC, 1962.)

NUCLEAR POWER—URANIUM AND NUCLEAR FISSION

The burning of conventional fossil fuels such as coal and oil are *chemical* reactions that proceed with the emission of heat. Energy is released as a result of changes in the bonds between the electron shells of the atoms. Chemical reactions involve only the transfer or sharing of electrons so that the nuclei are unaffected and the chemical elements retain their integrity. In contrast, nuclear energy is generated by changes in the bonding that holds the nucleus together—forces that are roughly a million times greater than the electron energies.

Early chemists believed that the chemical elements could never be created or destroyed and that the atom could not be split. However, in 1896, Becquerel discovered that certain chemical elements (notably uranium) undergo a spontaneous disintegration with the emission of energy in the form of particles or rays, a process that was named **radioactivity**. Subsequently, it was found that all elements with atomic number greater than 83 are radioactive. In effect, their nuclei are so large that they are unstable, and they break down or decay with the emission of energy in the form of rays or particles. These decays are spontaneous nuclear reactions, which result in the transformation of the element into one or more other elements. There are also a small number of elements of low atomic number that have one naturally occurring radioisotope (for example, $^{14}_{12}C$, $^{40}_{19}K$, $^{87}_{37}Rb$). The energy emitted is associated with holding or binding together the nucleus. As can be seen from Figure 6.2, the binding energy of a nucleus varies as a function of the total number of protons plus neutrons making up that nucleus (the mass number). The curve of mass number versus binding energy is such that the lightest and heaviest elements have lower nuclear binding energies. The breakdown of a large nucleus such as uranium into two smaller nuclei such as barium and krypton is called **nuclear fission.** Another way of releasing energy is by the joining of the nuclei of very light elements, such as hydrogen and lithium, to form heavier elements, a process called **fusion.** In either case, a small amount of matter has been converted directly into a large amount of energy, because whenever a nucleus is formed, its mass is slightly less than the sum of the masses of the individual protons and neutrons that comprise it. For example, helium (He) contains two protons and two neutrons in the nucleus and should weigh 4.03303 atomic mass units. In fact, helium only weighs 4.00260 units. The missing mass was converted into energy when the protons or neutrons joined to form the nucleus (that is, it is the binding energy). Before this century, it was believed that matter could be neither created nor destroyed, but in 1905, Einstein postulated the equivalence of matter and energy. His famous equation ($E = Mc^2$, where E = energy, M = mass, and c = velocity of light) related that conversion of a very small amount of matter to the production of very large amounts of energy (because c^2 is a very large number). In chemical reactions, such as those occurring when coal or oil is burned, the conversion of matter into

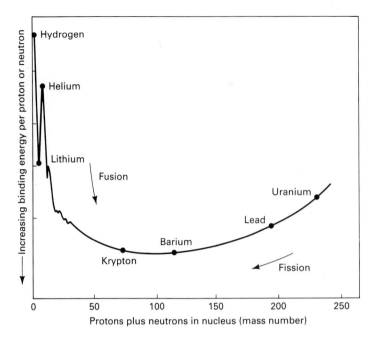

FIGURE 6.2. Binding energy, produced by conversion of some of the mass of an atomic nucleus, varies with the number of protons and neutrons. The higher an atom sits on the curve, the more energy will be given off when protons and neutrons combine to form its nucleus. The arrows indicate the directions of movement along the binding energy curve during fusion and fission.

TABLE 6.1

Naturally occurring isotopes of uranium

Uranium Isotope	Percentage of All Uranium	Half-life, Millions of Years
^{234}U	0.0054	0.247
^{235}U	0.7110	710
^{238}U	99.283	4510

energy is so small as to be undetectable. In nuclear reactions, the energies involved are so much greater that this conversion can be measured.

Nuclear Fission

The decay of natural radioactive materials, such as minerals containing uranium or thorium, takes place very slowly and over a great span of time (millions of years). We cannot slow the natural fission process, but we can accelerate it by bombarding radioactive nuclei with neutrons or by bringing together enough radioactive nuclei that their natural rate of neutron emission is sufficient to cause an increase in the rate of decay. Uranium occurs in three naturally occurring isotopes, each with markedly different abundances and half-lives (Table 6.1); however, the only naturally occurring atom that is readily fissionable is the isotope of uranium with mass number 235 (^{235}U). Many reactions occur during the fission of ^{235}U. One example is the bombardment of this atom with neutrons (n). When this occurs, ^{235}U may split into isotopes of barium (^{141}Ba) and krypton (^{92}Kr) (Figure 6.3) with the release of further neutrons and energy.

$$^{235}_{92}\text{U} + \text{n} \rightarrow ^{141}_{56}\text{Ba} + ^{92}_{36}\text{Kr} + 3\text{n}$$

$$+ \text{ energy (200 million electron volts*)} \qquad (6.1)$$

The released neutrons can penetrate the nuclei of adjacent atoms of ^{235}U so that the reaction can continue, provided a sufficient amount (the **critical mass**) of uranium is present. This is called a **chain reaction** (Figure 6.3). If this chain reaction is allowed to proceed uncontrolled, then the result is the explosive release of enormous amounts of energy, in other words, an atomic bomb. However, if the fission of uranium proceeds under carefully controlled conditions, the energy released can be extracted and used to generate power. If we note that reaction (6.1) releases 200 million electron volts for every atom of uranium that spontaneously decomposes, we find that the energy from just one gram of ^{235}U (a cube that would be only 4 millimeters on each side) is equivalent to 2.7 metric tons of coal or 13.7 barrels (12 metric tons) of crude oil (Figure 6.4). In addition, there is no smoke and no CO_2 released to pollute the environment—but there is some radiation. Obviously,

* 1 million electron volts = 1.6×10^{-13} joules

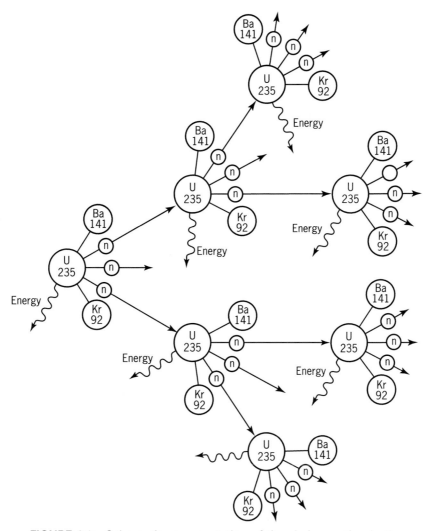

FIGURE 6.3. Schematic representation of the chain reaction in the fission of uranium. When a high-energy neutron (n) is absorbed by the nucleus of a uranium atom, it results in nearly spontaneous fission of the uranium nucleus producing more neutrons and a large release in energy. The released neutrons cause the fission of other uranium nuclei and the reaction proceeds in a rapidly expanding step-like, or chain, reaction.

uranium is a very attractive fuel to consider for power generation, and the technology necessary to exploit uranium fission has developed rapidly since World War II.

Thorium, which in nature is almost entirely made up of the isotope ^{232}Th, is an alternative source of fissionable material. Although ^{232}Th is not itself capable of sustaining a nuclear chain reaction, it can absorb neutrons from the controlled fission of ^{235}U to eventually become ^{233}U after passing through various fairly short-lived isotopes and emitting β particles.

$$^{232}_{90}\text{Th} + \text{n} \rightarrow {}^{233}_{90}\text{Th};\ {}^{233}_{90}\text{Th} - \beta^- \rightarrow {}^{233}_{91}\text{Pa};$$

$$^{233}_{91}\text{Pa} - \beta^- \rightarrow {}^{233}_{92}\text{U} \qquad (6.2)$$

The isotope ^{233}U is fissionable and can be made or "bred" from thorium in a nuclear reactor. However, the vast majority of nuclear power programs are based on uranium as a fuel, so the use of uranium as a source of energy will be emphasized here.

Uranium and How It Is Used—The Nuclear Reactor

The controlled fission of uranium for power generation takes place in a **nuclear reactor.** However, uranium extracted in mining operations is dominantly made up of the ^{238}U isotope (99.3 percent); the fissionable ^{235}U isotope comprises only

Uranium Fuel Pellet has as much energy available as ...

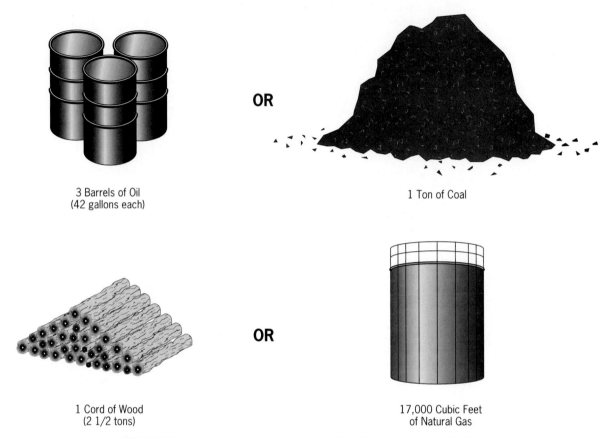

3 Barrels of Oil
(42 gallons each)

OR

1 Ton of Coal

1 Cord of Wood
(2 1/2 tons)

OR

17,000 Cubic Feet
of Natural Gas

FIGURE 6.4.   A uranium-bearing pellet that is placed in the fuel rod of a nuclear reactor contains only about one-third of a gram of uranium-235 but releases as much energy as the burning of much larger amounts of fossil fuels or wood.

0.7 percent of the total uranium and another isotope, ^{234}U, comprises only 0.005 percent (Table 6.1). Although reactors using natural uranium were among the first developed, particularly in England, many modern reactor designs require a fuel with ^{235}U at concentrations much higher than 0.7 percent. This necessitates a costly process of separation and concentration before the mined uranium can be used as a fuel. In fact, uranium differs from fossil fuels in that complex processing operations are often involved both before and after it is "burned" in the reactor, and these operations form a sequence known as the **nuclear fuel cycle** that we shall discuss before looking at the reactors.

The Nuclear Fuel Cycle.   The first stage in the cycle is the mining of uranium deposits. Mining involves standard open-pit and underground operations employing

methods similar to those used for the mining of other low-grade ores (see page 60). Because many uranium ores contain an average of much less than 1 percent of U_3O_8 (conventionally, grades and production figures are expressed in terms of this oxide), extensive **beneficiation** is needed (Figure 6.5). This involves mechanical concentration of size-reduced ore, perhaps making use of the high specific gravity of uranium minerals, followed by chemical methods such as leaching and solvent extraction to form an end product called **yellowcake,** a crude oxide containing 70–90 percent U_3O_8. However, after this processing, the yellowcake still only contains uranium with 0.7 percent ^{235}U, the isotope needed for conventional nuclear reactors.

The *enrichment* of the uranium to produce a fuel containing approximately 4 percent ^{235}U is a very difficult and expensive process, because it involves separating two iso-

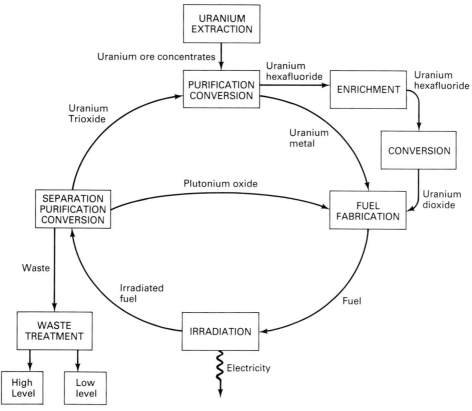

FIGURE 6.5. The nuclear fuel cycle schematically illustrates the steps involved in the conversion of uranium ore into nuclear fuel and ultimately into nuclear waste.

topes (^{235}U and ^{238}U) that have essentially no chemical difference and very little mass difference. The most common method used is gaseous diffusion, which is based on the fact that a gas diffuses through a porous membrane at a rate inversely proportional to the square root of its mass. The U_3O_8 is converted to gaseous uranium hexafluoride (UF_6) before being passed through thousands of porous barriers to separate $^{235}UF_6$ from $^{238}UF_6$. The enrichment process accounts for roughly 30 percent of the nuclear fuel costs. Following enrichment, the UF_6 is converted to a ceramic powder such as an oxide (UO_2) and compacted into small pellets that can be loaded into metallic tubes to form **fuel rods** or **fuel elements.**

The fuel elements, which are typically rods about 5 meters (about 16 feet) in length, are loaded into the reactor core where they are irradiated ("burned") and produce energy for 3–5 years. Eventually, the fissionable content of the rods drops to levels that will no longer sustain a chain reaction, and they are removed and replaced by new rods. Because the old fuel rods contain an abundance of dangerous but relatively short-lived radioactive isotopes, they are placed in tanks of water to allow some of these isotopes to decay. After several months, the fuel rods may be taken to a more permanent storage or may undergo reprocessing to recover the remaining uranium and some of the other isotopes.

Long-term storage of nuclear waste has been the subject of intense debate since the first reactors began operating. Several European countries have made decisions regarding their storage facilities, but the United States will not have any permanent repository until well beyond the year 2000. The most likely site will be Yucca Mountain in southern Nevada. The subject of radioactive waste disposal is discussed at greater length in Chapter 4.

The Nuclear Reactor. To understand the role of nuclear power at present and its potential in the future, it is necessary to know something about nuclear reactors. The different types and designs are many and varied, but certain major categories can be defined.

The first experimental and commercial reactors employed natural (unenriched) uranium as a fuel. A substantial fission chain reaction normally cannot be produced in a simple block of natural uranium,* because not enough

---

* A probably unique exception is the fossil natural fission reactor described from a uranium mine at Oklo in the Gabon Republic of West Africa (G.A. Cowan, *Scientific American* 235, p. 36, 1976). Here, scattered pockets of rich ore achieved the necessary (critical) conditions in unusual geologic conditions at a time in Earth history (about 2000 million years ago) when the natural relative abundance of ^{235}U was greater (about 3 percent of total uranium).

UNITED STATES NUCLEAR WASTE STORAGE—YUCCA MOUNTAIN

One of the principal problems, if not the single largest problem, for the nuclear power industry has been the ultimate disposal of spent nuclear fuel rods. Although the typical nuclear fuel rod containing enriched ^{235}U (about 4 percent is ^{235}U; the rest of the uranium is ^{238}U) has very low levels of natural radioactivity, the same fuel rod when extracted from the nuclear power plant at the end of its useful lifetime (3–4 years) exhibits very high levels of lethal radiation. Ever since the advent of commercial power generation by nuclear plants (first in England in 1956 and then in the United States in 1957), there have been numerous studies and unending debates as to what to do with the spent fuel rods. The very slow rates of decay of the radioisotopes requires that the rods be effectively isolated from human intrusion for about 10,000 years so that the radiation drops to safe levels (see Figure 4.30).

Several countries made relatively rapid decisions on storage sites—Germany decided to use salt beds, Sweden chose granite—but the United States has struggled with choices. The major criteria for a storage site were (1) distance from population centers; (2) security; and (3) prevention or minimization of environmental impact, especially with regard to ground or surface waters. The first and third criteria limited the United States to portions of the West and led to the investigation of the Hanford Facility in Washington (use of basalts), the WIPP site in New Mexico (Waste Isolation Pilot Project using salt beds), and Yucca Mountain, Nevada (using volcanic tuff). After years of debate, Yucca Mountain was chosen as the best site for development of a permanent facility. Yucca Mountain lies in an arid, unpopulated region of southern Nevada about 100 miles northwest of Las Vegas (see Figures 4.32 and 4.33 and Plates 26 and 27) on a Bureau of Land Management facility.

Geologically, Yucca Mountain overlies a 300-meter (1000-foot) thick sequence of volcanic tuffs which have been solidified into a rather solid mass as a result of the action of the volcanic heat and fluids that occurred when the beds were deposited more than 13 million years ago. Although there has been much faulting in southern Nevada, the block that constitutes Yucca Mountain is free of major faults. Several small volcanic cones occur in the area but none appear to have shown any activity in the past 10,000 years. The water table lies at a depth of 450–600 meters (1500–2000 feet), which is 200–400 meters (660–1300 feet) below the level of proposed nuclear storage.

The proposed facility will be developed as a series of galleries tunneled into the body of the volcanic tuff with the *hot* nuclear fuel rods set into cylindrical storage cavities in the floors of the galleries. Heat buildup should be minimal and the absence of percolating groundwater is expected to prevent any groundwater contamination. Debates still occur about the appropriateness of Yucca Mountain as the United States' nuclear storage facility, but the government expects it to meet all criteria for operation. A considerable dilemma exists because the United States government will begin accepting spent nuclear fuel by 1998, but the debates and construction delays have now pushed the opening date of the Yucca Mountain facility to 2010. In the meantime, nuclear power plants continue to hold increasing numbers of spent fuel rods, and there will be another major problem—how to get the rods to Yucca Mountain. The general public does not like to see rods building up in temporary storage sites, but home owners also do not want to see fuel rods transported past their homes.

neutrons emitted by the fission process would be *captured* by the small number of ^{235}U nuclei available. However, these neutrons are travelling at high velocities, and if they can be slowed to very low velocities, then the probability of the collision (more correctly termed **capture**) with other ^{235}U nuclei is greatly increased, and a sustained chain of fission reactions is possible. The neutrons are slowed by allowing them to collide with nuclei of light elements and transfer some of their energy in the same way a moving billiard ball does when it strikes a stationary ball. The light elements are known as **moderators.** Two elements that have been widely used as moderators are carbon in the form of **graphite** and **deuterium** (the isotope of hydrogen with mass number 2) in the form of deuterium oxide or *heavy water*. Development of the graphite-moderated natural uranium reactor for power generation was pioneered in Britain where the world's first large-scale nuclear power station at Calder Hall first produced electricity in 1956. From this prototype the first generation of nuclear power stations in Britain was developed on the *Magnox* reactor (Figure 6.6).

In a nuclear power station, the reactor simply acts as a source of heat and so replaces the furnace in a conventional power station. Different reactors employ different methods of extracting the heat and, in the Magnox reactor, pressurized carbon dioxide gas is blown through the core and the hot gas is then passed through heat exchangers to heat water and produce steam that can drive turbines and generators as in conventional power stations. The reactor must be operated under conditions that can maintain a fission chain reaction and a constant power output—a condition known as **criticality.** In the Magnox reactor, this condition is maintained using boron steel control rods that strongly absorb slow neutrons and are lowered into the core to slow the fission reaction or raised to increase reactivity and power output. The other type of reactor that has been developed to use natural uranium as a fuel is a heavy-water-moderated system pioneered by Canadians (in the so-called Candu program).

If natural uranium can be used as a fuel for power generation, why bother with the costly process of fuel enrichment? The answer is that if natural uranium is enriched even to a modest degree by the addition of fissionable isotopes, many of the problems of reactor design found in natural uranium reactors are overcome, and there are important gains in manufacturing and operational efficiency. For example, ordinary water or organic liquids may be used to moderate neutrons, the moderator and fuel may be intimately mixed to form a *homogeneous system* (although serious corrosion problems arise), and with high enrichment, it is even possible to completely dispense with the moderator. Other advantages arise from much greater freedom in the choice of constructional materials; for example, maximum operating temperatures can be increased. For reactors using enriched uranium, the number of possible types becomes very large. However, existing and planned types of reactors can be roughly divided into four groups.

1. heterogeneous graphite-moderated, gas-cooled reactors, for example, the advanced gas-cooled reactor (AGR);
2. heterogeneous water-moderated and cooled reactors, for example, light water reactors such as the boiling water reactor (BWR) and pressurized water reactors (PWR);
3. homogeneous reactors, for example, the homogeneous reactor experiment (HRE); and
4. fast (unmoderated) reactors.

The AGR is an example of the first type and represents the second generation of reactors in Britain following the Magnox reactors that uses fuel with a 2.5 percent fissile material. As Figure 6.6 shows, graphite is still used as a moderator with carbon dioxide coolant and a system of control rods, but

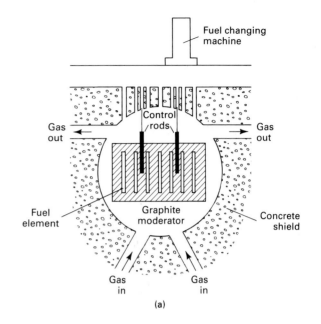

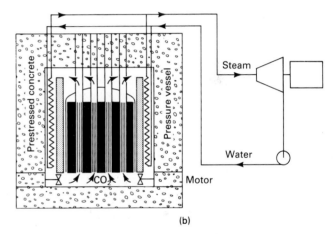

FIGURE 6.6. Schematic diagrams of gas-cooled reactors that used carbon as the moderator. (a) The Magnox reactor, the first generation of nuclear power plants, employed carbon dioxide as the means of transferring the heat from the reactor core to a heat exchanger where electricity is generated. (b) The advanced gas-cooled reactor was an advanced form of a gas-cooled reactor that used more enriched fuel and could operate more efficiently and at much higher temperatures.

enrichment allows a considerable increase in operating temperature and, consequently, in efficiency.

The second major reactor type uses water instead of a gas as a means of extracting heat from the reactor. Reactors of this type have been developed in the United States. They require fuel with 2–5 percent fissionable material (namely ^{235}U that has been enriched to 2–5 percent of the total uranium) and include the BWR in which the water, acting as both moderator and coolant, is allowed to boil inside the reactor vessel, and the PWR in which the pressure inside the reactor vessel is high enough to prevent boiling (Figure 6.7). The prototype PWR Yankee was built in Massachusetts and became fully operational in 1961, and the prototype BWR Dresden was constructed at about the same time in Illinois. The Dresden core consisted of 57.5 tons of uranium oxide enriched to 1.5 percent ^{235}U and produced 200 megawatts of electricity. The water was maintained at a pressure of 70 atmospheres, which allowed boiling at 300°C, so that this high-temperature steam could be used to directly drive turbines before being condensed and returned to the reactor vessel.

The use of enriched fuels enables systems to be designed in which the fuel and moderator are intimately mixed. Small experimental **homogeneous reactors** have been developed, such as the HRE of the Oak Ridge Laboratories in the United States. Systems like this may involve fused salts of the fuel and moderator or a solution of uranium salt in water. They have not been successfully developed on a large scale, partly because of the serious corrosion problems that arise.

The last main category of reactor types has been regarded as very important for the longer term future of nuclear fission as a source of energy; these are the so-called **fast reactors.** When the uranium fuel is highly enriched, it is possible to maintain the chain reaction using high velocity (*fast*)

neutrons and to dispense with the moderators entirely. In such a system, the core can be quite small, and a high proportion of neutrons can be allowed to escape through the surface. If a blanket of the nonfissionable ^{238}U is wrapped around this core, then these emitted neutrons can be used to make or *breed* a fissile isotope of plutonium.

$$^{238}_{92}\text{U} + \text{n} \rightarrow {}^{239}_{92}\text{U}; \; {}^{239}_{92}\text{U} - \beta^- \rightarrow {}^{239}_{93}\text{Np};$$
$$^{239}_{93}\text{Np} - \beta^- \rightarrow {}^{239}_{94}\text{Pu} \qquad (6.3)$$

In this way, more fissile material can be made in the blanket than is consumed in the core. Such fast reactors are known as **fast-breeder reactors.** The implications of this development for nuclear power generation are considerable because the reactor is capable of breeding its own fuel by converting the vastly more abundant ^{238}U isotope to a usable isotope (Figure 6.8).

A prototype fast-breeder reactor first became operational at Dounreay in Scotland in 1959 (Figure 6.9). The central core of 220 kilograms was enriched to 46.5 percent ^{235}U, and the heat output (60 megawatts) of a volume the size of a small garbage can was immense (roughly comparable to that of 60,000 100-watt light bulbs). The coolant was molten sodium and potassium, a much more efficient coolant than water or the gases used in other systems. An additional 12 megawatts of power was produced from fission processes in

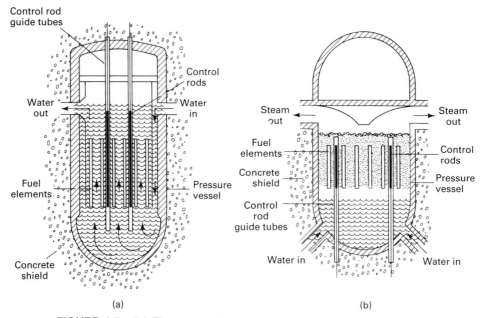

(a)   (b)

FIGURE 6.7. (a) The pressurized water reactor uses water under high pressure as both the moderator and the means of transferring heat from the reactor core to the electricity generating plant. (b) The boiling water reactor is maintained at a pressure of only about 70 atmospheres, which allow boiling at about 300°C. The steam thus generated is used to directly drive turbines to generate electricity.

The Formation of Plutonium

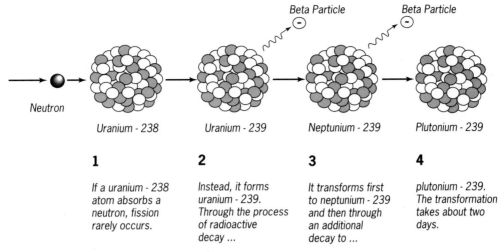

1

If a uranium - 238 atom absorbs a neutron, fission rarely occurs.

2

Instead, it forms uranium - 239. Through the process of radioactive decay ...

3

It transforms first to neptunium - 239 and then through an additional decay to ...

4

plutonium - 239. The transformation takes about two days.

FIGURE 6.8. The uranium-238 used as fuel in a fast-breeder nuclear reactor is converted to uranium-239, which then decays twice to form neptunium-239 and finally forms plutonium-239.

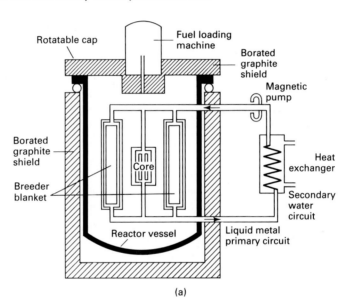

(a)

FIGURE 6.9. Schematic diagrams of fast-breeder nuclear reactors in which a blanket of nonfissionable U-238 is placed around the core. The U-238 is converted to Pu-239, a fissionable isotope, at a rate faster than the core is consumed. (a) In the loop-type fast-breeder reactor, the heat is carried out of the reactor vessel by a molten metal to a heat exchanger. (b) In the molten salt breeder reactor, salt transports the heat to a series of heat exchangers so that electricity can be generated.

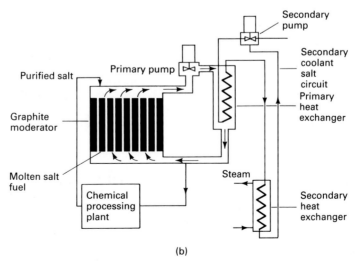

(b)

the blanket of 20 tons of depleted uranium. The molten metal coolant, in turn, generated steam to drive the turbines and generators. This prototype reactor operated successfully until 1977 when it was replaced by another fast breeder of improved design. The largest fast-breeder reactor in the world is the Super Phenix at Creys-Malville in France, having an output of 1200 megawatts. Other developments in this field include work in the United States on a modified core for the PWR with a breeder blanket and molten salt (Figure 6.9). Here, features of the thermal reactor with its moderator are combined with a breeder cycle.

Nuclear Reactor Safety—After Chernobyl.

There are few subjects in the whole area of resources and energy that cause greater public concern than the potential for accidents at nuclear power plants. In spite of the very stringent safety precautions that are taken in the design, construction, and operation of nuclear plants, major accidents have occurred in recent years. It is therefore important for us to examine the risks associated with nuclear power as objectively as possible when decisions concerning energy policy are made.

In all commercial nuclear reactors, a fission chain reaction is sustained at the level of criticality, which means constant power output. To maintain the balance in most reactor types, rods of material that capture neutrons very strongly and compete with the fission process can be lowered into the reactor core to slow the reaction or raised to speed it. These control rods are usually made of cadmium or boron and are inserted or removed automatically in response to power fluctuations. Clearly, a first hazard is the failure of the system, which would result in continued increase in power output. To guard against this, reactors are equipped with ancillary control rods designed to respond automatically in such a situation (or other dangerous situations) and to bring about a reactor shutdown, or *scram*, as it is commonly called. If these devices fail, the reactor can rise above criticality in a runaway in which the rate of reaction would increase in an unchecked manner. Fortunately, this situation could not produce a nuclear explosion like that of a nuclear weapon, but it could allow the temperature to rise to a level that would melt or even vaporize parts of the reactor. The damage to the reactor would probably render it no longer critical, and power would eventually fall. The greatest hazard would be the escape of gaseous radioactive iodine (^{133}I), an isotope (half-life of eight days) that is readily taken up in the human thyroid gland. Radioactive xenon and krypton gas and solid isotopes of strontium (^{90}Sr) and cesium (^{137}Cs) are lesser dangers. To prevent escape of dangerous fission products into the environment, reactors are enclosed in steel and concrete vessels.

In the heavy-water-moderated reactors of the Candu program, an additional safety feature is a dump tank into which the moderator can be readily emptied, should all else fail to prevent a runaway. However, in the PWR, the loss of

moderator, which also acts as a coolant, is a further hazard. Loss of coolant or coolant flow is probably the most serious hazard in most reactor types; thus, coolant flow is always carefully monitored. Fast-breeder reactors present their own safety problems. For example, if the core should melt, it could form into a mass in such a way as to be even more reactive. Diverters positioned beneath the core ensure separation of the core materials to prevent this if melting should occur. It should be emphasized that a nuclear reactor cannot explode like a nuclear bomb; the danger arises from the escape of highly poisonous or toxic fission products into the environment.

Up until 1979, the nuclear industry worldwide could claim an impressive safety record. The only significant release of radioactive material had been in Britain at Windscale in 1958; it involved a graphite-moderated, air-cooled reactor that was shut down at the time. The release, mainly of radioactive iodine (^{131}I), did not endanger life, but milk produced in an area of 300 square miles around the reactor (780 square kilometers) was unusable for a time. More recently, two serious accidents have significantly increased public concern and damaged the image of industry. They occurred at Three Mile Island, Pennsylvania, in the United States in March 1979 and Chernobyl in the Ukraine in April 1986 (described on page 176).

The Three Mile Island facility, located on an island in the Susquehanna River near Harrisburg, Pennsylvania, is a pressurized water reactor (PWR). Such reactors have both a primary cooling system to carry the fission heat to the steam generator and a secondary cooling system to carry steam from the steam generator to the turbine. Each system has its own pumps, the reactor cooling system pumps and the feed water pumps, respectively. Both cooling systems carry heat from the reactor core to areas outside. At 4:00 A.M. on 28 March 1979 the main feed water pump failed, and automatically, three reserve pumps (two electric and one steam-driven) went on. However, in the 15 seconds required for these pumps to build to normal pressure, the primary system heated and increased in pressure such that the automatic reactor shutdown procedure went into operation. A pressure relief valve in the primary system also opened to release pressure—all of these responses were quite proper and designed to occur. Unfortunately, unknown to the operators, valves that connected to the reserve pumps and were supposed to have been open at all times were closed. As a result, the steam generators soon boiled dry. In addition, the pressure relief valve in the primary system failed to reset properly and began to leak. In the long, complex series of events that followed, the pump valves were opened and eventually the leaky valve was blocked, but the operators were misled into thinking that there was too much water in the primary system instead of too little. As a result, the core lay uncovered for several hours, and substantial damage occurred before the situation was finally brought under control. The factors leading to the Three Mile Island accident involved three main ingredients: a temporary, abnormal situation aggravated by human error; a small loss-of-coolant accident; and misreading of the situation by the operators. Although very costly damage was done to the reactor itself, the dangers to the public were ultimately very small. In the early stages of the accident, radioactive xenon (^{133}X) was released; actual exposure is calculated to have the potential to cause the death by cancer of less than one person in the next 30 or 40 years.

Although there was no reported physical harm to any individual arising from the Three Mile Island (TMI) incident, it did undermine confidence in the nuclear power industry. Prior to 1979 there was the expectation that nuclear power would ultimately serve as the United States' and many other nations' principal energy source. At the time of the TMI incident, there were about 70 reactors operating in the United States, producing about 11 percent of the electrical power. There were immediate calls for new reactor designs with fail-safe backup systems, leading to long construction delays and soaring costs. Plans for many of the hundred or so planned nuclear plants were immediately scrapped, and decisions on many others were delayed (only to be canceled later); only plants that were close to completion were allowed to continue with construction. Projected construction periods of five years stretched on to 15 years, and original estimated costs of $500 million for plants became $5 billion. The power once prophesied to become so cheap that electric meters would not even be put on houses turned into the most expensive form of energy.

Over the 15 years that followed TMI, hitherto unimaginable events unfolded. The Washington Power Supply System went bankrupt because of its investment in nuclear power plants; a nearly completed plant in Ohio was converted to burn fossil fuel; the Seabrook plant in New Hampshire was prevented from operating for many years because it was 8 miles from the Massachusetts state border, and that state refused to approve a 10-mile radius emergency evacuation plan; and the Shoreham plant on Long Island, built at a cost of $6 billion, was sold to New York State for $1.00 and will never operate.

Nuclear power has, however, continued to be a major energy source as shown in Figure 6.10. As new plants came on line, the number of operating nuclear plants in the United States rose to a maximum of 110 in 1994. They are widely distributed (Figure 6.11), but with clusters of installations in the Northeast, near Chicago, and in California. Their electricity output reached about 20 percent of the United States' total in the mid-1990s. Nuclear power plants have finite operational lives—usually about 30–40 years—and many of the plants built in the 1960s will soon be subject to decisions on major refitting or shutdown. The first plant in the United States to face this was the Yankee Rowe in Massachusetts in 1994, and the decision was to shut it down. It is likely that the same choice will be made for several other of the older

plants. This creates new problems because the dismantling of nuclear plants has never been attempted and methods have not been devised for the disposal of the radioactive components. A footnote on the TMI incident is that 15 years after the meltdown, no human being has entered the containment area because of the high levels of radioactivity. It has been surveyed and some material has been removed by robots carrying TV cameras, but most of the highly radioactive material remains in place.

Although the United States and many other western countries have probably seen the peak of their nuclear power industries, nuclear power-generated electricity is going to be important for many years to come. Interestingly, nuclear power, once very much opposed by major environmental groups, is being reevaluated because it does not create acid mine runoff or acid rain or contribute CO_2 to the atmosphere. Other countries have responded to citizens' concerns and the problems of TMI and Chernobyl in various ways. Sweden has decided to use its existing nuclear plants but to build no more; France and Japan are actively building new plants and are committed to nuclear power as their major source of electricity; Austria completed a plant but decided never to use it; and Russia and the Ukraine have acknowledged grave safety concerns about their old plants but continue to use them because they have no other energy sources to produce power. The one part of the world where nuclear power is still the most popular option for future energy generation is the Far East. Of the 125 reactors still under construction or in planning stages in 1995, the vast majority were in Taiwan, Japan, China, South Korea, and other countries in the area.

What then can we say about the risks associated with nuclear power generation? It is still fair to say that the risk of death or serious injury to a member of the public as a result of a nuclear accident is very small, particularly when compared to many of the risks taken by people in everyday life (for example, compared to the one-in-fifty risk of death or serious injury in a motor accident in an average life span, the risk associated with nuclear power would be one in many thousands). Nevertheless, the lessons of Three Mile Island and Chernobyl must never be forgotten. To quote from the magazine *Nature* (editorial, vol. 323, no 6083, 1986), "The difficulty is that what went wrong at Chernobyl on 26 April could have happened anywhere. That is the plain truth which no amount of technical comparison of different reactor types can possibly conceal. Moreover, there have been several occasions in the recent past when nuclear accidents, luckily smaller in scale, have been brought about, because operators have chosen to disregard the regulations they are supposed to live by, or have been deserted by common sense and elementary caution." It is also important to remember that other aspects of safety and security, such as the hazards associated with nuclear waste disposal and the relationship that may exist between nuclear energy programs and the proliferation of nuclear weapons, must be considered in the overall formulation

Nuclear and Total Net Generation of Electricity 1957-1993

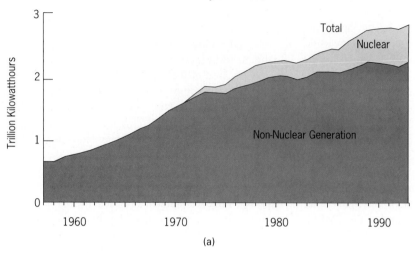

(a)

Operable Units, 1957-1993

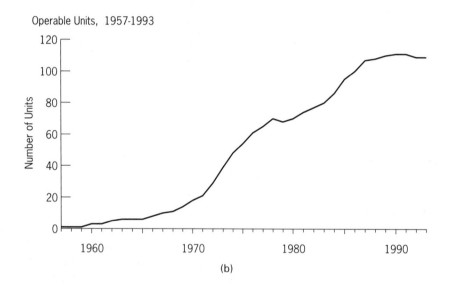

(b)

Nuclear Portion of Domestic
Electricity Net Generation, 1957-1993

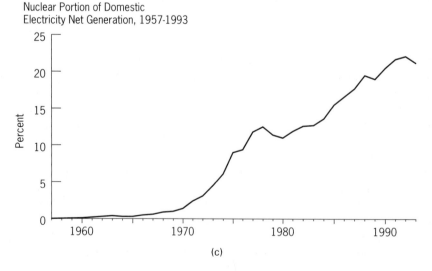

(c)

FIGURE 6.10. Nuclear power generation in the United States since 1957. (a) Total kilowatt-hours generated per year by nuclear and non-nuclear sources. (b) Number of operational nuclear units in the United States. (c) Percentage of electricity generated by nuclear plants. (From *1994 Energy Annual Review,* U. S. Energy Information Administration.)

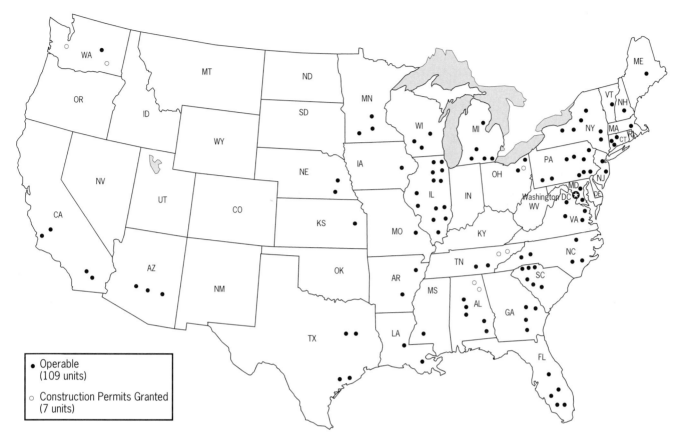

FIGURE 6.11. Nuclear generating units in the United States in 1994.

of policies regarding nuclear power. At the same time, it is important to realize that each of the competing energy sources creates its own problems and has its own costs. After all, most of the world's electricity is produced by burning coal and, worldwide, hundreds of coal miners are killed each year. However, because their deaths are not at the sites of power generation, we do not draw the same connection that we do about deaths at nuclear power plants.

Uranium in the Earth

Uranium is a rare element with an average concentration in Earth's crust of only about two parts per million. Although it can occur in trace amounts in a variety of minerals, the large size of the uranium atom tends to exclude it from the early crystallizing minerals in magmas. Hence, uranium is commonly concentrated in the final (*residual*) melts and fluids and in silica-rich rocks such as granites that are rich in alkali elements such as sodium and potassium. In these rocks, uranium concentrations may range up to tens or even a hundred or more parts per million. This uranium may be located in certain rare minerals that occur in such rocks as minor components (for example, zircon, sphene, and apatite), or it may occur as the most important ore mineral of uranium, urani-

nite (UO_2, also called **pitchblende**). Here, the uranium is in the uranous (U^{4+}) state. Occasionally, within or close to such igneous rocks, very high concentrations of uranium minerals occur either in veins or as more irregularly distributed *disseminations*. Such deposits were among the first uranium ores to be found and exploited and were the source of much of the uranium used by Pierre and Marie Curie for their pioneering work on radioactivity.

Most of the uranium at the surface of Earth probably formed in association with igneous rocks as described. However, a very important feature of uranium in the U^{4+} state is that it is readily oxidized to the uranyl (U^{6+}) state. Whereas U^{4+} compounds are highly insoluble, U^{6+} combines with oxygen to form the uranyl ion $(UO_2)^{2+}$, which, in turn, can form soluble complex compounds with species such as carbonate, sulfate, and fluoride. Near-surface groundwaters are commonly oxidizing in nature and hence provide a ready means of leaching and carrying uranium. Although much of this uranium may then be dispersed, the groundwaters are commonly oxidizing in nature and hence provide a ready means of leaching and carrying uranium. Although much of this uranium may then be dispersed, the groundwaters carrying the metal may pass into rocks in which reducing substances (commonly decaying organic matter) convert the

CHERNOBYL

The most tragic of nuclear accidents was that at Chernobyl in the Ukraine in April 1986; it resulted in loss of life and in significant contamination over a very large area. The accident centered around attempts to test a system for providing the necessary cooling water in the event of a reactor shutdown; these tests were to coincide with the actual closing of the reactor for its annual maintenance. In attempting to create the necessary conditions for this poorly planned test, automatic systems for operation of the control rods, emergency core-cooling systems, and various other fail-safe devices were overridden by the operators. When the test began to go wrong, both to save the test and to prevent damage to the reactor, further actions by the operators that were totally against regulations led to a complete loss of control. In the words of Academician Legasov, reporting to an international group of nuclear scientists in Vienna, the reactor was "free to do as it wished." Control rods were leaping up and down and water and steam were sloshing around uncontrollably. In less than 1 second, the power surged from 7 percent to several hundred times its normal level. The effect was like setting off half a ton of TNT in the core, and two explosions lifted the roof of the reactor, throwing red-hot lumps of graphite and pieces of uranium oxide fuel over the immediate area.

Over the next ten days, while the Russians struggled to quench the fire, roughly 10 percent of the core material was dispersed into the atmosphere to fall out over Russia and Europe. Large areas of Russia, Poland, Sweden, and Finland (Figure 6.12) were particularly affected, but significant increases in radiation levels were recorded as far away as Norway, Italy, and Britain where fallout from Chernobyl led to restrictions on the sale of crops and livestock. In the immediate area of Chernobyl, one person was apparently killed within the reactor and about 20 severely irradiated (17 of whom died within six weeks), but many thousands more face an increased risk of death from cancers associated with the radiation. The helicopter pilot who flew numerous missions dumping lead and sand on the burning reactor in the first few days allowed himself to be exposed to massive radiation, but his selflessness no doubt saved many others. He was praised for his heroism but has died of leukemia resulting from the exposure.

The nightmare of Chernobyl has continued to unfold in the years since the event as more information has become available and as death counts have risen. In 1995 the government of the Ukraine blamed the accident for a nearly 16 percent rise in the death rate in the northern Ukraine and for a rapid rise in thyroid and organ cancers. More than 140,000 citizens had to abandon homes because of high levels of radioactivity and about 500,000 more continued to live in contaminated areas. The number of deaths resulting from the disaster is not known, but by 1995 figures ranging from 8000–125,000 had been released. Furthermore, doctors feared that the peak of cancers and deaths would not appear until more than 10 years after the Chernobyl accident.

The Soviet government continued to operate the two other nuclear units at Chernobyl because of its need for electrical power. After the breakup of the Soviet Union, the Ukranian government found the same problem. A decision was finally made to shut down the other units by the end of 1993, but was reversed because there was no other adequate power supply for Kiev. In early 1995, the Ukranian government announced that it would shut down the two operational Chernobyl units by early in the year 2000 because other western countries had agreed to help finance the construction of a $3 to $5 billion natural gas power plant that could supply the needed electricity.

It appears that the legacy of the Chernobyl disaster will remain with us for many years to come.

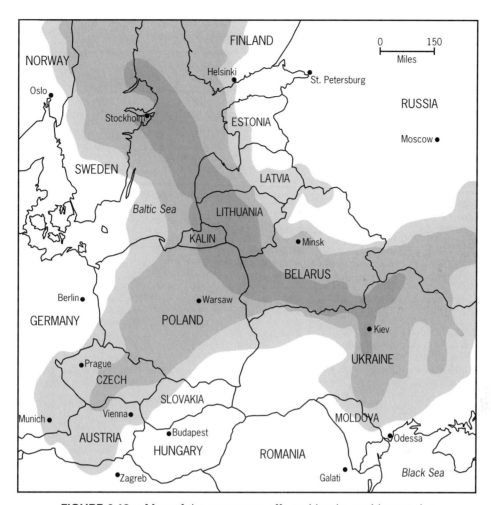

FIGURE 6.12. Map of the area most affected by the accident at the Chernobyl nuclear reactor near Kiev in the former Soviet Union in late April 1986. The shading shows simulation of the integrated dose of I-131 to adult thyroid glands accumulated from 26 April to 1 May 1986 (based on calculations done at the Lawrence Livermore National Laboratory in California). The central, darkest area had doses in excess of 1 rem, the intermediate zone had doses between 0.1 and 1 rem, and the outer zone had doses between 0.01 and 0.1 rem. (See Tables 3.3 and 3.5 for information on units of radioactivity and dosages experienced from other sources.)

soluble U^{6+} ion to the insoluble U^{4+} form, thus resulting in its precipitation. Other reactions involve absorption of the uranium by another mineral such as apatite, $(Ca_5(PO_4)_3(OH, F)$, in which U^{4+} replaces some Ca). The leaching, transportation, and precipitation of uranium in this way can lead to the formation of large bodies of rock enriched in the metal, and deposits produced by these second stage processes are the most important sources of uranium.

The most important types of uranium ore deposits are listed with examples in Table 6.2. The igneous deposits include various types of ores disseminated in alkali rocks and granites, although these are not very substantial contributors to world uranium resources. Deposits of the metamorphic

group include the concentrations (known as **skarns**) that have formed at the contact between molten igneous rocks and the rocks into which they have been emplaced. The ores that originally formed deeper in Earth's crust when heating caused some melting and the migration of material are in this general category.

Some of the most famous and important of all uranium deposits are detrital in origin, for example, those of the Witwatersrand in South Africa and Elliot Lake (also called Blind River) in Canada. Characteristically, ores of this type occur in very ancient (Precambrian) conglomerates that were deposited in former stream channels. The Witwatersrand area is better known as the world's greatest gold-producing region

TABLE 6.2
Important types of uranium ore deposits

Deposit Type		Characteristic Elements	Examples
Igneous	In pegmatites, alkali igneous rocks, carbonatites and related rocks (pegmatites)	U, Nb, Th, Cu, P, Ti, Zr, rare earths	Prairie Lake, Ontario, Canada Pocos du Coldas, Brazil Ilimaussaq, S. Greenland Rossing, S.W. Africa
Metamorphic	In contact areas between igneous and host rocks (skarns) or from the partial melting of rocks deep in the earth	U, Th, Mo, rare earths, Nb, Ti	Rossing, S.W. Africa
Detrital	Deposited in the bottoms of ancient rivers, lakes (fossil placers)	U, Th, Ti, rare earths, Au, Zr, Co	Witwatersrand, S. Africa Elliot Lake, Ontario, Canada
Unconformity	Occur close to a conspicuous Mid-Proterozoic unconformity	U ($\pm$Ni, rare earths, Ti, etc.)	N. Saskatchewan, Canada (Rabbit Lake, Key Lake, etc.) Northern Territory, Australia (Jabiluka, Nabariek, etc.)
Hydrogenic (deposited from fluids and waters)	From high-temperature water or fluids (hydrothermal) forming disseminations or veins (vein type)	U, Th, rare earths, ($\pm$Cu, F, Be, Nb, Zr)	Bokan Mt., Alaska, U.S.A. Rexspor, B.C., Canada
	U deposits formed at the same time as host shales, limestones, phosphate rocks, etc.	U, P, V, Cu, Co, Ni, As, Ag, C	Ronstad, Sweden Kitts, Labrador, Canada
	U deposited from low-temperature waters introduced into sandstones, conglomerates and forming disseminations or, sometimes, veins (sandstone type)	U, C ($\pm$Cu, V, Mo, Ag, Ni, As, Co, Au, Se, Bi)	Colorado Plateau area and Wyoming, U.S.A. Cypress Hills, Saskatchewan, Canada Beaverlodge, Saskatchewan Port Radium, N.W.T., Canada
	As an encircled cap at the surface of other deposits	U, Cu, Ag, Ni, As	Eldorado, Saskatchewan, Canada Rossing, S.W. Africa

(see Chapter 8), but in recent years about 10 percent of the known world production of uranium has also come from this area. Although the processes by which these ores formed remain controversial, it is widely believed that the gold and uranium were carried along the bottoms of stream channels as detrital grains. These grains would have been washed into the streams from source areas upstream and concentrated by virtue of their high density (in much the same way gold is concentrated in the prospector's pan). The persistence of the detrital uranium minerals is taken as evidence of an early Earth atmosphere with little or no oxygen; if oxygen had been present, the uranium would have dissolved. The deposits at Elliot Lake in Ontario, Canada, exhibit all the features shown by the Witwatersrand region, but a marked difference is that these ores do not contain significant quantities of gold.

The deposits categorized in Table 6.2 as hydrogenic include all those in which the uranium appears to have been deposited from water, either as a high-temperature fluid or a much lower temperature fluid such as groundwater. The boundaries between the different subcategories shown here are not always clear, but the divisions indicate the different processes at work. The veins formed by deposition from high-temperature fluids always show a fairly close spatial link with granites or similar rocks from which the fluids could have been derived. Such vein deposits are no longer a major world source of the metal. The richest uranium deposits in the United States are of the type found in Jurassic and Triassic sandstones in the Colorado Plateau area of western Colorado, eastern Utah, northeastern Arizona, and northwestern New Mexico. Similar deposits in younger rocks occur in Wyoming and are forming today in Texas. These deposits have formed through the precipitation of uranium from groundwaters that carry the metal in solution as uranyl complexes. The precipitation occurs as a result of reduction where the solutions encounter organic matter, as evidenced by the replacement of fossil logs by uranium or where the solution reacts with trapped H_2S. The deposits owe their characteristic shape, as

FIGURE 6.13. Many of the uranium deposits in the western United States are of the roll-type as shown in cross section. Oxidizing groundwaters dissolve the low concentrations of uranium and reprecipitate it further down an aquifer where reducing conditions are encountered. This results in a progressive accumulation of uranium and the movement of the arc-shaped deposit along the aquifer.

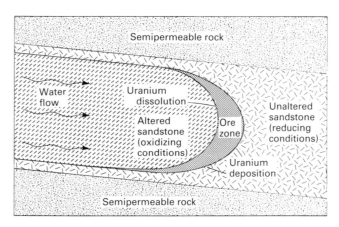

shown in the cross section in Figure 6.13, to the movement of fluid through the porous sandstones and the dissolution and reprecipitation of uranium and other metals along a moving front. Uranium is also concentrated in organic-rich black shales, such as the Chattanooga Shale of Alabama and Kentucky, but it is generally at much lower levels.

The Search for Uranium Deposits

From 1945 into the 1960s, uranium was the subject of the most intense mineral exploration activity ever undertaken for any metal, involving both government agencies and private companies. This search employed all of the standard exploration techniques but also made use of techniques that detect the same radiation exploited in nuclear power plants. The emission of the radiation is helpful in locating uranium, but it is also a potential health hazard in the following methods.

Gross Count Surveys. The simplest technique, which was widely used in early exploration, is to survey the ground using portable detectors that record total radiation levels without determining the nature of the radiation. Such simple Geiger-Muller and scintillation counters are of low sensitivity but have the advantage of being relatively inexpensive. They may be hand-held, mounted on a vehicle, or may be airborne, in which case they form a useful method of rapid reconnaissance. One problem is that the penetration of gamma rays through rocks and soils is limited to a distance of 10–20 centimeters; thick overburden may obscure the signal.

Gamma-Ray Spectrometry. This involves equipment capable of determining the strength of radiation of different energies. Gamma rays characteristic of uranium (1.76 million electron volts), thorium (2.61 million electron volts), and potassium-40 (1.46 million electron volts) that are emitted over an area can be measured and linked to other geologic information. The basic technology can be incorporated into hand-held, vehicle-mounted, or airborne systems, with con-

siderable sophistication being possible in airborne systems that have on-line computer processing of data. The overall costs of gamma-ray spectrometry may be five to 10 times greater than gross count surveys, and, like the latter, gamma-ray spectrometry is limited to measuring only surface radiation. Water, vegetation, snow cover, and even the air can also absorb and shield gamma radiation. Hence, airborne surveys need to be flown at low altitude to ensure detection.

Radon Measurement. Radon (^{222}Rn) is a radioactive gas given off by the decay of uranium (^{238}U). It is chemically unreactive, so it remains a gas and tends to move upward through soils above uranium-bearing rocks. As noted in Chapter 4, the accumulation of radon in homes in areas underlain by uranium-bearing rocks is a recently recognized health hazard. Various techniques have been developed to sample and measure radon gas in the air and in soils, using instruments such as the radon emanometer. Radon also enters streams, lakes, and spring water in areas around uranium deposits, and methods of measuring its concentration in natural waters have been devised. Although helpful in uranium exploration, radon is considered a major health hazard, and the discovery that it has built up to significant levels in many homes is prompting much concern (see Chapter 4).

Uranium Reserves and Resources and the Future of the Fission Reactor

Reserves of rich deposits of uranium are widespread but are not large (Table 6.3). The figures are probably conservative because an element of secrecy surrounds the subject of uranium (Figure 6.14). Substantial deposits that are economically recoverable now or in the foreseeable future are known on all of the continents. Assessment of the potential of lower grade deposits is difficult because the necessary data are not available. Within the United States, the kinds of source materials available have been broadly evaluated, as illustrated in Figure 6.15. It has recently been argued by Deffeyes and MacGregor in the United States that the distribution of

TABLE 6.3

Estimated uranium resources in ores rich enough to be mined for use in uranium-235 power plants, together with estimated rates of production for 1990. Data are reported as the oxide U_3O_8. No distinctions are drawn between reserves and resources, and no data are reported by the Communist countries (or the former USSR)

Country	Reasonably Assured Resources (m.t. of U_3O_8)	Estimated Production Rate, 1990* (m.t. of U_3O_8 per yr)
Australia**	1,600,000	9000
United States**	894,000	6000
Republic of South Africa***	391,000	6000
Canada***	235,000	13,000
Niger***	160,000	?
Namibia***	133,000	4000
France***	55,300	?
Other***	608,000	5000

*Production rate estimate from *Mining Annual Review*, 1983.
**Resource data from *American Association of Petroleum Geologists*, Bulletin Vol. 67, pp. 1999–2008, 1983.
***Resource data from *Mining Annual Review*, 1980. Much of the large "other" category is in low-grade deposits in Sweden.

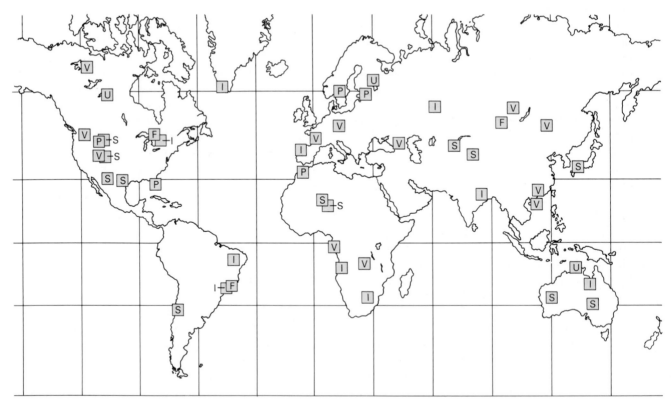

FIGURE 6.14. Major uranium deposits occur worldwide as shown on this map.

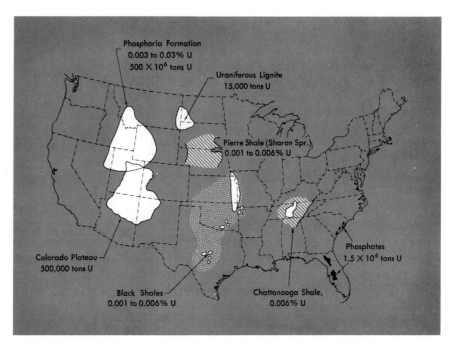

FIGURE 6.15. Long-term, low-grade resources of uranium occur in phosphate deposits, lignites, and black shales. Richer deposits, for which reserve estimates can be made, occur mostly in and around the Colorado Plateau. (From M.K. Hubbert, "Energy Resources." Publication 1000-D, Committee on Natural Resources, National Academy of Sciences—National Research Council, Washington, DC, 1962.)

uranium in Earth's crust follows a log-normal abundance curve with a 300-fold increase in recoverable uranium for each 10-fold decrease in ore grade (Figure 6.16). Such a trend would guarantee an ever-increasing uranium supply, as rising uranium prices would justify mining lower grades of ores. Others have put forward a less optimistic view suggesting that uranium reserves are not large enough to support future extensive use of power stations that use ^{235}U. If all of the reserves and resources listed in Table 6.3 were used solely for their ^{235}U content and if the conversion of heat energy to electricity were 40 percent efficient, the total energy produced would be only 8×10^{20} joules. On the other hand, an equally efficient fast-breeder reactor would be capable of extracting 1140×10^{20} joules because it can utilize the much more abundant ^{238}U. Stockpiled ^{238}U and known reserves could supply energy through a fast-breeder reactor system for many hundreds of years.

The world's first commercial nuclear reactor at Calder Hall in Cumbria, England, started to supply electricity in 1956. About 40 years later, in 1995, over 420 reactors in 25 countries were providing over 300,000 megawatts of the world's electricity. The global distribution of reactors shows the anticipated concentration of nuclear plants in the United States, western Europe, and Japan. A breakdown of nuclear generating capacity in terms of reactor type (Figure 6.17) illustrates both this point and the dominance of the light-water reactors that are so extensively employed in the United States. However, the nuclear generating capacity is often only a relatively small proportion of the total demand for electricity or that estimated until the end of the century. In a number of countries (Sweden, for example), decisions have been made to reduce or phase out nuclear power over the next few decades. Furthermore, the world is using less than half as much nuclear power as anticipated in 1970, and projections for future use have shrunk even more. The largest cutbacks have been in the United States, although most other countries have curtailed their programs. In 1983, *The Financial Times Energy Economist* reported that "The day when nuclear power will be the world's leading electricity source now seems to have been postponed indefinitely." Although the unresolved problems surrounding safety, waste disposal, and nuclear weapons proliferation may have contributed to this lack of anticipated growth, the main reason is much simpler. In most countries, nuclear power is no longer economically attractive, both because of rising construction and operating costs and a much smaller growth in the demand for electricity than had been anticipated. Indeed, many alternative energy sources are now becoming economically viable.

ALTERNATIVE ENERGY SOURCES

Solar Energy

The sun is essential to life and has been the major source of our energy throughout history (Figure 6.1). This has been mainly through its role in biological growth and therefore in the formation of fuels such as wood, coal, and oil. These fuels (see Chapter 5) provide us with ways of indirectly harvesting energy from the sun. Other indirect ways of harvesting this energy come from the influence of the sun on the atmosphere and hydrosphere; it causes the wind and rain,

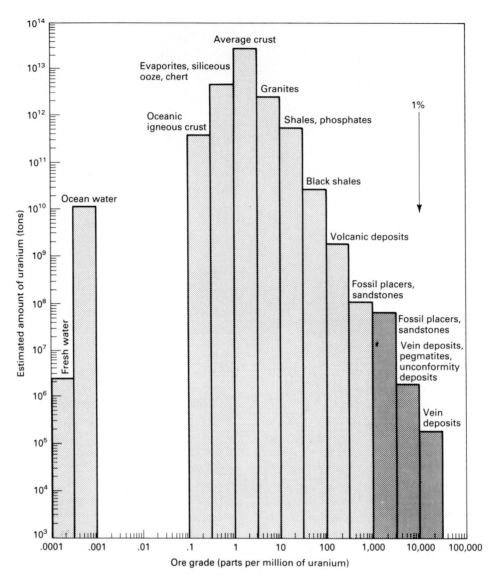

FIGURE 6.16. Diagram showing the distribution of uranium in Earth's crust as a log-log plot of estimated amount of uranium versus ore grade in parts per million of uranium. Bars represent various categories of uranium deposits or repositories of uranium in descending order of uranium content and define a log-normal global abundance curve. The three bars on the left represent deposits of the type now being mined specifically for uranium. The diagram shows that for approximately every ten-fold decrease in grade there is a 300-fold increase in the amount of recoverable uranium. (From K.S. Deffeyes and I.D. MacGregor, *Scientific American*, vol. 242, p. 66, 1980.)

ocean currents, and temperature differences in the oceans that are discussed as sources of energy in later sections of this chapter. The relationships between direct and indirect energy from the sun are summarized in Figure 6.18.

The term **solar energy** generally refers to the direct utilization of the sun's rays to generate energy in forms that can supply the needs of mankind. This energy can be best considered in two categories: **low-quality energy**—ordinary

diffuse sunlight that is used to produce low temperature forms of energy; and **high-quality energy**—solar energy that has been concentrated or changed by a physical or chemical process to produce electricity or a fuel such as hydrogen.

The sun has a surface temperature of about 5500°C. From its distance of 1.5×10^8 kilometers, approximately 4×10^{24} joules per year of energy reach the surface of Earth. This energy is mainly infrared and visible light radiation with

FIGURE 6.17. A map to illustrate the worldwide utilization and anticipated future development of nuclear power (in the mid-1990s). Countries involved in nuclear power generation are shown with the number of operating commercial nuclear reactors, reactors on order but not yet operating, and percentage of total electricity generated by nuclear energy.

lesser amounts of ultraviolet radiation (Figure 6.19). The amount of each type of radiation reaching Earth's surface depends on the distance the sun's rays have to travel through the atmosphere, because direct radiation from the sun is partly scattered and partly absorbed by molecules of various gases, by water vapor, and by dust in the air. Absorption at infrared wavelengths (>700 nanometers, Figure 6.19) is due largely to water vapor and, to a lesser extent, carbon dioxide. Absorption at ultraviolet wavelengths (<300 nanometers) is principally due to ozone (O_3). As noted in Chapter 3, depletion of the ozone in the atmosphere would result in more ultraviolet radiation passing through the atmosphere and in increases in the incidence of skin cancer. At around noon on a clear day in the mid-latitudes, direct radiation from the sun is reduced about 30 percent by these processes. Very cloudy conditions may reduce direct radiation to less than 1 percent

of the value above the atmosphere, but even under cloudy conditions there is appreciable diffuse radiation derived from scattered direct radiation.

Expressed in units of power, solar energy arrives at the surface of the earth at an average rate of 180 watts per square meter, but the range and distribution of the incident solar power in different parts of the globe varies greatly, primarily as a function of latitude (Figure 6.20). This energy constitutes such a large potential energy resource, that if only 20 percent of this average incident power were collected, a land area of approximately 7×10^4 square kilometers (less than one-fifth the size of California) would be sufficient to supply the entire energy requirements of the United States.

Low-Quality Solar Energy. The simpler systems used for the direct collection of (unconcentrated) solar energy

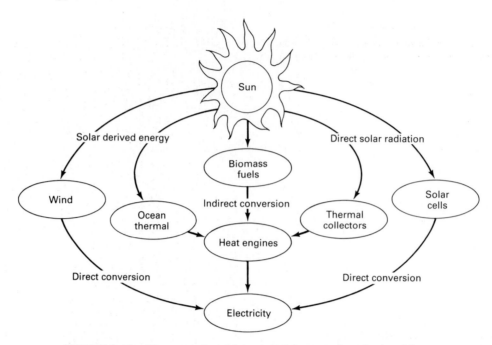

FIGURE 6.18.   The ways in which electricity may be obtained from the energy of the sun, either directly or indirectly.

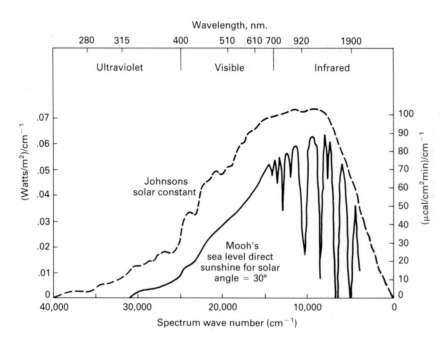

FIGURE 6.19. Energy from the sun (shown both in watts and in microcalories on the vertical scales) as a function of the wavelength of the sun's radiation expressed in both reciprocal centimeters (cm^{-1}, bottom scale) and in nanometers (nm, top scale). The dashed line shows the total flux of solar energy incident outside the atmosphere of Earth (Johnson's solar constant) and amounts of 178×10^{12} kilowatts continuous for the whole globe (or 1.5×10^{18} kilowatt-hours/year). The solid line represents the solar flux at sea level in direct sunshine for a solar attitude of 30°. The energy is depleted on passing through the atmosphere due to absorption by water vapor, carbon dioxide, oxygen, nitrogen, ozone, and dust particles (in some cases at very specific wavelengths). The average solar energy is reduced in this way to 2.16×10^{17} kilowatt-hours per year. (From *Task Force Report—Solar Energy*, U.S. Federal Energy Administration, 1974.)

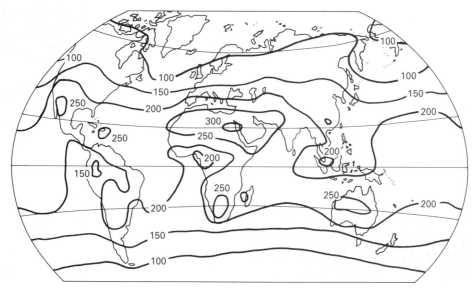

FIGURE 6.20. Map of the world to show the variation in annual mean solar energy flux (on a horizontal plane). Contours are in watts per square meter.

produce thermal energy of low quality in the sense that the temperatures produced are low (under 100°C) and the amounts of energy collected by any one system are small. In the United States, the thermal energy available for an average day varies from about 5400 kilocalories per square meter in southwestern states such as New Mexico to about 27 kilocalories per square meter in the Northeast and Great Lakes states. This low-quality thermal energy is well suited to many applications, particularly the heating of water and interior space.

A south-facing window is the simplest type of solar collector. The sunlight that passes through the glass is absorbed by objects in the room and by the wall, from which it radiates to warm the air of the room. Provided that good insulation reduces heat losses as much as possible, windows exposed to direct sunlight can maintain comfortable temperatures in a room even on a cold winter day. These simple principles are increasingly being used in the design of buildings—first, by arranging windows to capture sunlight and, second, by providing thermal storage facilities. Thermal storage is accomplished using massive objects, such as rocks, concrete, or containers filled with water, that are warmed by sunlight and then slowly release heat after sunset. The combination of solar heating and thermal storage can substantially reduce the heating fuel needs of a building but will rarely provide the sole means of heating.

All heating systems involve the transfer of heat energy, and it is important to recall that this can involve one or more of three mechanisms. Heat can be transferred (1) by **radiation,** in which waves (that may be visible light and infrared radiation) from a hot object such as the sun are absorbed by matter and reconverted into heat; (2) by **convection,** in which heat is carried by the motion of hot masses of matter (for example, hot water circulating through pipes in a building); and (3) by **conduction,** in which heat is transferred by contact between particles of matter (for example, from hot water to the metal pipe through which it passes). More elaborate systems for the heating of buildings and water involve purpose-built solar collectors, a heat-transfer fluid such as air or water, and a heat-storage system such as a large mass of rock or water. The collector is normally a large panel with a blackened collecting surface to trap a layer of air above it and reduce heat loss by conduction. This air itself may be used as the heat-transfer fluid, or water circulated through tubes that form part of the collecting surface may be used. An example of such a system is shown in Figure 6.21. Here, water that is heated in the solar panels is circulated through a heat exchanger to transfer this energy (by conduction) to a storage water tank that directly provides the supply to space-heating radiators or to the supply of running water. Such a system is nearly always coupled with conventional heaters and is controlled by a system of thermostats, valves, and timers to permit the most efficient use of solar and conventional energy. Although solar heating systems such as this are not technically complex and operating costs are negligible, they tend to be costly to install. Also with the savings in conventional fuel costs, it may take many years to repay the investment in a system. Taking an average for the rate at which solar energy arrives at Earth's surface and assuming that the collector is about 50 percent efficient, its daily energy output per square meter will be roughly equivalent to burning one-tenth of a gallon of heating oil in a 70 percent efficient furnace.

One obvious problem in using solar energy for heating buildings is that the greatest needs occur when and where the

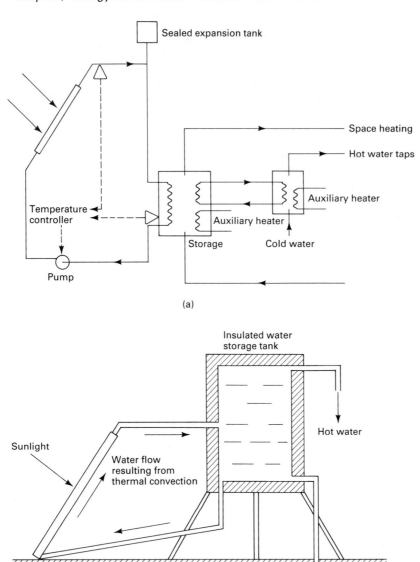

FIGURE 6.21. Domestic solar heating systems providing (a) both space-heating and (b) a supply of hot water and hot water only.

available sunlight is least. This disadvantage does not apply to solar heating of water for domestic and commercial use, because it is needed throughout the year, regardless of climate. A solar water heater of the type shown in Figure 6.21 can be placed on top of flat-roofed buildings and will provide domestic hot water needs throughout the year in a hot climate.

These few examples serve to illustrate the uses of low-quality solar energy. When one considers that in countries of North America and Europe about one-third of all the energy consumed is used for space heating and water heating, the potential of this resource becomes clear. Also, the limitations of climate are not as great as may be imagined. Even in countries such as England and Germany that are at relatively high latitudes with cool temperate regimes and considerable

cloudiness, it would be possible to provide 50 percent of domestic heat by solar energy in most areas. Such systems are not more widely used because conventional sources of energy are still readily available and are fairly inexpensive, and the initial cost of changing to any form of solar energy system is high. There is insufficient incentive for the home owner to invest in such a system, even though it is both inexpensive to run and pollution free, but future increases in the cost of conventional resource fuels could bring about much more use of solar heating.

High-Quality Solar Energy. The generation of temperatures much above 100°C or of the substantial amounts of energy required by many industrial operations involves more sophisticated means of collecting solar energy than those described so far. Two main approaches may be used: the sun's rays may be concentrated using lenses or focusing mirrors, or, alternatively, the rays may produce a chemical reaction or an electric current when they interact with specific materials.

The concentration of sunlight is based on the age-old principle of the burning glass in which a pocket lens can be used to burn a hole in paper by focusing the sun's rays on it. This principle was known even in ancient times, as is shown by the story of Archimedes constructing a great burning mirror to set fire to the ships of the Roman fleet attacking Syracuse in 212 B.C. One system undergoing development today involves a central collecting receiver mounted on top of a high tower. As shown in Figure 6.22, the sun's rays are reflected up to the receiver by a group of mirrors, called **heliostats,** which are programmed to automatically track the sun and keep its rays focused on the receiver. Temperatures of approximately 1000°C can be generated at the receiver. This receiver could simply be a boiler that generates steam to drive a turbine, or it could be a liquid metal such as sodium that is used to transfer the heat to a thermal storage system, which in turn produces the steam for driving a turbine and generating electricity. Such a thermal storage facility (for example, tanks containing salts or hydrocarbon fluids) could maintain steam to drive the turbine during brief periods of cloud cover or extend the operating day for the plant. A prototype facility with 2000 mirrors, each about 20 feet square, has been constructed at Barstow, California (Figure 6.23), and can deliver 10^7 watts of electricity during daylight hours. Plants of this type con-

vert the intercepted solar energy to electricity at about 20 percent efficiency. Full-scale plants would be 10 or more times the size of the Barstow plant and would probably be located in desert regions where land costs are minimal and the quantity of available solar energy is higher than in other regions. The costs of constructing such plants are much higher than for conventional fuel-burning power stations, with the large costs being involved in the mirrors and their control systems. However, as fossil fuel prices increase and design techniques for such large solar power stations improve, they become commercially more attractive.

Another type of solar energy concentrator generally suitable for smaller power plants is the **parabolic reflector.** This employs a cylindrical reflector (Figure 6.24) to focus the sunlight onto a small diameter collecting element, through which a heat-transporting medium such as a hydrocarbon or liquid metal is passed. This medium may circulate to a heat storage facility where heat exchangers extract the energy to make steam and drive turbines. Less complex movements are involved in tracking the sun, and the whole system can be constructed on a smaller scale suitable for a community-sized power generation system. Parabolic reflectors and other types of mirror systems have also been used to construct solar furnaces, for example, the solar furnace in the French Pyrenees at Odeillo, where temperatures of up to 400°C can be reached in a 50 square centimeter hot spot.

Solar energy can be converted directly into electrical energy by **photovoltaic cells.** In these devices, the light energy interacts directly with the electrons of a semiconductor to produce an electric current. These photovoltaic or **solar**

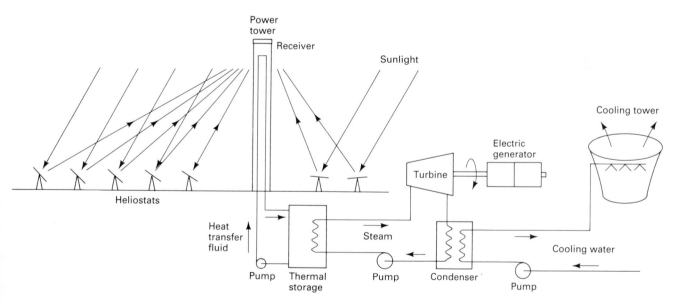

FIGURE 6.22. The basic design of a central tower solar electric power plant in which heliostats direct the sun's rays onto a central receiver. The heat generated is transferred via a fluid to some form of thermal storage facility and is used to raise steam and drive turbines.

FIGURE 6.23. Solar One, on the desert floor near Barstow, California, is an array of 1818 heliostats, each with a surface area of 40 square meters (430 square feet). Computers aim the sun-tracking mirrors to reflect sunlight on the central receiver 100 meters above ground. The receiver absorbs solar heat and converts water to steam that drives a turbine to make electricity. (Courtesy of Southern California Edison Company.)

cells are manufactured by processes similar to those used in making transistors. A variety of materials can be used, and a common one is silicon (see page 243). The manufacture of solar cells is a fairly complex and costly business because the compositions of the materials must be carefully controlled, and very thin wafers of appreciable surface area (at least several square centimeters) must be fabricated.

The economics of large-scale power generation using photovoltaic cells is not very attractive at present. The conversion efficiencies of the cells are fairly low: 12–15 percent for single crystal silicon cells and 4–6 percent for the cheaper, but less reliable, cadmium sulfide/copper sulfide cells. Solar cells have the advantage of using both direct and diffuse radiation and of converting solar energy directly to electricity.

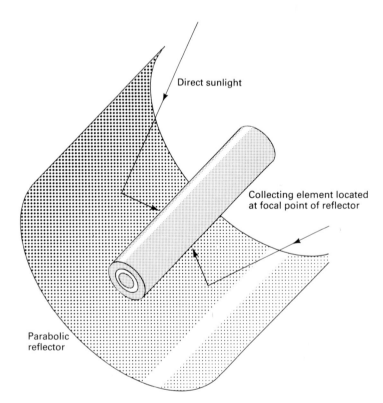

Direct sunlight

Collecting element located at focal point of reflector

Parabolic reflector

FIGURE 6.24. A focusing collector in which a parabolic reflector directs the sun's rays onto a heat transfer fluid located within an evacuated tube to minimize heat losses.

The direct current electricity produced may be used directly or it may be converted to alternating current. It may be attached to storage systems so that power can be supplied even when there is insufficient solar radiation to produce electricity. A typical commercial silicon cell with a diameter of 7 centimeters would have an output of about 0.4 watts when operating in direct sunlight on a clear day. Obviously, very large numbers of these cells have to be mounted together to generate substantial output, and the cost of manufacture and installation is very great. Assuming an overall conversion efficiency of 10 percent for the complete collection-storage-conversion system, a 1000 megawatt power station in an area such as the southwest United States would require roughly 40 square kilometers of cell surface. Indeed, for certain types of solar cell, the energy expended in its manufacture is comparable to that provided by the cell during its working lifetime of a few years. It is not surprising that these cells have mainly been employed as power sources in remote locations (Figure 6.25) and in specialist applications such as solar-powered calculators. Perhaps the most spectacular success of the solar cell in energy generation has been in the powering of both manned and unmanned space vehicles. More widespread use in routine power generation will only come as new manufacturing methods and designs reduce the cost compared with more conventional methods. Nevertheless, major advances in efficiency and reliability of photovoltaic cells have been made in the last decade, and costs have been falling dramatically along with greatly increased production.

The first major photovoltaic project in the third world was installed in Saudi Arabia in 1981. It generates 350×10^3 watts to meet the electricity needs of 3600 people in three villages. Indeed, it is in providing electricity for small isolated communities that this technology may make its greatest contribution. At the other end of the scale, there are plans to complete a 100 million watt power plant near Sacramento, California, in the 1990s. Judging from present and planned power schemes, the total generating capacity at the end of the century may be 5000–10,000 megawatts—only a small fraction of the world's electricity. However, based on the evidence of present growth rates, some experts predict that photovoltaics may be providing 20–30 percent of the world's electricity by the middle of the twenty-first century. One futuristic proposal for massive power generation involves Earth satellites in stationary orbit with very large arrays of photovoltaic cells that collect solar energy, which is then transmitted to Earth by microwave beams (Figure 6.26).

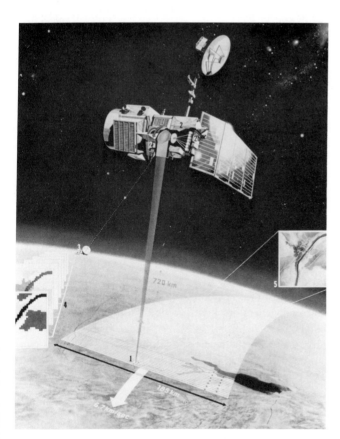

FIGURE 6.25. Solar cells are finding increasing use in remote locations on Earth and on communications satellites. The wings of the satellite shown above are arrays of solar power cells. (Courtesy of COMSAT.)

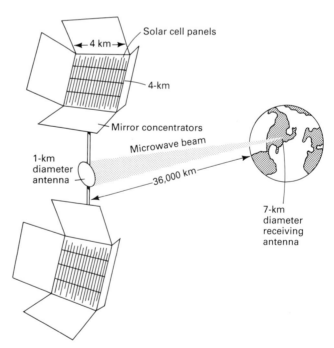

FIGURE 6.26. Schematic illustration of a satellite solar power station. Solar radiation is collected by large arrays of photovoltaic cells, and the electrical energy generated is transmitted to Earth by a microwave beam.

Certain chemical reactions, known as **photochemical reactions,** take place when light energy is supplied, just as many reactions only occur when energy is supplied in the form of heat. The energy used in photochemical reactions may then be held within the products of the reaction as part of the bond energy and may be released later when, for example, these products are combusted as a fuel. The best known example of this is **photosynthesis,** the process in which carbon dioxide from the atmosphere and water are combined to form carbohydrates and more complex organic molecules with the liberation of oxygen. The resulting plant material, such as wood or the fossilized products of this vegetation (coal), can be burned as fuels. Other ways in which biological materials may provide energy are discussed in a later section of this chapter. However, recent research has concentrated on using energy from the sun to bring about chemical reactions in simpler systems and to synthesize fuels. The ideal reaction, if it could ever be made to work in this way, is the breakdown of water.

$$2H_2O \text{ (liquid)} \rightarrow 2H_2 \text{ (gas)} + O_2 \text{ (gas)} \qquad (6.4)$$

The hydrogen gas (H_2) produced would provide an excellent fuel for burning to generate electricity and, of course, the starting material is abundantly available! However, the heat energy required to break down water involves temperatures of 2500°C (which can be achieved in solar furnaces). Research workers have been looking for compounds that could be added to the water to cause the breakdown to occur simply by absorption of the sun's rays (namely, to **catalyse** the reaction). Promising materials (such as a ruthenium complex resembling chlorophyll, the key compound in biological photosynthesis) have been found but require more development. Other researchers are attempting to reproduce photochemical reactions using molecules much more like those used by biological systems. Whether any of these methods will ever become commercially significant will depend not only on their workability but also on their efficiency and the complexity and cost of producing the necessary chemicals.

A potential method for the transformation of solar energy directly to electrical energy, and which involves photochemical processes, is **photoelectrochemical conversion.** This involves directing the sun's rays onto an electrochemical cell, rather like the wet battery cell used to store electrical energy in an automobile. In the normal electrochemical cell the electrical current is generated solely by chemical reactions, but in the **photogalvanic** cell, a photochemical reaction is involved. A photogalvanic cell can also be used to bring about the breakdown of water and to produce hydrogen. All of these cells are still the subject of research and development; that the problems are considerable is illustrated by the fact that the French chemist Becquerel, grandfather of the man who discovered radioactivity in 1895, first discovered the photovoltaic effect in 1839, but it has yet to find a significant technological application.

Hydroelectric, Wind, Wave, Ocean, and Tidal Power

Nature transforms the solar energy reaching the earth into several other forms of energy. About 23 percent of incoming solar radiation is consumed in evaporating the water that subsequently falls as rain and snow (Figure 6.1). In effect, the sun acts as a great pump drawing water from the sea and dropping it onto the land, where it runs downward to the sea. Flowing water is therefore a renewable resource. An additional 46 percent of incoming solar energy is absorbed by the oceans, the land, and the atmosphere. This energy warms the seas and produces ocean currents, winds, and waves. At least some of this can be considered a renewable, potential energy resource.

Water and wind power have both been used in small ways, such as water wheels and windmills, for many thousands of years. Water wheels were known to the ancient Greeks, but the capacity of those water wheels was very small. Toward the end of the eighteenth century, the largest water wheels for industrial use did not exceed 10 horsepower. Nevertheless, they were a major source of power prior to development of the steam engine, which heralded the start of the industrial revolution in Europe. However, it was only at the beginning of the twentieth century that large-scale damming of rivers commenced for generation of electricity.

Hydroelectric Power.   **Hydroelectricity,** the electricity generated by the force of flowing water, is usually produced at large dams (see page 192). Dams are constructed to increase the height from which the water drops (or the *head* of water) and to provide a constant flow of water through turbines, which, in turn, drive electrical generators. Because falling water is a form of mechanical energy directly used to drive the turbines, the two-stage process involved is 80–90 percent efficient in converting that energy to electricity. In fuel-powered generating stations, the heat produced by burning the fuel has to be first converted to mechanical energy by raising steam to drive turbines, which are then used to drive electrical generators; the efficiency of this three-stage process is much less (approximately 40 percent for fossil fuels, approximately 30 percent for nuclear fuels). Where the construction of a dam is not always practical, water may be routed to turbines via canals or large pipes, as in the power plant at Niagara Falls, New York. Hydroelectric power stations are generally very large because large quantities of water are needed to produce even modest amounts of energy. For example, for an elevation change of 50 meters (approximately the height of Niagara Falls), 8 metric tons of water must flow through a turbine to produce 1 kilowatt of electricity.

If a reservoir is present as part of a hydroelectric system, the impounded water acts as a form of stored energy.

Because hydroelectric systems can be started almost instantaneously, this energy can be made available in the form of electricity at very short notice and can serve as a very effective backup system for plants that use other sources of energy. An extension of this idea, now used in a number of countries, is the **pumped-water storage system** (Figure 6.27). When excess electricity is available within a linked network of power plants (often at night), water is pumped from a lower reservoir or storage area to a higher one and is then available to drive turbines and produce electricity when needed.

The installed hydroelectric generating capacity around the world has been steadily increasing throughout this century (Table 6.4). In certain countries, it accounts for a substantial proportion of the electrical energy produced. In the United States, 15 percent of electrical energy is produced from hydroelectric plants, and three times as much water flows daily through hydroelectric plants as is discharged by all rivers into the sea (because of pumped storage and the presence of more than one dam on many rivers). The United States government noted in 1994 that major hydroelectric dam construction in the United States has ended; hence, only through changes in turbine efficiency will any greater production of electricity through hydropower be realized. However, the percentage of this energy source currently developed worldwide is still very small. Evaluation of this resource involves an assessment of the amount of water flowing in streams and rivers and the distance it flows downhill before reaching the sea. The United States Energy Information Administrator's estimate of the world's potential for generating electricity by water power is 29×10^{12} watts, and the distribution of this worldwide is shown in Table 6.4. At present, only about 20 percent of this power has been developed. If it were fully developed, the energy produced each year would be 0.9×10^{20} joule—about one-third of the total energy now consumed and larger than the world's presently installed electrical generating capacity.

Even if the world's community would accept the total damming of its great river systems, the dams have finite and sometimes rather short lifetimes. All rivers carry large masses of suspended sediment that is deposited as soon as the stream is dammed. Depending on the sediment load, many reservoirs will be completely filled by sediment in periods ranging from 50–200 years. For example, the Great Aswan High Dam on the Nile, built in the 1960s, will be at least half silted by the year 2025. Hydroelectric power may be renewable, therefore, but the sites for its generation are nonrenewable. The second point, which is favorable, can be seen from Table 6.4. The world's largest undeveloped potential lies in South America and Africa. Although these continents have small fossil fuel resources, it is fortunate that their water power is so plentiful. The long-term future for hydroelectric power in the Southern Hemisphere must be considered very promising.

Despite the fact that the hydroelectric power generation is renewable and nonpolluting, its generation can create major environmental problems due to resulting changes in river systems. Hydro-Quebec, a Canadian power company, has dropped plans for one of the world's largest hydroelectric facilities east of Hudson Bay in Canada because of public criticism and because the State of New York, expected to be the largest customer, canceled its contracts on the grounds that adequate environmental impact assessments had not been carried out. In 1995, the Chinese, delayed by internal debate and external criticism for decades, finally began construction of the great Three Gorges hydroelectric dam. This will cost more than $25 billion, require 20 years to complete, and displace more than 1 million people, but it will be the world's largest facility and provide power that China believes it needs for its growing population.

Wind Power. Wind has been tapped as an energy source for thousands of years, both through sails on ships and through windmills to lift water and to grind grain. Among the largest windmills were those used in Holland (Figure 6.28a), which have become the picturesque symbol of that country. Smaller windmills were extensively used throughout the United States for pumping water before electricity became available and are still used in many parts of the world (Figure 6.28b). However, the power output under optimal conditions of even the large Dutch-type windmills is considerably less than that produced by a small automobile engine.

In 1895, the first wind-electric system was built in Denmark. By 1910 several hundred small wind-powered generators (5000–25,000 watts) were in operation in that country. It was not until 1931, however, when the former Soviet Union built a 100,000-watt unit near Yalta, that a really large wind turbine expressly designed for producing electricity was constructed. The United States built a two-bladed, 175-foot (53-meter) diameter, propeller-like turbine at Grandpa's Knob, Vermont, that produced 1.25×10^6 watts in a 30 miles per hour (13.4 meters per second) wind—a machine that was tested between 1941 and 1945. Since that time, a great variety of windmill designs have been proposed and some tested using models and prototypes. An example is a machine with a blade nearly 70 meters in diameter and rated at 2×10^6 watts (at 11.5 meters per second) that was built in North Carolina in 1979. An unexpected problem developed, however, when this unit generated a low frequency hum that kept many people in the nearby community awake at night. Efforts to stop the sound were never successful, and the windmill was shut down and dismantled after a mechanical failure. A very different design, sometimes called the Darrieus wind turbine, is a vertical axis machine (Figure 6.29) that is less efficient but can be built to an even larger size. The small (17-meter diameter) machine shown is rated at 3×10^5 watts. The United States, Canada, and many of the northern European countries have programs for the development and installation of larger machines. Indeed, in the United States, the wind Energy Systems Act of 1980 initiated an eight-year, $900 million

FIGURE 6.27. Hydroelectric pump storage facilities such as this one in Bath County, Virginia, generate electricity when water falling through large tunnels in the dam turns turbines. At times of low electricity demand, excess electricity generated in other fossil fuel or nuclear power plants is used to pump water into the reservoir so that it is available to generate power at peak demand times. (Courtesy of Virginia Power.)

TABLE 6.4

International hydroelectric power generation

Area	Total Runoff Potential* watts × 10^11	Exploited Potential watts × 10^11	Potential Exploited percent	Power Generation in 1991** kilowatt hours × 10^12
Europe and Former USSR	5.4	2.4	44	727
Africa and Mid East	7.8	0.2	3	66
South and Central America	5.8	0.9	16	370
North America	3.1	1.6	52	607
Oceania and Far East	6.5	1.3	20	432
TOTAL	28.6	6.4	22	2202

*From M.K. Hubbert, "Energy Resources, A Report to the Committee of Natural Resources." National Academy of Sciences-National Research Council, Publication 1000D, 1962; division of Asia and Far East estimated.
**From Energy Information Administration, *Annual Energy Review,* 1993.

(a)

(b)

FIGURE 6.28. (a) The traditional windmills of Holland have been used to harness wind energy for grinding grain and sawing wood since the middle of the thirteenth century. They also played an important role in shaping the Dutch landscape because from 1414 to the present they have been used to pump lakes dry and lower the water table to create the low-lying agricultural areas known as polders. (Courtesy of Royal Netherlands Embassy.) (b) Simple windmills, such as this one in Patagonia in southern Argentina, are used worldwide to pump water for agricultural and domestic use. (Photograph by J. R. Craig.)

FIGURE 6.29. Modern windmills or wind turbines for use in generation of electricity. In the foreground, the so-called Darrieus wind turbine is a vertical axis machine, whereas the propeller-type machine in the background is a more conventional design. (Courtesy of Southern California Edison Company.)

program to develop wind power systems. A consequence of this has been the sudden growth in **wind farms**—clusters of turbines connected to the electric grid—in parts of the United States. Although the world's first commercial wind farm began generating power in New Hampshire in 1981, the major developments since then have been in California, a state blessed with mountain passes that provide ideal wind farm sites. With farms like the one at Altamont Pass (Figure 6.30), where over 10,000 machines generate up to 142×10^6 watts, the goal is to supply 8 percent of the state's electricity from wind power by the end of the century.

What is the likely future of wind power for large-scale energy generation? There are certainly a number of problems with this technology. The most obvious is that winds blow intermittently and do not readily lend themselves to large-scale power schemes in many parts of the world. Windmills typically operate between 35 and 60 percent of the time. What makes this problem more acute is that a wind turbine has to be designed for maximum output at a particular sustained wind speed. A turbine designed for producing a maximum power output with a wind speed of 10 meters per second, for example, would have an output only one-eighth of this at half the wind speed (5 meters per second). Furthermore, above 10 meters per second wind speed the output would not be increased because the unit already would be at maximum power. At about double the optimum wind speed the blades are "feathered" and power generation cuts out altogether. Further problems, both technical and environmental, are associated with the siting of windmills. Because of the problems of land costs in the more populated areas where electric power is required, problems with radio and television

FIGURE 6.30. The U.S. Department of Energy operates an experimental wind farm with more than 10,000 windmills at Altamont Pass, near San Francisco. (Courtesy of U.S. Department of Energy.)

interference, problems of noise generation, and general disruption of the environment by these large machines, it has been suggested that they might be erected at sea (as, for example, in one British plan to create offshore farms in the windy North Sea). The number of windmills required for a major power generation program would be very large; for example, the generation of 4×10^6 watts in California (8 percent of state requirements) will require between 10,000 and 100,000 machines occupying an estimated 615 square kilometers of land. Despite these problems, the future appears good for wind power, with experts predicting that wind farms will have an economic advantage over coal and nuclear power plants in many parts of the world by the late 1990s. The smaller scale uses of wind power, as in transportation at sea, recreation, and farm use, have long had many applications, and experts also predict a resurgence of small-scale windmills and related devices in the future. We may see a rebirth of the large sailing ship in forms that use not only sails but wind turbines designed to drive propellers (Figure 6.31). Indeed, a Japanese prototype cargo ship employs computer-controlled sails made of canvas on steel frames that can provide 58 percent of the power when the fully laden ship is travelling at 12 knots in a 30 knot wind.

Wave Power. Wave power is closely related to wind power because waves arise from winds blowing over the ocean. Waves contain much more energy than winds of equal velocity because the mass of water involved is more than 800 times that of the same volume of air. A single wave that is 1.8 meters high, moving in water 9 meters deep, generates approximately 10^4 watts for each meter of wavefront. Vast amounts of energy (estimated to be as much as 2.7×10^{12} kilowatt hours per year) are continuously being dissipated on the shorelines of the world. Although wave power has been used to ring bells and blow whistles for navigational aids for many years, large-scale energy recovery has only recently been considered. Over the past decade, many research groups have developed designs and tested small-scale prototypes that they have claimed could generate electricity at costs competitive with conventional power stations. One example is the Sea Energy Associates (SEA) Clam (Figure 6.32), which consists of a series of flexible air bags mounted along a long hollow spine of reinforced concrete. Passing waves compress the bags and force the air into and out of the spine through a turbine. The *self-rectifying* turbine, which turns in the same direction whether the air is moving in or out, drives a conventional electric generator. Other devices involve floating rafts that transmit the mechanical energy of wave motion to hydraulic pumps that power a generator, and rigid concrete structures in which a column of air is trapped in such a way that the volume changes as waves pass, forcing the air through a turbine.

FIGURE 6.31. The Minilace is an experimental cargo ship that uses a sail as well as a conventional engine. The sail can increase speed and decrease fuel consumption, significantly increasing efficiency. (Courtesy of the Wind Ship Development Company.)

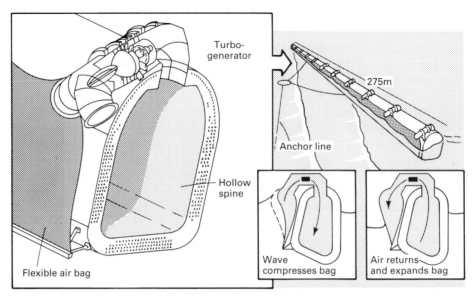

FIGURE 6.32.   The SEA Clam wave energy converter, one of the proposed systems designed to harness wave energy in power generation. The diagram shows how wave motion compresses a flexible bag and forces air through a small self-rectifying turbine into the hollow spine; the air then expands back out. Large numbers of individual units would be assembled in line to form a generating station.

There is no shortage of ideas on how to harness wave power for the generation of electricity. At present, however, the funds to put these ideas into full-scale operation are not available. It has been estimated, for example, that a 2×10^9 watt wave power SEA Clam system, comparable to a large conventional power station, would require 320 SEA Clams along 130 kilometers of coastline. The cost would be considerable, estimated at more than $7 billion at 1995 prices. Because of the cost and because the ultimate potential of wave power is still unclear, many groups and companies that supported the relatively low cost, early development of wave power devices have not yet provided the funds to build more costly prototypes.

Ocean Power.   The term *ocean power* usually refers to a system of **Ocean Thermal Energy Conversion** (OTEC). The sun warms the surface waters of the ocean, and this water, being less dense than the deeper cold water, remains near the surface. A temperature gradient is created as shown in Figure 6.33, and if the water at the two temperatures can be brought together, there is the basis for a heat engine that can generate electricity. The difficulty is the relatively small temperature difference involved—only about 20°C from top to bottom even in the tropics. Although the thermal efficiencies would only be 2–3 percent, the very large reservoir of heat in the oceans should make this feasible. Small pilot plants have been set up and operated earlier this century in Cuba and on the West African coast, demonstrating that OTEC is possible in principle.

Most of the recent development efforts have centered on using a closed-cycle turbine that employs a fluid such as ammonia that boils at a low temperature (25°C) but at a much higher pressure than water. As shown in Figure 6.33, the warm surface water is used to heat the fluid and vaporize it so that it expands through the turbine; it is then condensed back to liquid by contact with cold water pumped from the ocean depths. A power plant would probably be enclosed in a submerged unit floating beneath the ocean surface. Electric power generated from the turbine could be transmitted ashore via submarine cables and possibly used at the site of the plant to produce hydrogen by the electrolysis of water, and the hydrogen could then be shipped in tankers.

Whether large-scale schemes using OTEC are economic remains uncertain; cost estimates vary widely. Unresolved problems include technical aspects of construction, problems of corrosion and encrustation of the machinery with marine organisms, and the environmental impact of OTEC plants. Supporters say that bringing cold nutrient-rich water to the surface would increase fish catches in the area around a plant. But surface sea temperatures play a major role in Earth's climate, and the effects of a large network of OTECs would need careful investigation. If all of these problems were to be solved, a very large source of energy would be made available. Just how large is difficult to estimate because it depends on the efficiency of the generating plant. Even if it were less than 1 percent efficient, the ocean's thermal energy potential exceeds the potential from fossil fuels. Another novel use of the ocean's deep cold waters (approxi-

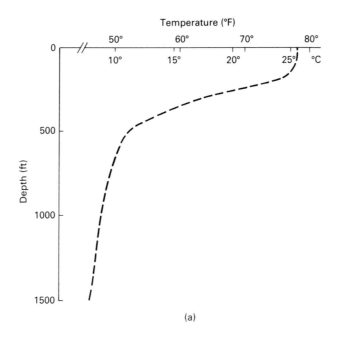

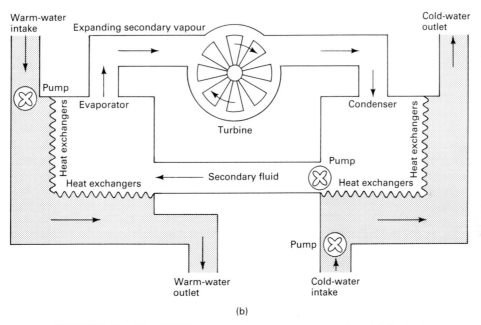

FIGURE 6.33. The OTEC approach to energy generation. (a) Typical temperature variation with depth in the ocean in equatorial regions. This difference is used as the basis for a heat engine cycle of the type illustrated (b).

mately 4°C) does not involve electrical generation but makes use of the water's low temperatures as a refrigerant to preserve foods such as flour and corn and to serve as a tropical air-conditioning system.

Tidal Energy. Tidal energy differs from the other energy sources discussed because it is not derived ultimately from the heat of the sun. The ocean's tides are the result of the gravitational pull of both the moon and sun on Earth and its oceans. The changes in ocean height resulting from the rhythmic rise and fall of tides can be used to drive a water turbine connected to an electric generator. However, only in certain parts of the world is the tidal rise and fall sufficient to justify constructing a power plant. The best areas, where tidal ranges exceed 10 meters, include the Bay of Fundy, the English Channel, the Patagonian coast of Argentina, the Murmansk

FIGURE 6.34. The dam built across the Rance estuary on the French coast is equipped with flood gates and turbines, visible at the right side. As the tides rise and fall, the flow of water in and out through the turbines generates electricity. (Photograph courtesy of Electricite de France.)

coast (Barents Sea), and the coast of the Sea of Okhotsk (north of Japan). Large tidal ranges occur because the effect of ocean bottom shape and contours of the shorelines enhances tidal rise and fall; elsewhere, the range is generally much less.

The harnessing of tides is not a new idea. For several centuries, beginning in 1580, 6.5-meter diameter water wheels installed under London Bridge used the tidal rise and fall of the River Thames to pump water for London. At present, the only large-scale tidal power station in the world is at

the Rance Estuary on the Britanny coast of France (Figure 6.34). This site has a peak electricity-generating capacity of 240×10^6 watts, but because of the rhythmic nature of tides, the average capacity is only 62×10^6 watts. The system involves isolating the estuary from the ocean by a barrage containing turbines and floodgates. At high tide a reservoir behind the barrage is allowed to fill; then the floodgates are closed as the tide goes out. At low tide the elevation of water in the reservoir exceeds that of the ocean by roughly the tidal range. The water can then be used to drive a water turbine and generate electricity in much the same way as a conventional hydroelectric plant. The reservoir level then drops to that of the ocean at low tide, and, if the turbine passages are closed as the tide comes in, the difference in elevation between the high ocean and lower reservoir water levels can also be used to generate power by opening the turbines to fill the reservoir. In this way, power is obtained at high and low tides roughly four times a day.

Tidal power is limited in the number of sites around the world that could be developed and in the total amount of energy potentially available. Development of all of the suitable sites would only generate about 16×10^6 watts, or less than 1 percent of the world's present total usage of electric power.

The oceans contain other sources of energy in the form of the great surface currents. The Gulf Stream, for example, has mechanical power from its flow equal to 2.2×10^{14} watts (or 7×10^{21} joules) per year. Speculative proposals have been put forward for harnessing this vast renewable resource, such as the mooring of massive (170-meter diameter) turbines in the ocean off the coast of Florida (Figure 6.35). The flexible turbine blades would rotate at one revolution per

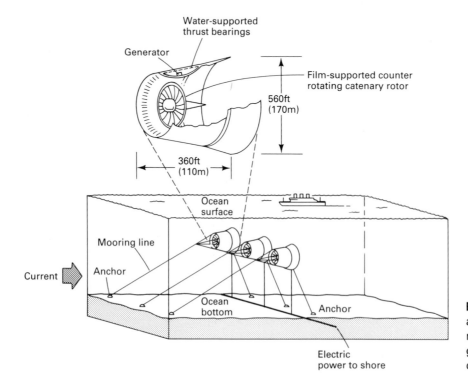

FIGURE 6.35. Proposed design and mooring arrangements of rim-driven turbines for use in generating electrical power from ocean currents.

minute, and it is estimated that 230 such turbines could extract 1×10^{10} watts, enough to supply Florida's electricity needs. Another, as yet totally unexploited, source of energy in the oceans involves salinity, namely, the salinity difference between fresh (river) and salt (ocean) water. The difference in **osmotic pressure** between these two natural waters can produce a positive flow through a suitable membrane that could be used to raise the height of salt water in a column, which could then be discharged through a turbine to generate power.

Geothermal Energy

Except for the near-surface rocks where weather and groundwater conditions exert major influences, temperatures increase with depth in the earth. The rate of temperature increase varies from place to place. Measurements made in deep drill holes around the world show **geothermal gradients** ranging from 15°C to 75°C (with an average of 25°C) per kilometer beneath the surface. Temperature increases are believed to level off at depths of about 100 kilometers with estimates of temperatures in Earth's mantle being around 1000°C and in the core around 5000°C or more. From this it is clear that a vast amount of heat energy is stored within Earth.

The slow but continuous outward flow of heat from Earth averages 6.3×10^{-6} joules per square centimeter per second, or 32.3×10^{12} joules per second (32.3×10^{12} watts) over the entire surface of Earth. The total amount is vast but is very diffuse, and the quantity reaching the surface is equivalent to little more than one three-thousandth (0.003) of the heat received from the sun. If all the heat escaping from 1 square meter could somehow be gathered and used to heat a cup of water, it would take four days and nights to bring it to a boil.

Despite the heat loss, Earth is not cooling; new heat is added continually. Several naturally radioactive isotopes, principally uranium-238, uranium-235, thorium-232, and potassium-40, occur in trace amounts throughout Earth. Each time a radioactive atom disintegrates, a very small amount of heat is released. For example, atoms in an average igneous rock in the continental crust release 9.4×10^{-8} calories (3.93×10^{-7} joules) per gram per day. Although this is not much, summed over the whole Earth it is enough to maintain a nearly constant average temperature distribution. The rate at which new heat is added is so low that we could never harness it, but the accumulated heat from millions of years can be used. However, if it is used at a faster rate than it is replenished, geothermal heat must be considered a nonrenewable resource.

How can geothermal energy be recovered? In certain special circumstances, nature has already provided the answer to this question. In some areas, such as in the vicinity of active volcanoes, abnormally hot rocks are found close to the surface. Groundwater slowly seeping downward is heated

and may reemerge as geysers or hot springs (Figure 6.36). Regions where this occurs are known as **geothermal fields** and are of three types. The first is a field of low-temperature water (≤85°C) that cannot be used efficiently in the generation of power but can be used for space-heating in homes, industry, and greenhouses. Resorts specializing in hot baths, as in the famous "Spa" towns that were popular in eighteenth and nineteenth century Europe, have long used geothermal hot springs. In Hungary and France, geothermal water is still used to heat homes, and in Reykjavik, Iceland, the entire city is heated by geothermal hot water. Although more than 10^9 watts of low-temperature thermal power is derived from geothermal wells worldwide, nearly half of this is in Iceland.

The geothermal energy that is used today as a source of power occurs in either **dry-steam** (vapor-dominated) or **wet-steam** (liquid-dominated) fields. Dry-steam fields occur in geothermal settings where the temperature is high and the water pressure is just above atmospheric pressure. The water boils underground, making steam that fills fractures and pores in the rock, and the steam can be tapped directly by wells drilled into the field. Examples of major dry-steam fields are Larderello in northern Italy that has been producing power since 1904 and the Geysers field in California [about 145 kilometers (90 miles) north of San Francisco] where the first geothermal power plant in the United States was commissioned in 1960 (Figure 6.37). In the 1980s, 17 geothermal power plants were providing over 1×10^9 watts capacity. In the more common wet-steam fields, the reservoir of hot water is under high pressure and may reach temperatures approaching 400°C without boiling. The most famous wet-steam field is at Wairakei in New Zealand.

The use of geothermal fields in electricity generation is shown in Table 6.5. In the 1980s, more than 130 geothermal power plants were operating in over a dozen countries and were producing in excess of 3×10^9 watts. Thus, the total amount of power generated in this way is very small compared to world needs, and the areas where geothermal power has been developed are those of volcanic activity chiefly, areas ringing the Pacific, in Iceland, and in the central Mediterranean. No doubt, other sources will be developed, but they are likely to be localized in areas of active volcanism.

A number of systems are being used or have been proposed for the conversion of geothermal energy into electricity. Two of them are illustrated in a simple way in Figure 6.38. The first is a direct steam cycle of the type used at dry-steam fields such as Larderello and the Geysers; steam brought out of the ground at these sites is clean enough to go directly into the turbine, after which it is condensed and may simply be returned to the ground. The flash steam approach is used in most of the wet-steam fields. In this method, the release of pressure in the flash chamber results in the spontaneous generation of steam to drive the turbines, and the condensed steam is returned to the ground. Two more advanced cycles have been developed for maximum efficiency at lower temperatures. In the flash binary system, the

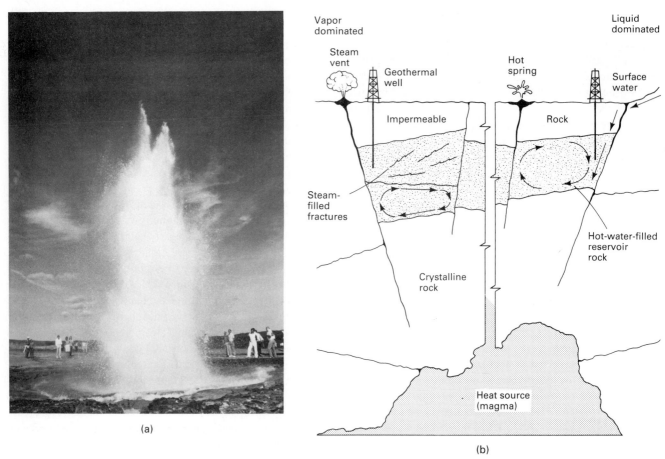

(a)

Vapor
dominated

Liquid
dominated

Steam
vent

Geothermal
well

Hot
spring

Surface
water

Impermeable

Rock

Steam-
filled
fractures

Hot-water-filled
reservoir
rock

Crystalline
rock

Heat source
(magma)

(b)

FIGURE 6.36. (a) Geothermal energy is locally evidenced by natural geysers such as those in Yellowstone National Park, Wyoming. (Courtesy of J.D. Rimstidt.) (b) Schematic diagram to show the geological features of dry-steam and wet-steam geothermal fields.

FIGURE 6.37. The Geysers power plant north of San Francisco, California, is the largest complex of geothermal power plants in the world. The plant began operation in 1960 and is now generating two million kilowatts. The steam rising from stainless steel lined drill holes reaches the surface at more than 355°F and is used to spin turbines to generate electricity. (Courtesy of Pacific Gas and Electric Company.)

TABLE 6.5

Geothermal electricity capacity installed worldwide as of 1992

Country	Total Megawatts
United States	2979
Philippines	894
Mexico	725
Italy	635
New Zealand	286
Japan	270
Indonesia	143
El Salvador	105
Nicaragua	70
Iceland	50
Kenya	45
Others (10 countries)	74
TOTAL of 21 COUNTRIES	6276

From I.B. Fridleifsson and D.H. Freeston, "Geothermal Energy Research and Development," *Geothermics*, v. 23, no. 2, p. 175 (1994).

wet-steam is flashed and vaporizes a working fluid (usually a hydrocarbon) that is expanded through the turbine in a closed circuit, maintaining a clean, long-life turbine. In the liquid-liquid binary system, the brines are not allowed to flash, and heat is transferred to a working fluid to drive the turbine. This reduces some of the problems caused by flashing the brine and also isolates the hydrogen sulfide (H_2S), commonly found in such brines, from the atmosphere. In both cases, the condensed brine is returned to the ground. The practice of simply discharging the condensed brine is a wasteful one that is gradually being replaced by the use of flash distillation to desalinate and produce usable fresh water, or even by the extraction of valuable salts and minerals from the brines.

Several other potential geothermal resources exist, but the technology to exploit them has yet to be developed. The first, sometimes called **geopressured zones,** involves pockets of hot water and methane trapped under high pressure and at fairly high temperature (approximately 175°C) in deep sedimentary basins. Examples occur in the United States along the coasts of Louisiana and Texas at depths of 1200–8000 meters. It is hoped that energy could be extracted from this resource via three routes: the geothermal heat of the water, the hydraulic energy of the water under high pressure (approximately 2000 pounds per square inch at the surface), and the gas dissolved in the water. However, test wells drilled between 1979 and 1981 proved disappointing in terms of water temperatures, gas content, and the extent of this resource. The second potential geothermal resource is usually called **hot dry rock** and, as the name implies, involves extracting the heat from dry rocks at depth. Unlike geopressured

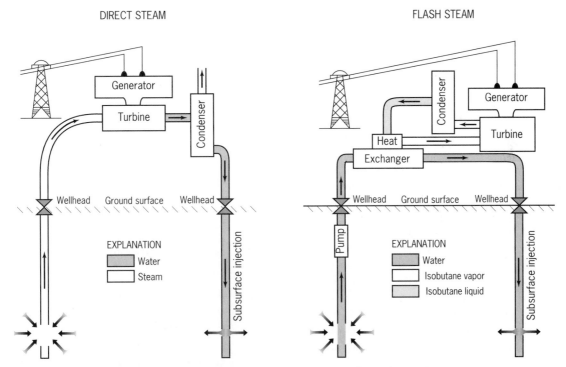

FIGURE 6.38. Systems for the conversion of geothermal energy into electricity. Steam from the geothermal well may be directly used to drive turbines or may be produced by release of pressure in a flash chamber and then directly used. Alternatively, heat from the geothermal fluid may be used to vaporize a working fluid that drives the turbine.

zones, which are limited in extent, the hot dry rock resource is potentially very large worldwide and does not require the rather exceptional geological conditions associated with geothermal fields.

Many parts of Earth's surface are underlain by rocks such as granite that generate more heat than the average rock because of the relatively greater amounts of radioactive atoms they contain or the igneous intrusions that still retain excess heat from the time of their emplacement. The most probable means of exploiting the heat energy involves drilling two boreholes into a mass of granite and then explosively or hydraulically fracturing the zone between the bottoms of the two holes. As water is pumped down the first hole, it passes through the fractured rocks, taking heat from them, and is returned through the second hole to be used for electricity generation when it reaches the surface (Figure 6.39). This method of power generation is not as simple as it sounds. To reach regions with temperatures greater than 200°C generally requires wells around 5–7 kilometers deep that are expensive and difficult to drill. Furthermore, the transmission of fluids between the input and output wells has been plagued with problems, and at the low steam temperatures involved, present turbines are only about 10 percent efficient. Nevertheless, the technical problems can, in some cases, be overcome as shown by a full-depth pilot plant at Los Alamos that generated 6×10^4 watts from granite at 3000 meters. For the ultimate future of geothermal energy, it is also possible to consider drilling into molten magma chambers or exploiting dry rocks at greater depth in areas of only average geothermal gradient.

The extraction of energy from geothermal fields is well established, but as we have seen, it is a resource that is limited geographically and probably also limited in terms of worldwide reserves. The U.S. Geological Survey estimates that down to a depth of 3 kilometers, which seems to be a limit for the occurrence of big geothermal fields, the worldwide reserves are 8×10^9 joules. Such a small amount suggests that this type of geothermal energy will be locally important, but globally insignificant. The total heat energy in the pools is, of course, much larger than 8×10^9 joules, but the estimate takes into account the low efficiency with which electricity can be generated from geothermal steam. Experience in Iceland, New Zealand, and Italy suggests that not more than 1 percent of the energy in a pool can be effectively recovered.

Reserves of energy in geothermal fields represent only a tiny fraction of all geothermal heat. Experts cannot agree how much of the remainder should be considered a potential resource. A map of the United States showing areas and types of potential geothermal resources suggests a very large amount (Figure 6.40). However, the technological problems involved in exploiting even a very small fraction of this geothermal energy are likely to be considerable and the costs prohibitive. In the case of England, for example, it has been estimated that to meet between 1 percent and 2 percent of the

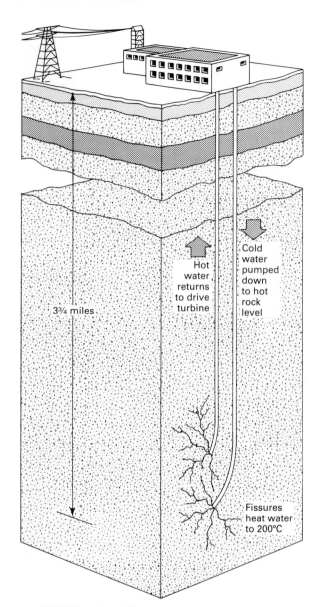

FIGURE 6.39. The generation of electricity using hot dry rock geothermal energy. Cold water is pumped down the well, heated in passing through fissures in the fractured hot rocks at depth, and then is returned to the surface to be used to drive turbines.

national demand for electricity by the year 2000 would require 120 pairs of holes 6000 meters deep costing nearly $2 billion for drilling alone.

Energy from Biological Materials and Waste Products

The staple energy sources in many parts of the developing world are not the fossil fuels or nuclear power plants of the developed nations but are wood and animal dung. In

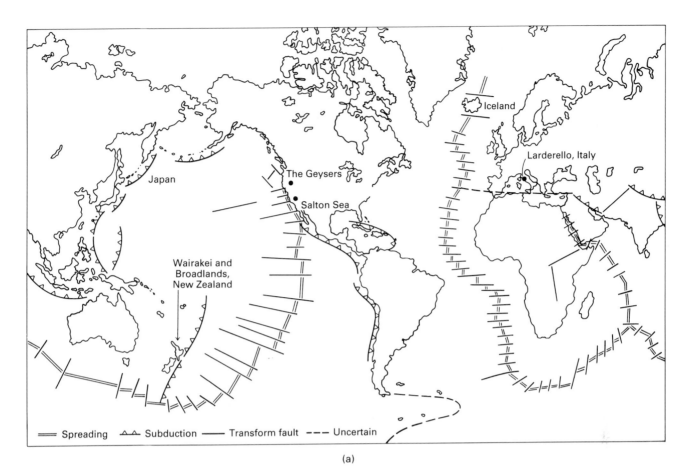

Spreading   △△ Subduction   —— Transform fault   --- Uncertain

(a)

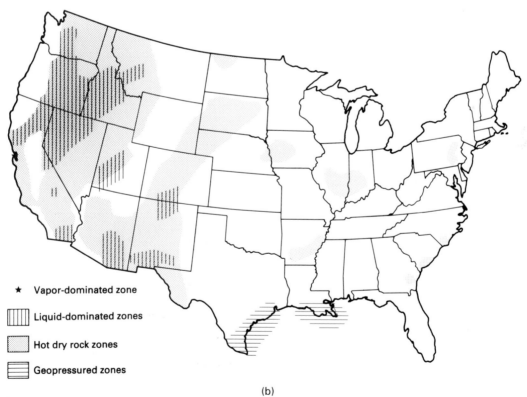

★ Vapor-dominated zone

|||| Liquid-dominated zones

Hot dry rock zones

Geopressured zones

(b)

FIGURE 6.40. (a) The major geothermal areas of the world occur along the major continental plate boundaries. (b) A map of the United States showing the location and types of geothermal resources.

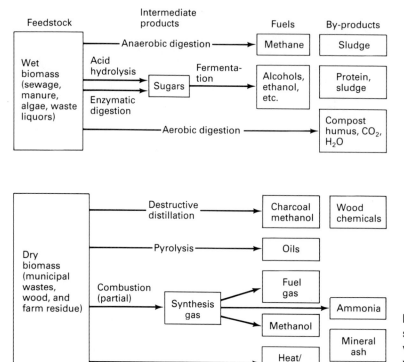

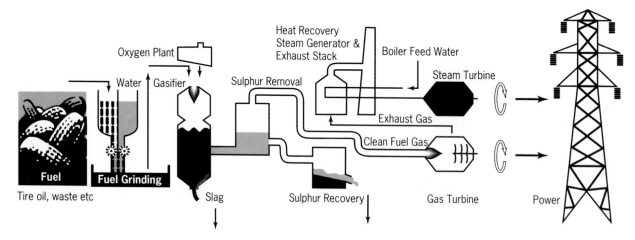

FIGURE 6.41. Block diagram to show how biomass can be converted into fuels, the processes involved, types of fuels produced, and by-products of the operation.

advanced societies, methods are being developed to convert organic wastes and otherwise useless plant materials into more usable forms for energy production. The name given to these wastes, which include manure, sewage, forms of urban refuse, and waste products from crop cultivation and forestry, is **biomass** (Figures 6.41 and 6.42). Considerable quantities of biomass wastes generated by technologically advanced societies are illustrated by the estimated annual figures for

the United States shown in Table 6.6. (The methods of extracting energy from wastes other than biomass have already been discussed in Chapter 4.)

A variety of processes are being developed for the conversion of biomass into fuels, and Figure 6.41 illustrates several of the basic routes. For example, a fermentation process known as **anaerobic digestion** can be used to convert biomass into methane, which can be directly substituted for

FIGURE 6.42. Much waste material (including tires, municipal solid waste, organic debris, etc.) can be used to generate gases that can be burned to generate steam to make electricity or to be used as chemical feed stocks. The nonburnable slags may be useful, and the sulfur in the materials can be recovered.

TABLE 6.6

Approximate values of waste biomass collected in the United States

Sources	Millions Dry Tons/Yr
Municipal	200
Raw sewage	60
Forestry	120
Field crops processing residues	64
Manure	174
TOTAL LAND BIOMASS	618

natural gas. The technology is now available to produce methane gas in this way at costs similar to those involved in the gasification of coal. It is also possible to produce liquid fuels such as alcohols from biomass by a process called **pyrolysis,** which involves heating the organic material in an oxygen-deficient atmosphere. One use of this liquid fuel, much publicized in the United States, is as a partial substitute for gasoline in automobile engines. A mixture of roughly 10 percent ethyl alcohol derived from biomass and 90 percent unleaded gasoline produces a fuel named **gasohol.** Although the energy savings in using gasohol appear to be marginal, if any, precious resources of petroleum are conserved. This is particularly important for countries such as Brazil that have to import large amounts of oil and have, therefore, concentrated in recent years on alternative energy sources.

Brazil produces large amounts of anhydrous ethyl alcohol from sugar cane, sugar beet, cassava, and sorghum. This alcohol is blended with gasoline to produce a gasohol. The amount of alcohol added has been increased gradually up to the 20 percent maximum that can be burned in a conventional engine. Cars that run entirely on alcohol have also been developed, and by early 1983 a majority of new cars purchased in Brazil had alcohol fuel engines. The shift from gasoline to alcohol as a fuel has been particularly attractive in Brazil—a nation with large expenses for oil imports and vast sugar cane producing areas in the depressed northeastern part of the country. Through the efforts of the Brazilian government, alcohol production rose from 1 million barrels/ year in 1976 (providing 1 percent of fuel for automobiles) to 34 million barrels in 1983 (around 25 percent of automotive fuel needs) and to nearly 100 million barrels in the 1990s.

The example of Brazil draws attention to the use of biomass as an energy source, not just as a waste product of other activities. It has been proposed, for example, that single cell algae that are particularly efficient in producing hydrocarbons by photosynthesis could be grown in ponds, harvested, and fermented in a digester to produce methane. This could either be used as a substitute for natural gas or used on site to generate electricity. In the latter case, the carbon dioxide produced from methane combustion could be returned to the growing pond to promote the growth of the algae. The Nobel prize-winning scientist Melvin Calvin be-

lieves that by the end of this century a significant contribution to world energy requirements could be made by plants. He envisages the use of currently unproductive land (thereby avoiding competition with food crops) to grow plants that would be mechanically harvested and dried. This material would be treated with chemical solvents to dissolve out sugars and other hydrocarbons; the sugars could be fermented to produce alcohol. Suitable plants for use as feedstock for such a *green factory* have been identified and include the gopher plant (*Euphorbia lathyris*). From 1000 metric tons of plant material, Calvin suggests it is possible to obtain 80 metric tons of hydrocarbons, 260 metric tons of sugars (that could yield 100 metric tons of alcohol on fermentation), and still have 200 metric tons of woody residue, which can be used as a fuel. The important feature of the green factory is not its energy efficiency, but the fact that it produces liquid fuels and other chemicals (such as feedstocks) that currently depend heavily on oil supplies. The principles involved in the green factory can be extended to a wide range of farming activities both on land and in the sea.

In countries such as the United States, cultivated plants and grains are unlikely to provide a major future source of energy. For example, to satisfy the current United States consumption of natural gas using methane derived from plants would require a land area roughly equivalent to the total presently under cultivation (1.1 million square miles or 2.85 million square kilometers). Nevertheless, recent decades have seen a major resurgence in the fuel that sustained the early development of America—wood. This is largely being used for heating of homes and small industries and in the small-scale generation of steam and electricity. Wood, however attractive as a renewable resource, cannot begin to produce enough energy to be of more than local importance. If wood were substituted for all other fuels, all of the forests in the United States would be cleared in less than five years, so great is the demand for energy. Over a much shorter time span, this would repeat what happened to the forests of Great Britain before coal became the principal energy source.

Nuclear Fusion—the Ultimate Energy Source?

The energy that is emitted by the sun and by other stars throughout the universe results mainly from the process of **nuclear fusion,** in which nuclei of light atoms combine to form heavier atoms. The most promising candidates to provide fusion energy on Earth are heavy isotopes of hydrogen known as deuterium ($^2_1$H) and tritium ($^3_1$H) that can be fused to produce the heavier element helium (He) as $^4_2$He or $^3_2$He. The fusion of two deuterium atoms can produce helium, a free neutron (n), and a great deal of energy.

$$^2_1H + {}^2_1H \rightarrow {}^3_2He + n$$

$$+ \text{ energy (3.2 million electron volts)} \qquad (6.5)$$

A related reaction results in the formation of tritium by fusion of deuterium atoms.

$$^2_1H + ^2_1H \rightarrow ^3_1H + ^1_1H + n$$

$$+ \text{ energy (4 million electron volts)} \quad (6.6)$$

These two reactions are about equally probable when fusion of deuterium atoms occurs, but, whereas in the first case a stable product is formed, in the second the tritium atom reacts with another deuterium atom.

$$^2_1H + ^3_1H \rightarrow ^4_2He + n$$

$$+ \text{ energy (17.6 million electron volts)} \quad (6.7)$$

Therefore, the net result of these three reactions can be written as

$$5\,^2_1H \rightarrow ^4_2He + ^3_2He + ^1_1H + 2n$$

$$+ \text{ energy (24.8 million electron volts)} \quad (6.8)$$

and the energy released per deuterium atom in these fusion reactions is 4.92 million electron volts. The fusion of deuterium and tritium to produce helium and release very large amounts of energy has already been achieved by humans but only in the most uncontrolled and explosive manner imaginable. It is, in fact, the basis of the nuclear weapon known as the hydrogen (H) or thermonuclear bomb. In the H-bomb, the conditions needed for fusion are created by first detonating an atomic bomb. The problem of using nuclear fusion as an energy source for the benefit of humankind consists entirely in the *controlled* and sustained production of such fusion reactions.

The technical problems involved in producing controlled fusion reactions are so great that, despite several decades of research already undertaken, it is most unlikely that commercial fusion reactors could be in operation before the next century. To initiate a fusion reaction such as that involving two deuterium atoms, temperatures greater than 100 million degrees have to be reached. At such temperatures, a gas is so hot that its atoms have been torn apart by collisions into their component electrons and nuclei, and it is known as a **plasma.** This plasma has to be confined to allow collision and fusion, and one means of achieving this is to hold it within a magnetic field that is toroidal in shape (like a doughnut). The success of a Russian toroidal magnetic confinement machine called *Tokamak* has been followed by work along these lines in the United States and England (Figure 6.43). An alternative to this approach is called **inertial confinement** and involves firing a large amount of energy, which may be in the form of laser beams, electron beams, heavy ion beams, or even fragments of discrete matter, into small fragments consisting of a mixture of hydrogen isotopes. Such beams, focused from different directions, can create shock wave compression and heating effects and at the same time confine the plasma. This method aims at producing fusion as a series of small explosions, perhaps several a second, whereas in magnetic confinement systems, a more continuous reaction is the objective. The plasma would have to be heated to the temperature of ignition when, as in putting a match to a flammable material to start a fire, the reaction would begin and the energy released would maintain the temperature and, in turn, would maintain the reaction. Methods of heating the plasma, in addition to compression within an enormous magnetic field, have included shooting beams of neutral atoms into the plasma that collide with particles and raise the temperature, and the use of radio frequency heating—the principle employed in the domestic microwave oven. The system used to confine and heat the plasma must

FIGURE 6.43. Fusion reactors such as the Tokamak reactor, shown in an artist's rendering, generate power by fusion occurring in the central doughnut-shaped chamber. By mid-1986, plasma temperatures above 200 million degrees kelvin had been generated in this chamber for short periods of time. (Courtesy of the Princeton Plasma Physics Laboratory.)

be capable of controlling the three critical factors for fusion: temperature, plasma density, and time. A fusion reactor would, of course, generate energy as large amounts of heat that could be extracted using conventional systems, probably based on those used in fission reactors.

Assuming that the great technical problems involved in controlled fusion can be overcome, what will be the fuel for such power plants and its cost and availability? If a reactor were to be constructed that utilizes the deuterium-deuterium reaction, then seawater would provide a vast supply of this fuel. Seawater contains one deuterium atom for every 6500 atoms of hydrogen, so that one cubic meter of water contains 1.028×10^{25} atoms of deuterium, which, if utilized in deuterium-deuterium fusion, has a potential fusion energy of 8.16×10^{12} joules. This is equivalent to the heat of combustion of 269 metric tons of coal or 1360 barrels of crude oil. If we extend this calculation to estimate the energy that would potentially be derived from one cubic kilometer of seawater, this would be the equivalent to 269 *billion* metric tons of coal or 1360 *billion* barrels of crude oil. The latter figure is of the same order as some estimates of ultimate world resources of crude oil. Therefore, deuterium-deuterium fusion holds the possibility of generating the same amount of energy from a cubic kilometer or so of seawater as would be provided by all of the world's remaining oil; comparable estimates suggest that the world's remaining coal could be matched in energy by a few tens of cubic kilometers of seawater.

However, these calculations assume that the fusion reactor is based on the deuterium-deuterium reaction, whereas much current research is aimed at a controlled deuterium-tritium reaction (as in equation 6.7), which requires far less stringent experimental conditions. Tritium, however, is very much rarer than deuterium and has to be produced by neutron bombardment of another light element, lithium (Li).

$$^{6}_{3}\text{Li} + \text{n} \rightarrow {}^{4}_{2}\text{He} + {}^{3}_{1}\text{H} + \text{energy (4.8 million electron volts)}$$

$$(6.9)$$

and

$$^{7}_{3}\text{Li} + \text{n} \rightarrow {}^{4}_{2}\text{He} + {}^{3}_{1}\text{H} + \text{n}$$
$$+ \text{energy (2.5 million electron volts)} \qquad (6.10)$$

This tritium would then combine with deuterium as in reaction 6.11, and the net result would be equivalent to

$$^{6}_{3}\text{Li} + {}^{2}_{1}\text{H} + \text{n} \rightarrow 2\,{}^{4}_{2}\text{He} + \text{n}$$
$$+ \text{energy (22.4 million electron volts).} \qquad (6.11)$$

Unfortunately, lithium is not available in great abundance (in seawater, for example, it occurs as only one part in 10 million), and the isotope ^{6}Li constitutes only 7.4 percent of natural lithium. It is an element that can be extracted from certain brines and is mined in the form of the mineral spodumene ($\text{LiAlSi}_2\text{O}_6$), which occurs in pegmatite deposits. It is much more limited as a resource, and estimates suggest that if used as a major energy source, it may only last a few hundred years.

The ultimate fuel for fusion reactors would be hydrogen itself, the supply of which is virtually unlimited. It is hydrogen fusion that is chiefly responsible for energy production in the sun and stars, but it requires still greater temperatures, and the technical problems involved in harnessing hydrogen fusion for energy generation are even greater than for the other fusion reactions.

In 1989, two distinguished scientists working in the field of electrochemistry claimed to have achieved a nuclear fusion reaction at room temperature by passing a small electrical current through palladium electrodes immersed in water. In their experiments, they claimed that helium and excess heat were generated by a fusion reaction involving deuterium. Unfortunately, this phenomenon, known as cold fusion, could not be satisfactorily reproduced by other scientists.

Nuclear fusion can potentially provide humankind with an energy source that is almost limitless. A further advantage of nuclear fusion is that hazardous radioactive wastes are not produced as by-products of reactor operation; thus, there is neither the problem of transport nor storage of dangerous fissionable materials. Neutron radiation is produced in fusion, however, as the above equations show, but some scientists believe that reactors could be developed employing reactions such as that of deuterium-^{3}He. Although requiring much higher temperatures than deuterium-deuterium or deuterium-tritium reactions (namely, about 300 million degrees), deuterium-^{3}He reactions produce 10–50 times less neutron radiation. The potential of nuclear fusion as an energy source of the future is obvious, and its limitations lie not in the availability of fuel but in our ingenuity in developing the necessary technology.

THE FUTURE

There is not an energy shortage. Vast amounts of energy are available on Earth—more than we could ever use. Any energy crisis is of our making because we rely too heavily on relatively inexpensive and convenient fossil fuels. There are many alternatives to the fossil fuels as we have shown in this chapter, but each of the alternatives also has drawbacks.

Nuclear energy is still the most likely future energy source in many of the industrialized societies, if only because of the considerable amount of money already spent on research, development, and plant construction. But nuclear energy brings with it great problems. Wastes from nuclear power plants remain lethally radioactive for periods of thousands to tens of thousands of years, and there is still no consensus on how to safely dispose of these wastes. Furthermore, breeder reactors produce more and more fissionable materials that could be used for nuclear weapons.

The other forms of alternative energy discussed in this chapter range from well-established sources such as hydroelectric power to the highly speculative sources such as ocean power and nuclear fusion. Some have obviously limited potential, many are being actively developed on a small scale, and still others require a great deal of research and development before they could ever make a significant contribution.

Which of these alternative sources will replace the fossil fuels will depend on a whole range of economic, social, and political factors, some of which may be undreamed of as yet. Only two points about the future seem now to be certain. Energy needs will continue to rise for at least the near future, and energy sources will have to change. It is vital for many of the technologically advanced societies to prepare for that change, because it will surely involve changes in the need for many other resources and in the lifestyles of future generations.

FURTHER READINGS

BRAUN, G. W., "Commercial wind power." *Annual Reviews of Energy and Environment* 17 (1992) pp. 97–121.

GRAY, T. J. and GASHUS, D.K., *Tidal Power.* New York: Plenum Press, 1972.

HUNT, S. E., *Fission, Fusion and the Energy Crisis,* 2nd ed. New York: Pergamon Press, 1980.

MERRICK, E. (ed.), *Energy, Present and Future Options.* New York: John Wiley and Sons, 1984.

National Academy of Sciences, *Energy in Transition 1985–2010.* San Francisco: W. H. Freeman and Co, 1979.

Office of Civilian Radioactive Waste Management, "Nuclear Waste." U.S. Department of Energy (DOE/RW-0361TG), 1992.

Office of Civilian Radioactive Waste Management, "Ionizing Radiation." U.S. Department of Energy (DOE/RW-0362TG), 1992.

Office of Civilian Radioactive Waste Management, "The Waste Management System." U.S. Department of Energy (DOE/RW-0363TG), 1992.

Office of Civilian Radioactive Waste Management, "The Nuclear Waste Policy Act." U.S. Department of Energy (DOE/RW-0364TG), 1992.

RINEHART, J. S., *Geysers and Geothermal Energy.* New York: Springer Verlag, 1980.

RUEDISILI, L. C. and FIREBAUGH, M.W., *Perspectives on Energy,* 2nd ed. New York: Oxford University Press, 1978.

WOHLETZ, K. and HEIKEN, G., *Volcanology and Geothermal Energy.* Berkeley, University of California Press, 1992.

7 ABUNDANT METALS

The bridge at Ironbridge, constructed between 1775 and 1779 on the Severn River in England, was one of the first major structures constructed of iron. It remains today as a monument to the Industrial Revolution. (Courtesy of the Ironbridge Gorge Museum Trust.)

If we remove metals from the service of man, all methods of protecting and sustaining health and more carefully preserving the course of life are done away with. If there were no metals, men would pass a horrible and wretched existence in the midst of wild beasts; they would return to the acorns and fruits and berries of the forest. They would feed upon the herbs and roots which they plucked up with their nails. They would dig out caves in which to lie down at night, and by day they would rove in the woods and plains at random like beasts, and inasmuch as this condition is utterly unworthy of humanity, with its splendid and glorious natural endowment, will anyone be so foolish or obstinate as not to allow that metals are necessary for food and clothing and that they tend to preserve life?

Georgius Agricola, De re metallic, 1556 . Translated by H.C. Hoover and L.H Hoover, 1912. Dover Publications Inc, New York, 1950.

FOCAL POINTS

- Metals are extracted from ores derived by mining of *ore deposits;* the mineability of such deposits depends upon such factors as their mineralogy, grade, size, and location.
- The abundant metals, those which have an average concentration in Earth's crust of 0.1 percent or greater, are magnesium, aluminum, silicon, titanium, manganese, and iron.
- Iron accounts for more than 95 percent of all the metal used today.
- Iron deposits occur in all types of rocks; the primary minerals from which iron is extracted are hematite (Fe_2O_3), magnetite (Fe_3O_4), and goethite ($FeOOH$).
- The largest iron deposits in the world are the *banded iron formations;* these formed as chemical precipitates in the Precambrian oceans, probably coinciding with the generation of oxygen by the first photosynthesizing plants.
- Iron smelting is carried out by reducing iron oxides to iron metal by reaction with carbon monoxide gas, usually derived from coke.
- World steel production has risen steadily since 1950, although production in the United States and other western countries has remained approximately constant; thus, for example, the United States proportion has dropped from nearly 50 percent to about 10 percent.
- Manganese, a metal vital to steel production, is mined in many countries (although not the United States); it also occurs as ferromanganese nodules on many parts of the deep ocean floor.

- Aluminum, derived from bauxite (a soft heterogeneous mass of aluminum hydroxides occurring as a "soil" in some areas), has become the second most widely used metal because of its light weight, ability to conduct electricity, noncorrosive nature, and workability; the major drawback of aluminum is the large amount of energy needed to extract it from its ores.
- Titanium, although used in many advanced technologies, is used primarily in the preparation of white paint pigment.
- Magnesium, the lightest of the abundant metals, is used in the preparation of refractories and in lightweight alloys with aluminum.
- Silicon, the most abundant metal in Earth's crust, has long been used in steel manufacturing and is being increasingly used in new technologies, for example, in solar cells and computer chips.

METALS AND THEIR PROPERTIES

Metals are unique among the chemical elements in being opaque, tough, ductile, malleable, and fusible and in possessing high thermal and electrical conductivities. Approximately half of the chemical elements possess some metallic properties, but all true metals have two or more of the special metallic properties. Our early ancestors were drawn to the use of metals because they are tough (but not brittle as stone), malleable, and can be melted and cast. These same properties are important today, but we also rely heavily upon the special electrical and magnetic properties of metals and their machinable characteristics. Without metals, technology as we know it could not have come into being, nor could it be continued.

Today, approximately 30 metallic elements are made commonly available through mining and processing of their ores. Although many metallic elements are used in their pure forms because of unique properties, modern society commonly finds that chemical mixtures (**alloys**) of two or more metals, or metals and nonmetals, have superior characteristics. The alloys are also metallic but usually have properties of strength, durability, or corrosion resistance that exceed the properties in the component pure metals. Examples of common alloys are steel, brass, bronze, and solder. **Steel** is an alloy in which the main constituent, iron, is combined with other metallic elements such as nickel, vanadium, or molyb-

denum or a nonmetallic element such as carbon. Steels are tougher, less brittle, and more resistant to wear than iron alone. Brass is an alloy of copper and zinc. It melts at a lower temperature than copper, the metal it most nearly resembles, and it is much easier to cast. Bronze was the first alloy used by our ancestors and was developed about 3500 B.C. This alloy of copper and tin melts at a relatively low temperature, is very easily cast, is harder than pure copper, and is corrosion resistant. Common solder is an alloy of lead and tin that has an especially low melting temperature. The molten alloy has the property of melting or combining with certain other metals. This property allows a solder, when cooled and solidified, to effect a joint between two pieces of the same metal, or, in some cases, two fragments of different metals.

THE NATURE OF ORE DEPOSITS

Metals can be separated into groups, as discussed in Chapter 1, on the basis of their abundances in Earth's crust (see Figure 1.6). The abundant metals are those that individually make up at least 0.1 percent by weight of Earth's crust. There are only six such metals—silicon, aluminum, iron, magnesium, manganese, and titanium (Table 7.1). Silicon, though significantly different in physical properties from other metals, is included in the following discussion because of its importance in iron smelting. All other metals occur in much

TABLE 7.1

The abundant metals

Element	Symbol	Atomic No.	Atomic Wt.	Crustal Abundance (%)	Specific Gravity (g/cc)	Melting Point (°C)
Magnesium	Mg	12	24.31	2.3	1.74	649
Aluminum	Al	13	26.98	8.2	2.70	660
Silicon	Si	14	28.09	28.2	2.33	1410
Titanium	Ti	22	47.90	0.57	4.50	1660
Manganese	Mn	25	54.94	0.095	7.20	1244
Iron	Fe	26	55.85	5.6	7.86	1535

lower concentrations and are thus categorized as scarce metals; these are discussed in Chapter 8. Many kinds of common rocks contain significant quantities of several of the abundant metals and small amounts of the scarce metals, but few of these rocks can now, or ever will, be considered as resources or ores from which we will extract the metals. It is helpful to recall the discussion in Chapter 1 that defined ores (reserves) as deposits that can be worked profitably for *economic* or *strategic* reasons. Thus, there are important distinctions between average rocks, in which the concentrations of elements are too low to be profitably extracted, local concentrations that may be rich but too small for consideration, and **ore deposits** that may be economically exploited.

Many factors determine whether or not a given rock is an ore, not only of the abundant metals but of any metals; these have been discussed at length in Chapter 4, but it is worthwhile to recall that the most important are

1. mineralogy
2. grade
3. grain size and texture
4. size of the deposit
5. depth of the deposit
7. geographic location
8. possible by-products

The mineralogy, or the form in which a metal is held, and the grade or proportion of metal content are the most important factors because they determine the process and the energy that must be used to extract the metal and the value of the extracted product. Each of the abundant metals occurs in a wide variety of minerals, but it is only the few listed in Table 7.2 that serve as **ore minerals** for these metals. Iron is present in large quantities in minerals such as fayalite (Fe_2SiO_4) and pyrite (FeS_2), but neither is mined primarily as an iron ore because of the large amounts of energy needed to extract the iron from the fayalite and the pollution problems resulting from extraction of the iron from the pyrite make use of these minerals noneconomical. Similarly, aluminum is present in many silicate minerals, but the extraction is generally prohibitively expensive relative to that for the minerals listed.

The grain size and texture determine the methods of processing and extraction and may, in the case of very fine grain size, actually make rich ores unworkable. The size and depth of the deposit control the mining method and, hence, much of the cost. Geographic location influences accessibility, environmental conditions, and even the tax or royalty changes incurred in mining.

The recovery of by-products commonly helps make the mining of mineral deposits profitable; in fact, some important metals (for example, cadmium, gallium, germanium) are recovered almost only as by-products. The abundant metals are generally recovered from ores in which they are the only metal refined, but many ores of the scarce metals yield a variety of useful by-product metals. The by-products are not present in sufficient grades to warrant their being mined alone, but they are recovered at little or no additional cost when mining the major metal, and their sales help pay for the total mining operation. In many instances, the by-products (that may also include waste rock products such as sand or agricultural limestone as well as metals) have helped make

TABLE 7.2

The abundant metals and their principal ore minerals

Metal	Important Ore Minerals	Amount of Metal in the Ore Mineral
Silicon	Quartz (SiO_2)	46.7
Aluminum	Boehmite ($AlO \cdot OH$)	45.0
	Diaspore ($AlO \cdot OH$)	45.0
	Gibbsite ($Al(OH)_3$)	34.6
	Kaolinite ($Al_2Si_2O_5(OH)_4$)	20.9
	Anorthite ($CaAl_2Si_2O_8$)	19.4
Iron	Magnetite (Fe_3O_4)	72.4
	Hematite (Fe_2O_3)	70.0
	Goethite ($FeO \cdot OH$)	62.9
	Siderite ($FeCO_3$)	62.1
	Chamosite ($Fe_3(Si,Al)_2O_5(OH)_4$)	45.7
Magnesium	Magnesite ($MgCO_3$)	28.7
	Dolomite ($CaMg(CO_3)_2$)	13.1
Titanium	Rutile (TiO_2)	60.0
	Ilmenite ($FeTiO_3$)	31.6
Manganese	Pyrolusite (MnO_2)	63.2
	Psilomelane ($BaMn_9O_{18} \cdot 2H_2O$)	46.0
	Rhodochrosite ($MnCO_3$)	39.0

mining operations profitable when major metal prices have fallen or when the grades of the major metals have been insufficient alone to keep a mine profitable.

Our attention in this chapter will be focused on the **abundant metals,** which are used in great quantity in our society; in the following chapter, we shall consider the important **scarce metals.** The ore minerals of the abundant metals are listed in Table 7.2. Note that the minerals are all simple oxides, hydroxides, or carbonates. Even though silicate minerals are by far the most abundant in Earth's crust, they are rarely used as the sources for metals because they are difficult to handle and extremely expensive to smelt. However, it may be that the future will see many silicate minerals being used, but at present only two silicate minerals, kaolinite and anorthite, are viewed as potential ore minerals. Where geochemically scarce metals are concerned, silicate minerals are sometimes used under special circumstances. Examples are beryl ($Be_3Al_2Si_6O_{18}$), which is used as a source of beryllium because there are few other minerals containing this metal, and willemite (Zn_2SiO_4), which was mined for zinc in one locality where the high grade of the ore warranted its recovery.

IRON: THE BACKBONE OF INDUSTRY

Iron is the third most abundant metal in the crust, but historically it has been the workhorse of industry. Today it accounts for more than 95 percent by weight of all metals consumed and a significant proportion of the remainder—most of the nickel, chromium, molybdenum, tungsten, vanadium, cobalt, and manganese—are mined principally for use in the steel industry. The reasons for iron's dominance are not hard to find—the first is the abundance and ready accessibility of rich iron ores; the second is the relative ease with which the smelting process can be carried out; the third, and most important, is the special property of iron and its alloys that allows it to be tempered, shaped, sharpened, and welded to give a product that is exceptionally strong and durable. No other metal enjoys the same range of versatile properties. Rudyard Kipling in his brief poem "Cold Iron" captured the versatility of iron in a striking way.

> Gold is for the mistress—silver for the maid
> Copper for the craftsman, cunning at his trade.
> 'Good!' Said the Baron, sitting in his hall,
> but iron—cold iron—is master of them all.

Iron is the most extensively used metal in the world, and there is virtually no part of our society that does not make use of iron and steel products in some manner. In recent years, total world production of iron and steel has exceeded 1 billion (10^9) metric tons, and in countries such as the United States more than 600 kilograms per capita are used. Although the end products of iron and steel are nearly countless, the major categories for use in industrialized societies today (and their approximate percentages of total use) are construction (30 percent), transportation (25 percent), and machinery (20 percent). Other important uses include grocery cans, home appliances, and oil, gas, and water drilling equipment. Today, we take for granted the ready availability of iron and steel in a large variety of forms. It was not always so, and we need go back only about 250 years to recount the advances that have led iron and steel to their positions of prominence today.

Iron Minerals and Deposits

Iron, because of its crustal abundance and its chemical reactivity, occurs in hundreds of different mineral forms. However, like the other abundant metals, it is economically extracted from only a few minerals (Table 7.2). The iron oxides, **hematite** (Fe_2O_3) and **magnetite** (Fe_3O_4), are the most important ore minerals and will no doubt continue to be for many years. The other ore minerals were important in the past and are still locally significant today.

Iron deposits occur worldwide (Figure 7.1) and have formed as a result of many different processes throughout geologic time. The behavior of iron in geologic processes, especially at Earth's surface, is strongly influenced by its ability to exist in more than one oxidation state. Under the reducing conditions that may exist beneath Earth's surface and in some deep relatively oxygen-free waters, iron may exist in the **ferrous** state, (Fe^{2+}). In this form, iron is relatively soluble, and it may form ferrous minerals such as siderite ($FeCO_3$), chamosite ($Fe_3(Si,Al)_2(O_5(OH)_4)$), and mixed ferrous-ferric minerals such as magnetite. At Earth's surface and wherever oxygen is abundant, the iron oxidizes to its **ferric** state (Fe^{3+}), an extremely insoluble form, and is deposited in ferric minerals such as hematite or **goethite** ($FeO \cdot OH$). Iron deposits have formed by **igneous, metamorphic,** and **sedimentary** processes. There are many distinct types of deposits, but nearly all of the major deposits mined today or in the recent past are of only a few types. These will likely continue to serve as our major sources of iron ore and are concisely described below.

Deposits Formed through Igneous Activity. Three major types of iron ores arise from igneous activity: (1) accumulation in large **mafic** intrusions, (2) contact metamorphic deposits, and (3) ores formed through submarine volcanism.

Large mafic igneous intrusions, such as the Bushveld intrusion in the Republic of South Africa, commonly contain significant concentrations of magnetite. In these intrusions, much of the magnetite was precipitated in thick layers as it crystallized and settled out of the magma onto the floor of the

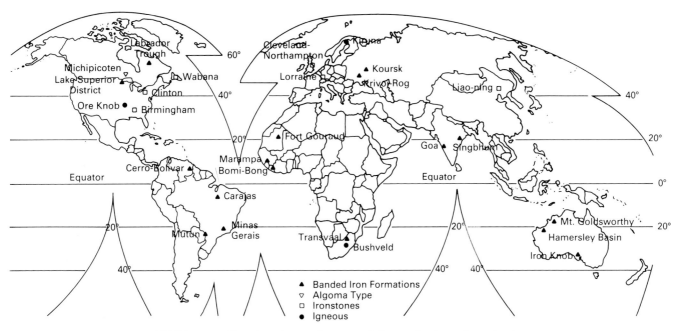

FIGURE 7.1. The locations of some of the major iron deposits in the world. The banded iron formations constitute the world's major reserves.

chamber. The total amount of magnetite in the igneous rock may be only a few percent, but its occurrence in nearly pure layers makes its mining convenient. Although these accumulations in basic igneous rocks are not presently mined for their iron content, in the Republic of South Africa they serve as important ores of the vanadium that is concentrated in the magnetite (see Chapter 8 and Figure 8.8 on page 256).

Contact metamorphic deposits form where iron-bearing fluids given off by igneous intrusions react with adjacent rocks, especially limestones (Figures 7.2 and 7.3). The hot fluids given off by the cooling intrusions react with—and sometimes completely replace—the wall rocks, leaving a mixture of coarse-grained iron oxides and a host of unusual metamorphic minerals. Most of these occurrences are too small to be economically recovered, but in the United States at localities such as Cornwall and Morgantown, Pennsylvania; Iron Springs, Utah; and Pilot Knob, Missouri, massive rock contact deposits were mined for many years.

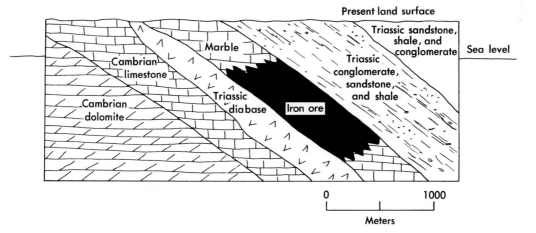

FIGURE 7.2. The Cornwall mine in Pennsylvania is an example of a contact metamorphic iron oxide deposit formed where iron-rich fluids from an intrusive Triassic diabase replaced part of a limestone bed with magnetite. The relationship of the ore to the limestone, converted to marble near the intrusion, is shown in the cross section.

FIGURE 7.3.   A view of the open pit mine at Cornwall, Pennsylvania, in which the massive magnetite ore (dark zone in the base of the pit) is visible below the white marble formed by metamorphism of the original limestone. (Photograph courtesy of Bethlehem Steel Corporation.)

Sea floor volcanism is almost always accompanied by submarine hot springs that issue forth solutions rich in iron and silica. The rapid cooling and oxidation of the solutions as they mix with seawater results in the precipitation of iron oxide and silica known as **Algoma-type** deposits, after the locality in the Canadian Shield where they were first recognized. A few of these deposits in Canada and elsewhere have proven rich enough to mine, but most are too small or too low in grade to be successfully worked.

Residual Deposits.   These deposits of iron minerals are formed where the weathering process oxidizes ferrous iron in rocks and leaves behind concentrations of the insoluble ferric minerals. This process accounts for the brown, yellow, and red colors that are familiar in most soils. Locally, especially in tropical regions where the chemical reactions are more rapid because of higher temperatures and abundant rainfall, the weathering process removes the more soluble compounds and leaves concentrated residues of iron oxides and hydroxides. These types of deposits, known as **brown ores,** have been forming since Precambrian times and are widespread. Most of the deposits are small, however, and although locally important in the past, are not considered economical in terms of today's large-scale mining operations.

In tropical regions, the intensive leaching process has left large areas of hard red residual soils known as **laterites** (Figure 7.4), a name derived from the Latin *latere* meaning *brick*. These soils are poor agriculturally and often become worse when they are used for farming because the exposure causes $Fe(OH)_3$ in the soil to irreversibly convert to $FeO \cdot OH$. This dehydration reaction is similar to the reaction that occurs when clays are baked to form bricks. The soils become so hard that they do not absorb moisture and become unworkable. Where most intensely developed, laterites may contain 30 percent or more iron and may represent large future sources of iron. The tonnages of iron potentially avail-

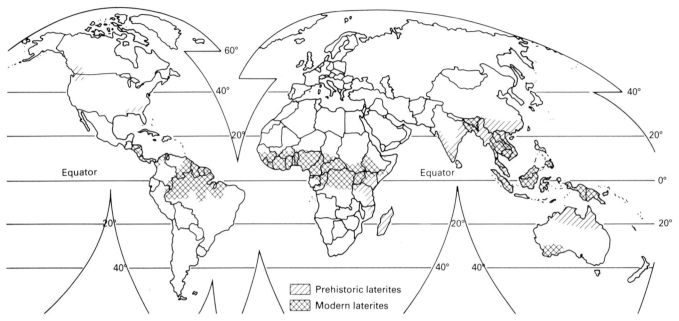

FIGURE 7.4. Laterites are hard, red, residual soils rich in iron minerals that formed in tropical to subtropical regions. The shaded regions on the map show where intense leaching has removed more soluble compounds and formed iron-rich lateritic soils.

able from the lateritic soils probably exceed those from all other sources by a factor of at least ten, but their mining would cause massive environmental problems.

Sedimentary Deposits. Three important types of iron ores have formed through sedimentary processes: **bog iron deposits, ironstones,** and **banded iron formations.** The bog iron deposits are the smallest of these types of sedimentary deposits. Although not mined today, they provided ore for many early European operations and the first iron ore to the fledgling American industries in the seventeenth and eighteenth centuries. These deposits form locally in glaciated regions and in coastal plain sediments where iron, originally put into solution by the reducing conditions created by decaying organic matter, is oxidized and precipitated as lenses and sedimentary cements (Figure 7.5). The deposits are generally quite local in extent and are highly variable in grade.

Ironstones are iron-bearing formations that are much larger and more important than bog iron deposits. The ironstones are continuous sedimentary beds that may extend for tens or even hundreds of kilometers and are a few meters to tens of meters in thickness. In many respects they are similar

to many other sedimentary rocks, containing cross-beds, abundant fossils, oolites, facies changes, and other sedimentary features. The main difference is that they contain significant amounts of goethite, hematite, siderite, or chamosite (a complex iron aluminum silicate) as coatings on mineral fragments, as oolites, and as replaced fossil fragments (Figure 7.6).

The origins of the ironstones are not clear, but they appear to represent shallow, near-shore marine, and rarely, freshwater sediments where the formation of the iron minerals occurred both as direct sedimentation and as a diagenetic replacement. The distribution of the individual iron minerals was controlled by the nearness to shore, the water depth, and the amount of oxygen in the water (Figure 7.7). In the shallowest areas, the abundance of oxygen resulted in oxidation of the iron to the ferric state and the formation of goethite, whereas in the deeper areas, richer in carbon dioxide but poorer in oxygen, the iron precipitated in the form of siderite or chamosite.

In both instances, the iron must have been transported to the sites of deposition in the more soluble ferrous state, either as groundwater or as deep basin fluids. The special

FIGURE 7.5. Bog iron ores form where reduced iron carried in groundwater is oxidized and precipitates as insoluble ferric iron compounds.

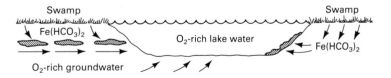

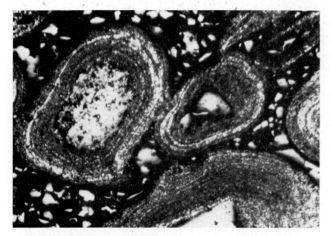

FIGURE 7.6. Ironstones consist of pellets, cements, oolites, and fossil fragments that have been infilled and replaced by iron hydroxides. This microscopic view is of an area 1 millimeter across.

conditions that led to the formation of the ironstones are believed to have resulted from generally warm and humid climates that permitted the generation of abundant organic matter. This resulted in significant amounts of organic acids and carbon dioxide in groundwater solutions that then readily reduced and dissolved iron minerals in the soils and rocks. The leached iron moved slowly via the groundwater system into lakes or shallow marine basins where iron accumulated. In some cases, the iron minerals precipitated directly on the seafloor or lake floor; in others, the iron minerals replaced calcium carbonate minerals, fossils, and oolites or were precipitated by diagenetic processes interstitially among the other minerals.

The ironstones have formed since the beginning of the Cambrian Period, a time span inclusively called the Phanerozoic Eon. Consequently, these ores have sometimes been referred to as the **Phanerozoic type.** Iron ores of this type have been very important in Europe where they are collectively referred to as the **Minette type** and where they supplied much of the ores for the iron and steel industries of the United Kingdom, France, Germany, and Belgium. In North America, where Appalachian examples of these ores are called the **Clinton** (or **Wabana**) **type,** they were important resources from the late eighteenth until the mid-twentieth century. Today, the importance of these ores is much diminished because the richest areas have been mined-out and because banded iron formations are more economical to work.

The largest concentrations of iron oxides are found in banded iron formations (commonly called BIFs), which today supply most of the world's iron ores and constitute the bulk of the world's iron ore reserves (Table 7.3). They are also known as **Lake Superior-type** ores after the large deposits that are mined in the United States. Formations of this type occur in the Precambrian rocks of all continents and are mined extensively in the United States, Canada, Brazil, Venezuela, Australia, India, China, and the former Soviet Union (Figure 7.1). A wide variety of terms has been applied to deposits of this type in different parts of the world. Commonly encountered names for silica-rich ores are **taconite** (in the United States), **itabirite** (in Brazil), or **banded jaspilite** (in Australia). They are from 30–700 meters in thickness and

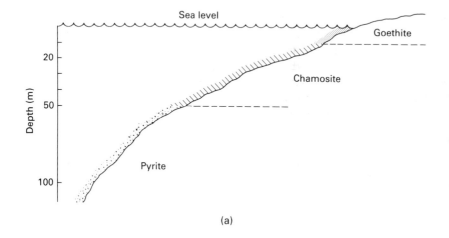

(b)

FIGURE 7.7. (a) Schematic diagram showing the relationship of water depth with different facies of iron minerals forming today. (b) Ironstones mined on the Yorkshire coast of eastern England were major sources of iron for the Industrial Revolution. Today, the old workings are visible along the rocky coast. (Photograph courtesy of F. M. Vokes.)

TABLE 7.3

World iron ore reserves and production in the early 1990s in millions of metric tons

	Mine Production 1993	Crude Ore		Iron Content	
		Reserves	Reserve base	Reserves	Reserve base
United States	55.2	16,100	25,000	3,800	6,000
Australia	120.0	16,000	28,100	10,200	17,900
Brazil	148.0	11,100	17,300	6,500	10,100
Canada	35.0	11,900	25,500	4,600	10,000
China	200.0	9,000	9,000	3,500	3,500
France	5.0	2,200	2,200	900	900
India	55.0	5,400	12,100	3,300	6,300
Liberia	2.0	900	1,600	500	800
Mauritania	10.3	400	700	200	300
South Africa	29.0	4,000	9,300	2,500	5,900
Sweden	20.0	3,000	4,600	1,600	2,400
Former Soviet Union	200.0	63,700	78,000	23,500	29,000
		2,000	3,300	1,200	1,700
Other countries	59.7	5,400	12,500	2,300	6,300
World total (may be rounded)	940.0	150,000	230,000	65,000	100,000

often extend over hundreds to thousands of square kilometers. Many of these deposits, including all in the United States and Canada, have been metamorphosed to some degree, so that they now consist of fine-grained magnetite and/or hematite in a matrix of quartz, iron silicates, and iron carbonate in a very compact, finely laminated rock (Figure 7.8). The BIFs, like the ironstones, commonly display strong facies development, indicating that at the same time differing conditions resulted in the formation of iron oxide-rich zones closest to shore and iron carbonate or iron silica zones farther out into the basin. The iron contents of the BIFs vary widely; the presently mined deposits typically have 20–40 percent iron.

The banded iron formations have produced billions of tons of ore and now are the world's major source of iron; however, their modes of origin remain somewhat enigmatic. Banded iron formations, which are present on all continents, have several major characteristics in common. The most important is that most, if not all, of them formed during the period of 2.6 to 1.8 billion years ago. They all exhibit the typical banding visible in Figure 7.8, and all are very low in aluminum content and are nearly free of common detrital sedimentary debris. They resemble the Algoma-type deposits in that they consist of fine layers of silica and iron oxide minerals, but the BIFs are much broader in extent and do not show any apparent relationship to submarine volcanism. Detailed studies of the BIFs indicate that they were formed in broad sedimentary basins following prolonged periods of continental weathering and erosion and the inundation of the land surface by shallow seas. The erosion had previously removed most detrital debris so that deposition in the basins was largely that of chemical precipitates. The origins of the

iron are not clear, but it is likely that it was derived from several different sources including weathering of continental rocks, leaching of marine sediments, and submarine hydrothermal systems that discharged iron-rich fluids onto the seafloor. Today it would be impossible to transport the huge quantities of iron from eroding land surfaces in rivers and streams or to disperse it widely from submarine vents because it would be quickly precipitated in the insoluble ferric

FIGURE 7.8. Banded iron formations (BIFs) may have very regular layering or display irregular banding as shown. The light-colored bands consist of nearly pure iron oxides (hematite and magnetite), whereas the darker zones are nearly pure silica.

form. However, during the Precambrian period when the BIFs formed, there was probably little free oxygen in Earth's atmosphere or dissolved in surface waters. The carbon dioxide content of the atmosphere was probably much higher and gases such as methane (CH_4) could have been present. Under these conditions, rainwater, stream and lake waters, and ocean waters would have been slightly acidic and much less oxidizing—conditions that would have allowed for the ready transport of iron in solution in the soluble ferrous form. The iron accumulated in the broad shallow basins and gradually precipitated as iron oxides and hydroxides. The cause of the repetitive precipitation of layers of alternating iron oxides and silica has been a point of much debate. Annual climatic changes, cyclical periods of evaporation, the effects of microorganisms altering silica availability and releasing oxygen, and episodic volcanism are some of the many suggested causes. Whatever our final understanding of the origins of these important deposits, their formation was apparently directly controlled by the nature of the Precambrian atmosphere. As the atmosphere changed, so did the capacity of the ocean to serve as a transporter of iron. When photosynthesis started contributing large quantities of free oxygen to the atmosphere, banded iron deposits no longer formed; therefore, we have no analogous processes active in the world today.

Banded iron formations typically contain 20–40 percent iron, values that were long considered too low for economic recovery. In some areas, however, surface chemical weathering has removed the associated siliceous or carbonate minerals and left enriched residual ores containing 55 percent or more iron. The initial mining efforts of the mid- to late-1800s in the great Precambrian iron deposits of the world such as the Lake Superior District of the United States (Figure 7.9a and page 220) and in the 1950s and 1960s in the Laborador Trough in Canada, Cerro Bolivar in Venezuela, Minas Gerais in Brazil, the Hamersley Range in Australia, and Krivai Rog in Russia were all for the enriched ores. In the early parts of this century there was concern, echoed by the words of Andrew Carnegie reproduced on page 221, that these rich ores were nearing depletion in places such as the Lake Superior District. Initial efforts in the early 1900s to concentrate the lower grade ores, the taconites, were only moderately successful, but renewed interest in the 1940s led to the development of economical concentration techniques. This new technology opened the way for exploitation of billions of tons of ores previously considered waste and led to the present iron ore mining industry. Since that time, the technology for processing the lean ores of the BIFs has spread worldwide, and these ores have become the world's dominant source of iron ore, a position they will certainly hold for many years to come. The Lake Superior District alone had produced more than 5 billion tons of ore by 1990 and still possesses reserves several times greater than the ore so far mined.

Mining and Beneficiation

Iron ore mining on a small scale dates back several thousand years. The earliest operations obtained ores locally by digging in a wide variety of shallow pits and underground tunnels. However, as better means of transportation evolved, many smaller mines closed and iron mining became concentrated in larger, more efficient operations.

Today, about 85 percent of the world iron ore production is mined from open pit operations; in the United States and Canada, open pits account for 97 percent of the total. Surface mining has become dominant because the iron ore bodies have large lateral dimensions and many of them lie relatively close to the surface. Furthermore, open pit mines have larger production capacities, are generally cheaper to operate per ton of ore, and are easier and safer to maintain than underground mines. As a result, the underground iron mines have found their ability to compete with open pit mines continually reduced; this is evidenced by a drop in the number of underground iron mines in the United States from about 30 in 1951 to one in the 1980s and 1990s. United States open pit mines operate at a disadvantage relative to many foreign mines because they must mine 5–6 metric tons of rock (about 3 metric tons of ore and 2–3 metric tons of overburden waste) for each metric ton of iron oxide produced. In contrast, the large Brazilian and Australian mines only have to mine 1.5–2 metric tons for each ton of iron oxide produced.

Mining in open pit mines is done primarily with large power shovels and with trucks having capacities of 120–150 tons. The ore is removed in a series of steps, called **benches** (Figure 7.9b), by drilling 30–38 centimeter (12–15 inch) diameter blast holes that are charged with an explosive mixture of ammonium nitrate and fuel oil; individual blasts can break up 1.5 million metric tons of ore at a time.

The richest iron ores, those that consist almost entirely of the iron ore minerals listed in Table 7.2, are referred to as **direct shipping ores.** These usually contain more than 50 percent iron by weight and can be effectively processed at the smelter after only being crushed. Unfortunately, such ores usually constitute only a portion (often a small one) of most iron ore deposits, and these areas are usually mined first. Once these ores are exhausted, the mines must close or adapt to the processing of lower grade materials. Thus, for example, the original mining of the ores in the Lake Superior District of the United States was based on the direct shipping ores, as mining and recovery methods had not yet been developed to handle the lower grade ores. Andrew Carnegie, pioneer of the American steel industry, lamented that the depletion of the richer ores could spell disaster for the American iron mining industry. In his address to the Conference of Governors at the White House, 13–15 May 1908, he said:

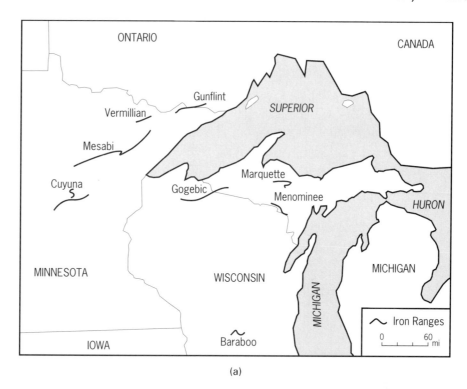

(a)

FIGURE 7.9. (a) The great banded iron formation-bearing ranges of the Lake Superior District occur as linear belts as much as 150 kilometers (90 miles) in length in Michigan, Wisconsin, Minnesota, and Ontario. (b) Open pit mining of the banded iron formations (locally called taconites) in the Lake Superior District. The ore is blasted out in a series of benches and is then transferred by large power shovels into trains or large trucks for transport to the processing plant. (Photograph courtesy of U.S. Steel Corporation.)

(b)

THE IRON RANGES

The principal metal of the modern era is iron, and the principal deposits of iron in North America are those of the Lake Superior District (Figures 7.9 and 7.10). These deposits have yielded more ore than those of any other district in the world and provided the iron and steel on which the American Industrial Revolution was built.

The first European settlers in eastern North America had to rely totally upon iron shipped from Europe. Within a few decades, a fledgling American iron industry developed and drew upon a variety of small, and often relatively low grade, ores scattered on the coastal plain and along the Appalachians. Through the first half of the nineteenth century, explorers were opening up the central and western parts of what now constitutes the United States and Canada. On 19 September 1844, a surveying party working on the Upper Peninsula of Michigan suddenly noted that their compasses displayed great variations with north needles commonly pointing WSW. Subsequent examination of the rocks in the area known as the Marquette Range revealed that they were composed of high-grade iron ore containing magnetite (Fe_3O_4). Within one year, the Jackson Mining Company was incorporated and purchased one square mile (640 acres) of land for $2.50 per acre. Mining commenced and the first loads of ore were shipped in 1848; however, the lack of any major transportation system delayed large-scale development until 1855 when completion of a shipping port at Sault Ste. Marie opened the way to Lake Superior.

The discovery of the Marquette iron ores led to exploration for additional deposits around Lake Superior and resulted in the discovery of the Menominee Range in 1849, the Gogebic Range in 1884, the Vermilion Range in 1885, the Mesabi Range in 1890, and the Cuyuna Range in 1903. Not only were the discoveries numerous, but their extent was almost beyond belief. The Marquette Range is 53 kilometers (33 miles) long, the Menominee District is 80 kilometers (50 miles) long, and the Mesabi Range is 177 kilometers (110 miles) long. Furthermore, the thicknesses of the ore-bearing zones are high by any standard, 105–230 meters (340–750 feet) in the Mesabi and up to 760 meters (2500 feet) in the Marquette Range. Previously discovered ore deposits were considered large if they were measured in millions of tons, but these ores were gigantic, being measured in the billions of tons.

Despite the enormity of the iron ore deposits of the Lake Superior District, a major problem remained—transportation. To get the ores from the isolated areas around western Lake Superior, it was necessary to construct canals and railroads to provide the low-cost transportation of millions of tons of ores to shipping terminals on the Great Lakes. This allowed the Lake Superior mines to become the primary suppliers of ore for the great steel centers of Pittsburgh, Pennsylvania, and Gary, Indiana, and resulted in the closure of the smaller eastern mines. The large quantities of high-grade iron ore that became available provided the backbone for American Industry as the Industrial Revolution transformed the United States from a rural country to an industrial giant. Iron ore production, which was only about 100 thousand metric tons in 1860, increased 20 fold to more than 2.5 million metric tons by 1885, to 20 million metric tons in 1900, and, ultimately, to nearly 100 million metric tons in 1951. In all, nearly 600 individual mines produced ore from the iron ranges with nearly 300 mines lying along the Mesabi Range.

By 1990 the total production of iron ore from the Lake Superior iron ranges had exceeded 5 billion tons, far surpassing any other district for any kind of ore in the world. Although the original high-grade ores that ran as high as 65 percent Fe have been mined out and foreign production has reduced the market, the iron ranges are still the heart of the iron and steel industry in the United States, providing nearly 50 million metric tons of ore per year. Today's ores, referred to as taconites, average only about 25 percent Fe, but the reserves exceed 50 billion tons and it appears that they will continue to serve as major sources of iron for the United States for many years to come.

I have for many years been impressed with the steady depletion of our iron ore supply. It is staggering to learn that our once-supposed ample supply of rich ores can hardly outlast the generation now appearing, leaving only the leaner ores for the later years of the century. It is my judgment, as a practical man accustomed to dealing with those material factors on which our national prosperity is based, that it is time to take thought for the morrow.

The lower grade materials of the Lake Superior District and most other important iron ore districts are called

(a)

(b)

FIGURE 7.10. (a) After the iron ores have been mined, they are finely ground to liberate the iron oxides. The powdery oxides are then formed into pellets, which are then transported to and charged into the blast furnaces. (Photograph courtesy of U.S. Steel Corporation.) (b) The iron ore pellets are transported across the Great Lakes in large ships such as the *Burns Harbor*, shown here loading up for its voyage. (Photograph courtesy of Bethlehem Steel Corporation.)

taconites and consist of admixed, often banded, iron oxides and silicates. They commonly contain only 50 percent iron oxide and average only 30–40 percent iron. Fortunately, the technology to effectively process these ores has been developed, and Andrew Carnegie's fears for the exhaustion of iron ores are no longer relevant. In order to use these ores, they must be upgraded by **beneficiation,** which concentrates the useful iron minerals and removes problem impurities such as minerals containing phosphorus and sulfur. The final product is powdery to fine sand-sized grains of iron oxides; but the grains are difficult to handle and cannot be fed directly into blast furnaces without being blown out the top. Therefore, the iron oxide grains are formed into 1–2 centimeter pellets (Figure 7.10) by adding a binder, usually bentonite, fine volcanic ash, or a clay and then fired so that they are strong enough to be transported and easily handled. These pellets have proven very useful to the iron and steel industries because they are easy to handle and have uniform compositions of 63–65 percent iron. Also, their natural porosity allows them to react rapidly with the carbon monoxide gas in the blast furnace during the smelting process.

Iron and Steel Smelting

The very first iron objects were hammered pieces of iron meteorites that did not need smelting. But meteorites are rare, and the use of terrestrial iron ores, which consist of iron combined with other elements, required **smelting,** the technique of separating the pure metal by melting the ore. The origins of iron smelting are unknown but probably lay in the Middle East or Asia Minor more than 3000 years ago. The **Iron Age** is usually dated as beginning about 1200 B.C. when the use of iron tools spread rapidly across the Middle East and across Asia to China. Iron making was subsequently spread throughout Europe by the Romans who learned the technique from the Greeks. European colonization then disseminated iron smelting to other parts of the world, such as the Americas, where it was not yet known. The modern blast furnace had its basic origins in about 1340 A.D. and slowly evolved into its present form as shown in Figure 7.11. It consists of a refractory-lined cylindrical shaft that allows the charge to be introduced into the top and the molten iron and slag to be drawn from the bottom.

To produce 1 metric ton of iron, 1.6 metric tons of iron ore pellets must be mixed with 0.7 metric ton of coke and 0.2 metric ton of limestone. This mixture is introduced into the blast furnace where it reacts with 3.6 metric tons of air at temperatures of about 1600°C (3000°F). The chemical reactions are complex, but the two principal reactions are the controlled combustion of the coke to produce carbon monoxide and the reduction of the iron oxides to iron by the carbon monoxide, which is simultaneously oxidized to carbon dioxide.

$$2C + O_2 \longrightarrow 2CO$$
(coke)   (air)   (carbon monoxide gas)

$$3CO + Fe_2O_3 \longrightarrow$$
(carbon monoxide gas)   (iron ore)

$$2Fe + 3CO_2$$
(free iron)   (carbon dioxide gas)

The limestone aids in the formation of a slag that absorbs undesirable elements from the charge. Molten iron, referred to as **pig iron,** is tapped from the bottom of the blast furnace into a transfer ladle that delivers it to the steel-making furnace (Figure 7.12). The slag is tapped separately and either dumped or cooled. Its uses include concrete aggregate, railroad ballast, and soil conditioner.

Approximately two-thirds of all the pig iron produced is subsequently used in the manufacture of **steel,** an alloy of

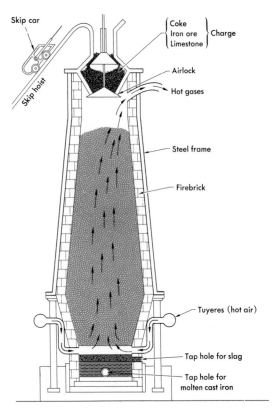

FIGURE 7.11. Diagrammatic representation of the interior of a blast furnace. The production of each metric ton of pig iron from an ore containing 60 percent iron requires approximately 250 kilograms of limestone as a flux and a metric ton of coking coal. Electrical and oxygen furnaces require different mixes and are noteworthy for being more efficient in their use of coke, but the same three ingredients are used. The production of iron illustrates how interdependent are the uses of the different metals. (From Skinner, *Earth Resources*, New York: Prentice-Hall, 1986.)

iron with one or more elements that give the resulting metal specifically desired properties. Carbon steel, the most easily produced and most widely used steel, is produced by adjusting the amount of carbon left after original smelting. Today, as shown in Table 7.4, a wide variety of different metals is added to iron to produce steels with different properties for specific uses. The actual steel production usually takes place in a separate furnace where the alloying elements are carefully admixed. After the steel is refined, it is cast, rolled, or otherwise shaped into the useful forms we see around us every day.

Iron and Steel Production

Since the Industrial Revolution, the quantity of iron ore mined and the amount of iron and steel produced have far surpassed the production of all other metals combined. Indeed, iron and steel production has sometimes served as a general measure of the economic well-being of a nation.

The iron ores that fed the fledgling European iron industry at the beginning of the Industrial Revolution in the 1700s were taken from large deposits in England, in the Alsace-Lorraine area along the French-German border, and in Sweden. The first European settlers in eastern North America had to import iron products from Europe; however, as they explored the Atlantic coastal plain, they discovered local accumulations of iron hydroxides, known as **bog irons,** in the swamps and bogs. Such ores had been mined in earlier times in Europe but were used up by about 1700. As the American settlers moved westward, they found sedimentary ironstones in the high ridges of the Appalachians from New York to Alabama. Although these formations contain significant quantities of iron oxide minerals wherever they occur, iron concentrations only locally reached economical levels (40–50 percent Fe). The largest district was that near Birmingham, Alabama, which remains an iron and steel center today.

Westward expansion in the United States eventually resulted in the discovery of extremely large iron deposits near the western end of Lake Superior in 1845. Production from the vast deposits there gradually displaced that from all others. Furthermore, the discovery of similar deposits in many parts of the world and the development of techniques for bulk mining and processing of these ores, which in places have only 30–40 percent iron, have resulted in the Lake Superior-type ores becoming the dominant source of iron in the world today, a position they are likely to retain for many years to come.

The modern steel industry traces its origins to the development of blast furnaces in central Europe in the fourteenth century. Growth was slow and production limited in quantity and quality until Abraham Darby found the way to use coke in iron smelting in 1709 in Shropshire, England. Europe, and England in particular, were the centers of iron and steel production and technology until the mid-nineteenth century when the combined effects of the discovery of the

FIGURE 7.12. Iron, melted in a blast furnace, is transferred by a large ladle into a steel-making furnace where it will be converted to a specific steel alloy prior to processing into finished products. (Photograph courtesy of U.S. Steel Corporation.)

Lake Superior ores, the development of the Bessemer smelting process (in England), and the rapidly expanding American economy shifted the focus across the Atlantic. Before the turn of the century, the United States had become the world's dominant steel producer, a position it held until the 1970s. The United States was well supplied with high-grade ores, abundant coal, and limestone. An effective lake and rail transport system was developed to bring the ores to places such as Bethlehem and Pittsburgh, Pennsylvania, and Gary, Indiana, where the major iron and steel centers grew.

Iron and steel production surged worldwide in the first years of the twentieth century but then were reduced in continental Europe by the effect of World War I. Production began to expand in the 1920s, only to stagnate during the Great Depression of the early 1930s. By the late 1930s, production once again began to increase as economies improved and as Germany and Japan began preparations for World War II. The war drastically reduced European and Japanese capacity for iron and steel production but left the United States with an intact industry and a large world market.

Thus, in 1950 the United States was the preeminent steel producer, supplying 47 percent of the world's total (Figure 7.13). Since that time, there has been a very marked change in the industry as Japan and western Europe were

TABLE 7.4

Elements added to iron to give desirable properties to steel

Element	Function in Steel
Aluminum	Remove oxygen; control grain size
Chromium	High temperature strength; corrosion resistance
Cobalt	High temperature hardness
Niobium	Strength
Copper	Corrosion resistance
Lead	Machinability
Manganese	Remove oxygen and sulfur; wear resistance
Molybdenum	High temperature hardness; brittleness control
Nickel	Low temperature toughness; corrosion resistance
Rare earths	Ductility; toughness
Silicon	Remove oxygen; electrical properties
Sulfur	Machinability
Tungsten	High temperature hardness
Vanadium	High temperature hardness; control grain size

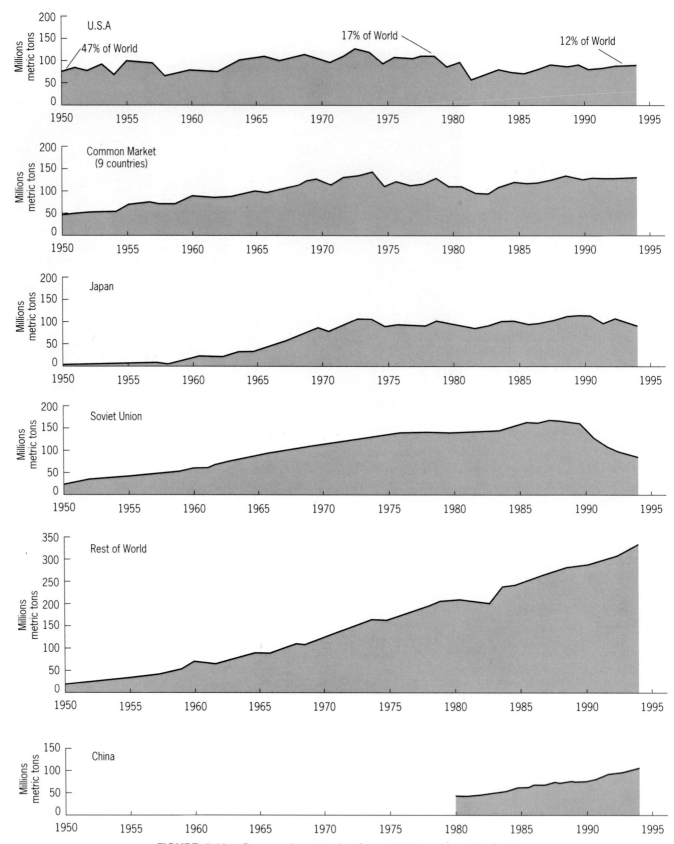

FIGURE 7.13. Raw steel production from 1950 into the 1990s for the United States, the European Common Market, Japan, the Soviet Union (Russia and the Ukraine after 1991), and the rest of the world. (Modified and updated from *Mineral Facts and Problems*, U.S. Bureau of Mines, 1980.)

rebuilt and as larger and more effective means of transport were developed. Japan and the European countries that once bought American steel could make their own steel more efficiently and less expensively than the United States because their plants were new and their operating costs less. Japan, in particular, benefited from the new, large, low-cost ocean transport of raw materials and the opening of huge, low-cost deposits in western Australia. In spite of having very limited reserves of iron ore, coal, or even limestone, Japanese industrial efficiency overcame difficulties arising from having to import all the raw materials and export most of the products. Japan's costs were lower than those that had abundant domestic supplies of all of the materials, namely, the United States and the countries in Europe. Consequently, as shown in Figure 7.13, since 1950 world steel production has increased more than six-fold while that of the United States has

declined so that the United States' total is now only 12 percent of the world's. The decline in total United States iron and steel production, combined with cost-cutting efforts in an attempt to remain competitive, has resulted in a reduction in the number of jobs at the blast furnaces and steel mills from more than 700,000 from 1976–1979 to less than 300,000 in 1995 (Figure 7.14). There are no indications that this trend will change in the years ahead. The situation is very similar in a number of European countries, especially Great Britain, where the iron and steel industry has experienced a large loss of markets and jobs because it cannot compete effectively with Japan.

While the American and British iron and steel industries struggle, two other nations in particular are expanding theirs—the former Soviet Union and South Korea. The Soviet Union placed great emphasis on the production of more

FIGURE 7.14. The United States labor force involved in iron ore mining (lower curve, left-hand scale) and in the steel industry (upper curve, right-hand scale) has dropped dramatically since the late 1950s, reflecting the decline in production and the increase in efficiency. (From U.S. Bureau of Mines.)

iron and steel from its own resources to meet growing domestic needs. In contrast, South Korea, resource-limited like Japan, developed an extremely modern and efficient industry that competes very effectively with Japan in terms of iron and steel exports.

Today, the problems for the iron and steel industry in the United States are not those of resource adequacy but rather of economic competitiveness. Thus, mines and mills are operating far below capacity; even so, the United States now imports more and more iron and steel because it is cheaper than producing it domestically. Since 1980, iron ore imports have ranged from 19–37 percent of consumption, and steel imports have ranged from 15–23 percent of consumption. Canada has been the largest foreign supplier of iron ore, whereas the European Economic Community, Brazil, and Japan have been the largest sources of imported steel (Figure 7.15). This has resulted in the number of jobs in the United States' iron ore mining business decreasing from more than 20,000 in the mid-1970s to less than 8,000 in the mid-1990s. Unfortunately, there is no evidence that this situation will change in the foreseeable future.

The automotive industry has been a major consumer of iron and steel for many years and has also become a major supplier of the scrap metal that is now recycled as noted on page 227 and Figure 7.16. The recycling of vehicles has evolved into a major industry because of the development of efficient shredders, the large mass of iron and steel in each vehicle, and because there is no convenient or acceptable other means of deposit.

Iron Ore Reserves and Resources

The world's reserves of iron ore today are both large and widespread as shown in Figure 7.1 and the data in Table 7.3. Considering that annual world production is now about 900×10^6 metric tons, the known world reserves of about 150×10^9 metric tons will be sufficient to last for more than 150 years. Furthermore, the United States Bureau of Mines estimates world iron ore resources to be at least 800 billion tons, containing more than 230 billion tons of recoverable iron. It is apparent that sufficient iron ore is available to meet our needs far into the future.

MANGANESE

Manganese is a metal that is little known to the general public but that is very important to modern society because it is

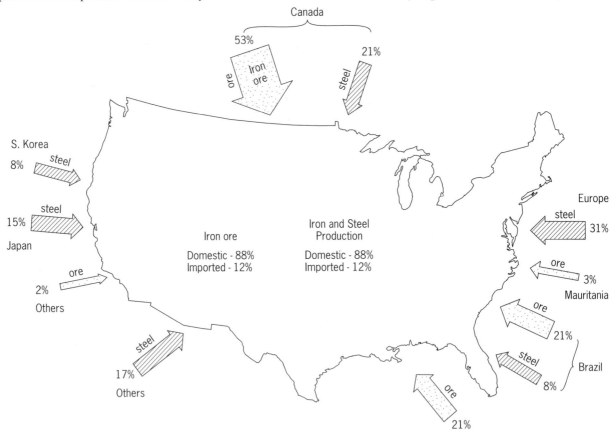

FIGURE 7.15.   The United States domestic production and its importation of iron ore and steel from major foreign sources in the early 1990s. (From the U.S. Bureau of Mines.)

MAKING AND RECYCLING AUTOMOBILES

There is probably no item more characteristic of modern developed societies in general, and the United States in particular, than the automobile. In the mid-1990s there are approximately 145 million registered automobiles in the United States; in addition, there are approximately 45 million registered trucks and buses. Thus, approximately 5 percent of the human population living in the United States operates approximately 35 percent of the world's 550 million registered motor vehicles. There are, of course, many tens of millions of additional vehicles unregistered—some operating and many in new and used car inventories.

The motor vehicle manufacturing industry represents one of the major consumers of many kinds of resources, especially iron and aluminum, and the fuel for the vehicles they manufacture constitutes the principal use of petroleum products. In 1992, a total of approximately 9,701,000 motor vehicles (5,663,000 cars and 4,038,000 trucks and buses) were manufactured in the United States. An additional 3,615,000 cars and 777,000 trucks and buses were imported, thus bringing the total of new vehicles in the United States to about 14,093,000 in one year. At the same time, about 12,781,000 cars, trucks, and buses were retired from service and about 10,000,000 of these were recycled (Figure 7.16).

The manufacture of the average new automobile consumes more than 0.97 metric tons (2100 pounds) of iron and steel; hence, more than 9 million metric tons of these metals went directly into just the new vehicles manufactured domestically (Table 7.5). In addition, more than 800,000 tons of aluminum, 185,000 tons of copper, 70,000 tons of zinc, and more than 1 million tons of glass were also incorporated into new vehicles. Each of the new vehicles also had a battery and at least four tires, but these two items are replaced at fairly frequent intervals. Hence, there is the total manufacture and disposal (in approximately equal numbers) of 80 million batteries and 250 million tires each year.

For many years, old automobiles and their batteries and tires were often discarded in junk yards, in fields, or along back roads (see Plate 12). This resulted in unsightly litter from the automobile chassis and tires and pollution from the lead batteries, engine fluids, and burning tires. Some waste sites have accumulated many millions of tires as shown in Plate 11. Today, the old vehicle bodies, tires, and batteries are still viewed as eyesores, but they are viewed as potential resources as well, because approximately 10 million automobiles are being shredded and sorted into usable metals every year. The recovered iron and steel represents about 20 percent of the total scrap of these metals reused per year in the United States, and the lead from the old batteries provides about 60 percent of the domestic need for new lead products. The quantity of platinum used in the exhaust system catalytic converters is small relative to other metals, but it is of high value and is being recycled in large proportion. The extensive recycling of automobile components provides an important source of metals, decreases the need for landfill space, and reduces pollution. The principal vehicular components not yet being recycled in large proportions are the tires, but there is considerable potential for the use of tires, or tire derivatives, for fuels and certain types of oils.

essential for the production of iron and steel. Manganese, like iron, exists in nature in more than one oxidation state; these oxidation states (Mn^{2+}, Mn^{3+}, Mn^{4+}) control its geological behavior and distribution. Manganese tends to be concentrated by chemical sedimentary processes, and important manganese resources in the world are sedimentary rocks, mixed sedimentary and volcanic rocks, or residual deposits formed by leaching of primary deposits. Like iron, manganese is very soluble in acidic or reducing solutions that carry it as Mn^{2+}, but it is very insoluble when it becomes oxidized, precipitating as minerals such as pyrolusite (MnO_2) or psilomelane ($BaMn_9O_{18} \cdot 2H_2O$). Manganese has little use on its own as a pure metal because of its brittleness and is rarely used even as an alloy in steels. However, there is no other substitute for its use as a scavenger of minor detrimental impurities such as sulfur and oxygen during the smelting of iron. Although the distinctive purple colors of manganese compounds and strong oxidizing properties of manganese had been utilized for centuries, manganese was not isolated as an element until 1774, and it did not become important industrially until its importance in steel making was discovered in the middle 1800s. After that, it was soon

FIGURE 7.16. Crushed automobiles being placed on a conveyor belt in preparation for shredding, which will allow separation of the various components for recycling. Approximately 10 million automobiles are shredded and recycled each year in the United States. (Photograph courtesy of the Institute of Scrap Recycling Industries, Inc.)

found that the most useful form of manganese is as **ferromanganese,** an alloy of iron and manganese containing 78–90 percent manganese. Up to 7 kilograms of manganese are necessary for the production of each metric ton of iron or steel. Although more than 90 percent of the world's manganese consumption is in the iron and steel industry, there are also important uses for manganese oxides in the chemical industry. Two of the best known uses are as potassium permanganate, a powerful oxidizing agent used for water treatment and purification, and as manganese dioxide, a necessary component in dry cell batteries.

Manganese ores usually consist of dark brown to black oxides, especially pyrolusite (MnO_2) and romanechite ($BaMn_9O_{16}(OH)_4$), that range from hard and compact to friable and earthy. Locally, the carbonate rhodochrosite ($MnCO_3$) and the silicate braunite ($MnSiO_3$) are important ores. The largest and most important sedimentary deposits include Groote Dylandt on the north coast of Australia, the Molango District in Mexico, the Kalahari Field in the Republic of South Africa, and the Bol'shoy Tokmak, Chiatura, and Nikopol' deposits within Russia. Important residual deposits include the Sierra do Navio in Brazil, the Moanda in Gabon, and several deposits in India. At present, only deposits containing 35 percent or more manganese constitute reserves (Figure 7.17). If deposits with manganese contents down to approximately 30 percent are also considered in the reserve base, the available manganese increases about four times. When world reserves are compared against total annual production, it is apparent that there will be sufficient manganese to meet human needs for many years to come. However, despite the relative abundance of manganese on a global scale, the distribution is irregular, and the United States, Japan, and western Europe are all lacking in economical deposits of this important metal. Relatively small de-

TABLE 7.5

Materials used in manufacturing motor vehicles in the United States in 1992

Material	Average 1994 Automobile		Total U.S. Automotive (metric tons)	Total U.S. Use (metric tons)	Percent Use Vehicles
	lbs	kg			
Conventional steel	1388.5	630.0 ⎫			
High-strength steel	263.0	119.3 ⎪	7,651,360	84,300,000	9.1
Stainless steel	45.0	20.4 ⎬			
Other steels	42.5	19.3 ⎭			
Iron	408.0	183.1	1,776,070	9,869,000	18.1
Aluminum	182.0	82.6	801,220	5,725,000	14.0
Zinc	16.0	7.3	70,810	1,276,000	5.5
Lead*	25.0	11.3	864,628*	1,277,000	66.3
Platinum	—	2.7g	26.36 m.t.	65.0	40.6
Glass	245.5	111.4	1,080,580	—	—
Copper	42.0	19.1	185,270	2,311,000	8.0
Natural rubber }	134.0	60.8	⎰ 680,406	910,212	74.7
			⎱ 1,129,342	1,946,920	58.0

*Approximately 80,000,000 batteries are produced each year with most serving as replacements.
Data from General Motors Corporation and Statistical Abstract of the United States.

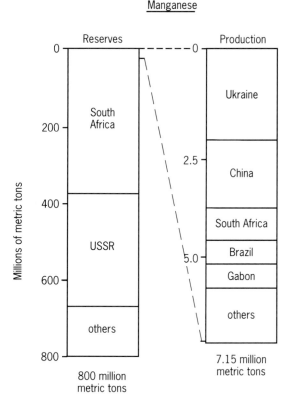

FIGURE 7.17. South Africa and the nations of the former Soviet Union contain the world's principal reserves of manganese. At present rates of production, these reserves will last about 40 years. The seafloor nodules and lower grade terrestrial ores will be sufficient to meet needs for hundreds of years. (From the U.S. Bureau of Mines.)

posits were mined in the United States as early as the 1830s, and this continued until the end of World War II, but the most significant remaining domestic deposits have average grades of less than 20 percent. This has led to a concern about the adequacy of stable long-term supplies from foreign producers, but the presence of large reserves in many countries will probably ensure adequacy of imports.

There is yet another potentially exploitable manganese resource—the deep ocean floor. The ship *Challenger,* sent around the world by the Royal Society (of London) between 1873 and 1876 to gather data about the waters, rocks, plants, and animals of the oceans, found that some parts of the deep ocean floor are covered by quantities of black nodules up to several centimeters in diameter (Figure 7.18a). Subsequent studies have found that these nodules, generally referred to as **ferromanganese nodules** or **manganese nodules,** are widespread on the ocean floor and are complex mixtures of iron and manganese oxides and hydroxides with minor but potentially important amounts of other metals (Table 7.6). The nodules consist of onion-like concentric layers that have

grown over a central nucleus of rock or shell material (Figure 7.18b). Growth appears to be very slow—on the order of 1 millimeter per 1000 years—and may well be influenced by bacterial activity. The manganese and other metals are probably derived both from the land, as terrestrial weathering and erosion slowly liberate metals and transport them to the oceans, and from submarine hydrothermal and volcanic vents that occur along midocean ridges. The total quantity of manganese recoverable in the form of nodules is not well known, but the United States Bureau of Mines conservatively estimates the richest deposits alone to be more than 16×10^9 metric tons, approximately 20 times the known terrestrial resources and more than 800 years' worth of production at present rates of use.

The ultimate exploitation of the seafloor nodules presents economic, technological, and legal challenges. American and Japanese companies have recovered nodules from the Pacific Ocean floor on a trial basis, but commercial processing appears to be many years away. Possible recovery methods, shown schematically in Figure 7.19, make use of simple drag dredges, a continuous bucket line, or a vacuum cleaner-like device in which air bubbles injected at the base provide the suction. Regardless of the technique employed, the recovery of nodules from depths of 4000 meters (12,000 feet) is difficult and expensive. The exploitation of nodules on the deep seafloor raises two additional questions: what are the possible environmental effects and who has the right to mine on the ocean floor? Little is known of the deep-sea life forms and the extent, if any, to which they could be harmed by sediment disturbance caused by seafloor mining. The international Law of the Sea conference of the United Nations worked for many years to try to define ownership of, and access to, midocean resources. It resulted in the general recognition of exclusive economic zones covering the continental shelves but did not resolve the problems of mining manganese nodules and other deep ocean resources. Serious international problems remain, and a legal framework for the recovery of manganese nodules has yet to be worked out and accepted by all countries. For some time, there was reluctance by the United States to sign a treaty because of disagreements about the deep sea resources. When the United States finally signed the treaty in 1994, it was agreed that the industrial countries would have significant control over resources, such as manganese nodules, that they might ultimately mine.

ALUMINUM, THE METAL OF THE TWENTIETH CENTURY

Aluminum is the second most abundant metallic element (after silicon) in Earth's crust, where it occurs at an average concentration of 8.2 percent. However, it is so difficult to free the metal from its minerals that aluminum has been

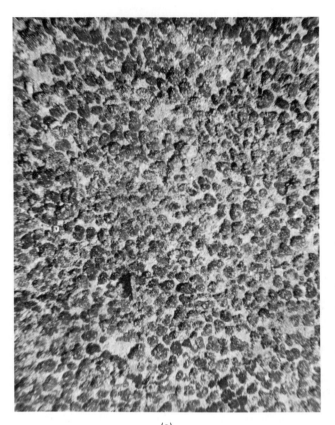

(a)

FIGURE 7.18. (a) Manganese nodules are common on many parts of the deep ocean floor. These nodules in the Pacific Ocean are 5–10 centimeters in diameter. (Photograph by W.T. Allen, Deep-Sea Ventures.) (b) A cross section cut through a manganese nodule shows the concentric nature of the manganese and iron oxides within the manganese nodule. (Photograph by B.J. Skinner.)

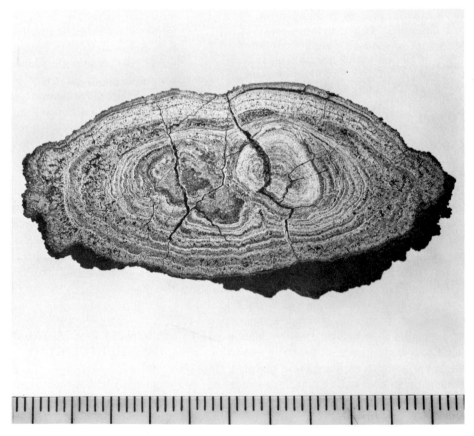

(b)

TABLE 7.6

Average elemental compositions of ferromanganese nodules from the major oceans

Element	Atlantic	Indian	Pacific	Pacific*
Manganese	15.5	15.3	19.3	24.6
Iron	23.0	13.4	11.8	6.8
Nickel	0.3	0.5	0.9	1.1
Copper	0.1	0.3	0.7	1.1
Cobalt	0.2	0.3	0.3	0.2
Zinc	—	—	—	0.1

*A 230 km² area at 8°20′N and 153°W.

produced commercially for a little over 100 years. Despite its relatively recent appearance on the industrial scene, aluminum has proven to be a remarkably useful metal. It weighs only about one-third as much as either iron or cop-per, it is malleable and ductile, it is easily machined and cast, it is corrosion resistant, and it is an excellent conductor of electricity. This versatility has resulted in such wide-spread use that today the only metal with a greater consumption worldwide is iron.

Rubies and sapphires have been valued since Biblical times, but it was not until the end of the eighteenth century that they and corundum were recognized as oxides of aluminum (Al_2O_3) and were collectively called *alumina*. From this, the metal was named *aluminum* in 1809, but it was not isolated in its free state until 1825. Because of the difficulty in producing the metal and its novelty, it was valued more highly than gold for a short time. Napoleon III, nephew of Napoleon Bonaparte and emperor of France from 1852 until 1871, even had a baby rattle for his infant son and his most prized eating utensils made of aluminum. The breakthrough that permitted commercial production, and hence the wide-scale

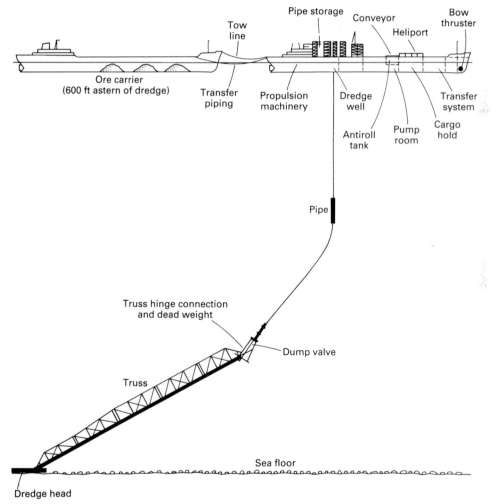

FIGURE 7.19. Recovery of manganese nodules will be accomplished by vacuum cleanerlike systems such as shown here or by bucketlike systems. The major problem is maintaining continuous and economic recovery in ocean depths of 3300–5000 meters (10,000–15,000 feet). (Courtesy of DeepSea Ventures.)

use of aluminum, came in 1886 when Charles Hall in the United States and Paul Heroult in France developed an electrolytic process to release the metal from the oxide. At about the same time, Karl Bayer from Austria developed a chemical process to produce alumina in large quantities from bauxite. The Hall-Heroult and Bayer processes laid the foundations of the modern aluminum industry. Commercial production began in 1888, and the processes continue to be used in only slightly modified forms today.

Aluminum Products and Usage

Because of its versatility, aluminum now finds a wide range of uses in our daily lives. The annual usage of aluminum metal in the United States exceeded 6 million metric tons by the mid-1990s or about 24 kilograms (53 pounds per person). No other country uses so much aluminum in total, nor so much per person, as the United States, but the use of aluminum is increasing significantly in nearly every country. In the United States, the major uses are packaging and containers (33 percent), transportation (23 percent), and building (17 percent); other important uses include electrical (9 percent) and consumer durable goods such as refrigerators (8 percent). The principal packaging use is aluminum beverage cans, 100 billion of which were being produced in the United States by the early 1990s. Transportation uses continue to be important because aluminum's light weight affords more efficient use of fuels and because aluminum is resistant to corrosion. Approximately 70 kilograms (150 pounds) of aluminum are used in the average car built in the United States today; and the quantity is projected to ultimately reach 90 kilograms (200 pounds). Aluminum is widely used in construction because of its light weight and resistance to weathering, and it seems likely that there will be increased consumption in this area. Although copper is nearly always used for household wiring, aluminum serves in virtually all of the high power transmission lines that extend across the countryside. It is the light weight and relatively high strength-to-weight ratio of aluminum that allow the construction of the long spans between towers.

Less visible than the uses of aluminum metal are the uses of aluminum compounds. The most important of these are alumina and aluminum hydroxide $Al(OH)_3$, which is also called activated bauxite. Both activated bauxite and alumina are widely employed in the petroleum industry as absorbents in oil and gas refining; other important uses are as fire retardants and as fillers in plastics and paper. Alumina has long served as a major component in refractories for the steel industry because it has a very high melting point and is relatively unreactive. Alumina is an important grinding and polishing compound, but increasingly it has to compete with harder materials such as synthetic diamond and silicon carbide. A quantitatively small, but very important and growing use of alumina is in the production of synthetic rubies and sapphires, which are used in the construction of lasers, as jewel bearings in precision mechanisms, and as synthetic gemstones.

Aluminum Ores

Aluminum, like iron, is such an abundant element that it is a constituent of many common minerals. The most important are feldspar (the most abundant mineral in Earth's crust), mica, and clay. To date, and probably for the near future, most aluminum production has been from **bauxite,** a name derived from the southern French village of Les Baux where it was first recognized in 1821. Bauxite is a heterogeneous material composed chiefly of the aluminum hydroxides gibbsite $(Al(OH)_3)$ and boehmite and diaspore (both $AlO \cdot OH$). These relatively uncommon minerals are formed by the breakdown of aluminum-bearing rocks under special conditions of lateritic weathering. The conditions occur most frequently in subtropical to tropical climates where there is abundant rainfall and the groundwater is neither too acid nor too alkaline, where there are aluminous parent rocks, and where there is subsurface drainage but low relief so that mechanical erosion is slow relative to chemical leaching.

During the intense chemical weathering characteristic of lateritic conditions, the three least soluble components are SiO_2, Al_2O_3, and Fe_2O_3. After the more soluble constituents such as Na, K, Mg, and Ca have been removed in solution, the residue is mainly iron hydroxide plus clays such as kaolinite $(Al_2Si_2O_5(OH)_4)$. Percolating waters, made slightly acid by the decay of organic debris, slowly dissolve the clays and carry the silica and some of the iron. What remains are aluminum and iron hydroxides. Where the ratio of aluminum hydroxides to iron hydroxides is high, the resulting rock is the aluminum-rich laterite bauxite. Successive solution and precipitation commonly results in a characteristic pisolitic texture of the type shown in Figure 7.20 and Plate 32.

Aluminum-rich rocks at times serve as the parent rock for some deposits, and bauxites can form from the weathering of any rock that is aluminum-bearing. In fact, some important bauxites, those known as the terra rosa type, develop on limestones that contain very little aluminum. In these cases, the calcium carbonate of the limestones is relatively rapidly dissolved in the acid groundwaters found in tropical climates. This leaves a clay residue that can be altered to form discontinuous and localized, but rich, lenses of bauxite. Most major commercial bauxite deposits have formed during the past 60 million years, and all of the largest have formed in the tropics over the past 25 million years. Deposits such as those in Arkansas or France, areas that are presently temperate, formed in earlier geologic times when the climates of those areas were tropical. No doubt, many additional bauxites have formed during Earth's history, but because they are

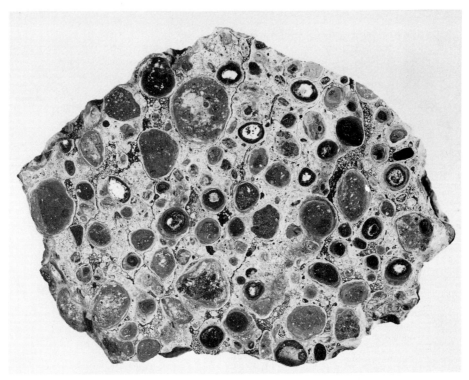

FIGURE 7.20. Bauxite, the ore of aluminum, commonly exhibits a characteristic pisolitic texture. (Photograph by B. J. Skinner.)

surface deposits, they have been destroyed by erosion. Bauxites are unknown in arctic regions because they would not form there today and because it is likely that any deposits formed in the geologic past would have been removed or covered up by glaciation.

Aluminum Smelting and Production

The conversion of raw bauxite into alumina and aluminum metal is a multistep process, as shown in Figure 7.21. Bauxite mining is relatively easy and inexpensive because the deposits lie on or near Earth's surface and the ores are usually soft and easily removed. In contrast, the processing, and especially the production of metallic aluminum, is complex and extremely energy intensive. Unfortunately, the bauxite deposits that supply the raw material, the sources of abundant inexpensive energy needed to process the ore, and the markets for the end products tend to be widely separated. Most mining of bauxite takes place in tropical regions that have neither abundant inexpensive electricity nor large markets for the aluminum products. To maximize the efficiency of shipping to processing sites, the bauxite is first crushed, washed to remove impurities, and then dried as shown in Figure 7.21. The washed concentrate is shipped to countries such as Norway, Canada, and the United States where there is now (or *was* when plants were established) abundant in-

expensive electrical power. In each of these countries, the source of the power for processing is principally hydroelectric plants.

The production of aluminum metal is accomplished by the electrolytic reduction of alumina in a molten bath of natural or synthetic cryolite (Na_3AlF_6) that serves both as an electrolyte and a solvent. The actual metal production takes place in a series of large bathtublike vats called a **pot line,** where hundreds of aluminum ingots, each weighing up to a metric ton, are produced simultaneously. The metal reduction process uses very large amounts of electricity because temperatures must be maintained at 950°C or more and because the electrical currents and voltages must reach as much as 150,000 amperes and 1000 volts, respectively. In the United States, the growth of the aluminum industry in the first half of the twentieth century coincided with the development of regional power networks and the building of major hydroelectric facilities. The availability of the large amounts of inexpensive electricity generated in the Columbia River basin and the Tennessee Valley led to the construction of major aluminum smelters in these areas. This situation worked well because the aluminum companies, while getting the cheap power they needed, provided a use for the surplus electricity generated by the hydroelectric dams. Consequently, United States' aluminum metal production rose rapidly from the beginning of the century until 1973

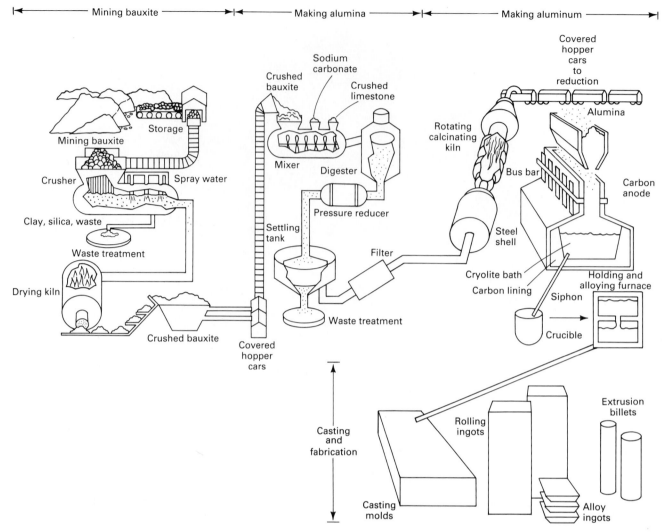

Mining bauxite ⟷ Making alumina ⟷ Making aluminum

FIGURE 7.21. Schematic diagram showing the steps in mining, processing, and smelting of aluminum. (Courtesy of The Aluminum Association.)

when it exceeded 4100 million kilograms (Figure 7.22). At that time, the oil embargo raised energy prices and ended the period of growth of the aluminum industry in the United States. As a result of rising energy costs, production in the United States has leveled off to 3500–4000 metric tons per year and is expected to gradually decrease in the future. Other countries that were dependent upon expensive imported energy sharply curtailed or, in the case of Japan, terminated primary aluminum production deciding that it was more economical to import aluminum metal than to refine it. This underscores what is generally recognized as the major problem of aluminum refining—it is energy intensive.

The amount of energy needed to refine aluminum relative to the amount needed for several other metals is shown in Figure 7.23. It is apparent that the energy required to extract a ton of aluminum from typical bauxites is approximately five times that required per ton of iron extracted from

taconites or of copper extracted from sulfide ores. Also shown are the amounts of energy that would be required if we were to refine aluminum from other common aluminum-bearing minerals such as clay or plagioclase feldspar.

A concern for aluminum resources and the energy-intensive extraction of the metal has led to a great deal of recycling of aluminum. By the early 1900s, the recycling of aluminum scrap in the United States had reached 1.6 million tons, equal to 30 percent of American aluminum production. This quantity was second only to iron in terms of recycled metal. It consists of new scrap, which is waste material generated in the production of new aluminum products, and old scrap, which consists of old aluminum products that have been discarded (can, foil, engine parts, wire, etc.). In 1970, 3 billion (3×10^9) aluminum beverage cans were recycled in the United States; in 1983, that had risen to 27.5 billion (27.5×10^9) cans, and in 1993 it was 63 billion (63×10^9).

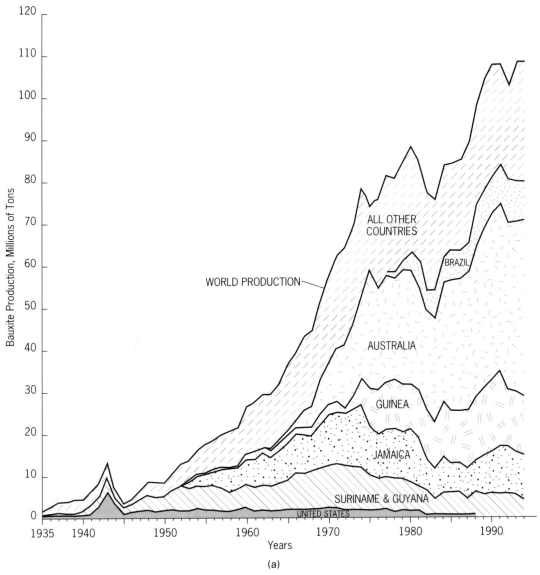

FIGURE 7.22. (a) World bauxite production increased rapidly in this century between 1950 and 1980 but dropped with the high energy prices in the early 1980s. Production increased again from the mid-1980s. (b) Aluminum production in the United States paralleled the world production of bauxite until about 1980 but has now stabilized at about 4000 metric tons per year. (From the U.S. Geological Survey and the U.S. Bureau of Mines.)

As noted in Chapter 3, recycling of these cans, and all aluminum scrap, is important because it represents not just a saving of resource, but also a large saving of energy. The remelting and forming of a new aluminum can from an old one requires only 5 percent of the energy needed to make the can from bauxite in the first place. Thus, the recycling of aluminum represents a 95 percent energy saving. One way to picture the energy saved in recycling an aluminum drink can is to see it about one-third full of gasoline. This is the equivalent amount of energy lost if the can is discarded and has to

be replaced using newly produced metal. When Japan announced the closing of its primary aluminum production facilities in 1985, the country decided to step up the importation of aluminum scrap for reprocessing because it is economically more efficient and saves the large costs and problems involved in the importation of the fossil fuels and bauxite needed for primary production. In a very real sense, the importing of the aluminum scrap represents the importing of energy, the energy that some other country had supplied to initially refine the metal.

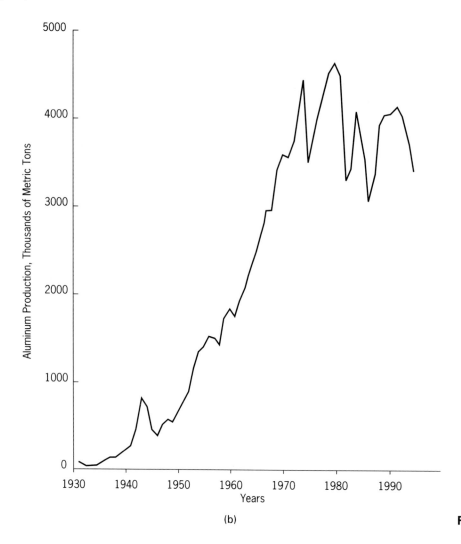

(b)

FIGURE 7.22. *(cont.)*

Bauxite Reserves

The specification of bauxite reserves is complicated because the quality of deposits is not judged solely on the accessibility and aluminum content, but also on other chemical properties such as iron and silica content, upon local factors such as energy costs, and on the proximity of markets. Typical bauxites mined in Jamaica contain 49 percent Al_2O_3 (on a dry basis), and high-grade ores in South America, Guinea, and Australia contain 50–60 percent Al_2O_3, whereas mineable reserves in Arkansas and western Australia have only 40 percent Al_2O_3. Most European bauxites have 45–65 percent Al_2O_3.

World bauxite reserves (Figure 7.24) are concentrated in tropical and semitropical regions (Figure 7.25). Exploration over the past 50 years has greatly expanded reserves from 1×10^9 metric tons in 1945, to 3×10^9 metric tons in 1955, to 6×10^9 metric tons in 1965, to 21×10^9 metric tons in 1985, and to 23×10^9 metric tons in 1995. Guinea and Australia together have about one-half of world reserves;

more than 25 percent occurs in the western hemisphere in Brazil, Jamaica, Guyana, and Surinam. The principal United States deposits are about 20 million metric tons in central Arkansas plus 2–3 million tons that occur in Alabama and Georgia. At the present world mining rate of approximately 100 million metric tons of bauxite annually, the reserves identified would last more than 200 years. Estimates of total world bauxite resources that may one day be mineable are 40–50×10^9 metric tons and would allow for bauxite mining for a much longer period of time. From this, a quantity of 9–11×10^9 metric tons of aluminum metal can be extracted. This quantity is indeed large, but it is very much smaller than the amount of iron that will ultimately be recoverable from Earth's crust.

Concerns over the sufficiency of bauxite as the source of aluminum, especially in countries like the United States that have limited bauxite reserves, have led to the consideration of other types of materials as potential sources of aluminum. The former Soviet Union produced alumina from nepheline $((Na, K)AlSiO_4)$ and alunite $(KAl_3(SO_4)_2)(OH)_7$.

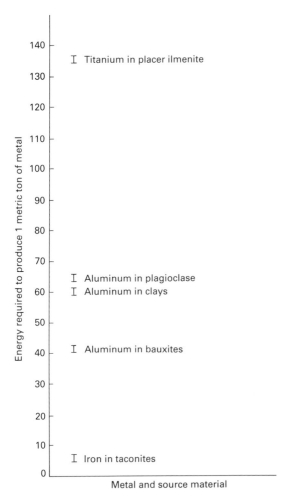

FIGURE 7.23. Energy requirements for the recovery of iron, titanium, and aluminum from different types of ores.

TITANIUM

Titanium, the least common of the abundant metals, comprises only 0.56 percent of Earth's crust. Like several other of the abundant metals, it has found application only in the modern world. Although titanium was recognized as a chemical element in 1790, more than 100 years passed before any commercial potential was realized, and it has only been used on a large scale in the past 50 years. Today, titanium has two major applications. The first is in a variety of alloys where it imparts a high strength-to-weight ratio, a high melting point, and great resistance to corrosion. These properties have led to its widespread use in aircraft engines and air frames, electricity generating plants, welding rods, and a wide variety of chemical processing and handling equipment, and to its designation as a strategic metal. The second use, which accounts for approximately 95 percent of the world's consumption of titanium minerals, is the preparation of white titanium oxide pigment. Because of its whiteness, opaqueness, permanence of color, and low toxicity, titanium oxide is now the principal white pigment used in paint, paper, plastic, rubber, and many other materials (see Chapter 9). Formerly, white lead oxide had been widely used, but this resulted in numerous cases of lead poisoning. In addition, white lead is more susceptible to changes in coloration when subject to air pollution. The use of titanium is relatively inconspicuous; nevertheless, the amounts used every year are very large. For example, in the late 1980s and early 1990s, the United States annually produced approximately 25,000 metric tons of titanium metal worth about $180 million and about 1 million metric tons of titanium dioxide pigment valued at more than $2 billion.

Titanium occurs in minor amounts in most types of rocks as the oxide minerals **rutile** (TiO_2) and **ilmenite** ($FeTiO_3$); locally, **leucoxene,** an alteration product of ilmenite, is also present. Generally, these minerals are widely dispersed in igneous and metamorphic rocks as accessory minerals. Locally, however, the igneous processes involved in the formation of **mafic** rocks (**gabbro** or **anorthosite**) have concentrated large amounts of iron and titanium oxides, especially ilmenite, into lenses or thick layers. When the iron oxide present is magnetite (Fe_3O_4), separation of the titanium minerals into a relatively pure concentrate is usually possible because the minerals are coarse grained and the magnetite is magnetic. In contrast, mixtures of ilmenite with hematite are usually very fine-grained intergrowths as shown in Figure 7.26b and are nearly impossible to separate into pure concentrates by mechanical means. The only way to thoroughly separate the titanium from these ores is by expensive chemical processes in which the ores are dissolved.

Most sedimentary rocks contain minor amounts of titanium oxide minerals derived from igneous or metamorphic rocks by weathering and erosion. The ilmenite and rutile are hard (5–6.5 on the **Moh's scale**) and resistant to solution or

In addition to nepheline and alunite, particular interest has been focused upon clays (especially kaolinite), oil shales (the aluminum-rich waste after processing for oil), and anorthosite (composed primarily of the **plagioclase feldspar** anorthite, $CaAl_2Si_2O_8$). The potential resources of clays and anorthite are large and widespread; unfortunately, as is evident in Figure 7.23, the processing of these materials for aluminum requires even more energy than needed to process bauxite. The potential use of oil shales would also depend on the economical extraction of the oil—something that seems unlikely in the foreseeable future.

In summary, the total bauxite reserves appear to be adequate for many years, but several other mineral commodities will continue to be investigated as possible aluminum sources. It is hoped that their processing costs can be made competitive with that of bauxite and that many industrial nations will become less dependent upon foreign sources for the aluminum raw materials.

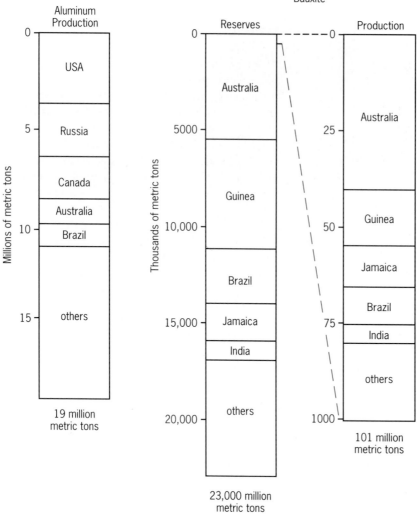

FIGURE 7.24. Annual world production in the mid-1990s and the reserves and production of bauxite. At present rates of production, identified reserves will last more than 200 years. (From the U.S. Bureau of Mines.)

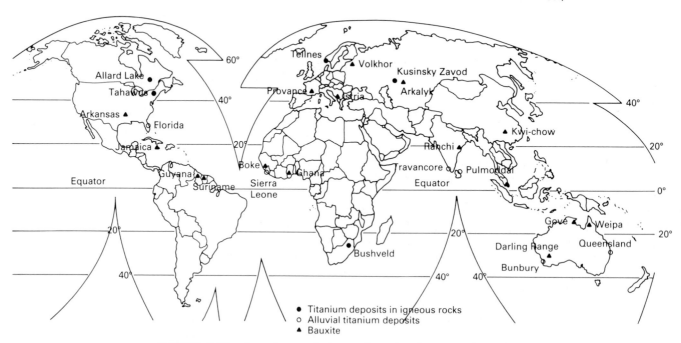

FIGURE 7.25. Locations of the major aluminum and titanium deposits.

(a)

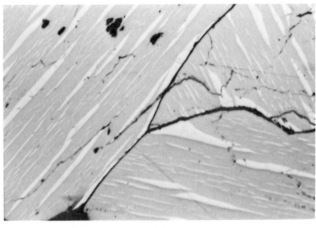

FIGURE 7.26. The principal mineralogical sources of titanium are rutile (TiO_2) and ilmenite ($FeTiO_3$). (a) Placer rutile grains concentrated from beach sands. (b) Microscopic view of intimate lamellar intergrowth of ilmenite (dark gray) with hematite (white) in the hard rock ores at Tahawus, New York. (Photographs by J.R. Craig.)

(b)

chemical attack, and thus survive the weathering and erosional processes intact (Figure 7.26a). Because their densities (rutile = 4.25 and ilmenite = 4.8) are higher than those of common constituents of river and beach sands (quartz = 2.65 and feldspar = 2.6–2.7), the titanium minerals may be selectively concentrated into specific zones or sedimentary horizons (known as **placer deposits**). The gold panner makes use of the same properties by concentrating black sand and gold in a pan; in fact, the black sand is often largely ilmenite and rutile. The TiO_2 content of the ilmenite in placer deposits varies as a function of the initial composition of the ilmenite and the degree of weathering because the slow alteration can result in preferential leaching of iron. Thus, placer ilmenite concentrates from South Africa average only 48 percent TiO_2, whereas those from Florida and New Jersey have 61–65 percent TiO_2. Rutile concentrates are usually 93–96 percent TiO_2, and leucoxene concentrates contain up to 90 percent TiO_2. Even though the grade of the titanium may not be as rich as that in igneous deposits, the unconsolidated nature of the sediments makes processing both simple and economical.

Titanium minerals are mined today from both deposits in igneous rocks (*hard rock* mines) and from placer sand occurrences. Until about 1942, nearly all commercial ilmenite and rutile production came from placer deposits; today, rutile production still comes only from placers, but nearly 40 percent of the ilmenite comes from hard rock mines. The worldwide production of titanium is derived from the mining of about 4 million metric tons of placer ilmenite and 500,000 metric tons of rutile. The total world reserves are estimated at about 300 million metric tons of contained TiO_2, and world resources are at least 1.2 billion metric tons of TiO_2 content. Consequently, there will be sufficient titanium to meet our needs for many years to come. Furthermore, recent investigations of the detrital deposits of the continental shelves have revealed the presence of much larger potential resources of placer titanium minerals that could be exploited if those on land are exhausted.

TABLE 7.7

Energy requirements to produce aluminum and titanium oxides and metals (per metric ton) in btu

	Aluminum	Titanium
Mining	1.1–3.3	5.1
Shipping	0.5–3.3	0.5–3.6
Production of alumina (per ton)	52.8	—
Production of TiO$_2$ pigment (per ton)	—	75–112
Production of aluminum metal (per ton)	70.7–102.0	—
Production of titanium metal (per ton)	—	453–522
Total energy requirement in btu	125–161	534–643

Data from U.S. Bureau of Mines, 1985.

Titanium, like silicon, aluminum, and magnesium, requires large amounts of energy for processing from its source mineral forms to produce either pigment or metal. The energy required to produce titanium metal from ilmenite and rutile is shown relative to several other metals in Figure 7.23. Most titanium is used to produce pigment and does not require as much energy for its production; comparison of the amounts of energy needed to form oxides and metals of aluminum and titanium is shown in Table 7.7.

Titanium occurs in small amounts in all types of rocks worldwide, but economically viable deposits are much less common. The most important hard rock ilmenite reserves are those at Allard Lake (Quebec), Tahawus (New York), Tellnes (Norway), and Otanmaki (Finland). Important placer deposits are worked in Australia, India, the Republic of South Africa, Russia, Sri Lanka, and Sierra Leone. World production of rutile, ilmenite, and titanium metal are summarized in Figure 7.27. The difference between the large production of the titanium minerals and the limited production of the metal reflects the fact that most of the minerals are converted into TiO$_2$.

The mining of titanium minerals does not create any unusual environmental problems because the mining is usually carried out in simple shallow open pit operations or on

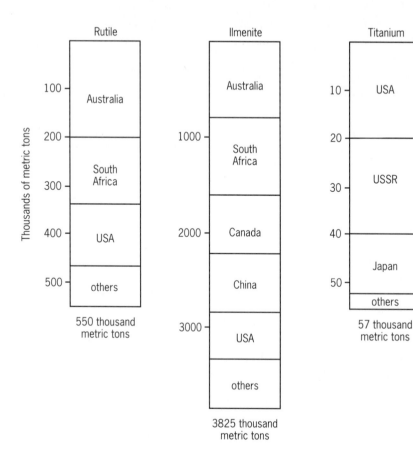

FIGURE 7.27. The world's production of rutile and ilmentite is dominated by Australia and South Africa, whereas the production of titanium metal is carried out primarily in the United States, the countries of the former Soviet Union, and Japan. (From the U.S. Bureau of Mines.)

(a)

(b)

FIGURE 7.28. Titanium sand mining. (a) A small dredge, at the left, digs the sands and sends them into the concentrator where the 5 percent of the titanium minerals present are separated. (b) Mining of beach sands for the titanium minerals is carried out along the coasts in parts of Australia. (Photographs courtesy of RGC (USA) Minerals Sands Inc.)

beaches (Figure 7.28). After scooping up the loose sands, the recovery is usually accomplished by the use of spiral separators or jigs that separate the titanium minerals on the basis of specific gravity. Hence, there is no blasting and no use of chemicals. The economical sedimentary deposits usually contain 6–8 percent titanium minerals; consequently reclamation returns 92–94 percent of the material and there is often no evidence of the previous mining activity. However, the processing of ilmenite to produce pigment generates up to 3.5 metric tons of toxic sulfate and sulfuric acid waste per ton of product. Previous methods of disposing of such wastes into streams and oceans have now been replaced by acid neutralization plants; unfortunately, the runoff of sulfates from the waste sites of older

plants has seriously polluted streams and continues to cause problems locally.

MAGNESIUM

Magnesium, the eighth most abundant element in Earth's crust, is the lightest of the abundant metals. Like most of the other abundant metals, its common occurrence and its important uses are not usually realized by most people. Magnesium finds its largest use not as the metal but as the oxide MgO (called **magnesia**) and as the silicate mineral, **forsterite** (Mg_2SiO_4), both of which are used as **refractories** (see Chapter 9) in the steel and some base metal industries.

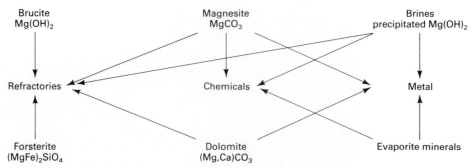

FIGURE 7.29. The uses of the principal raw materials of magnesium. (From *U.S. Geological Professional Paper 820,* (1973).)

As a metal, magnesium is commonly mixed with aluminum to produce lightweight corrosion-resistant alloys that are widely used in beverage cans, automobiles, aircraft, and machinery. In addition, magnesium compounds are used in such varied materials as cement, rubber, fertilizers, animal feed, paper, insulation, and pharmaceuticals.

Magnesium-bearing raw materials are abundant and geographically widespread. They consist of several minerals, brines, and seawater (Figure 7.29). The first magnesium resources exploited in the mid-eighteenth century were **magnesite** ($MgCO_3$) deposits in the former Czechoslovakia, Austria, and Greece. Similar deposits were subsequently discovered in California, and mining began there in 1887. During World War I, a process was developed whereby magnesium-bearing refractory materials could be extracted from dolomite ($CaMg(CO_3)_2$), a very common sedimentary rock, by intense baking (called **calcining**) to drive off the CO_2 (Figure 7.30).

Magnesium is unique in being the only metal to be extracted directly from brines and from seawater. The recovery of magnesium metal from deep-well brines that contain several thousand parts per million magnesium began in Michigan in 1917. There, brines are trapped in the thick sequence of evaporite minerals that underlie the Michigan Basin (see Figure 9.12). Recovery of magnesium from seawater, in which it is the third most plentiful dissolved element (1350 parts per million), began in 1940. The extraction process, shown schematically in Figure 7.30, is relatively simple

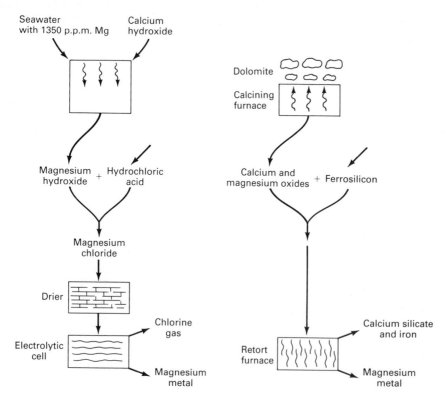

FIGURE 7.30. Magnesium metal is prepared from seawater by reaction with calcium hydroxide and hydrochloric acid followed by electrolytic refining or by reacting calcined dolomite with ferrosilicon in a high-temperature or retort furnace.

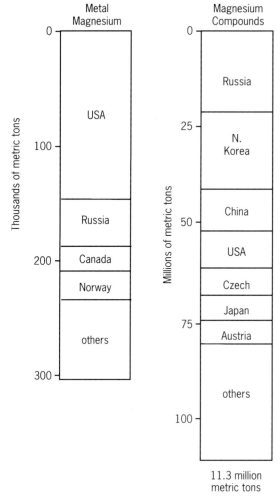

FIGURE 7.31. World production of magnesium metal and magnesium compounds in the 1990s. The reserves of magnesium in seawater, brines, and dolomite are virtually inexhaustible. (From the U.S. Bureau of Mines).

SILICON

Silicon is the second most abundant element in Earth's crust and is an essential constituent of all the common silicate minerals that comprise many of the common rocks. Because of its very strong affinity for oxygen, with which it is combined in quartz (SiO_2) and all silicate minerals, free silicon only occurs in nature under the most unusual circumstances. The only confirmed occurrence is in Michigan where an intense lightning strike fused some glacial debris, producing temperatures of about 2000°C and reducing some quartz to native silicon.

In spite of its abundance in oxide forms all around us and its importance in modern technological applications, silicon metal is relatively unfamiliar to most people. Pure silicon is a lightweight, silvery substance that has a lustrous semimetallic appearance. Although the use of silicates such as clay minerals dates from prehistoric times, and the use of glass made from silicates began at least 12,000 years ago, free silicon was not prepared until 1824. In the late 1800s, the use of silicon as a deoxidizing (oxygen removing) agent for steels was discovered, and this led to a large demand in the growing steel industry. Today, silicon (or an iron-silicon alloy called **ferrosilicon**) is prepared by melting clean quartz, usually coarse-vein quartz or well-cemented quartzite (Figure 7.32a), with iron or steel scrap and coal, coke, or charcoal (as a reductant) in a large electric arc furnace. These furnaces, up to 13 meters in diameter and 13 meters high, can prepare 150–200 metric tons per day. Periodically, the furnaces are tapped and the molten silicon or ferrosilicon is cast into elongate bars called ingots. The ferrosilicon is mixed with the molten iron or steel to remove oxygen and to serve as an alloying agent. The addition of up to 17 percent silicon in cast iron reduces scaling and corrosion at high temperatures. Silicon is also added into aluminum and copper alloys in amounts up to 25 percent because it improves the casting properties, adds strength, and reduces corrosion.

In recent years, silicon has found many additional uses outside of metallurgy. The best known of these began in 1949 when E. I. du Pont de Nemours and Co. produced the first silicon pure enough for use in transistors and other semiconductors. Today, the **silicon chip** (Figure 7.32b) is the basis for many electrical devices in computers, calculators, and communications equipment. The chips are prepared by first producing ultrapure single crystals of silicon and then by introducing into these crystals specific amounts of certain chemical elements to produce desired electrical properties. Another important use is as photovoltaic devices, commonly called **photocells** or **solar cells** (Figure 7.33), in which thin layers of silicon, either as single crystals or as amorphous films, and other compounds convert sunlight into electrical energy. Today, photovoltaic cells are in broad use from pocket calculators to earth-circling satellites, and their application will probably continue to expand rapidly.

chemically but requires large quantities of electricity. In the 1990s, magnesium metal and other compounds were being produced in the United States from seawater in California, Delaware, Florida, and Texas, from the lake brines of the Great Salt Lake in Utah, and from well brines in Michigan. World production of magnesium and magnesium compounds in the 1990s is summarized in Figure 7.31.

Resources from which magnesium metal and its compounds can be recovered are globally widespread, and estimates range from very large to virtually unlimited. The reserves of the highest quality raw materials, such as the magnesite mined in Nevada, exist in quantities sufficient to meet human needs for a very long time. Furthermore, the amounts of magnesium available in the form of dolomite and in seawater and brines are so large that they will never be exhausted.

(a)

(b)

FIGURE 7.32. Quartz in the form of (a) sand, quartzite, and crystals serves as the source of silicon that now finds broad applications as (b) chips in many modern technological applications. (Photograph of silicon chips courtesy of ITT; photograph of silica sources by S. Llyn Sharp.)

Silicon is also used to produce compounds such as **silanes** (silicon-hydrogen compounds, for example, SiH_4), which are used in the manufacture of numerous kinds of silicone resins, rubbers, lubricants, adhesives, antifoaming agents, and water-repellent compounds. In 1891, E. G. Acheson failed in his attempts to synthesize diamonds, but he accidentally discovered silicon carbide (SiC), also known as carborundum. This substance, with a Moh's hardness of 9.5 (compared with 9 for corundum and 10 for diamond), is now one of the most widely used commercial abrasives and is commonly found on some of the better grades of sandpaper.

The world's resources of silicon in the form of silica (SiO_2) in quartz and other silicates is virtually unlimited. The constraints on the production of silicon or ferrosilicon are those of purity, which is reasonably met by quartz from many **quartzites,** pegmatite masses, and gravel deposits, and the availability of electrical power. The world production of about 3.5 million metric tons of silicon per year represents the efforts of many countries (Figure 7.34). However, the large increases in electrical power costs in recent years have seen a shift in silicon production from countries such as Japan and the United Kingdom to countries with lower power costs.

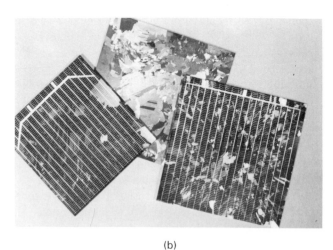

(a)

(b)

FIGURE 7.33. Modern solar cells produce electricity for an increasing variety of applications. These contain layers of crystalline or amorphous silicon in which the incident solar radiation produces electricity. (Photographs courtesy of Solarex Corporation.)

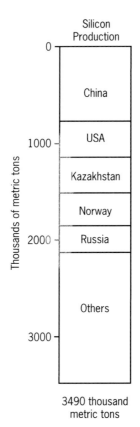

Silicon
Production

FIGURE 7.34. The annual world production of silicon in the mid-1990s. It is likely that production will continue to rise, and there is an inexhaustible supply of quartz from which to prepare silicon. (From the U.S. Bureau of Mines.)

ABUNDANT METALS IN THE FUTURE

It is now apparent that Earth's crust contains vast quantities of the abundant metals in concentrations and forms that will be exploitable by current technologies. Their geochemical abundance coupled with increasingly diverse uses ensures that they will remain the principal metals of society in the foreseeable future. Iron will no doubt remain the dominant metal because of its low cost, availability, and broad range of uses. Manganese will be needed because it is essential to the production of all steels. Aluminum, magnesium, titanium, and silicon will no doubt find expanded use, especially in construction and transportation where they permit weight and energy savings. However, because these latter metals are energy intensive in terms of their extraction, their use could be affected by the availability and costs of energy. We now turn our attention to the scarce metals, which though constituting only trace proportions of Earth's crust, serve modern society in a wide range of important roles.

FURTHER READINGS

BROWN, R., "Iron and Steel Scrap." *U.S. Bureau of Mines Annual Report, 1990* (1992).

CUNNINGHAM, L. D., "Silicon." *U.S. Bureau of Mines Annual Report, 1990* (1992).

DIXON, C. J., *Atlas of Economic Mineral Deposits.* New York: Cornell University Press, 1979.

EDWARDS, R. and ATKINSON, K., *Ore Deposit Geology.* London: Chapman and Hall, 1986.

GUILBERT, J. M. and PARK, C. F., *The Geology of Ore Deposits.* New York: W. H. Freeman and Co., 1986.

HOUCK, G. W., "Iron and Steel." *U.S. Bureau of Mines Annual Report, 1990* (1992).

HUTCHISON, C. S., *Economic Deposits and Their Tectonic Setting.* New York: John Wiley and Sons, (1983).

KUCK P. H., "Iron Ore." *U.S. Bureau of Mines Annual Report, 1990,* (1992).

PATTERSON, S. H., KURTZ, H. F., OLSEN, J. D., and NEELEY, C. L., "World Bauxite Resources." *U.S. Geological Survey Professional Paper 1076-B,* 1986.

PLUNKERT, P. A. and SEHNKE, E. D., "Alumina, Bauxite, and Aluminum." *U.S. Bureau of Mines Annual Report, 1990,* (1992).

WILBURN, D. R., "Aluminum Availability and Supply." *U.S. Bureau of Mines Information Circular 9371.*

Consequently, Norway, with abundant hydroelectric power and only a small domestic steel industry, has become a major exporter of ferrosilicon. China has increased its production of ferrosilicon so that it is now the world's leading producer of total silicon forms. The growth in demand for silicon will be almost totally dependent upon the world's steel industries because they account for most of the consumption. It is likely that semiconductor usage will continue to rise, but this accounts for less than 1 percent of the total.

8 THE GEOCHEMICALLY SCARCE METALS

The Quebrada Blanca Mine in Chile is an example of a modern gold mine. The low grade gold ore is extracted from a large open pit mine (out of sight to the right of this scene), crushed, and then stacked in large rectangular heap leach piles visible in the background. Dilute cyanide-bearing solutions, sprayed onto these piles, drain through them dissolving the gold. The solutions drain onto large impermeable plastic liners and are collected into the ponds visible in the center of the photo. Gold is finally extracted using chemical reactions and electrolytic processes conducted in the building in the central part of the operation. (Courtesy of Cominco.)

The total volume of workable mineral deposits is an insignificant fraction of the earth's crust, and each deposit represents some geological accident in the remote past. Deposits must be mined where they occur—often far from centers of consumption. Each deposit has its limits; if worked . . . it must sooner or later be exhausted. No second crop will materialize. Rich mineral deposits are a nation's most valuable but ephemeral material possession—its quick assets.

T.S. Lovering, "Mineral Resources from the Land." In P. Cloud (ed.), *Resources and Man*. San Francisco: W.H. Freeman and Co., 1969, pp. 109–134.

FOCAL POINTS

- There are more than 30 geochemically scarce metals, defined as metals that occur in Earth's crust at average abundances below 0.1 percent.

- The geochemically scarce metals commonly occur dispersed in common minerals; only when they are much concentrated (25–1000 or more times) do they form their own specific minerals and, in turn, mineable deposits.

- The four major groups of geochemically scarce metals are (1) ferro-alloy metals, (2) base metals, (3) precious metals, and (4) special metals.

- The ferro-alloy metals—especially Ni, Cr, Co, Mo—are used to alloy with iron to provide special steels (stainless, tool, high-temperature, etc.).

- Nickel, chromium, and cobalt occur primarily associated with large mafic or ultramafic igneous rock bodies; molybdenum occurs in felsic, porphyritic rock bodies.

- The base metals—such as Cu, Pb, Zn, Sn, Hg—occur primarily in deposits formed by precipitation from hydrothermal fluids; they are used in a broad range of technologies.

- Copper, the most widely used base metal, was one of the first metals known to humans and today serves as the most important metal for the electricity industry.

- The precious metals—Au, Ag, and the platinum group—today serve as monetary standards and are used in jewelry and as important technological metals.

- The search for gold has been the driving force for much of human exploration and colonization and continues to be the object of exploration activities.

- The special metals are a broad group with the common characteristic of playing increasingly important roles in new technologies; their use is likely to increase in the future.

PRODUCTION OF THE GEOCHEMICALLY SCARCE METALS

The backbone of industry is built from the geochemically abundant metals. But it is the geochemically scarce metals that keep industry efficient, effective, and healthy because it is the scarce metals, used in small amounts, that control the properties of alloys of the abundant metals, that carry electric currents, and that allow automobiles to run and planes to fly. Consider iron, which is so widely used that it accounts for about 95 percent by weight of all metals used. The properties of pure iron are so limited that iron alone could not possibly satisfy all the requirements of modern industry. For some uses, iron must be hardened, for others it must be made more flexible or more ductile, more resistant to abrasion, or more resistant to rust. All such changes can be accomplished by the addition of small amounts of geochemically scarce metals as alloying agents. Consequently, several of the geochemically scarce metals—nickel, chromium, molybdenum, tungsten, vanadium, and cobalt—are mined and used principally as alloying components for special steels.

The **geochemically scarce metals** (Figure 8.1 and Table 8.1) are those that are present in Earth's crust in such trace amounts that none exceeds 0.1 percent of the crust by weight. Indeed, some metals are so geochemically scarce that they make up a millionth of a percent or less of the mass of the crust. Examples are gold, which has a crustal abundance of 0.0000004 percent by weight, and ruthenium, which only has a crustal abundance of 0.00000001 percent! Despite their extreme geochemical scarcities, both gold and ruthenium have special properties that make them important, or even essential, commodities for industry. Approximately 35 geochemically scarce metals are now mined and used for special industrial purposes. No other group of natural resources fills such a wide and varied range of needs. Things happen more rapidly, more efficiently, and more effectively. In a sense, the geochemically scarce metals are similar to the enzymes that make our bodies work effectively and help carry out the complex chemical processes needed to keep us healthy. The geochemically scarce metals are, in a sense, the enzymes of industry. It is their special properties that have led to such technological marvels as the generation and distribution of electricity, the telephone, radio and television, automobiles, aircraft, and rockets. Yet it is in this same group of metals that many experts believe shortages and restrictions of natural resources might first appear. When shortages do appear, it is not entirely clear whether or not they will affect the way we use all of the technological innovations of the past, but it is almost certain that shortages will retard future technological developments.

There are many differences between the geochemically scarce and geochemically abundant metals in addition to the ways in which they are used. Although the world's annual production of iron has, for many years, been 100 million tons or more, only four of the geochemically scarce metals—chromium, copper, lead, and zinc—have ever been produced at rates that exceed a million tons a year. The production rate of many scarce metals is still less than a thousand tons per year (Table 8.1). One might well ask how, with such small annual rates of production, material shortages could possibly develop? The answer lies in the way the geochemically scarce metals are distributed through the crust, in the difficulty of finding new ore deposits, and in the difficulty of extracting these metals from the host minerals.

DISTRIBUTION OF SCARCE METALS IN THE CRUST

Eighty-eight different chemical elements have been identified in Earth's crust. The average concentrations of individual elements range from as low as 10^{-8} percent to as high as 45 percent by weight, but only nine major elements account for 99 percent of the mass of the crust (Table 8.1). The combined total of the remaining 79 elements accounts for only 1 percent of the mass of the crust. Most of the 79 minor elements fulfill the definition of geochemical scarcity in that their individual abundances are less than 0.1 percent by weight.

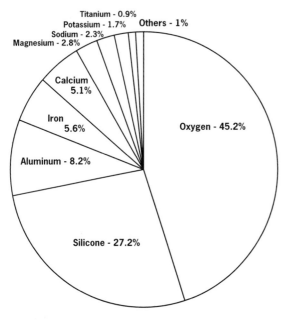

Composition of the Continental Crust

Titanium - 0.9%
Potassium - 1.7%
Sodium - 2.3%
Magnesium - 2.8%
Calcium 5.1%
Iron 5.6%
Aluminum - 8.2%
Others - 1%
Oxygen - 45.2%
Silicone - 27.2%

FIGURE 8.1. Nine chemical elements account for 99 percent of the mass of the continental crust of Earth. The geochemically scarce metals are nearly all present in abundances of less than 0.01 percent as shown in Table 8.1.

TABLE 8.1

Geochemically scarce metals. Abundance and approximate production in the mid–late 1990s

Metal	Chemical Symbol	Crustal Abundance (wt%)	World Production (m.t./yr.)	Major Producers
Antimony	Sb	0.00002	75×10^3	Bolivia, South Africa, Mexico
Arsenic	As	0.0002	50×10^3	China, Ghana, Chile, Mexico
Beryllium	Be	0.0002	330	U.S.A., China, Brazil, Russia
Bismuth	Bi	0.000004	3.5×10^3	China, Mexico, Peru, Canada
Cadmium	Cd	0.000018	20×10^3	Japan, Canada, Belgium, U.S.A.
Chromium	Cr	0.0096	9.5×10^6	Kazakhstan, South Africa, India, Finland
Cobalt	Co	0.0028	22×10^3	Canada, Zambia, Russia, Zaire
Copper	Cu	0.0058	10×10^6	Chile, U.S.A., Canada, Russia
Gallium	Ga	0.0017	38	Germany, Hungary, Japan
Germanium	Ge	0.00013	50	U.S.A., Japan, China, Spain
Gold	Au	0.0000002	2.3×10^3	South Africa, U.S.A., Australia, China
Indium	In	0.00002	150	Canada, Japan, France, Italy
Iridium	Ir	0.00000002	2	South Africa, Russia, U.S.A., Canada
Lead	Pb	0.0010	3×10^6	Australia, China, U.S.A., Peru
Mercury	Hg	0.000002	2.5×10^3	China, Spain, Algeria
Molybdenum	Mo	0.00012	110×10^3	U.S.A., China, Chile, Iran
Nickel	Ni	0.0072	900×10^3	Russia, Canada, New Caledonia, Indonesia
Niobium	Nb	0.0020	13	Brazil, Canada, Zaire
Palladium	Pd	0.0000003	164	Russia, South Africa, U.S.A., Canada
Platinum	Pt	0.0000005	140	South Africa, Russia, Canada, U.S.A.
Rare Earth Elements		~0.002	65	China, U.S.A., Russia, Australia
Rhenium	Re	0.00000004	24	U.S.A., Chile, Peru, Canada
Rhodium	Rh	0.00000001	13	South Africa, Russia, U.S.A., Canada
Ruthenium	Ru	0.00000001	6	South Africa, Russia, U.S.A., Canada
Silver	Ag	0.000008	14×10^3	Mexico, U.S.A., Peru, Canada
Tantalum	Ta	0.00024	320	Australia, Brazil, Zimbabwe, Canada
Tin	Sn	0.00015	180×10^3	China, Indonesia, Brazil, Bolivia
Tungsten	W	0.00010	30×10^3	China, Russia, Portugal, Bolivia
Vanadium	V	0.017	30×10^3	South Africa, Russia, China, U.S.A.
Zinc	Zn	0.0082	7×10^6	Canada, Australia, China, Peru
Zirconium	Zr	0.014	800×10^3	Australia, South Africa, Ukraine, U.S.A.

Data From Mineral Commodity Summaries 1995, U.S. Bureau of Mines

The nine major elements are the ones that form the common minerals found in all common rocks. Only the most common of the geochemically scarce metals—copper, zinc, and chromium—form minerals that can be found in common rocks, and even those minerals are of very limited occurrence. Nevertheless, careful analyses reveal that essentially all naturally occurring chemical elements are present in trace amounts in all common rocks. However, most rocks contain, at most, three or four major minerals plus an equal number of minor ones. Both the major and minor minerals are generally compounds of two to five of the nine major chemical elements. There is a simple explanation for the seemingly contradictory statement that all common rocks consist of minerals that contain the nine major elements, but that the same rocks also contain trace amounts of all of the geochemically scarce elements. The explanation is that the geochemically scarce elements are all present in the common minerals by **atomic substitution** or, as it is sometimes called, **solid solution.** Atoms of nickel, for example, can substitute

for atoms of magnesium in the magnesium silicate mineral olivine (Mg_2SiO_4), and atoms of lead can substitute for atoms of potassium in orthoclase feldspar ($KAlSi_3O_8$). The properties that control solid solutions are like those that control liquid solutions. Hence, when the saturation limit of a liquid solution is exceeded, crystals of the solute start to grow. So too, when a solid solution becomes saturated, a new mineral must form. When the limit is exceeded for substitution of Pb for K in potassium feldspar, a lead mineral must form. The reason that minerals of geochemically scarce metals do not occur in common rocks—or do so only in rare circumstances—is that the amounts of the scarce metals present in the crust do not exceed the conditions of saturation of the solid solutions in common minerals.

There is no single rule concerning the concentration levels at which geochemically scarce metals form separate minerals because of the differences between the properties of the various metals. However, a rough rule of thumb is that at concentrations above about 0.1 percent, a mineral will form.

TABLE 8.2

Calculated value of geochemically scarce metals in solid solution in a metric ton of average granite

Element	Concentration in Average Granite* (%)	Price of Metal (1995)[†] ($US/kg)	Value of Metal in a Metric Ton ($US)
Thorium	0.002	107	2.14
Beryllium	0.0002	500	1.00
Lithium	0.003	52	1.56
Niobium	0.002	8.2	0.16
Tantalum	0.0002	58	0.12
Uranium	0.0005	39	0.20
Zinc	0.005	1	0.05
Tungsten	0.0002	5.7	0.01
Gold	0.0000002	12,860	0.03
Copper	0.0024	2.4	0.06
Lead	0.0039	0.8	0.03
Molybdenum	0.001	7.7	0.08
Silver	0.0000036	170	0.01
			$5.45

*After Wedepohl (1978).
[†]Some values estimated because not quoted as metal.

Below that level, scarce metals occur only in solid solution. The rule is approximately correct for many metals including copper, lead, and zinc, but it is too low for a few metals such as gallium and germanium, and it is too high for a few others such as gold, molybdenum, and uranium.

Suppose we were to attempt to mine **granite,** a common igneous rock, and after crushing the rock to a powder, we attempted to break down the solid solutions to recover the most valuable of the geochemically scarce metals. The result, as shown in Table 8.2, would be economically ludicrous. It costs $15 to $30 a metric ton just to mine and crush granite to a fine powder that is suitable to start the necessary chemical treatments. The final cost of extraction would be hundreds of dollars a ton. Rather than attempting to mine metals from common rocks, therefore, society has always sought ore deposits, those localized geological concentrations of ore minerals that carry unusually high contents of a desired scarce metal, and that can be mined at a profit. Many of the geological processes active in ore deposit formation have been discussed in Chapter 2.

As described in Chapters 4 and 7, many factors determine whether or not a local concentration of such minerals can be considered an ore deposit. Presuming all factors such as grade, size, depth, and so forth are favorable, the minimum grade that a scarce metal ore deposit must reach is shown in Figure 8.2. The ratio of that minimum grade to the grade of that metal in average, common rocks is the concentration factor that must be attained by geological processes. Some of the concentration factors are enormous. Mercury, for example, must reach a local concentration 100,000 times greater than the crustal average for an ore deposit to be economical. The circumstances required for this happen very rarely indeed.

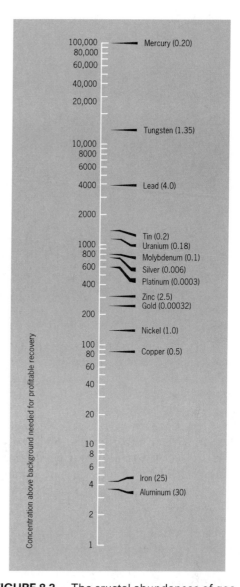

FIGURE 8.2. The crustal abundances of geochemically scarce metals are so low that large concentrations above background averages are needed before deposits can be profitably mined. The abundant metals require lower concentration factors to produce rich ores. The bracketed percentages are the minimum metal contents an ore must have before it can be mined under the most favorable circumstances with present-day technology. Note that as the price of a metal goes up or down, its position will move on the diagram. Between 1969 and 1990, for example, the concentration factor needed for a viable gold deposit dropped from about 4000 to about 250 as a result of technological advances and a rise in the price of gold. (Adapted from Skinner, 1986.)

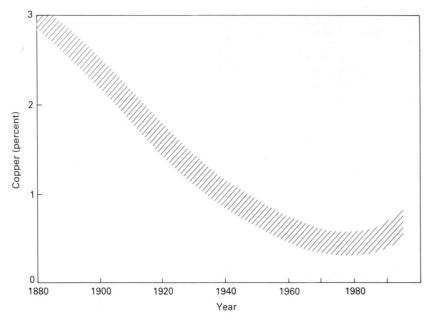

FIGURE 8.3. The minimum grade of copper that could be mined profitably dropped steadily from about 1880 to 1970 largely as a result of increased efficiencies in mining practices and the low cost of energy. Lower metal prices and higher energy costs caused the curve to flatten after about 1970.

Not surprisingly, ore deposits of geochemically scarce metals tend to be small and rare by comparison with ore deposits of geochemically abundant metals. The minimum concentration factors can change as the prices of metals change or as technological developments occur. Over the last 200 years, the minimum concentrations have tended to decline because great advances have occurred in mining and metallurgical technologies. It is not known how low concentration factors can be pushed, but if copper can be taken as an example, it is possible that an end to declining grades has already been reached (Figure 8.3).

ORE MINERALS OF THE SCARCE METALS

Between 99.9 and 99.99 percent of the total amount of any given scarce metal is present in the crust in atomic substitution in common silicate minerals. Therefore, only a tiny fraction—between 0.01 and 0.1 percent—of a given metal occurs in ore minerals. Fortunately, the ore minerals tend to be found in localized concentrations rather than being scattered and disseminated. Fortunately, too, the geochemically scarce metals tend to form ore minerals that are sulfide or oxide compounds, or in a few cases, native metals, and it is relatively easy to separate these ores from the associated and valueless silicate gangue minerals. Even so, some of the scarce metals (for example, gallium, germanium, cadmium) never occur in sufficient concentrations to be the objective of a mining operation. Instead these elements, occurring in small but extractable concentrations as solid solutions in more abundant minerals, are only recovered as by-products (see Box on page 279). Consequently, their availability for use in technology is controlled by the mining of minerals primarily for other metals. If the mining for the other major

metals were to cease, we would also lose the supply of the by-product metals.

The most important geochemically scarce metals and the classes of ore minerals they form are listed in Table 8.3.

TABLE 8.3

Kinds of ore minerals formed by the geochemically scarce metals

Sulfide Minerals	Examples of Ore Minerals
Metal:	
Copper	Chalcocite (Cu_2S), chalcopyrite ($CuFeS_2$)
Lead	Galena (PbS)
Zinc	Sphalerite (ZnS)
Mercury	Cinnabar (HgS)
Silver	Argentite (Ag_2S)
Cobalt	Linnaeite (Co_3S_4), Co-pyrite ((Fe,Co)S_2)
Molybdenum	Molybdenite (MoS_2)
Nickel	Pentlandite ((Ni,Fe)$_9S_8$)
Oxide Minerals:	
Beryllium	Beryl ($Be_3Al_2Si_6O_{18}$)
Chromium	Chromite ($FeCr_2O_4$)
Niobium	Columbite ($FeNb_2O_6$)
Tantalum	Tantalite ($FeTa_2O_6$)
Tin	Cassiterite (SnO_2)
Tungsten	Wolframite ($FeWO_4$), scheelite ($CaWO_4$)
Vanadium	V in solid solution in magnetite (Fe_3O_4)
Native Metal:	
Gold	Native gold
Silver	Native silver
Platinum	Platinum-palladium alloy
Palladium	Platinum-palladium alloy
Iridium	Osmium-iridium alloy
Rhodium	Solid solution in osmium-iridium alloy
Ruthenium	Solid solution in osmium-iridium alloy
Osmium	Osmium-iridium alloy

FIGURE 8.4. An alchemist (right) and his assistant testing formulas for the transmutation of base metals into gold. Even though the search for a successful transmutation was futile, many chemical processes were successfully developed by alchemists. (From a woodcut by Hans Weiditz, 1520.)

CLASSIFICATION OF GEOCHEMICALLY SCARCE METALS BY USAGE

All of the important geochemically scarce metals can be divided into four major groups based on their properties or the way they are used. The first group of metals is known as the **ferrous** or **ferro-alloy metals.** It is a group of metals that are mined and used principally for their alloying properties, especially in the preparation of specialty steels. Examples of the ferrous metals are chromium, vanadium, nickel, and molybdenum.

The second group of metals are variously called **nonferrous metals** or **base metals.** The term *base metal* is an old name that arose in the middle ages during the days of **alchemy.** Metals such as copper, lead, zinc, tin, and mercury were less valuable and less desirable—and hence base—so the ancient alchemists tried to convert them into the precious metals, gold and silver (Figure 8.4). The ancients were not successful in their efforts, and it is possible that today we might well argue that copper, zinc, and tin are actually more important than gold and silver because of their importance in industry and technology. Nevertheless, the terms *precious* and *base* remain with us. There is, however, an alternate designation for base metals. Because the principal uses of the base metals are for purposes other than alloying agents with iron, base metals are also known by the term *nonferrous metals.* Neither base nor nonferrous is a completely correct description, but both terms are nevertheless widely used.

The third group, but almost certainly the first group of scarce metals to be used by our ancestors, is the **precious metals** (Table 8.4). The precious metals of antiquity, gold and silver, were called **noble metals** because they are not readily debased by forming compounds with other chemical

TABLE 8.4

Analyses of hydrothermal solutions, weight percent

Chemical Element	(1)	(2)	(3)	(4)
Chlorine	15.50	15.70	15.82	4.65
Sodium	5.04	7.61	5.95	1.97
Calcium	2.80	1.97	3.64	0.750
Potassium	1.75	0.041	0.054	0.370
Strontium	0.40	0.064	0.111	—
Magnesium	0.054	0.308	0.173	0.057
Bromine	0.12	0.053	0.087	—
Sulfur*	0.005	0.031	0.031	0.160
Iron	0.229	0.0014	0.030	—
Zinc	0.054	0.0003	0.030	0.133
Lead	0.010	0.0009	0.008	—
Copper	0.0008	0.00014	—	0.014

*Sulfur analyzed as $(SO_4)^{-2}$.
(1) Salton Sea Geothermal brine (Muffler and White, 1969).
(2) Cheleken geothermal brine (Lebedev and Nikitina, 1968).
(3) Oil field brine, Gaddis Farms D-1 well, Lower Rodessa reservoirs, central Mississippi, 11,000 ft (Carpenter et al., 1974).
(4) Fluid inclusion in sphalerites, OH vein, Creede, Colorado (Skinner and Barton, 1973).

elements and hence are little subject to corrosion. In more recent times, platinum, palladium, osmium, iridium, rhodium, and ruthenium (the so-called platinum group elements) have also come to be called precious or noble metals because they too exhibit nonreactive properties.

The fourth and final group, the **special metals,** does not fit into the previous three categories but has unusual properties that make it important for industry. Tantalum, for example, is widely used for electronic purposes because of its desirable electrical properties. Beryllium, on the other hand, is a very useful metal in nuclear technology and high-speed aircraft. Production and use of the special metals are recent; most special metals have only come into use in the twentieth century. It is not surprising that the special metals do not readily fit into the traditional grouping of precious, base, and ferrous metals because the uses to which they are put have only been developed as a result of twentieth century technology.

THE FERRO-ALLOY METALS

The ferro-alloy metals are products of twentieth century technology. Although the individual chemical elements were all known and had been separated into their elemental forms well before the dawn of the twentieth century, their widespread use as alloying metals for special steels only started in this century.

Chromium

Chromium was first discovered in 1765 through analysis of a chromate mineral found in Siberia. The metal was first separated as a pure chemical element in 1797. Chromate compounds have long been used in the tanning industry and in the manufacture of pigments for textiles, and they are still used for these purposes today. The properties of chromium as a valuable alloying metal were discovered as early as 1820, but the widespread use of chromium alloys only started in 1899 when ferrochromium, an iron-chromium mixture produced by chemically reducing the mineral chromite ($FeCr_2O_4$), was first produced in an electric furnace. Ferrochrome is still the way chromium is added to a batch of molten iron to make a chromium steel.

Chromium is one of the most visible yet least recognized metals in our modern industrial society. Chromium plating on steel and chromium-containing alloys, such as **stainless steel,** are the shiny, noncorroding metal surfaces we find on automobiles, in kitchens, on faucets, and in the cutlery we use. Chromium is also one of the so-called strategic metals, which means it is a metal considered to be vital to national defense and the continued operation of industry. This designation results from the widespread use of chromium-steel alloys in aircraft engines, military vehicles, weapons, and the chemical industry.

Chromium finds important uses today in three broad fields—metallurgy, chemistry, and refractories. As discussed above, metallurgy is an essential usage because of chromium's unique alloying properties. A steel containing between 12 percent and 36 percent chromium by weight has a greatly reduced tendency to react with oxygen and water—that is, a chromium-bearing steel corrodes very slowly. Chromium is also added to the steel used to make various machine tools because it increases hardness and resistance to wear.

The principal use of chromium as a chemical continues to lie in the production of pigments. Chromium pigments range in color from deep green and intense yellow to bright orange. Such pigments are widely used in paints, inks, roofing materials, and textile dyes. A lesser known, but still very important, chemical use of chromium compounds is in the tanning of animal skins. The lightweight leathers used for furniture, clothing, shoes, wallets, and similar objects are produced by bathing raw hides in solutions of chromium sulfate under controlled conditions of temperature and acidity. Chromium in solution forms chemical bonds with the amino acids in the leather, and this stabilizes the organic material by reducing its tendency for biological decay and increasing its resistance to heat.

In the refractory industry, the ore mineral **chromite** has proven to be ideal for making the bricks used to line very high-temperature smelter, blast, and gas furnaces. Chromite is a member of the spinel family of minerals, for which the general formula $A^{2+}B_2^{3+}O_4^{2-}$ can be written. The letter A designates any of the divalent ions Fe^{2+}, Mg^{2+}, and Mn^{2+}, while B designates the trivalent ions Fe^{3+}, Al^{3+}, and Cr^{3+}. Chromite thus has the formula $(Fe,Mg)(Cr,Al,Fe)_2O_4$. Chromites preferred for the production of ferrochrome have high contents of Cr^{3+} and Fe^{2+}, whereas chromites preferred for refractory bricks contain more Mg^{2+} and a little Al^{3+} as well as Cr^{3+}. Chromites of suitable composition are usually mixed with MgO to impart strength and to increase the resistance of refractory bricks to thermal and chemical attack.

Geological Occurrence. Chromium is present in small amounts in all **mafic** and **ultramafic** rocks—that is, rocks rich in iron and magnesium but poor in silica. Chromite is the major ore mineral of chromium, and its occurrence is essentially restricted to ultramafic rocks. It occurs in two major types of ore bodies, **podiform** and **stratiform.** The podiform deposits appear as irregular pods or lenses that may range in mass from a few kilograms to several million tons and that occur nearly always in highly faulted and deformed portions of tectonically active zones. A common feature of these deposits is the appearance of the chromite as rounded or eyelike granules (Figure 8.5). The pods are enclosed in deformed masses of **dunites, serpentinites,** and related ultramafic rocks that are believed to be solid fragments from the upper mantle that were squeezed up during tectonic collisions between continents. Typical podiform deposits occur in the Ural Mountains of the former Soviet Union, the Appalachian and Pacific Coast ranges of the United States, Cuba, the Philippines, and the countries around the eastern end of the Mediterranean. The bodies, though small, contain chromites with very desirable compositions.

Stratiform chromite deposits are, as the name indicates, discrete, sharply bounded strata of essentially pure chromite (Figure 8.6) that occur in large, mafic intrusions where the layering developed as an artifact of the processes of cooling and crystallization. Individual monomineralic layers of chromite are known to range up to several meters in

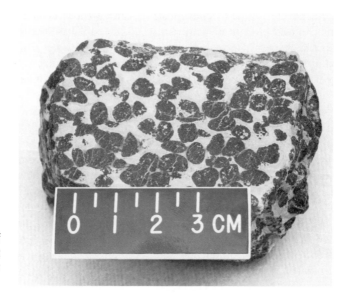

FIGURE 8.5. Pelletal grains of chromite in a podiform deposit from Greece. (Photograph by S. Llyn Sharp.)

thickness in the largest layered intrusions, but such thick layers are very rare. More commonly, chromite layers are a meter or less in thickness. Whether thick or thin, however, the chromite layers may extend laterally up to tens of kilometers, and in the largest known layered intrusion, the Bushveld Igneous Complex in South Africa, the layers extend up to hundreds of kilometers. Stratiform chromite layers contain most of the world's known chromite resources, although in many cases the compositions of the stratiform chromites are not as desirable for metallurgical or refractory purposes as the chromites from podiform deposits.

The origin of stratiform layers of chromite remains in question. For many years, geologists accepted the idea that the layers formed when dense chromite grains crystallized from cooling bodies of **magma,** then settled to the floor of the magma chamber to form the monomineralic layers we see today. A dense mineral such as chromite was presumed to sink rapidly, while a less dense mineral such as pyroxene would sink more slowly, and as a result a separation would be effected. Recently, this simple picture based on crystal settling has been questioned and found wanting. The textures of the chromite grains, and indeed the sequence of minerals in the layers, suggest that the minerals actually grew on the bottom of the magma chamber and that little or no settling was involved. The thick, economical layers of chromite formed during long periods of time when chromite was the only

FIGURE 8.6. Stratiform layers of chromitite, a rock comprised almost entirely of chromite, exposed along the banks of the Dwaars River, South Africa. The chromitite is interlayered with anorthositic norite (white) in the lower portion of the Bushveld Igneous Complex. (Photograph by B. J. Skinner.)

mineral crystallizing from the magma. We now believe that the periods of chromite formation were brought about by relatively large-scale, but temporary, changes in the composition of the crystallizing magma as a result of contamination by overlying or underlying rocks. Such contamination would have altered the chemistry of the magma just enough so that, for a period, only chromite crystallized; after that period, the normal sequence of igneous minerals would again crystallize.

By far, the most important stratiform deposits of chromite in the world occur in the Bushveld Igneous Complex of South Africa. This enormous complex of layered intrusions covers 66,000 square kilometers, is 12 kilometers thick in places, and is also host to the world's largest known resource of vanadium and the platinum group metals.

Production and Reserves. The production and reserves of chromite are dominated by the Republic of South Africa, which holds about 70 percent of the world's reserves; South Africa and Kazakhstan are the largest producers (Figure 8.7). The United States and all of Europe, except Finland,

are without economically viable chromite deposits. The United States does have large, low-grade stratiform deposits in the Stillwater Complex, Montana, but the chromite has a composition that is difficult to process and expensive to use. As a result, the industrial countries of the world depend for their supplies on stratiform deposits in South Africa and Zimbabwe and podiform deposits in the former Soviet Union.

Because of the strategic importance of chromium, there is continuing concern about the potential for supplies to be cut off from the major suppliers either due to civil unrest or political considerations. The data in Figure 8.7 indicate that the known world reserves of chromite are certainly adequate to meet needs for many years to come; furthermore, it seems likely that the Bushveld Igneous Complex has additional large resources, not included in the reserve number in Figure 8.7, that can also be exploited in the future. Chromium is thus one of the important commodities where future availability may well be more dependent on political and social issues than on the physical limits of resources.

The widespread use of chromates as coloring agents in paints, in fabrics, and on paper means that chromium compounds are all around us. Concerns about the toxicity of some chromium compounds has led organizations such as the Environmental Protection Agency (EPA) and the Occupational Health and Safety Administration of the United States to introduce regulations regarding its use. Of particular concern has been the release of chromium into groundwater from leachates derived from old landfills and old industrial sites where the disposal of chromium compounds was accomplished by dumping or burial.

Vanadium

Vanadium was identified as a chemical element in 1830, and like chromium, its salts soon found uses in the tanning of leather and in preparation of colored pigments for textiles, pottery, and ceramics. The use of vanadium as an alloy came much later. In 1896, French scientists found that vanadium so toughened steel that it could withstand the impact of bullets and could be used to make armor plate. It was soon discovered that vanadium steel also toughened the cutting edges of knives, improved swords, and greatly increased the strength of certain constructional steels. This later discovery led the United States automobile industry to start using vanadium steel, and by 1908 its use was advertised as a special feature of Ford motor vehicles.

Vanadium steels continue to be very widely used in automobiles and in industry in general because the incorporation of as little as 0.2 percent vanadium in an ordinary carbon steel greatly increases its strength, high-temperature abrasion resistance, ductility, and even the ease with which steels can be welded. The use of high-strength vanadium steel allows a minimum weight of steel to be used in an automobile, and this, in turn, leads to increased efficiency and to a reduction in the amount of fuel needed.

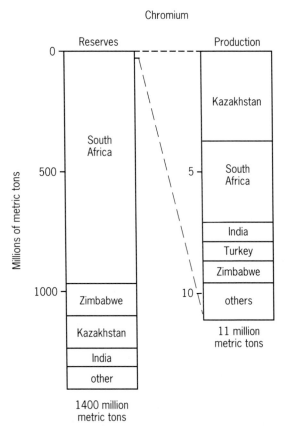

FIGURE 8.7. The world's 1400 million metric tons of chromium reserves are held primarily in South Africa, but the major producers are Kazakhstan and South Africa. At present rates of production of about 11 million metric tons per year, the world's reserves will last more than 125 years. (From the U.S. Bureau of Mines.)

The ease and reliability with which vanadium steel can be welded has led to its widespread use in gas and oil transmission pipelines. The 1288-kilometer Alaskan pipeline, which brings oil from the Prudhoe Bay to the port of Valdez, incorporates 650 tons of vanadium.

Geological Occurrence. Despite a crustal abundance of 0.017 percent, which makes vanadium one of the most common of the geochemically scarce elements, vanadium ore deposits are rare. The reason deposits are rare is that vanadium readily substitutes for ferric iron (Fe^{3+}) and therefore readily enters into solid solution in common minerals such as magnetite (Fe_3O_4). The solid solution of vanadium is so extensive that the limits are rarely exceeded, and thus local concentrations of vanadium minerals are rare. The most important ore deposits of vanadium are vanadium-rich magnetites (containing approximately 2 percent V_2O_5). These are found as monomineralic stratiform layers of magnetite in certain layered intrusions of mafic igneous rock. The most important of the vanadiferous magnetite deposits discovered so far are in the Bushveld Igneous Complex in South Africa. The stratiform layers of vanadiferous magnetite, of which there are about ten, are near the top of the Bushveld Igneous Complex, while the stratiform chromite layers that they closely resemble (Figure 8.8) are near the base. The vanadium magnetite layers, like the chromite layers, appear to have formed as a result of monomineralic crystal growth on the floor of the magma chamber.

When separate deposits of vanadium minerals do occur, they apparently form as a result of weathering. When igneous rocks that contain vanadium-bearing magnetites or other vanadium-bearing minerals are weathered in arid climates, the vanadium is oxidized from the trivalent V^{3+} state to the more soluble pentavalent V^{5+} state. Pentavalent vanadium can be transported long distances in solution. Precipitation of vanadium minerals can occur through evaporation or, as in the Colorado Plateau region of the United States, through contact with organic matter, which serves as a reducing agent that causes the vanadium in solution to be converted to the less soluble V^{3+} state. Uranium and copper also have more than one valency state and exhibit a behavior similar to vanadium. Uranium and vanadium are sometimes found concentrated together as a result. The region of Colorado, Wyoming, Utah, and New Mexico where deposits of this kind are found is known as the **Uravan district** because of the co-occurrence of uranium and vanadium. For many years in the early part of this century, deposits in the Uravan district were worked for vanadium. From the time of World War II and the development of atom bombs and nuclear power, attention in the region has been focused almost entirely on uranium.

Vanadium tends to be concentrated, at least to a small degree, whenever concentrations of organic matter occur. The vanadium content of coal averages about 0.02 percent, while that of crude oil is about 0.005 percent. Certain very

heavy oils (tars) have much higher vanadium contents. The tar in the Athabasca Tar Sands of Canada contains up to 0.025 percent vanadium, while that from the Orinoco Tar Sands of Venezuela contains 0.05 percent. In Peru and Argentina, veins of solid bitumen, believed to have formed by distillation of petroleum, contain 0.1 percent and 0.85 percent vanadium, respectively.

The role of vanadium in fossil fuels is not well understood. It is clear that much of the vanadium must enter the deposits after sedimentation because the vanadium content of living plants and animals is not high. The vanadium appears to enter during degradation of the original organic matter in the sedimentary pile, perhaps brought in by groundwater, and is locked up in compounds called **porphyrins.** The atomic structures of the vanadium porphyrins found in crude oils resemble cages, with the vanadium atoms at the center. The cages are nearly identical to the structures of the chlorophylls (magnesium-centered porphyrins) of green plants and the hemoglobins (iron-centered porphyrins) of blood. Vanadium probably changes place in the structures with magnesium and iron during **diagenesis.**

Because many vanadium compounds are considered to be toxic to humans, there is much care taken in working with ores or products rich in vanadium. In all practical applications, the concentrations are quite low, and the metals are found in inert alloy forms; hence, there have been no reports of health problems.

Production and Reserves. The bulk of the vanadium produced today (about 60 percent) comes from the vanadiferous magnetite deposits of South Africa, Russia, and China (Figure 8.9). Lesser amounts are recovered as by-products from the slags of iron smelters and smelters producing elemental phosphorus. In the western United States, the ores of the Uravan District of the Colorado Plateau are mined for uranium, and vanadium is recovered as a by-product. Thus, the economic viability of the deposits is primarily dependent upon the price of uranium. The decline in the demand and price of uranium, as a result of the nuclear accidents at Three Mile Island and at Chernobyl (see Chapter 6), has severely curtailed production of vanadium from the major deposits in the United States.

The recovery of vanadium by-products from the ash of burned fuel oils during petroleum refining and from spent catalytic converters used in oil refining now accounts for 1510 metric tons of metal, or about 5 percent of the world's annual production. In the United States, this type of recovery accounts for more than 26 percent of total production. The distillation of petroleum concentrates the tiny quantities of metals of the oil into the solid residue referred to as petroleum coke. Increasingly, this coke is being used to generate so-called synthesis gas (a mixture of CO, CH_4, and H_2), which becomes a chemical feedstock or is burned to generate electricity. In the process, the metals, especially vanadium, are again concentrated and deposited in a residual slag;

FIGURE 8.8. Dark-colored stratiform layer of magnetite in the upper portion of the Bushveld Igneous Complex, South Africa. The layers are almost entirely comprised of magnetite and have the same origin as the chromitite layers in Figure 8.6. The magnetite contains vanadium in solid solution and is one of the world's major sources of this valuable alloy metal. (Photograph by Craig Schiffries.)

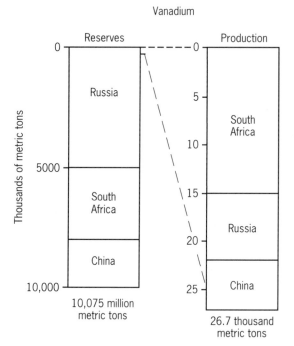

FIGURE 8.9. The world's primary reserves of vanadium are held in Russia, South Africa, and China and are sufficient to last nearly 400 years at present rates of production of about 27,000 metric tons per year. Today, much vanadium is also being recovered from the materials left after petroleum refining. (From the U.S. Bureau of Mines.)

this slag may contain up to 40 percent vanadium and can be readily processed as an ore of the metal.

It is apparent that known world reserves of vanadium will last for at least another hundred years. Furthermore, it has been estimated that if the price of crude oil rises sufficiently to permit mining of the rich oil sands of the world, those in the Athabasca region of Alberta alone could supply well over 2 million tons of vanadium, sufficient for an exceedingly long time into the future.

Nickel

Nickel has been used for millenia. Small amounts of nickel are present in some of the ancient copper coins dug up in the Middle East. It is probable that the use of nickel in this case was accidental and that it came about because nickel was present in small amounts as an unrecognized contaminant in the copper ore used to make the coins. Nickel really entered the cognizance of the Western world when it was encountered during the seventeenth and eighteenth centuries by copper miners in Saxony, in what is now eastern Germany. Certain nickel minerals so resemble copper minerals in their color and in other properties that the Saxon miners attempted to smelt the ore to recover copper. What they ob-

tained were specks of a shiny white metal that could not be worked into useful objects, so they named the material *kupfernickel*, or *Old Nick's* copper. They believed that the devil, Old Nick, and his mischievous gnomes had bewitched the copper ore. The frustration of those old miners lives on in the name nickel. Early in the eighteenth century, a Swedish chemist, Axel Cronstedt, showed that nickel is actually a separate chemical element, but it was not until 1781 that pure, metallic nickel was prepared.

The first practical use of metallic nickel was in a nickel-silver alloy, the so-called German silver, that is used for trays, tea pots, and other household utensils. Extensive demand for nickel arose as a result of discoveries by the English scientist and inventor Michael Faraday, who developed the process of **electroplating.** In this process, metal is dissolved into solution from a metal plate connected to one terminal of a battery and then deposited on another metal object connected to the other terminal. Nickel dissolves when connected to the anode (the positive terminal of the battery), it moves as a result of the electrical current, and then is deposited as a thin layer on the metal object connected to the cathode (the negative terminal). Because nickel resists corrosion and can be polished to a high luster, nickel plating soon became very popular, and by 1844 a plating industry was firmly established in England. Soon thereafter, nickel was added to copper coins to harden them. Belgium did so in 1860, and the United States followed in 1865. Use of the term *nickel* for the five-cent piece in the United States and Canada soon followed, even though the alloy of the coin contains 75 percent copper and only 25 percent nickel.

The use of nickel as an alloying agent with iron came about in the twentieth century. Nickel and chromium steels do not corrode or rust—they are stainless. Used alone, or in combination with chromium and other alloying agents, nickel-bearing steels find many uses in the manufacture of aircraft, trucks, railroad cars, and other structures that require great reliability and high strength. It is probably not an overstatement to say that nickel has proved to be the most versatile of all the ferro-alloying metals.

Nickel is still widely used as a plating metal, is still used in coinage, and is still used to harden copper and make versatile alloys with metals other than iron. But the major use of nickel today, accounting for about half of the world's total production, is as an alloying agent with iron.

Geological Occurrence. All of the important nickel deposits in the world are found in, or adjacent to, mafic and ultramafic igneous rocks. Nickel is one of the chemical elements that is depleted in the crust but enriched in the **mantle.** Thus, mafic and ultramafic igneous rocks derived from magmas generated in the mantle tend to have high nickel contents. Whereas the average nickel concentration in the continental crust is only 0.0072 percent by weight, many mafic and ultramafic igneous rocks contain as much as 0.1

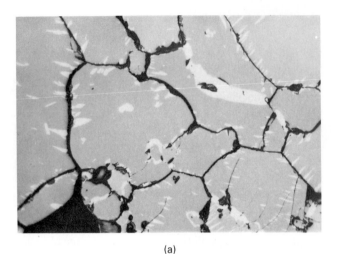

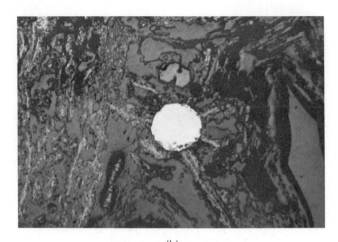

(a)   (b)

FIGURE 8.10.   (a) Droplet of iron and nickel sulfides in basalt from midocean ridge. (Photograph by J. R. Craig.) (b) Pentlandite (white) exsolved from pyrrhotite due to cooling. (Photograph by D. J. Vaughan.)

percent nickel. The nickel is present in mafic igneous rocks in solid solution in **pyroxenes** and **olivines,** where it substitutes for magnesium and iron.

Ordinary mafic and ultramafic igneous rocks are not sufficiently enriched in nickel to be considered ores. Concentrations occur in two entirely different ways. The first is a form of magmatic segregation involving **liquid immiscibility.** When a magma cools and starts to crystallize, minerals such as olivine and pyroxene form and grow in the liquid. The growth of crystals of pyroxene in the magma indicates that the liquid has become saturated in pyroxene. Suppose, however, that the cooling magma becomes saturated in a compound but that the temperature is still above the melting temperature of that compound. That is what sometimes happens in the case of the iron sulfide mineral **pyrrhotite.** Instead of a crystal of pyrrhotite forming in the cooling magma, tiny drops of a molten iron sulfide liquid form. The silicate magma and the iron sulfide liquid do not mix and are said to be immiscible, like oil and water (Figure 8.10a). The immiscible liquid is not pure iron sulfide but tends to scavenge atoms of nickel, copper, platinum, and certain other chemical elements in the magma, so it is really an iron-nickel-copper-sulfide liquid. The immiscible sulfide droplets are more dense than the silicate magma, so they tend to sink and form sulfide-rich zones near the base of the magma chamber. When the sulfide liquid eventually crystallizes, the main mineral that forms is pyrrhotite ($Fe_{1-x}S$), but intergrown with the pyrrhotite are grains of the only important sulfide ore mineral of nickel, pentlandite (($Ni,Fe)_9S_8$) (Figure 8.10b), together with chalcopyrite ($CuFeS_2$) and tiny grains of metallic platinum and other platinum group minerals. By the processes of concentration through liquid immiscibility and magmatic segregation, nickel contents as high as 3 or 4 percent can be reached.

The world's richest and most important nickel ore bodies are all sulfide ores that formed as a result of magmatic segregation. The most famous nickel ore deposits are at Sudbury, Ontario, where intrusive, mafic igneous rocks form an elliptical ring 56 kilometers on the long axis and 26 kilometers on the short axis. Around the outer edge of the basin, near the base of the intrusion, a number of large, rich deposits occur (Figure 8.11). One of the strange features about Sudbury is that the intrusion has the shape of a cone rather than a flat sheet, as is usual for most dikes and sills. The probable reason for the conical shape was realized in the 1960s as a result of investigations associated with space research. Many features on the surface of the moon and other bodies in the solar system result from large meteorite impacts. As the properties and characteristics of impact structures on Earth were studied, it became apparent that the Sudbury ring might be an ancient (1.9 billion year) impact structure, and that the magma carrying the immiscible sulfide droplets probably rose from the mantle along fractures created by the impact event. Other rich and important sulfide ores of nickel are found in Canada in the Thompson Lake district of Manitoba, Kambalda in western Australia, Botswana, Zimbabwe, and Russia.

The second important way that nickel can be concentrated in a mafic or ultramafic rock is through weathering. When mafic igneous rocks are subject to chemical weathering under tropical or semitropical conditions, the silicate minerals (pyroxene, olivine, and plagioclase) break down to form hydrous compounds, and iron is oxidized to the ferric state. The small amount of nickel present in solid solution in the olivines and pyroxenes is released in the process, and it either forms nickel silicate minerals, or it is incorporated into the structure of other minerals formed during weathering. The weathering minerals, such as chlorite and serpentine, sometimes contain 1 percent or 2 percent of nickel; under

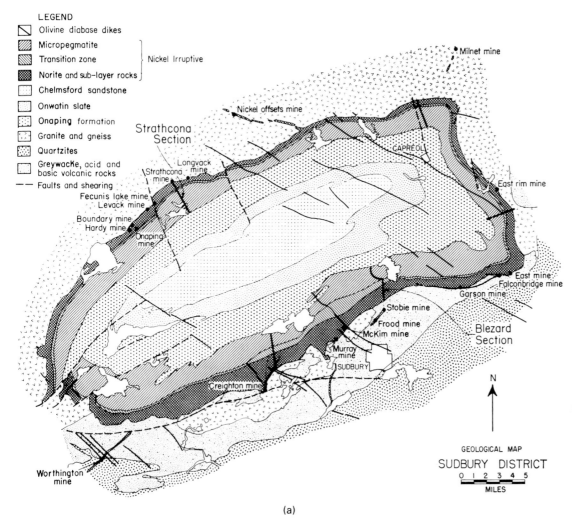

LEGEND
◻ Olivine diabase dikes
▨ Micropegmatite
▨ Transition zone ⎫
▨ Norite and sub-layer rocks ⎬ Nickel Irruptive
◻ Chelmsford sandstone
◻ Onwatin slate
▦ Onaping formation
▦ Granite and gneiss
▦ Quartzites
◻ Greywacke, acid and basic volcanic rocks
— — Faults and shearing

Strathcona Section
Nickel offsets mine
Longvack mine
Strathcona mine
Fecunis lake mine
Levack mine
Boundary mine
Hardy mine
Onaping mine
Milnet mine
CAPREOL
East rim mine
East mine
Falconbridge mine
Garson mine
Blezard Section
Stobie mine
Frood mine
McKim mine
Murray mine
SUDBURY
Creighton mine
Worthington mine

N

GEOLOGICAL MAP
SUDBURY DISTRICT
0 1 2 3 4 5
MILES

(a)

FIGURE 8.11. (a) Map of the Sudbury Intrusive, the largest nickel district in the world. (From E. Gaspartini and A. J. Naldrett, *Economic Geology*, vol. 67, no. 605 (1972). Used with permission.) (b) A shatter cone produced by the passage of impact-induced shock waves through the Mississagi Quartzite, near Sudbury, Ontario. Similar shatter cones can be found at many places outside the Sudbury ring. The long axes of the cones all point to the same place—a point several kilometers above the center of the ring that is believed to have been the now-eroded point of impact. (Photograph by B. J. Skinner.)

certain circumstances the nickel silicate minerals, collectively called **garnierite,** may form and produce ores as rich as 4 percent or 5 percent. Residual weathering ores are referred to as **laterite ores.** The most famous laterite ore is in New Caledonia, where French interests have been mining garnierite-rich bodies for most of this century. There, a nickeliferous **peridotite** has weathered to form lateritic garnierite ore (Figure 8.12). Rich garnierite deposits are rare, but lateritic weathering of mafic igneous rocks is widespread around the world. As a result, there are a great many low-grade lateritic deposits. Such ores are difficult to process, but some are worked today in Cuba, the Dominican Republic, the Philippines, and Indonesia.

Production and Reserves. Nickel is one of the strategic minerals for which the United States has very limited resources of high-grade deposits. It does have very large, low-grade deposits, however. These sulfide ores are in the Duluth Gabbro, Minnesota, and average about 0.21 percent nickel.

For many years, a large fraction of the world's nickel has come from the Sudbury and Thompson Lake districts of Canada. A steady increase in the mining of nickel from the Norils'k deposits in Russia has now brought the production there to the same level as Canada (Figure 8.13). Important production of sulfide ore also comes from Australia, Botswana, Finland, Republic of South Africa, and Zimbabwe,

FIGURE 8.11.   (*cont.*)

(b)

while mining of lateritic ore is carried out in Cuba, the Dominican Republic, Greece, Indonesia, New Caledonia, the Philippines, and the United States.

Molybdenum

Molybdenum is a versatile and highly important member of the ferro-alloy family of metals, but it is relatively unknown outside of metallurgical circles. This is because molybdenum, like several other metals, is scarcely ever used in its pure elemental form. Nevertheless, it is an extremely versatile metal that is used in a wide assortment of products.

The name molybdenum comes from the Latin word *molybdaena* and from the older Greek word *molybdos,* which actually refer to the lead mineral galena and metallic lead, respectively. There are a number of soft, easily deformed, grey minerals that look like lead and galena. Among those confusing minerals are graphite (C) and the mineral we now call **molybdenite** (MoS_2). From the time of the Greeks and Romans, all of the leadlike minerals were called *molybdos.* The confusion was only resolved in the eighteenth century when, in 1778, molybdenite was identified as a sulfide compound of a new chemical element, and in 1782, the element was separated as a metal. The chemistry required to prepare the metal is difficult, and it was not until 1893 that pure metal was produced.

As soon as pure molybdenum was available, its alloying properties were tested by French scientists. It proved to make a very tough and resilient steel that was ideal for armor plating. By 1898, molybdenum tool steel had also been developed. However, neither of these uses created much demand. A few small mines were opened in the latter years of the nineteenth century, but those in the United States had all ceased to operate by 1906. Production in those days was satisfied by molybdenum ores worked in Norway, Australia, and Canada.

Molybdenum finally found a market in World War I when it was discovered that molybdenum steels could be substituted for the widely used tungsten steels in high-speed cutting tools and armaments. As a result, large deposits were opened at Climax, Colorado, and Questa, New Mexico. When World War I ended, military demand for molybdenum slumped and production at Climax and Questa was stopped. Starting about 1920, new uses were found for molybdenum

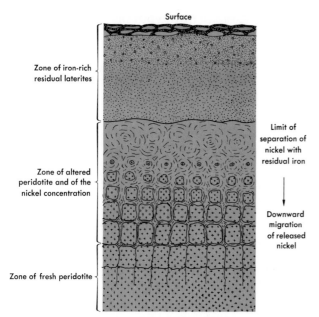

FIGURE 8.12. Chemical weathering of nickeliferous rocks, such as peridotite, releases nickel trapped in the olivine; the breakdown products of the olivine are then redeposited in the form of minerals such as garnierite. Residual ores of this kind are valuable resources of nickel and are worked in New Caledonia and Cuba. (From E. de Chetalat, *Bull Soc Geol France* Ser. 63, Vol. XVII, 129, Fig. 4, (1967).)

steels, and in the electrical industry, it was found that molybdenum alloys made desirable heating elements. These new markets led to a resumption of full-scale mining by 1924.

About 90 percent of the molybdenum mined today is still used as an alloying element in steels, cast irons, and **superalloys** where it imparts hardness, toughness, resistance to corrosion and abrasion, and adds strength at high temperatures. Its content in steel ranges from 0.1 percent to 10 percent by weight, and it is usually employed in combination with other of the ferro-alloy elements. The steels produced are now used in all segments of industry but find special demand in cutting tools, transportation, and oil and gas production equipment. The anticorrosion properties imparted by molybdenum have led to the increasing application of its steels in severe chemical environments and in seawater.

Nonmetallic applications for molybdenum include lubricants, catalysts, and pigments. Molybdenum disulfide (MoS_2) has a well-defined layer structure somewhat like mica, is exceedingly soft and slippery to the touch, and resists breakdown even at high temperature and pressure. Consequently, it is widely used as an additive to oils and greases where it helps significantly to reduce friction and wear in automobile engines. Molybdenum catalysts are also used in the production of petroleum-based chemicals and alcohols.

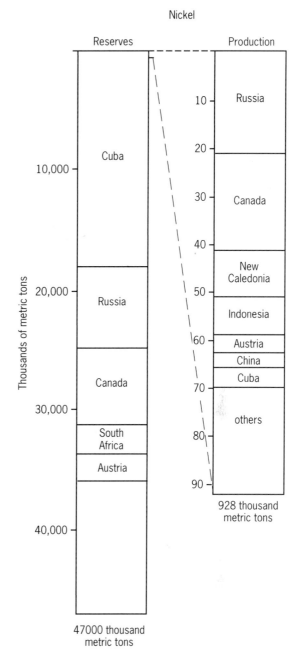

FIGURE 8.13. Cuba, Russia, and Canada hold the greatest reserves of nickel. At present rates of production, known reserves will last about 50 years. (From the U.S. Bureau of Mines.)

Molybdenum orange (MoO_2) is an important pigment in paints, dyes, and inks.

Geological Occurrence. Nearly all of the known molybdenum ores consist of molybdenite (MoS_2) a lead-gray metallic mineral that occurs in **porphyry-type** igneous intrusions of the type described under copper. The large porphyry-type deposits, closely related to subduction zones at the edges of continental plate boundaries (Figures 8.24 and 8.25) and

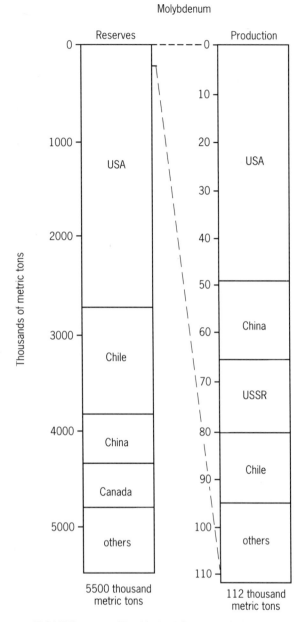

FIGURE 8.14. The United States holds about 50 percent of the world's reserves of molybdenum and produces about 45 percent of the world total each year. At present rates of production, the known reserves will last about 50 years. (From the U.S. Bureau of Mines.)

commonly rich in copper minerals, usually contain minor amounts of molybdenite as well. A significant fraction of molybdenum production comes as a by-product from porphyry copper mining. A few large deposits such as those at Climax and Urad, Colorado, and Questa, New Mexico, contain molybdenite plus minor tin and tungsten minerals, almost to the exclusion of copper sulfides. The molybdenite occurs as disseminations and thin coatings in cross-cutting fractures in the igneous intrusions and surrounding rocks as are evident in Figure 8.23. It was deposited along with large

amounts of quartz by **hydrothermal** solutions that were episodically released from the crystallizing magma.

Molybdenite also occurs in much lesser, and usually uneconomical, quantities in **contact metamorphic** zones adjacent to silica-rich igneous rocks, in quartz vein deposits, and in pegmatites. Molybdenite is usually recovered as a by-product from these deposits.

Production and Reserves. The United States dominated the world molybdenum market for many years with the bulk of production coming from the large deposits at Climax, Colorado, and Questa, New Mexico. In recent years, however, production has increased in the former Soviet Union, Chile, Canada, Mexico, and Peru. The decline in the United States steel industry, long the principal market for American production, combined with increasing competition from other western hemisphere producers, has resulted in at least temporary closings of the Questa mine and major cutbacks in the mining at Climax and Urad, Colorado.

The known reserves of molybdenum (Figure 8.14) are clearly adequate for many years to come. It does appear, however, that there will be a continuing shift in production away from the United States as the dominant world source to Chile, China, Mexico, and Peru.

Cobalt

The earliest uses of cobalt as a brilliant blue coloring agent date from antiquity. Egyptian and Babylonian potters used cobalt oxide, known as cobalt blue, to color glass and ceramics. Chinese craftsmen extensively developed the art of cobalt coloring during the Ming Dynasty (fourteenth to seventeenth centuries), and in Europe, Venetian artisans of the fifteenth and later centuries were renowned for their cobalt-colored glassware.

The name *cobalt*, like that of nickel, has an association with old German miners. During the sixteenth century, arsenic-bearing silver-cobalt ores were mined in the Harz Mountains (now in eastern Germany). The roasting of these ores released poisonous arsenical fumes that caused ulcers on the bodies of the miners tending the furnaces. The miners believed the source to be silver-stealing goblins called *Kobolds,* who replaced good silver minerals with useless cobalt arsenides that look somewhat like silver.

Cobalt was shown to be a separate chemical element in 1780, and the modern history of cobalt dates from this time. The principal uses of cobalt continued to be in coloring agents and chemical compounds used in various industrial processes. In 1910, the use of cobalt as an alloying compound was finally demonstrated by an American, Elwood Haynes, who showed that the addition of about 5 percent cobalt to a steel containing chromium and tungsten greatly improved its qualities as a tool-steel. This alloy and other chromium-cobalt alloys were the forerunners of today's **superalloys** that retain their mechanical strength at high temperature and are resistant to the corrosion of hot gases. The recognition of the importance of cobalt and its marked increase in superalloys employed in jet engines, rocket nozzles, and gas turbines after World War II has led to cobalt being designated a strategic metal. Cobalt alloys also have remarkable magnetic properties—the magnetism is very strong and is retained forever. The magnets used in the loudspeakers of high-fidelity sound systems are almost all cobalt-based magnets.

Geological Occurrence. Most of the world's cobalt is produced as a by-product from the mining and metallurgical treatment of the ores of copper, nickel, and silver. The most important cobalt ores are **stratiform** copper sulfide ores, which are found in the *copperbelt* in Zaire in central Africa. This type of deposit consists of copper sulfide minerals, such as chalcopyrite ($CuFeS_2$), together with cobalt sulfide minerals such as linaeite (Co_3S_4) and cobaltiferous pyrite $(Fe,Co)S_2$ enclosed in fine-grained **clastic** strata. The origin of the deposits is problematic, but the sulfide minerals appear to have been introduced into the sedimentary strata soon after deposition by warm saline solutions circulating in subsurface aquifers.

Cobalt also tends to be concentrated wherever nickel is concentrated. Thus, cobalt is an important by-product from the exploitation of both magmatic segregation nickel sulfide ores and lateritic nickel ores.

Production and Reserves. Two countries, Zaire and Zambia, produce about twice as much cobalt as all the other countries of the world combined (Figure 8.15). These are the only countries where mines are worked principally for cobalt; elsewhere, cobalt is simply a by-product.

The world's largest reserves lie in the stratiform ores of central Africa. The large Canadian reserves nearly all occur with the rich nickel ores in the Sudbury basin; the cobalt is produced as a major by-product of the nickel mining. In addition to the known reserves, there are probably at least another 4,500,000 metric tons of cobalt as identified resources. The largest resources are in Cuba in the nickel-laterite ores. Large resources have also been identified in Zaire and in the United States, principally associated with the low-grade nickel deposits of the Duluth Gabbro in Minnesota. Further very large deposits are believed to lie on the ocean floor, where some of the ferromanganese nodules (described in Chapter 7) contain up to 1 percent cobalt (see Table 7.5). Thus, even though definite reserve figures cannot be quoted for cobalt, the long-term future for the metal appears to be assured.

Tungsten

Tungsten is a grayish-white colored metal that has many alloying properties similar to those of chromium and molybdenum. It has the distinction of being the metal with the highest melting temperature (3400°C) and the further distinction of being the metal with the highest tensile strength.

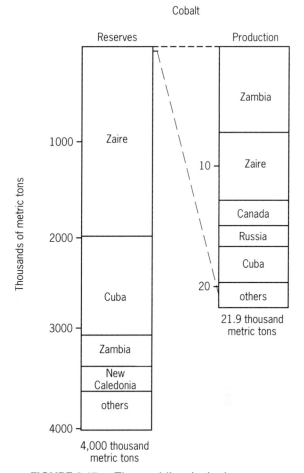

FIGURE 8.15. The world's principal reserves of cobalt are in Zaire and Cuba, but Zambia and Zaire are the principal producers in the 1990s. At present rates of production, the known reserves of cobalt will last about 180 years. (From the U.S. Bureau of Mines.)

Alloys of tungsten are therefore extremely hard and extremely stable at high temperatures.

Metallic tungsten and the ore minerals of tungsten are all very dense. The name *tungsten* recognizes this property and comes from two Swedish words, *tung,* meaning heavy, and *sten,* stone. Until the middle of the eighteenth century, the mineral we know today as scheelite ($CaWO_4$), but then called tungsten, was thought to be an ore mineral of tin. In 1781, the Swedish chemist K. W. Scheele showed that tin was not present, and that a new chemical element was probably involved. Two years later, two Spanish chemists, the d'Ellhuyar brothers, prepared metallic tungsten for the first time. The name *tungsten* was thereafter reserved for the element, and the mineral was named *scheelite* in honor of Scheele. The first use of tungsten as an additive to steel occurred in France in 1855. Within a few years, the toughness of tungsten steels came to be appreciated, and by 1868 small amounts of tungsten were added to train rails made in France. Today tungsten steels are used in many circumstances where toughness, durability, and resistance to impact are needed.

The single most important use of tungsten is not for its alloying properties—although these uses are certainly very important—but for the manufacture of tungsten carbide (WC), a compound with a hardness approaching that of diamond. Tungsten carbide can be sintered into intricate shapes, and it is widely used in the preparation of tungsten carbide tools, drill bits, cutting edges, and even armor-piercing projectiles.

The high melting temperature of tungsten facilitates its use in such places as the filaments of electric light bulbs, the distributor points of automobiles, and various heating elements. When the overall uses of tungsten are considered, approximately 45 percent of the annual production is used to make tungsten carbide, 25 percent for ferro-alloys, 18 percent for tungsten metal and alloys in which tungsten is the major metal, and 11 percent for nonferrous alloys. All other uses total only 1 percent.

Geological Occurrence. Tungsten has a geochemical abundance of 0.001 percent by weight and is therefore one of the scarcest of the geochemically scarce metals. It forms only two minerals of economic importance, scheelite ($CaWO_4$) and wolframite ((Fe,Mn)WO_4). The most important tungsten deposits were formed by hydrothermal solutions. These fluids are widespread in Earth's crust, and indeed, more ore deposits are formed through their agency than any other deposit-forming agency. The origin and chemistry of hydrothermal solutions are discussed more fully in the section on copper. Such solutions deposit small amounts of wolframite or scheelite, together with tin minerals, in quartz-rich **veins** that are usually closely related to intrusive igneous rocks that are felsic in character. Much of the world's tungsten production comes from quartz veins and closely spaced quartz stringers called **stockworks.** A small amount of production arises as a by-product of gold, tin, or copper mining. Tungsten deposits also occur where igneous rocks have been intruded into limestones or marbles to form **contact metamorphic** deposits (sometimes called **skarn ores**). The ore mineral in these deposits is usually scheelite, and the deposits, although often rich, are generally small. Several deposits of this kind are worked in the United States in Nevada, Utah, and California.

Production and Reserves. By far, the largest producers of tungsten in the world are China and the members of the former Soviet Union. Most Chinese ores are quartz vein deposits, and resources are believed to be huge although they have not been completely explored and tested. Significant production comes, too, from Korea, Burma, and Thailand (Figure 8.16)—three countries adjacent to China that are endowed with mineralization similar to that in China.

Reserves of tungsten have not been adequately measured. Estimates shown in Figure 8.16 are possibly too low for China and Australia. As far as resources are concerned,

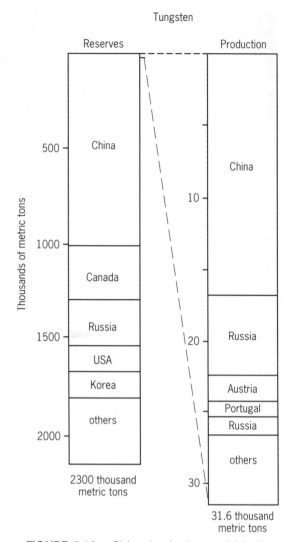

FIGURE 8.16. China leads the world in the reserves and production of tungsten. At present rates of production, the known reserves will last more than 70 years. (From the U.S. Bureau of Mines.)

estimates are practically meaningless because so little information is available.

THE BASE METALS

A **base metal** is commonly defined as a metal or alloy of comparatively low value and one that is relatively inferior in certain properties such as corrosion. Such a definition seems to suggest that the base metals are second-class citizens in the family of metals. Nothing could be further from the truth because the base metals are endowed with many important and unique properties. It was the base metals that our distant ancestors first learned to shape into useful objects. We still recognize those achievements in the terms *Copper Age* and

FIGURE 8.17. A 20-centimeter high, copper figurine of Gudea of Lagash, made approximately 4200 years ago. The inscription in Sumerian reads "For Bau, the good lady, the daughter of An, the lady of the holy city. His lady, Gudea governor of Lagash the man who built the temple E-Ninnu of the god Nigirsu, built her wall of the holy city." (Specimen from the Yale Babylonian Collection. Photograph by W. Sacco.)

Bronze Age. The Copper Age designates that first great step humankind took when it advanced from the Stone Age and learned to work and employ metals. The next step, into the Bronze Age, took humankind into the field of alloy metallurgy. Bronze is an alloy of two or more metals but is principally copper plus tin. From the time our ancestors first learned how to work copper into needles, axes, arrowheads, and other useful objects (Figure 8.17), the practical uses found for the base metals have expanded continually. When the first indoor plumbing was installed by the Romans, they used lead pipes. When the ordinary working man wanted something better than leather or wooden plates to eat from, pewter, an alloy of base metals, came into common use.

When it was shown to be possible to transmit and use electricity in the nineteenth century, electricians turned to a base metal, copper, to carry electricity from generating plants to people's houses. Is it possible to imagine how today's world of 5 billion people could operate without the widespread use of electricity? Nothing has changed our lives so much as this one great technological advance, and it is a base metal that has been the workhorse.

The base metals of antiquity were copper, lead, tin, and mercury. Several hundred years ago, zinc was added to the list. Zinc was actually used by the Chinese and Romans over 2000 years ago, as evidenced by its presence in bronze dating from those times. But the Chinese and Romans apparently could not smelt and prepare zinc metal, so the presence of the zinc in the alloy probably means that it was added as a sulfide or oxide mineral during smelting of the copper ore. The last of the base metals, cadmium, has properties similar to those of zinc. Like the ferro-alloy metals, use of cadmium is a product of twentieth century technology.

Copper

Nobody knows whether the use of gold preceded that of copper or whether both were used about the same time. Wherever and whenever the first use of metallic copper occurred, it is so far back in time that we will probably never find out who used it or for what purpose. It is not surprising that the use of copper should go so far back in time because copper, like gold, sometimes occurs as a native metal; thus, our ancestors did not have to first learn how to smelt ores to obtain the metal. What they had to learn was how to hammer native copper, rather than grind or chip it as they had been doing with stones, to make useful shapes. They had obviously learned to do so by 6000 years ago because excavations of the remains of civilizations that existed at that time yield finely wrought copper artifacts (Figure 8.17). The use of copper probably goes even further back in time; the smelting of copper ores seems to have started between 5500 and 6000 years ago, and it is reasonable to think that the use of native copper metal started much earlier.

The earliest underground mining activities, remains of which can still be seen today in several places in Europe, go back to the Stone Age and seem to have been for flints. The earliest underground mining for metal seems to have been for copper at least 6000 years ago.

The value of copper, from antiquity until the later years of the nineteenth century, was related to its **malleability** and the ease with which both copper and its alloys can be worked and cast. Copper metal and the main copper alloys, bronze and brass, are attractive to look at, durable, and relatively corrosion resistant. Copper and its alloys found innumerable uses in weapons, utensils, tools, jewelry, statuary, pipes, and architectural features.

The nineteenth century brought a great expansion in the use of copper because one of copper's most desirable properties is its high electrical conductivity. Not only can copper transmit electricity with a minimum loss of power, but the transmission wires are flexible and malleable, and they can be easily joined and soldered. The spectacular growth of the electrical power industry, plus all the industries using electricity, would certainly have been hampered without copper. Not surprisingly, the production of copper rose rapidly during the nineteenth century. In the early decades of the nineteenth century, average world annual production was less than 10,000 metric tons. We now produce more than double that amount each day! By the 1850s, production had risen to about 50,000 metric tons a year, and by the 1890s, when electric power and telegraph needs started growing rapidly, production reached about 370,000 metric tons. By the mid-1990s, the world's annual copper production had exceeded 9 million metric tons and was continuing to rise.

Geological Occurrence.   The geochemical abundance of copper is high—among the highest of the geochemically scarce metals. Its average content in the continental crust is 0.0058 percent, and in the oceanic crust it is still higher. It is not surprising for a metal that has been used for so long and in such large quantities that literally hundreds of thousands of copper deposits, large and small, have been discovered around the world. A great deal is known about copper deposits as a result, but many questions remain to be answered.

All of the important copper ore minerals mined today are sulfides; they are chalcopyrite ($CuFeS_2$), digenite (Cu_9S_5), chalcocite (Cu_2S), bornite (Cu_5FeS_4), enargite (Cu_3AsS_4), and tetrahedrite ($Cu_{12}Sb_4S_{13}$); in addition, there are many other less important minerals. Historically, ores containing native copper, the two carbonate minerals, azurite ($Cu(CO_3)_2(OH)_2$) and malachite ($Cu_2CO_3(OH)_2$), and the two copper oxide minerals, tenorite (CuO) and cuprite (Cu_2O), were also important. Native copper deposits such as the famous ores of the Keweenaw District on Michigan's northern peninsula are infrequent, and none is currently a

large producer on the world scene. Copper forms the oxide and carbonate minerals as a result of weathering interactions between the atmosphere and groundwater and a sulfide ore body. The oxide and carbonate minerals are found in secondary, oxidized cappings above primary sulfide ores. Beneath the oxidized cappings there is sometimes a blanket of very high-grade sulfide ore in a zone of secondary enrichment (Figure 8.18). Oxidized cappings and secondary enrichment zones are often very rich, and sometimes they contain spectacular mineral specimens (Figure 8.19). When found, such zones are soon mined, leaving a once rich mine to face a future dependent on the lower grade primary sulfide ores. Historically, the rich surface ores often provided a means to repay the initial costs of finding and opening an ore body. By the time the leaner sulfide ores were reached, it was possible to mine them because the cost of the initial investment had been repaid. Many of the famous ore bodies in the western Americas, both north and south, were developed in this fashion. Today, however, they all mine primary sulfide ores.

Copper sulfide deposits can be conveniently separated into three classes—magmatic segregation deposits, hydrothermal deposits, and sediment-hosted stratiform deposits. Each of the deposit classes deserves separate discussion.

Magmatic Segregation Deposits.   The least important class of copper deposit as far as current production is concerned is the magmatic segregation class. Such deposits have the same origin as the ores of nickel that formed by magmatic segregation of immiscible sulfide liquids. The ore bodies are therefore associated with large bodies of mafic or ultramafic igneous rocks. Sudbury, Ontario, discussed under nickel, is an example of a magmatic segregation deposit. Indeed, all of the magmatic segregation ores that are mined for nickel also produce important amounts of copper.

Hydrothermal Deposits.   Copper deposits (and deposits of many other metals) that are formed through the actions of **hydrothermal solutions**—hot aqueous solutions circulating through the crust (see Chapter 2)—are numerous. Most common are small veins, usually found close to bodies

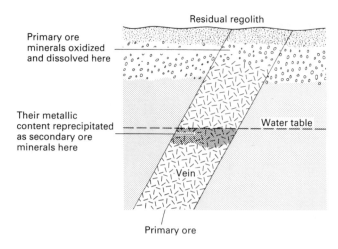

FIGURE 8.18.   Descending groundwater oxidizes and impoverishes copper ore above the water table, forming an acid solution that removes soluble copper compounds and leaves a residue of limonite. The descending acid solution deposits copper at and below the water table, producing secondary enrichment below.

FIGURE 8.19. Gossans, the oxidized cappings that form above sulfide ore deposits as a result of weathering, often contain spectacular mineral specimens. These crystals of cerussite (PbSO₄) formed in the limonite gossan above the ore at the Flagstaff Mine, Utah. The specimen is 16 centimeters across. See also Figure 2.10 and Plate 35. (Photograph by W. Sacco.)

of intrusive igneous rock but also found in metamorphic and sedimentary rocks far removed from known igneous intrusions. Such veins are usually quartz rich, and they almost always are secondary features formed long after the host rocks became lithified. They are confined in what were once open fractures through which the hydrothermal fluids flowed. Most vein deposits are small, containing only a few tons of ore, and therefore are not of much economic interest. When they are large and rich, as were the great veins that surrounded the granitic intrusions at Cornwall, England (Figure 8.20), and at Butte, Montana, they constitute some of the richest and most profitable deposits ever found. Such rich bonanza veins were very important historically, but today, many of the richest veins have been worked out, and they are of less importance than they once were. Nevertheless, investigations of vein deposits have been particularly informative in unraveling the complex questions that surround hydrothermal solutions.

Hydrothermal solutions are, as their name indicates, hot, water-based solutions. The water can come from two quite separate sources. First, the water may start as rainwater or seawater at Earth's surface. Such water trickles down the innumerable openings and fractures in surface rocks; below the water table, every opening is filled. At sufficient depth—a few thousand meters—the surrounding rocks are hot enough that the buried waters become effective solvents. Small amounts of material are dissolved from the enclosing rocks, and the hot water becomes a solution containing such

constituents as NaCl, MgCl₂, CaSO₄, SiO₂, and sometimes small amounts of one or more of the geochemically scarce metals (Table 8.4).

The second way a hydrothermal solution can arise is from a cooling magma. When rock melts and a magma forms deep in the crust or upper mantle, the magma assimilates any water that is present. Magmas formed in the crust, such as granites and diorites, generally have several weight percent water in them. When such magmas cool and crystallize, much of the dissolved water is released as a hot, aqueous solution that carries with it the same soluble constituents that deeply buried rainwater and seawater pick up.

Because hydrothermal solutions from the two different sources are so similar in chemical composition, it is exceedingly difficult to say what the origin of a given fluid is. The problem is complicated further because the major driving force that causes hydrothermal solutions to flow is heat. When heated, a solution expands and rises convectively, thereby creating fluid flow. The principal heat sources in the crust that cause convective flow are shallow bodies of cooling magma and piles of hot lava, the very bodies that release magmatic hydrothermal solutions. But the rocks into which magmas are intruded also contain rainwater- and seawater-generated hydrothermal solutions in the pore spaces. A magmatic heat source will start these solutions flowing, too. Once flow starts, both kinds of hydrothermal fluids became inextricably mixed. Hot springs in areas of active magmatic activity, such as those in Yellowstone National Park (Figure 8.21),

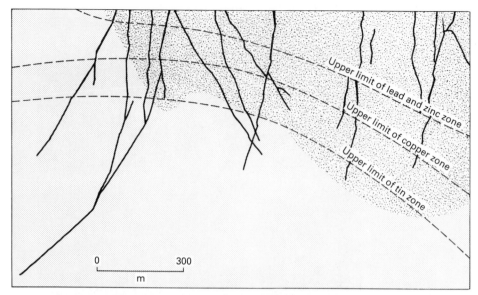

FIGURE 8.20. Mineral zoning developed in a system of veins formed around a granitic stock in Cornwall, England. Each of the veins (as shown in Figure 2.5 and Plate 39) is mineralized and contains the tin mineral cassiterite (SnO_2), copper minerals of which chalcopyrite ($CuFeS_2$) is the most important, and zinc and lead minerals sphalerite (ZnS) and galena (PbS). The zonation is believed to arise from a drop in temperature of the hydrothermal solutions as they flowed through the vein fractures.

FIGURE 8.21. A hot spring and geyser, Yellowstone National Park, Wyoming. Such hot springs are believed to be the surface expressions of large, deeply circulating hydrothermal systems of the kind that formed the veins in Cornwall (Figures 2.5 and 8.20 and Plates 38 and 39). (Courtesy of J. D. Rimstidt.)

FIGURE 8.22. Photograph of a tungsten-bearing vein at Panasqueira, Portugal, showing large quartz crystals (on the lower side), dark wolframite crystals, and arsenopyrite. (Photograph by A. Arribas.)

are the tops of convectively driven hydrothermal systems. At Yellowstone, scientists have been able to show that more than 90 percent of the hot water started as rainfall.

When a hydrothermal solution starts to rise upward, a number of things can happen: (1) the solution may start to cool; (2) it will react with rocks such as limestone because such a solution tends to be slightly acidic; (3) the pressure will drop; and (4) boiling may occur. Each of these changes, or more likely a combination of them, can cause the solution to reach saturation and start precipitating the dissolved constituents. If it is the sulfide minerals of the geochemically scarce metals that precipitate, usually with associated quartz, an ore deposit may result (Figure 8.22). A rising hydrothermal solution tends to change progressively as the dissolved ore and gangue minerals precipitate. As a result, a sequential or zonal pattern of mineral precipitation may develop as shown in Figure 8.20.

The major kind of hydrothermal copper deposit being worked today is closely related to vein deposits. Known as **porphyry copper deposits** because the intrusive igneous rocks with which they are always associated have porphyritic textures, the deposits consist of innumerable tiny fractures, usually no more than a millimeter or so thick, spaced every few centimeters through a body of intensely fractured rock (Figure 8.23). The geological setting of porphyry copper deposits and the rocks with which they are associated indicate that they represent subsurface conduits and chambers that once lay beneath volcanos. The formation process began with the intrusion of a magma. As nonhydrous minerals such as feldspars began to crystallize around the outer edges of the intrusion, the water content of the remaining magma increased until the pressure was so great that steam explosions shattered the crystallized rock. The escaping hydrothermal solutions—

FIGURE 8.23. Specimen of ore from the molybdenum-bearing porphyry deposit at Climax, Colorado. The sample shows the typical intense fracturing along which the ore minerals have been deposited. The specimen is about 15 centimeters wide. (Photograph by M. Fortney.)

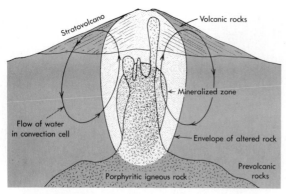

FIGURE 8.24. Idealized section through a stratovolcano showing convection cells of hydrothermal solutions, the limits of hydrothermally altered rocks, and the location of a mineralized zone in which a porphyry copper deposit is forming. (Adapted from Silitoe, 1973.)

carrying silica, potassium and sodium salts, and dissolved metal sulfides—moved outward, precipitating minerals and sealing the fractures. As cooling continued, this process was repeated several times, leaving many generations of small fractures, several of which contain small but significant amounts of copper ore minerals. When the volume of shattered rock is large, a porphyry copper deposit can also be very large—over 1 billion (10^9) tons of ore in some of the largest deposits. The deposits have distinctive zonal patterns that can be related to the fluid circulation system (Figure 8.24).

When porphyry copper deposits are mined, it is impractical to dig out the individual tiny veinlets. Instead, the entire body of shattered rock is mined. As a result, porphyry copper deposits tend to have lower grades (ranging from 0.25 percent to 2 percent copper plus small amounts of molybdenum and gold) than the richer bonanza vein deposits. What makes these porphyry-type deposits profitable at such low grades is their very large size and shape. Most are relatively near the surface and are approximately cylindrical bodies of mineralized rock that lend themselves to very large mining schemes. Indeed, it was at the porphyry copper deposit at Bingham Canyon, Utah (see Plate 37), where D. C. Jackling and R. C. Gemmell first proposed and demonstrated that large-scale bulk mining is more profitable than small-scale, labor-intensive, selective mining. They made their proposal in 1899. By 1907, they had installed an open-pit mining scheme capable of producing 6000 metric tons of low-grade copper ore per day. The daily capacity of Bingham Canyon in recent times was well above 100,000 metric tons and once achieved a maximum 24-hour production of 400,000 tons (360,000 metric tons).

Literally hundreds of porphyry copper deposits have been found, and today they account for more than half of the world's copper production. The deposits are concentrated around the rim of the Pacific Ocean basin, where they have

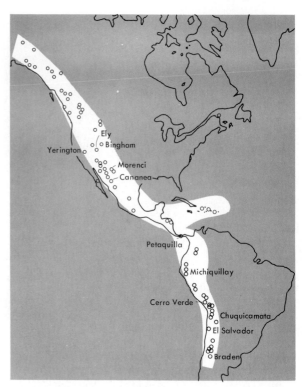

FIGURE 8.25. Porphyry copper deposits in the Americas define a remarkable metallogenic province that parallels the western continental boundary. Another belt of porphyry copper deposits is being exposed and developed in the Pacific Islands. (From Skinner, 1986.)

formed as a result of volcanism associated with the subduction of oceanic crust (Figure 8.25). The porphyry copper deposits around the Pacific are geologically young and related to the present phase of plate tectonics. Older deposits are known, and in all cases they seem to be related to ancient plate edges where subduction once occurred.

Two other kinds of hydrothermal copper deposits also deserve discussion because each is a significant producer of copper. The first is a **contact metamorphic** or **skarn** class of deposit. When granitic magma intrudes a pile of rock that contains limestone or marble, the acid solutions released by the cooling magma react with the $CaCO_3$ in the limestone. The reactions cause rapid precipitation of copper minerals and lead to very rich ores. Commonly, skarn ores form rich pockets associated with larger masses of porphyry-type ore. Examples are the Gaspé copper deposit in Quebec and the Yerington deposit in Nevada.

The final class of hydrothermal copper deposit is known as a **volcanogenic massive sulfide** deposit. The enclosing rocks are invariably volcanic in origin, and the volcanic rocks have features suggesting that they were erupted under the sea. The ore minerals are always sulfides, and the term *massive* reflects the fact that very little volcanic debris or silicate gangue minerals are present to dilute the sulfides.

Unfortunately, pyrite (FeS_2) is usually the most abundant sulfide mineral, but generally chalcopyrite ($CuFeS_2$), sphalerite (ZnS), and other useful sulfide minerals are present in small amounts, too.

Volcanogenic massive sulfide deposits are known in rocks as old as three billion years, and such deposits can be observed forming on the seafloor today. They are among the most common of all hydrothermal ore deposits, but most are too small to be of economic interest.

Deep diving submarines have, in recent years, discovered submarine hot springs along the volcanic rifts that mark the midocean ridges. The springs are places where hot sea-water erupts after it has been heated at depth in the piles of volcanic rock that make up the upper layers of the oceanic crust. The hot circulating seawater is apparently heated by the magma chambers that underlie the midocean ridge. It reacts with and alters the basaltic lavas it passes through, and by the time it rises again to the ocean floor it is a rapidly flowing jet of brine as hot as 350°C. When such a jet erupts into cold ocean water, it is quickly cooled; as a result, its dissolved load precipitates, sometimes as very fine sootlike sulfide minerals (thus giving the name *black smokers* to some vents) (Figure 8.26) and sometimes forming a blanket of massive sulfide ore around the vent. Only one of the modern

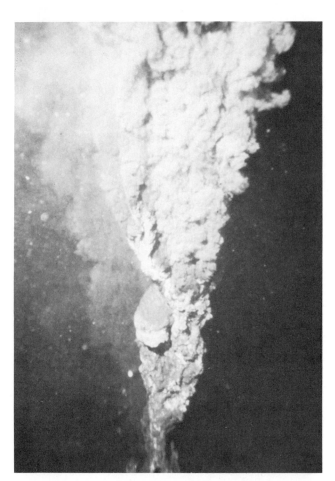

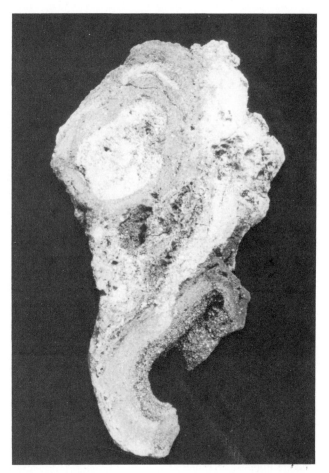

(a)   (b)

FIGURE 8.26. (a) A chimneylike structure of sulfide minerals built up around a vent from which hydrothermal solutions, at 350°C, are being emitted into the sea above the East Pacific Rise. The solution is colorless, but when it mixes with cold seawater a dense cloud of exceedingly fine-grained sulfide minerals is precipitated. Such structures and precipitates are colloquially referred to as chimneys and black smokers. (Photograph by R. Ballard.) (b) Section of a chimney recovered by a deep-diving submarine from a depth of 2500 meters at 20°N latitude on the East Pacific Rise. The principal sulfide mineral present is pyrite, but small amounts of chalcopyrite and sphalerite are also intermixed. (The specimen is about 22 centimeters across.) (Photograph by Brian Skinner.)

deposits so far discovered, in the Red Sea, is large enough to be of potential interest for mining. More than a hundred others have been found in the eastern Pacific and mid-Atlantic, but all are small. Furthermore, the known deposits are all at 1500 meters or greater depths of water.

It may well be that other large, rich, modern massive sulfide deposits will someday be found on the ocean floor. For the present, the only massive sulfide deposits that are being mined are in ancient fragments of oceanic crust found on the continents. Such massive sulfide deposits have been mined since ancient times as on Cyprus, and the word *copper* comes, in fact, from the Greek word *cyprus*.

Sediment-Hosted Stratiform Deposits. The final group of copper deposits all share distinctive and puzzling features. They are always in **clastic,** marine sedimentary rocks, usually shales, that contain a certain amount of organic matter and calcium carbonate, and they are usually stratiform, which means the mineralization occurs in stratalike layers. The ore minerals are either native copper or, much more commonly, sulfide minerals. Because neither copper metal nor sulfide minerals are known to precipitate directly from present-day seawater—and it is not likely that ancient seawater had the composition for this to happen either—a puzzle surrounds the origin of such ores.

One group of theories concerning the origin of stratiform deposits suggests that the deposits are related to volcanogenic massive sulfide deposits and that the sulfide minerals were precipitated from submarine hot springs. The trouble with such theories is that hot springs usually produce massive ores, but the sediment-hosted stratiform ores always contain very large proportions of clastic silicate mineral grains. A second group of theories, which the authors of this volume prefer, ascribes the origin to hydrothermal solutions that circulated in coarse, clastic sedimentary layers beneath the now mineralized shales. Such theories ascribe the origin of the ores to reactions between the solutions and mineral constituents in the shales. The reactions seem to have occurred soon after the sediments were deposited and, in certain cases, before they were consolidated into solid rock. The most famous of the sediment-hosted stratiform copper deposits are enclosed in the **Kupferschiefer,** a Permian-aged shale found through much of northern Europe (Figure 8.27). The Kupferschiefer deposits, which average only about 20 centimeters in thickness but extend laterally over more than 6000 square kilometers, have been mined continually since the fourteenth century. Larger and richer stratiform deposits, discovered in the twentieth century, are now worked in Zambia and Zaire in central Africa (Figure 8.28). In the United States, there are deposits at White River, Michigan, and at Creta, Oklahoma, that are of this class.

Production and Reserves. About 60 percent of the world's copper production comes from porphyry copper

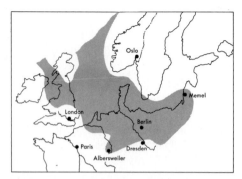

FIGURE 8.27. Extent of the shallow Zechstein Sea, in which the thin sedimentary bed now known as the Kupferschiefer was laid down during the Permian period. (After R. Brinckmann, 1960. From Skinner, 1986.)

and associated skarn deposits. An estimated 20 percent comes from sediment-hosted stratiform deposits, and about 12 percent comes from volcanic-hosted massive sulfide deposits. The remainder comes as a by-product from the mining of nickel, lead, and zinc ores and from chemical leaching of old mine dumps. Copper is so widely produced around the world that in 1994, 60 countries reported production. It is not surprising for such a widely used and widely exploited metal that both the reserves and resources of copper are very large (Figure 8.29).

The production and reserve situation for copper since the end of World War II is illustrated in Figure 8.30 and is

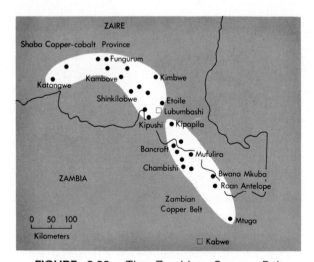

FIGURE 8.28. The Zambian Copper Belt and adjacent Shaba Copper-Cobalt province in Zaire contain a remarkable series of stratabound copper deposits. Deposits in the Zambian Copper Belt are contained in sediments laid down along an ancient Precambrian shoreline. Those in Zaire are similar in age but are not shoreline sediments. (From Skinner, 1986.)

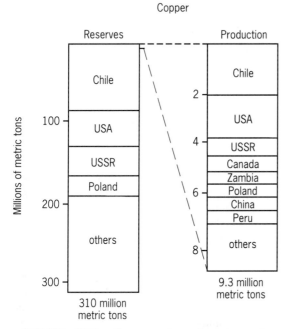

FIGURE 8.29. Copper deposits occur in many countries, but Chile, the United States, and the nations of the former Soviet Union contain the largest reserves and are the greatest producers today. The world's proven reserves will last more than 30 years at present rates of production, but the reserve base of likely mineable ore doubles that time. (From the U.S. Bureau of Mines.)

representative of most of the base metals. The figure demonstrates that cumulative production of copper since 1946 would long ago have exhausted the copper reserves known in the world at that time. However, the figure shows that copper reserves have been discovered more rapidly than mined, even though mining rates have markedly increased and are now at their highest levels ever. This has developed primarily because increased understanding of the geology of copper deposits has resulted in successful exploration strategies. This example is for copper, but similar situations exist for lead, zinc, and several other base metals.

Resources of copper in large deposits that are below today's mining grades are very large—several times larger than the reserves. In the United States, large quantities of copper exist in magmatic segregation deposits in the Duluth Gabbro, Minnesota. Very large stratiform resources also exist in the late Proterozoic Aged Belt Series rocks of Montana. But the largest copper resources of all do not belong to any country. They are in the ferromanganese nodules that lie on the deep seafloor. In areas of slow sedimentation, such as the central Pacific Ocean, ferromanganese nodules average more than 1 percent copper (See Table 7.6), and many are known to contain as much as 2 percent. The same nodules also carry important amounts of nickel and cobalt. Some estimates put the total copper resources in recoverable manganese nodules in excess of 1 billion (10^9) tons of copper. This suggests, therefore, that the seafloor resources of copper are about the same size as the on-land resources. Despite the fact that copper is mined at such a high annual rate, the world's reserves and resources appear adequate for a century or more. The big

FIGURE 8.30. The cumulative world production of copper metal since 1946 has been about 270 million metric tons, but the reserves (reserve base has been used in recent years) have increased dramatically since the 1960s as exploration and recovery techniques have improved. (From the U.S. Bureau of Mines.)

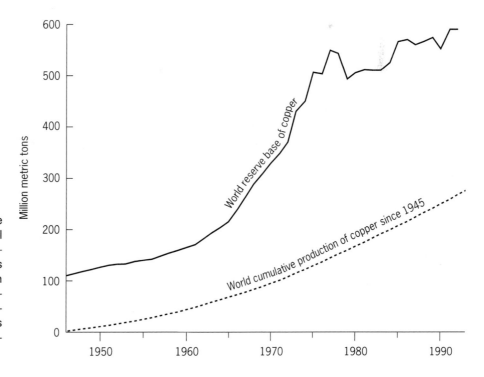

LEAD IN THE ENVIRONMENT

Lead is an ancient metal creating modern problems. Its usage dates back to ancient times when early metallurgists or potters, who learned how to refine it from galena (PbS), found that the lead was easily cast, molded, or otherwise shaped into pipes and storage vessels. It also served well in ceramic glazes, solders, and even glasswares. It was heavy but resisted corrosion reasonably well and hence became widely traded and extensively used. Lead became the common metal of water pipes, and new alloys were used for printer's type, munitions (especially small bullets and shot), and paints. With the advent of the automobile, lead storage batteries became the primary means of providing power to start engines and the additive tetraethyl lead became the primary means of increasing octane and preventing engine preignition, or *knocking*.

Until the second half of the twentieth century, lead seemed a most ideal, useful, and benign metal; only a few precautions had been offered. Gradually, however, evidence began to accumulate that although lead metal is not poisonous (many people lived for long periods with lead pellets or bullets in their bodies), many lead compounds are. Lead, like many metals, does not necessarily remain in the form in which it was used; it is readily dissolved in acidic solutions and slowly oxidizes to form lead oxides with properties and solubilities different from lead metal. Furthermore, the body eliminates lead only very slowly; thus, prolonged exposure results in gradual buildup. This buildup can be especially harmful in children because the lead inhibits production of hemoglobin, interferes with normal growth and development of the central nervous system, and locks on to essential enzymes in the brain. The effects of lead poisoning, or *plumbism*, include anemia, reduced hearing abilities, lack of coordination, drowsiness, cramps, and paralysis.

Mounting evidence of lead poisoning and the recognition that lead is widespread in our environment—as fumes from leaded gasoline, as paints used in tens of millions of homes, and as lead hunting shot—have resulted in a series of actions designed to limit lead exposure. In the 1970s, the government began to require that automobiles operate on unleaded gasoline; by the end of the 1980s the United States had virtually eliminated leaded gasoline and many other countries were preparing to do likewise. These actions have sharply reduced exposure to lead, but government estimates in 1992 projected that the United States still has more than 40 million homes containing old lead-based paints and that more than 3 million children have been affected. The principal problem is the ingestion of dust and fragments of old, flaking lead-containing paints. A second source is drinking water that may contain low levels of lead that gradually dissolved (especially by acidic waters) from lead pipes or solders used to join copper pipes. In 1992 the U.S. Environmental Protection Agency initiated a long-term program to remove lead from all public drinking water supplies.

Lead compounds have long been used in ceramic glazes on tableware and in lead glass sometimes used as decanters for wine. Only recently, it has been learned that the contact of food and the acid nature of wine can actually extract enough lead from the dishes or glassware to create a potential health hazard. Consequently, some types of tableware have been banned from sale and warnings have been issued not to store wines for long periods in lead glass containers.

During the 1970s, it also became apparent that there was widespread poisoning of water fowl that ingested some of the hundreds of thousands of tons of lead shot that lay on the bottoms of lakes and wetlands. This led to the banning of lead shot in favor of steel shot for hunting. Unfortunately, this provides for no means of recovering the massive amounts of lead that remain in the wetlands from some two hundred years of hunting. Accordingly, lead exposure has been much reduced but not eliminated.

question to be answered in the future concerns the cost of working presently uneconomical resources.

Lead and Zinc

Lead and zinc are discussed together because their ore minerals so commonly occur together. Their uses as metals are rather different, however. Lead is another metal with a history that stretches back to antiquity. It rarely occurs in the native state, so the use of lead metal only commenced when our ancestors learned how to smelt lead ores. Lead was used in weights, sheet metal, solders, ceramic glazes, and glassware by the ancient Egyptians, the Phoenicians, Greeks, and Romans. The Phoenicians worked lead mines in Cyprus, Sardinia, and Spain and traded the metal around the Mediterranean. The famed mines at Laurium in Greece produced both silver and lead and supplied the ancient Greeks with much revenue. The great quantities of silver that enriched Rome and paid for so many of its conquests and much of its high living were derived from lead smelting and from refining operations carried out in Spain, Sardinia, and Britain. In recent years, we have come to realize that the Roman smelting of lead and silver ores resulted in very widespread lead pollution throughout several parts of Europe.

An unusual combination of properties has given lead a wide range of industrial uses. The metal is soft and easily worked, it is very dense, it has a low melting temperature, it possesses very desirable alloying properties, it resists corrosion, and it is an excellent shield against harmful radiations. The principal use of lead today is for automobile storage batteries; it is also used in crystal glass, for flashings in building construction, in ammunition, in various alloys (especially solder), in bearings, and in printer's type. But lead also has unpleasant properties. It is toxic, and this has led to a reduction in its use in situations where humans might ingest lead or lead compounds. Thus, the use of lead in paints and gasoline has been drastically curtailed. For a number of years now, all new automobiles sold in North America have been designed to use unleaded gasoline; presumably, leaded gasoline will eventually cease to be sold.

Zinc is a relatively soft, bluish-white colored metal. It is more difficult to produce zinc metal by standard smelting practice than it is to produce copper or lead. Therefore, zinc was a relatively late addition to the family of base metals used by humankind. The first commercial production of the metal is claimed to have been in China some 600 years ago, but details are poorly recorded. The first reliable record of zinc smelting was from Bristol, England, in 1740. As demand grew, other smelters were opened in Belgium, Germany, Russia, and in 1860 in the United States.

The largest part of the world's zinc production is used in galvanizing, a process by which protective coatings are put on steel and iron, mainly by a hot-dipping process in which the object to be coated is dipped into a bath of molten zinc.

Because zinc resists corrosion and does not rust, even a thin coating prevents rust from forming on iron and steel. Zinc also has desirable alloying properties, and many die-cast objects that are not subject to abrasive wear are made from zinc-based alloys. Zinc is a constituent of brass, and it is used in its oxide form (ZnO) in paint pigments, ointments, lotions, and creams to prevent sunburn. Zinc became more prominent, if not more conspicuous, in the United States when the copper penny was replaced in 1982 by a zinc penny that is copper coated.

Geological Occurrence.   Lead and zinc minerals are formed in deposits that resemble copper deposits in many ways. There are four important kinds of deposits, and in all of them the same two minerals occur—galena (PbS) and sphalerite (ZnS).

The first kind of deposit is a hydrothermal vein type. As with copper, lead and zinc minerals are very common in veins; but also as with copper, most of the veins are too small to be of much interest. Nevertheless, in many countries, including Peru and the United States, vein deposits still contribute to the production total.

Volcanogenic massive sulfide deposits, the second kind of deposit, are often rich in zinc or in zinc plus lead. The famous Kuroko deposits of northern Honshu, Japan, are of this type, and they have a long production history of both lead and zinc. In New Brunswick, Canada, large massive sulfide ores have been known for many years. Many of the New Brunswick ores are so fine grained that it is not possible to separate the galena and sphalerite to prepare concentrates suitable for smelting, so even though the deposits are large and easily mined, they cannot be exploited profitably.

The third and most important class of hydrothermal lead-zinc deposit is known as the **Mississippi Valley type** (MVT), after the remarkable metallogenic province stretching from Oklahoma and Missouri to Kentucky and Wisconsin—a region that includes most of the drainage basin of the Mississippi River (Figure 8.31). Deposits with similar affinities have been discovered in Canada, northern Africa, Australia, Russia, and Europe. MVT deposits always occur in limestones where the ore minerals have either replaced the limestone beds or have been precipitated between fragments and limestone **breccia.** The solutions that form the MVT deposits develop in sedimentary basins and flow laterally outward until they come in contact with limestones around the margins of the basins (Figure 8.31). There, the solutions may dissolve the limestone and precipitate the galena and/or sphalerite. The rich zinc deposits in Tennessee have formed where groundwaters had first dissolved much limestone, leaving a well-developed cave system. The ore-bearing solutions then deposited the ore minerals, sometimes as large spectacular crystals, between **breccia** blocks that developed either from cave collapse or tectonic fracturing (Figure 8.32). Other important deposits of this kind are the lead deposits in

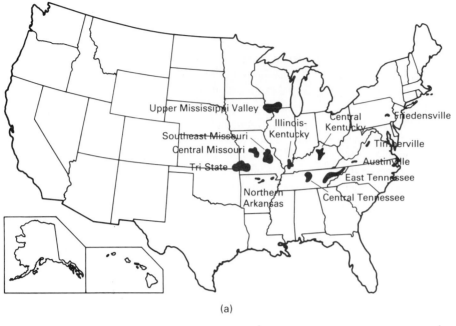

(a)

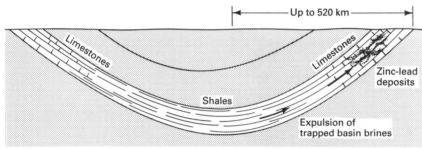

Up to 520 km

Limestones

Limestones

Shales

Zinc-lead
deposits

Expulsion of
trapped basin brines

(b)

FIGURE 8.31. (a) Map showing the principal Mississippi Valley-type (carbonate-hosted) lead-zinc deposits in the United States. (b) Cross section of a large sedimentary basin showing expulsion of metal-bearing fluids from shales with subsequent deposition in the limestones on the flanks of the basin.

(a)

(b)

FIGURE 8.32. (a) Typical example of Mississippi Valley-type breccia ore from east Tennessee. The sphalerite was precipitated around the edges of the irregular and disoriented limestone and dolomite blocks; the white is late-stage white dolomite that filled the remaining voids after the deposition of the sphalerite. (Photograph by J. R. Craig.) (b) Example of well-developed crystals of sphalerite, fluorite, and barite from a cavity in the central Tennessee zinc deposits. (Photograph by S. Llyn Sharp.)

southeast Missouri and the great zinc deposits of Pine Point in Canada.

An increasingly large production of lead and zinc now comes from deposits of the fourth kind, sediment-hosted stratiform deposits. As with stratiform copper deposits, the origin of these deposits is problematic. The clearest example is the Kupferschiefer, where a zonal pattern of lead and zinc mineralization occurs around the copper deposits. The origin of the ores is, most likely, deposition in the Kupferschiefer by hydrothermal solutions that circulated in coarse, clastic sediments below the shale.

Most of the large, stratiform lead-zinc deposits are Precambrian in age. One very large and very rich deposit, the Sullivan body, occurs at Kimberley in British Columbia. But the largest bodies of this kind have been found in Australia. A deposit at Broken Hill in New South Wales is one of the richest ore bodies ever found. The second, at Mount Isa in Queensland, is also very large, and besides lead and zinc, it has large copper reserves, too. In the early 1990s, the Red Dog mine in Alaska was brought into production and has become the world's largest zinc producer. The deposits at Broken Hill, Mount Isa, Sullivan, and Red Dog are so rich that the ores contain combined values of lead plus zinc in excess of 20 percent—in fact, the ores are so rich, they closely resemble massive sulfide deposits.

Production and Reserves.   The world's production of lead and zinc is dominated by six countries (Figures 8.33 and 8.34), but significant lead and zinc production is reported from about 50 countries.

World reserves of lead and zinc present a situation similar to that of copper; that is, increased geological understanding has led to increased discoveries of reserves. Furthermore, world demand for zinc is expected to only increase slowly, and world demand for lead, because of environmental concerns, could stabilize or decrease. As long as lead storage batteries are needed for automobiles and trucks, the demand for lead will continue to increase. The increased use of electric vehicles to reduce pollution in cities would also increase the need for lead. However, if the efforts to develop alternative, lighter-weight batteries is successful, it would dramatically reduce the world's use of lead.

Tin

Tin shares the distinction with copper and lead of having been used by humankind for more than 5000 years. Where and when tin was first used is not known, but it was probably either in the Middle East or in southeast Asia. Most likely, the earliest use was as an alloying agent. Two tin-bearing alloys have been used since very ancient times. The first is bronze, a copper-based alloy in which tin serves as a hardening agent for the copper. Bronze is tougher and more durable than pure copper, and thus bronze tools last longer and are more effi-

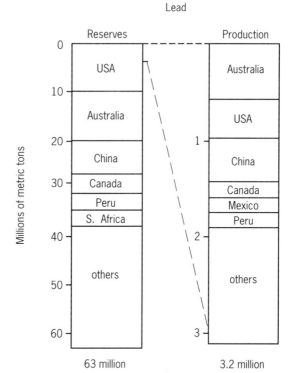

FIGURE 8.33.   Lead reserves are located in many countries, with the United States and Australia holding the largest quantities. World reserves will last about 20 years at the present rates of production. (From the U. S. Bureau of Mines.)

cient than copper tools. The discovery of bronze was one of the great milestones in the technological history of the human race. The second alloy of antiquity is pewter. Tin itself is too soft to be worked into spoons, knives, plates, and similar utensils, but when lead is added to tin, an inexpensive, harder, and very useful alloy—pewter—is the result. By the addition of small amounts of antimony or copper, pewter can be made even stronger and more durable than a straight tin-plus-lead pewter.

Tin is a soft, white metal with a low melting temperature. It does not corrode or rust, and so is an effective coating agent to cover metals that do corrode. The method for plating tin on copper was developed at least 2000 years ago, and tin-plated iron was first manufactured in the sixteenth century. Although the use of steel, aluminum, and plastic cans is rising rapidly and supplanting tin-plated cans, tin plating is still an important process.

The low melting temperature of tin and alloys of tin and lead make tin the prime constituent of solders. The principal use of tin today is in solders, consuming approximately 35 percent of all tin mined. Bronze is used in certain soft-metal bearings, in ornamentation, automobiles, and aircraft.

Geological Occurrence.   There are many tin minerals, but almost all production comes from cassiterite

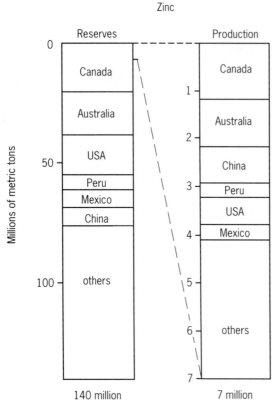

FIGURE 8.34. Zinc reserves commonly occur with the reserves of lead, hence the similarity of this figure to Figure 8.33. World reserves of zinc will last about 20 years at present rates of production. (From the U. S. Bureau of Mines.)

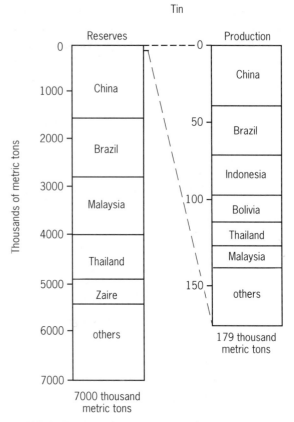

FIGURE 8.35. The world's tin reserves are concentrated in China, Brazil, and southeast Asia. At present rates of production, the reserves will last about 40 years. (From the U. S. Bureau of Mines.)

(SnO_2). A small amount of tin is produced as a by-product from the mining of other base metals, and in such cases, tin is usually present in the ore as the sulfide mineral stannite (Cu_2FeSnS_4).

Cassiterite is sometimes found in **pegmatites** associated with granitic rocks, but more commonly, it is found in hydrothermal deposits related to andesitic or rhyolitic volcanism. The hydrothermal deposits may be veins, disseminations in altered rocks, or even **skarns.**

Cassiterite is a dense, chemically stable mineral that does not alter or dissolve in stream waters. As a result, cassiterite is readily concentrated in **placers,** and worldwide, more tin is produced from placers than from hard-rock mines because placer mining is inexpensive compared to hard-rock mining.

Production and Reserves. Seven countries dominate the tin market (Figure 8.35). Tin produced in Malaysia, Thailand, and Indonesia—three of the world's largest producers—comes almost entirely from placers. The remaining countries report both placer production and hard-rock production.

The reserves of tin are reasonably large—more than ten times the annual production rate—and resources are even

larger. The United States Geological Survey has estimated that tin resources might be as high as 30 million metric tons. Whether or not all the tin in the estimated resources can actually be found and mined is an open question. Present reserves will last for at least 40 years and could last much longer.

Mercury

Mercury is the only metal that is a liquid at room temperature. It combines readily with other metals to form alloys—in the case of mercury, such alloys are called *amalgams.* One common use for a silver-mercury amalgam is filling cavities in teeth.

There is only one important ore mineral of mercury, cinnabar (HgS). It is a soft, blood-red-colored mineral found in hydrothermal vein deposits at a few places around the world. Small quantities of metallic mercury are often found with cinnabar. Mercury is produced both by primary mining and as a by-product from zinc and copper mining. The principal producing countries, in order of importance, are China, Mexico, Algeria, and Spain (Figure 8.36). Between them, they account for about 75 percent of the world's production. Italy, although not presently a producer, has large reserves of mercury. The best estimates of mercury resources suggest

MORE THAN ZINC FROM A ZINC MINE

What do you get from a zinc mine? The question seems straightforward enough and most respondents would say "zinc." That answer is certainly correct, but it is commonly far from complete. In fact, zinc mines, like most metal mines today, may yield a variety of resources, many or most of which are by-products of the primary resource for which the mine is operated. By-products are defined as *secondary or additional products,* but they often play a critical role in the economic viability of a mine. Furthermore, there are several important resources that are derived almost entirely as by-products; that is, we would lose access to some metals if we were to stop mining for others.

Zinc mines exemplify this relationship between primary products and by-products very well. The world's only source of zinc is the mineral *sphalerite*, which has the nominal idealized composition of ZnS. Sphalerite may form in a variety of types of ore deposits but is especially well known in *carbonate hosted zinc* or *Mississippi Valley-type* deposits. The deposits, named for their occurrence in limestone or dolomite beds along the Mississippi Valley, contain crusts of sphalerite that have precipitated in fractures and around the edges of fragments of carbonate (Figure 8.32).

Natural sphalerite is never pure and always contains one or more of several other metals that can fit in place of the zinc atoms in the crystal structure. When the zinc, which was originally distributed in sediments and rocks in just a few parts per million, was dissolved in slowly moving, heated groundwaters, trace quantities of other metals were also dissolved. Iron is nearly always present in sphalerites and often contributes to the darkening of its color but is of no economic value in these ores. In contrast, some sphalerites, especially those from the Mississippi Valley-type deposits, contain a few tenths of one percent gallium, germanium, cadmium, and even indium. Although the concentrations are small relative to the zinc (which is over 60% in pure ZnS), the selling price of each of these metals is greater than zinc. The price of cadmium is about two times as much as zinc, indium about 250 times as much, gallium about 500 times as much, and germanium about 1000 times as much. Hence, once the ore has been mined and the sphalerite concentrated, most of the effort and cost has been expended; relatively little added cost is required to extract the other metals, and they may add significantly to the profitability. Gallium and germanium are components in light-emitting diodes and lasers; indium is important in solders, solar cells, and electronic coatings; and cadmium is widely used in nicad batteries. There are no mines in the world where these are the principal metals mined; accordingly, if the zinc mines closed, we would lose not only a supply of zinc but also a supply of gallium, germanium, cadmium, and indium.

One other important by-product not to be overlooked is the limestone or dolomite. Usually the sphalerite, with its by-product metals, constitutes less than 5 percent of what is actually mined. As a result, once the mill processes the ore, 95 percent or more of the rock is left over as *waste.* Nearly all mines will sell this limestone or dolomite for construction or agricultural purposes. It is low in value but it is a free *leftover* and selling it means that it brings in some revenue and that it does not have to be stored. In fact, there have been times when the price of zinc has been depressed, and it has been the extra revenue generated by selling the limestone or dolomite that has kept the mines profitable. Indeed, there is much more than zinc extracted from a zinc mine.

that the world's needs will be met for at least another 100 years. The principal uses of mercury are in batteries (33 percent), for chemical production (30 percent), and in scientific measuring devices (40 percent).

Cadmium

Cadmium is a soft, malleable, silver-white metal that was discovered and first separated as a pure metal in 1817 by a German scientist who was investigating impurities in zinc minerals. Cadmium minerals are rare, but cadmium itself is widespread in trace amounts in the principal zinc ore mineral sphalerite (ZnS). Cadmium replaces zinc by atomic substitution, and in the smelting of zinc, the cadmium can be recovered. All cadmium production now comes as a by-product of zinc mining (see above).

For about 60 years after discovery of the chemical element cadmium, its only use was in chemical compounds as

FIGURE 8.36. The mercury collection system used at Almaden in Spain for more than 200 years, from 1720–1928. The cinnabar-bearing ore (see Plate 36) was roasted in the chambers at the left and the mercury vapor condensed as it passed through the terra cotta pipes. A hole in the pipe at the low point allowed the liquid mercury to drip into a channel and flow to a collection site at the far end. Modern systems operate in the same manner but are enclosed to prevent exposure to the mercury vapor. (Photograph by J. R. Craig.)

pigments for paints. Cadmium compounds have very bright and intense colors—yellows, reds, blues, and greens. By the 1830s, they were being used by French artists and, in the 1840s, by English watercolor painters. Starting about 1890, cadmium found new uses as a metal in low-melting alloys and in chemical reagents. In 1919, a cadmium-electroplating process was developed; cadmium plating is similar to zinc plating, and this accounts for the bulk of the cadmium used today. Other uses are in batteries, pigments, and alloys.

Because cadmium is produced as a by-product of smelting zinc ores, the large zinc smelting countries, Japan, the United States, and Canada, are the main producers. In the 1990s, the world's total production of cadmium has been about 20,000 metric tons per year. It is somewhat meaningless to talk about cadmium reserves, which are estimated to be about 500,000 metric tons, because the production of cadmium is dependent upon the mining of zinc.

In recent years, the Occupational Safety and Health Administration of the United States has determined that cadmium can be toxic to humans. This has increased workplace safety regulations and brought about special concerns regarding cadmium in paints and in the leachate from landfills.

THE PRECIOUS METALS

The **precious metals** owe their name to their high values. Two of them, gold and silver, have been known and prized since antiquity. The other precious metals, the six platinum group metals, joined the select list in more recent times. The metals are precious (and expensive) for several reasons, but two are paramount. First, they are all rare and costly to find and recover. Second, to varying degrees, the precious metals resist corrosion and have great lasting qualities. Their resistance to chemical reaction is said to be due to their nobleness, hence their alternate name—**noble metals.**

Gold

Metallic gold is soft and malleable, but also extremely resistant to chemical attack, and it is corrosion-free. Indeed, gold is so stable and has so little tendency for corrosion that most of the gold that has ever been mined is still in use. The gold that was present in the bracelets that adorned Cleopatra's arms could possibly now be residing in someone's teeth, a wedding band, or a gold coin. Once gold has been recovered from the ground, it can be melted down repeatedly and used again and again.

Gold was possibly the first metal used by our ancestors; in all likelihood, the first uses were for ornamentation. Gold's rarity and imperishability soon made it a medium of exchange, and eventually it became an accepted measure of value around the world (Figure 8.37). To a certain extent, it still fills this role, although few countries still back their issue of paper currency with gold. In addition, as the use of gold for monetary purposes has declined, its use for industrial purposes has grown so large that more than half of the world's annual production is now used in electronic products, aerospace applications, special alloys, and dentistry.

Geological Occurrence. Gold deposits are formed by hydrothermal solutions. By far, the most important

FIGURE 8.37. Stacks of gold bullion bars in the Federal Reserve Bank vault. Gold has often served as a monetary standard and remains a measure of wealth. (Photograph courtesy of the Federal Reserve Bank of New York.)

mineral in such deposits is native gold, but in a few instances the telluride minerals, calaverite ($AuTe_2$) and sylvanite (($Au,Ag)Te_2$), are also important. Hydrothermal gold deposits are commonly veins, in which the associated gangue mineral is generally quartz. Disseminated deposits of gold are also known, particularly in the western United States (for example, the Carlin and Cortez deposits in Nevada), but production from them is a small fraction of the production from vein deposits.

Gold is a dense, indestructible mineral. It is therefore readily concentrated in streams where the action of flowing water washes away the less dense sand grains and leaves the gold concentrated behind barriers and near the base of the stream channel (Figure 8.38). Alluvial **placers**, as these deposits are called, were almost certainly the first deposits to have been worked by our ancestors, and they are still important producers. Many of the great gold rushes were started when prospectors discovered alluvial gold. Not only was the gold in the alluvial deposits worth recovering, but there was always the hope that prospecting upstream would lead to the Mother Lode from which the gold was derived. The great gold rush to California in 1849 is an example (as discussed on page 286; see also Figure 3.7), and from that rush, many interesting things followed. The great Mother Lode of California was discovered, but other parts of American heritage grew from the gold rush, too.

The greatest gold deposits that have ever been discovered, the Witwatersrand deposits in the Republic of South Africa, are ancient placers. These famous deposits were dis-covered in 1886, and they soon became the main gold producers in the world, a position they continue to fill today. The extreme mining depths now being reached and the rapidly escalating costs of mining suggest, however, that these famous deposits may not see a second century of production.

The Witwatersrand deposits are ancient conglomerates that were laid in a shallow marine basin (Figure 8.39). Into the basin ran ancient rivers, and at the mouth of each river a delta slowly built up. The gold and other heavy minerals are found in the coarse clastic sediments—the **conglomerates**—that make up the deltas (Figure 8.40), and they are presumed to have been brought into the basin as clastic particles by the same streams that brought the pebbles into the conglomerates. The deposits are very old, between 2.3 and 2.8 billion years, and they are enormous—more than twenty times larger than any other single gold district in the world. The source of the gold and how it came to be in the ancient conglomerates has been the subject of fierce debate for a century. The actual source of the gold is not known and is presumed to have been eroded away. The presence of large amounts of rounded placer pyrite grains and significant quantities of placer uranium minerals has led to the interpretation by most researchers that the erosion of the original source rocks and subsequent deposition in the Witwatersrand deltas took place when Earth's atmosphere contained very little or no free oxygen. If oxygen had been present, the pyrite would have oxidized (as it does today) and the uranium would have dissolved. Hence, the presence of pyrite and uranium in these ores, like the great banded iron formations discussed in the

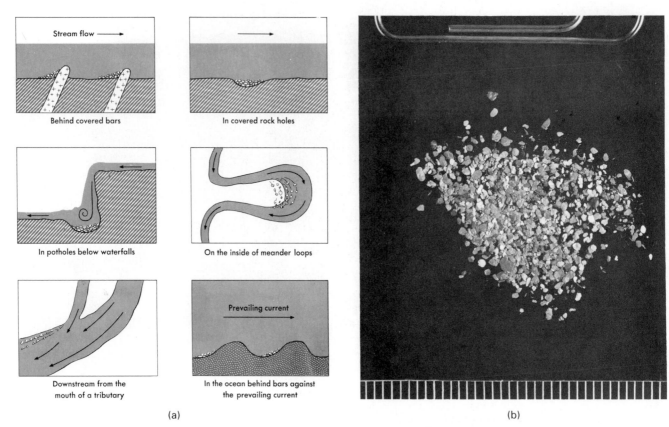

(a)   (b)

FIGURE 8.38. (a) Typical sites of placer accumulations where obstructing or deflecting barriers allow faster moving waters to carry away the suspended load of light and fine-grained material while trapping denser and coarser particles that are moving along the bottom by rolling or partial suspension. Placers can form whenever there is moving water, although they are most commonly associated with streams. (b) Grains of placer gold from California. By continual pounding in fast-moving streams, malleable gold is freed from brittle quartz and other valueless minerals. The tiny but dense gold grains accumulate in placers. It was gold such as this that the forty-niners mined in the streams of California. The grains are 1–2 millimeters in diameter. (Photograph by W. Sacco.)

previous chapter, is consistent with views that the early Earth atmosphere did not contain free oxygen. The Witwatersrand deposits are certainly unique in their size; similar but smaller deposits occur in similar age rocks in the Elliott Lake region of Canada and the Jacobina region of Brazil, but none has been found to be as rich as South Africa's basin.

The gold mines of South Africa are the world's deepest. By the 1990s, the deepest mining activity was being carried out 3600 meters (11,800 feet) below ground level. Plans are being laid to carry mining activities even deeper, to 4500 meters (14,700 feet). Whether it will be possible to mine safely and profitably at these extreme depths remains to be seen, but on that question rides South Africa's hope of continuing as the world's major producer of gold.

Gold is present in at least small amounts in a great many hydrothermal deposits of copper. The amount is rarely sufficient to warrant mining for gold alone, but when copper is being mined, gold can be recovered during smelting. Gold is one of the major by-products of porphyry copper mining and also from the mining of volcanogenic massive sulfide deposits.

Production and Reserves. There are two widely used units in the production of precious metals—the Troy ounce and the gram. One ounce (Troy) is equal to 31.104 grams. The total world production of gold for 1994 was 73,624,000 ounces (Troy). This is equal to 2,290,000,000 grams, or 2290 metric tons of gold! The total amount of gold ever produced is estimated at approximately 130,000 metric tons with more than 70 percent of that produced since 1900.

We have better records for the production of gold than for any other metal because of its long-held status of high value, and, consequently, we can construct a reasonable estimate of the production of gold over the past 8000 years (Figure 8.41). There are two major times when worldwide

FIGURE 8.39. The place where the fabulous Witwatersrand gold conglomerates were discovered by two prospectors, George Harrison and George Walker, in 1886. The conglomerate is somewhat weathered due to oxidation of pyrite (compare Plate 40). The man in the photograph is Dr. Desmond Pretorius, one of the great authorities on the geology of this remarkable deposit.

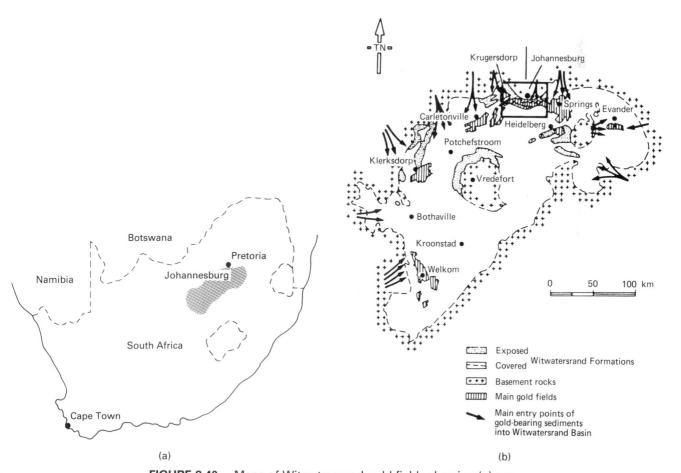

(a)

(b)

FIGURE 8.40. Maps of Witwatersrand gold fields showing (a) general location in South Africa and (b) the basin with the major gold fields with arrows indicating the directions of transport of the conglomerates into the basin. (Courtesy of Geological Society of South Africa.)

283

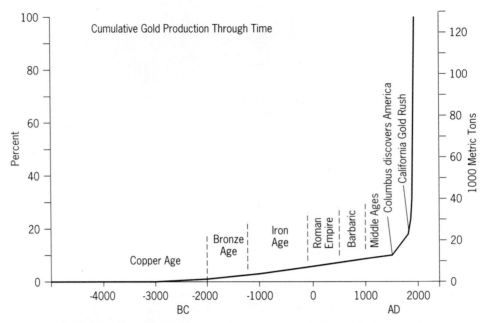

FIGURE 8.41.   Gold was one of the first metals found and mined by humans. Rates of production were low through most of human history, but rose significantly after Columbus' voyage to the New World. The California Gold Rush marked another major increase in the rate of gold production. Total world gold production throughout all human history until the mid-1990s is estimated to be about 125 thousand metric tons.

production sharply increased: the discovery of the New World in 1492 and the California Gold Rush in 1849. The California gold fields increased world production many fold, but the most important gold source for the past 100 years has been South Africa, as is evident in Figure 8.42. The price of gold was held fixed at various levels for many years, most notably at $35 (U.S.) from 1934 until 1968. This may have stabilized currency markets, but it lessened the value of gold because the value of everything else rose with inflation while gold remained fixed. In 1968, as a result of growing world pressures, the price of gold was allowed to float freely on world markets. Despite much expectation for very rapid price changes, the value of gold at first only rose slowly. The volatility of economic markets has subsequently led to an irregular pattern, as shown through 1994 in Figure 8.43. The large price surge in 1980, when gold actually peaked at near $900 per troy ounce, actually resulted primarily from efforts by some individuals to corner the world's silver market (the prices of gold and silver often move together). There are two important points to remember about gold prices: no one has been able to make accurate long-term predictions, and not everyone sees the value of gold remaining the same or even changing in the same direction because it is always quoted in U.S. dollar values, and there are constant changes in the dollar relative to the currencies of other countries. At a time when Americans see

steady gold prices, someone in England may see the price rising (as the pound loses value against the dollar), while someone in Japan sees the price falling (as the dollar loses against the yen).

Gold is so widely produced that more than 60 countries reported production in the 1980s and 1990s. Almost certainly, there were small productions in other countries, too, but they were not reported. Despite the wide extent of gold mining around the world, production is dominated by seven countries (Figure 8.44). South Africa has remained the world's largest producer, but both its production and its percentage of the total has been declining in recent years. The Vaal Reefs Mine of South Africa remains the world's largest single producer, but its importance wanes as total world production continues to rise and will likely reach 2500 metric tons per year by 2000 A.D. There is a lesson to be learned from the curves in Figure 8.42 besides the lesson of the influence of metal price on production. The lesson concerns exhaustion. No matter how large, how rich, or how carefully a deposit is mined, every ore body has a finite lifetime. South Africa's gold mining days are far from finished, but the declining production curve at a time of high prices is an early warning that the end must come someday.

What are the world's reserves and resources of gold? Because reserves are not reported by all countries, an accurate report is not possible. The mineable grades of gold ores

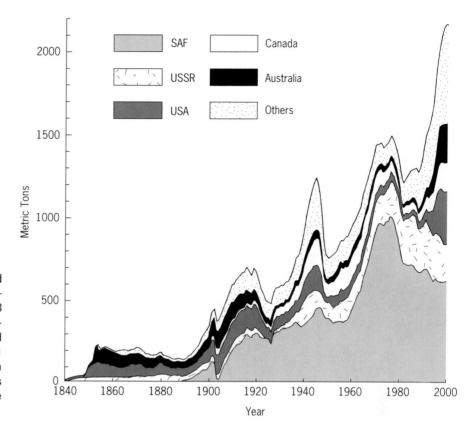

FIGURE 8.42. Annual world gold production since 1840. The discovery of gold in California in 1848 dramatically increased world production rates; this was followed by Australian discoveries in 1851 and the great discoveries in South Africa in 1886. South Africa has dominated world production since shortly after 1900.

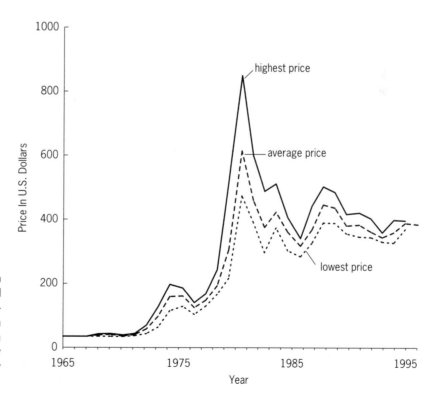

FIGURE 8.43. The variation in the average yearly price of gold since 1967 when the price was allowed to move freely. Prediction of the price of gold has proven very difficult despite the efforts by many workers in a wide variety of fields.

GOLD EXTRACTION USING MERCURY AND CYANIDE

For as long as humankind has valued and sought gold, one of the principal concerns has been how to efficiently recover the gold from the sediment or solid rock in which it occurs. The ancient gold discoveries were no doubt mostly placers, where the grains of gold have weathered out of the rock and become somewhat concentrated by the winnowing action of the water. Although large nuggets could be extracted by hand, it required the invention of the gold pan to provide an efficient means of concentrating and recovering the very small grains (see Figures 2.12 and 8.38). However, even with a gold pan, many small grains are easily lost. To increase the efficiency of recovery, someone, somewhere, in antiquity realized that gold will readily stick to and amalgamate with liquid metallic mercury forming an alloy.

For many centuries, amalgamation was a widespread method of gold recovery. A small amount of mercury was placed in the bottom of a gold pan; agitation of the pan brought the mercury in contact with gold grains, which also sank to the bottom because of their high density. After removing the amalgam from the pan, the mercury was separated from the gold by squeezing it through a finely woven cloth and/or by heating the amalgam to vaporize the mercury. In larger operations, mercury was placed on a sloping copper plate and a watery slurry of crushed ore (Figure 8.45a) was allowed to pass over the plate. The gold grains stuck to the mercury while the other rock fragments washed away. As a result of the development of other better technologies for extraction and recognition of health problems (especially nerve damage) caused by mercury, commercial extraction of gold by mercury is no longer practiced.

The accidental loss of mercury through inefficient methods and by heating amalgams has left small amounts of mercury in many areas that were prospected for gold in the 1800s and early 1900s. The mercury occurs in the sediments as small droplets that are slowly converted into a variety of compounds, some of which (like methyl mercury) are poisonous. In addition, many *week-end panners,* who pan for gold as a hobby and who continue to use mercury amalgamation, lose small amounts of mercury into streams. Despite government regulations, mercury amalgamation remains widely used in several areas of the Amazon River basin where Brazilian panners known as *garimpeiros* today suffer widespread mercury poisoning. Brazilian officials estimate that the panners have released at least one kilogram of mercury into the environment for every kilogram of gold recovered—an incredible total of nearly 2000 tons of mercury—in the past 10 years.

Today, commercial gold extraction is carried out using cyanide because the cyanide is cheaper, more efficient, and safer than mercury. Cyanide is very poisonous and must be used with great care to protect workers and wildlife. Gold, early referred to as a *noble metal* because it was so unreactive and insoluble in most solutions, even strong acids, is extremely soluble in cyanide solutions (as $NaAu(CN)_2$). As a consequence, modern gold mines where ore grades may be as low as about 1 part per million (0.03 troy oz per ton) or 0.0001 percent, can efficiently extract gold. The gold-bearing rock, once mined, is crushed to a size just small enough to allow the tiny gold grains (often no larger than 0.01 millimeter across) to become exposed, and then it is piled on large impermeable sheets of plastic. Water solutions, containing only about 0.05 percent sodium cyanide and maintained at a pH above 10 to prevent generation of poisonous gases, are allowed to percolate down through the crushed rock to dissolve the gold (Figure 8.45b). When the solution flows out of the bottom of the pile, it is collected and allowed to pass through filters of activated charcoal onto which the gold is adsorbed. The gold is then redissolved and precipitated electrolytically and the cyanide solutions are reused or rendered harmless so they do not damage the environment. One commonly used variation to heap leaching is called *carbon-in-pulp.* In this method, the activated charcoal is mixed directly with very finely ground ore in the dilute cyanide solution in large tanks. The mixture is agitated to promote gold solution and its absorption by the charcoal; then the charcoal and fine ore particles are separated, the ore discarded, and the charcoal taken for processing to recover the gold.

The carbon-in-pulp treatment is more expensive to operate but allows for much faster treatment of the ore (hours instead of months) and can be used where it is not possible to construct large leach pads. The efficiency of the cyanide technique is so great that much of the gold recovered today commonly comes from rocks where the gold is not even visible to the unaided eye and where the gold panners of old never dreamed that gold could be recovered.

have been dropping as recovery technology has improved and are now less than 1 part per million (see page 286 and Figure 8.45). Any further improvements could substantially increase reserves beyond the present estimates of about 44,000 metric tons.

Silver

Silver, like gold, was one of the earliest known metals. It was probably first used for simple ornaments and utensils in the Middle East, where silver objects more than 5000 years old

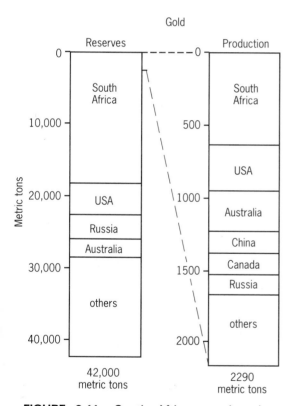

FIGURE 8.44. South Africa contains the world's largest reserves of gold and is the world's leading producer in the mid-1990s. The United States is now second in reserves and production. At current rates of production, the known reserves will last nearly 20 years; however, intense exploration efforts around the world are constantly finding new, usually low-grade, deposits that will certainly provide gold far into the future.

have been excavated. Like gold, silver occurs as a native metal. But, unlike gold, the native metal is not the most common mineral form. Much more common are silver-bearing sulfide minerals.

Silver was in wide use before the emergence of the Greek city-states, but it was one of those city-states, Athens, that showed the value of a good silver mine. The most famous of the ancient silver mines at Laurium belonged to Athens, and, with the wealth it produced, Themistocles built the fleet of ships that defeated Xerxes and saved Europe from Persian domination. Athens then grew to leadership among the city-states, and the Athenians became famous for their wealth and leisure. The mines at Laurium were worked for several centuries and are estimated to have produced over 250 million ounces (7.5 billion grams or 7500 metric tons) of silver. In recent years, it has also been recognized that the smelting of these lead-rich ores resulted in widespread lead pollution throughout much of the Mediterranean area.

The Greeks, Phoenicians, and other people from the countries bordering the Mediterranean used silver in their coinage, but it was the Romans who really brought it into wide usage. They made silver the basis of their monetary system (Figure 8.46) and expanded their empire to control sources of silver and other metals. When the power of Rome weakened and the empire finally fell, the mines of Europe closed. The Dark Ages descended on Europe. The mining of metals, particularly silver, which had formerly been mined in Europe and sent east to the Asian and Middle Eastern countries, slowed to a trickle and finally ceased. For 500 years, there was little or no mining. When Charlemagne came to power near the end of the eighth century, he opened the old mines of central Europe to build his revenue. Discoveries of new deposits followed in Germany, Bohemia, the Tyrol, and the Harz Mountains. Most significantly, very rich silver deposits were found at Rammelsberg and Frieberg in Germany in 920 and 1170 A.D., respectively, at Joachimsthal in Czechoslovakia in 1200, and at Schneeburg in Germany in 1460. From these deposits, the flow of precious metals restored Europe's wealth and helped its emergence from the Dark Ages. Trade routes were reopened and new routes were established. The land routes through the Middle East were particularly troublesome because of the taxes extracted by the Saracens and others on all materials passing through. This led Spanish and Portuguese sailors to seek sea routes; Vasco de Gama opened the routes around Africa, and Columbus sailed west and found the Americas.

The discovery of South and Central America with their enormous mineral wealth probably saved Europe from a new dark age. The mines of Europe were unable to cover the debts of the crowned heads and ambitious bankers. The vast flood of silver and gold from Mexico, Peru, Bolivia, Ecuador, and Brazil filled Europe's coffers again. The greatest production came from Bolivia, where the fabulous deposits of Potosi gave forth a flow of silver that seemed to never end. Spanish treasury records show that between 1503 and 1650, nearly 17 billion (10^9) grams (more than 540 million ounces) of silver had been shipped from the New World to Spain. By 1700, Bolivia alone had produced over 1 billion ounces of silver. The countries of South America were the main producers of silver until the 1870s, when the great deposits of Nevada, Utah, and the other western states pushed the United States into leadership (Figure 8.47). The United States held that position until 1900, when Mexico took over. Mexico continues as the world's leading producer of silver to the present day.

Silver has many technical and industrial uses, but two of its properties account for about 75 percent of the consumption. The first property is its high electrical conductiv- ity. Silver metal has the least resistance to electricity (the highest conductivity) of all metals. As a result, it is widely used in electrical contacts and conductors where the highest reliability is necessary. About 25 percent of all silver used in industrial countries is consumed in this manner. The second important property of silver—rather, of silver in certain compounds such as silver iodide—is that it is light sensitive. This is the property used in photography, and as a result, half of all silver consumed is used in photography. Other uses are in coins, sterling ware such as eating utensils and trays, jewelry, solders, and batteries. Silver was long used in 10-, 25-, and 50-cent coins in the United States but was withdrawn after the minting of the 1964 coins.

Geological Occurrence. Silver is a chemical element that resembles copper in many ways. As a result, silver can readily proxy for copper, by atomic substitution, in most copper minerals. Not surprisingly, much of the silver now mined comes as a by-product from copper mining. Silver also has an affinity for lead, and a great deal of the world's silver is also produced as a by-product of lead mining. Today,

(a)   (b)

FIGURE 8.45. (a) The Chilean Mill, such as this one at Gold Hill, North Carolina, was pulled by a horse so that it rotated about a central post. The large wheels, cut from quartzite, crushed gold-bearing ores so that the ore could be passed over mercury-coated copper plates where the gold would stick to the mercury. (Photograph by J. R. Craig.) (b) Most of the gold produced in the world today is recovered by heap leaching as shown here at Quebrada Blanca, Chile. The low-grade ore is reduced to less than 1–2 centimeters in large steel crushers and then piled on large plastic liners. Then dilute sodium cyanide solutions are sprayed on top and allowed to slowly percolate through the ore piles dissolving the gold. The gold is recovered by the methods described in the text. (Courtesy of Comico, Ltd.)

(a)

(b)

FIGURE 8.46.   Silver dinarius from Rome, in the time of Augustus (27 B.C.–14 A.D.). (a) The head of Augustus appears on the front. (b) Augustus' title (Caesar) and the name, together with two laurel trees, appear on the back. (From the Numismatic Collections, Yale University. Photography by W. Sacco.)

FIGURE 8.47.   The rich silver ores discovered at Eureka, Nevada, were one of the many rich deposits that made the United States the world's leading silver producer during the second half of the nineteenth century. The KC Mine as it looked in 1873 was one of several operating mines at Eureka. The entrance to the mine was a horizontal tunnel covered by the shed in the center of the photograph. Mined ore was tipped down the covered chutes to the processing plant just visible to the lower right. (From the collections of Beinecke Library, Yale University.)

more than 75 percent of all the silver produced is by-product silver. Inasmuch as both copper and lead deposits are largely of hydrothermal origin, the by-product silver is also of hydrothermal origin.

A number of deposits around the world are still worked principally for silver. The minerals recovered are mainly argentite (Ag_2S) and tetrahedrite (($Cu,Ag)_{12}Sb_4S_{13}$), but a number of other silver minerals are also recovered. The deposits in which all of these minerals are found are hydrothermal veins, and the geological settings in which the veins are located are principally volcanic rocks of andesitic and rhyolitic affinity. Because the great mountain chain that runs down the western edge of the Americas is made up of andesitic and rhyolitic volcanoes, it is from here that most of the world's silver has been found. More than three-quarters of all the silver that has ever been produced has been mined in the Americas.

Production and Reserves. Silver resembles gold in that a large number of countries (more than 55 in the mid-1990s) report production. Unlike gold production, no single country dominates silver production the way South Africa dominates gold production. But five countries do produce about 60 percent of the new silver each year (Figure 8.48).

It is apparent from Figure 8.48 that the annual world production of silver of about 15,000 metric tons vastly exceeds the world's production of gold. There is, nevertheless, a real problem concerning silver. In recent years, the consumption of silver has often exceeded the production of silver. Because silver is subject to a certain amount of corrosion and is not recoverable in many of the uses to which it is put, there is a small but steady loss of silver. To make up the difference between the silver consumed and produced, silver is withdrawn from inventory, from coinage, and from private hoards. Eventually, if consumption continues to exceed production, the hoards of silver will be depleted. The production of silver is not likely to rise very much, however, because so much of the production is a by-product. If copper and lead productions rise, silver production rises, too. If copper and lead productions fall, silver production falls. Because the amount of copper in porphyry copper and in volcanogenic massive sulfide deposits is very large, silver production will not cease, but someday it may well decline. A drop in production would cause a rise in prices, and this, in turn, would make some of the uses for silver too expensive. Reduced consumption would then follow. However, the development of digital photography is considered by some to be the first step in the decline in the photographic processes that have consumed so much silver. If this occurs, the demand for silver will significantly decrease.

Platinum Group Metals

The six platinum group metals—platinum, palladium, rhodium, iridium, ruthenium, and osmium—always occur together. They occur in the same geological setting, and to a certain degree they can substitute for each other in minerals by atomic substitution. Many of their chemical and physical properties are similar, too, so it is convenient to discuss these metals as a group rather than individually.

The group takes its name from its most abundant member, platinum. Each of the metals is silvery white in color, and, although the metals are all malleable to a certain degree, both platinum and palladium are sufficiently malleable that they can sometimes be mistaken for silver. Indeed, the first uses of platinum probably occurred as a result of such a misidentification. Platinum metal occurs in the native form in placers. Grains of platinum, intermixed with silver grains, were used by ancient Egyptian artisans in certain works of ornamentation. The artisans must have realized platinum was more difficult to work than silver, but because it could be soldered, they probably regarded the platinum as just an impure form of silver.

When the Spanish conquistadors conquered South America, they discovered finely wrought objects of a strange, white metal among the Indian treasures they looted. The Indian metalsmiths had learned to shape, solder, and even

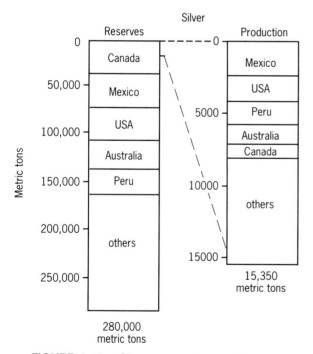

FIGURE 8.48. Silver occurs in, and is produced by, many nations today, but five countries account for about 50 percent of reserves and production. At present rates of production, known reserves will last about 18 years. (From the U. S. Bureau of Mines).

alloy platinum. The Spaniards lacked these skills and did not attempt to learn from the Indians. They considered platinum to be valueless because they could not work it as they could silver. Consequently, they called the metal *platina,* a degrading term meaning *little silver.* Furthermore, the importation of platinum into Europe from the New World was banned so that it would not degrade gold and silver, and much platinum was thrown into rivers and the sea.

The first precise separation of platinum as a chemical element and the first clear statement of its properties arose from the work of an English scientist, William Lewis. He published the results of his studies in 1763, and soon thereafter, other chemists in Germany and France learned how to purify the metal; as a result, they discovered many of platinum's alloying properties. During the purification of platinum, it was discovered that other platinum-like metals were also present in many of the ores. In 1803, the English scientist Wollaston separated and identified palladium. In 1804, Wollaston described rhodium, while his countryman, Tennant, isolated and named osmium and iridium. Forty years were to pass until a German named Claus, working in Russia, discovered the last of the platinum group metals. He named it *ruthenium* in honor of his adopted country. *Ruthenia* is the latinized name for Russia.

All of the platinum group metals are resistant to corrosion, each has a high melting temperature, and each has interesting properties as a **catalyst.** Speeding chemical reactions through catalysis, plus the use of the metals in highly corrosive environments and in very high-temperature situations, accounts for the main uses of all of the platinum group metals.

Of particular importance is the use of platinum group elements in automobile catalytic converters (Figure 8.49), where platinum deposited on the inner surfaces of the sieve-like openings of the ceramic base converts harmful exhaust gases into inert ones. These converters have long been mandatory on automobiles and trucks in the United States and are being increasingly required on such vehicles around the world as concern for clean air rises.

Geological Occurrence. The platinum group metals are found as native metals and as sulfide and arsenide minerals. There are only two important geological settings in which these minerals are found in economical quantities. The first is in mafic and ultramafic rocks where the platinum group metals are concentrated in both chromite horizons and sulfide-rich layers in layered intrusions. As a result, production of platinum group metals comes from the same deposits, such as Sudbury, Ontario, and the Bushveld Igneous Complex in South Africa, that produce nickel, copper, and chromium from magmatic segregation ores.

The second geological environment in which the platinum group metals are concentrated is in placers. Like gold, the metals are dense and very resistant to corrosion. They

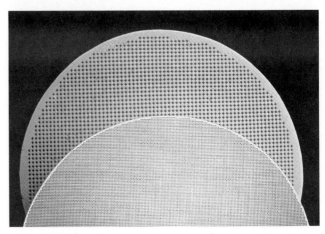

FIGURE 8.49. Automotive catalytic converters are prepared of cordierite ($Mg_2Al_4Si_5O_{18}$) in the form of narrow square tunnels and are coated with platinum-group metals, which convert hot noxious gases into harmless compounds as the exhaust passes through. (Courtesy of Corning, Inc.)

concentrate readily in alluvial sediments. Commonly, the source of the metals in placers is ultramafic rocks such as serpentine and peridotites. The great placer deposits of Russia have this origin. Serpentine in the Ural Mountains contains small amounts of platinum group metals, so that streams that carry debris from weathering of serpentine from the Urals have valuable placers associated with them. These provided sufficient platinum that Russia minted and circulated large numbers of platinum coins from 1828 to 1841.

Production and Reserves. Separate production figures are not reported for all of the platinum group metals, but it is possible to estimate the approximate percentages from the amounts of metals consumed. Platinum and palladium each account for about 40 percent of the production. Rhodium accounts for 9 percent, iridium 6 percent, ruthenium 4 percent, and osmium 1 percent.

The world's production of platinum group metals is overwhelmingly dominated by two countries, Russia and the Republic of South Africa (Figure 8.50). Between them, they have been producing about 90 percent of all the platinum group metals mined in the 1980s and 1990s. Between them, too, they own most of the world's reserves. Of particular importance are two horizons within the Bushveld Complex in South Africa. One horizon is the 0.5-meter-thick Merensky Reef that has served as the major source for platinum for many years and that contains reserves estimated at 500–600 million troy ounces ($15–19 \times 10^9$ gram). The other horizon, a meter-thick layer of massive chromite known as the UG-2, lies below the Merensky Reef and is estimated to contain reserves of 800–1350 million troy ounces ($25–41 \times 10^9$ gram). In the United States, large resources of platinum group met-

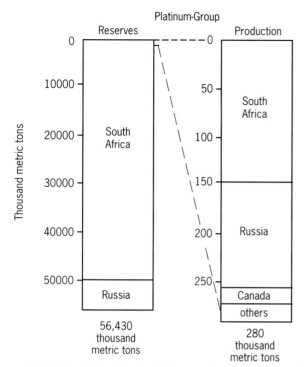

FIGURE 8.50. South Africa holds about 90 percent of the world's reserves of platinum group metals and is the largest producer. Most of the world's remaining reserves are in Russia, which is also the second largest producer. At present rates of production, the known reserves will last for 200 years. (From the U. S. Bureau of Mines.)

als are present in the Stillwater Complex, Montana. These deposits occur in a Merensky Reef-like layer in a layered intrusion that is smaller, but that resembles the Bushveld Complex. Mining began on this zone in the late 1980s, and the United States production has been steadily increasing.

THE SPECIAL METALS

The special metals earned their name because of their unique properties and the special roles they fill in our twentieth century technology. None of them is mined in large quantities, but each fills one or more special roles that make their continued availability of vital importance to society.

Niobium and Tantalum

Niobium (also called columbium) and tantalum have similar properties and commonly occur together in nature. They were identified as separate chemical elements in 1801, but for more than 125 years no use was found for them. Eventually, in the 1920s, tantalum came to be used in the chemical and electrical industries, but it was only at the time of World

War II that it found uses in electrical capacitors and in alloys for armaments. Niobium was first used about 1930 when it was added to steel to make very high-temperature alloys.

Niobium is still used for high-strength alloys needed in such demanding environments as gas turbines and the engines of jet aircraft. It is also used to make superconducting magnets. Most of the tantalum used is still employed in the electronics industry for capacitors and rectifiers. Other applications include tantalum carbide for high-temperature cutting tools and, because of their corrosion resistance, tantalum mesh and pins in the human body during surgical repairs.

The main minerals that contain niobium and tantalum are columbite $((Fe,Mn)Nb_2O_6)$ and tantalite $((Fe,Mn)Ta_2O_6)$. Columbite always contains some tantalum in solid solution, and tantalite always contains niobium, so the two metals are always produced together.

Tantalum and niobium minerals are found in several kinds of igneous rock. The first is an alkali-rich rock called a **nepheline syenite.** Such rocks are rarely rich enough to be mined, but in the Kola Peninsula of the former Soviet Union, they do reach mining grade and are being exploited. The second kind of igneous rock is a **carbonatite.** This rare and unusual rock consists largely of calcium carbonate, and it is known both as an intrusive and extrusive igneous rock. Carbonatites have been worked for their niobium and tantalum contents at Oka in Quebec and at Axana in Brazil.

The third type of igneous rock that often contains economic amounts of niobium and tantalum is the pegmatite. One of the major sources of tantalum in North America is the Bernic Lake pegmatite in Manitoba.

Both columbite and tantalite are chemically stable, hard, and dense. Therefore, the minerals tend to become concentrated in placers. Such deposits have been worked in Brazil, western Australia, and West Africa.

The total world production in the 1980s and 1990s has been about 15,000 metric tons of niobium per year and about 300 metric tons of tantalum per year. The major producing countries are Canada, Australia, and Brazil.

Arsenic, Antimony, and Bismuth

The three elements arsenic, antimony, and bismuth have similar properties and tend to occur in the same kinds of geological environments. Arsenic is little used in its elemental form. It is a brittle, grayish-colored substance that lacks the malleability usually associated with metals. For this reason, arsenic is often called a semimetal. The main use for arsenic is in chemical compounds, mainly as arsenates used in wood preservation, fungicides, insecticides, and pesticides. All of the arsenic produced comes as a by-product from base metal mining. The world's annual production in the 1980s and 1990s has been between 40,000 and 50,000 metric tons of arsenic trioxide (As_2O_3). The main producers are China, Chile, and Mexico.

Antimony, like arsenic, is really a semimetal, but it has useful alloying properties, so much of the production finds a use in the metallic form. Antimony metal is added to the lead plates in batteries to toughen the lead. It is also used as an alloying agent with other base metals besides lead to harden alloys and make them more resistant to corrosion. Antimony compounds find uses as pigments in paints and plastics, as fire-retarding agents, as stabilizers in glasses, and in many other circumstances. The world's annual production of antimony, stated as the metal, has been about 70,000 metric tons in the 1990s. The major producers, in order of importance, are China, Bolivia, Russia, and the Republic of South Africa.

Bismuth, the heaviest of the trio of semimetals, is also the most metallic in its properties. Most people know bismuth in its various chemical compounds used for medicinal purposes. The well-known antacid Peptobismol is a proprietary form of a medicinal bismuth compound. The two largest uses of bismuth are as medicinal and cosmetic compounds. The third major use of bismuth is as an additive to low-melting alloys. The world's annual production of bismuth is small, amounting to only about 4000 metric tons.

Arsenic, antimony, and bismuth are all produced as byproducts of smelting processes for more abundant metals such as lead, zinc, and copper, although antimony, the element used in the largest amount, is also produced directly at the Murchison Mine in South Africa. All of the producing deposits, whether direct or by-product, are hydrothermal, and all of the ore minerals are sulfides.

Germanium, Gallium, and Indium

Germanium, gallium, and indium are very much metals of the twentieth century. In each case, the major production is a by-product from the processing of major metals, principally aluminum and zinc, but to a lesser extent, lead and copper.

The total quantity of the three metals produced is relatively small, but the uses to which they are put are wide ranging. Germanium has a high electrical conductivity, and it is the material from which some of the semiconductors in computers are made. Gallium has the unusual property of expanding on crystallizing, and this leads to some most unusual alloying effects. Indium has a very low melting temperature and is very soft and highly malleable, so it too has very interesting, although highly specialized, alloy properties. The principal uses for all three metals are in the electronics industry.

The world's annual production of the three metals is not known, and because the uses to which they are put are so sensitive, most countries will not supply production figures. The reserves of germanium and indium are held almost entirely in the form of solid solutions in the zinc sulfide, sphalerite. Thus, the availability of these elements will be almost entirely dependent upon the primary mining of zinc. Potential resources of germanium would increase to millions of metric tons if it were to be recovered from fly ash and flue dusts that result from the burning of coal. Gallium also occurs in solid solution in some sphalerites but mostly is present in concentrations of about 50 parts per million in bauxites.

Beryllium

Beryllium metal is produced by a relatively young industry because many of its uses have arisen as a result of the nuclear and space industries, but a beryllium compound has been known and used since antiquity—the two gemstones, emerald and aquamarine, are species of the beryllium mineral, beryl (Figure 8.51).

The chemical element beryllium was first identified in 1797, but only in 1828 was the metal itself produced. It is a very light metal, reddish in color, very strong and stiff, and it has a very high melting temperature. Mixed with copper, beryllium produces a very hard and elastic alloy. The low

FIGURE 8.51. Beryl crystal from a pegmatite at Portland, Connecticut. Note the hexagonal shape of the crystal, which is about 4 centimeters in diameter. The emerald, shown in Plate 56, is a gem-quality beryl. (Photograph by W. Sacco.)

atomic weight of beryllium makes it almost transparent to X rays and thermal neutrons, so the metal is widely used for the windows in X-ray tubes.

There are two major sources of beryllium. The first is the mineral beryl that is found in many pegmatites around the world. Unfortunately, none of the deposits is particularly large or rich. The second important mineral is bertrandite ($Be_4Si_2O_7(OH)_2$), which occurs in certain hydrothermal deposits associated with rhyolitic volcanic rocks. The deposits at Spor Mountain, Utah, are the largest known deposits of this kind.

The world's annual production of beryllium metal has only been about 300 metric tons in the 1990s. Production has been a little larger at times, but at no time has beryllium ever been produced in very large quantities. The restriction on production is two-fold. First, deposits are small and very expensive to work. Second, the separation of beryllium from its ores is a very expensive and exacting process.

Rare-Earth Elements

The **rare-earth elements (REE)** really do not deserve their name because they are much more abundant than many other geochemically scarce metals. There are 15 REE (Table 8.5), starting with lanthanum (atomic number 57) and ending with lutetium (atomic number 71), and they all have very similar chemical properties. When first discovered, the REE were known only in their oxide forms, and because they resembled the oxides of the alkaline earths (CaO, BaO, etc.) and did not seem to form common minerals, they were labeled *rare earths.*

The REE are the basis of a small industry that started more than a century ago. The oxides are stable at high temperatures, and they were added to the thorium oxide lamp mantles used by our great-grandparents. In more recent times, they have found uses in such diverse applications as petroleum-cracking catalysts, opacifiers and coloring agents in the glass and ceramics industry, inhibitors of radiation in television tubes, lasers, and special optical glasses.

The REE are produced mainly from two minerals, monazite ($CeYPO_4$) and bastnaesite ($CeFCO_3$). Although the formulas of both minerals are written for cerium compounds, all of the REE substitute for Ce in the structures by atomic substitution.

REE minerals are found in small amounts in many igneous rocks, but principally in pegmatites, carbonatites, and granites. Some of these deposits are mined, as at Mountain Pass in California, but the main production comes from monazite concentrated in placers. It is recovered as a by-product from the mining of rutile, ilmenite, cassiterite, and other placer minerals.

The world's annual production of REE, reported as rare earth oxides, has been about 60,000 metric tons. In the past, much data regarding rare earths was considered proprietary; however, in recent years the data have been more freely disclosed, and the U.S. Bureau of Mines has made reasonable estimates of production and reserves (Figure 8.52).

TABLE 8.5

The rare-earth elements. The relative amount of each REE produced is in proportion to its geochemical abundance in the crust

Name	Chemical Symbol		Atomic Number	Geochemical Abundance (wt %)
Yttrium*	Y		39	0.0035
Lanthanum	La		57	0.005
Cerium	Ce		58	0.0083
Praseodymium	Pr		59	0.013
Neodymium	Nd	The light REE	60	0.0044
Promethium	Pm		61	Human-made
Samarium	Sm		62	0.00077
Europium	Eu		63	0.00022
Gadolinium	Gd		64	0.00063
Terbium	Tb		65	0.0001
Dysprosium	Dy		66	0.00085
Holmium	Ho		67	0.00016
Erbium	Er	The heavy REE	68	0.00036
Thulium	Tm		69	0.000052
Ytterbium	Yb		70	0.00034
Lutetium	Lu		71	0.00008

*Yttrium is commonly classed with the REE because its properties are so similar.

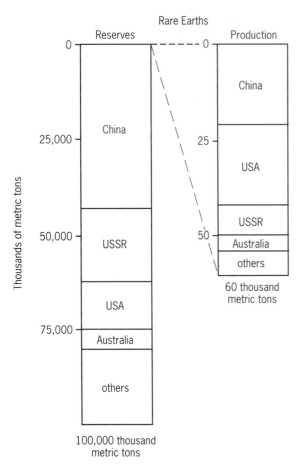

FIGURE 8.52. The world's production of rare-earth elements has been rising and has reached about 60,000 metric tons annually in the mid-1990s. At present rates of production, the world's reserves will last more than 1500 years. (From the U. S. Bureau of Mines.)

DISTRIBUTION OF DEPOSITS OF THE SCARCE METALS

There are literally hundreds of thousands of mineral deposits, large and small, that have been discovered, tested, and sometimes mined. As a result, geologists have long realized that certain kinds of deposits occur more commonly in some kinds of rocks than in others. For example, the association between mafic igneous rocks and nickel deposits, or the similar association with chromium deposits, has long been recognized. Despite such associations, it was only during the 1970s, when the consequences of plate tectonics and continental drift were being considered, that the possibility of a larger underlying pattern was realized. A great deal remains to be deciphered, but it is now apparent that many classes of ore deposits formed where and when they did as a consequence of plate tectonic motions.

Most volcanism around the world is associated either with plate spreading edges (midocean ridges) or with plate subduction edges (deep-sea trenches). The kinds of volcanism differ at the two edges, but each serves as a heat source to drive hydrothermal systems and to bring metal-rich magma up from the mantle or lower crust (Figure 8.53). Most of the young, active hydrothermal systems that have been discovered around the world can be shown to be directly related to the modern plate edges. We must conclude, therefore, that hydrothermal mineral deposits formed as a result of volcanism arose as a direct consequence of plate tectonics, and that present and past plate motions must control their distribution.

The origins of sediment-hosted stratiform deposits and even Mississippi Valley-type deposits can also be related to plate motions. Most stratiform deposits are located in

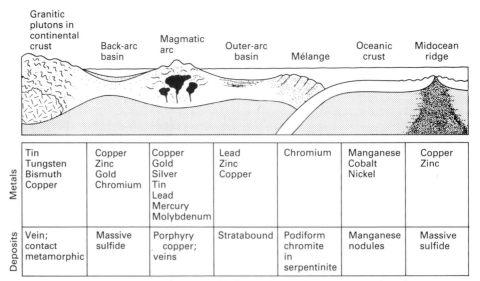

FIGURE 8.53. Diagram showing the kinds of mineral deposits and the most important metals concentrated in relation to tectonic plates.

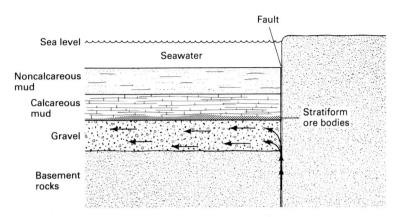

FIGURE 8.54. One way that stratiform ore bodies are believed to form in sediments is through hydrothermal solutions rising up faults and spreading laterally through a porous aquifer. If the sediment above the aquifer reacts with the solution, sulfide minerals such as chalcopyrite, sphalerite, and galena may precipitate.

grabens, which are sediment basins formed by blocks of crust dropped downward along normal faults (Figure 8.54). Grabens arise as a result of tensional forces, and those tensional forces are a consequence of plate tectonics. Mississippi Valley-type deposits form in sediments deposited on the shelves of large sedimentary basins. The basins form as a consequence of plate motions, so these deposits appear to be distributed in a way that suggests a plate tectonic control. We may eventually be able to understand and decipher the underlying controls on all mineral deposits, but, at present, only the broadest outline is visible.

PROSPECTING FOR DEPOSITS OF THE SCARCE METALS

Most of us have an overly romanticized image of the grizzled old prospector going about his work. The image usually includes a mule and a faithful dog who accompany the prospector as he works his way up and down hill slopes, tapping rock specimens or digging shallow holes, searching for the elusive nugget of gold or rich showing of copper minerals. The image may once have been correct, but it is no longer. The rich, easily discovered deposits that crop out at the surface, just waiting for some knowledgeable prospector to come along, have mostly been discovered. In some well-prospected areas, it has been many centuries since the last outcropping deposit was found. In the part of Europe that was once controlled by the Romans, for example, no new deposits of base or precious metals have been discovered since the Roman empire fell. Deeper extensions of known mineral districts have indeed been located, but prospectors have not found any entirely new mineral districts. Much more sophisticated techniques are now needed to find new mines.

The pattern of discovery just described for Roman Europe can also be discerned in other well-prospected parts of the world. The New England states—for example, Connecticut, Massachusetts, Rhode Island, Vermont, New Hampshire, and Maine—were all active mining states and were producers of important quantities of scarce metals at

some time in their histories. With the exception of Maine, those days are long gone, and prospectors have not turned up deposits of interest for many, many years. The situation in the southeastern United States is somewhat similar. Discoveries of placer gold in the early 1800s led to lode mines that operated until exhausted in the early twentieth century. Base metal deposits were discovered in the 1850s through 1880s and produced ores until the early 1900s, except for some Mississippi Valley-type zinc deposits in Virginia and eastern Tennessee that have survived until the present. The major recent activity has been large-scale gold mining in mines such as Ridgeway, Brewer, and Barite Hill in South Carolina. Although in areas where small placer occurrences have long been known, these ore bodies were defined on the basis of modern ultrasensitive geochemical exploration techniques.

Eventually, each country will have been thoroughly prospected by traditional means. But that does not mean that all deposits will have been found. More than half of Earth's surface is covered so deeply by soil and sediment that it is not possible to see the rock below. To prospect in such terrains, it is necessary to use indirect means. Three such means are employed. The first is geological interpretation. By knowing the kinds of rocks and geological settings in which ore deposits might be found, geologists can locate drill holes more carefully and get samples from as deep as 5000 meters. Such testing is expensive, though, and the ore deposit targets being sought are small. Even a large massive sulfide deposit is only a few hundred meters in diameter. What chance does a driller have of hitting such a body when it is 2000 or 3000 meters deep? The chances are poor, unfortunately. To increase the opportunity of making a hit, two additional methods are called into play. The first is geochemistry. Groundwater in contact with a buried ore deposit can sometimes produce a dispersed halo of trace elements around the ore. By carefully sampling water, soil, and even sediments in streams, faint imprints of trace elements such as mercury, zinc, or copper can sometimes be detected. The second method employs geophysics. Some ore bodies contain magnetic minerals, and others contain minerals that conduct electricity. By making very sensitive magnetic and electrical measurements on the ground surface, it is sometimes possible to detect buried ore bodies beneath as much as 500 meters of barren rock.

The future of prospecting depends not on the old prospector and his mule, but rather on the sciences of geology, geochemistry, and geophysics. On them, too, depend the future supplies of scarce metals that society will need.

THE LONG-TERM FUTURE FOR THE SCARCE METALS

The geochemically scarce metals are distributed in two ways in Earth's crust. More than 99.9 percent of the total amount of any given scarce metal is distributed by atomic substitution in common silicate minerals. The remaining tiny fraction is distributed in ore minerals. Let us consider the problem of recovering metals from ores versus recovering metals from common rocks, using copper as an example.

The energy used in mining a sulfide ore is a function of the grade of the ore and the difficulty of smelting the concentrate. It takes less energy to mine and produce a concentrate of sulfide minerals from a high-grade ore than from a low-grade one. As shown in Figure 8.55, a plot of grade versus energy rises steeply toward lower grades. Now consider the case of an ordinary rock. The energy used to mine a ton of rock is the same as that used to mine a ton of high-grade ore. But in the case of the rock, the copper is present in solid solution, so it is not possible to make a rich concentrate to send to the smelter. Instead, the entire rock must be smelted and processed, and that is a very energy-intensive process. The recovery curve for getting copper out of common rocks is on the left-hand side of Figure 8.55.

Note that the two curves in Figure 8.55 do not meet or overlap. This is because there is a lowest grade for sulfide ores, and below that grade, all copper is in solid solution. Similarly, there is a highest grade for copper in solid solution in the minerals of common rocks. If the day should ever be reached when all the sulfide ores of copper have been mined, we would have to find a way, technically, to overcome the mineralogical barrier and start mining common rocks. The cost in energy to produce copper from the highest grade common rocks will be ten times as much as the energy cost of mining the lowest grade sulfide ores. Whether society might wish to pursue this source is a decision for the future.

When might the mineralogical barrier be reached? Obviously, if prospecting beneath cover rocks is successful and efficient mining practices are conducted, there is a great deal of scarce metal ore still to be mined. But a century or more ahead, the day will be reached when both the exposed and buried rocks have been prospected, and common rocks may have to be considered as sources. It may well be that those

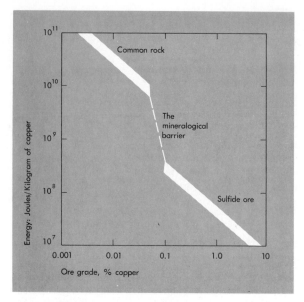

FIGURE 8.55. Energy used to extract metallic copper from ores containing sulfide minerals and from solid solution in silicate minerals in common rocks. The two curves are parallel but do not overlap. The gap represents a mineralogical barrier to the trend to mine increasingly lower grade ores. All geochemically scarce metals seem to display this relationship. (From Skinner, 1896.)

who follow us, and who have to face this prospect, will choose not to mine common rocks for scarce metals but instead will work to develop a technology based on the abundant metals such as iron, aluminum, and magnesium, for which there are no foreseeable supply limitations. What that future society will be and how technology of the day will cope with material demands are questions that can be answered only in the future.

FURTHER READINGS

Brobst, D. A. and Pratt, W. P. (eds.), "United States Mineral Resources." *United States Geological Survey Professional Paper* 820 (1973).

Edwards, R. and Atkinson, K., *Ore Deposit Geology: And Its Influence on Mineral Exploration.* London: Chapman and Hall, 1986.

Guilbert, J. M. and Park, C. F., *The Geology of Ore Deposits.* New York: W. H. Freeman and Co., 1990.

Neuharth, C. R., "Ferroalloys." *U.S. Bureau of Mines Annual Report 1990* (1992).

Sawkins, F. J., *Metal Deposits in Relation to Plate Tectonics.* Berlin: Springer-Verlag, 1984.

Skinner, B. J., *Earth Resources,* 3rd ed. Englewood Cliffs, New Jersey: Prentice Hall, 1986.

United States Bureau of Mines, "Minerals Yearbook," *Metals and Minerals,* vol. 1, published annually, 1994.

9 FERTILIZER AND CHEMICAL MINERALS

The ocean is used as a source of salt, one of the most widely used chemical minerals. This photograph of salt recovery operations in Bonaire in the Netherlands Antilles shows piles of salt that have been recovered by evaporating seawater. Ocean water with about 3.5 percent dissolved salts is pumped into large lagoons where it is allowed to evaporate using only the energy of the sun. Once the water has evaporated, the salt is harvested and shipped for use in a myriad of industries. (Photograph courtesy of AKZO NOBEL.)

Man can live without gold but not without salt.

Flavius Magnus Cassiodorus, A Roman Politician of the Fifth Century A.D.

FOCAL POINTS

- Three principal fertilizer components—nitrogen, phosphorous, and potassium—are necessary for plant growth and substantially increase crop yield.

- Humans began using animal wastes and ashes from cooking fires as fertilizers to increase food production in prehistoric times.

- World fertilizer production is presently about 300 million tons per year and will have to rise continually to feed a rising world population.

- Nitrogen-bearing fertilizers first became important in world trade in the early 1800s with the shipment of large quantities of bird guano from western South America to Europe.

- The supply of natural nitrates, shipped from what is now northern Chile, caused the War of the Pacific (1878–1883); the conflict resulted in Bolivia losing its coastline.

- Nitrogen fertilizers today are synthesized from atmospheric nitrogen.

- Phosphate fertilizers, originally made from bones, are now processed from phosphate rock using sulfuric acid to make soluble superphosphates.

- Potassium fertilizers, once derived from the "pot-ash" of hardwoods, are now extracted from evaporite deposits.

- Sulfur, sometimes included in fertilizers, is a widely used chemical product. It is extracted from underground deposits (associated with "salt domes") by pumping hot water into the deposits to melt out the sulfur. It is also increasingly extracted from fossil fuels.

- Halite, or "common salt," is the most widely used chemical mineral. It is extracted from underground mines in large evaporite beds, from natural brines, and from seawater.

- A long list of mineral-derived chemicals serves modern society in the manufacture of many thousands of materials.

INTRODUCTION

The general public often does not appreciate the importance of the mineral resources used in fertilizer and chemical industries because usually only the resulting products are seen, not the minerals themselves. For example, we see the copies emerge from a photocopier but not the selenium compounds that actually transfer the image, and we use soaps daily but never see the boron minerals from which they are made. These mineral groups are **nonmetallic minerals**, a general term used to describe Earth resources that are not processed for metal or fuel. They are mined and processed either for their nonmetallic elements or for their physical or chemical characteristics. Nearly everyone is familiar with fertilizers because they are widely used on home gardens, lawns, and large commercial farms. While the large number of minerals used in chemical processes have very specialized uses, the following account gives a general overview and shows the diversity of these important chemical minerals.

MINERALS FOR FERTILIZERS

The constant increase in world population requires a constant expansion in food production. Ten elements—hydrogen, oxygen, carbon, nitrogen, phosphorus, potassium, sulfur, calcium, iron, and magnesium—are required to grow food. The first three of these, which constitute 98 percent of the living plant, are supplied in water drawn up from the soil and carbon dioxide absorbed from the atmosphere. The other elements, although constituting only 2 percent of the plant matter, are vital to many growth processes. Plants directly extract these elements from mineral or organic matter in the soil or groundwater. It is not so much the absolute concentration of these elements in the soil that is important, but rather the concentrations that are available in a water-soluble form that the plant can absorb. Natural soil-forming processes, discussed in greater detail in Chapter 11, slowly decompose many of the primary rock-forming minerals into clays, oxides, and soluble salts from which the plants can extract these necessary elements. Long before our ancestors understood soil formation or knew anything about chemistry, they found that many organic wastes, such as animal dung and fish heads, would increase crop yields. A progression of events lead to our present resources we now use for fertilizers.

HISTORICAL OVERVIEW OF FERTILIZERS

Food supply depends on three resources—**soil**, **water**, and **fertilizer**. The earliest hunter-gatherers needed water directly for survival, but they gave little thought to soils and had no concept of fertilizers. However, when they became agriculturalists, planting and tending crops, they discovered that the yields in different areas were not always equal but were dependent on the availability of water and some unseen characteristics of the soils.

We shall never know who first fertilized crops or when this happened, but the earliest fertilizers were apparently manures—animal and possibly even human. Our ancestors did not know that these manures contain the three most important elements for plant growth—**nitrogen**, **phosphorus**, and **potassium**—but they did recognize the increased growth and yield caused by the applications of manure. By Greek and Roman times, manures were classified according to their richness, with that of birds being rated the best. Xenophon noted in about 400 B.C. that, "The estate has gone to ruin [because] someone did not know it was well to manure the land." Perhaps he gave the greatest compliment to this so often unappreciated product when he wrote, "There is nothing so good as manure."

Written records are sparse, but archeological evidence shows that the use of natural waste organic materials as fertilizers became a worldwide practice, nearly always on a local scale. An exception to this was the exploitation of the large Peruvian coastal **guano** deposits. This developed into a major element of commerce between Peru and Europe from 1808 until after 1880. These deposits, which had accumulated on coastal islands with almost no rainfall, were easily accessible and very inexpensive to mine. The Indians had exploited them for at least 60 years but had been careful not to disturb or dislodge the large bird colonies that generated the deposits. England, seeking fertilizer for its important, newly introduced turnip crop, was thus a ready market. English merchants rapidly took advantage of the decline of Spanish influence in the region, and shipments were sent to Germany and England before 1810. However, significant commercial development did not occur until 1840. From 1840 until 1880, more than 4,350,000 metric tons of guano were shipped to England peaking at 274,000 tons in 1858. In the decade 1855–1864, the value of Peruvian guano cargoes to Britain exceeded £20,000,000. A Peruvian exporter of that period, who first believed that there could be no viable trade of guano, later noted, "The base manure could well be transformed into the purest gold."

The demise of the great guano trade happened from 1878 to 1885 as two other fertilizer industries—nitrates in South America and phosphates in Europe—rapidly expanded. The nitrates and nitrate compounds, commonly referred to as **saltpeter** or **niter**, consist of potassium nitrate (KNO_3), sodium nitrate ($NaNO_3$), and calcium nitrate ($Ca(NO_3)_2$). They occur in the very dryest parts of the coastal regions of southern Peru, once western Bolivia, and northern Chile. They were mined on a small scale as early as 1810, and major shipments to Europe began about 1830. The nitrate exports rose to 21,300 metric tons in 1850, 106,000 metric tons in 1867, 535,000 metric tons in 1883, and peaked at

THE EARLY POTASH INDUSTRY AND U.S. PATENT NUMBER 1

Samuel Hopkins of Pittsford, Vermont, was only 25 years old when he received the very first U.S. Patent on July 31, 1790, for an improvement "in the making of Potash and Pearl ash by a new apparatus and process." The patent was signed by President George Washington, Secretary of State Thomas Jefferson, and Attorney General Edmund Randolph. The term *potash* aptly describes the general mixture of potassium hydroxides and carbonates that accumulate in hardwood ashes; *pearl ash* is a purer variety that slightly resembles the color of a pearl. Potassium was already valuable, but Hopkins improved the quality of the product, thus contributing significantly to what has been called the United States' first industrial chemical.

Farmers in many parts of the world recognized that the ash of some trees, especially the deciduous *hardwoods*, was rich in potash and served well as fertilizers to promote the growth of crops. The colonial world did not, however, seek the potash so much as a fertilizer, but rather because of its value in making soap and glass, dyeing fabrics, baking, and making saltpeter (KNO_3) for gunpowder. By about 1750, England had developed a great demand for soaps to wash wool before it was woven. Having largely exhausted its own forests in order to provide charcoal for steam engines and to make iron and steel, England turned to its colonies as a new source of potash. It was prepared by taking the black sooty ash that accumulated in the fireplace and leaching it with water in large pots (Figure 9.1). The soluble potassium salts dissolve and can then be reprecipitated when the water evaporates. Early small scale operations relied upon ashes they purchased from local residents, but these were inefficient because the amount and quality of the supply were irregular. Accordingly, commercial ventures developed across New England and southern Canada in the vast hardwood forests. The best potash yields came from elm, maple, ash, hickory, beech, and basswood; softwoods, such as pine, were of little value. Large steel pots were specially made for the leaching and boiling of the residue. The American revolutionary leader, Ethan Allen, worked with his brothers in the manufacture of potash kettles before he became the leader of the Green Mountain Men.

During the American Revolution, the need for gunpowder intensified the need for potash and hence further spurred the development of the industry. The potash was reacted with nitrogen-rich materials, such as bat guano, to make saltpeter, a vital constituent of gunpowder. A single large tree could yield forty pounds (18 kg) of potash worth four dollars when it was burned and the ashes leached.

Samuel Hopkins developed a technique of reburning the raw ashes to remove much of the unburned black wood char. This concentrated the potash and allowed for the production of higher quality potassium salts that commanded a much higher price. The United States became the world's leading producer of potash and remained as such until the discovery of the potassium-bearing evaporite beds in Germany in the 1860s. Although we no longer rely on Hopkins's methods, potash pots, or ashes, potassium serves as a vital mineral fertilizer resource and is still widely used in making soaps, glasses, and a vast array of chemicals.

3,100,000 metric tons in 1928. The total production of the area from 1830 has been estimated at a possible 23.4 million metric tons of contained nitrogen from about 140 million metric tons of raw ore. Chile has controlled all of the natural nitrates since the War of the Pacific (1879–1883). They met with competition from ammonia produced by a coal coking process beginning in 1892 and from nitrates prepared by fixing atmospheric nitrogen beginning about 1900. The rise in world nitrate demand and the rapid expansion of the by-product nitrate industries quickly reduced natural Chilean nitrate to a minor role in world production—67 percent of the world's nitrogen production in 1900, 22 percent in 1929, and 0.14 percent in 1980.

The earliest uses of **phosphates** parallel those of nitrates because many early fertilizer compounds contained both elements (Table 9.1). The earliest use of phosphate minerals was in about 1650 when English farmers applied ground bones to their fields. Usage gradually expanded, but the presence of phosphate in the bones was not recognized as the valuable component until 1835. In attempts to make bones more soluble, German chemist Justus von Liebig dissolved some in sulfuric acid in 1840. His experiment

FIGURE 9.1. Potash, mixtures of potassium and sodium carbonates and hydroxides, was extracted from the ashes of hardwood trees. The name is derived from the ashes and the large pots used to extract the salts. (From the Earl Palmer Collection at Virginia Tech.)

provided the basis for modern phosphate fertilizer, but he fused the phosphate with lime and produced a product that appeared to be worthless because it was not soluble in water. Within two years, English chemist John Lawes put Liebig's ideas to use and mixed sulfuric acid with bones and natural phosphate rock to produce what he called **superphosphate**. The value of this new fertilizer led to phosphate rock mining in France in 1846, England in 1847, Canada in 1863, and the United States in 1867.

Recognition of the value of potassium as a fertilizer component developed in the early 1800s and was finally confirmed by John Lawes and his co-worker, J. H. Gilbert, in 1855. Prior to this, many farmers had found that the application of wood ash, a material that can contain significant amounts of potassium, was beneficial to their crops. Although this **potash**, consisting of a mixture of potassium-sodium carbonates and hydroxides, served as a fertilizer, it was primarily valued for its use in making soaps and glass (see page 301). Significant world production of potassium salts began with the discovery of evaporite deposits at Strassfurt, Germany, in 1857 and in France in the early 1900s. These sources provided the relatively small world needs until World War I when the major German supplies were cutoff. This stimulated exploration for alternative sources and led to the beginning of potassium production in the United States, in 1917. The potassium was removed from subsurface brines at Searles Lake in California; this led to the discovery of large bedded deposits near Carlsbad, New Mexico, in the 1930s. During the 1920s and early 1930s, discoveries were also made and production begun in Poland, Palestine, Spain,

TABLE 9.1

Compositions of fertilizer materials

	(%)		
	Nitrogen (N)	Phosphate (P_2O_5)	Potash (K_2O)
Natural Materials			
Saltpeter ($NaNO_3$)	15.6–16	—	—
Fish scrap	8	5–8	—
Sewage sludge	5–7	2–3.5	—
Urea	46	—	—
Bones	3.5	20–25	—
Kainite	—	—	12–14
Seaweed ash	—	—	up to 30
Carnalite	—	—	8–10
Wood ashes	—	2	up to 6
Peruvian guano	13	12.5	2.5
Synthetic Materials			
Superphosphate ($CaH_4(PO_4)_2 \cdot H_2O$)	—	16–22	—
Triple superphosphate ($3CaH_4(PO_4)_2 \cdot H_2O$)	—	44–52	—
Ammonium nitrate (NH_4NO_3)	33–35	—	—
Ammonium phosphate (($NH_4)_3PO_4$)	11	60	—
Diammonium phosphate ($NH_4H_2PO_4$)	21	53	—
Potassium chloride (KCl)	—	—	48–62
10-10-10	10	10	10

and the Soviet Union. In the late 1940s, rich deposits were found in Saskatchewan, Canada, but commercial production did not begin until 1958.

Today, the world's fertilizer industry focuses on the extraction, manufacture, and distribution of the nitrogen, phosphorus, and potassium either in bags for home use or in bulk liquid or solid forms for commercial farming. The numbers such as 5-10-10 or 5-10-20 seen on fertilizer bags refer to the percentages of nitrogen as nitrate (NO_3) or ammonia (NH_3), phosphorus as phosphate (P_2O_5), and potassium as potash (K_2O). The remaining 65–75 percent is mostly inert material, such as clay, although 1 or 2 percent of sulfur, calcium, and magnesium can also be present. The total percentage of major fertilizer components may seem low—only 25–35 percent—but greater concentrations could lead to damage of the delicate growth hairs on plant roots or upset the delicate levels of dissolved substances in plant fluids.

The demand for fertilizers has been climbing rapidly (Figure 9.2), such that the total world consumption has doubled about every 15 years. Unfortunately, the effectiveness of increased fertilizer usage appears to be diminishing. The **Global 2000 Report to the President** notes that a 200,000,000 metric ton increase in grain production in the early 1960s was associated with a 20,000,000 metric ton increase in fertilizer consumption. This 10 to 1 increase dropped to about 8.5 to 1 in the 1970s, 7 to 1 in the mid-1980s, and possibly will be 5 to 1 by the year 2000. Clearly, world demand for fertilizers will continue to rise to produce food for the increasing world population. Fortunately, reserves are large; however, except for nitrogen, the reserves suffer from the same problems that beset many of the scarce metals—they are geographically restricted, and we have already used the richest and most accessible deposits.

NITROGEN

Nitrogen, found in all proteins and amino acids, is vital to plant growth. It is an integral part of the chlorophyll molecule responsible for **photosynthesis**, the food-making process in green plants. Most rocks and soils contain little or no nitrogen as discrete minerals, but many kinds of plants provide organic nitrogen, as ammonia or nitrate, for soils where it can readily bind to the surfaces of clay particles.

The earliest nitrate fertilizers were animal wastes spread on fields to stimulate plant growth. These locally

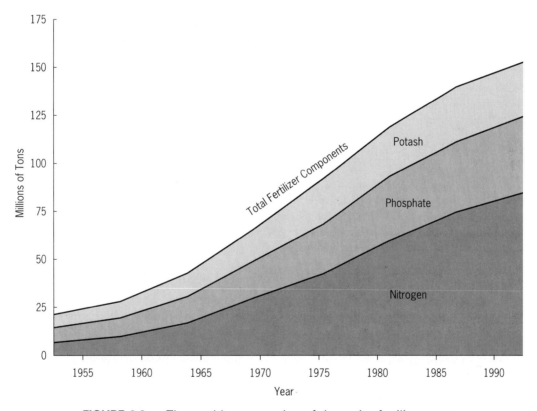

FIGURE 9.2. The world consumption of the major fertilizer components. The total amount of fertilizer components used in 1990 was about six times greater than that used in 1960. Potassium and nitrogen fertilizers are listed in terms of their K_2O and elemental nitrogen contents, respectively, because they are produced in a variety of forms. (From FAO Fertilizer Yearbooks.)

derived farm manures were a sufficient source of nitrogen for crops until about the middle of the nineteenth century. At that time, the expansion of agriculture outpaced these local sources, and Europe began importing guano from Peru to fulfill its nitrogen fertilizer needs. These guano deposits accumulated over many years on very arid coastal islands from huge colonies of nesting seabirds. The local Indians made use of the nitrogen and phosphate-rich guano (Table 9.1), but it did not become known to Europeans until von Humboldt described it after his visits in 1802. Some small shipments were made by 1810, but the major trade did not develop until 1840. It flourished for 40 years, but was then displaced by the production of nitrate minerals from what is now northern Chile.

Today the guano trade from western South America has practically ceased. The only significant guano industry remains in the island nation of Nauru in the South Pacific where annual production still averages about 2,000,000 metric tons. It is mined for its phosphate and nitrogen contents and shipped primarily to Australia and New Zealand.

Natural nitrate mineral deposits are rare because nearly all nitrate compounds are very soluble and easily washed away by rains and groundwater. They generally occur as efflorescences or crusts resulting from the oxidation of nitrogen-bearing substances in the presence of other salts. Potassium nitrate is the most widespread of these minerals. It occurs as crusts on the walls and in the soils of some caves, such as those in Kentucky and Virginia, where it has apparently accumulated as a result of the evaporation of groundwater that dissolved nitrogen compounds derived from organic matter in the overlying soils. In the 1700s and 1800s, the demand for the gunpowder ingredient saltpeter led to the development of saltpeter plantations, or nitriaries, in France and Germany. These plantations simulated the natural conditions of saltpeter formation by exposing heaps of decaying organic matter mixed with potash or lime to the atmosphere; the crusts of saltpeter were episodically gathered and processed. Calcium nitrate formed as a by-product when lime was added to the organic matter. It also commonly appeared as a crust on the walls of stables, formed from reaction of the nitrogen compounds in horse wastes with lime used to reduce odors and insects.

Sodium nitrate, or ordinary niter, though much more restricted geographically than the potassium or calcium forms, has been much more important as a source of nitrogen. This mineral occurs in very large deposits in the northern part of the Atacama desert in what are now the two northernmost provinces of Chile (Figures 9.3 and 9.4). This is one of the dryest places on Earth with no precipitation for many years at a time and an annual average rainfall of less than 2.5 centimeters. The nitrates originated in sea spray that precipitates on the soils from frequent fogs. The uncommon rains dissolve the very soluble nitrates and concentrate them as cements, or **caliches**, in the soils before the water evaporates. Mining of nitrate deposits began near the beginning of the nineteenth century; by 1812 there were at least seven operations in which caliches were boiled in water to dissolve the nitrates while the saltpeter settled out as the liquids cooled. By the 1830s the increased use of chemical fertilizers in European agriculture made the nitrates a useful return cargo for ships sailing to Europe. Although the mines were in the Tarapaca district of Peru and the Antofagasta district of Bolivia, the labor and the investments were dominantly Chilean. In response to Peruvian attempts to expropriate the mines and increase Bolivian taxation, Chile took the two provinces with a small army and naval forces in the War of the Pacific. This crippled the Peruvian economy and made Bolivia a land-locked nation, but it left Chile with a near monopoly on world nitrate production.

Chilean nitrates continued to be the world's principal source of nitrogen until about 1915 when nitrogen from coking ovens and atmospheric fixation processes became dominant. In 1892, a new type of coking oven that trapped expelled gases was introduced. Ammonia, one of the most abundant gases from this process, was immediately used in the fertilizer and chemical industries. About 1900 it was also discovered that ammonia could be prepared from atmospheric nitrogen. The **Haber-Bosch process**, used in a slightly modified form today, accomplished this task. Fritz Haber, a famed German chemist, found that the controlled combustion of a fossil fuel, coke, or gas with steam would yield carbon monoxide and hydrogen. With the aid of a catalyst, he could react this hydrogen with atmospheric nitrogen to form ammonia. Today, the hydrogen is usually supplied by natural gas. Ammonia could be used directly to make fertilizers, or it could be oxidized to make explosives such as glyceryl trinitrate (formerly known as nitroglycerin) and trinitrotoluene (TNT). Haber's discoveries were very important to the German military, which was cut off from Chilean nitrate supplies during World War I.

Today, the synthetic nitrate industry produces more than 99.8 percent of world nitrogen needs. Chile still mines nitrates at rates of more than 500,000 metric tons per year, but this constitutes only about 0.14 percent of world usage. Even the total Chilean nitrogen reserves of 2.5×10^9 metric tons (containing more than 7 percent $NaNO_3$) would not equal one-half of the world's present yearly consumption.

More than 75 percent of the nitrogen compounds produced in the world is used as fertilizer components. The United States, India, and Canada are the world's primary fixed nitrogen producers, but the process is widely used in many countries. This makes the world production close to 100 million tons of fixed nitrogen (Figure 9.5). Nitrogen compounds have a variety of other important uses—plastics, fibers, resins, refrigerants, detonating agents for explosives, and nitric acid. The availability of nitrogen from Earth's atmosphere for the production of fixed nitrogen is unlimited. Hydrogen is most commonly derived from natural

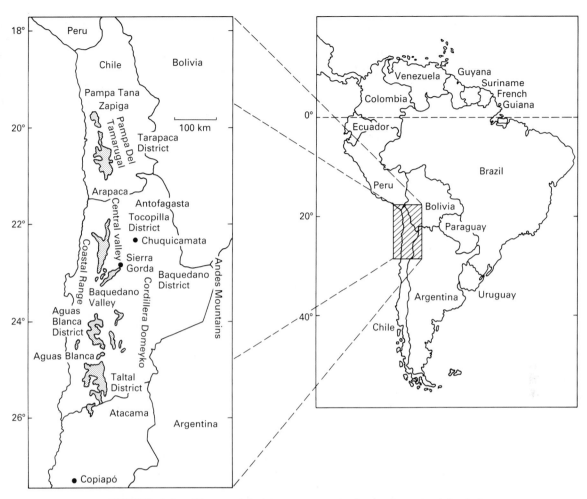

FIGURE 9.3. The world's largest natural nitrate deposits (shaded areas) lie in the Tarapaca and Antofagasta provinces in what is now northern Chile. The extreme aridity of this area that allows for the preservation of these deposits results from the cold Humboldt Current that flows northward along the western coast of South America. Tarapaca and Antofagasta were parts of Peru and Bolivia before Chile annexed them in the War of the Pacific, 1878–1883.

gas. Because of this, there is a strong price dependence of fixed nitrogen on the cost of fossil fuels. The natural Chilean nitrate reserves, containing more than 7 percent $NaNO_3$, are estimated to be 2.5×10^9 metric tons. The probable resources at grades less than 7 percent are thought to be more than 22×10^9 metric tons.

PHOSPHORUS

Phosphorus is indispensable for all forms of life because it is found in **deoxyribonucleic acid** (DNA), **ribonucleic acid** (RNA), and ADP/ATP molecules that store energy for the body cells. In natural ecosystems, the availability of phosphorus is usually life limiting.

Phosphorus is usually referred to in its oxide form, phosphate, P_2O_5. Earth's crust contains about 0.23 percent phosphate. Most of this is present as the mineral apatite, $Ca_5(PO_4)_3(F,Cl,OH)_2$. Apatite is a disseminated accessory mineral in many types of rocks, but its mineable concentrations may occur in igneous rocks or marine sedimentary rocks. Phosphorus is also present in the guano deposits left by birds or bats described earlier.

Bone is another natural occurrence of phosphate as apatite. English farmers had observed that applications of ground bone increased crop yield as early as the mid-1600s, and the Pilgrims learned from Indians that buried fish carcasses and bones helped corn grow. By the middle of the nineteenth century, European countries imported bones—possibly some from humans—from every available source.

FIGURE 9.4. The nitrate deposits of northern Chile, shown here being drilled for processing and shipping as fertilizers to North America and Europe in the 1930s, occurred as thick cemented portions of the desert soils.

However, there was a problem with apatite's insolubility. Attempts to find a more soluble phosphate fertilizer were unsuccessful until 1842, when John Lawes developed superphosphates. As a result of his success, there were 14 fertilizer plants in Great Britain by 1853, and production had reached 100 metric tons per day by 1862. Lawes's techniques were used with the development of phosphate-rock mining in

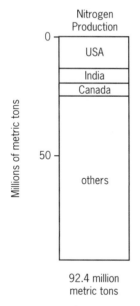

FIGURE 9.5. The world's annual production of more than 90 million metric tons of nitrogen in fertilizers is led by the United States, but many countries produce similar large quantities. The nitrogen in the atmosphere provides an inexhaustible resource.

France and England by 1850. In the United States, the first phosphate mining took place in South Carolina in 1867, but the major development of the industry dates from 1888 when massive phosphate deposits were discovered in Florida. Today, deposits can be found in several states (Figure 9.6), but nearly 90 percent of American production comes from the large deposits in Florida and North Carolina.

The techniques used today to convert natural phosphate minerals into usable fertilizer forms are still based on Lawes's experiments that use sulfuric acid. Much superphosphate is used, but some phosphate appears as liquid fertilizers, and some is even transformed into triple superphosphates with much higher P_2O_5 contents. Historically, sedimentary phosphorites have been the world's dominant phosphate sources, but igneous bodies containing large concentrations of apatite are slowly being exploited, especially in the former Soviet Union. The guano deposits of Chile and Peru, once major producers, have diminished in importance but still find demand among "organic" gardeners.

Phosphate rocks are found in many parts of the world (Figure 9.7), and major reserves are mined by many nations (Figure 9.8), but the major world suppliers of phosphate are the United States, China, Morocco, and Russia. Marine phosphorites, which constitute the principal reserves, presently supply approximately 80 percent of the world phosphate rock production and 100 percent of United States production. Although minor amounts of phosphates occur in nearly all marine sediments, major accumulations appear to have developed only where upwelling cool phosphate-saturated seawater moved across shallow platforms and into near-coastal environments. Here the phosphate precipitated, probably by complex microbiological processes, as microcrystalline muds, nodules, and hard crusts (Figure 9.9). In some areas, vast accumulations of fish bones and teeth (Figure 9.10) further contribute phosphate to the source. Partial replacement of some calcite shells by apatite suggests that phosphate-bearing solutions also percolated through the sediments after deposition.

The largest of the marine phosphorite deposits occur in the Miocene sediments of the North Carolina and Florida coastal plains and in Morocco. These phosphorites are relatively thin (2–10 m) beds that extend over broad areas (more than 2500 square kilometers in Florida and at least 1200 square kilometers in North Carolina). The sediments are mostly unconsolidated and are thus easily mined with large drag lines and dredges (Figure 9.11, Plate 43). The North American deposits will continue to be major sources of phosphate rock but are objects of increasing environmental concerns. The main problems are the vast amounts of groundwater pumped out of the mines and underlying formations to permit mining at greater depths, the release of trace amounts of radioactive elements from the ores, and the generation of mountains of very fine-grained gypsum as a by-product of the sulfuric acid treatment.

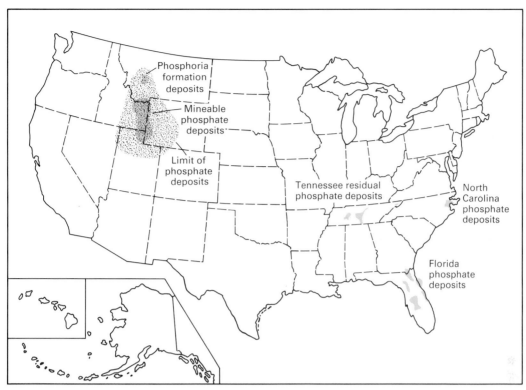

FIGURE 9.6. Major phosphate deposits have been worked in four areas of the United States. The beds of the Phosphoria Formation and those in North Carolina and part of Florida are primary marine sediments. The deposits in Tennessee and parts of Florida are residual accumulations that result from weathering. Although nearly 90 percent of present production comes from Florida and North Carolina, the largest recoverable phosphate resources occur in the Phosphoria Formation. (From U.S. Geological Survey Circular 888, 1984.)

Another particularly large, apparently unique deposit of this type was formed during Permian times in a shallow marine basin covering what are now parts of Idaho, Nevada, Utah, Colorado, Wyoming, and Montana. The phosphate-rich sediments, called the Phosphoria Formation, cover more than 160,000 square kilometers and reach thicknesses of as much as 140 meters. However, over most of the area the thickness of the phosphatic bed is only 1 meter or less; at best it can be considered only a potential resource. The tonnage, however, is enormous—estimated at more than 2,000,000,000 metric tons.

There is no substitute for phosphate fertilizers; the need for phosphate rock will continue to grow for at least the next 100 years to feed the increasing world population. The world's phosphate reserves are large and, with the likelihood of new discoveries and technological advances to permit mining of lower grade deposits, probably adequate for the next century. There will, however, be considerable change in world supply patterns because the relatively rapid depletion of the United States' richest mines will force the United

States to become a phosphate importer shortly after the year 2000. Unless there are major discoveries, phosphate production in Florida—the United States' principal phosphate producer—will begin dropping rapidly after 2000 A.D. North Carolina will continue to produce significant amounts of phosphate rock, however, and minor production will be available from the western states.

Potential resources of phosphorus are large. Prospecting for phosphate deposits has not been thorough enough to ensure that we have exhausted all the large deposits. In part, this is a recognition of the economic difficulties entailed in opening new deposits in competition with existing mines. It also stems from the difficulty of recognizing phosphorus-rich rock. Many phosphate rocks look like ordinary shales and limestones, even to experts. We can, therefore, probably anticipate discoveries of new, large deposits in the future.

One large potential resource has already been discovered. The U.S. Geological Survey recently announced the finding of phosphatic crusts and nodules in the off-shore continental shelf extension of the rich Florida phosphate beds.

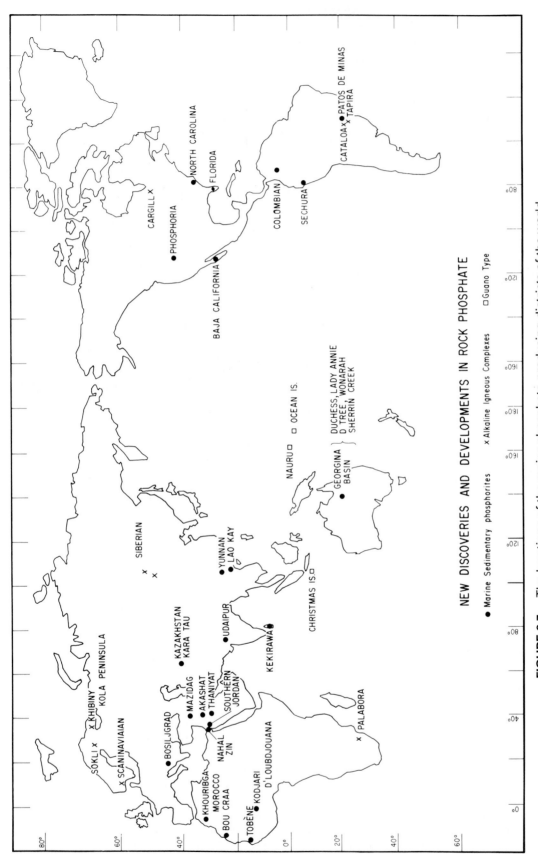

FIGURE 9.7. The locations of the major phosphate-producing districts of the world. (After P.F. Howard, *Economic Geology, 74* (1979), p. 193.)

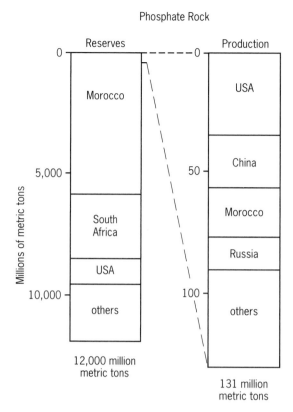

Phosphate Rock

FIGURE 9.8. The world's principal reserves of phosphate rock are in Morocco and South Africa, but the United States and China are the principal producers. Known reserves will last more than 90 years at present rates of production, and large resources have been discovered on several areas of the continental shelves. (From U.S. Bureau of Mines.)

FIGURE 9.10. The marine sedimentary phosphate deposits of North Carolina and Florida consist of unconsolidated pebbles and granules and contain abundant remains of fish, reptile, and mammal bones. (Photograph by J.R. Craig.)

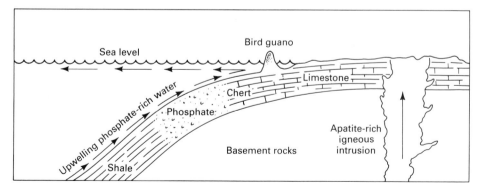

FIGURE 9.9. Marine sedimentary deposits such as those in Florida, North Carolina, and the Phosphoria Formation were deposited along continental margins where there was upwelling of phosphate-bearing ocean waters. The other major types of occurrences have formed from phosphate-rich igneous intrusions and from the accumulation of phosphate-rich bird guano on arid coastal islands.

FIGURE 9.11. The phosphate deposits of Florida and North Carolina occur in flat-lying, unconsolidated beds that are mined by the use of large mobile drag lines. After stripping the overburden (the upper 3 meters in this pit), the phosphate-bearing ores (the 4 meters above the floor of the pit) are removed, and the area is returned to its original form (see Plate 44). (Photograph by J.R. Craig.)

Unfortunately, the deposits are lower grade than their landward equivalents, but the tonnages are large—probably as large as the present reserves. The availability of phosphorus, like nitrogen and potassium, will not likely become a limitation to food production.

POTASSIUM

Potassium, the third of the important fertilizer elements, is the eighth most abundant element in Earth's crust. Potassium occurs in nearly all rocks and soils, although its quantity varies widely. It occurs in igneous and metamorphic rocks primarily as potassium feldspar ($KAlSi_3O_8$); weathering releases the potassium to be incorporated in clay minerals such as illite ($KAl_2(Al,Si)_4O_{10}(OH)_2$). The K^+ ion of the clay minerals is exchanged with plants by substitution of a hydrogen ion. Unlike nitrogen and phosphorus, potassium does not form an integral part of plant components, but it is vital as a catalytic agent in numerous biological functions such as nitrogen metabolism, synthesis of proteins, activation of enzymes, and maintenance of water content.

Although potassium occurs in most rocks, the only occurrences that can be economically extracted and processed into fertilizers are those from evaporite sequences. These special accumulations formed by the evaporation of large amounts of seawater in broad basins (Figure 9.12). Nearly complete evaporation results in the deposition of large amounts of halite (NaCl) and smaller amounts of several potassium salts; the most important are sylvite (KCl), langbeinite ($2MgSO_4 \cdot K_2SO_4$), kainite ($KCl \cdot MgSO_4 \cdot 3H_2O$), and carnallite ($KCl \cdot MgCl_2 \cdot 6H_2O$).

Because potassium salts are very soluble, they are only preserved in very arid regions or in salt beds buried below meteoric or groundwater zones. Evaporites generally occur as flat-lying beds that are now mined by rubber-tired diesel or electric mining machines. The salts are blasted or cut from walls in the mining areas and then brought to a surface refining facility where the ores are crushed and then separated into different minerals by a complex flotation system. The concentrates of potash minerals are then processed into a wide variety of solid and liquid fertilizers. The name *potash* was derived from the custom of leaching wood ashes and then boiling the solutions in large iron pots to crystallize the soluble potassium salts used in making soaps and glass.

Potassium, in the form of carbonates and hydroxides in wood ashes, was used as a fertilizer long before the 1840s when it was recognized as an element vital for plant growth. The first potash mining began in 1857 when evaporite-bearing potassium chloride was found at Strassfurt in Germany. These, and additional deposits found in the Alsace-Lorraine area, were controlled by a German cartel that had a virtual monopoly over the international potash trade until 1915. In January 1915, Germany imposed an embargo on potash exports, and prices in the United States rose from about $45 per ton to more than $480 per ton in 1916. Spurred by the shortage and high prices, the United States stepped up production from wood ashes and discovered potassium-rich subsurface brines near Searles Lake in California. Following World War I, exports from Europe again became available, but the shortages during the war period had stimulated exploration and resulted in significant discoveries in Poland, Palestine, Spain, and the former Soviet Union. In 1925, potash deposits were found near Carlsbad, New Mexico, by oil prospectors; mines were opened in the 1930s, and they soon not only supplied the United States but became major exporters. High-grade deposits of potash were discovered in the Canadian province of Saskatchewan in the 1940s while drilling for oil. These were not brought into production until 1958, but they now constitute the western world's major supplies and reserves.

The American deposits are part of a broad evaporite sequence that underlies parts of New Mexico, Texas, Oklahoma, and Kansas. In Permian times, a large, shallow sea deposited thick beds of evaporite salts over this 160,000 square kilometer area. In a 4800-square kilometer portion of the basin near Carlsbad, New Mexico, the sequence contains potassium salts in beds reaching 4 meters in thickness. These deposits, among the richest in the world but small in total volume, may have reserves totaling nearly 100,000,000 metric tons.

North America has two other large potassium reserves (Figures 9.12 and 9.13). The Paradox Basin of the Pennsylvanian Period in southeastern Utah and southwestern Colorado contains an estimated 12,600 square kilometers of potassium-rich salts, although much of it is too deep to warrant present recovery. In Saskatchewan, Canada, a huge and incompletely explored resource of potassium salts has been found in the Williston Basin (Devonian period). Estimates of as much as 4,000,000,000 metric tons of accessible K_2O have been published. Large reserves also exist in the Perm region of the former Soviet Union where beds containing KCl more than 30 meters thick extend over an area of 1000 square kilometers (386 square miles) and contain at least 3,000,000 metric tons of potassium salts. The existence of such large quantities of potash-bearing evaporites plus the very large quantities dissolved in the oceans ensure that we should not have any problem regarding future potash reserves.

SULFUR

Sulfur, one of the first known nonmetallic chemical elements, has many diverse uses. It is the fourth major fertilizer element, and the U.S. Bureau of Mines notes that "most products produced by industry require sulfur in one form or another during some stage of their manufacture."

Sulfur is abundant in Earth's surface as native sulfur, metal sulfides (especially pyrite, FeS_2), mineral sulfates (primarily **gypsum**, $CaSO_4 \cdot 2H_2O$), sulfate dissolved in the oceans, hydrogen sulfide (sour gas) in natural gas, and organic sulfur in petroleum and coal.

Sulfur was known in the ancient world as **brimstone**, "the stone that burns," and has been used for thousands of years as a fumigant, medicine, bleaching agent, and incense in religious ceremonies. During the Peloponnesian War between the Greek city-states of Athens and Sparta in the fifth century B.C., mixtures of burning sulfur and pitch (oil residue) were used to produce suffocating gases to incapacitate soldiers. The Romans advanced the use of sulfur in warfare by combining brimstone with pitch and other combustible materials to produce the first incendiary weapons. A thousand years later, in the tenth century, the Chinese developed gunpowder in which sulfur is a necessary ingredient. The subsequent introduction of gunpowder into European warfare four centuries later made sulfur an important mineral commodity for the first time.

It was, however, the development of chemistry in the 1700s and the growth of the chemical industries in the 1800s that brought sulfur to prominence in the modern world. Early chemists found that sulfuric acid, the most versatile of the mineral acids, was simple and inexpensive to prepare. Prior to the mid-1800s, world demand for sulfur was satisfied primarily by the native sulfur deposits in Sicily. The rise in both demand and price, controlled by the Sicilian monopoly, resulted in a shift to pyrite (FeS_2) as a major sulfur source. Pyrite, when roasted in air, yields sulfur oxide gases that readily react with water to form sulfuric acid. In 1894, the **Frasch process** for mining subsurface native sulfur deposits associated with Gulf Coast salt domes was introduced. This process (Figure 9.14) employs hot water to melt the sulfur from the host limestones and gypsum and to transport it to the surface. A series of concentric pipes are set in 25-centimeter holes drilled into the sulfur-bearing rock. Hot water passes down the outer pipe at 140°C to melt the sulfur; once molten, the sulfur is forced up the intermediate pipe by hot air forced down the inner pipe. The Frasch process remains an important method of sulfur recovery.

The native sulfur recovered by the Frasch process occurs with anhydrite ($CaSO_4$) or gypsum on top of salt domes and in certain evaporite beds. Salt domes occur in many parts of the world but are especially abundant along the Gulf Coast of the United States from Alabama to Mexico (Figure 9.15). Gypsum and anhydrite brought into a near-surface environment are attacked by certain anaerobic bacteria to form a cap on the salt domes.

These derive their oxygen from gypsum and their food from organic matter (commonly petroleum) and convert the gypsum into calcite ($CaCO_3$) and free sulfur. Only a small proportion of salt domes contain commercial quantities of native sulfur, but these account for more than 50 percent of the United States production and more than 25 percent of world production. If circulating subsurface waters locally dissolve gypsum beds in sequences of evaporite rocks, petroleum and bacteria can enter the resulting voids, leading to the formation of rich localized zones of sulfur. This has

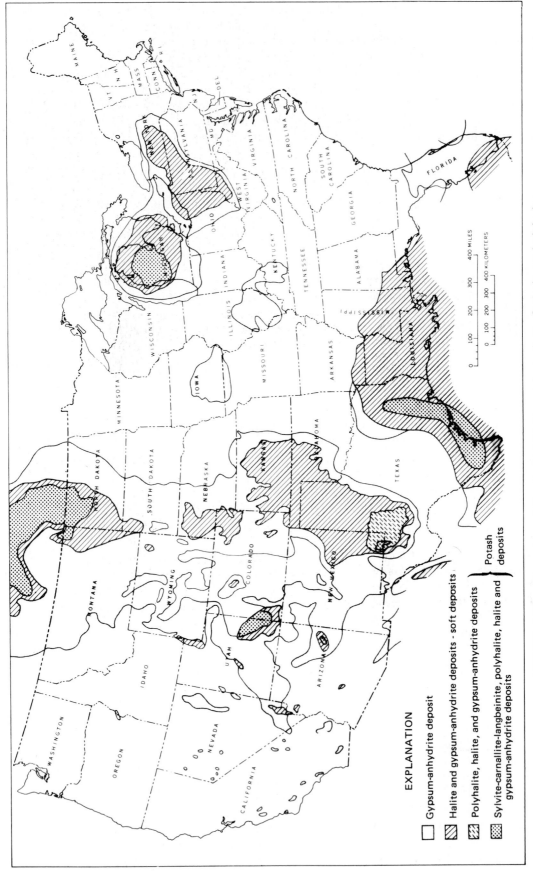

FIGURE 9.12. The areas of the United States and southern Canada underlain by major marine evaporite deposits of gypsum and anhydrite, halite, and potassium salts. (After U.S. Geological Survey Bulletin 1019-J and U.S. Geological Survey Professional Paper 820, 1973.)

EXPLANATION

Gypsum-anhydrite deposit

Halite and gypsum-anhydrite deposits - soft deposits

Polyhalite, halite, and gypsum-anhydrite deposits

Sylvite-carnallite-langbeinite, polyhalite, halite and gypsum-anhydrite deposits

Potash deposits

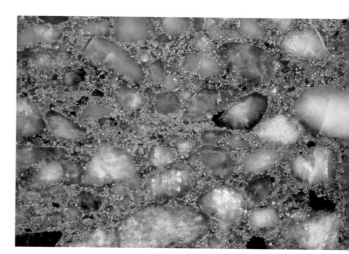

Plate 37. The large open pit at Bingham Canyon, Utah, is one and three-quarters miles across and is one of the largest mines in the world. It is mined primarily for copper but also produces several by-product metals, including gold and silver. (Photograph courtesy of Kennecott Corporation.)

Plate 38. The M-Vein, Casapalca, Peru, is a rich mass of sulfide minerals containing silver, lead, copper, zinc, and other minerals. The ore minerals were deposited by a hydrothermal solution that flowed through a preexisting fracture in volcanic rocks. (Photograph by B.J. Skinner.)

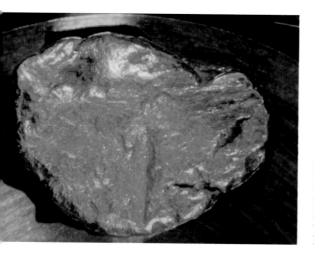

Plate 39. In contrast to the single vein at Casapalca, Peru, shown in Plate 38, many deposits contain multiple veins such as these at Cligga Head in southwest England. Alteration zones occur along the sides of the narrow tin- and tungsten-bearing veins as a result of the ore fluids reacting with the wall rocks. (Photograph by J.R. Craig.)

Plate 40. The Main Reef Leader, one of the rich, gold-bearing conglomerates mined in the Witwatersrand Basin, near Johannesburg, South Africa. The rounded quartz pebbles are set in a matrix of sand grains and rounded pyrite (FeS_2) grains, here seen as gold colored particles. Gold is present but too fine-grained to be seen. (Photograph by Carlos Pais; courtesy of Geological Society of South Africa.)

Plate 41. Small gold nuggets led to the discovery of most of the world's major gold districts prior to the development of geochemical exploration techniques in the past few decades. This 3.5 gram nugget, which is 1 cm in length, was recovered from a stream in Cabarrus County, North Carolina, where the first gold mine in the United States was located. (Photograph by J.R. Craig.)

Plate 43. A giant dragline scoops up rich photophate ore in Florida. The ore is then pumped via a slurry pipeline to the processing plant. The very fine-grained waste material that remains after processing is allowed to settle and dry in huge settling ponds such as the one visible in the upper left-hand corner of the photograph. (Photograph courtesy of IMC Corporation.)

Plate 42. The Barney's Canyon Mine in Utah is typical of modern operations. Low-grade gold ores are mined from the open pit in the background, crushed, and placed in large heap leach pads visible in the foreground. Cyanide solutions that soak through the piles of crushed rock dissolving out the gold are then treated to recover the gold. (Photograph courtesy of Kennecott Corporation.)

Plate 45. A line of fumaroles along a fault at Alae, on the southwest flank of Kilauea volcano, Hawaii. At the time this photograph was taken, volcanic vapors were depositing sulfur crystals in the fumarolic vents and laying down a yellow blanket of fine-grained sulfur on the countryside. (Photograph by B.J. Skinner.)

Plate 44. The reclamation of the land mined for phosphates, as shown in Plate 43, can produce productive wetlands and wildlife habitat within a few years of the mining operation. (Photograph courtesy of the Florida Institute of Phosphate Research.)

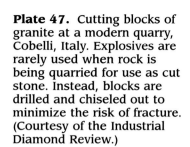

Plate 47. Cutting blocks of granite at a modern quarry, Cobelli, Italy. Explosives are rarely used when rock is being quarried for use as cut stone. Instead, blocks are drilled and chiseled out to minimize the risk of fracture. (Courtesy of the Industrial Diamond Review.)

Plate 46. River sediments such as these deposits laid down by the Pee Dee River in North Carolina often serve as important sources of sand and gravel used for construction. Similar sediments can contain significant placer accumulations of gold or titanium minerals. (Photograph by J.R. Craig.)

Plate 48. The Taj Mahal, Arga, India, is a breathtaking example of a building constructed with cut stone. The principal building stone is marble, but it is adorned with indicate insets of semi-precious stones, many in the form of passages from the Koran. The Taj Mahal is a mausoleum, completed about 1650 A.D. by Shah Jahan following the death of his favorite wife Mumtaz Mahal. The Shah and his wife are both buried in Taj Mahal. (Photograph courtesy of the Government of the India Tourist Office.)

Plate 49. The Yule marble quarry in Colorado produces some of the finest marble for statuary. Blocks are carefully cut and shipped around the world. (Photograph by J. Groeneboer; courtesy of the U.S. Bureau of Mines.)

Plate 50. The volcanic ash deposits in the Cappadocia region of Turkey have weathered into unique conical shapes and have been soft enough for inhabitants to carve complexes of rooms for thousands of years. The rock is strong enough to hold up, and the insulation properties of the rock are quite good in keeping the dwellings warm in winter and cool in summer. Göreme, Uçhisar. (Photograph courtesy of Embassy of Turkey.)

Plates 51. Concrete, an "instant rock," has become the most widely used construction material in the building of the infrastructure for modern western societies. The intersection of two interstate highways in Tennessee required huge amounts of concrete in the construction of the four levels of crossing road surfaces. (Photograph courtesy of U.S. Federal Highway Administration.)

Plate 52. Concrete and steel have become superior building materials for the construction of beautiful and functional structures such as the Sunshine Skyway Bridge across Tampa Bay in Florida. (Photograph courtesy of U.S. Federal Highway Administration.)

Plate 53. Sandstone and quartzite were cut into round disk-like millstones used to grind grains, such as wheat and corn, into flour in water-powered mills. These were widely used in the eighteenth and nineteenth centuries, but the mills and the craftsmen, such as Mr. W.C. Saville, who made the millstones, are nearly gone. (Photograph by Gene Dalton; courtesy of the *Roanoke Times*.)

Plate 54. Gems are among the most highly valued resources and are usually beautiful crystalline forms of minerals. (Left) The 128-carat yellow "Tiffany" Diamond. (Right) Natural pearls and mother of pearl, the lustrous material on the inside of seashells that is identical to the material that forms the pearls. (Photographs courtesy of Tiffany Inc., (left) and CISGEM of the Chamber of Commerce of Millan, Italy (right).)

Plate 55. Some gems reveal their natural beauty even before they are cut and polished. Natural and cut emeralds from Colombia. (Photograph by Bart Curren; courtesy of ICA Gem bureau.)

Plate 56. An intricate pattern of interesting circles produced by a spray irrigation system used in the midwestern states of the United States. The sprinkler system rotates around the water supply well at the center of the circle. (Photograph courtesy of Valmont Industries.)

Plate 57. The Central Arizona Project, a giant system of canals and pump stations, is designed to bring water from the sparsely populated drainage basin of the Colorado River system in northern Arizona to the heavily populated cities and irrigated farmlands of southern Arizona. (Photograph courtesy of U.S. Bureau of Reclamation.)

Plate 58. Subsidence in the Baytown area of Houston, Texas, has resulted form the subsurface extraction of oil and water and has led to regular flooding of residential areas by high tides and abandonment of many homes. (Photograph courtesy of Orin Pilkey.)

Plate 59. The Aral Sea, on the boundary between Uzbekistan and Kazakhstan, has lost 70 percent of its volume and has dropped 16.5 meters (54 feet), leaving ships and ports high and dry because the water that normally feeds the sea has been diverted for agricultural use. (Photograph courtesy of P.P. Micklin.)

Plate 60. Prolonged drought conditions can leave public water supplies, like the Gibralter Reservoir that serves Santa Barbara, California, dry. (Photograph courtesy of Santa Barbara County Public Works Department, Water Resources Division.)

(a)

(b)

Plate 61. (a) The Flood of 1993 inundated 11 million acres (17,000 square miles) of farmland for several months as heavy rains forced rivers out of their banks. (b) People in scores of towns, some more than 5 miles from the major rivers, were forced to evacuate. (Photographs courtesy of Federal Emergency Management Administration.)

Plate 62. Heavy rains in January 1995 flooded large parts of northern Europe. Areas such as Itteren (Province of Limburg) in The Netherlands were in great danger because much of the country lies below sea level. (Photograph by Aerophoto Schiphol BV; courtesy of The Royal Netherlands Embassy.)

Plate 63. Aqueducts, such as this one at Xiangao in China, have been used for thousands of years to transport water to major cities. Simple aqueducts are constructed so that the flow of water from source to users is controlled by gravity. (Photograph by J.R. Craig.)

Plate 64. Supplying the large quantities of water needed by large cities like New York requires a complex infrastructure of reservoirs, aqueducts, pump stations, and tunnels. The new Third Water Tunnel, presently under development, is 8–10 meters in diameter and lies 200–250 meters beneath the city. (Photograph by Ted Davey; courtesy of the New York City Department of Environmental Protection.)

Plate 65. The 710-ft (216 meter) high Glen Canyon Dam on the Colorado River northern Arizona has controlled the river flow and created Lake Powell. The water of the Colorado River is controlled by a series of dams and is distributed for use among the adjacent states by the Colorado River Compact. (Photograph courtesy of the U.S. Bureau of Land Management.)

Plate 66. Two soil profiles. (a) Layering is visible in the highly weathered soils such as those that underlie the stable land surface of the upper coastal plain of North Carolina. Technically, such soils are called plinthic paleudults. Iron has been leached from the upper layers, leaving them bleached and light colored. The leached iron is deposited about a meter below the surface in a pronounced reddish-color layer. (b) The soil profile at Poor Mountain, Virginia, formed above a base of sandstone and sandstone colluvium (brown). The uppermost, or A, zone is an organic-rich forest soil. Below it lies a thin, very dark Bh zone, rich in both iron and humus, and below that lies a bleached and leached E zone, where organic chelates have removed the iron oxides in solution. (Photograph by James C. Baker.)

(a)   (b)

Plate 67. Deflation near Meningie, South Australia. Grazing sheep removed much of the vegetation, leaving the sandy soil vulnerable to wind erosion. A large tussock, not touched by the sheep, stabilized a remnant of the original surface. Wind erosion has lowered the surface as much as 1.5 meters in places. (Photograph by B.J. Skinner.)

Plate 68. Uncontrolled erosion at Twin Ponies, Iowa, has cut a deep furrow and is rapidly removing top soil. The severe loss of good top soil will reduce the productivity of the area. (Photograph courtesy of the U.S. Department of Agriculture, Soil Conservation Service.)

Plate 69. Contour farming as this shown at Red Rock, Iowa, is conducted to minimize soil erosion by plowing across the slopes and by planting crops in sequences that help retain soil and mature at different times. (Photograph by Lynn Betts; courtesy of U.S. Department of Agriculture, Soil Conservation Service.)

Plate 70. Deforestation of several islands in the Caribbean, such as is shown on Nevis, has resulted from growing populations and shortages of fuels. The results are often barren and unproductive fields that will not support farming, offer no fuel wood, have no wildlife, and retain little water. Efforts to reverse these effects have met with limited success. (Photograph by and courtesy of Bonham Richardson.)

Plate 71. Miners swarm over the working face of the fabulously rich gold deposit at Sierra Pelada, Brazil. The Brazilian government did not allow mechanized mining operations, instead letting the small-time miner have a chance to make a fortune. The scene shown in the photograph, taken in 1985, has been repeated many times around the wold in recent years as poor peasants have sought a way out of poverty. Unfortunately, few have been successful and the environmental damages have been significant. (Photograph by Glenn Allcott.)

Plate 72. Earth, seen from space, will be the only source of mineral resources for many years to come. The blue ocean stands in marked color contrast to the brown landmass of Africa and the wispy, white cloud systems. The northeast corner of South America is visible and the Mediterranean Sea and Europe can be seen above Africa. (Photograph courtesy of European Space Agency.)

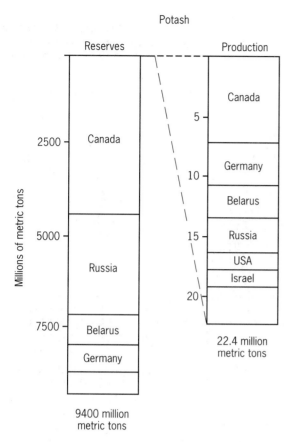

Potash

FIGURE 9.13. Canada and Russia hold the largest amounts of potash reserves in the world. Canada, Germany, Belarus, and Russia are the largest producers in the 1990s, and world reserves of 9400 million metric tons will last more than 400 years at present rates of production. (From U. S. Bureau of Mines.)

happened on a large scale in west Texas where more than 50,000,000 metric tons of recoverable sulfur have been found in one oil field alone.

Since the 1940s, by-product sulfur recovered from petroleum refining and natural gas treatment has become increasingly important. Sulfur was originally removed from oil and gas merely to produce cleaner petroleum products and odorless gas but is now very valuable. In the United States alone, more than 7,000,000 metric tons of sulfur were derived from oil and gas per year by the 1990s, more than 70 percent of domestic production. Sulfur production in the United States and other major suppliers is summarized in Figure 9.16.

Today, sulfur is used in a broad range of industrial applications and in a wide variety of chemical compounds. More than 80 percent of United States domestic sulfur is used as sulfuric acid. The acid is often used to convert very insoluble natural phosphates into superphosphates for agricultural applications. It is also used to make soaps, rubber, plastics,

acetate, cellophane, rayon, explosives, paper bleaches, white titanium oxide paint pigment, leachates for copper and uranium ores, and the **pickling** (cleaning) agent used on the surface of steel products prior to further processing (Figure 9.17). New uses still in the developmental stage include sulfur-asphalt paving for highways and sulfur concretes for use in acid and brine-rich environments where the salt often leads to significant deterioration of conventional materials.

The world reserves of native sulfur (Figure 9.16) represent only minimum values of the total extractable sulfur. These figures do not include sulfur available from natural gas and petroleum, extractable from metal sulfides processing, and the almost limitless amounts in gypsum and anhydrite. Also, at least 600×10^9 metric tons of sulfur are contained in coal, oil shale, and shales rich in organic matter. The sulfur in these sources is not yet available because we lack low cost extraction methods.

MINERALS FOR CHEMICALS

Many nonmetallic minerals are important raw material sources of elements or compounds used in the chemical industry. These are often little known to the public because the chemical products usually bear no resemblance to the original source mineral or because the minerals are only used in the processing and are not incorporated into the final product. The total list of chemical minerals is very long indeed, and includes the fertilizer minerals already discussed. Table 9.2 lists several important chemical minerals and summarizes their uses.

Halite (NaCl)

Halite, or common table salt, serves as a source of sodium, chlorine, soda ash (Na_2CO_3), hydrochloric acid (HCl), caustic soda (NaOH), and other compounds indispensable in the manufacture of hundreds of other products and chemical reagents. Salt itself is important in food production and preservation, water softening, and snow and ice removal. It is essential to our diets, but only small amounts of total production are used for human consumption. Also, the recent discovery that excessive salt usage is associated with hypertension has led to a reduction of salt levels in many foods. Much of the table salt used today contains about 0.01 percent potassium iodide as an additive to provide the body's needed iodine. Without sufficient iodine, the thyroid gland can enlarge into a goiter.

NaCl occurs naturally in seawater, in saline seas and lakes (such as the Dead Sea in Israel, Salton Sea in California, and the Great Salt Lake in Utah), and as thick sequences of marine evaporites. Evaporite deposits have formed throughout geologic time as a result of the evaporation of ocean and lake waters in large basins.

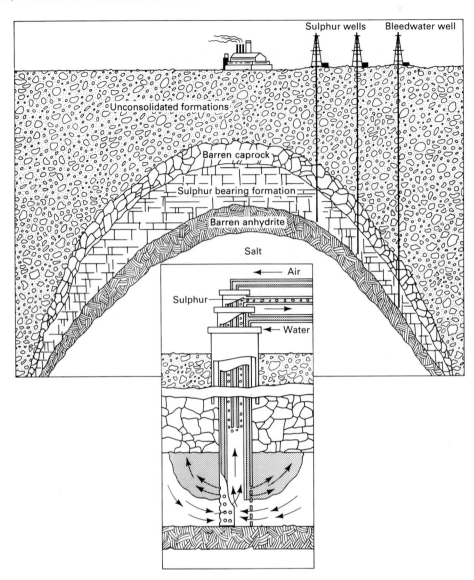

FIGURE 9.14. Sulfur often occurs in the cap rock overlying salt domes. The sulfur is extracted by the Frasch process, shown enlarged in the insert, whereby superheated water is forced down the outer shells of concentric pipes. The melted sulfur is then drawn up a center pipe and pumped to chemical plants for processing. (After a diagram courtesy of Freeport McMoRan, Inc.)

Dissolved constituents in seawater (Figure 9.18) can be recast into the constituents that precipitate from seawater by balancing the positively charged cations, such as sodium (Na^+), against negatively charged anions, such as (Cl^-), thus preserving electrical neutrality. Sodium chloride is by far the most abundant constituent. This is followed by magnesium chloride and magnesium sulfate, calcium sulfate, and potassium chloride. Evaporation of seawater, which normally contains about 3.5 percent total dissolved salts, will precipitate each salt when the brine becomes saturated with that salt (Figure 9.19).

Calcium carbonate is the first substance to precipitate, but the quantity is very small. Once the volume of seawater

has been reduced to only 19 percent of the starting amount, $CaSO_4$ or $CaSO_4 \cdot 2H_2O$ (depending on temperature) begins to precipitate. Halite ($NaCl$) begins to precipitate when the volume reaches about 9.5 percent of the original. When the volume is finally reduced to 4 percent, a complex magnesium and potassium salt called **polyhalite** ($K_2SO_4 \cdot MgSO_4 \cdot 2CaSO_4 \cdot 2H_2O$) begins to crystallize. More than half of the halite will precipitate during the reduction in solution volume from 9.5 to 4 percent, so the thickest layer formed during a single evaporation cycle will be the $NaCl$ layer. The sequence of minerals separating from the final 4 percent of the brine (called the **bitterns**) is complex and variable, depending on such factors as the temperature and

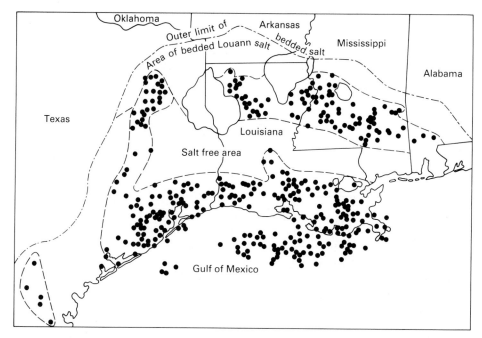

FIGURE 9.15. Salt domes in the Gulf Coast region of the United States. The individual domes may be 100 meters to more than 2 kilometers across and have risen through as much as 12 kilometers of overlying marine sediments. The domes lie in distinct zones where the surface is underlain by the Louann Salt bed that was deposited in an evaporite basin in Permian time. (Courtesy of Gulf Coast Geological Society.)

FIGURE 9.16. The world's largest sulfur reserves are held by the former Soviet Union, but seven countries hold reserves of more than 100 million metric tons. Known world reserves will last at least 25 years at present rates of production. The large quantities of sulfur held in petroleum, natural gas, and coal are not included in the reserves but will provide as much sulfur as Frasch procedures in the years to come. (From U. S. Bureau of Mines.)

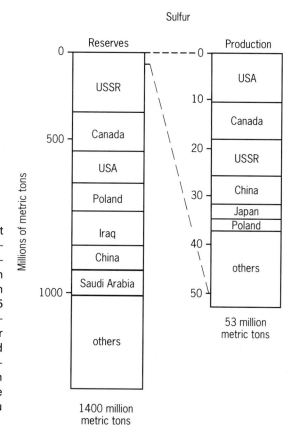

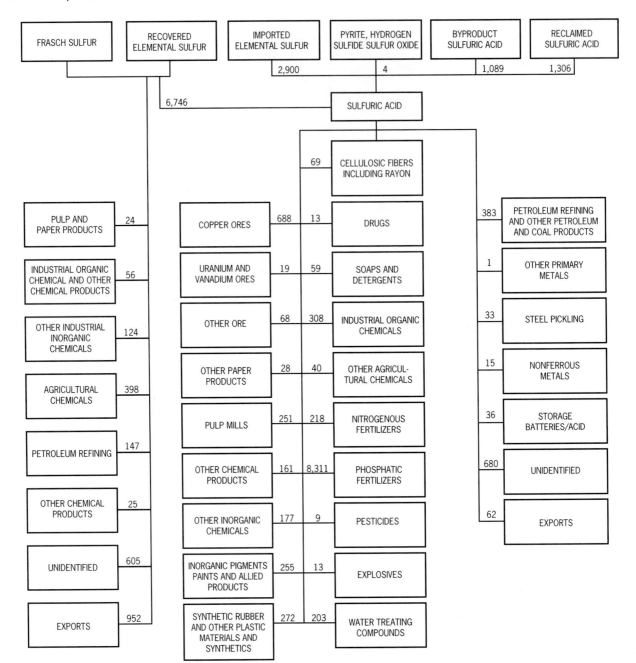

FIGURE 9.17. Sources and uses of sulfur in the United States in 1990. Sulfur, as indicated by the complexity of this diagram, is one of the most important and widely used industrial chemicals. Note that the largest single use, by far, is for the preparation of phosphatic fertilizers. The numbers are in thousands of metric tons of sulfur content per year. (From U.S. Bureau of Mines.)

whether or not the final liquid can react with the earlier-formed crystals. Two of the precipitates in the last stage, sylvite (KCl) and carnallite (KCl·MgCl$_2$·6H$_2$O), constitute the world's principal sources of soluble potassium used for fertilizers.

The complete evaporation of an isolated body of sea-water should produce this sequence. However, natural ma-rine evaporite sequences nearly always have greater amounts of calcite, gypsum, and halite and only rare presence of potassium and magnesium salts. Furthermore, complete evaporation of a body of seawater even as deep as the Mediterranean Sea, which averages about 1370 meters, would produce only 24 meters of halite and 1.4 meters of gypsum. However, beds of gypsum and halite from several

TABLE 9.2

A brief survey of some of the important mineral-derived chemicals and their uses*

Principal Element or Compound	Mineral Source	Chemical Products and Uses
Antimony	Stibnite (Sb_2S_3) Tetrahedrite ($Cu_{12}Sb_4S_{13}$)	Flame retardants, batteries, glass, ceramics
Arsenic	Tennantite ($Cu_{12}As_4S_{13}$) Arsenopyrite (FeAsS) Realgar (AsS)	Wood preservatives, agricultural herbicides and desiccants, semiconductors
Bismuth	Bismuthite (Bi_2S_3)	Pharmaceuticals
Boron	Borax ($Na_2B_4O_7 \cdot 10H_2O$) Kernite ($Na_2B_4O_7 \cdot 4H_2O$) Brines	Glass products, detergents, fibers
Bromine	Brines	Gasoline additives, flame retardants
Cadmium	Minor component of sphalerite ((Zn, Fe)S)	Batteries, pigments, plastics
Chlorine	Halite (NaCl) Brines	Plastics, water treatment, paper manufacture
Fluorine	Fluorite (CaF_2)	Steel and aluminum flux, welding rods, enamels, water fluoridation
Gallium	Minor component of sphalerite ((Zn,Fe)S)	Semiconductors, light-emitting diodes, lasers
Germanium	Minor component of sphalerite ((Zn,Fe)S)	Semiconductors, infrared optics, catalysts, phosphors
Indium	Residues from base metal refining	Alloys, nuclear reactor control rods, glass coating for liquid crystal displays
Iodine	Brines	Colorant in dyes, antibiotics, iodized salt
Lead	Galena (PbS)	Glass, paints, ceramics
Lime	Limestone ($CaCO_3$)	Agriculture, refractory
Lithium	Brine Lepidolite ($K(Li,Al)_3(Si,Al)_4O_{10}(F,OH)_2$)	Glass, ceramics, greases, batteries, aluminum production
Mercury	Mercury (Hg) Cinnabar (HgS)	Paints, fungicides, chlorine gas production
Nitrogen	Atmospheric (N_2) Nitre ($NaNO_3$)	Ammonia for fertilizers and chemical reagents, plastics, fibers, explosives (see text discussion)
Phosphorus	Apatite ($Ca_5(PO_4)_3(F,OH,Cl)_2$)	Phosphate fertilizers (see text discussion)
Potassium	Sylvite (KCl)	Potash fertilizers (see text discussion)
Rhenium	By-product of molybdenite (MoS_2)	Catalysts in gasoline production, thermocouples, flash bulbs
Rubidium	Minor element in lepidolite ($K(Li,Al)_3(Si,Al)_4O_{10}(F,OH)_2$)	Photochemical applications, medicines
Salt	Halite (NaCl) Brines	Basis for many chemicals including chlorine, caustic soda, soda ash (see text discussion); food products, deicing, water treatment, aluminum and steel manufacture, many other uses
Selenium	By-product of copper refining	Photocopiers, semiconductors, glasses, pigments, rubber compounds
Silver	Argentite (Ag_2S) Tetrahedrite (($Cu,Ag)_{12}Sb_4S_{13}$)	Black and white photographic film
Sodium	Halite (NaCl) Soda ash ($NaCO_3$) Mirabilite ($Na_2SO_4 \cdot 10H_2O$)	Detergents, glasses, pulp and paper manufacture
Sulfur	Sulfur (S) By-product of oil refining	Sulfuric acid for phosphate fertilizer production
Zinc	Sphalerite (ZnS)	Alloys, paints, medical compounds

*Although most materials used primarily for alloys or building materials are omitted, there is some overlap with other chapters where, for example, metals are used both in the chemical and metallurgical industries.

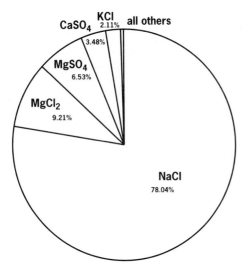

FIGURE 9.18. The major constituents of seawater. NaCl, also known as common salt or the mineral halite, constitutes more than three-quarters of the substances dissolved in seawater.

hundreds to thousands of meters thick are known from numerous localities. Many of these contain fossil and textural evidence of having formed in shallow water. It is thus apparent that these thick marine evaporite sequences did not form as a result of a single evaporative episode in very deep, totally isolated basins. Rather, they formed through the continuous evaporation of water from a partially isolated basin that was episodically fed with seawater for thousands of years (Figure 9.20). Water flows into the basin over a shallow barrier bar; as the water evaporates, the remaining brine becomes more concentrated and heavier, sinking to the bottom of the basin where it is trapped. Depending upon the rate of influx of additional seawater and the rate of evaporation, the brine in the basin may precipitate only calcite, calcite and gypsum, or calcite, gypsum, and halite. The distribution of evaporite sequences (Figure 9.12) reveals that in only a few places have evaporative concentrations resulted in the precipitation of potassium and magnesium salts as well as halite, calcite, and gypsum.

Evaporite deposits are widespread in the geologic record both in time and space. High temperatures are impor-

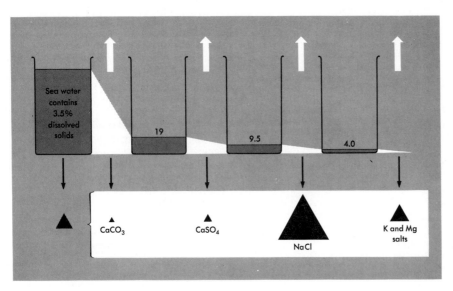

FIGURE 9.19. Schematic presentation of the sequence of minerals precipitated by the evaporation of seawater. When evaporation reduces the volume to 19 percent of the original, gypsum begins to precipitate; at 9.5 percent, salt begins to precipitate; and at 4 percent, potassium and magnesium salts begin to precipitate. (After B. J. Skinner, *Earth Resources*, 3rd ed., Prentice Hall, 1986.)

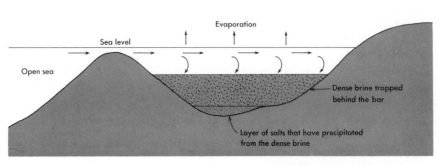

FIGURE 9.20. Cross section of a basin in which evaporite salts accumulate. Seawater containing approximately 3.5 percent dissolved salts flows into the basin through a shallow inlet and is concentrated by evaporation. The concentrated brine is heavier than the seawater and sinks below fresh, inflowing seawater. When the brine reaches a sufficiently high salinity, salts precipitate and accumulate on the floor of the basin.

tant but not necessary for the evaporative concentration of salts. Indeed, the largest evaporites forming today are within 30° of the equator, but there are several small lakes in which salts are depositing in Antarctica. Most of these lakes, which owe their evaporative concentration to high winds and very low humidities, are rich in sodium chloride. One small antarctic lake, Don Juan Pond (shown in Figure 2.13) is well known for being the only place on Earth where the evaporite mineral antarcticite ($CaCl_2 \cdot 6H_2O$) exists.

There are no modern evaporite basins comparable with the major ones found preserved in the geologic record. The largest evaporite area today is the 18,000-square kilometer Kara-BogazGol at the eastern edge of the Caspian Sea. At this site, waters spilling into the basin evaporatively concentrate so that sodium sulfate precipitates on large flats. Numerous small flats, where halite forms, exist along the shores of the Red Sea, and salt pans are adjacent to landlocked lakes such as the Great Salt Lake and the Dead Sea.

The Mediterranean Sea, with its narrow inlet at Gibraltar and its location in a relatively arid region, is almost an evaporite basin. Here, evaporation increases the salt content and the density of the surface waters so that they sink. However, the Straits of Gibraltar are deep enough to permit these heavier waters to escape out of the Mediterranean in a westward-flowing bottom current before they are concentrated enough for salt deposition. Above these concentrated heavy waters, less salty and less dense seawater flows into the Mediterranean as an eastward-moving surface current. If the channel at Gibraltar were shallower, the evaporatively concentrated water would not escape but would become further concentrated until salts precipitated.

Evaporite sequences containing halite occur worldwide. The problem is not one of availability but one of mining and shipping. Furthermore, the world's oceans contain essentially inexhaustible quantities (conservatively estimated at 46×10^{15} metric tons). In the United States, salt is mined (Figure 9.21) from flat-lying evaporite sequences, such as those in Michigan, Kansas, and New Mexico (Figure 9.12), and from large remobilized salt domes in the sediments of the Gulf coastal area (Figure 9.15). Most of the bedded salt in the Gulf coastal region is too deep to mine, but the salt has risen upward through the weak sediments as great columns in hundreds of places. This occurs because the salt has a slightly lower density than the overlying rocks and has slowly been buoyed toward the surface. The salt domes range from 100 meters (330 feet) to more than 2 kilometers (1.25 miles) across and have risen upward through the sediments by as much as 12 kilometers (7 miles).

Many areas of the world have salt domes, including Europe, South America, the Middle East, and the former Soviet Union. They are particularly abundant in the area on the north side of the Gulf of Mexico (Figure 9.15). Although the domes are obvious sites for salt mining, they also serve as major sources of sulfur extracted from the overlying cap rock

FIGURE 9.21. Salt mining from evaporite beds underlying the city of Cleveland, Ohio. Note the layering that probably represents annual cycles of salt deposition. The thicker white beds formed during the summers when there was more evaporation. The thinner beds represent periods of slower evaporation in winter; they are dark because of the presence of minor amounts of silt and weathered organic matter. (Photograph by Burke and Smith Studios; courtesy of International Salt Company.)

by the Frasch method and as major sources of petroleum that may occur trapped in upturned beds adjacent to the dome. The extraction of both oil and salt from the same dome has led to problems. In 1980, an oil drill operating from a barge in Lake Peigneur, a Louisiana lake that lies directly above a buried salt dome, penetrated a salt mine 430 meters (1410 feet) below. The entire lake drained into the salt mine, carrying the drill rig, several barges, many holly trees from a shoreline garden, and a tug boat with it. Fortunately, all drillers and miners escaped unharmed, but both the well and salt mine were lost.

In March 1994, a major collapse in the largest salt mine in the western hemisphere occurred at Retsof in western New York. After more than 100 years of continuous mining in a "dry mine," a major failure extended from the mine workings at a depth of 300 meters (1000 feet) to the surface, registering a 3.6 magnitude earthquake. No one was hurt, but the resulting fractures into the overlying water-bearing beds resulted in groundwater flow of nearly 75,000 liters (20,000 gallons) per minute into the mine. Potential long-term effects of the collapse include the loss of jobs of the miners and the widespread dispersal of salty water into fresh water aquifers and wells. The cause of the collapse is not known with certainty, but it may have resulted from a newer mining method that removed 90 percent of the salt, leaving only 6-meter (20-foot) pillars supporting the central portions of 90 meters (300 feet) by 365 meters (1200 feet) mined-out rooms.

LAKE PEIGNEUR: WHERE OIL AND SALT DID NOT MIX

It is unfortunate, but nevertheless true, that resource exploitation may have adverse effects on the environment; also, the search for one resource may impact on the availability of another. Such was the case at Lake Peigneur in southern Louisiana in November of 1980, providing an object lesson for the care to be taken when resources are sought and exploited.

This flat and marshy area has a gentle hill called Jefferson Island where a large pillar or "dome" of salt comes close enough to the surface to bow up the land (Figure 9.22). Adjacent to the hill lies shallow Lake Peigneur, which is connected to the Gulf of Mexico by a canal. In 1920, a mine shaft was sunk into the salt dome. By 1980, some 50 million tons of salt had been extracted, and the shaft had reached 600 meters (1800 feet) in depth, with many miles of mine workings. The upturned layers of sediment adjacent to salt domes are well known as oil traps (see Figure 5.31), and many millions of barrels of oil and gas have been produced from the flanks of domes similar to Jefferson Island. Oil drilling into the upturned rocks around the Jefferson Island Salt Dome began in November 1980 using a small platform located in Lake Peigneur. The operation was uneventful until about 5:00 A.M. on November 20 when the drill pipe became stuck at a depth of about 1250 feet. As the crew attempted to pull the pipe loose, the pipe bounced, shaking the drilling platform, which began to list. The drill crew loaded into small boats and reached shore just in time to see the drill platform fall over and disappear from sight—in a lake that was supposed to be only 1–2 meters deep!

At about the same time, the salt miners descended into the salt mine to begin the day's production. They soon found that the bottom levels of the mine were filled with a quickly rising level of muddy water. Responding to the danger, the miners safely exited the mine by 9:00 A.M. Apparently, the drill missed the upturned rocks beside the salt dome and instead penetrated the salt and the mine workings. Drilling fluids and lake water poured through the hole, enlarging it as the flow rapidly increased. The effect was much like that of pulling a plug in a bathtub full of water.

At about 11:00 A.M., two men enjoying early morning fishing in a small boat realized that the lake level suddenly dropped; they witnessed the development of a whirlpool into which water, fish, and several moored barges were being drawn. The fishermen escaped to shore. However, by the time the lake was completely drained, 12 barges had been pulled into the swirling hole like toys down the drain in a bathtub. Water normally flowed from the lake out into the canal and to the Gulf of Mexico, but the draining of the lake reversed the flow and began to draw shrimp boats moored in the canal. A small tugboat tried to block the water flow with a barge, but both the barge and the tugboat were drawn in and disappeared down the hole in the bottom of the lake; the crew escaped by diving overboard into the mud. The final loss also included 50 acres of the Live Oak Gardens, a botanical garden on the lakeshore, along with the owner's house, which slid into the lake as the shoreline collapsed. The disaster's last gasp was a short-lived geyser that spouted air and muddy water from the mine shaft at about 2:30 P.M.

Fortunately, no one was injured, but the sequence of events resulted in no oil recovery and the loss of the salt mine, one tugboat, three barges (nine of the original twelve resurfaced after about 3 days), 50 acres of botanical gardens, and one home. The drilling company also received a protracted lawsuit. Although the oil company never admitted blame, it did pay $45 million to those affected. Conflicts in resource exploitation are bound to occur, but many like the incident at Lake Peigneur are avoidable.

Salt production occurs in many parts of the world (Figure 9.23). The mining of salt in beds or salt domes is carried out by modern diesel equipment (Figure 9.21). In arid regions, including the southwest coastal areas of the United States, salt is harvested by evaporating seawater or brines in large fields or terraced ponds (Figure 9.24). Approximately 45 percent of the salt is used in the chemical industry for the manufacture of chlorine gas and sodium hydroxide; approximately 20 percent is used for deicing. Although the most visible use of salt is in salt shakers, the consumption of salt in food products represents less than 6 percent of total usage. Few data are available on actual

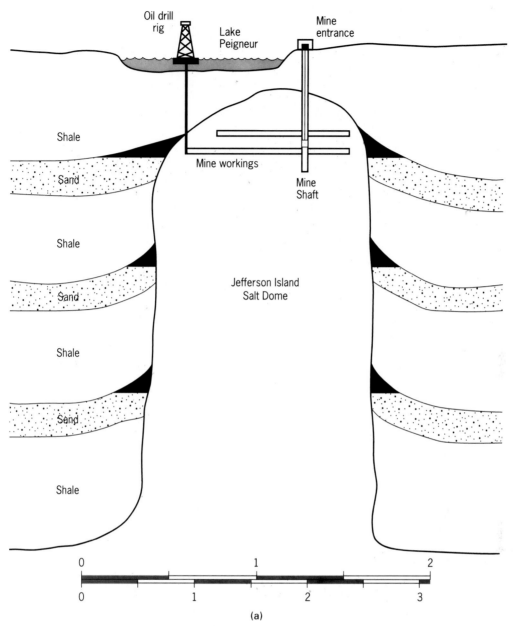

(a)

FIGURE 9.22. (a) The Jefferson Island salt dome, shown in schematic cross-section, is approximately one mile in diameter and has risen more than five miles above the top of the original salt bed. The Diamond Crystal Salt Mine operated in the uppermost 1500 feet of the salt dome, and the oil drill rig in Lake Peigneur was attempting to locate oil that might have occurred adjacent to the dome in the upturned beds. (b) Aerial photograph of Lake Peigneur after it had drained into the salt mine. The lake waters and drill rig have disappeared, leaving a mud bottom with some grounded barges. Portions of holly tree gardens that have slumped into the lake are shown in the foreground. The lake refilled within a few days, and several barges, which had disappeared down the hole at the drill site, resurfaced. (Photograph courtesy of Dr. J. D. Martinez.)

FIGURE 9.22.   *(cont.)*

(b)

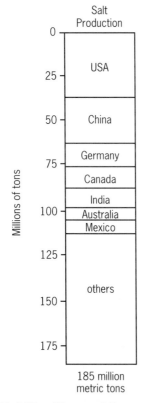

FIGURE 9.23. The world's annual production of about 185 million metric tons of salt in the mid-1990s is led by the United States and China, but many countries produce salt from mines, brines, and seawater. The world's salt resources are inexhaustible. (From U.S. Bureau of Mines.)

reserves, but all salt-producing countries are well-endowed. Because of the vast quantities of bedded evaporites, the enormous amounts dissolved in the oceans, and the simplicity of salt extraction, the world's salt supply is inexhaustible. A greater concern than the availability of salt is the environmental impact of salty waters released from chemical processing or as runoff into rivers and lakes when salt is used to deice highways.

Soda Ash (Na_2CO_3) and Sodium Sulfate (Na_2SO_4)

Sodium carbonate (trona) and sodium sulfate (thenardite) are widely used in the manufacture of glass, soaps, dyes, detergents, insecticides, paper, and in water treatment. Sodium bicarbonate ($NaHCO_3$) is common household baking soda. Natural **soda ash**, as the carbonate is commonly called, was probably first derived from mineral crusts around alkaline lakes in southern Egypt thousands of years ago. The early Egyptians and Romans used soda ash to make glass, as a medicine, and in bread-making. Until the eighteenth century, it was primarily obtained by leaching the ashes of burned seaweed, but a process was developed in 1791 to prepare it from halite and sulfuric acid. A more efficient process was developed in the 1860s to prepare soda ash from salt, coke, limestone, and ammonia. This process became a major source of soda ash for many years, but the discovery of large soda ash deposits in the western United States made the recovery of the natural materials cheaper than its synthesis. Sodium carbonate and sodium sulfate are evaporite minerals that form in some arid region lakes where weathering rocks release abundant sodium and,

(a)

(b)

FIGURE 9.24. Simple solar evaporation of brines and seawater has served as a source of salt for thousands of years. (a) Terraced evaporation ponds in the mountains of Peru. (Photograph courtesy of V. Benavides, Geological Society of America Special Paper 88, 1968.) (b) Salt being harvested in a broad evaporation pond in Colombia. (Photograph courtesy of the Colombian Government Tourist Office.)

sometimes, sulfur. Modern examples of such areas include the Searles, Owens, and Mono Lakes of California and Lake Magadi in Kenya. The lakes supply some of these sodium salts, but the bulk of production comes from bedded deposits formed from preexisting lakes.

More than 60 identified sodium carbonate deposits exist in the world, the largest of which is in southwestern Wyoming. One unit in the Green River Formation, Wyoming, contains 42 beds of trona, 25 of which have a thickness of 1 meter or more. Eleven of these beds are more than 2 meters thick and underlie an area of more than 2850 square kilometers. These beds alone contain more than 52×10^9 metric tons of soda ash; more than 22×10^9 metric tons of these are reserves. These reserves are large enough to meet the United States' needs for more than 700 years. Several alkaline lakes in eastern Africa contain large quantities of soda ash. These deposits and many others have been insufficiently evaluated in South America and Asia; they will likely supply the world's needs for many years.

The world's reserves of sodium sulfate are much smaller than those of sodium carbonate but are also sufficient to meet the world's needs for at least 600 years. Commercial sources in the United States include shallow subsurface

brines in west Texas, Searles Lake in California, and the Great Salt Lake in Utah.

Boron

Natural boron minerals are very much restricted in their geologic occurrence. Nevertheless, we find boron compounds in glass products, insulation, laundry detergents, food preservatives, fire retardants, ceramic glazes, and enamels. The trade in boron compounds dates from the thirteenth century when Marco Polo brought borax ($Na_2B_2O_4$) crystals from Tibet to Europe. The discovery of natural boric acid (H_3BO_3), also known as the mineral sassolite, in the hot springs of Tuscany, Italy, in 1771 led to the development of an industry that supplied most of the world markets from the 1820s into the 1870s. This market was superceded by Chilean production in the latter part of the nineteenth century. In 1864, borax crystals were found in springs north of San Francisco, California, but the modern United States boron industry is based upon large deposits subsequently discovered in Nevada and southern California. Deposits developed in Death Valley, California, between 1881 and 1889 had their borax minerals transported by the celebrated 20-mule teams (Figure 9.25).

FIGURE 9.25. The celebrated 20-mule team drawn wagons carried boron minerals from the deposits in Death Valley, California, in the 1880s. (Photograph courtesy of United States Borax & Chemical Corporation.)

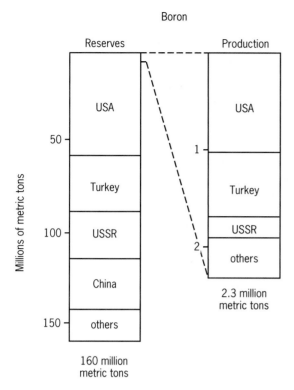

FIGURE 9.26. The United States and Turkey both hold the largest reserves and are the principal producers of boron. At present rates of production, known world reserves will last about 70 years. (From U.S. Bureau of Mines.)

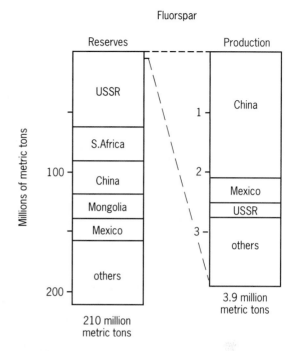

FIGURE 9.27. The former Soviet Union holds the largest reserves of fluorite, but China was the largest producer in the mid-1990s. At these rates of production, known reserves will last more than 50 years. (From U.S. Bureau of Mines.)

Although limited to a few deposits where volcanically-derived fluids have concentrated and formed boron-bearing minerals, there are economical deposits in the United States, the former Soviet Union, China, Turkey, Chile, and Peru with reserves of more than 150 million metric tons of boron oxide content. This will easily meet the world's needs far into the twenty-first century (Figure 9.26). The United States leads in reserves, but the nations of the former Soviet Union lead in production.

Fluorine

Fluorine compounds are vitally important to the production of most steel and aluminum and are used in the production of the uranium fuel in nuclear power plants. Fluorine compounds are also used in ceramics, water fluoridation agents, teflon, and experimental artificial blood substitutes for humans. Nearly all fluorine is derived from the mineral **fluorite** (CaF_2) that occurs in minor amounts in many hydrothermal ore deposits and relatively rich limestone-hosted deposits formed by low temperature, high salinity brines squeezed out of sedimentary basins. The fluorite in these latter deposits is commonly associated with lead and zinc min-

eralization and with barite. World fluorite reserves are widespread, totaling nearly 300 million metric tons, enough to last well into the twenty-first century (Figure 9.27). The United States, though processing large fluorite resources, has very limited reserves and currently relies heavily upon Mexico, the world's largest producer, for its fluorine.

Fertilizer and Chemical Minerals in the Future

The demand for fertilizer minerals will surely increase for the next 100 years or more to grow food for the expanding world population. It is also likely that the use of minerals in the chemical industry will continue to increase and diversify to include many applications in foods, supplements, toothpastes, and cosmetics (see page 326 and Table 9.3). Worldwide reserves of the mineral resources are large and certainly appear adequate to meet future needs. It is likely, however, that production patterns will change as less-developed countries become competitors for the advanced countries. Among nonmetallic resources, fertilizers and chemical minerals are the most vital, but their use is small when compared with that of the minerals used in construction and industry to which we now turn.

MINERALS IN FOODS, MEDICINES, AND COSMETICS

Many mineral commodities are very visible in their typical uses. We can all picture mineral products that have been merely roughly shaped or cut (e.g., stone walls and carved statues) and many that are processed (e.g., concrete in highways, glass, and steel). In addition to these uses, many other minerals are very widely used but nearly invisible to us. A diverse group of minerals and their synthetic analogues are used in the production of foods, medicines, and cosmetics (Table 9.3).

In foods, these minerals are used to enhance flavor, help preserve against spoilage, impart color, or modify physical characteristics. The most common mineral substance used in foods is halite, common salt (NaCl), which has been used as the widespread flavor enhancer for thousands of years. It was also widely used as a food preservative before refrigeration was developed. Although less commonly used in that manner today, many salted products remain available. Baking soda, $NaHCO_3$, (equivalent to the mineral nahcolite) is widely used in many types of baking to develop the desired porous texture of breads, cookies, or cakes. It is prepared from naturally occurring Na_2CO_3. More visible, but rarely recognized, is the use of synthetic anatase (TiO_2) in powdered sugar. The anatase possesses a very fine white opacity that is preserved even when adhering to a moist donut, but it has no flavor, no calories, and is inert in the human body. Several forms of aluminum silicates and silica (SiO_2) are widely used in materials such as nondairy coffee creamers and other powdered food preparation goods to prevent them from caking due to absorbed moisture.

Somewhat intermediate between foods and medicines are food additives, supplements, and toothpastes. Many stores today offer a vast array of supplements with individual elements (cobalt, iron, selenium, zinc, etc.). These elements are usually bound in some form of a soluble organic compound so they can be readily absorbed by the body. In contrast, calcium carbonate (known as limestone or calcite) and dolomite tablets, even if synthetically prepared, are virtually identical to the vast quantities of these minerals that occur worldwide. Toothpastes, carefully designed to be gentle on mouth tissues, typically contain abrasive materials to help remove organic deposits, stains, and bacteria from dental surfaces. Among the most commonly used abrasives today are silica, calcium carbonate, several forms of calcium phosphates, and sodium bicarbonate. Sparkle and brightness are sometimes added by including mica or TiO_2-coated mica. Fluoride, to help harden teeth, is added in the form of sodium fluoride (villiaumite) or sodium fluoro-phosphates.

Natural and synthetic mineral compounds, especially carbonates and bicarbonates, have been used in medicines to neutralize stomach acids and to generally control pH for years. Zinc oxide is widely used to promote healing either by itself or mixed with other compounds. Long before modern medicine, various peoples had discovered medicinal properties of some petroleum products. Today, petroleum jelly is commonly used on rashes, burns, and other minor skin irritations. Barite ($BaSO_4$) is not medicinal itself, but it has been widely used in X-ray images to enhance the visibility of some body organs and vessels.

Thousands of years before the development of the cosmetic industry, our ancestors adorned their faces and bodies with a variety of colored mineral pigments, especially red and yellow oxides and hydroxides of iron. Today's cosmetics are much more complex and contain an array of special organic oils, emulsions, dyes, and scents, but they still commonly contain clays (kaolin, bentonite, and montmorillonite), talc, calcium or sodium carbonate, calcium silicate, and silica to provide the body of the cosmetics and help in covering blemishes, absorbing oils, and controlling pH. In addition, they often contain titanium oxide, iron oxides, zinc oxide, ultra marines (originally prepared by powdering the gem lapis lazuli, but now usually synthetic), green chrome oxides, mica, and even powdered metals such as aluminum, copper, or bronze for coloring additives.

The minerals that we use in foods and medicines serve to enhance the quality and flavor or to promote health, but they are generally invisible. In contrast, minerals used in cosmetics are intentionally visible, but they generally remain unrecognized in terms of their true nature.

TABLE 9.3

Minerals used in foods, medicines, and cosmetics

Foods

NaCl—halite—common salt	Sodium and calcium phosphates
NaHCO$_3$—nahcolite—baking soda	SiO$_2$—silica
TiO$_2$—anatase	MgO—periclase
Al$_x$Si$_4$O$_2$Si$_y$O$_z$—aluminum silicates	CaSO$_4$—anhydrite

Supplements

CaCO$_3$—calcite	(Ca,Mg)CO$_3$—dolomite
KCl—sylvite	

Toothpaste

SiO$_2$—silica	CaCO$_3$—calcite
CaHPO$_4$ · 2H$_2$O—brushite	NaF—villiaumite
NaHCO$_3$—nahcolite	mica
TiO$_2$—anatase	

Cosmetics

kaolinite	zinc-oxide
montmorillonite	titanium oxide
bentonite	iron oxide
talc	mica
calcium carbonate	metal powders

FURTHER READINGS

BLAKEY, A. C., *The Florida Phosphate Industry.* Cambridge, Massachusetts: Harvard University Press, 1973.

Economic Geology, an issue devoted to phosphate, potash, and sulfur. Vol. 74, no. 2 (1979).

ERIKSEN, G. E., "The Chilean nitrate deposits." *American Scientist* 71 (1983) pp. 366–374.

REEDER, R. J., editor, "Carbonates: Mineralogy and Chemistry." *Reviews in Mineralogy,* Vol. 11. Washington, D.C.: Mineralogical Society of America, 1983.

TISDALE, S. L. and NELSON, W. L., *Soil Fertility and Fertilizers,* 3rd ed. New York: MacMillan Publishing Company, 1975.

U.S. Bureau of Mines, *Mineral Facts and Problems,* published annually.

WINES, R. A., *Fertilizer in America.* Philadelphia, Pennsylvania: Temple University Press, 1985.

10 BUILDING MATERIALS AND OTHER INDUSTRIAL MINERALS

The Sphinx and the great pyramids attest to the abilities of the early builders and to the durability of natural stone as a building material. (Courtesy of the Egyptian Tourist Authority.)

Stones make a wall, walls make a house, houses make streets, and streets make a city. A city is stones and a city is people; but it is not a heap of stones, and it is not just a jostle of people.

Jacob Bronowski, The Ascent of Man (1973)

FOCAL POINTS

- Building materials are the largest volume mineral commodities extracted from Earth.
- Most building materials have relatively little intrinsic value. Many different types of material are used, and local materials generally provide the main supplies.
- Treating building materials by cutting, polishing, refining, or calcining them markedly increases their value.
- Crushed stone, used primarily for roads, building foundations, and concrete, is the most widely used building material; limestone is the principal rock employed, but many other types are also used.
- Cement is the most important treated rock product and is prepared by heating limestone with small amounts of clay and silica. Although cement was used by the Romans, its formula was lost and not rediscovered until 1756.
- Gypsum is widely used in the manufacture of plaster of Paris and plasterboard.
- Clays of various types are used to prepare ceramic materials ranging from bricks to fine china.
- Glasses are made mainly from quartz, but a wide variety of materials, such as borax and alumina, are added to vary the properties.
- Asbestos is one of the most widely known industrial minerals because of its association with health problems. The six asbestos minerals form strong, flexible, and nonreactive fibers that have many industrial uses. The recognition of health problems has dramatically reduced the use of asbestos.
- Gemstones are particularly unusual and rare forms of relatively common substances.

- Natural diamonds are formed in Earth's mantle at depths greater than 150 km and have been brought to the surface in kimberlite pipes that formed as explosive vents.
- Synthetic diamonds are now produced on a large scale and are used in applications ranging from abrasives to electronic "chips."

INTRODUCTION

Building materials are the largest volume mineral commodity extracted from Earth. They rank second only to the fossil fuels in value. Almost every known rock type and mineral has contributed in some way to the construction of buildings, roads, bridges, dams, or similar structures.

Most building materials, unlike metals, fuels, fertilizers, and chemical minerals, have little intrinsic value; they are both abundant and widely distributed. It is only after they are removed from Earth and processed to more useful forms that their value increases. For example, the limestone and shale used to make cement may be worth $5 or less per metric ton in the ground, but after mining, crushing, firing, and conversion to a high-quality cement, the product may be worth $50 or more per ton. The processing of building stone or clays used in ceramic products adds even more to their value (Figure 10.1).

Because of their abundance, the factors controlling building material exploitation and marketing differ greatly from those for such expensive commodities as fuels or metals. Normally, mining operations are undertaken only to satisfy a local demand because the transportation cost for any great distance is rarely justified. For many of the materials discussed in this chapter, the volume of the trade is large, but it is conducted within nations on a local level. Only in the cases of special building stones is the expense of distant transport justified. Therefore, international trade is not relevant since demand is commonly satisfied internally. Reserves also tend to be large, and the potential resources are even larger. Commodities such as building stone are so abundant that it is pointless to even attempt putting numbers on reserves or discussing their geology in detail. This is not true, however, for a few of the more specialized building materials, such as vermiculite and perlite, or for some of the major industrial minerals.

In this chapter, major building materials are discussed, with emphasis on the character of the raw materials, problems of their extraction and processing, their uses, and their limitations. The building materials are separated for discussion into two groups—*untreated* and *treated* rock products. Other major industrial minerals that do not readily fall into the categories of fertilizers and chemical minerals are also discussed. These include minerals valued because of particular properties they possess, such as great hardness, resistance to high temperatures, inertness, distinctive color, asthetic quality, or high density.

UNTREATED ROCK PRODUCTS

It is necessary to distinguish between materials that have simply been quarried or mined to be cut or crushed and those that have been subjected to more complex treatments that change the finished product into something very different from the raw material. The former we shall call *untreated* rock products, and the latter, *treated*. The two major categories of untreated rock products are the various types of **building stone** and the **aggregates,** which include **crushed rock, sand** and **gravel,** and **lightweight aggregates.** Aggregates are used mainly in concrete, highways, railroad bases, ballast materials, or graded fill on construction sites.

Building Stone

Natural stone is one of the oldest building materials known to man. It has been widespread, available, durable, easy to maintain, and pleasing in appearance. Consequently, natural stone has been used throughout human history to provide shelter from the elements, safety from enemies and other dangers, facilities for transportation, and media for artistic expression. In the simplest of shelters, humans used natural

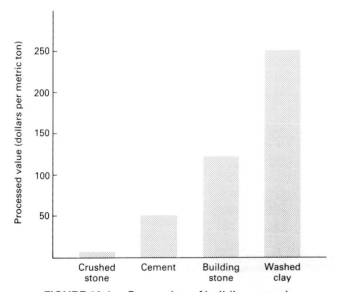

FIGURE 10.1. Processing of building materials adds greatly to their value. (After B.J. Skinner, *Earth Resources,* 3rd ed. Prentice Hall, 1986.)

FIGURE 10.2.   The volcanic ash in the Cappadocia region of Turkey is soft enough to carve, yet sturdy enough to last; this has been the site of hundreds of homes. (Courtesy of the Ministry of Tourism of Turkey.)

FIGURE 10.4.   Natural stone was the principal construction material used by the Romans. The durability of a structure built using carefully cut and shaped blocks is evident in this amphitheater constructed in Nimes, France, by the Romans in the first century. (Courtesy of the French Government Tourist Office.)

caves for protection. A natural progression of this was the carving out of shelters within rocks. Numerous dwellings have been cut into the thick glacial loess deposits in China, but perhaps the best examples are those carved into volcanic ash beds in Cappadocia, Turkey (Figure 10.2, Plate 51). Ancient peoples constructed dwellings and ceremonial sites from many materials, but generally only stone edifices have survived (Figures 10.3, 10.4, and 10.5). However, throughout the twentieth century, the use of natural stone has been declining in the face of competition from processed materials. In the United States, for example, more than half of the stone produced was so-called **dimension stone**—stone that was quarried, cut, and finished to a predetermined size—at the turn of the century. In the 1990s, dimension stone accounted for only 0.1 percent of the quarried stone. Before considering the types of rock that are commonly used for this purpose, consider the various categories of building stone.

Rubble and rough construction stone refer to large blocks of rough-hewn rock used in sea walls, bridge work, and many

FIGURE 10.3.   The great Stonehenge ring, constructed by the Wessex Culture peoples of Britain about 2000 B.C., has been interpreted as a ceremonial, astronomical, and burial site. The great stone blocks were originally shaped and then transported as much as 150 miles (240 km). The rocks appear today just as they did 4000 years ago. (Photograph by J.R. Craig.)

FIGURE 10.5. The castles of Europe, such as Kilchurn Castle on Loch Awe in Scotland, have survived for hundreds of years because of the durability of the local stone that was used to construct the walls. (Photograph by J.R. Craig.)

other applications. This must be very resistant. It also refers to smaller blocks used as wall-facing material.

Rip-rap is the name given to large, irregularly shaped stones (generally from around 7–70 kg) used in river and harbor work and to protect highway embankments from erosion.

Ashlar consists of rectangular stone pieces of nonuniform size set randomly in a wall. Ashlar blocks are generally 10 centimeters or more thick and up to a square meter or more in area; they may have rough-hewn or smooth faces (Figure 10.6).

Cut stone includes all building stone that is cut to precise dimensions on all sides, textured, smoothed, or polished. Most cut stone is used as a facing on exterior or interior walls of buildings and therefore applied in thin slabs as a veneer.

Monumental stone is that employed in gravestones, statues, mausoleums, or more elaborate monuments.

Flagstones, curbing, and paving blocks are used in paving pedestrian areas in town and cities.

Roofing slate refers to rocks used to cover a roof.

FIGURE 10.6. Ashlar, on the campus of Virginia Tech, is commonly used as a building facing. It consists of randomly set rectangular pieces of building stone. (Photograph by J.R. Craig.)

Mill-stock slate refers to smooth-finished slabs of slate used in electric switchboards, billiard tables, laboratory bench tops, blackboards, and other products.

Terrazzo is sized material, usually marble or limestone, that is mixed with cement for pouring floors; it is then smoothed to expose the chips after the floor has hardened.

Many kinds of rock have been used at some time or another as building stone. The important factors governing the suitability of any particular rock for use in building are its physical properties and whether or not it is pleasing to the eye. The most important rock types are as follows:

Granite is used commercially to include not only those coarsely crystalline igneous rocks made dominantly of **feldspars** and **quartz** (true granite and **granodiorite**), but also coarsely crystalline igneous rocks containing feldspars but devoid of quartz (**syenite**) and containing appreciable **ferromagnesian minerals (diorite)** or very high concentrations of these minerals (**gabbro, norite**) to form black granites. Granites, in this very broad and unscientific use of the term, may be ideal building stones for rough construction because they break easily along joints. They are also commonly used for curbstones because they resist abrasion and weathering, and they are often very attractive materials for use as cut stone and monumental stone. The scientific classification of the most important igneous rocks is shown in Table 10.1.

Sandstone is defined in commercial terms as consolidated sand in which the grains are chiefly quartz and feldspar cemented by various materials that may include silica, iron oxides, **calcite,** or clay. A conspicuous feature of these clastic sedimentary rocks is their bedding or stratification. Bedding planes are commonly planes along which the rock splits easily; when these planes are regular and evenly spaced, the rock may be a natural flagstone, flat rock used for walkways. **Sandstones** are also widely used for cut stone, ashlar, and rubble. For example, brownstone, a red sandstone of Triassic age, is used in the eastern United States as a building material.

Limestone is the other sedimentary rock most widely used in building. In commercial terms, it is a *rock of sedimentary origin composed principally of calcium carbonate or the double carbonate of calcium and magnesium* and therefore includes true limestones and **dolostones.** Like sandstone, limestone is a well-known building material used for ashlar and cut stone and may also form a natural flagstone. It has been widely used throughout Europe to construct large public buildings, cathedrals, and mansions. Many of the colleges of the Universities of Oxford and Cambridge were constructed from Jurassic age limestones quarried from central England (Figure 10.7).

Marble scientifically refers to a form of limestone that has been thoroughly recrystallized during metamorphism. Commercial marble includes these true marbles, other certain crystalline limestones, and some highly altered ultramafic igneous rocks made of hydrated magnesium silicate minerals known as **serpentines.** All of these marbles can easily be cut (Figure 10.8), carved, or shaped and take a good polish. They are the best known of all monumental stones

TABLE 10.1

Classification of some of the most important igneous rocks

	Abundance of quartz and/or light-colored (felsic) minerals			Abundance of dark-colored (mafic) minerals, especially ferromagnesian minerals (olivine, pyroxene)		
	FELSIC	INTERMEDIATE		MAFIC	ULTRAMAFIC	
	Mainly potash feldspar (KAISi$_3$O$_8$)		Mainly plagioclase feldspar (Na,Ca)(Al,Si)Si$_2$O$_8$		No feldspar	
	with quartz	little or no quartz	with biotite and/or hornblende	with pyroxene and/or olivine	without olivine	with olivine
Coarse grained (plutonic)	GRANITE (granodiorite has dominant Na-plagioclase)	SYENITE	DIORITE	GABBRO (also norite)	PYROXENITE	PERIDOTITE
		MONZONITE				
Medium grained (hypabyssal)	MICRO-GRANITE	MICRO-SYENITE	MICRO-DIORITE	DIABASE (dolerite)		
Fine grained (volcanic)	RHYOLITE	TRACHYTE	ANDESITE	BASALT		

FIGURE 10.7. The Radcliff Camera with All Souls College. Many of the university buildings at Oxford are built from limestones of the Jurassic age quarried in central England. (Photograph by D. J. Vaughan.)

and are greatly prized as facing materials for exterior and interior use (Figures 10.9 and 10.10).

Slate is a very fine-grained rock produced when shale has been compressed during metamorphism. As well as hardening the rock, this process imparts cleavage to the rock, allowing it to readily split into thin, parallel sheets. The dominant minerals are quartz with fine **micas** and other minerals that align with cleavage planes. Slate is best known as

FIGURE 10.8. High-quality marble used in construction may be mined in open quarries or in underground mines such as this mine in Vermont. The marble is cut into rough blocks in the mine and then shaped and polished for its final usage. (Courtesy of the Vermont Marble Corporation.)

FIGURE 10.9. The "Pieta" by Michelangelo is a classic example of sculpture from white marble quarried at Carrara, Italy. (Courtesy of the Italian State Tourist Office (E.N.I.T.), London.)

MARBLE FOR THE MASTERS

Sculptors are always very particular about the medium in which they work, desiring that the final work speak both in substance and style. For more than 2000 years, sculptors' rock of choice has been marble, and the single most highly sought marble comes from Carrara in the Apuan Alps of Northern Italy. Quarrying apparently began in the Carrara region by 500 B.C. and gradually expanded. Major development came with the Renaissance in the 1400s and 1500s, and ultimately more than 650 different quarries have been cut into the sides of the mountains to seek the marble that has been transported around the world. These quarries have yielded more marble than any other place on Earth and continue to be mined at a rate of more than one million tons per year.

It is widely held that Michelangelo, like sculptors before and after him, visited Carrara in order to select the best stone for his works (Figure 10.9). On Monte Altissimo, he found a *statuario* marble that was more uniform and white than any other in Italy. The Romans believed in a *living* Earth and supposed that the marble regrew after excavation and would never be exhausted. There was still so much that Michelangelo had plenty to choose from in the early 1500s, but today the best of the *statuario* is nearly gone. The remaining individual blocks of *statuario* are bought by sculptors from around the world at premium prices.

The marble at Carrara consists of calcite ($CaCO_3$) which initially formed as a submarine limestone. Subsequently, it recrystallized as a result of increasing temperature and pressure when the rocks of the Alps were deeply buried and intensely deformed. The individual grains of calcite increased in size from their original hundredths or tenths of a millimeter to several millimeters. This coarseness, along with the clarity of the individual crystals, allows light to penetrate and gives a special sheen to the finished product. Colored marbles, which occur all over the world, owe their shades to various amounts of impurities, such as iron oxides and clays.

Marble quarrying is tedious work because cracks and chips can weaken blocks and greatly reduce their value. From Roman times until the nineteenth century, most of the work was done by hand. Rows of holes were chipped to define the boundaries of blocks; then wooden wedges were driven into these holes. When soaked with water, the wedges expanded and gently cracked the blocks loose. Metal wedges were also employed. Explosives were once tried for this purpose, but soon were found to shatter and weaken the rock. Wire saws, which operate by continuously wearing their way through the soft marble, were introduced in the late 1800s. These saws reduced wastage and worked well until the 1970s when large diamond-studded circular saw blades came into use.

Although little *statuario* now remains, lesser quality marble is in high demand for ornamental construction. Consequently, Carrara remains a major supplier of the world's marble needs. Every year, Carrara hosts an annual marble fair. In 1991, for the first time in more than 50 years, there was a large block of marble on display from the Yule marble quarry in Colorado. The Yule quarry (Figure 10.10), the largest in the United States for many years and second only to Carrara in world production from 1909–1917, provided the stone for the Tomb of the Unknown Soldier at Arlington National Cemetery in Arlington, Virginia, and many other buildings in Washington, DC. The Yule quarry was closed in 1941, but it has been reopened again to ship large blocks of high-quality marble around the world.

a roofing material, and it is still regarded by many people as the highest quality and most permanent form of roof covering. However, as with the other building stones, its use has largely been superseded by less expensive processed materials. Many of the great slate quarries, like those in North Wales that once supplied most of England and Wales, have been abandoned (Figure 10.11).

Crushed Rock

Crushed rock constitutes the largest volume mineral commodity used in the United States and many other countries. Its principal use is the base for road construction, but very large quantities are also used in the foundations of buildings and as an aggregate in concrete. Enormous quantities are

FIGURE 10.10. The Yule marble quarry in Colorado produces fine marble widely used for statuary. After being closed for many years, the quarry was reopened in the early 1990s. (Photograph by J.G. Groeneboer; courtesy of the U.S. Geological Survey.)

FIGURE 10.11. Slate, widely used in the past as a roofing material and for a variety of other purposes, was mined in regionally metamorphosed terrains such as North Wales in the United Kingdom. The large Bethesda quarry is typical of slate-producing operations. (Photograph by B. J. Skinner.)

used. For example, the 45,000 mile (72,000 km) United States Interstate Highway System required 1.5 billion tons of crushed stone for its construction. The total used in construction of all the highways and cities in the United States probably exceeds 100 billion tons. Lesser amounts of crushed rock find a wide range of other uses in fertilizers, glass making, refractories, fillers, and terrazzo surfaces.

The best aggregate rocks are hard and inert but still easy to mine and crush. Specifications for crushed rock to be used for various purposes are usually established by national organizations and include properties such as resistance to abrasion, ability to withstand freeze-thaw conditions, size distributions of fragments, and absence of material that may react with the alkali substances in concrete mix. Depending on the specifications, crushed rock may be used for concrete, coarse or fine bituminous (asphaltic) concrete, **macadam** (black top), other road surfaces, road base, railroad ballast, fill, and a variety of other uses.

In the United States, limestone and dolostone make up more than two-thirds of the stone quarried for aggregate because they are widely available, easy to mine and crush, and strong (Figure 10.12). Granite and related light-colored igneous rocks make up about one-seventh of the stone

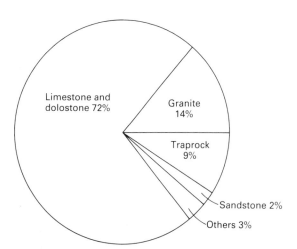

FIGURE 10.12. The rock types most widely used in the preparation of crushed stone in the United States. (From the U. S. Bureau of Mines.)

quarried. The only other rock types that significantly contribute to the United States' production are fine-grained, dark-colored igneous rocks such as basalt, known collectively as traprocks, and sandstones or quartzites.

In most countries, surface exposures of rock suitable for aggregate are common. Large quantities of rock are extracted by blasting and quarrying an open pit. The rock is then crushed at the site of mining operations, a location close to the user to lower transport costs. For these reasons, crushed stone is one of the lowest unit cost items of commerce, averaging no more than $5 per metric ton in the United States, a country that produces 1 billion tons of this commodity annually. It has been less than 150 years since Eli

Whitney Blake invented the modern rock crusher in 1858. This invention was to provide crushed rock for the "ambitious" project of a 2-mile long macadam road from New Haven to Westville, Connecticut. Before this, all rocks were crushed by hand, even those used for the construction of roads built using the methods pioneered by the Scottish inventor John McAdam in 1819. Today, concrete is primarily composed of crushed rock with cement as the binder. This is used as construction material for highways and large buildings. Its strength, resistance, and moldability also allow it to function well as road surfaces and sidewalks, in bridges (where it is reinforced by internal steel rods), walls, and statuary (Figure 10.13).

(a)

(b)

FIGURE 10.13. (a) Modern highway and bridge construction using large quantities of crushed stone, concrete, and steel have eliminated many of the problems of unpaved roads (b) and the need for massive amounts of timber to build trestles. (c) The Cowlitz River arch span in Washington, 520 feet (170 meters) long. (Photographs courtesy of the Portland Cement Association, the Forest History Society, and the Federal Highway Administration, respectively).

FIGURE 10.13. (*cont.*)

(c)

Sand and Gravel

Sand and gravel mining constitute the second largest non-fuel industry in the United States and many other parts of the world. Approximately 1 billion metric tons are mined in the United States at over 5000 locations, involving more than 3500 producers with a total product value of $3.5 billion. The principal uses of sand and gravel are as aggregates for concrete and the rock matter added to bituminous mixtures to make macadam road surface. Sand is classified as having particle sizes less than 2 millimeters in diameter. Those of gravel are larger and may range up to approximately 9 centimeters. In the United States, where the construction industry consumes more than 95 percent of the sand and gravel produced, the tonnage of gravel used is about twice that of sand.

Commercially, sand and gravel are obtained from many types of rocks, but the main sources are present-day or ancient river channels (Plate 46), their flood plains, or **alluvial fans.** Here, rounded pebbles are produced by the action of transport downstream, and often only the harder and more stable rock fragments survive. There is also some separation of different sized particles, with finer grains washed farther downstream or out to sea. The deposits that result may have the rounded, hard, and stable particles, properties desired for concrete aggregate, as well as being readily accessible and easily mined. The deposits of sand and gravel that were left behind following the retreat of the great ice sheets that once covered much of northern Europe, Canada, and the northern United States are also commercially important (Figure 10.14). Some beach deposits also have such materials.

FIGURE 10.14. Sand and gravel are the products of natural geological weathering processes, and exploitable deposits occur worldwide. Glacial outwash deposits, such as those near Trondheim, Norway, can provide excellent sources of naturally washed and sorted gravels and are very easily worked. (Photograph by J.R. Craig.)

As with crushed rock, sand and gravel are resources that are exploited in areas as close to the consumer as possible to reduce transport costs. However, some local resources are limited or have largely been consumed, as in the densely populated areas of Europe and North America. In these northern latitudes, extensive sand and gravel deposits occur beneath the sea on the **continental shelves,** having been deposited by rivers and glaciers during low sea level stands of the Ice Ages. These submarine deposits are now exploited by dredging off the west coast of Europe on a substantial scale and in a smaller way off the shores of New Jersey, New York, and New England. Gravel deposits are sparse or absent off many tropical coasts, and these areas may also have little surface exposure of rocks suitable for crushing. In the Gulf of Mexico, for example, although sands can be found in river deltas, gravels are almost unknown. The only available coarse-grade building materials are old shell beds and coral reefs, and when such supplies are used up, gravel or crushed stone will need to be imported into areas like southern Texas, Louisiana, and Florida.

Deposits of sand and gravel are generally simple to mine with power shovels, bulldozers, and draglines in dry pits or through dredging in rivers, off-shore, and natural or artificial lakes. The processing may involve no more than separating the different size fractions by washing and screening the materials. There may also be crushing operations or even some form of separation process to remove unwanted impurities such as particles of shale.

The crushed stone industry and the sand and gravel industries are both increasingly subject to land-use and environmental problems. These problems result primarily from the necessity of locating the quarries and pits near consumers, which are areas of rapidly expanding urban growth.

Vermiculite, Perlite, and Other Lightweight Aggregates

Lightweight aggregates include a variety of materials used chiefly in making boards, plaster, concrete, and insulation. Use of these materials is increasing because they are easily handled in construction work and the trapped air they contain makes them good insulators. Examples include such natural materials as volcanic cinders and **pumice,** which are simply crushed and sized after quarrying. There are also similar synthetic materials that are by-products of industrial operations, such as processed slag. Other lightweight aggregates involve treatment, usually by heating, of some product of mining operations. In some instances, clay or shale is sintered, or roasted, in kilns to drive off water and cause them to expand. Two particularly interesting natural substances that expand on heating are **vermiculite** and **perlite.** For both, the expansion is so great that the end product is an *ultra*-lightweight aggregate.

Vermiculite is a mineral with a layered structure like micas and clays. Although its composition varies, it is basically a hydrous magnesium-iron aluminum silicate. When it is rapidly heated to above 230°C, the layers separate as water between the layers converts to steam; this process is called **exfoliation.** It increases in volume eight to twelve times, although individual flakes may expand as much as thirty times to form wormlike pieces; the name vermiculite comes from the Latin *vermiculare,* which is to breed worms (Figure 10.15). Vermiculite occurs in many places throughout the world, although important deposits are found in the United States (Montana and South Carolina) and South Africa (Palabora, N.E. Transvaal). The Montana deposit is a large altered **stock** of mafic igneous rock (**pyroxenite**), and the Palabora deposit is also part of an altered igneous rock (**carbonatite**) complex. The brown or greenish flakes of vermiculite are mined in open pits. The total annual world production is about 500,000 metric tons. Of this, an estimated

(a)   (b)

FIGURE 10.15. Vermiculite exhibits the unusual characteristic of swelling when heated. The effect is shown here in the contrast of vermiculite as mined (a) and that which has been heated (b). (Sample courtesy of the Virginia Vermiculite Corporation; photograph by S. Llyn Sharp.)

200,000 tons is produced in the United States. The exfoliation plants are usually found close to the final markets to reduce transport costs; in the 1990s, there were 33 plants in 18 states in the United States. The U.S. Bureau of Mines estimates the total world reserves (excluding the former Soviet Union and China) at 50 million metric tons of which 25 million metric tons are in the United States and 20 million metric tons are in South Africa. Total world resources are estimated to be three times as much as the reserves.

Perlite is a glassy volcanic rock that contains a small amount of combined water that vaporizes upon rapid heating and also expands 4–20 times its original volume. The resulting material is a solid filled with bubbles and pores having a characteristic white color. Perlite ore is found in belts of volcanic rock in many parts of the world, but the major producers are Greece, Hungary, Italy, the former Soviet Union, and the United States. As with vermiculite, perlite deposits are mined by open-pit methods, and the ore is crushed, dried, and screened before shipment to expanding plants near the final markets. Annual world production is about 1,500,000 metric tons from estimated world reserves of at least 700 million metric tons.

TREATED ROCK PRODUCTS

Treated rock products are materials that must be chemically processed, fired, melted, or otherwise altered after mining so they can be molded and set into new forms before use. Important examples include the raw materials for the manufacture of cement, plaster, clay, and other materials needed in the production of bricks, a wide range of ceramic products, and the raw materials for the glass industry.

Cement

Cement, a chemical binder made chiefly from limestone, is one of the most important construction materials of the twentieth century. It is mixed with sand to produce mortar, used as the binding agent for brick, block, or other masonry, or mixed with sand and gravel to make concrete. The ancient Greeks and Romans first used cement and mortar by adding water to a mixture of quicklime (CaO made by heating or calcining limestone), sand, and a finely ground glassy volcanic ash. Because the volcanic ash came from the town of Pozzuoli, near Naples, it is known as **pozzolan cement.** The addition of water to this mixture causes a series of chemical reactions that leads to recrystallization and hardening of the cement when it dries. The end product is then stable in air and water, as we can judge from the fact that pozzolan cement was used to build the Roman Pantheon and the Colosseum; both still stand after more than 2000 years. However, the "art" of making such cements, although further developed by these ancient civilizations, was forgotten during the middle ages and was only rediscovered in 1756 when a British engineer named John Smeaton was commissioned to rebuild the famous Eddystone Lighthouse off the coast of Cornwall, England. He searched for a hydraulic cementing material that would set and remain stable under water. He is said to have found the formula when examining an ancient Latin document. Smeaton found that clay must also be present to produce hydraulic cement and that this could be introduced by using a limestone that is naturally rich in clay, hence known as **cement rock.** Such **natural cements** were further developed during the eighteenth century, but because the compositions of cement rocks vary widely, the cement was not uniform in strength or setting times. In an effort to improve the uniformity of cement, Joseph Aspidin patented a formula for **portland cement** in 1824. He called it portland because of a fancied resemblance to Portland stone, a limestone widely used in British buildings. It soon supplanted all other cements and became the basis of modern cements and concretes, the most common construction material in the world. Twice as much concrete is used than all the other structural material combined.

The raw materials needed for portland cement include lime (CaO), usually made from the $CaCO_3$ in limestone; alumina (Al_2O_3), usually from shale or clay; and silica (SiO_2), which may come from clay and shale or sand. Because limestone is the major ingredient, outweighing the others by roughly a factor of ten to one, cement works are usually located near limestone quarries. Sometimes, a natural limestone contains clay or shale impurities of the desired composition and is, therefore, a cement rock. Small amounts of iron-containing materials (iron ores or waste products from iron works) are also used, and gypsum or anhydrite is added later to control setting times. The winning of the major raw materials involves the same kinds of open-pit mining as for other forms of crushed rock.

The steps involved in the manufacture of portland cement require crushing and grinding the raw materials, then blending them either as dry powders or as slurries mixed with water (Figure 10.16a). This blend is then fed into a long rotating kiln with temperatures close to 1500°C. This drives off any carbon dioxide and water and partly melts some of the material to a glass. The resulting substance is ground to a powder with the addition of gypsum (approximately 5 percent of the bulk) and is then ready for use. Portland cements are, in fact, largely mixtures of complex silicates and aluminates of calcium that react when water is added. New compounds form and grow as hard masses of interlocking crystals (Figure 10.16b).

The raw materials needed for cement manufacture are widely available throughout the world, and over 100 countries produce significant amounts of their own cement. China has become the world's leading manufacturer of cement, producing more than 300 million metric tons per year; the world total is about 1.5 billion tons (Table 10.2).

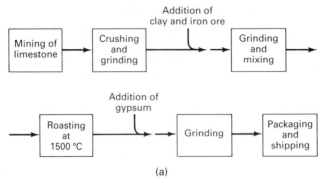

FIGURE 10.16. (a) The conversion of limestone into cement involves several steps. (Courtesy of the Portland Cement Association.) (b) The crystallization of cement begins when water is added to the clinker. The reactions result in the formation of calcium silicate crystals that interlock and give cement its durability and strength.

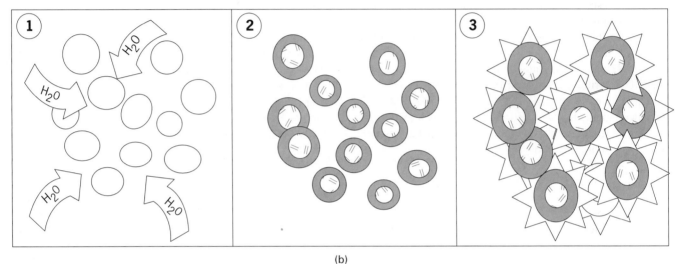

(b)

Not just any limestone is suitable for cement manufacture; only limestones that are extremely pure $CaCO_3$ with very low amounts of iron, magnesium, or manganese are suitable. Hence, cement-producing plants tend to be concentrated along specific geologic formations formed during the precipitation of pure limestones in warm tropical seas.

TABLE 10.2

Producers of cement, 1993

Country	Production* (m.t. × 10^6	Total (%)
China	335	24.0
Russia	143	10.2
Japan	100	7.2
United States	81	5.8
India	59	4.2
Korea	50	3.6
Italy	46	3.3
Germany	42	3.0
All others	540	38.7
WORLD TOTAL	1396	100.0

Data from the U.S. Bureau of Mines.
*The materials to make cement are available in many parts of the world in virtually unlimited quantities.

Plaster

Plaster is made by heating, or **calcining,** gypsum, which is the hydrated form of gypsum, calcium sulfate ($CaSO_4 \cdot 2H_2O$). When gypsum is calcined at 177°C, 75 percent of the water is driven off to form the new compound $CaSO_4 \cdot \frac{1}{2}H_2O$. This is commonly called **plaster of Paris** after the famous gypsum quarries in the Montmartre district in Paris that produce high-quality plaster. When plaster of Paris is mixed with water, it solidifies by rehydrating and reverting to a finely interlocked mass of tiny gypsum crystals. The earliest known use of gypsum and its plaster was 5000 years ago by the Egyptian civilization. The early Greek writer, Theophrastus, described the burning of gypsum to prepare plaster in a very common manner. Plaster of Paris was used in England as early as the thirteenth century, but the first British manufacture of plaster dates back to the late seventeenth century.

However, the use of plaster remained limited until about 1870 because of its very rapid setting time. Then the use of organic additives, such as glue and starch, to retard setting was discovered. This revolutionized the industry and permitted the first large-scale use of plaster in construction. Most early construction use was as hand-applied wet plaster spread over a wire screen or wooden laths to cover walls and ceilings. The development of prefabricated wall board in 1918 provided a way to greatly reduce labor costs while still using plaster. Today, **plasterboard** is by far the most widely used indoor wall covering in North America and Europe. It is prepared by feeding a slurry of plaster onto a rapidly moving, continuous roll of heavy paper. A second sheet of paper is fed onto the slurry in order to sandwich it. As the sandwich of paper and plaster travel several hundred meters on a conveyer system, the plaster sets sufficiently for the continuous slab to be cut into standard-sized sheets. These sheets are then sent slowly through a long kiln so that the plaster slurry hardens into solid gypsum and the boards are ready for use.

Gypsum occurs in marine evaporite sequences (see Chapter 9). It has now been recognized that calcium sulfate deposits can build up on hot saline tidal flats without developing thick salt accumulations. In fact, calcium sulfate occurs in evaporites not only as gypsum but also as anhydrite ($CaSO_4$), so called because it contains no water of crystallization. Which form of calcium sulfate precipitates depends on the temperature; anhydrite is favored at higher temperatures and is more commonly produced under the hot climatic conditions in which most evaporites initially form. However, this anhydrite is often converted to gypsum after rain-derived groundwater percolates through the deposits. Because of this relationship between the two minerals, most large deposits contain a mixture of gypsum and anhydrite. Anhydrite can-not be used to produce plaster of Paris; hence, materials from deposits rich in anhydrite are finely ground and soaked in water so that gypsum is formed prior to further processing into plaster of Paris. Some anhydrite is used directly in the cement industry or as a soil conditioner or mineral filler.

The United States, which possesses gypsum-producing areas that are widely distributed (Figure 10.17), is the world's largest producer and consumer of gypsum and anhydrite. In fact, as much as 10 percent of the land area in the United States is underlain by gypsiferous rock, indicating that the United States' potential resources are superabundant (over 20 billion tons). The U.S. Bureau of Mines has, in fact, stated that reserves are sufficient for 2000 years at projected rates of production. For example, gypsum deposits in Texas and Oklahoma extend for more than 320 kilometers over a width of 32–80 kilometers with a thickness of up to 7 meters. Culberson County, Texas, is underlain by a gypsum bed covering more than 1500 square kilometers up to 20 meters thick. The most picturesque gypsum deposits are in the 700-square kilometers of snow-white dunes at White Sands National Monument in New Mexico (Figure 10.18). The widespread geologic occurrence and extensive use of gypsum is shown by the fact that it is produced in over 60 countries, with the United States, Canada, Germany, France, the former Soviet Union, Great Britain, Spain, and Italy as the major producers. With deposits so widespread and transportation costs so high

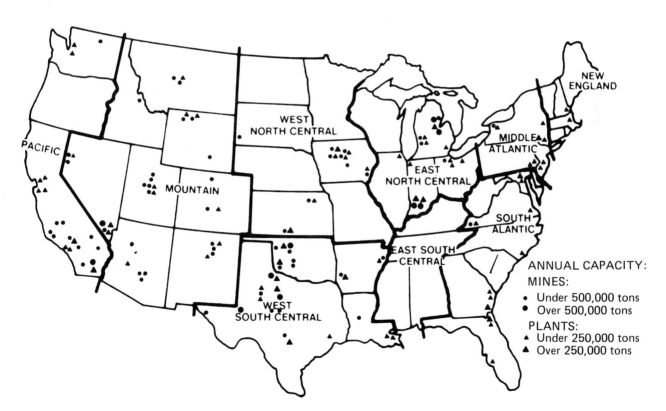

FIGURE 10.17. Gypsum is produced in a large number of areas in the United States. (From the U.S. Bureau of Mines.)

FIGURE 10.18.   The great sand dunes at White Sands National Monument in New Mexico are composed of gypsum that has weathered out of the nearby mountains and accumulated by the action of the wind. (Courtesy of White Sands National Monument, National Park Service.)

relative to the value of the commodity, there is only a limited world gypsum trade. The price of gypsum in the mid-1990s was about $15 per metric ton in the United States and about £10 per metric ton in Britain. In spite of the United States being the world's largest gypsum producer, it is also the world's largest gypsum importer, with most of the imports coming from Canada. Gypsum is mined using both open-pit and underground methods; apart from crushing and grinding, there is little processing of the ore prior to calcining.

Brick and Ceramic Products

A very large range of raw materials and a vast range of finished products are the province of the ceramics industry. The simplest of these are clay-rich muds, which are shaped and sun dried into adobe bricks (Figure 10.19). These bricks, often incorporating pebbles, straw, sticks, and other materials, decompose quickly in rainy areas but are quite durable in arid regions. In most of the developed world, the principal ceramic products are chiefly made from clays that can be molded into the desired shapes before firing. Struc-

FIGURE 10.19.   Sundried adobe bricks, as used in this building in a small town in Jujuy Province in northwestern Argentina, are widely used as construction materials in many arid regions of the world. The thatch helps to carry the rain, when it does occur, away from the the clay-rich bricks so that they do not break down. (Photograph by J.R. Craig.)

tural ceramics—such as bricks, tiles, sewer pipes, and related products—are a major part of that industry. We can do no more than mention a few examples of the raw materials used in this field, their availability, and their utilization.

Ceramic products require materials that make up the bulk of the product (skeleton formers or fillers), bonding agents to form glass, fluxes that aid in firing, and various materials that give special properties, such as color and durability, to the product. Clays are the usual skeleton formers, making up the major raw material used in the industry. The term **clay** refers to a group of very fine-grained minerals with hydrated layer structures at the atomic level. Many clays become plastic as they take up water, enabling them to be molded. Firing at high temperatures in kilns drives off the water and melts some of the particles, which then welds the material together. Rocks largely or wholly made up of clay minerals are mostly formed by weathering of those rocks (granites, basalts, gneisses) rich in alumino-silicate minerals, such as feldspar and mica. They may accumulate as residual deposits, or may be transported and deposited as sediments in lakes, seas, or oceans. Clays soon transform to other solid rocks when they are dehydrated and heated during burial, so they are found only near Earth's surface, not deeper in the crust. Like many of the other building materials, they are usually recovered by large quarrying operations in surficial deposits, with the quarries located as close as possible to the manufacturers and markets. In a number of pits, the clays are washed out by high pressure hydraulic water cannons (Figure 10.20). Some of the most important clay minerals are listed in Table 10.3 along with information on their compositions, properties, and geologic occurrences.

The clays used in the manufacture of bricks and tiles are very widespread, and reserves are so large that few countries make attempts to estimate them. The U.S. Bureau of Mines declares their deposits to be more than sufficient for another century of production at anticipated rates of growth. Potential resources are even larger. These structural ceramic products (bricks, tiles, sewer pipes, etc.) are normally manufactured by extruding the stiff plastic material, mixing the mined clay with 10–15 weight percent water, sending it through a die of appropriate shape, drying it under conditions of controlled humidity, and then firing it in a kiln. The dehydration and vitrification on firing results in a resistant material made of high silica glass, **mullite** ($3Al_2O_3 \cdot 2SiO_2$), pure silica, and other compounds welded together.

A relatively recent use of clays is the manufacture of catalytic converters for automotive exhaust systems (Figure 10.21). Clays, mixed with water and other silicate starting materials, is kneaded into a soft mass and extruded through a special die system to produce a continuous, roughly cylindrical tube with screenlike openings running its length. The tube is cut into proper lengths and fired at 1400°C (2550°F) to produce cordierite ($Mg_2Al_4Si_5O_{18}$), a mineral that has very

FIGURE 10.20. Clay pits, such as those in Cornwall in southwest England, provide a raw material used chiefly in the paper industry and also in the manufacture of fine china and ceramics. (Photograph courtesy of ECC Ltd.)

high thermal stability but expands very little when heated. This is then coated with catalytically active platinum by dipping it into solutions containing dissolved platinum salts.

There are also a number of special types of clays used in ceramics, deposits of which are more rare. **China clay,** or **kaolinite,** is a particularly pure hydrated aluminum silicate originally used for high-quality porcelain. This is now a relatively minor use compared to its importance as a filler.

Ball clay is largely made up of kaolinite and used in the manufacture of electrical porcelain, floor and wall tiles, and dinnerware. Deposits occur in Georgia, Tennessee, Kentucky, Devonshire, and India. In the manufacture of whiteware, ball clay is used to impart plasticity and dry strength; china clay imparts a whiter color. Finely ground silica, called potters flint, is also mixed with these clays to decrease the shrinkage that occurs during drying and firing; feldspar ($(Na, K, Ca)Al_{1-2}Si_{3-2}O_8$) is mixed as a flux to lower the firing temperature.

Glass

The glass industry uses substantial amounts of industrial minerals. Glass is actually made by melting together certain minerals that are cooled in such a way to prevent

TABLE 10.3

The names, compositions, structures, and some information regarding properties, occurrence, and uses of some industrially important clay minerals. Note that most mined clays are mixtures of several clay minerals.

Name	Composition	Structure	Properties, Occurrence, and Uses
Kaolinite Kaolinite Group or "Kandites" includes kaolinite, dickite, nacrite, and halloysite—see below.)	$Al_4[Si_4O_{10}](OH)_8$	One layer of linked SiO_4 tetrahedra bonded to a layer with Al in octahedral coordination (1 : 1)	Kaolinite can form the white high-purity material prized for porcelain making, as a filler in paper manufacture, and a wide range of other industries. May be of hydrothermal, residual, or sedimentary origin. Many refractory fire clays are essentially of kaolinite.
Halloysite	$Al_4[Si_4O_{10}](OH)_8 \cdot 8H_2O$	As above but with a single layer of water molecules between the (1 : 1) sheets	Halloysite occurs in residual and hydrothermal deposits. It is used for a variety of purposes including catalysis in the oil industry.
Illite (The Illite Group includes illite, hydro-micas, phengite, and glauconite.)	$K_{1-1.5}Al_4[Si_{7-6.5}Al_{1-1.5}O_{20}](OH)_4$	A sheet of octahedrally coordinated Al atoms sandwiched between two tetrahedral $(Si,Al)O_4$ sheets (2 : 1). K between these (2 : 1) sheets	Deposits are generally sedimentary in origin and contain other clay minerals. Used in common structural clay products such as bricks and tiles.
Montmorillonite (The Montmorillonite Group, or "Smectites," includes montmorillonite, nontronite, saponite, and hectorite—see below.)	$Na_{0.7}(Al_{3.3}Mg_{0.7})[Si_8O_{20}](OH)_4 \cdot nH_2O$	Again a (2 : 1) sheet with interlayer Na and H_2O	Montmorillonites are the essential clays in the "bentonites" produced by alteration of volcanic rocks. These are used in foundry clays and drilling muds. A moderate amount of montmorillonite is important in structural clay products to give plasticity. Also used in bleaching clays and adsorbents.
Hectorite	$(Ca,Na)_{0.66}Mg_{5.3}Li_{0.7}[Si_8O_{20}](OH)_4 \cdot nH_2O$	As above but with Mg and some Li instead of Al	Results from alteration of volcanic rocks. One use is in drilling muds.
Chlorite (The Chlorite Group includes "chamosite" and clinochlore.)	$(Mg,Al,Fe)_{12}[(Si,Al)_8O_{20}](OH)_{16}$	A (2 : 1) sheet with a further sheet of octahedrally coordinated Al,Fe,Mg. Hence a (2 : 1 : 1) sheet	Chlorite occurs as a component in many clays and shales mined for use in structural clay products.
Attapulgite (Members of this miscellaneous group include sepiolite and palygorskite.)	$Mg_5Si_8O_{20}(OH)_2 \cdot 4H_2O$	A chain-type structure. Double silica chains linked together by octahedral groups of oxygens and hydroxyls containing Al and Mg atoms	Deposits of sedimentary origin occur. Attapulgite is in the clays called fuller's earth (fulling is removal of grease from wool) valued for adsorbing properties.

crystallization. Consequently, glasses are made of atoms bonded without the repetitive ordering characteristic of crystals (Figure 10.22a).

The most important and common glass-forming material is silica, which is usually obtained from the quartz in sandstones. However, its high melting point (1713°C) and high viscosity in the liquid state make it difficult to melt and work; fused silica products are only used when their special properties (high softening point, low thermal expansion, resistance to corrosion, etc.) are essential. To lower the melting

temperature of silica to as low as 500°C (930°F), soda (Na_2O) is added. Because the resulting product, referred to as **water glass,** has no chemical durability and is soluble in water, lime is also added as a stabilizing agent. The first of these ingredients comes from sodium carbonate or sodium nitrate or from the processing of **rocksalt** (NaCl) and **limestone** ($CaCO_3$); the second comes from crushed limestone or dolostone. A few percent of alumina (Al_2O_3) is often also incorporated into the glass to further improve chemical resistance; feldspars from **pegmatites** and **aplites** are common sources of this ingre-

FIGURE 10.21. The substrate of the catalytic converter used to reduce automobile exhaust emissions is composed of synthetic cordierite ($Mg_2Al_4Si_5O_{18}$). The cordierite is made by baking a mixture of clays and additives at about 1500°C; platinum-bearing catalysts are added after synthesis. (Photograph courtesy of Corning, Inc.)

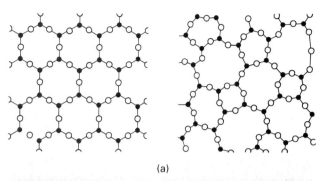

(a)

(b)

FIGURE 10.22. (a) Schematic diagrams illustrating the differences between a crystalline solid (left) and a glass (right). The crystalline material has a regular repeated atomic pattern, whereas the glass exhibits a more variable random pattern. (b) Glass is used to make thousands of items, including beautiful decorative pieces. (Courtesy of Corning, Inc.)

dient. The resulting product is the basic soda-lime-silica glass used for the bulk of common glass articles.

Smaller amounts of other minerals are used in glass manufacturing to give particularly desired properties or provide glass for more specialized applications. Borosilicate glass contains approximately 10–14 percent boron oxide (B_2O_3) derived from the mining of **borax.** The borosilicate glasses resist corrosion and withstand heating and cooling, so they are used in ovenware, tableware, and industrial glassware (such as the commercial product, Pyrex). High alumina glasses (15–30 weight percent Al_2O_3) are used in the manufacture of fibers and certain cooking utensils. Alumina for the glass industry is obtained from feldspar-rich rocks, such as pegmatites, aplites, and also **nepheline syenite,** an igneous rock made largely of feldspar and **feldspathoid** minerals. Lead crystal glass may contain as much as 37 percent lead oxide (PbO) for which red lead is the basic raw material, generally obtained as a by-product of base metal mining (see Chapter 8). This glass is used for high-quality tableware and certain optic uses (Figure 10.22b).

Small amounts of a wide range of substances are used to color glass; commonly, these are the oxides of metals such as chromium, cobalt, nickel, copper, iron, vanadium, manganese, and uranium. On the other hand, in producing high-quality colorless glass, iron oxide impurity in the sand and limestone raw materials may be a problem. This is overcome with a decolorizing agent, most commonly made up of selenium oxide, cobalt oxide, or certain other oxides of the rare earth elements. These additives absorb colors not absorbed by the iron oxides, hence canceling their effect to the observer. The decolorizing agents are among the most expensive materials used in the glass industry. Small amounts of chemicals, such as sodium sulfate (Na_2SO_4) and arsenic oxide (As_2O_3), and mineral products, such as fluorite (CaF_2) and rocksalt (NaCl), are also used as refining agents. The two basic raw materials used to make glass—sand and limestone—are widely distributed in Earth's crust and have low initial cost. Soda (Na_2O) is the most expensive of the major raw materials used to make the common types of glass, accounting for over 50 percent of the raw material cost per ton.

Glass production involves batch mixing of the raw materials and their melting together in pots and crucibles or large tanks, usually heated by burning oil or gas. After forming, it is slowly cooled, or **annealed,** to reduce internal stresses. During this stage, it may be rolled out to form plate glass or subjected to a wide variety of manufacturing processes that range from injecting the molten glass into molds to make bottles to the traditional mouth blowing and hand shaping techniques of art glass.

Today in the United States alone, glass production consumes about 15 million metric tons of high-purity silica sand, several million tons of limestone, more than 3 million tons of various sodium compounds, 500,000 tons of feldspar, and more than 350,000 tons of boron oxide containing minerals annually.

Glass occurs naturally in two forms: **fulgerites,** rare fused slender glass tubes that result from lightning strikes in sand, and **obsidians,** natural volcanic glasses formed when silicate magmas cool very quickly. Our ancestors found obsidian useful for making arrowheads, knives, and sometimes as jewelry or even money. The first human-manufactured glasses date back to about 3000 B.C. as glazes on ceramic vessels. By about 1500 B.C., glass vessels were produced, and by 50 B.C., glass blowing was an established art. Little is known about glass production after the fall of the Roman Empire, but it continued to develop in Italy, and an elaborate guild system of glass workers grew in Venice by the time of the Crusades in the twelfth century. Glass making remained primarily for artwork, containers, and drinking vessels well into the 1700s; it was not until the early 1800s that window glass became widely available, leading to a vast expansion in manufacturing facilities through the 1800s. The modern industry has continued to produce new types of glass with novel properties—fiberglass insulation, photosensitive glass, special reflective glass, and fiber optics. Fortunately, the abundance of most of the materials needed to produce glass will ensure its future availability, and the likely development of glasses with new properties should result in even wider applications.

OTHER MAJOR INDUSTRIAL MINERALS

All the substances discussed in this chapter and Chapter 9 could normally be classed as **industrial minerals.** This class of materials excludes metallic ores, mineral fuels, and even gemstones, but it includes many other substances not previously described. It would be impossible to discuss all of them, but a number of the more important examples will be chosen. As we have already noted, these will include minerals and rocks valued because of the particular properties they possess. **Asbestos** minerals are fibrous materials that are strong, flexible, inert, and heat resistant. Many rocks and minerals are capable of withstanding great heat and are used to make refractory products, whereas others enable melting

of material in furnaces at lowered temperatures providing **fluxes.** Other minerals and rocks are used simply as **fillers** or bulking agents in a wide range of products because they are inert and harmless. More specialized minerals are required for **pigments** or coloring agents, whereas a mineral such as **barite** finds industrial applications because of its high density combined with inertness, **diamond** because of its hardness, or **zeolites** because of their unusual crystal structures.

Asbestos

Asbestos is not a single mineral; the term refers to a number of silicate minerals that occur as fibrous crystals (Figure 10.23a). Hence, the definition of asbestos is complicated because the term is based upon mineral habit, or form. The U.S. Bureau of Mines, summarizing the definition given by the American Society for Testing and Materials in 1984, says, "Asbestos is a term applied to six naturally occurring minerals exploited commercially for their desirable physical properties, which are in part derived from their asbestiform [fibrous] habit. The six minerals are the serpentine mineral chrysotile and the amphibole minerals grunerite asbestos (also referred to as amosite), riebeckite asbestos (also referred to as crocidolite), anthophyllite asbestos, tremolite asbestos, and actinolite asbestos. Individual mineral particles, however processed and regardless of their mineral name, are not demonstrated to be asbestos if the length-to-width ratio is less than 20:1 (Table 10.4). The remarkable properties of asbestos minerals are chiefly the result of their crystalline structures. For example, chrysotile (Figure 10.23a) has a structure in which silica and magnesium hydroxide atomic layers are rolled up to form *scrolls,* with several such scrolls making an individual fiber (Figure 10.23b).

Asbestos is valuable because the strong, flexible fibers can be separated, spun, and woven like organic fibers, such as cotton and wool. They also make flexible materials when embedded in a suitable matrix. Unlike organic fibers, these products are fire and heat resistant, stable in many corrosive environments, and good electrical and thermal insulators. They are also wear resistant and strong (Table 10.4). Only some asbestos is suitable in length and flexibility for spinning; chrysotile has the best spinnability, amosite and crocidolite are fair, and the others are poor. The length and flexibility of fibers will also vary within and between particular asbestos deposits. Asbestos is classified commercially on the basis of length of fiber and the degree of openness, or separation, of the fibers.

Asbestos is used in a wide range of products. Some of the well-known uses are in the motor industry—brake linings, clutch plates, and other friction materials—and in asbestos textiles used in the electrical industry. The single greatest use is in asbestos cement products where the large volume of short fibers unusable for spinning are bound in portland cement to make pipes, jackets shingle, sheets, or

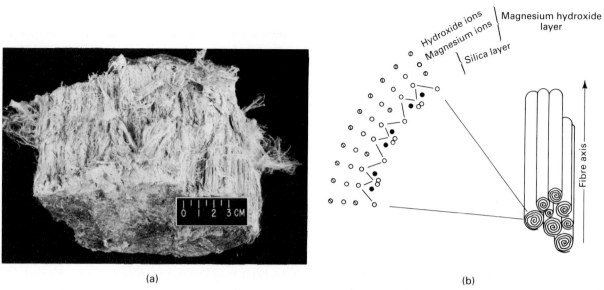

(a)   (b)

FIGURE 10.23. (a) Chrysotile asbestos has found many uses because it forms as long, flexible fibers. (Sample from Thetford, Ontario; photograph by S. Llyn Sharp.) (b) Schematic diagram of the structure of a fiber of chrysotile asbestos. Each crystal is in the form of a scroll made from a closely connected double layer with magnesium hydroxide units on its external face and silica units on its inner face. The details of a small section of the scroll show the structure of a double layer. Each fiber is made of several such scrolls. (Reproduced from A.A. Hodgson, "Chemistry and Physics of Asbestos" in L. Michaels and S.S. Chissick, *Asbestos*, vol. 1, Wiley and Sons, Ltd, 1979. Used with permission.)

TABLE 10.4

Types of asbestos fibers and their properties

Type	Formula	Color	Tensile Strength (p.s.i.)	Resistance to: Acids, etc.*	Heat**
Chrysotile	$Mg_6(Si_2O_5(OH)_4)_2$	White, gray, green, yellowish	80,000–100,000	Poor	Good
Crocidolite ("Blue asbestos")	$Na_2Fe_5(Si_4O_{11}(OH))_2$	Blue	100,000–300,000	Good	Poor
Amosite	$(Mg,Fe)_7(Si_4O_{11}(OH))_2$	Ash gray, brown	16,000–90,000	Good	Poor
Anthophyllite	$(Mg,Fe)_7(Si_4O_{11}(OH))_2$	Gray-white, brown, green	4000	Very good	Very good
Tremolite	$Ca_2(Mg,Fe)_{5-}(Si_4O_{11}(OH))_2$	Gray-white greenish, yellow blue	1000–8000	Good	Fair to good
Actinolite	$Ca_2(Mg,Fe)_{5-}(Si_4O_{11})OH)_2$	Greenish	1000	Fair	—

*Refers to resistance to dissolution in 25% HCl, CH_3COOH, H_3PO_4, and H_2SO_4 (and also NaOH) at room temperature for long periods and boiling temperature for short periods.
**Refers to weight loss on heating at temperatures of ~200–1000°C for 2 hours due to loss of OH.

corrugated and flat boards. The addition of asbestos increases the strength or flexibility of these products. It is also added to some papers, millboards, paints, putties, and plastics to provide desirable properties.

Chrysotile asbestos, which makes up the great majority of world production, is formed during the alteration of magnesium-rich (ultramafic) rocks, such as **peridotite** and **dunite.** This alteration by hydrous solutions produces the serpentine minerals antigorite, lizardite, and chrysotile, all of which are hydrated magnesium silicates. Many ultramafic rocks have undergone this process of **serpentinization,** but few contain workable deposits of chrysotile asbestos. Formation of such deposits requires an unusual combination of faulting, shearing, folding, serpentinization, and metamorphism of the host rocks. Many mountain belts around the world contain bodies of ultramafic rock that have been serpentinized. Commonly, these rocks are parts of **ophiolite complexes,** a name given to masses of mafic and ultramafic rocks with associated volcanic rocks originally formed as part of Earth's crust beneath the oceans, then thrust onto the continents during mountain building.

Because only a very small fraction of serpentine bodies contain commercially exploitable asbestos, the availability of this commodity is similar to that of scarce metals. World production is dominated by the former Soviet Union and Canada which contribute about three-quarters of the total tonnage (Table 10.5). The Republic of South Africa is a major producer of chrysotile and the only large producer of crocidolite and amosite. Total world reserves are estimated to be in excess of 100 million tons and will likely be adequate for the foreseeable future. Canadian production of chrysotile comes mainly from the eastern townships of Quebec where the deposits lie in a serpentine belt extending from Newfoundland down into Vermont. The deposits of the eastern townships are good examples of the location of asbestos ore within the serpentinized rocks of an ophiolite suite. Other

Canadian deposits occur in Ontario, within the Rocky Mountains in British Columbia, and in the Yukon. Major producing areas for chrysotile in Russia occur in the Ural Mountains (Bajenova District). Crocidolite and amosite are mined in South Africa where they occur in banded ironstones. Anthophyllite is mined in Finland; small deposits are worked for tremolite in Italy. Most asbestos mining is from open pits, with some underground mining of deeper deposits of unsuitable shape for surface exploitation. The ore is crushed and milled as a dry process with screening to separate impurities.

Asbestos has been known and used in small quantities for thousands of years, but it was not until the late nineteenth century that it became important to industry. The modern industry grew from processing Quebec-mined asbestos in England and Italy. In 1900, the total production was 200–300 thousand metric tons, and it has been estimated that the cumulative world total production to 1930 was about 500 million metric tons. After that time, the use of asbestos accelerated so rapidly that, in 1979 alone, world production was about 500 metric tons. However, the health hazards associated with asbestos have had a profound effect on its use in the United States, where consumption dropped from a high of 803 thousand metric tons in 1973 to only 31 thousand metric tons in 1993. World consumption reached a peak (about 5 million metric tons) in 1976 and remained above 4 million metric tons per year until 1990, but it has since dropped to less than 3 million metric tons (Figure 10.24).

Although the relationship between asbestos and various diseases has received attention in the last 20 years, health problems associated with asbestos were evident before 1900, within 20 years of the first factory production. Between 1890 and 1895, 16 of 17 workers in a French asbestos weaving factory died, and their deaths were attributed to the asbestos dust. Asbestosis, a disease resulting from the inhalation of very fine particles of asbestos dust, was first recognized in 1906 and completely described in 1927. The asbestos fibers in the lungs cause the formation of scar tissue (fibrosis) (Figure 10.25), resulting in fatigue and breathlessness after some years. Other diseases associated with asbestos exposure include lung cancer (which develops in about 50 percent of asbestosis sufferers) and mesothelioma, a rare cancer only associated with the presence of crocidolite. Smoking promotes the cancers in the lungs.

In most applications, asbestos fibers are totally encapsulated in various matrix materials, cannot be inhaled, and do not pose a health risk. However, when asbestos fibers are free during mining and processing, drilling and sawing, or deterioration of the matrix (e.g., breakdown and peeling of old asbestos-bearing paints), they constitute a major health hazard. The deadly consequences of asbestos exposure have led to increasingly stringent rules concerning its use. In 1985, the United States Environmental Protection Agency (EPA) proposed banning many asbestos-containing products (pipes, flooring, tiles) and phasing out the remaining uses of asbestos over a 10-year period.

TABLE 10.5

Producers of asbestos, 1993*

Country	Production (m.t. × 10^3)	Total %
United States	14	0.5
Russia	1000	36.0
Canada	515	18.6
Korea	400	14.4
China	240	8.6
Bulgaria	237	8.5
Zimbabwe	150	5.4
South Africa	100	3.6
All others	119	4.3
WORLD TOTAL	2775	

From the U.S. Bureau of Mines.
*Reserves are listed as large and resources are listed at 200 million tons.

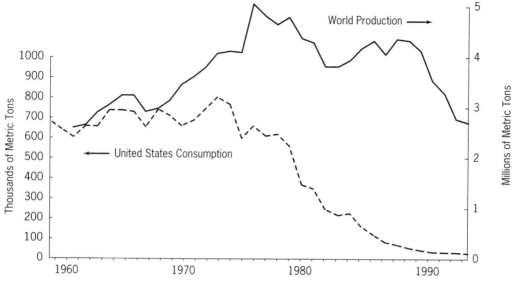

FIGURE 10.24. Worldwide production of asbestos peaked in 1976 but began to drop in the late 1980s. Consumption in the United States gradually rose until about 1973; it has since dropped dramatically because of concerns about its impacts on human health. (From the U.S. Bureau of Mines.)

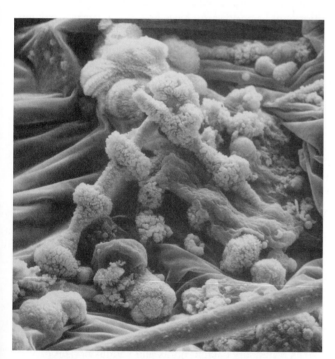

FIGURE 10.25. Scanning electron microscope photograph of asbestos fibers in an autopsied human lung. The asbestos fibers have been overgrown by iron-rich materials as the body tried to protect itself from the effects of the asbestos. (Photograph by Lesley S. Smith and Anne F. Sorling; from "Health Effects of Mineral Dusts," Mineralogical Society of America, *Reviews in Mineralogy*, vol. 28. Used with permission.)

Subsequently, there have been numerous additional EPA rulings banning the use of asbestos in various materials and some court orders overturning various regulations. One important ruling by the United States Occupational Safety and Health Administration (OSHA) in 1992 removed the non-asbestiform varieties of actinolite, anthophyllite, and tremolite from the list of materials covered by legislation on asbestos. Because of the widespread public concern over the asbestos health hazards and the large number of lawsuits brought on behalf of those exposed to asbestos, asbestos use will continue to decline. However, the health hazards of asbestos create a dilemma for some parts of the mineral industry because no other natural or synthetic material has been found to exhibit the qualities of strength, chemical inertness, and durability of asbestos and at such a low cost.

According to Dr. M. Ross of the U.S. Geological Survey, crocidolite and amosite have been shown to be far more dangerous than the chrysotile asbestos, which accounts for about 90 percent of total usage. Careful thought must be given to the costs of removal of asbestos-containing materials and the imposition of rigorous safety standards. For example, there is no evidence that ingesting asbestos in drinking water causes disease. Furthermore, the removal processes often liberate more asbestos dust than was present from its original applications.

Refractories, Foundry Sand, and Fluxes

Refractories are materials that can withstand high temperatures without cracking, spalling, or reacting despite contact with molten metals, slags, or other substances. Not only do refractories have to withstand such temperatures, but they also may be subjected to abrasion, impact, sudden temperature change, chemical attack, and high loads under extreme conditions. They provide linings for the furnaces used to smelt and refine metals and produce alloys, for the furnaces or kilns used in the ceramic industry and in glass and cement manufacture, and for coke ovens or boilers used in gas or electric plants. A host of other uses range from lining incinerators to manufacturing spark plugs for automobiles.

The industrial minerals now used in the greatest quantities to make refractories are clays that have traditionally been called **fire clays.** These are often found beneath coal seams in a sequence of sedimentary rocks. The dominant clay mineral present is kaolinite with various impurities that affect its properties, such as its plasticity. Fire clays can be molded and shaped to make bricks, tiles, or more elaborately shaped products before being fired. The heat resistance of such products ranges from 1500°C–1650°C, and they have a wide range of applications as furnace and boiler linings. Fire clays are also used in the manufacture of refractory cements. Important sources of these clays are found in England, Germany, Pennsylvania, Georgia, and Alabama. The United States production of fire clay is approximately 3 million metric tons; very large reserves of this material exist worldwide.

Silica (SiO_2) in its various natural forms is commonly used to manufacture refractories. Some sandstones are directly cut into bricks; alternatively, quartzite or quartz itself may be crushed and bonded with lime to make silica bricks. Such bricks do not soften at temperatures much below their melting point (approximately 1700°C) and are used in many metallurgical processes. Other refractories are made using bauxite and other forms of natural alumina, such as **diaspore** ($Al_2O_3 \cdot H_2O$). The aluminosilicate minerals (**sillimanite, andalusite, kyanite,** which are all **polymorphs** of Al_2SiO_5) are also used to make high-alumina refractories. These minerals are common in metamorphic rocks, and concentrations mined as commercial deposits occur in South Africa (andalusite), Sweden (kyanite), Australia (sillimanite), and the United States (in Virginia, California, and Nevada). High-alumina refractories can withstand temperatures up to 1800–2000°C. Magnesia (MgO), produced from magnesium in seawater and from quarried magnesite and dolomite, is an important component in many refractories used in the steel industry. Some of the best raw materials for high-temperature refractories are chromite and **zircon** ($ZrSiO_4$). Chrome refractories are widely used in steel mills, whereas zirconia (ZrO_2), which will withstand temperatures up to 2500°C, is used for refining precious metals. Zircon, providing the raw materials for these refractories, comes from beach sands in India, Brazil, Australia, and Florida.

Foundry sand is used to make the molds to cast molten metals. The most widely used foundry sand is a mixture of silica (SiO_2), clay, and water known as **greensand.** In some cases, the silica is clay-free and dredged from lakes or taken from dunes, then washed, graded, and dried. Clay (commonly **bentonite**), water, and some cellulose for binding properties are added. There are also natural molding sands that contain sufficient clay to be used directly in the foundry. Other minerals that are sometimes used instead of silica for foundry sands include **olivine** (($Fe,Mg)_2SiO_4$), zircon ($ZrSiO_4$), and chromite (($Fe,Mg)(Cr,Al,Fe)_2O_4$). The refractory properties of chromite vary with its exact composition of Fe/Mg, Cr/Al, and Cr/Fe ratios. The particular type of "sand" used will depend on the nature of the casting operation. In general, raw materials for producing foundry sands are widespread and not in short supply; annual production in the United States, for example, is about 30 million metric tons.

In contrast to the refractories and foundry sands that are valuable because they resist high temperatures and can be used to contain molten metals, **fluxes** help melt material during smelting or in operations like **soldering, brazing,** and welding. The fluxes used in smelting are aimed at efficiently separating the waste products from the metal in the form of a **slag.** The slag must have a relatively low formation and melting temperature, must be fluid at smelting temperatures, must have an appreciably lower specific gravity than the metal, and must not dissolve appreciable amounts of the smelted metal. Common fluxing materials include limestone, silica, and **fluorspar.** Limestone is a *basic* flux used in ferrous and nonferrous metallurgy; calcium oxide is formed when the limestone decomposes and produces slags of low specific gravity and low fusion temperatures during the smelting of copper and lead ores; it is also used in iron and steel making. Silica, an *acid* flux, is also used in steel making, whereas fluorspar is a *neutral* flux widely used to make slags more fusible and fluid. Limestones, quartzites, and sandstones suitable for use as fluxing agents are relatively widespread throughout the world. Fluorspar deposits, which have precipitated from relatively low temperature **hydrothermal fluids,** are widespread but often small and impure.

Soldering and **brazing** are metallurgical operations in which a joint forms using a filler metal of different composition and lower melting point than the joined pieces. Fluxes act to aid the spread of the solder or braze and mop up impurities, such as oxide coatings, that may hinder the formation of a successful joint. In soldering, which differs from brazing only in being done at a lower temperature (about 425°C), fluxes may contain various chlorides of zinc, ammonia, sodium, and tin along with various organic compounds and acids. Brazing fluxes commonly contain borax and various borates or various fluorides and chlorides of sodium, potassium, lithium, and zinc. Fluxes are also used in welding, the joining of metals by heating with or without a filler metal. In this case, the compounds used in the fluxes include silica and oxides of manganese, titanium, aluminum, calcium, and zirconium. All industries using metals for construction and fabrication (for example, automobiles, ships, aircraft, and household appliances) make use of these techniques.

Filler and Pigments

Mineral fillers are fine-particle, inert, and cheap substances that are added to a great range of manufactured products to provide bulk or to modify the properties of the product by giving weight, toughness, opacity, or some other characteristic (Table 10.6). As can be seen, these materials range from **talc,** a very soft hydrated magnesium silicate best known for its use in cosmetics, through a variety of clays, to rocks such as limestone or pumice. Some major industries that use fillers include paper, paint, plastic, rubber, pesticide, detergent, and fertilizer industries. Many mineral substances have other uses and are discussed elsewhere in this book.

Several of the clay minerals or rocks provide useful fillers because of their fine particle size. Kaolin, although originally used in the manufacture of fine porcelain, is now used in large amounts by the paper industry (see Box on page 352). The best quality clays, which are of high purity and whiteness, are used to coat high gloss papers (Figure 10.26). The United States and Great Britain are the world's principal producers of kaolin clays. The United States deposits occur as clay sediments and kaolinitic sands of late Cretaceous

TABLE 10.6

The more important mineral fillers

Substance	Composition	Useful Properties/Major Applications
Asbestos*	See page 346	Fibrous and strong; building materials, tiles, plastics, etc.
Barite*	$BaSO_4$	Dense and inert; rubber, paint
Bentonite	Clayrock, a mixture of clay minerals (montmorillonite dominant)	Pesticides and detergents
Diatomite SiO_2	Sedimentary rock, dominantly from shells of small organisms (diatoms)	Porous and light, absorptive; paints, paper, plastics, pesticides
Fuller's earth	Clayrock, a mixture of clay minerals (dominant montmorillonite and attapulgite)	Absorptive; pesticides, greases, paper
Gypsum*	$CaSO_4 \cdot 2H_2O$	Low cost; paints, paper, cotton goods, pesticides
Kaolin* (China clay)	A pure clay mineral $(Al_4Si_4O_{10}(OH)_8)$	White color, low cost; paper, paint, adhesives, plastics, rubber, ink, pesticides
Limestone*	Rock, dominantly $CaCO_3$	Soft particles, soluble in acids, abundant and cheap; asphalt, fertilizers, insecticides, paints, rubber, plastic
Mica (muscovite)	Layer silicate $(KAl_2(AlSi_3)O_{10}(OH)_2)$	Layer structure and electrical insulation properties; roofing material, paint, rubber, wallpaper
Perlite*	See page 338	Lightweight; fines used in paint, drilling muds, plastic
Portland cement*	See page 339	
Pumice*	Vesicular volcanic rock	Stuccos, plasters, paint
Pyrophyllite	$Al_2Si_4O_{10}(OH)_2$	Soft platey structure; asphalt roofing, paint, rubber battery boxes
Rock dusts	Variable; commonly carbonates	Low cost, strong; asphalts and cheap fillers
Quartz (+ other silica)	SiO_2	Low cost, hard, inert; quartz paints, bitumens
Slate*	Rock comprised of silica and micaceous minerals	Low cost, inert, compatible with bitumens; roofing, sealing compounds, paints, hard rubber
Talc	$Mg_3Si_4O_{10}(OH)_2$	Soft platey structure, good adhesion; paints, rubber, roofing, insecticides, asphalt, paper, cosmetics, textiles
Vermiculite*	See page 338	Fines used; fertilizers, pesticides

*Discussed in detail elsewhere in the book. See index for relevant sections.

WHAT IS THIS PAGE MADE OF?

Most readers of this book know that paper is made from wood, but many probably do not realize that much of this page is also mineral matter. Paper gets its name from papyrus, a reedlike plant the ancient Egyptians would cut into thin slices for use as a writing medium. Modern paper, however, is now produced using techniques first discovered by a Chinese worker. In 105 A.D., Ts'ai Lun found that he could pound fibers of the inner bark of the mulberry tree into sheets.

Much of the paper used today, especially for newspapers, is still composed of the fibers from a variety of trees. Logs are cut into 1–2 centimeter chips that are chemically digested in sulfite or sulfate solutions to liberate the cellulose fibers. The masses of fibers, called *pulp*, are poured out on special wire-cloth belts where excess water is drained and the mass of crisscrossing fibers is then pressed between steam-heated cylinders and wound into large rolls. This paper can then be used directly in printing presses.

High-quality glossy papers, such as that used in this book and many magazines, are much more complex and may contain as much as 30–50 percent mineral matter. Figure 10.26 shows a cross section of a piece of paper similar to the page you are now reading. The inner-most zone of the paper is cellulose fiber; the second zone is calcium carbonate; and the outer-most zone is the clay mineral kaolinite. These minerals provide strength, counteract acid decomposition, and provide a smooth surface that will accept the high-quality prints and inks used by publishers. If the surface were composed of cellulose fibers or of porous mineral matter, the printing inks would blur and not permit high-quality image reproduction. The addition of calcium carbonate and clay increases the quality and cost of the paper, but it reduces the recyclability of the paper because it is difficult to separate these minerals from the cellulose fibers. The presence of the mineral matter is also apparent when the paper is burned because much ash remains.

The application of the calcium carbonate and clay is accomplished by spreading a paintlike slurry of water, bonding agents, and mineral matter on the paper as it moves at a rate of several meters per second. The slurry-coated paper is then passed through a series of large metal rollers, called calenders, that flatten and polish the surface of the paper.

The use of mineral-coated papers has increased a great deal in recent years. Today, paper coating constitutes the second largest single use of clay minerals; the first is for the making of bricks. Before the development of papyrus, the Egyptians carved in stone or impressed cuneiform writing into clay tablets. Today, we do not use clay tablets, but we are returning to the use of clay on our reading and writing surfaces.

---

through early Tertiary age in Georgia and South Carolina. Kaolin was probably derived from deeply weathered bedrock and deposited by a system of rivers. The mined material is 90 percent kaolite with quartz as the main impurity. British deposits occur in Cornwall and Devon and come from the **hydrothermal alteration** of feldspars in granite bodies (Figure 10.20).

Clays, such as **fuller's earth** and **bentonite**, occur in sedimentary sequences and probably come from the breakdown and alteration of volcanic ash. Bentonite is chiefly made of **smectite** group clay minerals such as **montmorillonite, saponite,** and **hectorite** (Table 10.3). Most bentonites appear to have formed from volcanic ash that was transported considerable distances in the atmosphere and then deposited into the sea or lakes where it broke down to form the constituent clay minerals. Commonly, parent volcanic materials are thought to have been **rhyolite** or **andesite** (Table 10.1). Some bentonites appear to have formed by hydrothermal activity and occur as irregular bodies in rocks showing

other evidence of hydrothermal alteration. Some hectorite deposits in California are thought to have formed by alteration of volcanic ash, or **tuff**, as a result of hot-spring activity in alkaline lakes. Most fuller's earth deposits are, in fact, bentonites, although there are also some consisting largely of the minerals **palygorskite (attapulgite)** and **sepiolite** (Table 10.3). These may not have formed from alteration of volcanic materials, possibly having been precipitated from seawater evaporating in a tidal-flat environment. The name *fuller's earth* comes from the process of **fulling,** that is removing the grease from wool or other organic fibers. Such clays, as well as being used as fillers, therefore have important applications because of their absorptive properties; they are used as filters and purifiers of oils, fats, and various other chemicals. **Diatomite,** a sedimentary rock made up of the siliceous skeletons of microscopic organisms called diatoms, also has important applications in purification and filtration (Figure 10.27). The United States is the world's leading producer from deposits in California, Washington, and Oregon.

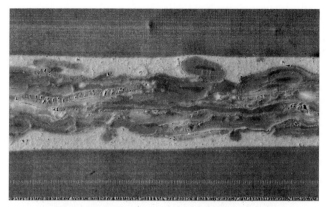

FIGURE 10.26. Scanning electron microscope photograph of a cross-section of coated paper such as that used in the production of this book and most magazines. The central wood pulp portion has been coated on both sides with minerals such as calcium carbonate, clays, and titanium dioxide. The minerals are applied in a paintlike slurry and then the paper passes through a large roller press, called a calender, which compresses and smooths it so it can receive high-quality images. (Courtesy of ECC Ltd.)

The addition of fillers commonly modifies the color of materials, whereas pigments are mineral-derived powders added solely to give color. From cave paintings of primitive humans to the modern production of paints for industrial and domestic use, mineral pigments have been employed to provide long-lasting color. Some pigments consist of untreated natural minerals; others are made by burning or subliming natural minerals. A third group is chemically manufactured. Natural pigments include the ochers, umbers, and siennas that come from iron oxides and hydroxides (**hematite, limonite**) sometimes mixed with clays and manganese oxides to provide permanent reds, yellows, and oranges. Roasting of some of these mixtures produces burnt umber or burnt sienna. Green colors result from silicates rich in iron and magnesium. White comes from gypsum, barite, and white clays. Chemical paints were once made with lead compounds; now little of this paint is used because of its high toxicity. Zinc oxide, barium sulfate, and titanium dioxide are all used in white paint manufacture, which consumes substantial amounts of these commodities. Natural pigments like the ochers, umbers, and siennas generally form as residual surface deposits through the alteration of ores and rocks. Certain areas are noted for particular pigments: yellow ocher comes from France and the United States, sienna comes from Italy; umber comes from Cyprus; and red oxides come from Spain.

Diamond and Other Abrasives

Abrasives, of which **diamond** is the most important, are materials used to cut, shape, grind, and polish modern alloys and ceramics. Diamond—the hardest, most dense form of carbon—is the hardest substance known. This hardness makes it essential for some uses and much more efficient than other abrasives. We think of diamonds most often as beautifully cut gemstones; however, most natural diamonds are small, poorly-shaped, and contain many imperfections, making them unsuitable for use as gems. In fact, only about 20 percent of natural diamonds are suitable gemstones; the remaining 80 percent are used in industry. Diamonds are classified using such terms as die stones, tool stones, dresser stones, drilling stones, bort, and diamond dust and powder. Their principal uses are in diamond saws, drilling bits, wire drawing bits, glass cutters, grinding wheels, and abrasives used for lapping and polishing.

For its formation, diamond requires pressures reached only at depths of 150 kilometers or more in Earth. Diamond-bearing rocks, called **kimberlites,** originate in the **mantle** of Earth and reach the surface in narrow pipelike vents, often no more than 50 meters in diameter (Figure 10.28). The reasons for the formation and location of the pipes remain a geologic puzzle.

Kimberlite pipes are rare; only about 1000 are known throughout the world (Figure 10.29). Of these, only about 500 are confirmed to contain diamonds and only 50–60 of them contain sufficient numbers of diamonds to justify

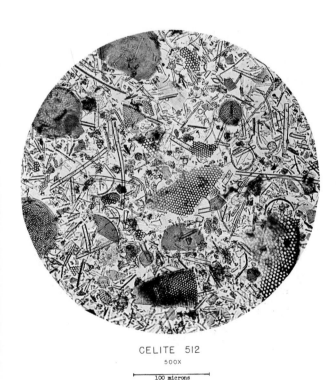

CELITE 512
500X

100 microns

FIGURE 10.27. Diatomite consists of the accumulated remains of siliceous shells of marine diatoms as shown in this photomicrograph from Lompoc, California. (Courtesy of the Mansville Sales Corporation.)

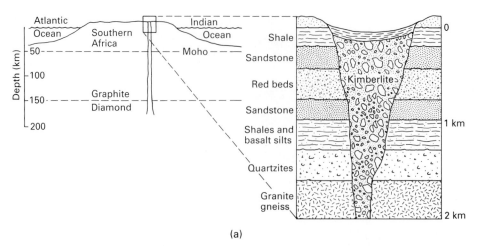

(a)

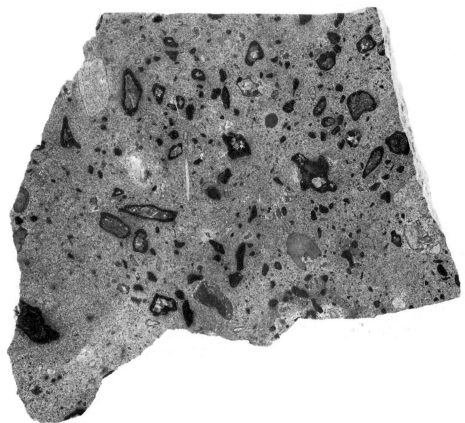

(b)

FIGURE 10.28.   (a) Kimberlite pipes are the only primary sources of diamonds. The pipes formed as violent gas-rich volcanic explosions carried mixtures of volcanic rocks and fragments of the surrounding rocks upward. Diamond-bearing pipes must have originated at depths of 150 kilometers or more because diamonds do not form at pressure conditions encountered at shallower depths (see also Figure 3.16). (b) Kimberlites consist of breccias with a wide variety of fragments representative of all rock types through which the pipe has intruded. Diamonds are recovered by crushing and carefully processing the Kimberlite. (Photograph by B.J. Skinner.)

FIGURE 10.29. Diamond-bearing kimberlites occur in all continents, but the greatest number of pipes are in central and southern Africa. The size of the circles shows, in a relative sense, the size of the deposits. In recent years, Australia has become the largest producer of industrial diamonds; new discoveries in Canada may lead to higher production in that country.

mining. South Africa remains the best known location for diamond pipes because of its long and interesting history (see Fig. 3.16), but it has now been surpassed in diamond production by several other countries (Table 10.7). The economic viability of a kimberlite pipe depends both upon the

TABLE 10.7

The principal producers of natural and synthetic industrial diamond

Country	Production (millions of carats)	
	Natural	*Synthetic*
United States	–	100.3
Australia	21.0	–
Botswana	5.0	–
Brazil	0.9	–
China	0.8	15.0
Ireland	–	60.0
Japan	–	30.0
Russia	8.0	60.0
South Africa	6.0	–
Zaire	12.0	–
All others	2.0	13.0
WORLD TOTAL	55.7	278.0

number of carats of diamond per ton of rock and the percentage of the diamonds that are of gem quality. The kimberlites of South Africa average only about 0.3 carats per ton, but about 20 percent of the stones are of gem quality. In contrast, the Argyle mine in Australia, the world's largest diamond producer with greater than 20 million carats per year, has a grade of 6 carats per ton, but it contains only about 5 percent gem-quality stones.

Because diamonds are very hard and resistant to weathering, they also accumulate in **placer** deposits. In fact, about 40 percent of the diamonds mined today come from placers. Although placers can occur anywhere that rivers drain from kimberlite-bearing rocks, today's largest lie along several hundred miles of the coast of Namibia in southwestern Africa. The overall grades are low, but the percentages of gem-quality stones are high (up to 95 percent), and recovery is very easy because the stones are simply mixed in with normal quartz beach sand. Diamond recovery from any source relies upon its high specific gravity of 3.52, its ability to stick to grease, and its characteristic visible fluorescence when exposed to X rays.

Diamond production figures are divided into two categories: (1) industrial and (2) gems. The industrial stones include virtually all small stones (called micros if they are less

SYNTHETIC DIAMONDS

"Diamonds Are a Girl's Best Friend," sang Marilyn Monroe. The same sentiment is being expressed by many scientists and engineers who have discovered that diamonds are more than just beautiful. Diamond is the hardest substance known, it has the highest thermal conductivity at room temperature, it is virtually inert to attack from chemicals, it is an excellent electrical insulator, it is transparent to light and X rays, and it is a superior semiconductor for electronic devices. The drawbacks to its widespread use have been its high cost and low availability in the forms desired. Natural diamonds vary widely in size and degree of perfection and are so valued as gemstones that their extensive use in electronics is impractical.

Recognizing that both high temperature and high pressure must have been required to form natural diamonds found in kimberlite pipes arising from Earth's mantle, scientists began serious efforts to synthesize diamonds in the early 1900s. Success came in 1954 when General Electric scientists in Schenectady, New York, heated graphite (another form of pure carbon) in the presence of a nickel or iron metal catalyst to about 1500°C and kept it at a pressure of 50,000–60,000 atmospheres. Under these conditions, carbon dissolves in the metal and regrows as crystals along the edges. After several hours, layers of small crystals up to 1 millimeter thick and 9 centimeters across could be formed. Unfortunately, the crystals were small and randomly shaped (Figure 10.30) and of little value for electronics. They are, however, quite inexpensive with production costs averaging much less than $1.00 per carat in the early 1990s. This has led to such a large scale production of this material, commonly called bort, that the world now produces many times more synthetic diamonds for industrial use than are mined (Table 10.7).

Scientists began to search for other methods of synthesis that could produce larger, sheetlike diamonds. Guided by a few initial successes in the 1960s, Japanese scientists in the 1980s began to solve the problems associated with a synthesis method known as chemical vapor deposition (CVD). In this technique, hydrogen gas is mixed with a hydrocarbon gas, such as methane, and heated to more than 2000°C using microwaves. The hydrocarbon gas decomposes and carbon precipitates out on a substrate as a single crystal film suitable for electronics. General Electric scientists announced in 1990 that they had successfully made diamond sheets up to 30 centimeters long and 4 centimeters wide using CVD. The cost of CVD synthesis was more than 100 times that of high-pressure synthesis, but it is expected to drop as techniques are perfected. CVD synthesis takes advantage of the fact that minerals can sometimes form even when they should not. Diamonds are actually only stable under the high temperature and pressure conditions of Earth's mantle. However, catalysts can sometimes promote crystallization under metastable conditions, that is, conditions under which some other mineral structure should form. Hence, CVD diamonds are created under conditions where graphite should form.

The development of new synthesis procedures, yielding larger diamonds at lower prices, has scientists and engineers anticipating the use of diamonds in integrated circuits in computers, on tweeters in stereo speakers, and even as scratch-proof coatings on glasses. In the early 1990s, two other diamond synthesis breakthroughs were also announced. (1) General Electric produced gem-quality synthetic diamonds larger than one-half carat, and DeBeers made a synthetic 5-carat gem diamond. (2) Scientists synthesized ultrapure diamonds, which are 99.9 percent composed of the isotope Carbon 12 (natural stones are 99 percent Carbon 12 and 1 percent Carbon 13) and have superior hardness and conductivity properties compared to natural stones. Diamonds may, indeed, be far more than just a girl's best friend.

than 0.45 millimeters) and many larger ones (if impure, cracked, or discolored). Industrial diamond production today is dominated by Australia and Zaire (Table 10.7), but South Africa, Russia, and Botswana are also major producers.

Diamond synthesis was a longtime goal for many scientists. Once it was realized that diamonds only formed within

Earth's mantle, there were many attempts to make diamonds using very high pressures and high temperatures. In 1955, General Electric announced the development of a process for the synthesis of industrial diamonds. This first commercially viable process for the manufacture of diamonds involved subjecting graphite to pressures greater than 1 million pounds per square inch (70,300 kilograms per square centimeter) and temperatures up to 2000°C in a sealed reaction vessel. The problem of promoting the transformation of graphite to diamond was solved by using molten nickel to dissolve the graphite; then they could recrystallize the carbon as diamond. This process spawned an industry that, by the mid-1990s, produced over 100 million carats a year, far in excess of world production of natural industrial diamonds (about 55 million carats in the mid-1990s). About two-thirds of all abrasive diamond grit now used is produced, with production taking place not only in the United States, but also in Sweden, South Africa, Ireland, Japan, and Russia. Although other diamond synthesis techniques have been developed, including some using explosive charges to generate very high pressures for very short times, most methods result in small diamonds (Figure 10.30). Larger gem-quality crystals have been made since about 1970 using processes that employ seed crystals. However, these processes are difficult and costly since growth must take place slowly to produce a quality, flaw-free crystal. The natural diamond is still preferred as a gemstone.

In recent years, very effective techniques to synthesize diamond films from carbon-bearing gases (especially methane) have been developed at low temperatures using radio frequency waves. This creates a whole new series of applications because a protective diamond coating could give many surfaces nearly unlimited lifetimes. Furthermore, diamond has very useful electrical properties, leading to many potential applications of thin diamond films as semiconductors and even computer chips.

Gem diamonds are priced arbitrarily according to human desires and range from hundreds to thousands of dollars per carat, depending on size, color, and clarity. In contrast, the prices of the industrial stones (bort) reveal the real value, which had dropped to less than $0.60 per carat in the mid-1990s. Larger stones needed for special cutting dies are, of course, more expensive and may range up to $80 per carat.

Other important natural abrasives include **corundum, emery,** and **garnet.** Corundum, or hexagonal aluminum oxide, is the second hardest natural substance. It is used almost exclusively as a finely crushed material for lapping and polishing optical glass and metals. As with diamond, methods have been developed for the synthesis of corundum, most particularly by heating bauxite in an electric arc furnace with small amounts of coke to reduce impurities, especially iron.

Corundum could be completely replaced by many other abrasives, but it retains some usage because it can cut with a chisel-like edge rather than by scratching. The United States has no reserves of corundum, and the small amounts used are imported primarily from South Africa. Emery is a gray to black granular mixture of variable amounts of corundum, magnetite, spinel, hematite, garnet, and other minerals. It has been widely replaced by synthetic abrasives because of its variability, but it is still used in coated abrasive sheets, nonskid pavements, and in stair treads. Garnet remains a popular sheet abrasive for dressing wood and soft metals. However, much more garnet is used in sandblasting and as a powder for optical grinding and polishing. Garnet is almost exclusively an abrasive, with the United States contributing more than 95 percent of its world production and more than 80 percent of its use. This cubic silicate mineral that has no cleavage is extracted from metamorphic rocks, especially the very coarsely crystalline gneisses at North Creek, New York; here, individual garnet crystals are often 10–20 centimeters or more in diameter (Figure 10.31).

The development of lower-cost synthetic abrasives, such as α- and β-alumina, and various carbides and nitrides (materials of uniform quality, superior hardness, and comparable price to many natural abrasives) threatens the economic future of the natural abrasive industry.

Barite (BaSO$_4$)

The consumption of **barite** reflects the state of the world economy because barite is almost entirely used by the petroleum industry. Approximately 90 percent of world barite production is finely ground for drilling mud, which lubricates the drill stem, cools the drill bit, and seals off the walls of the hole. The remaining 10 percent is used for a variety of chemical applications, glass making, and medical and pharmaceutical purposes. Barite has long been used to enhance the visibility of body organs and vessels in X-ray images, but this use is slowly declining as new imaging procedures have been developed. Barite is very well suited for oil and gas drilling because its high density helps prevent blowouts that can occur when high pressures are encountered. World barite production has soared during this century, especially since the

FIGURE 10.30. Synthetic diamonds now constitute the world's major source of abrasive diamonds. There have been reports of the synthesis of gem-quality diamonds of more than one carat in size, but these have not yet appeared on the market. (Courtesy of General Electric Company, Specialty Materials Department.)

FIGURE 10.31.   Garnet is a common mineral in many metamorphic rocks. It serves as an important abrasive material because it develops and retains sharp cutting edges when it is broken. Only rarely, however, are the crystals abundant or large enough to be economically exploited. This crystal is from Gore Mountain, New York, where crystals as large as 20 centimeters or more in diameter were long mined for use in abrasives. (Photograph by R.J. Tracy.)

1940s, as oil demands and oil drilling have rapidly increased (Figure 10.32). Barite occurs worldwide in vein and cavity-filling deposits, in weathered residual surface deposits, and in bedded accumulations. The origin of these deposits is not entirely clear, but most barite appears to have been deposited from hydrothermal solutions as fracture fillings or as chemical precipitates on the seafloor near volcanic vents. The world's principal producer is China with nearly 2 million metric tons per year in the 1990s. Barite is mined in many countries, often for their own local oil industries. The United States has long been the major consumer of barite, but the slowing of the United States domestic oil exploration and drilling program has seen a drop in the demand for barite from more than 2 million metric tons in 1983 to less than 1 million metric tons in 1993.

Zeolites

The **zeolites** compose a group of hydrous aluminum silicates of sodium, calcium, potassium, and, to a lesser extent, barium and magnesium. They have tetrahedral crystal structures in which clusters (SiO_4 and AlO_4) of atoms are joined together to form frameworks within which are large cavities containing water molecules (Figure 10.33). These cavities may be interconnected in up to three directions. When zeolites are

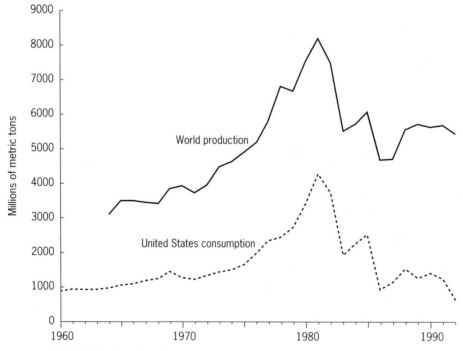

FIGURE 10.32.   The production of barite, which is used primarily in drilling for oil, follows the price of oil. Barite production peaked in the early 1980s when the high prices of oil stimulated additional reserve drilling. Since that time, the world production of barite has remained about 5 million metric tons, and the U.S. production has declined. (Data from the U.S. Bureau of Mines.)

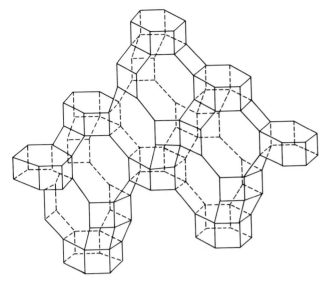

FIGURE 10.33. Schematic representation of the crystal structure of the zeolite mineral chabazite. The framework outlined consists of silicon and aluminum tetrahedra. Each framework unit contains a cavity connected to adjacent cavities by channels. (After Breck and Smith, *Scientific American,* 200 (1959) p. 881.

TABLE 10.8

Important zeolite minerals

Name	Formula
Analcime	$NaAlSi_2O_6 \cdot H_2O$
Chabazite	$(Ca,Na)_2Al_2Si_4O_{12} \cdot 6H_2O$
Clinoptilolite	$(Na_2K_2Ca)_3Al_6Si_{30}O_{72} \cdot 24H_2O$
Erionite	$(Na_2K_2Ca)_{4.5}Al_9Si_{27}O_{72} \cdot 27H_2O$
Faujasite	$(Na_2Ca)_{1.75}Al_{3.5}Si_{8.5}O_{24} \cdot 16H_2O$
Ferrierite	$(K,Na)_2(Mg,Ca)_2Al_6Si_{30}O_{72} \cdot 18H_2O$
Heulandite	$(Ca,Na_2)_4Al_8Si_{28}O_{72} \cdot 24H_2O$
Laumontite	$Ca_4Al_8S_{16}O_{48} \cdot 16H_2O$
Mordenite	$(Na_2K_2Ca)Al_2Si_{10}O_{24} \cdot 7H_2O$
Phillipsite	$(K_2Na_2Ca)_2Al_4Si_{12}O_{32} \cdot 12H_2O$

dehydrated by heating to approximately 350°C, a crystal permeated with a system of channels results. The sizes of these channels (apertures are approximately $2.5–7.5 \times 10^{-8}$ centimeters) are such that they allow certain smaller molecules to pass through them, but not larger ones. Hence, zeolites have great commercial importance as molecular sieves.

Zeolitic tuffs, which are altered volcanic ash deposits, have been used for more than 2000 years as lightweight building materials and in pozzolan cement. However, since the 1950s, zeolite minerals have been extracted to make use of their unique **ion exchange** and adsorption properties. Early zeolite applications included water softening agents to extract calcium and magnesium from drinking water and replace it with sodium. Subsequently, applications have greatly increased and include the selective extraction of radioactive elements, such as cesium-137, from contaminated water, poisonous ammonium ions from sewage and agricultural effluent, sulfur and nitrogen oxides from smokestack gases, and CO_2 and H_2S from natural gas.

Far more important today than the natural zeolites are the hundreds of thousands of kilograms of synthetic zeolites prepared from solutions of sodium hydroxide, sodium silicate, and sodium aluminates. Synthetic zeolites have larger structural cavities and may be prepared with structural sites allowing them to be used to break down large organic molecules in oil refining. As a result, these synthetic zeolites now serve as cracking catalysts at every major oil refinery. The use of zeolites is more efficient than using simple thermal cracking (merely heating the oil to break it up into smaller

hydrocarbon units) and may be used to add hydrogen to the oil. This process of hydrogenation results in an increased yield of gasoline from every barrel of oil.

Zeolites (Table 10.8) occur in a wide variety of rock types although, prior to about 1950, most examples came from fractures, or **vesicles,** in igneous rocks. In these environments, zeolites form good, readily identifiable crystals that are sought by museums and collectors, but they do not occur in the quantities necessary for economical recovery. In recent years, zeolites have been recognized as important constituents in a variety of sedimentary rocks and in metamorphic rocks formed under conditions of relatively low temperature and pressure. Clay minerals, feldspars, and feldspathoids can react with pore waters during metamorphism or in buried sediments to form zeolites. In sediments, the breakdown and reaction of **volcanic glass** appears to have been the way in which zeolites formed, although processes related to weathering or alteration by hydrothermal solutions may also occur.

Commercial interest centers on the bedded, near-surface sedimentary zeolite deposits. These include deposits formed from volcanic material in saline lakes a few centimeters to a few meters thick that commonly contain nearly monomineralic chabazite and erionite. Deposits formed in marine environments or from groundwater systems may be several hundred meters thick and are characterized by clinoptilolite and mordenite. Zeolites are mined in the United States, Japan, Italy, Hungary, Yugoslavia, Bulgaria, Mexico, and Germany. The use of natural zeolites continues to increase as new applications are developed, but synthetic zeolites that can be tailored for special purposes will provide competition.

Bituminous Materials

Bitumen is the general name for a group of materials made up of mixtures of hydrocarbons and includes petroleum, asphalts, asphaltites, pyrobitumens, and mineral waxes. Petroleum, a fossil fuel, is important as the source of a wide range of organic products including plastics and other polymers widely used in industry, often in conjunction with many other mineral products. **Asphalt** is a solid or near solid hydrocarbon found in native form in fissures and pore spaces in rocks and as lakes. It probably formed by slow natural fractionation of crude petroleum at or near Earth's surface. Because of its glue-like nature and waterproofing ability, it is widely used in road construction, flooring, roofing, and more specialized sealing compounds. Although most asphalt is refined from crude petroleum, rock asphalts (bituminous sandstones and limestones) are mined in parts of the United States (e.g., Kentucky, Texas, Oklahoma, and Louisiana) and certain European countries (France, Germany, Italy, and Switzerland) where they are used for local industries. Bitumen content is generally 3–15 percent. The best known of the rich lake deposits is on Trinidad, West Indies, where the lake covers 114 acres and reaches 285 feet deep.

Asphaltites, pyrobitumens, and mineral waxes are other natural bitumens. The first two are dark solids mostly found in veins and fissures; mineral waxes are softer, as the name suggests. These relatively uncommon materials have a variety of uses ranging from paints, inks, and varnishes to rubber and plastic manufacturing.

GEMSTONES

The first uses of gems date back to ancient times; gems are thought by some to have been worn before clothes. The designation *gemstone* is generally accepted to refer to materials appropriate for personal adornment. Gems are a unique type of resource because their very small amounts have extremely high values. Hence, gems are the most valuable Earth resources per unit size or unit weight. A flawless diamond no more than a centimeter across can cost many tens of thousands of dollars, while a beautiful emerald can be even more expensive.

The most important properties of gem materials are color, luster, transparency, durability, and rarity. Size alone is not of great importance; thus, a perfect small stone is commonly worth far more than a large imperfect or poorly cut stone.

Of the 3000 or so known mineral species, only about 100 have attributes that allow them to be considered gems (Table 10.9). Gems are commonly designated as precious (diamond, ruby, sapphire, emerald, and pearl) or semiprecious (all others) on the basis of market price, but all species exhibit wide variations in quality. Long used in jewelry because of their beauty (Plate 55), gems have also been viewed as endowing their wearers with mystical powers. Diamond, with a hardness greater than any other substance, was considered a symbol of strength. Sapphire has been viewed both as a symbol of heavenly bliss and faithfulness and as protection for its owner against poverty and snake bites (Figure 10.34). Ruby was believed to bring peace, love, and hap-

TABLE 10.9

Principal types of precious and semiprecious gems

Name	Composition
Amber	Hydrocarbon (fossil resin)
Beryl:	$Be_3Al_2Si_6O_{18}$
Aquamarine	"
Emerald	"
Chrysoberyl:	$BeAl_2O_4$
Catseye	"
Corundum:	Al_2O_3
Ruby	" (with trace of Cr)
Sapphire	" (with trace of Ti)
Diamond	C
Feldspar:	$KAlSi_3O_8$
Amazonstone	"
Garnet	$(Ca,Mg,Fe)_3(Al,Fe,Cr)_2(SiO_4)_3$
Jadeite	$Na(Al,Fe)Si_2O_6$
Peridot	Mg_2SiO_4
Opal	Hydrous silica
Pearl	$CaCO_3$
Quartz:	SiO_2
Agate	"
Amethyst	"
Jasper	"
Onyx	"
Spinel	$MgAl_2O_4$
Topaz	$Al_2SiO_4(F,OH)_2$
Turquoise	$CuAl_6(PO_4)_4(OH)_8 \cdot 5H_2O$

piness to its possessor, and emerald was thought to confer riches, fame, and wisdom to its wearer. In contrast, some well-known gemstones have stories of curses that befall those who own or wear them.

Gems are measured by weight; the unit of weight employed by jewelers is the carat (0.2 grams). Small stones are also commonly measured in points, each point being $\frac{1}{100}$ of a carat. The size of gems ranges from the small chips to crystals measured in hundreds of carats. The largest cut gem known is the Brazilian Princess, a 21,327-carat (about 9 ½ lb), light blue topaz found in eastern Brazil in the 1960s. Many large and beautiful diamonds have been found; among the most famous are the Hope Diamond (a blue, 44-carat stone from India now in the Smithsonian Institution's Museum of Natural History) and the Star of Africa (a colorless, 530-carat stone from South Africa) that is held in The Crown Jewels in London.

For thousands of years, gems were used as they were found without cutting or polishing; however, from about 4000 B.C., gemstones have been engraved, drilled, and cut. Until the late middle ages, most gems were cut as flat slabs or rounded into a low dome shape called a *cabachon*. In the fifteenth century, the cutting power of diamond was discovered by gem workers in France and the Netherlands; soon modern cutting and polishing techniques were employed, and diamond abrasives were developed. Today, virtually all crystalline gems are cut and polished in order to provide the most effective display of light and color. Thus, diamonds are

(a)

(b)

FIGURE 10.34. (a) Naturally occurring sapphire in its typical six-side, barrel-like crystal. (b) Sapphire cut and polished into a form ready for mounting. (Photographs by Bart Curren; courtesy of the International Colored Gemstone Association.)

transformed from fragments and roughly equant crystals into lustrous and strikingly cut stones (Figure 10.35). The form into which a gem is cut depends upon its original size, shape, and impurities (Figure 10.36). The most favored cut for diamond is the *brilliant* cut with 58 facets, developed in Venice about 1700. This cut promotes the internal reflection of light to enhance the appearance of the diamond.

Since about 1900, techniques for the synthesis of several types of precious and semiprecious gems have been developed. Examples are sapphire, ruby, emerald, and spinel.

Millions of carats of diamonds are now synthesized for industrial purposes, but no procedures have yet proven economical for the production of gem-quality stones. Although several techniques for gem synthesis are now available, the most commonly used, particularly for sapphire and ruby, are fusion processes in which a carrot-shaped single crystal, known as a boule, is grown to several centimeters across and ten or more centimeters long. Many modern gemstones, both natural and synthetic, are treated to enhance their appearance. These processes include bleaching, staining, heat

(a)

(b)

FIGURE 10.35. (a) Uncut gem diamonds as recovered from diamonds in South Africa. Many of the crystals exhibit a crude octahedral shape. (b) *Brilliant* and *marquise* cut diamonds ready for jewelry mounting. The diamonds are cut to take advantage of their ability to reflect light internally to increase their sparkle. (Photographs courtesy of De Beers Consolidated Mines, Ltd.)

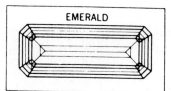

EMERALD

BRILLIANT

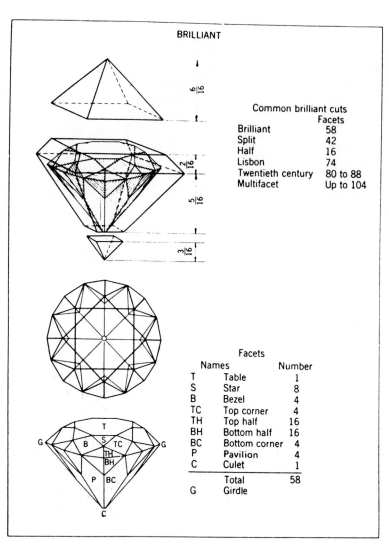

Common brilliant cuts

	Facets
Brilliant	58
Split	42
Half	16
Lisbon	74
Twentieth century	80 to 88
Multifacet	Up to 104

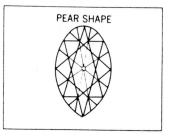

MARQUISE

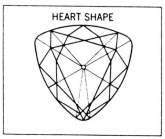

PEAR SHAPE

Facets

	Names	Number
T	Table	1
S	Star	8
B	Bezel	4
TC	Top corner	4
TH	Top half	16
BH	Bottom half	16
BC	Bottom corner	4
P	Pavilion	4
C	Culet	1
	Total	58
G	Girdle	

HEART SHAPE

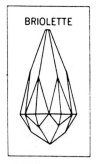

BEADS

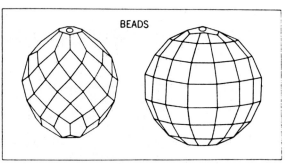

BRIOLETTE

UNCOMMON CUTS

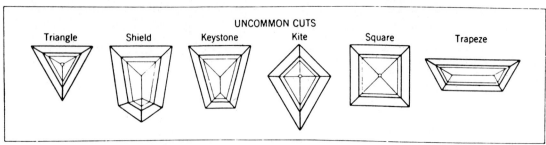

Triangle   Shield   Keystone   Kite   Square   Trapeze

FIGURE 10.36. The principal gemstone cuts used in jewelry today. The most popular cut for diamond is the brilliant. (From the U.S. Bureau of Mines, *Mineral Facts and Problems*, 1985.)

treating, and radiation treating. Other means of enhancement include using foils or dyes on the backs, gluing stones together, and using gels to fill in cracks and pits.

Gemstones occur in many parts of the world and have formed in such diverse environments as Earth's mantle (diamond), high grade regional and contact metamorphic rocks (ruby and sapphire), pegmatites (emerald), oysters (pearls), and trees (amber). So far as commerce is concerned, diamonds are by far the most important of gems, and South Africa has been the most important source of gem diamonds since their discovery there in the 1860s. These discoveries were of placer diamonds weathered out of diamond pipes, volcanic vents that have brought up material from Earth's mantle.

The largest diamond ever recovered was the Cullinan, which was found in 1905 in South Africa's Premier mine; it weighed 3106 carats (621.2 grams or 1.4 pounds) before cutting. Only one-half of the Cullinan was found because it had suffered breakage along natural cleavage planes. Despite all efforts, the other portion has never been found.

Placer diamonds are still being recovered, but the major mines today are the diamond pipes themselves, such as that at Kimberley (see Figure 3.16). In recent years, however, Botswana, Zaire, the former Soviet Union, and Australia have all become major and growing producers (Table 10.10). Diamonds were discovered at Argyle, Australia, in 1967 and production began in 1981. By the 1990s, it had become the largest producer in the world. There is no commercial diamond production in the United States; however, the Crater of Diamonds State Park near Murfreesboro, Arkansas, is open to the public and yields several gem-quality stones to visitors every year. Diamond-bearing kimberlite pipes have been known to exist in northern Colorado for some years, but their grades have never been sufficient to warrant mining.

Many diamonds have been found in the glaciated territories of North America, but their original sources, lying beneath the glacial tills, were not identified until 1990. Then a geologist, who had studied them for 10 years by tracking the glacial dispersal patterns of the kinds of minerals found

with diamonds, discovered a kimberlite pipe near Lac de Gras in the northern Northwest Territories of Canada. Subsequently, at least 25 additional pipes have been found in what appears to be one of the world's richest clusters of kimberlites. Some of the pipes are twice as rich as the typical South African pipes and contain good percentages of gem-quality stones. This discovery led to a claim-staking rush that rivaled the California Gold Rush. Canada could become the next South Africa in terms of diamond production, but the area must be evaluated and then the appropriate infrastructure (roads, power, water supplies, etc.) must be developed before diamond production can begin. Few data exist on the world's reserves of gemstones, but production has grown larger throughout the twentieth century and will likely continue to increase in the beginning of the next century.

Pearls are as unique as mined gems because they are a truly renewable gem resource. They form within the shell of oysters as the result of the deposition of concentric layers of calcium carbonate (in the form of the mineral aragonite) around a sand grain or other irritant. The occurrence of natural pearls is extremely unpredictable because only some oysters contain sand grains, and there is no way to know if a pearl is in an oyster except when it is opened. Cultured pearls result from the intentional placment of sand grains into oysters; the oysters are then allowed to live in ideal conditions for several years. Recently, this process has been accelerated by using seed spheres cut from oyster shells instead of small sand grains (Figure 10.37). In this way, the oysters require much less time to produce a pearl of larger size and, once the seed material has been coated by aragonite, the interior

TABLE 10.10

International production of gem diamond in 1993

Country	Production (millions of carats)	Total (%)
Australia	21.0	40.6
Botswana	10.0	19.3
Russia	8.0	15.5
South Africa	5.0	9.7
Zaire	3.0	5.8
Namibia	1.5	2.9
Angola	0.8	1.5
Brazil	0.6	1.2
All others	1.8	3.5
WORLD TOTAL	51.7	100

FIGURE 10.37. Cultured pearls are produced by placing a sand grain, or even a small sphere of oyster shell, into an oyster and allowing the oyster to precipitate calcium carbonate layers over the grain. The external layers are identical to natural pearls, and they are produced much faster and more reliably than natural pearls. (Photograph courtesy of CISGEM of the Chamber of Commerce of Milan, Italy.)

material is not visible. Pearls are softer than any of the other gemstones, requiring gentle handling so that they are not damaged. Cultured pearls, especially those that have relatively thin veneers of aragonite over a seed material, are even more easily damaged.

THE FUTURE FOR BUILDING MATERIALS AND INDUSTRIAL MINERALS

The mineral commodities discussed in this chapter are essential, directly or indirectly, to nearly all modern industries. The construction of roads, bridges, dams, and all kinds of buildings; the extraction of fuels and metals; and the manufacture of chemicals, plastics, ceramics, glass, paper, and processed foodstuffs all require them. They are essential to the complex system of dependencies on which modern industrial societies are built.

The reserves of most of the minerals and rocks discussed in this chapter are large, and the potential resources are even larger. Commodities such as building stone are so abundant that it is pointless even to attempt to estimate the reserves. Because of this abundance, some experts have suggested finding ways of using these nonmetallic minerals to replace commodities that are in short supply, such as scarce metals. Such a solution requires the innovation of new technologies and calls for the undertaking of appropriate research programs.

FURTHER READINGS

BARKSDALE, R. D., editor, *The Aggregate Handbook*. Washington, DC: National Stone Association, 1991.

BATES, R. L. and JACKSON, J. A., *Our Modern Stone Age*. Los Altos, California: Wm. Kaufmann, Inc., 1982.

BRUTON, E., *Diamonds*. London: NAG Press, 1978.

CIPRIANI, C. and BORELLI, A., *Simon and Schuster's Guide to Gems and Precious Stones*. Edited by K. Lyman. New York: Simon and Schuster Inc., 1984.

GUTHRIE, G. D. and MOSSMAN, B. T., editors, "Health Effects of Mineral Dusts." *Reviews in Mineralogy*. Vol. 28, Washington, DC: Mineralogical Society of America, 1993.

HARBEN, P. W. and BATES, R. L., *Geology of the Nonmetallics*. Cornwall, UK: Robert Hartnoll Ltd., 1984.

LANGER, W. H. and GLANZMAN, V. M., "Natural Aggregate: Building America's Future." *U.S. Geological Survey Circular* 1110 (1993).

LEFOND, S. J., editor, *Industrial Rocks and Minerals*, 5th ed. New York: Society of Mining Engineers of the American Institute of Mining, Metallurgical and Petroleum Engineers, 1983.

MICHAELS, L. and CHISSICK, S. S., *Asbestos: Volume I, Properties, Applications, and Hazards*. New York: Wiley Interscience, 1979.

O'NEIL, P., *Gemstones*. Alexandria, Virginia: Time-Life Books, 1983.

SKINNER, H. C. W., ROSS, M., and FRONDEL, C., *Asbestos and Other Fibrous Materials, Mineralogy, Crystal Structure and Health Effects*. New York: Oxford University Press, 1988.

U.S. Bureau of Mines, *Mineral Facts and Problems*, published annually.

WINES, R. A., *Fertilizer in America*. Philadelphia, Pennsylvania: Temple University Press, 1985.

11 WATER RESOURCES

Three major components of Earth's hydrologic cycle are the oceans, which contain the vast majority of all water; glaciers and ice caps, which contain most of the fresh water; and the atmosphere, which serves as a conduit to transport water. These are all visible in this photograph of the Muir glacier on the coast of Alaska. (Courtesy of Andrew Maslowski.)

A nation that fails to plan intelligently for the development and protection of its precious waters will be condemned to wither because of its shortsightedness. The hard lessons of history are clear, written on the deserted sands and ruins of once proud civilizations.

President Lyndon B. Johnson, 1968

FOCAL POINTS

- Water is the most vital *mineral* resource because it is essential for human survival.
- 97.2% of the water of Earth's hydrosphere is contained in the oceans; this water is saline, containing 3.5% salts and is unusable for most purposes.
- The largest store of fresh water available for human use occurs as groundwater.
- The hydrologic cycle describes the constant movement of water from the oceans to the atmosphere by evapotranspiration and to the land surface and back to the oceans as precipitation.
- The world's principal rainfall belt lies along the equator, whereas the main desert regions lie 25°–30° north and south of the equator and in the polar regions.
- Flooding occurs as a natural consequence of heavy rainfall but is aggravated by human construction on floodplains and by human activities that increase surface runoff.
- Attempts to control flooding usually involve the construction of dams to hold back water and channelization to promote rapid water flow away from the area.
- Supply systems to provide potable water for communities date from prehistory and are used on a massive scale today.
- United States per capita water usage averages about 5070 liters (1340 gallons) of fresh water per day.
- In the United States, electricity generating plants use the greatest amounts of water, most of which is recovered, but irrigation consumes the greatest amount of water.
- Extraction of groundwater can lead to a lowering of the water table, ground surface subsidence, and even saltwater intrusion into aquifers in coastal areas.
- The importance of water as a resource will inevitably grow as world population increases.

INTRODUCTION

Earth has been described as the *water planet* because the dominant scene of Earth from outer space is water in the form of blue oceans and white clouds (Figure 11.1). Indeed, no resource is more abundant or more necessary to us than the water that covers nearly three-quarters of Earth's surface and that moves constantly about us in visible and invisible forms. From earliest times, the oceans, rivers, lakes, and springs have served us in many ways—as gathering points, as routes of transportation, and as either the means of, or barriers to, our migrations. Indeed, the availability of clean water is as important for the development and maintenance of our modern technological societies as it was for the most primitive of early societies. In spite of the vast global abundance of water, its very uneven distribution constantly creates problems of there being too much or too little of it to satisfy our needs. These problems are often compounded by our desire to use ever increasing amounts of water, by our modification of natural water systems, and by our contamination of surface waters and groundwaters. These factors highlight our need for a thorough knowledge of the distribution of water, an understanding of the effects of our activities on water availability and purity, and for long-range planning of water requirements. Indeed, water is viewed by many as the most critical resource for the early twenty-first century. The rising world population, especially in areas of limited fresh water,

will strain the capabilities of supply systems; this is occurring at the same time that there is an increasing awareness of the need to leave huge quantities for preservation of the environment. Consequently, there is a rising political importance to fresh water and it will only grow in the years to come.

THE GLOBAL DISTRIBUTION OF WATER

The total amount of water available in Earth's hydrosphere is approximately 1.36×10^{10} cubic kilometers or 1.36×10^{21} liters (326×10^6 cubic miles) that is distributed in a variety of forms and locations (Figure 11.2). The overwhelming proportion of the water, 97.2 percent, lies in the oceans; an additional 2.15 percent is held in polar ice caps and glaciers. The oceans are saline and not directly usable for most human needs; the glacial and polar ice is fresh but inaccessible. Consequently, the vast majority of our requirements must be met by the remaining 0.65 percent. The distribution of this small proportion of Earth's water at any given time is a function of the hydrologic cycle and the natural storage capacity of the rocks and surface land forms. Thus, the problems of water supply are more complex than mere total abundance; they also include local distribution patterns, the rates of recharge and natural loss, and, increasingly, cleanliness. The availability of **potable water** (namely, water suitable for drinking), more than any other factor in the future, will determine the number of people who can live in any geographic province as well as their use of natural resources and their overall lifestyle.

The Hydrologic Cycle

The free water on Earth's surface, though essentially unchanging in quantity, is constantly in motion in the hydrologic cycle (Figure 11.3). Earth's atmosphere is a great solar-powered heat engine that draws up water by evaporation, transports water as a vapor and as clouds, and discharges water after condensation as rain and snow. The precipitated water may complete its cycle by flowing via the rivers and streams and groundwater systems back to the oceans or may be short-circuited back into the atmosphere by evaporation from the land surface or by transpiration from plants. Each region of the world has a natural water budget in terms of precipitation, **evapotranspiration,** and runoff; the effects of human alteration of the budgets in many areas are discussed later in this chapter.

Water has the highest heat capacity—or ability to absorb and hold heat with minimal temperature change—of any substance known. Consequently, the movement of massive amounts of water in the atmosphere and in ocean currents also represents movement of large quantities of thermal energy that play very direct roles in the control of the world's

FIGURE 11.1. Earth, the *water planet*, as seen from the Apollo 17 spacecraft. The abundance of water in the oceans, clouds, and ice caps gives Earth an appearance that is unique among the planets. (Photograph from NASA.)

	Location	Water volume (liters)	Percentage of total water
Surface water			
	Fresh-water lakes	125×10^{15}	.009
	Saline lakes and inland seas	104×10^{15}	.008
	Average in stream channels	1×10^{15}	.0001
Subsurface water			
	Vadose water (includes soil moisture)	67×10^{15}	.005
	Ground water within depth of half a mile	$4,170 \times 10^{15}$	.31
	Ground water—deep lying	$4,170 \times 10^{15}$	.31
Other water locations			
	Icecaps and glaciers	$29,000 \times 10^{15}$	2.15
	Atmosphere	13×10^{15}	.001
	World ocean	$1,320,000 \times 10^{15}$	97.2

FIGURE 11.2. The distribution of water in various forms and locations on Earth. (From the U.S. Geological Survey.)

climates. This effect is probably best seen in the North Atlantic Ocean where the Gulf Stream, warmed by the sun in the Caribbean, flows northeastward as the North Atlantic Current, giving up heat to provide the mild climate of northern Europe. Without the Gulf Stream to transport this heat, England and Scandinavia would likely be as cold as northern Canada or Siberia, which lie at the same latitude.

The evaporation of water from any wetted surface requires the input of 540 calories for every gram of water that is changed from a liquid to a vapor state. Because this heat comes from the surrounding environment (for example, remaining water, soil, air, etc.), there is a tremendous cooling effect. The melting of ice to form water requires much less energy—80 calories per gram—and hence is also effective for cooling. The condensation of water vapor to liquid water reverses this process and liberates 540 calories per gram of liquid water produced.

Precipitation and Evaporation Patterns

Precipitation around the world is very unevenly distributed (Figure 11.4). The highest precipitation zone is the equatorial belt where annual precipitation generally exceeds 100 centimeters (40 inches) and commonly exceeds 200 cen-

timeters (80 inches). This zone is flanked by two zones at approximately 25°–30° north and south latitude that contain many of the world's major deserts and commonly receive less than 25 centimeters (10 inches) precipitation. Precipitation generally increases in the temperate regions of 35°–60° north and south latitude and then decreases to less than 20 centimeters (8 inches) in the polar regions. These zones result from Earth's reception of solar energy and the movement of the major atmospheric cells (Hadley cells) (Figure 11.5). The high precipitation equatorial zone results from the rising of warm, damp air into the upper atmosphere where cooling reduces its capacity to hold water and thus produces rain. The arid regions that flank the equatorial zone result from the descent of the cooler and much drier air from the upper atmosphere. As the air descends, it is warmed by Earth's surface, and its ability to hold water rapidly increases. Thus, instead of releasing water, the air is absorbing water and creating arid regions. The world's precipitation patterns may also be significantly affected by major ocean currents (for example, the Humboldt current, which results in the extension of desert conditions up the west coast of South America) and by major mountain chains (for example, the desert regions of the western United States that lie on the eastern flank of the Rocky Mountains).

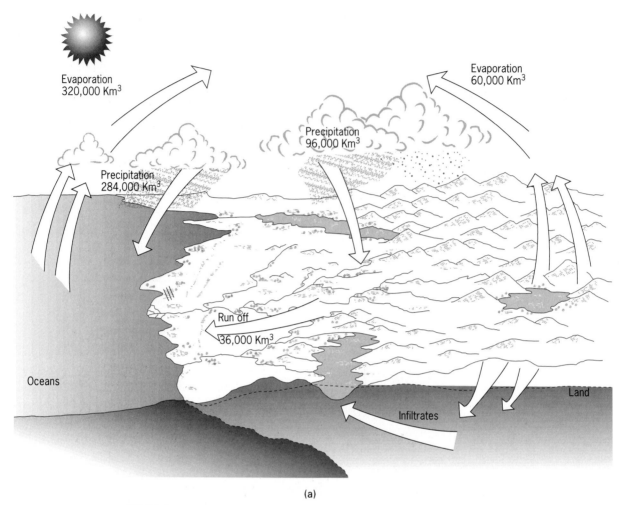

(a)

FIGURE 11.3. The hydrologic cycle for (a) all of Earth (After A.L. Bloom, *The Surface of the Earth*, Prentice Hall, 1969) and (b) the continental United States (From *The Nation's Water Resources 1975–2000*, The Water Resources Council, 1968.)

The United States is, in general, an example of a relatively rich country in terms of water resources because it receives an average of about 75 centimeters (30 inches) of rainfall per year. The rainfall is, however, quite irregularly distributed with annual values ranging from more than 250 centimeters (100 inches) in some mountainous areas of Washington, Oregon, and North Carolina, to less than 10 centimeters (4 inches) in some desert regions of the Southwest (Figure 11.6a). The actual amounts of precipitation vary significantly about the average with the highest percentage variations occurring in the areas of lowest average precipitation. The eastern United States, thanks largely to the Gulf of Mexico, enjoys an abundant supply of water and receives 65 percent of the total precipitation in the continental states, whereas the western part of the country, due largely to high mountains, is subject to a deficiency of water. This geographic variation is compounded by temporal variations tied to long-term weather fluctuations such as those created by the episodic appearance of the *El Niño* phenomenon in the Pacific Ocean. Thus, although water is a renewable resource,

the rate of renewal is neither uniform nor totally predictable. Accordingly, the long-term availability of water to satisfy national needs requires that we have both efficient storage systems and effective distribution systems.

Water is returned to the atmosphere from land or standing water by evaporation and by **transpiration**—the loss of water by plants directly to the atmosphere. The average annual evaporation rate (commonly called pan evaporation because it is measured by using water in an open pan) for a site is calculable on the basis of weather conditions, is readily tested by simple experiments, and thus is well established for many areas (Figure 11.6b). The rates are highest where solar insolation (radiation) and winds are greatest, especially where humidity is least; the rates are lowest where temperatures are lowest. Transpiration is a function of the type of plants involved as well as weather conditions and can vary markedly, depending upon the vegetation cover of an area. Nevertheless, the effects of both processes—evaporation and transpiration—are to return water into the atmosphere, to cool the surface where they occur, and to reduce the

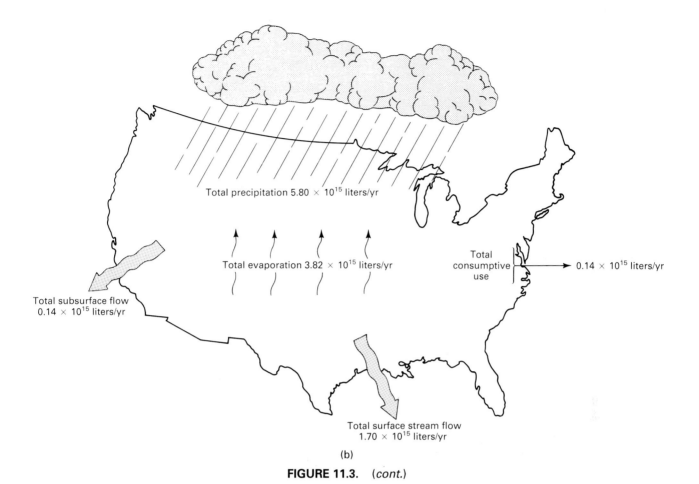

Total precipitation 5.80 × 10^{15} liters/yr

Total evaporation 3.82 × 10^{15} liters/yr

Total subsurface flow
0.14 × 10^{15} liters/yr

Total
consumptive
use

0.14 × 10^{15} liters/yr

Total surface stream flow
1.70 × 10^{15} liters/yr

(b)

FIGURE 11.3.   (*cont.*)

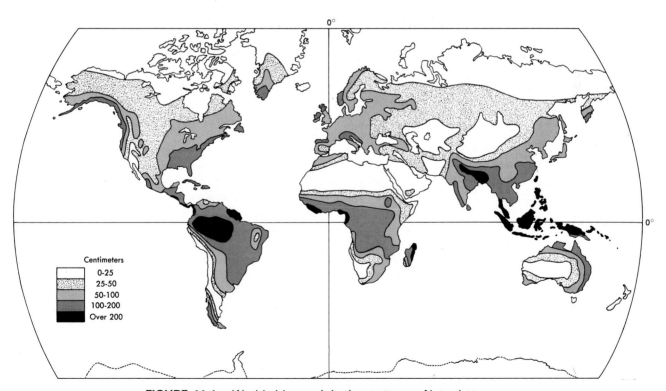

Centimeters
0-25
25-50
50-100
100-200
Over 200

FIGURE 11.4.   Worldwide precipitation patterns. Note that a zone
of high rainfall lies along the equator and that more arid zones lie
along belts that are 25°–30° north and south of the equator. (From
B.J. Skinner, *Earth Resources*, 3rd ed., Prentice Hall, 1986.)

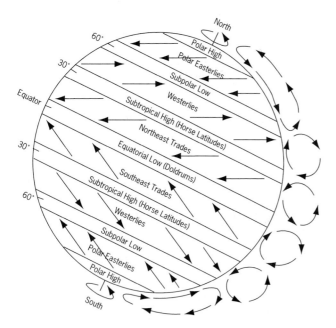

FIGURE 11.5. Idealized circulation of Earth's atmosphere showing the locations of, and air movement in, the Hadley Cells. In general, the low-pressure areas are zones of high rainfall and the high-pressure areas are zones of low rainfall.

availability of free water for agriculture, domestic or industrial use. For the world, the combined evapotranspiration rate is about 62 percent (Figure 11.3) and for the United States it is about 70 percent. The percentages are much greater in areas of low rainfall and high temperature and much lower in areas of high rainfall and cooler climate. In arid countries, such as Australia, the fraction of water lost to evapotranspiration is very large; in humid climates, such as that in Great Britain, the fraction lost to this process is relatively small.

The type and density of natural vegetation commonly reflect the availability of water in a region. In areas of low rainfall, plant cover will develop to a point where all precipitation is used in evapotranspiration and none is left for stream flow; additional plant growth can only occur if there is groundwater to support it. Ephemeral (or temporary) streams may, of course, flow during periods of high rainfall. In several parts of the southwestern United States, introduced pest plants, such as mesquite, have become such major consumers of both surface water and groundwater that they threaten the meager supplies available and are the objects of major eradication programs.

Evapotranspiration is a significant contributor to problems of surface water and soil quality in many arid parts of the world, including the desert of the southwest United States. There, the very high evaporation rates, exceeding 250 centimeters (100 inches) over large areas, result in the loss of very large quantities of water in reservoirs created by dams.

These losses reduce the availability of water for any use and the capacity to generate hydroelectric power. In addition, the evaporation from rivers and reservoirs leads to a deterioration of the water quality because of the residual concentration of salts (see page 411). The buildup of salts on the surface of irrigated fields in areas of high evapotranspiration has resulted in the deterioration or loss of millions of acres of previously productive crop land worldwide (see page 411).

Surface Water—Rivers and Lakes

The presence of rivers and lakes is an indication that the precipitation in an area exceeds the losses of water to evapotranspiration and groundwater seepage. In a very general sense the annual runoff pattern for the United States (Figure 11.6c), therefore, reflects the combined effects of precipitation (Figure 11.6a) and evaporation (Figure 11.6b). Thus, the areas of high rainfall are areas of high runoff, and large areas of low rainfall, such as parts of the western states, have essentially no runoff at all. It is, of course, important to remember that many areas in which the average annual evaporation exceeds average annual precipitation still have significant stream flow, at least for part of the year. This occurs because neither rainfall nor evaporation is constant during all seasons of the year or all times of the day. Precipitation may be seasonal but usually can occur at all hours of the day, whereas evaporation increases sharply during summer months and during afternoon hours. Furthermore, in periods of high rainfall much of the water may flow out of an area before there is time for it to evaporate.

The U.S. Water Resources Council has found, on the basis of available surface water and water demand, that the eastern portion of the United States constitutes an area of water surplus, whereas the western (and geographically larger) region is generally an area of water deficiency (Figure 11.6d). This pattern of water availability has played, and will continue to play, an important role in population distribution and in the manner of land use and resource exploitation. To permit accurate assessment of the regional water supply and demand, the continental United States has been subdivided into 18 Water Resources Regions by the U.S. Water Resources Council, primarily on the basis of major surface water drainage systems. The 30 percent of precipitated water shown as flowing in rivers and streams into the oceans in Figure 11.3 is a bit misleading because it does not show that considerable water, ultimately lost to evapotranspiration, actually first travels long distances as stream flow. In fact, much of this water has already been used in domestic water supplies and in industry before it returns to the atmosphere.

Groundwater

Earth's near-surface rocks and soils serve as the storage site for quantities of water estimated to be 3000 times larger than

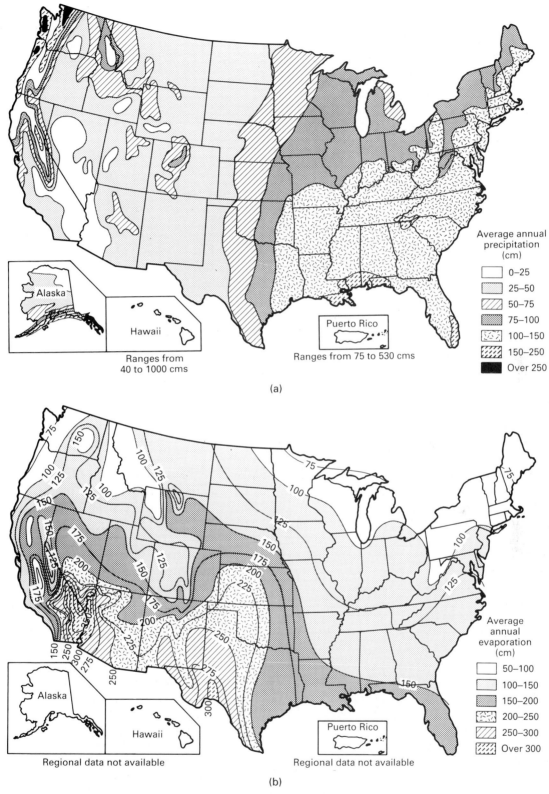

FIGURE 11.6. (a) Annual precipitation patterns for the United States. (b) Annual pan evaporation pattern for the United States. (c) Annual runoff patterns for the United States. (d) General water surplus-deficiency relationship in the United States. (From *The Nation's Water Resources, 1975–2000,* The Water Resources Council, 1968.)

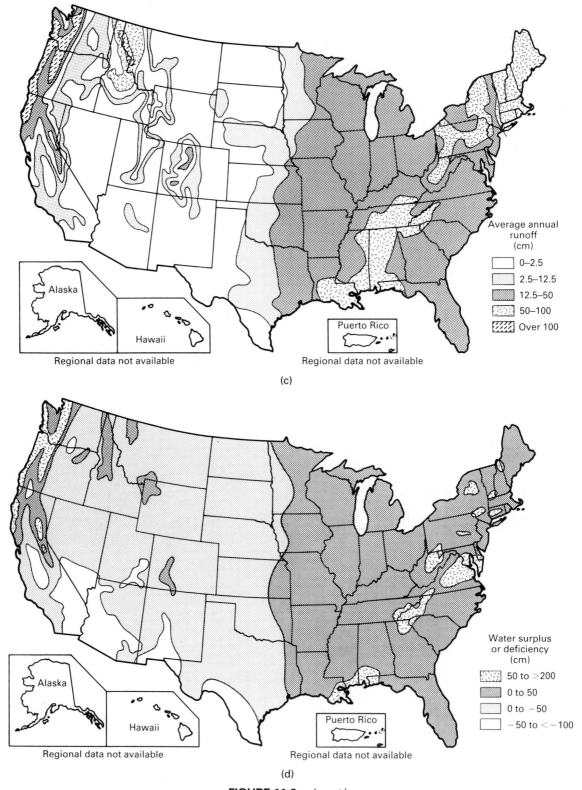

(c)

(d)

FIGURE 11.6. (*cont.*)

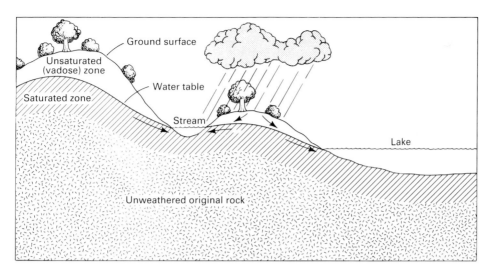

FIGURE 11.7. Cross section of a typical soil zone showing the relationship of the water table to the ground surface, streams, and lakes.

the volume of water in all rivers at any given time and 35 times larger than the volume of all inland lakes and seas. Although this water represents, by far, the largest quantity of accessible fresh water, it often represents a nonrenewable resource because the natural rates of recharge are so slow relative to the rapid rates at which we withdraw it. Deep groundwater often consists of water trapped and isolated in sediments some time in the geologic past. In contrast, shallow groundwater supplies are often intimately related to surface water as shown in Figure 11.7. Depending upon the land surface slope, vegetation, soil depth, and rock type, widely varying amounts of precipitation and runoff may percolate into the intergranular pore spaces and fractures. In most areas, the water percolates downward until it reaches the **water table.** The pores and fractures in the surface below the water table are water-filled. The water table is not flat but usually has a shape that is similar to, but smoother than, the topography of the land surface.

Above the water table is an unsaturated or **vadose** region of the soil. The upper part of this zone fills with water when it rains but then drains relatively quickly, leaving some water that adheres to mineral surfaces. However, even this small amount of water is very important because it is the principal water supply for most plants. During periods of drought, this upper soil zone can also lose much water directly to evaporation; under these conditions some moisture actually moves upward by means of capillary action. Somewhat deeper is a zone in which the flow of water through the unsaturated soil or rock is downward toward the water table. The soil and vadose water zones do not constitute direct resources of water but are essential for the replenishing of the groundwater zones.

It is important to recognize that most streams and lakes in equilibrium with their surroundings represent the inter-

section of the groundwater table with the surface topography. It is the slow lateral seepage of groundwater that provides the water for stream flow when there has been no rain and there is no surface runoff. In humid areas, streams will continue to flow, although with reduced volumes, even in long periods of drought. In arid regions, where the groundwater table may lie far below the land surface, streams will often flow after rainstorms only until the water has either evaporated or percolated into the subsurface. In these areas, the high rates of evapotranspiration commonly result in the return of most water to the atmosphere. The shallow penetration of the rainfall before being evaporated often allows the water to pick up dissolved salts that are then left as a near-surface soil cement (referred to as **caliche** or hard pan) that makes the soil less permeable and reduces the value of the soil for agriculture (see Chapter 12).

Aquifers, geologic formations that possess sufficient porosity and permeability to allow for movement of the water contained within them, underlie large areas of the United States (Figure 11.8). In fact, more than 50 percent of the people of the United States are presently dependent upon groundwater from aquifers for their domestic supplies. In many arid parts of the world, aquifers constitute the only significant source of water. Even in more humid parts of the world where surface water is present, aquifers are commonly utilized as major water sources because they provide a relatively constant flow of good quality water.

The major problems in the utilization of groundwater are rate of water flow, rate of recharge, and water quality. The surfaces of many parts of the continents are underlain by metamorphic or igneous rocks, and the only available groundwater is the meager quantities that lie in the fractures of joint systems or along faults. Interconnectedness of the joints allows ready movement of the water, but

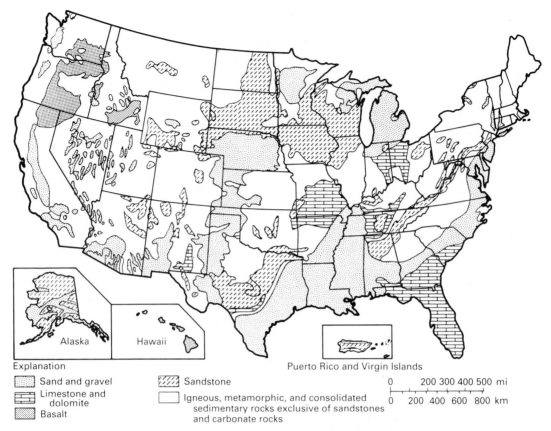

FIGURE 11.8. General occurrence of the principal types of water-bearing rocks in the United States. (From R.C. Heath, "Ground Water Regions of the United States," *U.S. Geological Survey Supply Paper* 2242, 1984.)

the quantities are often very limited. Even in many areas underlain by sedimentary rocks, porosity or permeability is too low to allow for a worthwhile rate of water flow. If an aquifer is to have a sustained yield, there must be a constant replenishment from surface water through the generally slow process of percolation. It has been estimated that 150 years would be required to totally recharge all of the groundwater in the United States to a depth of 750 meters (2460 feet) if it were all removed. The problem of the slow recharge of aquifers is becoming evident in several parts of the world, including the western United States where withdrawal rates up to 100 times those of the recharge rates are rapidly lowering the water table (see page 405). In these areas, the water is considered as being *mined* because it is being extracted just as any other nonrenewable mineral commodity. The effect of the loss of water on land value is being recognized, so that the farmers who own the land are permitted to depreciate the land value as the water table falls. Even in humid regions where there is abundant rainfall, the withdrawal of water from aquifers at rates exceeding those of recharge creates problems such as the draining of wells by depression of the water table and the movement

of salt water into previously freshwater beds. The third problem of aquifers is water quality. As groundwater moves through the rocks, it dissolves the more soluble constituents. The problem varies with rock type and flow rate and has been greatly aggravated in recent years by the introduction of contaminants from agricultural, domestic, and industrial sources. In general, water with less than 0.05 percent (500 parts per million) total dissolved solids is considered suitable for human consumption (specific requirements for potable water are listed in Table 11.1); however, water with up to 1 percent dissolved solids can be used for some purposes. Bacteria present within the soil may cleanse slow moving water of harmful natural biological contaminants. Unfortunately, complex synthetic chemical contaminants have seriously limited the usefulness of some aquifers, particularly when there is a rapid rate of water movement that spreads the contaminants much more rapidly than they can be filtered or decomposed by bacteria.

Another problem resulting from the withdrawal of water from aquifers is land subsidence. This is a local, but increasingly observed, phenomenon that can have serious consequences. This is discussed in greater detail on page 405.

TABLE 11.1

National drinking-water regulations*

Constituent	Maximum Concentration, p.p.m.
Arsenic	0.05
Barium	1
Cadmium	0.010
Chromium	0.05
Lead	0.05
Mercury	0.002
Nitrate (as N)	10
Selenium	0.01
Silver	0.05
Fluoride	1.4–2.4
Turbidity	1–5 turbidity units
Coliform bacteria	1/100 mL (mean)
Endrin	0.0002
Lindane	0.004
Methoxychlor	0.1
Toxaphene	0.005
2,4-D	0.1
2,4,5-TP Silvex	0.01
Total trihalomethanes [the sum of the concentration bromodichloromethane, dibromochloromethane, tribromomethane (bromoform) and trichloromethane (chloroform)]	0.10
Radionuclides: (for units, see p. 36)	
Radium 226 and 228 (combined)	5 pCi/L
Gross alpha particle activity	15 pCi/L
Gross beta particle activity	4 mrem/yr

Constituent	Maximum Level, p.p.m.
Chloride	250
Color	15 color units
Copper	1
Dissolved solids	500
Foaming agents	0.5
Iron	0.3
Manganese	0.05
Odor	3 (threshold odor number)
pH	6.5–8.5
Sulfate	250
Zinc	5

Data from the U.S. Environmental Protection Agency, 1982.

*The U.S. Environmental Protection Agency's National Interim Primary Drinking-Water Regulations and National Secondary Drinking-Water Regulations are summarized here. The primary regulations, which specify the maximum permissible level of a contaminant in water at the tap, are health related and are legally enforceable. If these concentrations are exceeded or if required monitoring is not performed, the public must be notified. The secondary drinking-water regulations control contaminants in drinking water that affect the esthetic qualities related to public acceptance of drinking water. These secondary regulations are intended to be guidelines for the states and are not federally enforceable.

Ice Caps and Glaciers

More than 70 percent of the world's nonsaline water is held in ice caps and glaciers. This water is primarily contained within the ice caps and glaciers of Antarctica and is unavailable for virtually all practical purposes (Figure 11.9).

Proposals to tow large icebergs to water-deficient areas such as the Middle East have been discussed episodically but have not yet resulted in any significant financial backing or serious efforts. In the short term, the amount of water held in glaciers and ice caps may be considered constant, but in the not-too-distant geologic past—the Pleistocene or Ice Ages—the

FIGURE 11.9.   The world's ice caps and glaciers such as these in Victoria Land, Antarctica, contain most of the world's nonsaline water. (Photograph by J.R. Craig.)

amount of water held as ice was as much as 50 percent greater than at present. During the major glacial advances, more of the snowfall over polar and cold temperate land masses built up and persisted with the result that glaciers advanced and sea level dropped as much as 100 meters (330 feet) below its present level. In contrast, during warmer interglacial periods, sea level has risen significantly to about present levels. One of the greatest concerns about global warming, if human activities were to bring it about, is the potential for sea level to rise. This would inundate many of the world's major coastal cities as well as much prime agricultural land.

Surface Runoff, Floods, and Flood Control

Most rainfall produces some **surface runoff.** The amount of this runoff is a function of the amount of rainfall, the slope and length of the drainage basin, the rock and soil type of the drainage basin, the vegetation cover, and the extent of any impermeable areas in the basin. The runoff may range from zero to more than 90 percent of total rainfall in a given basin; the remainder evapotranspires back into the atmosphere, percolates into the groundwater system, or is held back in storage facilities.

Surface runoff may be characterized in terms of a **hydrograph** or **lag-time diagram** (Figure 11.10). This depicts both the quantity and time of rainfall and the subsequent runoff from a drainage basin. Small drainage basins may have lag times measurable in minutes or hours, whereas large ones may have lag times of hours to days. Once the runoff characteristics have been determined for a basin, it is possible to predict water flow levels and to estimate potential flood conditions.

Activities, such as mining, timbering, farming, and construction, frequently promote an increase in the amount

and rate of surface runoff as shown in Figure 11.10b. Consider, for example, the effects of urbanization of a previously tree- or grass-covered area. Construction of a typical suburban community makes 10–30 percent of the area impermeable (streets, driveways, houses, sidewalks, etc.) and construction of a city environment or large shopping center may make 50–100 percent of an area impermeable. Most of the water from the impermeable area runs off onto permeable areas, thereby subjecting the permeable sections to water conditions equivalent to added rainfall. The result of natural rainfall plus the effect of the added water is then the **equivalent rainfall.** Much of the added runoff water does not actually drain onto adjacent land but is carried by storm drains into streams or rivers; nevertheless, that extra water will appear in some part of a drainage basin. Unfortunately, as more water runs off more rapidly, less of it is able to percolate into the soil to be added to the groundwater system. Assuming uniform rain distribution in a basin and 100 percent runoff of water from impermeable areas (this is never true but suffices for the demonstration here), the conversion of 25 percent of a basin to an impermeable condition would result in a 33 percent increase in equivalent rainfall for the permeable portion, conversion of 33 percent to impermeable condition would raise equivalent rainfall by 50 percent, and 50 percent impermeability would raise equivalent rainfall by 100 percent. Of course, even in rather permeable soils, there can be some runoff during very heavy rainfall; thus, the actual increase in runoff resulting from pavement or construction also depends on the intensity and duration of the rainfall.

The increase in runoff that will inevitably result from increases in impermeable area due to urbanization can either be permitted to contribute to normal stream flow or can be controlled. An example of such control is found on Long Island, New York, where the runoff from impermeable areas is diverted into shallow catchment basins from which the water seeps downward, enriching the groundwater supply. Another environmental benefit is that excessive amounts of fresh water do not pour into the brackish estuaries where its dilution effects can be detrimental to the marine life.

Flooding occurs when surface runoff exceeds a normal stream channel's capacity and the water spreads out onto the floodplain or beyond. Flooding is a natural phenomenon brought on by intense or prolonged rainfall or rapid melting of snow cover. It is of little or no consequence in undeveloped areas, but our tendency to build homes, businesses, and factories on floodplains has brought us into conflict with nature and often into peril. Floodplains are widely used as farmland because they are flat, provide ample water, and are fertile as a result of the soil deposited by episodic flooding. Relatively short duration flooding of farm fields, except at planting and harvest time, is usually not a great problem because the plants are tolerant of brief submersion. More intensive flooding can result in extensive erosion, burial of

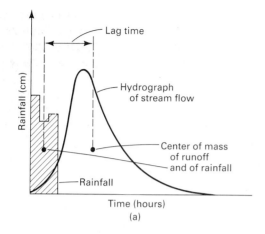

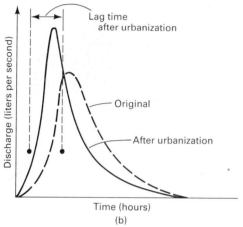

FIGURE 11.10. Hydrographs showing the relationships of rainfall, lag time, and runoff in an area (a) prior to and (b) after urbanization. Note that after urbanization the lag time is decreased and the rate of discharge is, for a while, greater than before urbanization. (From *U.S. Geological Survey Circular* 554, 1968.)

crops by too much new silt, or rotting of the crops. Although the extent to which our activities actually cause flooding is not completely understood, it is evident from the previous discussion that the removal of vegetation from large parts of the drainage basins and the subsequent expansion of impermeable surfaces increases runoff and contributes to the potential for flooding. Once hydrographs (Figure 11.10) have been defined, they can serve as valuable aids in predicting floods and the time of their rise, crest, and fall.

The United States, like many nations, suffers some local flooding every year. Usually, it is the result of intense but brief storms that drop large quantities of rain where cold and warm air masses meet or around the center of a low-pressure zone. Whether the flooding is brief and local or extensive and of considerable duration, this energy of the flowing water

(with a mass more than 800 times greater than air) often causes great damage to human structures (Figure 11.11). Widespread flooding often results from hurricanes that strike the southeastern United States from September to November and which are common sources of very large quantities of rainfall. In Southeast Asia, the seasonal monsoon rains create massive flooding of low-lying areas every year. In the spring and summer of 1993, the central United States suffered some of the most massive and extended flooding in the country's history. The Flood of 1993, as it became known, resulted from the persistence of a stationary front that allowed for the convergence of warm, moist air moving northward from the Gulf of Mexico and cooler air from the northwest along a band extending from Colorado to Michigan (Figure 11.12). This type of weather phenomenon is common for brief periods, but in 1993, it persisted for approximately five months. Many areas received rain virtually every day and totals through the period exceeding 200 percent of normal. There was no evaporation because the humidity was commonly 100 percent. The soils were saturated, so runoff was nearly 100 percent, but the dams to control flooding were full. Consequently, the river banks over an area of greater than 17,000 square miles (44,000 square kilometers) overflowed onto floodplains and hundreds of communities and more than 10 million acres (15,000 square miles; 38,000 square kilometers) of farmland were under water (Plates 61 and 62). Barge traffic along the Mississippi River had to be halted, railway lines were blocked, interstate highways were under water, and the rain kept falling.

Over the years, the Army Corps of Engineers had constructed levees along many stretches of the Mississippi and other rivers to prevent flooding of towns and farmland, but the flooding in 1993 was so extensive and the water levels were so high that many levees were topped and some breached. This resulted in flooding of areas previously viewed as safe and that were unprepared for flooding. In some areas, homes as far as 11 kilometers (7 miles) from the major rivers were flooded. There was major loss of crops from the area, at least 48 deaths, and damages estimated to be at least $10–$12 billion. Rains finally ended in August of 1993 and floodwaters gradually subsided, but some of the effects will be permanent. Many individuals moved, fearing they might face similar flooding again, and in a few instances entire towns have relocated on higher ground. The effectiveness of the levees and the value of the dams as flood control devices have been questioned. It has been recognized that the levees of many areas held the water in the main channels and thus allowed it to flow more rapidly downstream where, in several cases, the flooding became worse. Consequently, a decision was made not to rebuild all of the levees because the absence of the levees upstream would have allowed the floodwaters to spread laterally. This would have reduced the highest water flows in the major river channels and made the flooding downstream

(a)

(b)

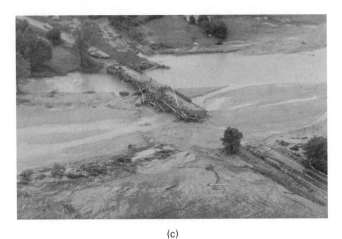

(c)

FIGURE 11.11. (a) A sudden flood in late 1938 swept through Louisville, Kentucky, toppling a row of houses but otherwise doing little damage to the structures. (Photograph from The American Red Cross.) (b) A brief, but intense, storm dropped heavy rains and resulted in a devastating flood in Big Thompson Canyon, Colorado, in 1976. Many campers were killed and numerous houses, such as the one shown, were torn apart. (Photograph from the U.S. Geological Survey.) (c) Heavy rains, such as occurred in June 1995 in central Virginia, may overwhelm river and stream channels and erode the supports for roads and bridges making rescue and repair efforts difficult. (Photograph courtesy of Virginia Department of Transportation.)

significantly less. Such decisions are not easy because minimizing flood damage downstream means increasing the flood damage upstream. The entire situation highlights the problems encountered when human activities come in conflict with natural environmental processes.

In an effort to reduce the vast amounts of damage and the scores of deaths and injuries that occur annually as a result of flooding, the two procedures now most widely used are the construction of dams and the channelization of rivers (Figures 11.13a and 11.13b, respectively). These processes operate on different principles but attempt to achieve the same result. **Dams** serve as temporary water barriers to hold back high flow before it reaches an area and thereby prevent it from causing a flood. **Channelization,** in contrast, provides an efficient means by which water may be carried out of an area so quickly that it does not rise to flood levels. The construction of levees, as noted in the discussion of the Flood of 1993, serves to dam waters from lateral movement while also serving as a formal channel for downstream movement.

Dams, of course, serve many other purposes, such as water storage for irrigation, electric power generation, recre-

ation, and livestock watering, but in the United States a significant proportion of the more than 58,000 dams are used, at least in part, for flood control. The dams range from earthen barriers used for farm ponds, to the 250-meter (770-foot) high Oroville Dam in California, and to the 23-kilometer (14.5-mile) long Watkins Dam in Utah. Dams have been effective in the reduction of flooding and have provided the added benefit of generating very large amounts of electricity. They have also provided many new lakes for recreational purposes. Unfortunately, the water requirements for these activities are often incompatible. Flood control calls for the emptying of reservoirs, at least before anticipated heavy precipitation, so there is ample storage capacity for the runoff; power generation calls for a steady water flow or one that is cycled to match electricity demand; and recreation calls for lakes to remain at a constant high level. A contribution that is frequently overlooked is the enrichment in the quantity of groundwater around dam sites; as dams fill, groundwater tables generally rise as more water percolates into the subsurface.

Against the advantages of dam construction some disadvantages must be weighed, such as sediment catchment,

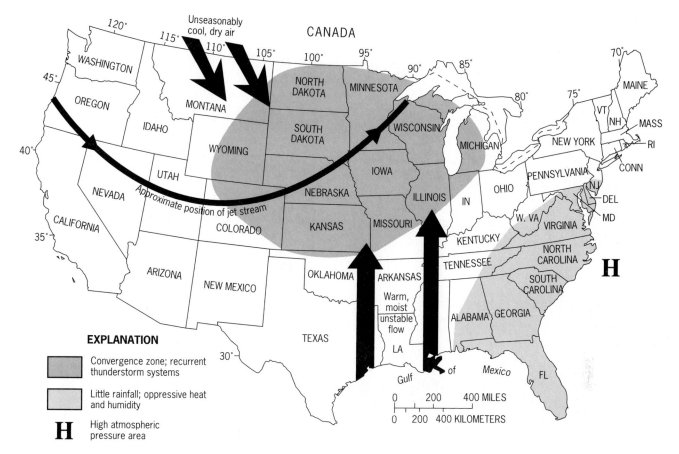

FIGURE 11.12. The dominant weather patterns in the spring and early summer of 1993 brought warm moist air from the Gulf of Mexico into convergence with unseasonably cool, dry air along the jet stream over the American Midwest. The area of convergence (diagonal shading) experienced much heavier than normal rainfall and extensive flooding (see Plate 61) while a portion of the Southeast (dotted area) experienced severe drought.

increased evaporation, loss of inundated land, interruption of river transport and fish migration, and environmental alteration. Construction of the Aswan High Dam in Egypt on the Nile River in the 1960s ended the annual flooding of the Nile Valley and has provided electricity generation facilities, but the reservoir that formed is now filling with the sediment that served as natural fertilizer for the agriculture for thousands of years in the Lower Nile Valley. This has markedly reduced soil fertility along the Lower Nile and is rapidly leading to **eutrophication** of the reservoir behind the dam. In all arid regions, the damming of rivers provides water for many uses but at the same time promotes evaporative water loss and the buildup of salts in the remaining waters. The construction of nearly every new dam meets with opposition from those whose land will be inundated and from those who do not want to see further change of the natural environment. In the 1970s the concern for endangered species of both fish and plants in the United States nearly prevented the completion of massive dams in Tennessee and Maine. The discovery of

the snail darter, a 3-inch minnowlike fish found only in the area to be flooded by the $116 million Tellico dam in Tennessee, provided the basis for halting construction for more than one year until it was determined that these fish could and do live in other rivers of the area. The finding of the Furbish lousewart, a wild snapdragon-like plant that was thought to be extinct, in the valley to be flooded by the $600 million Dickey-Lincoln dam in Maine provided grounds to delay the construction for many months until it was determined that additional colonies of the plants existed.

The United States governmental agencies responsible for major dam construction and supervision have now determined that few, if any, additional major power or flood control dams will ever be constructed in the country. Other countries, especially developing ones, are, however, considering new projects to provide electrical power for economic development and to control common flooding problems. Thus, Brazil is considering construction of major dams on the Amazon, and China broke ground in late 1994 for the

(a)

FIGURE 11.13. The principal methods of flood control are the construction of dams and channels. (a) Dams such as the Tennessee Valley Authority's Fontana Dam in western North Carolina have been used for flood control, recreation, and hydroelectrical power generation. (Photograph courtesy of Tennessee Valley Authority.) Channelization has frequently been used as a way to reduce flooding. (b) A plan-view schematically shows the change from the original meandering channel (curved solid lines) to a reworked straight channel (dashed lines) to allow for more rapid water movement. (c) A profile shows that the straightening and shortening of the channel results in a steeper gradient and hence a more rapid flow of water.

Three Gorges Dam on the Yangtze River in central China. This dam, scheduled to require more than 20 years for completion, would be the world's largest hydroelectric facility and would alleviate nearly annual flooding downstream. It has met with widespread opposition ever since it was first suggested in 1919 because it would alter the river ecology, flood hundreds of square miles of farmland, and displace more than 1 million people from their homes. In Canada, Quebec Hydro has developed plans for major hydroelectric

dams on the rivers that drain the sparsely inhabited area east of Hudson Bay. Even here, environmental concerns raised in Canada and New York, which would have been a major customer for the electricity, as well as pressure from Native American tribes has brought about cancellation of major parts of the project.

Channelization has provided an expedient means of flood control in many areas. The principle, illustrated in Figure 11.13b, is straightforward; replacement of a natural sinu-

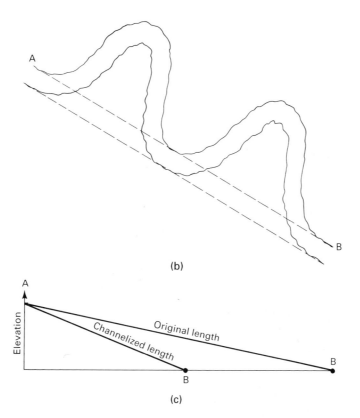

(b)

(c)

FIGURE 11.13. (*cont.*)

ous channel by a shorter and straighter one allows for more rapid water flow out of a flood-prone area, thereby reducing the likelihood of a flood. The rate of water flow is increased because the straighter channel offers less resistance and because the gradient of the new shorter channel is steeper. Frequent secondary effects have included the lowering of the water table and drainage of swamp land adjacent to the river; such land then usually has considerable real estate value.

Although often effective and carried out in hundreds of areas, channelization has also been found to have significant drawbacks, such as increased erosion, transfer of flooding, reduced natural filtering of groundwater, and the loss of wetlands habitat. Unless the channelization extends to a flood control reservoir or to the ocean, the rapid transport of water through one part of a river basin, only to dump it back into its original channel further downstream, merely transfers the problem of flooding downstream. An example of this in the United States is the Blackwater River in Johnson County, Missouri, where channelization did reduce local flooding but created extra flooding in adjacent counties downstream. The decrease in channel length from 53.6 to 29 kilometers (33.5 to 18 miles) nearly doubled the gradient and increased the water velocity, which, in turn, increased stream channel erosion. The original channel was 15–30 meters (45–90 feet) wide, but erosion broadened the channel up to 70 meters (200 feet) and resulted in the collapse of several bridges. The much greater rate of water flow tended to scour the channel

and reduced the total amount of **biomass** production (fish, plants, algae, insects, etc.) in the river by about 80 percent.

The channelization of the Kissimmee River in central Florida in the 1960s and the decision in the 1980s and 1990s to restore the river to its original state provide an informative lesson on the relationships between channelization, commercial interests, water needs, and environmental concerns.

OUR USE OF WATER

Water Usage and Consumption

Water is more widely used and more essential than any other resource. The amount used per capita, however, has varied widely as a function of each society's lifestyle and standard of living. In discussing water usage, it is important to distinguish between **withdrawal** (sometimes called usage), which is the water physically extracted from its source, and **consumption,** which is the withdrawn water that is no longer available because it has been evaporated, transpired, incorporated into products or crops, consumed by humans or livestock, or otherwise held from returning to its source.

Withdrawal uses of water are generally subdivided into (1) domestic-commercial; (2) industrial-mining; (3) thermoelectric power; and (4) irrigation-livestock, as illustrated in

RESTORING A RIVER: THE KISSIMMEE

The rapid growth of Florida's population from fewer than 3 million in 1950 to more than 14 million in 1995 has resulted in a variety of problems in terms of water resources. The Kissimmee River, which flows from the Orlando area southward to Lake Okeechobee (Figure 11.14) is a prime example, which can provide insight, not just in Florida, but in many parts of the world. Prior to the 1960s, the Kissimmee flowed slowly in a meandering channel bordered by more than 20,200 hectares (50,000 acres) of marshy wetlands. Episodic rains, some resulting from hurricanes, created large fluctuations in the water flow of the Kissimmee and would turn the river's floodplain into a broad sheet of shallow water. To control the flooding, between 1961 and 1971 the U.S. Corps of Engineers converted the original 163-kilometer (102-mile) meandering river into a 93-kilometer (58-mile) long, 10-meter (30-foot) deep channel with a series of dams, water control structures, drainage canals, and navigation locks. The elimination of the flooding problem and the construction of drainage devices to divert water for use by farmers, orchards, and the growing cities resulted in the conversion of 18,200 hectares (45,000 acres) of natural marshlands into pasture lands. The value of the land rose from $400/acre to more than $4000/acre. At the time of completion, the cost of $32 million was considered a reasonable cost for the benefits returned.

However, by the middle 1970s it became apparent that the channelization of the Kissimmee had many other effects. The wetlands had served as an important water filter to remove nitrogen and phosphorous from sewage and fertilizers. In addition, they had played a key role in supplying much of the water that evapotranspired into the atmosphere to provide frequent rainstorms. With the removal of the wetlands, rainfall decreased, water levels fell, water purity decreased, and the water flow in the Kissimmee and the productivity of Lake Okeechobee declined. The spawning sites for bass and other fish along the river were lost and 90 percent of the migratory and resident bird population disappeared. Thorough studies of the hydrology of Florida also revealed that the Kissimmee River and Lake Okeechobee were integral parts of the broad flow of water that created and supported the Everglades. With the decrease in the flow of water, the Everglades began to rapidly deteriorate.

It became clear that the only way to restore the quality of the water in Lake Okeechobee, and perhaps to save the Everglades, was to return the Kissimmee River to its original state. Although the state authorized such action as early as 1976, lack of funding and the Corps of Engineers' view that restoration was not a high priority resulted in little action until 1985 when the state sponsored a demonstration project. The project blocked a portion of the artificial channel and forced water back into the original river bed. The test had dramatic and rapid effects—water quality improved and natural plant and animal life returned to the floodplain.

The final 1945-page report and plan, which was approved by the Army Corps of Engineers in December 1994, calls for restoring the entire Kissimmee River system and could become the most ambitious environmental restoration project ever attempted. The plan calls for filling in 47 kilometers (29 miles) of the newer river channel, rebuilding 19 kilometers (11.6 miles) of original river channel moving more than 50 million cubic yards (38 million cubic meters) of soil to fill in up to 2000 miles (3200 kilometers) of canals, and return 14,000 hectares (35,000 acres) of original floodplain wetlands to their natural condition. The cost is high because some 30 percent of the drained pastureland was sold to private hands and had risen a great deal in value. Unfortunately, the price tag to complete the restoration keeps rising with each year of delay; the original price estimate of about $100 million had risen to $300 million by the 1980s and to much more than $2 billion by 1995. Consequently, when the project is completed in about 2015 there will have been the expenditure of perhaps $3 billion to have what we had originally for free.

(a)   (b)

FIGURE 11.14. (a) Location map of the Kissimmee River in south central Florida. (b) Photograph of the Kissimmee River showing the difference between the original meandering course in the foreground and straightened channel in the background. (Photograph courtesy of South Florida Water Management District.)

Figures 11.15a and 11.15b. Hydroelectric power generation, in which water is actually withdrawn only to the extent that it is diverted through turbines to generate electricity, is considered a special category and is discussed separately. The amount of water withdrawn and its division between surface sources and groundwater varies according to the population, the type of society, and the climatic conditions in an area. In the United States, approximately three-quarters of water usage is supplied by surface sources (Figure 11.15), but major agricultural states such as Nebraska and Kansas and the arid state of Arizona draw most of their water from underground sources (Figure 11.16). Not surprisingly, California, by virtue of size, population, and agricultural production, uses the most water, and Alaska, with its small population and very small agricultural production, uses the least.

Total water usage in the United States currently amounts to about 6130 liters (1620 gallons) per person per day when all of the usages are considered. If only the domestic household use (delivered by public supply systems) is considered, the figure is about 400 liters (105 gallons) per person per day. The use of water by our society is largely taken for granted, and we often overlook the large quantities required to support modern lifestyles. Table 11.2 presents some data on the water usage required for particular purposes by modern western society.

Rural water withdrawn from private wells constitutes only about 1 percent of United States water usage but in many sparsely populated areas this represents the dominant water supply. The use at any one site varies from the small amounts withdrawn for a single house to very large quantities used to supply large herds of livestock. In many less developed parts of the world the rural water supply commonly constitutes the major water source for large segments of the population (Figure 11.17). Because rural water is used for many agricultural purposes as well as for household needs, a somewhat larger proportion of the rural water is consumed.

Domestic and Commercial—Supplying Our Cities

Domestic and commercial water usage includes that needed by normal households and the water for motels, hotels, restaurants, offices, stores, businesses, and governmental and military establishments. Although it is only about 11.5 percent of total usage, it is the part that most of us see directly each day. More than 80 percent of what we use is returned to the water systems, and most of that is through public water treatment plants.

The growth of cities has always required the availability of continuous supplies of fresh water. As a result, virtually all ancient and most modern cities were established along

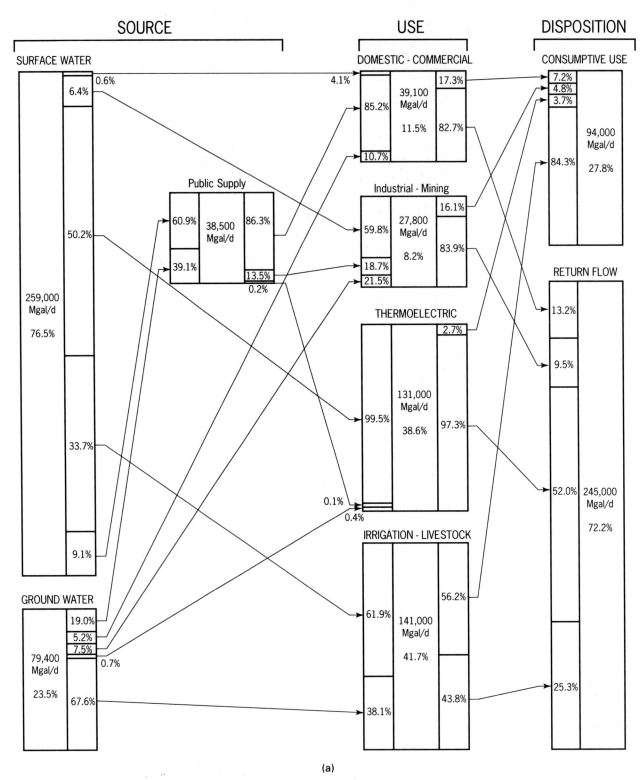

FIGURE 11.15. (a) Schematic presentation of water use in the United States in 1990 showing the source, type of use, and disposition (From U. S. Geological Survey Circular 1081) (b) Water use and availability in the United States in 1990. Groundwater withdrawal is shown by the lowest curve; surface water withdrawals are represented by the area between the two lower curves. Instream hydrologic power usage of water is actually about 2.5 times greater than the average flow of all rivers. For comparison, the United States population from 1950 to 1990 is also shown (right-hand scale).

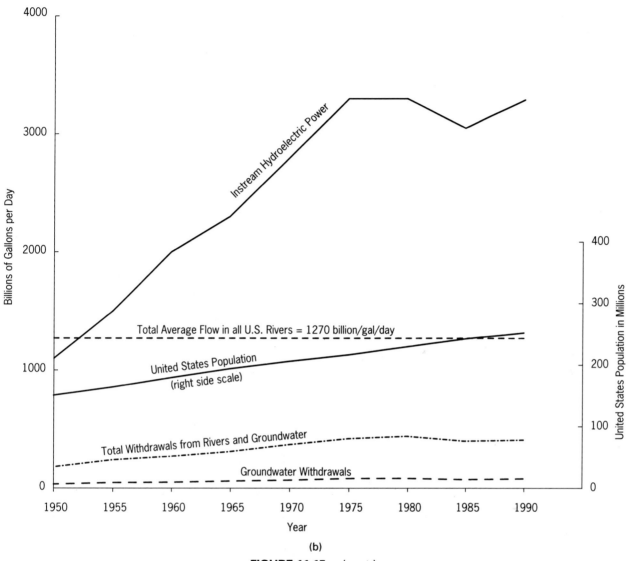

FIGURE 11.15. (cont.).

rivers or where there were ample springs. As cities grew, so did their needs for water. When these needs exceeded local supplies, it became necessary to find additional water and to develop means to transport it to urban distribution centers.

The earliest constructed water transportation systems, or **aqueducts,** were probably stream channels that were altered or extended so that they flowed into more accessible areas. Biblical Jerusalem was served by an aqueduct consisting of limestone blocks through which a 38-centimeter (15-inch) hole had been drilled by hand. The Greeks bored tunnels—up to 1280 meters (4200 feet) long at Athens—and built masonry structures to carry water. The ancient masters of the construction of aqueducts were, however, the Romans who built nine major aqueducts that brought 322 million liters (85 million gallons) of water a day to Rome in 97 A.D. All told, the Romans constructed aqueducts (Figure 11.18) to service nearly 200 of their cities and some of their

mining efforts throughout their empire. Few additional aqueducts were built until the late 1500s when Sir Francis Drake, then mayor, had one constructed that was 39 kilometers (24 miles) long for Plymouth, England. In 1609, a 61-kilometer (38-mile) aqueduct called the New River was built to bring water to London.

In the era of modern cities, even though the demand for water has increased, the large scenic aqueducts of the past have been nearly completely replaced by buried steel pipes and pumping stations. A prime example is New York City where a complex system of aqueducts links 15 major reservoirs containing more than 1860×10^9 liters (approximately 490×10^9 gallons), some of which are as much as 200 kilometers (125 miles) from the city (Figures 11.19 and 11.20). In spite of the vastness of the system used to supply New York City, there is little problem because the abundance of rainfall in the northeastern United States provides more than

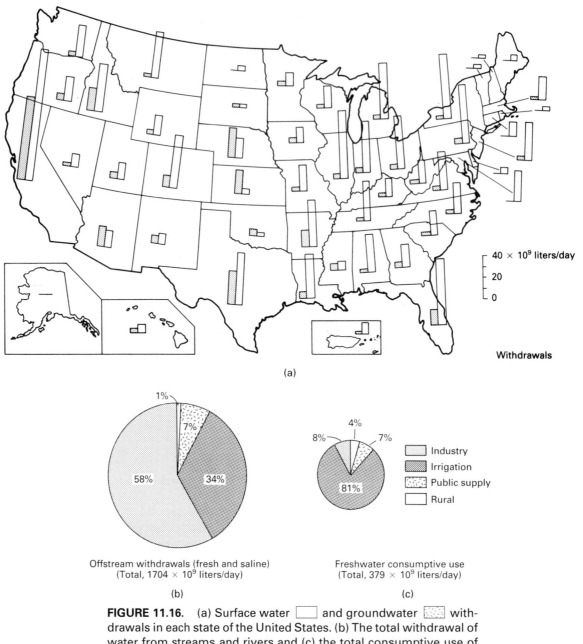

FIGURE 11.16. (a) Surface water ☐ and groundwater ▨ withdrawals in each state of the United States. (b) The total withdrawal of water from streams and rivers and (c) the total consumptive use of water in the United States for industry/mining, irrigation, domestic/commercial, and thermoelectric use. (Updated from *U.S. Geological Survey Circular* 1001, 1983).

adequate water for all other users as well as those in New York. However, New York City, like many long-established cities, faces critical problems with its aging infrastructure as described in the Box on page 390.

Some of the water problems of the western United States are also being addressed by means of aqueducts. Thus, the Central Arizona Project (see page 399) is a major supplier of water for cities such as Phoenix and Tucson, and the state of California has constructed a complex system to supply its major cities. One of these extends more than 1100 kilometers (685 miles) in California to bring water from many parts of the state to Los Angeles; it is discussed later in this chapter (see "Water for Drinking—The Los Angeles Aqueduct System").

TABLE 11.2

Water requirements for modern western society

Activity or Product	Water Required (liters)	(gallons)
Home use:		
Shower (per minute)	19	5
Bath	114	30
Toilet flush	15	4
Automatic washing machine	114	30
Hose flow per hour of		
lawn watering or car washing	1,136	300
Food production:		
Sugar per ton	946,000	250,000
Corn per ton	946,000	250,000
Rice per ton	9,460,000	2,500,000
Milk per gallon	61,000	16,000
Beef per pound	14,000	3,700
Nitrate fertilizer per ton	568,000	150,000
Industrial:		
Paper	23,700	62,500
Bricks per ton	950–1900	250–500
Oil refining per 42-gal barrel	1,770	468
Synthetic rubber per ton	2,500,000	660,000
Aluminum per ton	1,325,000	350,000
Iron per ton	113,600	30,000
Human survival:		
70 kg (154 lb) person per year	720	190

U.S.G.S. pamphlet *Scientific American,* September 1963, World Book Encyclopedia, and Water & Industry.

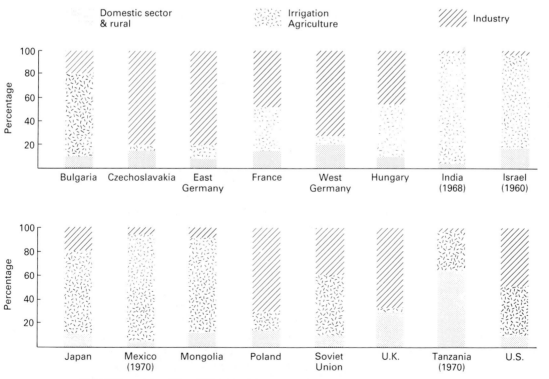

FIGURE 11.17. The differences in water usage in 16 countries reflect different types of economies (From *The Global Report 2000,* 1980.)

FIGURE 11.18.   Supplying water to cities has been a major concern since the Romans built aqueducts, such as the Pont du Gard at Nimes, France, to transport water to nearly 200 cities. This was built in the first century A.D. and carried water from two springs to Nimes. It is one of the best preserved of Roman structures. (Photograph courtesy of the French Government Tourist Office.)

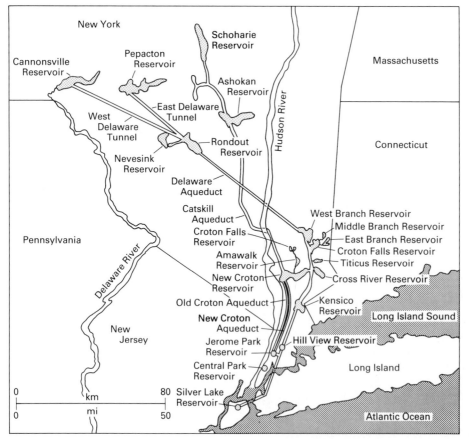

(a)

FIGURE 11.19.   (a) The water supply system for the city of New York links 15 major reservoirs—some as much as 200 kilometers (124 miles) away—to meet the needs of approximately 10 million people. (After a map, courtesy of the City of New York Department of Water Resources.) (b) Existing and projected New York City water supply tunnels. (Courtesy of Department of Environmental Protection of the City of New York.)

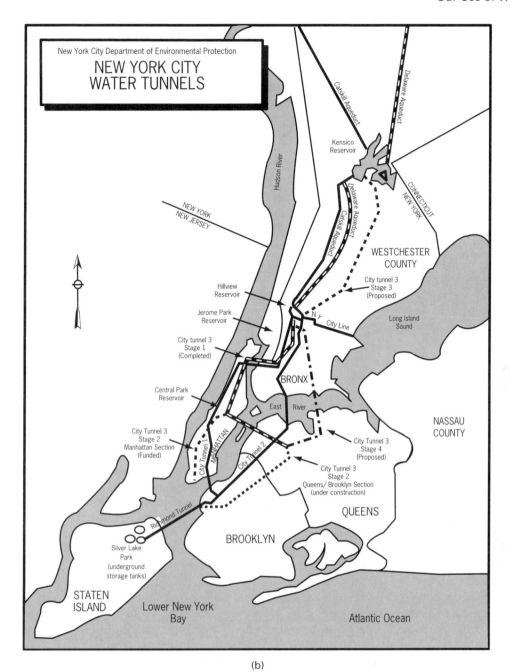

New York City Department of Environmental Protection
**NEW YORK CITY
WATER TUNNELS**

(b)

FIGURE 11.19. (*cont.*)

Irrigation

Irrigation has become an essential requirement for farming in large areas of the world where soils are sufficiently fertile, but rainfall is too low or too irregular to support the types of crops being grown. Water demand for irrigation has been rising rapidly and is now approximately 42 percent of total United States usage and as much as 80–90 percent of usage in India and Mexico (Figure 11.17). In the United States as in many countries, the withdrawal of water for irrigation takes place on a very irregular geographic distribution pat-

tern depending upon rainfall. Thus, the eastern part of the United States uses only approximately 5 percent of its water withdrawal for irrigation, whereas the western United States uses 90 percent of it water for this purpose. Irrigation systems range from simple siphons (Figure 11.21), in which gravity carries water from a main water course into the furrows, to large mechanized walking systems (Figure 11.22a) that may systematically distribute water from a central well in a circular pattern up to 1.6 kilometers (1 mile) in diameter (Figure 11.22b). Depending upon the weather conditions and the crops raised, irrigation may consume very large quantities of

WATER FOR NEW YORK CITY

How do you supply more than 1.5 billion gallons (5.7 billion liters) of clean water to more than 8,000,000 people who live over an area of 300 square miles (780 square kilometers) including two major islands (Manhattan and Staten Island)? The answer, of course, is with an incredible series of reservoirs, aqueducts, tunnels, and pump stations with an aggregate value of about $8 billion. The situation is somewhat similar for every major city in the developed world and is going to grow even larger and more complex as world population continues to increase.

It all began in a relatively simple manner when the first Dutch immigrants founded a small New York city on the top of Manhattan Island in the early 1600s. They met their water needs by relying on ponds, springs, and a few private wells. In 1667, shortly after the British seized the city, the first well was dug to serve as a public water supply. By the early 1700s, the combined effects of population increase, contamination by sewage and garbage, and saltwater intrusion into some wells forced the inhabitants to begin to haul in fresh water from the unspoiled springs in Brooklyn. Continued growth made these supplies inadequate and contributed to the city's inability to control major fires such as one that destroyed one-quarter of the buildings in 1776 and a cholera epidemic that killed 3500 people in 1832.

Citywide efforts to install an adequate water supply really began in 1799 when the State Legislature gave water delivery rights to a company that sunk new wells, built new storage ponds, and installed distribution systems of wooden pipes. The company was headed by the American Patriot Aaron Burr and used its excess funds to start the Chase Manhattan Bank. More and more water was needed, so 4000 immigrants were set to work in 1837 to develop drains, reservoirs, and a 41-mile (66-kilometer) aqueduct to bring water from the Croton River north of the city. The aqueduct, which carried water largely by gravity, delivered its first water to New York City during a celebration on 4 July 1842. The new water system seemed large enough for years to come, but more people meant more demand. By the 1880s, it was necessary to build newer larger dams and reservoirs and to begin the construction of the first large underground tunnel.

More clean water allowed the population to continue to grow. That growth, combined with the new flush toilets and household faucets, demanded yet more water. The city then looked outward again and purchased large watershed areas in the Catskill Mountains more than 100 miles to the northwest. This vastly enlarged the total capacity of reservoirs and the daily supply but required the construction of two large tunnel systems, 200–700 feet (65–225 meters) beneath the city streets, that were placed in service in 1917 and in 1936.

Today New York City is looking ahead again with the construction of another tunnel, No. 3, to improve the adequacy and dependability of the whole system. It ranks as one of the world's great engineering feats being 60 miles (100 kilometers) long, 24 feet (8 meters) in diameter, and, in places, lying 450–800 feet (140–250 meters) below the ground surface in solid rock (Figures 11.19, 11.20, and Plate 64). When completed soon after the year 2000, this tunnel will not only help in water delivery, it will permit the first maintenance of some of the older tunnels and pipe systems in more than 100 years and the first testing of some vital valve systems that have not been closed for more than 50 years. No resource is more vital than water, but most of us take the incredible infrastructure required for its delivery totally for granted.

water. For example, whereas irrigation constituted only 42 percent of total United States water used in 1975, it accounted for 84 percent of water consumed. The demand for irrigation water has resulted in the building of elaborate surface water catchment and transport systems, as seen in the Lower Colorado River region (page 398). Irrigation demand has also resulted in severe drainage of groundwater from parts of some aquifers, such as the Ogallala, where 150,000 wells now draw water (page 406) for farms along the eastern flank of the Rocky Mountains.

Water for Industry and Mining

Industrial water use includes water for processing, washing, and cooling with some of the major users being the steel, chemical, paper, and petroleum industries. Environmental

(a)

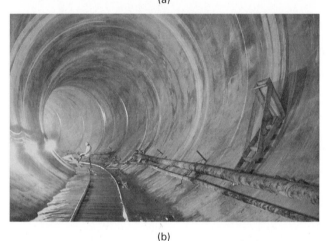

(b)

FIGURE 11.21. Simple gravity siphon irrigation system in which the water flows from a feed canal into furrows across the field. (Courtesy of R.B. Ross.)

FIGURE 11.20. (a) One of the pump stations required to supply 1.5 billion gallons (5.68 billion liters) of water per day to New York City. (b) A portion of the new 24-foot (8-meter) diameter Tunnel No. 3 being constructed to carry water under New York City. (Photograph by Carl Ambrose; courtesy of Department of Environmental Protection of the City of New York.)

concerns about industrial water usage usually do not center upon the quantities of water used because about 85 percent of the water is returned, but instead focus on the cleanliness of the water. Prior to the 1970s, industrial pollution was widespread, but the increasingly stringent water quality regulations in most western countries (notably the United States and countries of the European Union) now require that most industries return clean water to the environment.

Mining uses water for the extraction and milling of minerals and, except for these purposes, most water at mine sites is an impediment to operations. Open-pit mines can collect large quantities of water during heavy rains, and both surface and underground mines commonly have problems of groundwater inflow. Consequently, most mines produce all

the water needed on site, and many must dispose of excess water by pumping it into rivers. Modern mining and water regulations commonly require that all water discharged from mining sites be clean enough to support fish growth and meet strict water standards. Because many chemicals used during mineral processing (especially cyanide used to extract gold) are very toxic, modern mining companies generally adhere to *zero discharge* rules and recycle all of the chemical-bearing solutions. This avoids problems of public relations and environmental impact and saves the costly chemicals. The total water usage by mining operations in the United States is only about one-eighth of the combined industry and mining figure and, hence, only about 1 percent of total United States water usage.

Thermoelectric Power

Thermoelectric power plants use water in the generation of electricity from fossil fuel, nuclear, and geothermal sources. Most of the water is used for condenser and reactor cooling, and about 98 percent of the fresh water withdrawn is returned

(a)

(b)

FIGURE 11.22. (a) Walking irrigation system used to disperse water over large fields. (b) Aerial view of a large center-well walking irrigation system, in which a central well supplies water sprinklers that continuously proceed in circular paths up to 1 mile (1.6 kilometers) in diameter. (Photographs courtesy of Valmont Industries, Inc.)

to the rivers from which it comes. Thermoelectric power generation actually uses approximately 50 percent more water than is shown in Figure 11.15—the total is about 740 million liters or 195 million gallons per day, and the extra water is salt water withdrawn from coastal estuaries. The large water requirements of thermoelectric plants necessitate that they be located where there are abundant water supplies—nearly always on large rivers or at the coast.

The water used in thermoelectric plants passes rapidly through the cooling systems; thus, there is almost never any problem of contamination. The main environmental impact results from the return of the heated discharge water into rivers and estuaries. Unless carefully monitored and remixed with sufficient quantities of cool water, the warmer water can adversely affect normal aquatic life.

Hydroelectric Power

The total amount of water used to generate hydroelectric power in the United States dwarfs all other usage with the value of about 12.5×10^{12} liters per day (3.3×10^{12} gallons per day), which is about 2.6 times more than all of the water that runs off the country in all rivers and streams. This apparent impossibility results from the repeated reuse of water within pumped-storage power plants (where excess electricity generation capacity is used to pump back into a reservoir so that it can be used another time), from the repeated reuse that occurs in successive hydroelectric plants along the same river, and from the use of some water before it is evaporated or consumed in irrigation. The process of hydroelectric power generation itself consumes very little water, but the ponding of large reservoirs behind power dams, especially in arid regions, results in the evaporative loss of significant quantities of water.

Hydroelectric power is generated in all parts of the United States but, by far, the principal producing area is the Pacific Northwest where the tremendous flow of the Columbia River passes through several dams. Hydroelectric power generation has often been promoted as a nonpolluting alternative to fossil fuel and nuclear plants. Although this statement is true, the dams do have a large environmental impact on the areas they flood and in the modification of fish habitats and migration paths. There has been much concern about the major dams playing a role in the decline of salmon in the Columbia River and its tributaries. In attempts to increase the numbers of salmon, special lock systems, fish ladders, and other novel techniques have been used. However, it is clear that as long as major dams block the flow of rivers containing migratory fish, there will be conflicts between the needs of power generation and such environmental concerns.

The potential for hydroelectric power generation in a country such as the United States has been largely developed. Although the potential generating capacity for the world is approximately seven times that presently generated, the development of additional hydroelectric capacity will be hampered by the remoteness of suitable areas from population centers (see also Chapter 6).

The United States is a relatively water-rich nation, but because of its size and variable climate it has an irregularly distributed water supply. The differences in supply and consumption of the various water regions are considerable, but it is apparent that the nation is withdrawing only about one-third of available runoff and consuming only about one-third of that withdrawn. In spite of the remaining large capacity for development, local supply problems are becoming increasingly apparent and careful decisions will be needed in future years to ensure a constant high quality supply.

As early as 1978, **The Global 2000 Report to the President** summarized the world water supply situation and noted that there apparently will be adequate water available on earth to satisfy aggregate totals of projected water withdrawals in the year 2000. This conclusion has been reiterated by reports issued by the World Bank in 1995. However, because of the regional and temporal nature of water resources and the local demands that do not always correspond to the abundances, shortages will probably be more frequent and more severe than those experienced today.

Water Composition and Quality

The waters of Earth range widely in composition and suitability for human use. The purest spring water or rainwaters may have as little as 0.003 percent (30 parts per million) dissolved materials, whereas the most saline waters, such as found in the Dead Sea or Great Salt Lake, may have nearly 30 percent (300,000 parts per million) dissolved substances (Table 11.3). Seawater, which constitutes more than 97 percent of Earth's water, is remarkably homogeneous, with about 3.5 percent (35,000 parts per million) dissolved salts. In general, waters with more than 0.05 percent (500 parts per million) dissolved salts are considered unsuitable for human consumption and those with more than 0.2 percent (2000 parts per million) are unsuitable for most other human uses. The dissolved constituents in surface water and groundwater are derived from the atmosphere and from the soils and rocks with which they come in contact (see Chapter 12). Rainwater and snow generally contain a predominance of bicarbonate (from the solution of atmospheric carbon dioxide) but only a few parts per million of salts, dominantly sodium chloride carried in the winds from ocean spray. Other natural sources of atmospheric salts are volcanic eruptions that can release significant amounts of sulfates and chlorides into the atmosphere, wind blown dust from continental areas, and organic aerosols released by vegetation. In recent years, there has been a growing concern about the effects on the quality of rainwaters of both gases and particulate matter released by industrial processing and fossil fuel combustion. Numerous studies have demonstrated an increase in the acidity of

TABLE 11.3

Compositions of some typical river waters in the United States and ocean water

Substance (ppm)	Kootenai River, Roxford, MO	Mississippi River, Cape Graidean, MO	Arkansas River, Derby, KS	Chicorrea Creek, Hebron, NM	Colorado River, Hoover Dam, AZ	Delaware River, Philadelphia, PA	Ocean Water
Silica (SiO_2)	6.9	6.8	13	11	8.7	45	—
Iron (Fe^{2+})	0.06	0.18	—	—	0.01	—	—
Calcium (Ca^{2+})	46	47	107	225	92	18	413
Magnesium (Mg^{2+})	14	14	26	129	30	5.0	1288
Sodium (Na^+)	3.8	11	355 }	3.2	106	13	10,717
Potassium (K^+)	1.0	4.0	13 }		5.3	2.1	385
Bicarbonate (HCO_3^-)	160	138	249	380	159	28	—
Carbonate (CO_3^{2-})	0	0	0	0	0	0	—
Sulfate (SO_4^{2-})	45	64	217	1300	322	39	2863
Chloride (Cl^-)	2.0	12	505	48	104	19	19,275
Fluoride (F^-)	1.2	0.4	1.0	0.6	0.4	0.2	—
Nitrate (NO_3^-)	0	7.9	9.3	17	2.0	13	—
Total Dissolved Solids	215	254	1375	2220	763	128	35,000
pH	7.9	7.5	8.0	7.4	8.0	7.3	8.1

Data from "Quality of Surface Waters of the U.S.," Geological Survey Water Supply Paper 2141–2150, 1969.

rainfall in certain areas (so-called **acid rain;** see also page 82 and Figure 4.26). Acid rain has been found to be harmful to vegetation, fish, and many terrestrial organisms and promotes the weathering of building materials and natural rocks. In recent years, the pH of rainfall has dropped to 4.5–4.2 over large parts of southern Norway, southern Sweden, and the eastern United States; the most extreme case was a rainfall of pH 2.4, equivalent to the acidity of vinegar, in Scotland in 1974. Two primary causes of acid rain appear to be sulfur dioxide (SO_2) and nitrogen oxides (NO_x), which are generated by the burning of fossil fuels in power plants, industries, and motor vehicles.

Most of the dissolved substances in terrestrial waters are derived from the associated rocks, but the degree of concentration varies not only with rock type but also with the duration of contact and the amount of evaporative concentration. Compositions of waters in several rivers in the United States that are typical of waters worldwide are listed in Table 11.3. The differences demonstrate the effects of evaporative concentration (higher salt levels in rivers from Kansas, Arizona, and New Mexico) that occur in arid parts of the world. The partial dissolution of limestone leads to higher concentrations of calcium, magnesium, and bicarbonate; evaporation leads to higher concentrations of all substances, especially sodium chloride. Most surface waters are usable directly for most purposes, but the evaporative concentration has caused significant deterioration in some waters in arid regions. An example is the problem of the high salinity of the

Colorado River as it passes from the United States into Mexico (see page 398).

The U.S. Public Health Service and World Health Organization have established recommended maximum limits for the concentrations of many mineral, organic, and synthetic substances in public water supplies (Table 11.1). Of particular concern is the accidental introduction of synthetic organic chemicals into water supplies because many have toxic effects even in extremely low concentrations. The maximum total dissolved solids should not exceed 500 parts per million, but numerous public and private water supplies, especially in arid regions and many developing countries, yield waters that are above this limit (usually containing excess sodium chloride) because better water is not available or because costs to purify the water to meet these standards are prohibitive. There will be increased difficulty both in maintaining old and in developing new clean water supplies in future years as population pressures mount and as the number of complexity of possible chemical contaminants grows.

Water Ownership

The ownership of most mineral resources is relatively straightforward because they are static materials lying on or below the land surface in some relatively easily definable form. In most areas of private land ownership, the resources are considered a part of the land and may be exploited at the discretion of the owner, subject to state and local zoning regulations. Frequently, however, mineral rights have been separated from land ownership or have been sold or leased by the landowners to companies; the companies may exercise these rights to extract mineral resources if they comply with state and local laws regarding disturbance to overlying or adjacent properties.

The ownership of water, in its constant movement in visible surface waterways and invisible subsurface aquifers, has commonly been much less well defined. The present rules of ownership and use differ from one country to another, but the complexities are perhaps best shown by considering the example of the United States, where the existence of a relatively water-rich East and a relatively water-poor West has resulted in the enactment of different types of laws. It is impossible to briefly and thoroughly discuss the complexities of water law; hence, the following is intended to serve as an overview and to demonstrate the basis of modern water laws in the United States.

Riparian Rights in the Eastern United States. Basic **riparian** law may be summarized as the right of every landowner to make reasonable use of a lake or stream that flows through, or borders on, his or her property as long as this use does not damage the similar rights of other landowners. Although now locally much modified by regulatory statutes to provide for cities or public utilities, the riparian principle still basically governs the use of surface water in most of the eastern states. It has generally functioned in a proportional manner with the understanding that when water is plentiful, all have plenty, and when water is scarce, all share the hardship. The major exception to this is that municipal water supplies are now usually given protection of the right of eminent domain; hence, in times of shortage, cities get their quantities of water first, and riparians share what remains. The sale of riparian rights to those who do not border on streams has been allowed in some states but is not common. Because the eastern United States generally has large and continuous water supplies, the riparian system has worked well.

Prior Appropriation in the Western United States. The law of **prior appropriation** grew out of the California gold rush when the forty-niners staked claims for placer gold and for the water to wash the gold from the gravel. The rights to both the gold and the water were "First come, first served." This concept grew into the formalized laws that allowed the settlers in an area to make an appropriation of a specific quantity of water for any "beneficial use," and that protected the appropriations on the basis that the oldest are honored first and the newer appropriations are honored as long as there is sufficient water. Thus, in times of shortage the more recent appropriations would be denied water, whereas the earliest appropriations would always have some water unless there was none at all. In contrast to the riparian rights, which are generally held only by the landowner adjacent to a stream, appropriation rights have generally been available for sale to anyone who would pay, even if the buyer is a long distance from the stream. The consequences of this are seen in California; cities such as Los Angeles were very far-sighted in the early 1900s and bought up water rights in areas hundreds of miles away in anticipation of their needs decades later. Today, Los Angeles exercises its appropriation right to secure water that is transported by a complex series of aqueducts. Protests over the removal of water from the source regions, such as the Owens Valley east of San Francisco, to Los Angeles have led to numerous lawsuits, small pitched battles, and even bombings of the aqueducts. Nevertheless, Los Angeles bought the water appropriations and will have the rights to use them until or unless the courts rule otherwise.

Just as many riparian principles have been altered, appropriation rights have now been modified or overlaid by various compacts, agreements, or legislature decrees in many areas to allow for either more equitable or more economical use to be made of the water. Nevertheless, the original stamp of the appropriative right is still clearly visible in the water laws of many western states.

Groundwater

However difficult or arbitrary the decisions on surface water rights have been, the decisions on groundwater rights have been even more difficult because the water's source, its quantities, and its movements have generally been unknown. Clarification of groundwater rights is extremely important because this is the source of the water used in more than 50 percent of U.S. homes. Most courts in the past, and some today, follow the "English rule of absolute ownership," which states that groundwater, like the rocks, belongs to the property and thus is the possession of the owner of the surface, who may extract as much as he or she desires for any purpose. As long as wells were widely spaced and pumping relatively limited, there were few problems. However, the advent of modern high-capacity pumps and the decision by many large cities to use groundwater for portions of their water supplies have resulted in the drying up of many shallow wells. This led to widespread application of the "American rule of reasonable use," which permits unlimited extraction of groundwater for use on a plot of overlying land but does not allow the removal of water to distant places for sale (for example, to cities) without compensating farmers whose wells go dry as a result. In the western United States, many states have simply applied the law of prior appropriation to both groundwater and surface water. However, increasingly the western states have placed groundwater usage under the control of water commissions so that this valuable resource is not subject to excessive or wasteful withdrawals. Fortunately, in recent years, courts have increasingly considered our growing knowledge of the limits of groundwater resources and the manner in which groundwater moves rather than solely relying upon previous rulings that assumed the presence of unlimited quantities.

There are widespread misunderstandings about the amounts and the flow of groundwater. Studies usually report the saturated thickness of an aquifer, the specific yield, and the safe yield. The groundwater in aquifers actually only occupies the cracks or pores of the sediment or rock unit; only in some karst limestones (caves) are there actual underground rivers. Most aquifers in sedimentary rocks only contain 15–30 percent open pores, and fractured igneous rocks usually only have a few percent of their volumes as open fractures. Furthermore, much of the water does not drain out but is retained as films between grains or along fractures by capillary action (this is called specific retention); it may ultimately evaporate, but it will not drain out due to gravity. As a result, an aquifer that may have a reported thickness of 100 meters (330 feet) may contain only the equivalent of 25 meters (82 feet) of water of which only 12–15 meters (40–49 feet) is extractable. The withdrawal of groundwater depends not only on how much is present but also on how fast it can move through the pores. The specific yield is the maximum rate at which one can continuously pump water from an aquifer; the safe yield, usually a much lower value, is the maximum rate at which water can be pumped without lowering the water table. Fractured igneous or metamorphic rocks usually contain much less water because the volume of the fractures is small, but the water will often flow more quickly because the fractures are more continuous and intersecting. Furthermore, if they intersect areas of flowing streams they may be more rapidly recharged than typical sedimentary aquifers.

Environmental Water Rights

Over the past 20 years there has been an increasing awareness and emphasis on the water needs of wildlife; the result in the United States has been the development of many new regulations regarding environmental water rights. Although many policies, even into the 1950s, actively sought to drain wetlands to make them into farmland and to build diversionary canals to move water to farms and cities, today the situation is almost the reverse. The Endangered Species Act and the Wetlands Act of the 1970s are specifically aimed at preserving populations of animals and the habitats necessary for their survival. The effects of withdrawing surface waters are reasonably obvious and the effects on wildlife can be clearly linked with water loss (for example, fewer fish, beavers, water birds). On the other hand, groundwater withdrawal has less immediate and obvious effects but may be equally important as stream levels begin to drop, springs dry up, and marshy wetlands gradually convert to meadows. The combined effects of surface drainage and groundwater with-

drawal were especially evident along the Mississippi flyway, the migratory path for water birds, where duck populations dropped dramatically from the 1950s to the 1980s. The restoration of wetlands beginning in the 1980s had beneficial effects as breeding and feeding areas reappeared. The population of ducks has been rising steadily through the 1990s.

Effects such as these have introduced environmental water rights into the complicated factors governing water use throughout the United States and many other countries. No longer is it sufficient to merely point to increased needs or desires for water to raise crops or serve cities. Every new major use or transfer of water, from surface or subsurface sources, must be considered in terms of environmental impact as well. The result is a much more careful consideration of water needs, much better conservation practices, and frequently, higher water prices.

Desalinization of Water

Samuel Coleridge in his "Rime of the Ancient Mariner" identified a problem faced by large numbers of coastal cities and islands when he wrote "Water, water everywhere nor any drop to drink." Such localities have access to vast quantities of water, but it cannot be used because it is saline. In fact, four principal methods have been developed to permit the use of the seawater, or other brines, for human consumption. The general process, called **desalinization** or **desalting,** may be accomplished by any one or a combination of the following methods: (1) distillation, (2) electrodialysis, (3) reverse osmosis, or (4) freezing, which are shown in very simple schematic form in Figure 11.23. Distillation of a brine for potable water is identical to the process long used in school chemistry labs to produce high-purity water. In this process, salty water is boiled and the evolving steam is condensed into fresh water. The dissolved salt is left behind, making the remaining brine even saltier. Electrodialysis uses two special membranes that will selectively allow for the passing of sodium (Na^+) or chloride (Cl^-) ions. As salty water passes between the membranes, the sodium ions are drawn through one membrane to the cathode and the chloride ions are drawn through the other to the anode. The result is a flow of fresh water from the center of the cell and saltier brine from the lateral parts containing the electrodes. Reverse osmosis produces fresh water from salty water by forcing water molecules through a semipermeable membrane when high pressure is placed on the salty water. The membrane has pores that will allow for the relatively small free water molecules to pass through but will not allow the larger hydrated salt ions (Na^+ and Cl^-) to pass through. In a continuous process, about 30 percent of the original salty water passes through the membrane to produce fresh water and the remainder, now saltier, is discharged. The freezing process takes advantage of the fact that when salty water freezes, the ice formed is fresh water and the salt concentrates in the re-

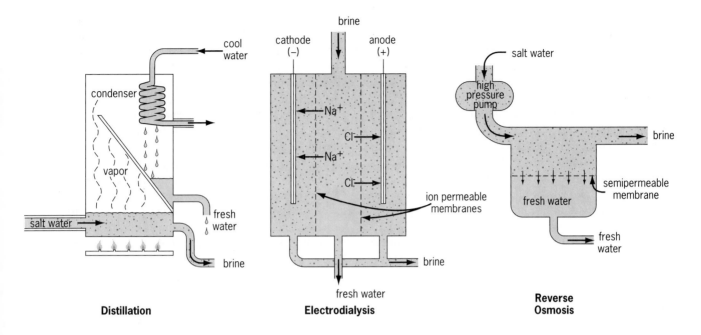

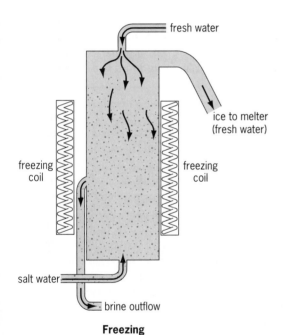

FIGURE 11.23. Fresh water can be prepared from seawater or other brines by many processes. The four most commonly used today are (a) distillation, (b) electrodialysis (c) reverse osmosis, and (d) freezing.

maining brine. In simplistic form, salty water is fed into a freezing chamber where the ice crystals that form are forced out into a melter to form fresh water. The saltier brine is rinsed off the ice crystals by use of a small amount of fresh water and is allowed to drain away. Regardless of the desalinization process employed, one of the products is a salty brine that can be toxic and corrosive. Safe disposal of this brine must be considered when desalinization plants are designed.

Each of the desalinization procedures requires the input of considerable amounts of energy and each is relatively expensive relative to the usual groundwater or surface water supply systems that serve most communities. Consequently, desalinization is usually undertaken only if other alternatives are not available. As freshwater supplies become more and more committed, countries and cities in arid regions and islands are increasingly looking to desalting as a viable, if expensive, source of potable water. This is especially true in countries such as Saudia Arabia along the Persian Gulf where oil for energy is plentiful and inexpensive, but water is scarce. During the Persian Gulf War in 1990–1991, much effort was made to protect some of the world's largest desalting plants from oil spilled in the Persian Gulf. In the United States, coastal cities in Florida and California are looking to the ocean or subsurface brines to provide increasing proportions of their future water supplies. Catalina Island off the coast of southern California has turned to desalting because of increased population but now sees a problem of more people wanting to come because of the success of the desalting plant.

POTENTIAL WATER PROBLEMS

Water, like most other mineral resources, is irregularly distributed over Earth's surface. Unfortunately, this distribution often does not correspond to our needs or desires for water at a given place and time. These inconsistencies have frequently led to problems of supply and quality and clearly suggest that such problems will increase in the years to come. In general, humid regions with more than about 75 centimeters (30 inches) of annual precipitation have sufficient surface water available in the forms of lakes, rivers, and permanent streams to meet water needs. However, in areas of intense population concentration, especially those without neighboring large rivers, the local demand can easily exceed supplies. Arid regions are constantly plagued with inadequate surface water supplies, the water quality is deteriorating due to the evaporative concentration of salts, and in some areas, groundwater supplies are dwindling. In some regions, water has become as important politically as it has economically because the control of water governs many other activities (see page 399 for an example and see Figure 11-24).

It is not possible to chronicle here examples of all current and potential water problems, but the following pages do attempt to discuss some of the major problems with which we must contend in the near future.

Limited Surface Water Supplies—The Colorado River Project

Deserts, by virtue of the absence of life-sustaining water, have always been some of the most inhospitable areas of the world for humankind (Figure 11.25). We have partly overcome the aridity of the desert by diverting rivers into it and by pumping up groundwater that occurs in underlying aquifers. Ancient irrigation systems brought about the spread of civilization from the Fertile Crescent—the valleys of the Tigris and the Euphrates in what is now Iraq—across Iran, Afghanistan, Pakistan, and India. More modern systems have allowed the spread of agriculture through arid regions of many lands and have converted parts of deserts in Israel and in California into some of the most productive regions in the world. The introduction of additional water supplies has allowed for the development of large population centers where naturally available surface water would not have permitted it.

The low latitude desert regions of the world have offered good sites for large-scale agriculture and development because many of them permit year-round growth of crops. The extensive agricultural development of these areas does, however, call for the consumption of very large quantities of water. The high evaporation rates mean that the water becomes a nonrenewable resource because there can be little recycling, and there must be a constant influx of the water to maintain these activities. The sources of the massive amounts of water needed to develop and sustain our activities in arid regions have been twofold—water imported from rivers in more humid adjacent areas and groundwater. Water provision schemes for arid regions have met with considerable success as evidenced by the creation of millions of hectares of agriculturally productive land. Unfortunately, even some of the largest and most carefully planned projects have the potential for major problems. An example is the well-known Colorado River Project that supplies water to seven western states and Mexico (Figure 11.26a and Plate 65). Since the late 1800s, farmers have tapped the Colorado for its water. By the 1920s, it became apparent that the water of the Colorado was too valuable a resource to allow uncontrolled exploitation. Therefore, in 1922 the Colorado River Compact (Figure 11.26b), signed by the states in its drainage basin, decreed that the upper basin states of Wyoming, Colorado, New Mexico, and Utah should forever get 7.5 million acre feet (9×10^{12} liters; one **acre foot** of water is equivalent to about 1.2×10^6 liters or 3.26×10^5 gallons) of water to share annually. The lower basin states of Arizona, California, and Nevada would draw the same. In 1944, a treaty guaranteed Mexico 1.5 million acre feet (1.8×10^{12} liters) of water annually; although the original treaty did not specify the quality of the water reaching Mexico, a subsequent agreement established that it should not contain more than 0.09 percent (900 parts per million) dissolved solids. The problem that has arisen is threefold. The Colorado River does not generally carry as much as 16.5 million acre feet of water (Figure 11.26B); the water reaching Mexico has contained as much as 0.15 percent (1500 parts per million) salt; and the Navajo Indian reservation, never considered in allotment schemes, has proposed a project that would claim a significant part of the Colorado River to irrigate its crops.

The original allocations of water between the upper and lower basin states were based upon water flow estimates

WATER IN THE MIDDLE EAST

When one thinks of critical resources and the Middle East, the thought generally focuses on oil. After all, this is the area of the world's greatest oil reserves, the home for several members of OPEC, and the site of the Persian Gulf War of 1991. But it is another resource, often taken for granted, that has been emerging as critical to development and peace in the region—water. The need for water in this arid and semiarid region has been apparent since Biblical times and its truth is clear in the recent Israeli comment, "Water is like blood; you can't live without it."

The dual problems of water availability and agreement on equitable distribution have grown more acute in the past 10–50 years because of large population increases resulting from immigration into some areas (for example, Israel), high birth rates in other areas (for example, Palestine), the need to intensively irrigate, and the desire to extract hydroelectricity. Solutions to finding and distributing the water have been made even more difficult by a series of Arab-Israeli conflicts and several border and resource disputes between Arab neighbors. The water resource problems of the Middle East are briefly described here but, in many ways, reflect the problems of water availability in several parts of the world.

Water was early recognized as a vital resource for Israel and, by the early 1950s, a regional agreement was being planned with Jordan to share the waters of the Yarmouk River and the Sea of Galilee (Figure 11.24). The 1956 Suez War, followed by the 1964 damming of the southern outlet of the Sea of Galilee, and finally the 1967 war effectively killed the plans. The Israeli annexation of the West Bank and the Golan Heights provided not only a military position, but also control of the runoff areas that now supply two-thirds of Israel's water. The Israelis control most of the Yarmouk River flow while the Jordanians contend that they have never been provided with 100 million cubic meters (130 million cubic yards, 26 billion gallons) of water annually from the Sea of Galilee as promised. Drought, combined with the extraction of water primarily for irrigating water-intensive crops, lowered the level of the Sea of Galilee in 1991 to its lowest level ever and raised its salinity to levels that threaten its aquatic life. Jordan has been forced to rely more than ever on groundwater but anticipates exhaustion of those supplies by 2011.

Slightly north and east, another water resource drama is unfolding. Turkey, which controls the headwaters of both the Tigris and Euphrates Rivers, began an ambitious plan in the mid-1980s that could ultimately include some 20 dams and 15 hydroelectric power plants. The biggest dam, the Ataturk on the Euphrates River, would be the fifth largest in the world and would reduce downstream flow to Syria and Iraq by half. The total project is designed to generate sufficient electricity to modernize Turkey and provide irrigation water to transform more than 4 million acres (16,200 square kilometers) of semiarid land into a Middle Eastern bread basket.

Turkey has said it will send return flow back to the Euphrates, but the Syrians fear contamination of the river—their main source of drinking water—by salts, fertilizers, pesticides, and other pollutants. Predictably, tensions are high but solutions are few. Water has no rival as a resource in an arid region or anywhere in the world.

from 1896 until 1922. Unfortunately, these estimates were made during a wet period during which the average annual flow was about 16.8×10^6 acre feet (20.6×10^{12} liters). Since 1931, however, the flow has only averaged about 13.1×10^6 acre feet (16.1×10^{12} liters), and in 1934 the flow was only 5.6×10^6 acre feet (6.9×10^{12} liters).

To smooth annual and seasonal fluctuations and to retain waters, an elaborate scheme has been built for trapping and tapping the Colorado River as is shown in Figure 11.26A. The dams store water for use but also bring about an increase in the salinity by allowing extra evaporation. The problem of supply has not been fully felt because some states have not yet demanded their total allocation and the Navajo Indians have not pressed their demands. However, the completion of the Central Arizona Project (Figure 11.27) in the 1980s results in Arizona using its allocation and California having to give up the extra million acre feet over its allocation that it has been taking to satisfy the water needs of San Diego and Los Angeles. Furthermore, projections for future water demand for agriculture and for processing of energy

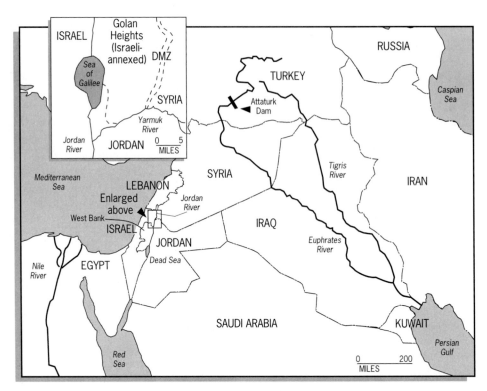

FIGURE 11.24.   Map of the Middle East showing the locations of the Sea of Galilee, the Dead Sea, and the Tigris and Euphrates Rivers.

resources (coal, oil, and perhaps oil shale) in the Colorado Basin exceed the river's flow.

The solution to the problem of the quality of water being passed on to Mexico has been the construction of a large desalinization plant at Yuma, Arizona, to be operational in the late 1990s. This $350 million facility operating by **reverse osmosis,** will deliver 1.5 million acre feet (1.8×10^{12} liters) of water with only about 0.08 percent (800 parts per million) impurities to Mexico for its irrigation needs. The saline by-product water from the plant, with about 0.82 percent (8200 parts per million) dissolved salts, will be channeled in a diversionary canal into the Gulf of California. The cost of the

FIGURE 11.25.   The droughts that have been experienced in several parts of Africa have killed large numbers of cattle and severely limited the capabilities of many peoples to raise crops. (Photograph from the United Nations.)

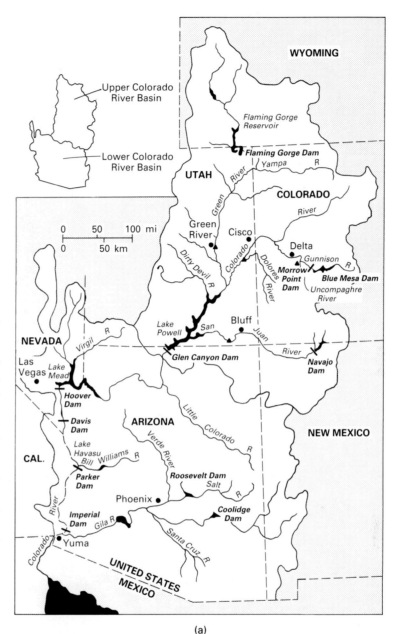

FIGURE 11.26. (a) The Colorado River basin, showing the location of the major dams and lakes and the areas of the upper and lower basins. (b) The top curve represents the total flow of the Colorado River—measured at Yuma, Arizona, before Hoover Dam was constructed in the 1930s and calculated as the flow at Hoover Dam plus the Gila and Bill Williams Rivers after that. The actual flow reaching Yuma since 1934 is the lower curve; the rest of the water has been diverted for irrigation and municipal water supplies. The dashed lines indicate the total amounts of water promised to the Colorado River Basin states and Mexico. (Data from U.S. Geological Survey, Yuma, Arizona.)

(a)

desalinated water to be delivered to Mexico to meet our treaty obligations has been estimated at 30 times the cost of irrigation water in California.

Additional conflicts have arisen along the Colorado River basin over the function of the dams that hold back the large reservoirs. The dams have eliminated the problems of flooding that had previously occurred periodically along the lower Colorado; however, the dams are now often so filled with water being held for irrigation that they no longer have the excess capacity necessary to stop floodwaters. Furthermore, the floodplains below the dams are now heavily populated; this prohibits the rapid release of water, which is sometimes needed to create the excess capacity for flood control. Compounding these problems is the need to be able to generate hydroelectric power to meet the increasing energy demands to pump water to the various areas served by the basin.

Groundwater Depletion and the Problem of the High Plains Aquifer

Under normal conditions, the quantity of groundwater and the level of the water table exist in a long-term equilibrium in which the recharge is balanced by the discharge. If pumping begins, the equilibrium is disrupted and, in general, the groundwater levels fall. If pumping is only of small

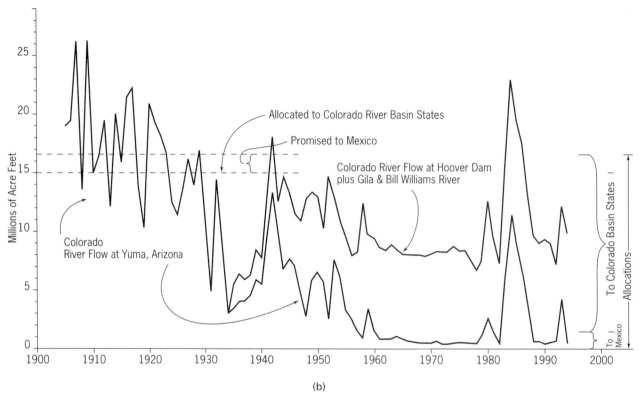

FIGURE 11.26. (cont.)

FIGURE 11.27. The Central Arizona Project carries water from the Colorado River to the major population centers in Arizona. (Photograph courtesy of the U.S. Bureau of Reclamation.)

quantities, the decline may be local, as a **cone-of-depression** around a single well; on the other hand, if large quantities are pumped from many wells, the fall may be very widespread. Pumping may also bring about decreases in the natural discharge to streams and to the sea, or in the rates of evapotranspiration.

A safe or a sustained yield is the amount of groundwater withdrawal that may be pumped for long periods of time without a continuing drop in the water table. Withdrawals in excess of that quantity result in *water mining* and a progressive drop of the water table and, at some point, a decrease in the rate at which water can be pumped. Water mining is thus much like the mining of any other mineral resource except that there is often at least some replenishing of supplies by natural recharge.

As noted previously, commonly 15–25 percent of the thickness of an aquifer is actually extractable water. Furthermore, as the water table drops and the saturated thickness decreases due to pumping, the rate of additional extraction also decreases because more of the water moves laterally instead of flowing directly downward in response to the pull of gravity.

The pumping of groundwater has increased rapidly in this century in response to larger populations, increased industrial demands, the expansion of irrigation into semiarid regions, and the development of high-capacity pumps. An example of this increase in the United States since 1950 is shown in Figure 11.28; the present rate of pumping (more than 80×10^9 gallons per day; 300×10^9 liters per day) approaches 10 percent of the estimated 10^{12} gallons per day

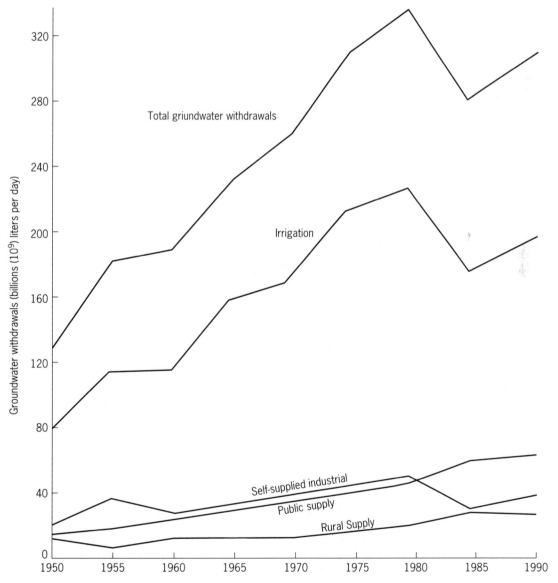

FIGURE 11.28. Trends in groundwater withdrawals in the United States 1950–1990. (From *U.S. Geological Survey Water Supply Paper* 2250 and *U.S. Geological Survey Circulars* 1004, 1988 and 1081, 1993.)

(38×10^{12} liters per day) of water estimated to be passing through the aquifers. Unfortunately, the demand for groundwater is very unevenly distributed and often does not correspond to the rates of recharge. Therefore, groundwater mining with a resultant fall in the water table has indeed occurred in many parts of the United States as shown in Figures 11.29 and 11.30.

The aquifers of the Atlantic and Gulf coastal plains are recharged by relatively high rainfalls (more than 92 centimeters; 40 inches per year), but the heavy demands of dense population and industry have resulted in areas where there has been a fall in the water table in every Coastal Plain state. An example of this decline is the area near Houston, Texas, where the water table dropped nearly 100 meters from 1940 until 1970 when stabilizing measures were taken. Groundwater levels in the upper Midwest and the western parts of the United States display marked declines in many areas because the lower rates of precipitation have been unable to recharge the aquifers as rapidly as pumping for irrigation withdraws water. This problem is especially prevalent in California, the nation's principal user of groundwater. The California Department of Water Resources has determined that large drops in the groundwater are occurring in 11 basins, eight of which are in the San Joaquin Valley, where agricultural irrigation is greatest. In the mid-1980s, the water table was declining as much as 2 meters (6 feet) per year and averaged about 0.8 meters (2.5 feet) per year. The coastal basins, serving cities as well as irrigation schemes, experienced water table drops of as much as 65 meters (200 feet) from 1950 to 1983. Another prime example of water table decline is in Arizona, in an area southeast of Phoenix, where water has been withdrawn for agricultural and municipal use since 1930. The average annual drop is now about 2.7 meters (8 feet) per year, and the total fall is nearly 130 meters (400 feet).

The southern High Plains of the United States, although commonly dry, hot, and windswept on the surface, is the location of one of the major groundwater accumulations in the United States—the Ogallala aquifer (Figure 11.31). This Miocene deposit contains more than 24,000 cubic kilometers (5800 cubic miles) of gravel, much of which is saturated with high quality groundwater. The southern High Plains, with an annual rainfall of 50–75 centimeters (20–30 inches) and an evaporation rate of 150–250 centimeters (60–100 inches) was the site of poor dry land farming until the water of the Ogallala was discovered in the 1930s. Since that time, some 150,000 wells have penetrated the aquifer to draw out millions of acre feet per year for use in irrigation. By the late 1960s, it became apparent that the water table in several parts of the aquifer was being depressed at rates as

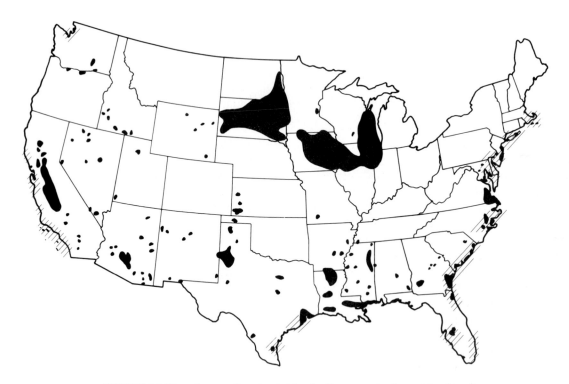

FIGURE 11.29. Areas of water table decline or artesian water level decline in excess of 12 meters (40 feet) in at least one aquifer since predevelopment are shown in black. Areas of salt water intrusion into aquifers along coastal margins are shown by the striping. (From *U.S. Geological Survey Water Supply Paper* 2250, 1984.)

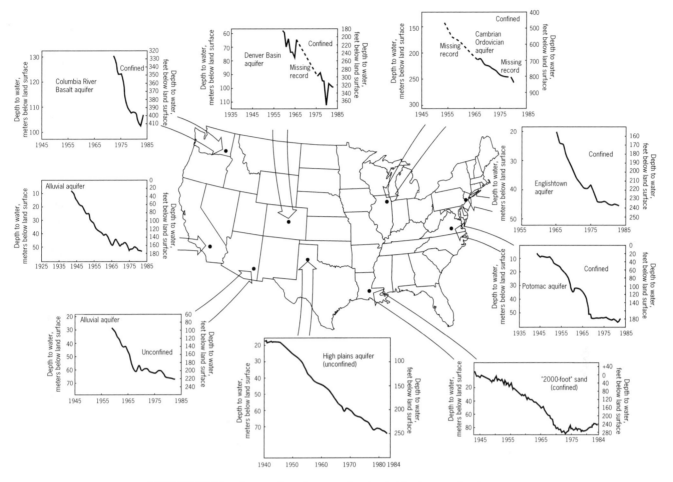

FIGURE 11.30. Examples of groundwater table depression in many parts of the United States as a result of major groundwater withdrawals. (Compiled from data in *U.S. Geological Survey Water Supply Paper* 2275, 1985.)

great as 1.5–2 meters (5.0–6.6 feet) per year. A few parts of the aquifer have actually registered a rise in the water table due to the addition of irrigation water, but large areas in the Texas Panhandle, Nebraska, and western Kansas have seen a drop in the water table of 30 meters (100 feet) or more in a span of less than 50 years. Accurate records only exist for the past 30 years, so the predevelopment levels are often estimates. After 1980 the records are very detailed, and it is apparent that the areas estimated to have suffered the greatest drop in water table to 1980 have continued to suffer in this way. The mining of this water at present rates, in an area where recharge is effectively nil, will leave many parts of the Ogallala dry within a few years. At stake are some 5 million acres (20 thousand square kilometers)—an area as large as the state of Massachusetts—in six Great Plains states, which have been major agricultural producers. The inevitability of the draining of the Ogallala and the nearly valueless nature of the land when there is no more water has even led the Internal Revenue Service to grant Texas High Plains farmers a depreciation on their land as the water table drops.

The examples of groundwater depletion discussed here are representative of a problem that is growing in magnitude both in the United States and worldwide. We shall either have to find ways to live with the amounts of continuously available water in each area or be willing to pay for massive water transport systems; we shall never find a way to live without water.

Land Subsidence Due to Groundwater Withdrawal

The removal of large quantities of groundwater in some areas has resulted not only in the lowering of water tables but also in the local and significant subsidence of the land surface as shown in Figure 11.32a. Extraction of groundwater from most aquifers has little or no effect on the land surface because the water is only interstitial to the grains of the rock that support the entire rock column. However, in some confined or semiconfined aquifers containing fine-grained sediments, the trapped water actually partially supports the rocks. Hence,

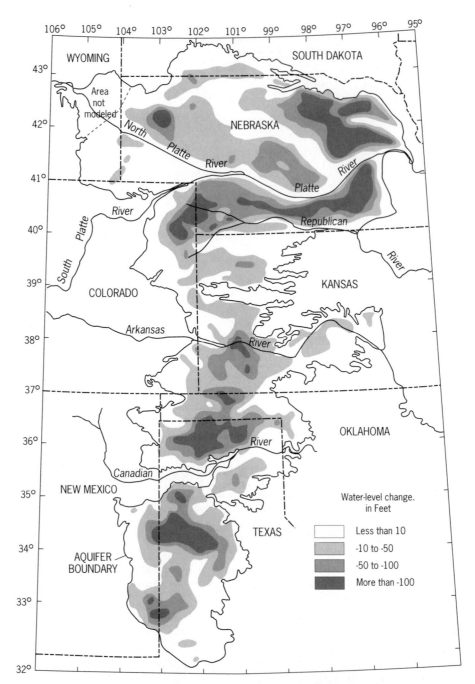

FIGURE 11.31.   Groundwater level changes in the High Plains Aquifer, the Ogallala Formation as measured and projected from predevelopment to the year 2020. Note that there are large areas, especially in Texas and Nebraska, where the decline is in excess of 30 meters (100 feet). In some small areas, the decline is projected to reach 5 meters (250 feet). On average, the water is moving at a rate of about 18 meters (60 feet) per day and only 15 percent of the total amount of the water in the aquifer is extractable. (From *U.S. Geological Survey Professional Paper* 1400 A and B, 1988.)

(a)

(b)

FIGURE 11.32. (a) Areas of significant land surface subsidence caused by the withdrawal of groundwater. (From *U.S. Geological Survey Water Supply Paper 2250, p. 66, 1984.*) (b) The *December Giant* sinkhole, which collapsed in December 1972, left a hole 130 meters (425 feet) across and 45 meters (150 feet) deep. This and 1000 other sinkholes in Shelby County, Alabama, are believed to result, in part, from natural and human-induced groundwater table lowering. (Photograph from the U.S. Geological Survey.)

when the water is pumped out, there is a slow and generally irreversible subsidence of the land surface. Occasionally, there are even sudden collapses as shown in Figure 11.32b.

Although subsidence rates are rarely dramatic, the effects and damages can be considerable and include (1) damage to well casings; (2) structural damage to buildings, roads, and bridges; (3) damage to buried cables, pipes, and sewers; (4) changes in the grades and efficiencies of canal and irri-

gation systems; and (5) increased susceptibility of flooding in low-lying coastal areas. There was great fear that New Orleans, much of which lies 2–3 meters (6.5–10.0 feet) below sea level as a result of subsidence, could suffer catastrophic inundation when Hurricane Andrew hit the Gulf Coast in 1992. Fortunately, the worst part of the storm passed west of New Orleans, but most informed scientists and officials feel that sooner or later a large hurricane with a strong tidal surge could swamp New Orleans, causing tremendous damage and loss of life. At this point, it is impossible to raise the level of New Orleans, so the only realistic protection would be the construction of massive seas walls and levees. Subsidence in the Santa Clara Valley of California has lowered the land surface below sea level, and has resulted in costs estimated at more than $30 million. In the Central Valley of California, subsidence began in the 1920s as groundwater was utilized for irrigation. By 1964, annual groundwater withdrawals had exceeded 20 million acre feet (24 × 10⁶ liters) and subsidence had affected about 13,500 square kilometers (5200

square miles). By 1970, the water table had dropped as much as 110 meters (350 feet) and the land surface had subsided as much as about 8 meters (26 feet) (Figure 11.33); the combined effect even reversed the direction of water flow in the aquifer.

The extraction of groundwater to meet the growing needs of the Houston-Galveston area since 1915 has resulted in subsidence of 2.5 meters (8 feet) in the Brownwood subdivision of Baytown. As a consequence, most of the 450 houses of this coastal subdivision have become permanently inundated by sea water (see Plate 58).

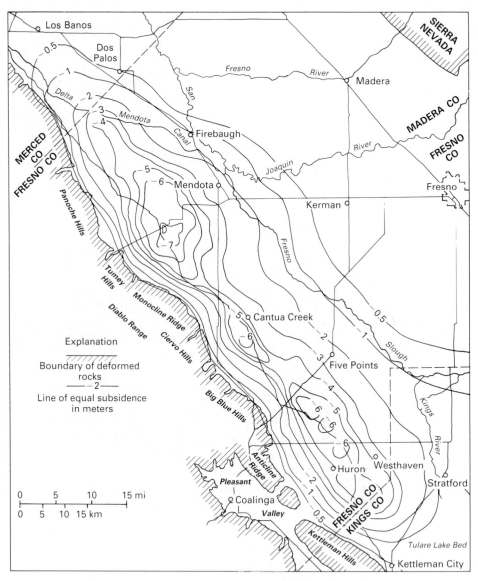

FIGURE 11.33.   An example of land surface subsidence as much as 8 meters (26 feet) in the Los Banos-Kettleman City area of California between 1920 and 1966 as a result of groundwater withdrawal. Further subsidence has been prevented by reinjection of groundwater and the use of alternative sources. (From *U.S. Geological Survey Professional Paper* 437-F, 1970.)

Saltwater Intrusion to Aquifers

Under normal conditions, the slow but steady percolation of groundwater in response to the pull of gravity is sufficient along most coastal areas to keep marine saline waters from seeping inland into the aquifers. The location of the boundary—the freshwater saltwater interface (Figure 11.34)—varies from one shoreline to another depending upon the rainfall and the permeability of the rocks and sediments and changes slightly in any given area as a function of annual, or longer term, climatic conditions.

Since the 1960s, it has become apparent that the extraction of large quantities of water from many aquifers to serve growing metropolitan areas has altered the natural hydrologic balance. The consequence of removing vast quantities of water that previously held back the saline waters is the landward movement of the freshwater saltwater interface, resulting in **saltwater intrusion** into the previously freshwater aquifers. This phenomenon has been observed in many places but is especially well documented along the coastal ar-

eas of the United States (Figure 11.29). Thus, freshwater wells have been abandoned near Atlantic City, New Jersey, Savannah, Georgia, New York City, and Los Angeles, and increases in salinity threaten usable water supplies near many rapidly growing sites. One example of the problem, as shown in Figure 11.35, results from the effects of heavy pumping of fresh water from an aquifer near New York City. The increase in salinity resulting from saltwater intrusion into the aquifer parallels the increase in pumping activity.

Although saltwater intrusion occurs primarily in coastal areas, similar problems may occur in other areas. Thus, in the Central Valley of California, an extensive body of saline water containing up to 6 percent (60,000 parts per million) dissolved solids lies below the freshwater aquifers. There is considerable concern about the potential upward movement of this saline water into the aquifers. In Mississippi, the reinjection of saline waste water from oil production has led to the contamination of normally freshwater wells in areas far removed from the coasts. The saline water was reinjected to avoid polluting surface waters; unfortunately,

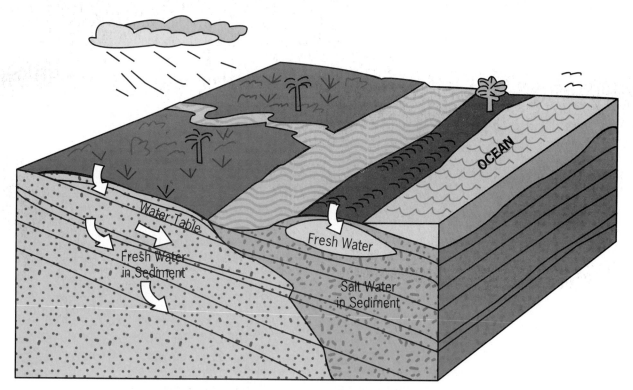

FIGURE 11.34. Groundwater conditions along a typical coastal region. The land surface, as well as a region under the barrier island, is underlain by rocks and sediments, which are saturated with fresh water recharged by rainwater. The ocean and bays behind the barrier island are underlain by sediments saturated with salt water. The boundary between the regions saturated with fresh water and salt water may move inland (saltwater encroachment) if the recharge of the fresh water is reduced or if excessive amounts of fresh water are removed by pumping.

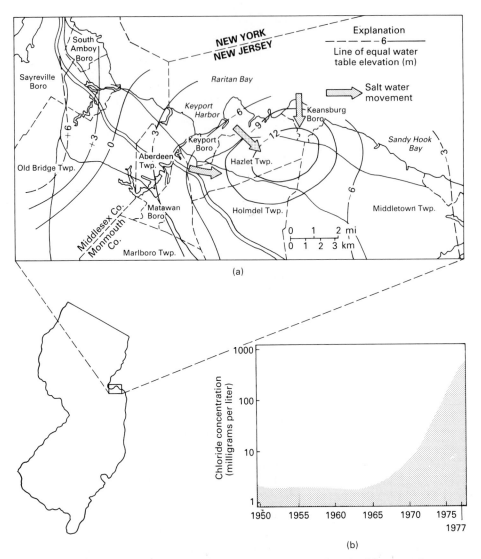

FIGURE 11.35. (a) Groundwater table depression in Monmouth County, New Jersey, as a result of increased pumping to meet the needs of a growing population. (b) The rise in chloride concentrations in water samples from the Union Beach Borough well field from 1950–1977 has forced abandonment of the wells. (From *U.S. Geological Survey Water Supply Paper* 2184, 1984.)

the directions of movement of underground waters, especially those under increased pressure, are often not well known.

It is apparent that the movement of saline water, especially when promoted by our activities, poses a threat to many important water supplies. Our increasing demands on groundwater supplies are likely to intensify the problems and, hence, require careful consideration of the most efficient uses of this valuable resource.

Soil Deterioration Due to Waterlogging, Salinization, Alkalinization

Irrigation in arid regions, although intended to bring unused or low-productivity land into full agricultural production, has

unfortunately also caused the deterioration or loss to production of an estimated 125,000 hectares (300,000 acres) of land every year. The problems arise in arid regions where irrigation systems supply water to soils faster than drainage can remove it. The excess water raises the water table to near the soil surface, causing **waterlogging,** and it permits evaporation to concentrate dissolved salts. Waterlogging is a problem by itself because most crop plants are not able to survive if their roots are under water; rice is the major exception. The buildup of mineral crusts (Figure 11.36) of the halite salts (**salinization**) or alkali salts (**alkalinization**) impairs plant growth; furthermore, runoff of salt-laden waters into streams reduces the usefulness of that water for irrigation elsewhere. The deterioration of soils by salt buildup occurred as early as

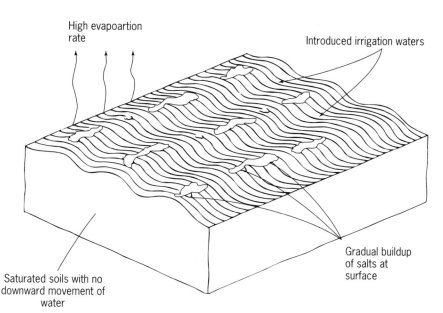

High evapoartion rate

Introduced irrigation waters

Gradual buildup of salts at surface

Saturated soils with no downward movement of water

FIGURE 11.36. Salts may build up in soils as a result of evaporation of water brought in for irrigation. Ultimately, the soils may become so salt rich that they can no longer be used to grow foodstuffs.

2400 to 1700 B.C. and is believed to have caused the collapse of ancient civilizations in Mesopotamia and in the Upper Nile Valley in Egypt. In 1959, it was estimated that 60 percent of Iraq's agricultural land was seriously affected by salinity. In the 1960s, the same problem arose in the Sind, one of Pakistan's major provinces, when 49 percent of all agricultural land was waterlogged. Furthermore, 50 percent of the irrigated land of the Sind was highly saline, and 25 percent was moderately saline. Argentina has 2 million hectares (5 million acres) of irrigated land affected in this way, Peru 300,000 hectares (740,000 acres), and the United States potentially faces the same problem in more than 1 million hectares (2.5 million acres) of the rich San Joaquin Valley in California. In the west central San Joaquin Valley, selenium weathering out of the adjacent formations has been concentrated by evaporation of water on the farmland soils. The selenium, mobilized by irrigation drainage, has accumulated in wetland ponds of the Kesterson National Wildlife Refuge, where closed basins have further concentrated the selenium to the point that it is causing very high rates of deformation of waterfowl (see page 435).

The land can be reclaimed by the installation of expensive subsurface drainage systems that allow the irrigation water to percolate downward through the soil. This downward movement is similar to the water movement in soils in humid areas and eliminates the buildup of the soluble salts at the soil surface. Such reclamation, however, has only been carried out in local areas because it is very expensive to install the drainage systems, it requires even larger amounts of water to flush out the salt-rich soils, and the salts that have been washed out may reach groundwater supplies or merely be deposited in downstream areas.

Desertification is a relatively recent term used to describe the deterioration of previously useful land adjacent to a desert region. The deterioration is at least partly in response to human activities such as farming and grazing. It frequently occurs in semiarid regions in response to changes in precipitation patterns but remains primarily a problem of soil usage and therefore is discussed in greater detail in Chapter 12.

LARGE-SCALE TRANSPORTATION AND DIVERSION SYSTEMS

Although we live on a planet 70 percent covered by water, we continually find that, in many areas, either the quantity or the quality of water is not sufficient for our needs. Consequently, we have deepened, dammed, and diverted rivers and streams so that they deliver the water in more useful places or provide better avenues for transportation. Schemes that alter or divert the flow of rivers have, in this time of environmental awareness, also become emotional issues that commonly bring those who desire to keep the status quo into opposition with those who see benefit from change. Because water, as a measurable and often limited resource, is considered in terms of municipal service, industrial production, power generation, or crop growth, its availability has broad economic implications.

It is, of course, not possible to begin to evaluate all of the types of water transportation and diversion schemes that have been constructed. The following discussion treats only three major examples.

Water for Transportation— The Tennessee-Tombigbee Waterway

When we think of water as a resource, we generally consider only the water that is actually used or consumed in daily life, in industry, or in irrigation. Water is no less an important resource when it serves as an avenue for transportation. The oceans and the world's rivers have served as trade routes since before recorded history. In Italy, coastal rivers and estuaries were modified into canals for commerce and, as in England, a wide-reaching canal system was built to facilitate transport of the coal and iron ore needed to fuel the Industrial Revolution. In the United States, the famed Erie Canal and many others like it were built to provide efficient and inexpensive means of large-volume transport. In a similar manner, the great St. Lawrence Seaway, a channel with a series of locks, was constructed to permit the direct movement of commodities from the Great Lakes to the Atlantic along an otherwise nonnavigable river.

Perhaps the two most famous water transport systems are the Suez and the Panama Canals. The Suez Canal, opened in 1869, provided a short sea route to the Far East from southern European ports. The Panama Canal, completed in 1914, reduced the length of the route from American Atlantic to Pacific ports by more than 15,000 kilometers (9400 miles).

Within the United States, the construction of canals, dams, and diversions has, in this century, commonly been referred to as *pork barrel* politics and has been the purview of the U.S. Army Corps of Engineers. The latest, largest, most expensive, and most controversial of these projects has been the Tennessee-Tombigbee Waterway (Figure 11.37). First discussed in the early 1800s, a plan was formulated in 1874 and finally authorized by Congress in 1946. Construction began in 1971; in January 1985 the 433-kilometer (234-mile) waterway with 10 locks that can lift ships 104 meters (341 feet) was opened to traffic at a cost of nearly $2 billion. The Tennessee-Tombigbee, as it is called, greatly reduces the distance and time of river transport from the Ohio Valley to the Gulf Coast and has been heralded as one of the nation's great achievements. It has also been considered an environmental disaster and an economic dilemma. The great canals noted previously have had both political and economic impact; the effects of the Tennessee-Tombigbee remain to be seen.

Water for Drinking— The Los Angeles Aqueduct System

Out of the desert with its rocks, heaven-hued and awe inspiring, its cactus-like sentinels of solitude, rose this Los Angeles—your city and mine. The magic touch of water quickened the desert into its flowering life—our city. And

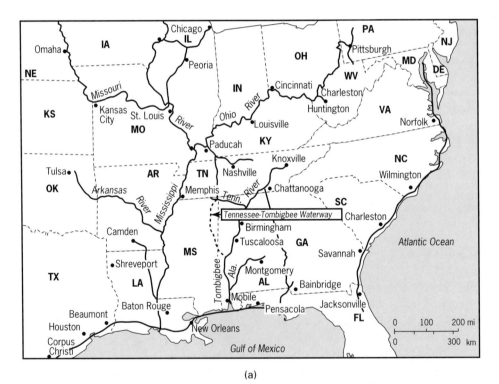

(a)

FIGURE 11.37. The Tennessee-Tombigbee water system, the largest project ever undertaken by the U. S. Army Corps of Engineers, has been both praised as an aid to economic development and criticized as a major waste of money. (From K.D. Underwood and F.D. Imsand, "Hydrology, Hydraulic and Sediment Considerations of the Tennessee-Tombigbee Waterway," *Environmental Geology*, vol. 7, 1985. Used with permission.)

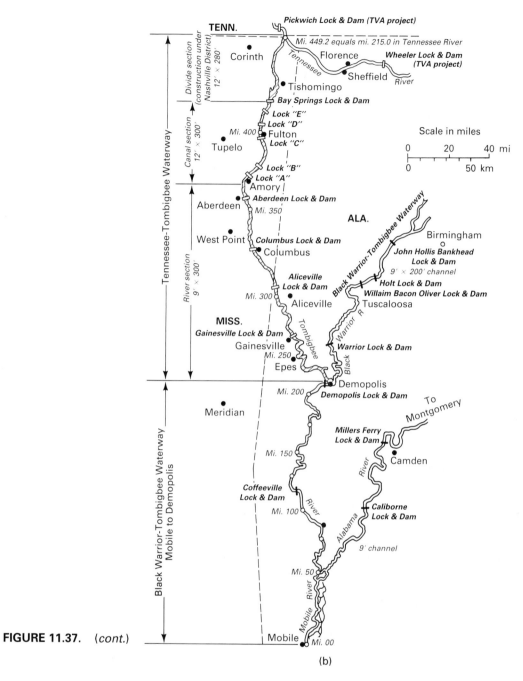

FIGURE 11.37. *(cont.)*

(b)

lest our city shrivel and die, we must have more water, we must build a great new aqueduct to the Colorado.

This statement by William Mulholland, the longtime water czar for Los Angeles, succinctly summarized the recurring plight of that city, this time in 1925, when it was realized that further growth could not occur without additional water supplies. Similar statements have, no doubt, been made in many other cities with various responses; the response in Los Angeles has been the construction of one of the world's largest, most complex—and controversial—aqueduct systems (Figures 11.38 and 11.39).

When Los Angeles was founded as a pueblo on a small river in 1781, no one envisioned that it would one day grow into a major city, covering more than 1165 square kilometers (450 square miles) with an overall population of over 7 million. The river served as an adequate source for 120 years, but by 1904 the city began to search for additional supplies to accommodate anticipated growth. Surface waters and groundwaters in adjacent areas were already in use, so city officials turned their attention to the Owens Valley on the eastern flank of the Sierra Nevada Mountains 400 kilometers (250 miles) to the east. Land and water rights were acquired, sometimes by subterfuge,

FIGURE 11.38. The water supply system of southern California involves the transport of water by aqueducts from various parts of the state. (From the Los Angeles Department of Water and Power.)

FIGURE 11.39. Aqueducts such as this one transport water from the well-watered mountains of California to the agricultural and urban areas of southern parts of the state where needs far exceed the local supply. (Courtesy of the Los Angeles Department of Water and Power.)

and construction began; by 1913 the $25,000,000 aqueduct was completed and Owens Valley water flowed into Los Angeles.

By 1923, the growth of the population to more than one-half million brought the realization that yet more water was needed. This time the Colorado River aqueduct system reached east and began to tap water dammed in Lake Havasu; the project was completed in 1941. Because Arizona did not use its full share of water as authorized by the Colorado River Compact (see page 398), Los Angeles was allowed to temporarily take Arizona's unused portion. With continued growth, more water was needed, and a second Owens Valley aqueduct was added in 1970.

In the 1980s, two circumstances forced Los Angeles to again look for more water, this time to the north where there are plans for a $5 billion Peripheral Canal that would take water from the Sacramento River and pass it south via the California Aqueduct. Firstly, population has continued to grow and to require increased amounts of water; secondly, in 1985, Arizona completed the first part of the Central Arizona Project to supply Colorado River water from Lake Havasu to Phoenix and Tucson. Consequently, Arizona is reclaiming the Colorado River water it had allowed Los Angeles to use since 1941; its right to do so was upheld in the Supreme Court.

Although the water supply system for Los Angeles has some similarities with that for New York City (page 390), the legal and emotional ramifications for Los Angeles are far greater. Because of the abundance of water in the northeastern United States, New York's use of water has negligible impact on the availability of water for others. In contrast, Los Angeles' needs and claims on water supersede the availability of water for many others, including those who live where the surface waters originate. This has resulted in scores of lawsuits, bombings of aqueducts, and, in recent years, concern about severe environmental effects. The continued growth of major cities such as Los Angeles in relatively water-poor areas is going to place greater demands on scarce or distant water supplies in the years ahead.

Water for Irrigation—The Russian Water Diversion Scheme

The steppes of central Asia are similar to the Great Plains of North America in that they represent a great agricultural belt that in large areas receives insufficient water for the region to produce to its full potential. This, coupled with constantly falling water levels and increasing salinities in the Caspian and Aral Seas in the 1980s, has led to renewed consideration of a water diversion scheme in the former Soviet Union that would have been the largest engineering project of all time. The diversion would have reversed the flow of a dozen or more rivers that now flow north into the Arctic Ocean and de-

liver approximately 38 billion cubic kilometers (9.1 billion cubic miles) of water to south European Russia and 60 billion cubic kilometers (14 billion cubic miles) to southern Siberia. Such a plan (Figure 11.40) would require at least 50 years to complete and would displace tens of thousands of people from farms and towns along flooded valleys. The environmental effects of diverting so much water into arid areas and away from the Arctic Ocean are not known and are strongly debated; subsequently, the Russian government is reconsidering the diversion plan. Nevertheless, the Aral Sea continues to decline and will likely be reduced to a series of shallow hypersaline lakes.

FIGURE 11.40 Russia has proposed a major water diversion scheme that would reverse the direction of flow of water in rivers now flowing into the Arctic Ocean and take it into the drier steppe region and the Caspian Sea. The breakup of the Soviet Union has delayed construction of this scheme, but it exemplifies the large-scale types of diversions that are being more commonly considered to redistribute water resources.

THE DEATH OF A LAKE: THE ARAL SEA

The Aral Sea, located astride the border between Kazakhstan and Uzbekistan in the central Asian part of the former Soviet Union, has been referred to as "one of the planet's most serious environmental and human tragedies." In 1960, the Aral Sea was the world's fourth largest lake—a beautiful body of water with a surface area of about 67,000 square kilometers (26,000 square miles) that supported a commercial shipping and thriving fishing industry. By 1993, the sea level had dropped more than 13 meters (40 feet), the surface area had decreased by about 50 percent, the volume had decreased by 73 percent, salinity had tripled, shipping had ended, the fish had died, and the sea had been split into two much smaller bodies (Figure 11.41 and Plate 59). What happened and why?

From time immemorial the Aral Sea had been fed by the waters of the Syrdarya and Amudarya Rivers. However, in the 1950s and 1960s, the Soviet Union decided to dramatically increase cotton production by expanding the area of central Asia that was under irrigation and cultivation. The first step was to build an 800 mile (1280 kilometer) long canal to divert large quantities of water from the Amudarya River to the southern part of the Kara Kum Desert. This was subsequently expanded into a complex network of 20 reservoirs and 60 canals that fed the water of the Amudarya and Syrdarya Rivers into 19 million acres (7.7 million hectares) of cropland in one of the driest regions of Asia. The rivers, which sustained the Aral Sea by feeding it 50–60 cubic kilometers (12–14 cubic miles) of fresh water per year, had, by 1985, become totally dry. Subsequently, small amounts of inflow have occurred but they have not been sufficient to reverse the effects of the diminished supplies.

The devastating effects of the diversion of the inflow are most visible in the change in the size and shape of the Aral Sea as shown in Figure 11.41. Former ports, with now useless ships (Plate 59) now lie as much as 20 miles (32 kilometers) from the shrinking shoreline. The rich schools of fish, which yielded 160 metric tons (176 short tons) per day and supplied 10 to 15 percent of the former Soviet Union's freshwater catch, are now totally gone because the salinity is nearly equal to that of ocean water. The volume has decreased approximately 75 percent as the water level has dropped more than 16 meters (50 feet) in the main body. The exposed seafloor, subject to strong winds, has been the source of vast clouds of dust and salt, which have blown onto and damaged the irrigated crops. Table 11.4 summarizes several of the data from 1960 extrapolated through 2000.

The devastation of the Aral Sea was completely predictable and demonstrates how easily and rapidly human activities in the pursuit of a resource can disrupt the environment. Many scientists hope that the lessons learned in the shrinking of the Aral Sea will not be repeated in other areas. In the United States, diversion of water from Mono Lake in eastern California to supply growing cities resulted in many of the same effects. However, in the mid-1990s, the water supplies were returned to Mono Lake to restore the lake to previous conditions.

TABLE 11.4

Changes in the Aral Sea from predevelopment (1960) of irrigation projected to the year 2000

Year	Surface level meters	Area (sq. km)	Volume (cu. km)	Annual inflow Ave of previous 5 yrs. (cu. km)	Salinity (grams/liter)
1960	53.41	66,900	1090	56.8	10
1971	51.05	60,200	925	45.0	11
1976	48.28	55,700	763	25.3	14
1993	—	33,642	300	5.0	—
large sea	36.89	30,953	279	—	37
small sea	39.91	2,689	21	—	30
2000	—	24,154	185	?	—
large sea	32.38	21,003	159	—	65–70
small sea	40.97	3,152	24	—	25

Data from P. Micklin, *The Shrinking Aral Sea, Geotimes* April 1993, p. 16 except for inflow which is from P.H. Glerck, *Water in Crisis,* Oxford Univ. Press 1993, p. 313.

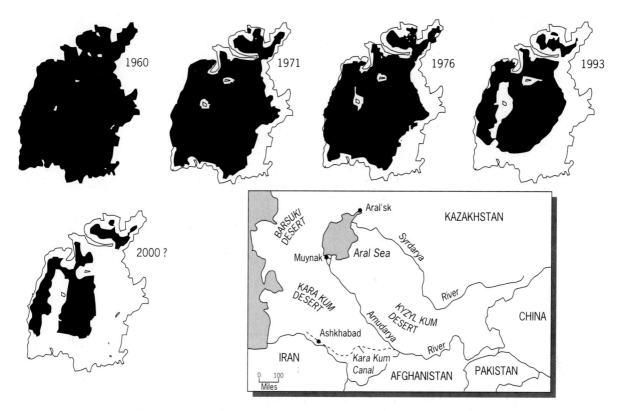

FIGURE 11.41. The surface area of the Aral Sea (black) has shrunk dramatically since 1960 and is projected to continue shrinking because of the diversion of the water from the Amudarya and Syrdarya Rivers for irrigation. (From "The Shrinking Aral Sea," P. Micklin, *Geotimes*, April 1994. Used with permission.)

FURTHER READINGS

AMBROGGI, R. P., "Water." *Scientific American* 243 (1980) pp. 101–115.

DUGAN, J. T., McGRATH, T. and ZELT, R. B., "Water Level Changes in the High Plains Aquifer—Predevelopment to 1992." *U.S. Geological Survey Water Resources Investigations Report* 94-4027 (1994).

GLEICK, P. H., *Water in Crisis: A Guide to the World's Fresh Water Resources.* New York: Oxford University Press, 1993.

MICKLIN, P. P., "The Shrinking Aral Sea." *Geotimes,* (April, 1993) pp. 14–18.

PEIXOTO, J. P. and KETTANI, M. A., "The Control of the Water Cycle." *Scientific American* 228 (1973) pp. 46–61.

PLATT, A. E., "Dying Seas." *World Watch.* (Jan./Feb. 1995) pp. 10–19.

SOLLEY, W. B., CHASE, E. B. and MANN, W. B., "Estimated Use of Water in the United States in 1980." *U.S. Geological Survey Circular* 1001 (1980).

SOLLEY, W. B., PIERCE, R. R., and PERLMAN, H. A., "Estimated Use of Water in the United States in 1990." *U.S. Geological Survey Circular* 1081 (1993).

TOBIN, G. A. and MONTZ, B. E., *The Great Midwestern Floods of 1993.* New York: Saunders College Publishing Co., 1994.

UNITED STATES GEOLOGICAL SURVEY, "National Water Summary 1983—Hydrologic Events." *U.S. Geological Survey Water Supply Paper* 2250 (1984).

UNITED STATES GEOLOGICAL SURVEY, "National Water Summary 1984—Hydrologic Events." *U.S. Geological Survey Water Supply Paper* 2275 (1985).

UNITED STATES GEOLOGICAL SURVEY, "National Water Summary 1985—Hydrologic Events." *U.S. Geological Survey Water Supply Paper* 2300 (1986).

UNITED STATES GEOLOGICAL SURVEY, "National Water Summary 1986—Hydrologic Events." *U.S. Geological Survey Water Supply Paper* 2325 (1988).

UNITED STATES GEOLOGICAL SURVEY, "National Water Summary 1987—Hydrologic Events." *U.S. Geological Survey Water Supply Paper* 2350 (1990).

UNITED STATES GEOLOGICAL SURVEY, "National Water Summary 1988–1989—Hydrologic Events." *U.S. Geological Survey Water Supply Paper* 2375 (1991).

UNITED STATES GEOLOGICAL SURVEY, "National Water Summary 1990–1991—Hydrologic Events." *U.S. Geological Survey Water Supply Paper* 2400 (1993).

WEEKS, J. B., GUTENTAG, E. D., HEIMES, F. J., and ZELT, R. B., "Summary of the High Plains Regional Aquifer System Analysis in Parts of Colorado, Kansas, Nebraska, New Mexico, Oklahoma, South Dakota, Texas and Wyoming. *U.S. Geological Survey Professional Paper* 1400-A (1988).

12

SOIL AS A RESOURCE

The fragile nature of the soils on which we depend for food supplies is illustrated by the severe wind erosion and deposition that occurred during the Dust Bowl days in the central and western United States during the 1930s. This photograph, taken in Gregory County, South Dakota, in 1936, shows a buried car and farm machinery on a previously prosperous farm. (Courtesy of Soil Conservation Service, U.S. Department of Agriculture.)

We abuse land because we regard it as a commodity belonging to us. When we see land as a community to which we belong, we may begin to use it with love and respect.

Aldo Leopold, A Sand County Almanac, 1968

FOCAL POINTS

- Soils form by the decomposition of all types of rocks in response to climate, vegetation, slope, and time.
- Physical weathering reduces the size of rock fragments and separates mineral grains, whereas chemical weathering changes the chemical nature of minerals.
- Soils are composed of residual quartz grains, clay minerals, iron oxides, and organic matter.
- Clays are the most important minerals that provide nutrients to plants because the clays loosely bond to nutrient cations, readily introducing them into the plants.
- Soils are characterized according to color, texture (mineral grain size), consistency, and structure. Distinctive soil horizons form over time and may have very different characteristics.
- The potential use of a soil, including agricultural production, depends upon its properties.
- Most of the United States' land area is forest, pasture, range, or crop land; the total amount used for dwellings, cities, roads, and mines is less than 4 percent.
- Natural erosion rates vary widely depending upon topography and climate; human intervention, such as cultivation, commonly increases soil erosion.
- Desertification, the transformation of productive land into deserts, occurs in many semiarid regions as a result of overgrazing and deforestation.

INTRODUCTION

Most of Earth's land surface is covered by a continuous layer of **soil** that is commonly less than 2 meters thick. *Soil* refers to a naturally formed earth surface-layer containing living matter capable of supporting the growth of rooted plants. Soil results from the weathering of underlying rocks by physical and chemical processes involving the **hydrosphere** and **atmosphere,** but living organisms of the **biosphere** also play a key role in soil formation and devel-

HOW FAST DOES SOIL FORM?

Although soil development is part of the long, complex process of weathering, a soil profile can form in a regolith much more rapidly than it takes to break down the underlying bedrock.

In some environments, a soil profile can form quickly. For example, a study in the Glacier Bay area of southern Alaska showed that an A horizon develops on a newly revegetated landscape within a few years of the glacial retreat (Figure 12.1). In this environment, rapid leaching of parent material occurs because of the high rainfall and moderate temperatures. Also, as the plant cover becomes more dense, the soil becomes more acidic, causing the leaching to be more effective. After about 50 years, a B horizon appears; the combined thickness of the A and B horizons is about 10 cm. Over the next 170 years, as a mature forest develops on the landscape, the A and B horizons increase in thickness to 15 cm, and iron oxides accumulate in the developing B horizon.

Rates of soil formation are much slower in less humid climates, taking sometimes thousands of years for a detectable B horizon to appear. Thus, the ice-free polar deserts of Antarctica are so dry and cold that sediments more than a million years old have only very weakly developed soils (entisols). The deep red-colored ultisols of temperate and subtropical regions probably date back to the Tertiary period, taking many millions of years to form.

The great length of time needed to develop a mature, productive soil highlights the potentially disastrous consequences of soil deterioration and erosion in agricultural regions. Once agricultural soils are destroyed, they can only be replaced over geologically long time intervals. Although ultimately renewable in the long run, over the lifetime of individuals—or nations—they must be viewed as nonrenewable resources requiring careful utilization and preservation.

opment. Where underlying rocks are covered by broken, unconsolidated materials devoid of living matter (as on the surface of the moon, for example), the surface material is not considered a soil according to soil science. Such a surface covering is described by the more general term, **regolith.** Soil comprises inorganic (mineral) matter and both living and dead organic matter. It is, therefore, a complex geological *and* biological system; there are many different types of soil. Although soils only make up a minute fraction of the material of the whole Earth, they are essential to life and a *vital* resource. Because soils support the growth of rooted plants, they are at the base of the human life support system. They are an Earth resource that we exploit through agriculture, and they can be renewable in the sense that they can be preserved through the careful use of fertilizers and crop rotation schedules. However, although soils can be made agriculturally productive through irrigation and fertilization, they can also be destroyed or irreparably damaged by natural agencies or careless human intervention. In the natural cycle of weathering, soil formation and soil erosion—to which man has introduced the utilization of soil for agriculture—balance very delicately. It is much easier for humans to damage or destroy soils than to create them.

In this chapter, the formation of soils, their chemistry, characteristics, classification, and distribution are reviewed; then their utilization and conservation are considered. Certain types of soils are exploited as sources of metals (e.g., aluminum is derived from bauxites), but these soils are technically considered ores (see Chapter 7).

SOIL FORMATION AND DISTRIBUTION

In order to understand the types of soil and their distribution, consider how soils form and the factors that lead to all their diverse soil types.

Formation—The Major Factors

The type of soil found at any given place results from many processes on many different materials. However, five major factors can be identified in soil formation.

1. parent material (the underlying rock or rock debris)
2. climate
3. vegetation
4. slope of the ground (which determines how quickly rainwater will drain and how deeply it will penetrate into the ground)
5. time (in the sense of the extent to which the various processes have progressed)

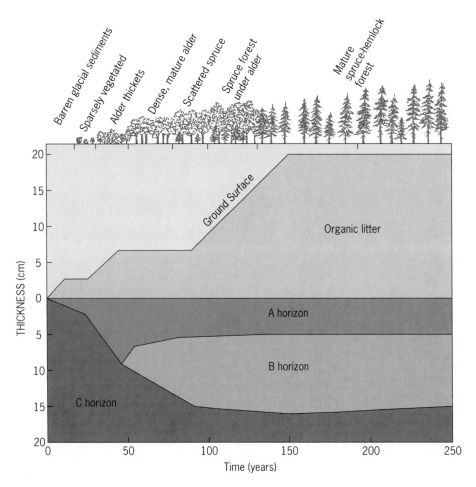

FIGURE 12.1. Soil development in the area of Glacier Bay, Alaska, over the past 250 years. During the first 40 years, the organic litter increased and the A horizon began to develop directly on the C horizon. The B horizon began to develop after about 40 years and reached a stable thickness after about 100 years. (Adapted from data from F. C. Ugolini.)

Formation Processes

Most rocks exposed at Earth's surface are not chemically stable and are constantly undergoing **weathering,** a process that involves both mechanical disintegration (physical weathering) and chemical decomposition (chemical weathering). Weathering is the first stage in soil formation.

In physical weathering, rocks are broken down to smaller pieces by various natural agents, the importance of which depends on the type of rock being weathered and the climate under which the weathering occurs. Wind, rain, frost action, and the differential expansion and contraction during rapid heating and cooling all contribute to the breakdown of rocks. Most rocks already contain internal fractures and planes of weakness. When material originally formed underground is exposed at the surface, the release of the confining pressures causes expansion, fracturing, and joint-formation. Joint planes also form when igneous rock cools. Bedding planes (original sedimentary layers) in sedimentary rocks or fracture planes introduced into rocks during major earth movements (**tectonism**) or minor movements are other examples of planes of weakness. In the broad temperate belts, frost wedging is probably the most important physical

weathering agent. When water trapped in fractures or pore spaces in rocks at the surface freezes, its volume increases by about 9 percent. Confined water that freezes can generate a possible 2100 tons per square foot, which is about 40 times greater than the force needed to break granite. Although this maximum amount of pressure is rarely reached, frost wedging produces stresses capable of disintegrating many rocks. This process is extremely visible in the wintertime when road surfaces disintegrate to form potholes. The frequent freezing and thawing of water in small cracks in the road surface breaks it down in the same way that rocks form soils. Plants and animals can also contribute significantly to physical weathering through the wedging action of plant and tree roots and the burrowing of animals.

Chemical weathering involves the breakdown of the *primary* minerals in the original rock to *secondary* minerals that are more stable in the surface environment or to material that may be carried away in solution. The extent to which the breakdown has occurred is expressed as the **index of weathering,** the ratio of a common element like aluminum or iron present in the secondary mineral compared to the total present in the soil. Water is the essential agent in chemical weathering; it either reacts with the minerals directly or carries dissolved species that can react with the minerals. Although there are many complex reactions, they can be grouped into major categories.

Hydrolysis, a reaction with water that decomposes minerals, is common in the major rock-forming silicate minerals.

$$Mg_2SiO_4 + 4H^+ + 4OH^- \rightarrow$$

$$2Mg^{2+} + 4OH^- + H_4SiO_4 \qquad (12.1)$$

(olivine + 4 ionized water molecules $\rightarrow$

magnesium and hydroxyl ions + silicic acid)

Hydration is the addition of an entire water molecule to the mineral structure. This is especially common in clay minerals and plays an important role in rock disintegration because the addition of the water causes the material to swell, resulting in a progressive spalling off from the weathering rock surfaces.

Carbonation is the reaction with carbonic acid, which forms when carbon dioxide from the atmosphere dissolves in rainwater.

$$CO_2 + H_2O \rightarrow H_2CO_3 \qquad (12.2)$$

(carbon dioxide gas + water $\rightarrow$ carbonic acid)

Carbonic acid reacts with minerals, in particular the carbonate minerals (calcite, dolomite), the principal components of limestones.

$$CaCO_3 + H_2CO_3 \rightarrow Ca^{2+} + 2HCO_3^- \qquad (12.3)$$

(calcite + carbonic acid $\rightarrow$

calcium ions + bicarbonate ions)

Oxidation is the bonding of oxygen to metallic elements (potassium, calcium, magnesium, and iron) of the primary minerals. A common example of oxidation is the formation of the rusty brown-orange hydroxides of iron on the surfaces of iron-containing rocks. In the case of the olivine mineral, fayalite, iron released by hydrolysis undergoes oxidation to ferric oxide.

$$Fe_2SiO_4 + 2H_2CO_3 + 2H_2O \rightarrow$$

$$2Fe^{2+} + 2OH^- + H_4SiO_4 + 2HCO_3^- \qquad (12.4)$$

(fayalite + carbonic acid $\rightarrow$

iron + hydroxyl ions + silicic acid + bicarbonate ions)

The ferrous iron (Fe^{2+}) rapidly oxidizes in solution because of the oxygen in the atmosphere and soil waters and usually forms iron hydroxide as follows:

$$4Fe^{2+} + O_2 + 6H_2O \rightarrow 4FeOOH + 8H^+ \qquad (12.5)$$

(iron ion + oxygen + water $\rightarrow$

iron hydroxide mineral + hydrogen ions)

The hydrogen ions generated by the oxidation of the iron help to promote more weathering.

Ion-exchange involves the transfer of **ions,** charged atoms, of metals like calcium, magnesium, sodium, and potassium between waters rich in one of the ions and a mineral rich in another. It is particularly important in the alteration of clay minerals (e.g., illite, a potassium-rich clay mineral, may lose potassium into solution and take up magnesium ions to form montmorillonite).

Chelation, a process in which hydrocarbon molecules absorb metals, is a biological process that takes place in soil formation. The different primary minerals weather at different rates, such that their **weatherability** is highly variable (Figure 12.2). Although variable, it is systematic, and the resistance to weathering of the primary silicates can be explained in terms of their crystal structures. For example, olivine, a mineral that contains SiO_4 tetrahedra linked by Mg or Fe ions, is much less resistant than quartz, which is made up of SiO_4 tetrahedra linked by their corners to form a complete framework of these stable units. Thus, quartz has a very low solubility. Because it is also hard, resists abrasion, and is commonly a primary mineral in many rocks, quartz is a common constituent of soils.

The secondary minerals resulting from weathering processes depend directly on the nature of the primary minerals and the type of underlying bedrock. Therefore, rock type (parent material) exercises a major control over the kinds of soils that form. In chemical weathering of granite, many reactions take place simultaneously (Table 12.1). Many of the rocks exposed at the surface of the earth are sediments made largely of the secondary minerals redeposited after one (or more) weathering cycles.

Climate is second only in importance to parent material as a controlling factor in soil formation. The climate directly controls weathering and soil formation through the amount of precipitation and temperature. It also works indirectly through the kinds of vegetation that cover the land. The importance of climate can be illustrated by considering four contrasting examples.

Humid tropical climates lead to intense chemical weathering to produce soils largely made of insoluble residues—iron oxides (laterites) and aluminum oxides (bauxites). The removal of metal atoms in forming bauxite from an original igneous rock may follow a specific sequence.

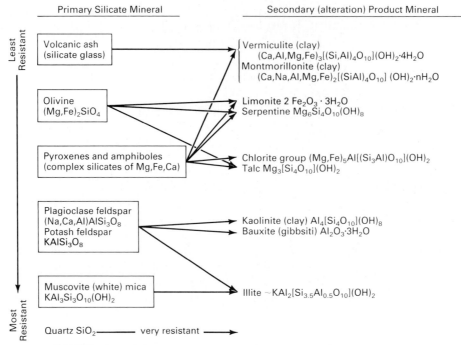

FIGURE 12.2. Weatherability of the major (primary) silicate minerals and their common (secondary) alteration products.

$$4KAlSi_3O_8 + 4H^+ 18H_2O \rightarrow$$

$$Al_4Si_4O_{10}(OH)_8 + 8H_4SiO_4 + 4K^+ \qquad (12.6)$$

(feldspar + hydrogen ions + water $\rightarrow$ kaolinite + silicic acid + potassium ions)

$$Al_4Si_4O_{10}(OH)_8 + 7H_2O \rightarrow$$

$$2Al_2O_3 \cdot 3H_2O + 4H_4SiO_4 \qquad (12.7)$$

(kaolinite + water $\rightarrow$ gibbsite (bauxites) + silica)

Humid mid-latitude climates with seasonal freezing allow much greater accumulations of vegetational debris—a **humus** layer—and dissolved species may not be removed but can recombine to form stable clay minerals.

Hot arid climates allow for the growth of little vegetation and provide too little water to permit much chemical weathering. Consequently, such regions rarely develop true soils. Instead, salts may be left at or near the surface from the evaporation of the little available water, or may form a variety of rocklike crusts such as caliche, a calcium carbonate cement (Figure 12.3). Weathering involves rapid mechanical and chemical breakdown of the less-resistant silicates. Clays may blow away, leaving only quartz sands.

Cold climates, such as Antarctica, may also be very dry because all the water has turned into snow, ice, and frost and is useless for chemical weathering. The biological activity of plants and microorganisms is also much reduced, although the slow rate of decay of organic material can lead to its accumulation forming peat bogs and thick peat accumulations, such as those found in Canada known as **muskeg.** Mechanical breakdown (by frost wedging) is the major weathering process.

The degree to which biological processes, chiefly involving vegetation and microorganisms, contribute to soil

TABLE 12.1

Products of weathering of a granite (idealized)

Mineral Component	Chemical Composition (idealized)	Products of Weathering	
		Soluble	Insoluble
Orthoclase feldspar	$KAlSi_3O_8$	K^+ (minor), soluble silica	Clay with K^+
Plagioclase feldspar	$(Na, Ca) Al_2Si_2O_8$	Na^+, Ca^{2+}, soluble silica	Clay with some Na^+, Ca^{2+}
Biotite	$K(Mg, Fe)_3(Al, Fe)Si_3O_{10}(OH, F)_2$	K^+ (minor), Mg^{2+}, soluble silica	Clay minerals, hematite (Fe_2O_3)
Muscovite	$K Al_2(AlSi)_3O_{10} (OH)_2$	K^+, soluble silica	Clay with K^+ and/or limonite (FeO, OH)
Quartz	SiO_2	None	Quartz grains

FIGURE 12.3. A white, one-meter thick layer of caliche (calcium carbonate) has formed in the upper soil horizon in much of Patagonia. The high rate of evaporation relative to precipitation in this part of Argentina results in calcium carbonate accumulating near the surface when the calcium-bearing groundwater evaporates. (Photograph by J.R. Craig.)

formation depends on the temperature and available moisture. Living plants take up certain chemical elements as essential **nutrients,** but these are returned to the surface soil when the plant sheds its leaves or dies. Plants also control the moisture content of the soil by transpiring water, and they protect soils from erosion. Animals burrowing through the soil may also play an important role. For example, earthworms rework the soil by burrowing and passing soil through their intestinal tracts. These biological processes are, in turn, influenced by climate and by the parent rock material from which the soil forms. These processes control the development of vegetation, which may permit animals to flourish. A soil is, therefore, complex and constantly changing—a dynamic system in which many interacting physical, chemical, and biological processes occur at the same time.

Soil Chemistry

Soils are both complex mixtures of chemical compounds and complicated systems within which chemical reactions constantly take place. Reactions occur chiefly as a result of water and air that are present. The air present in pore spaces provides atmospheric gases (oxygen, nitrogen, carbon dioxide) that dissolve in the water and play important roles in reactions. The water in soils contains a large number of dissolved atoms, usually in the form of positively charged **cations**—Al^{3+} (aluminum), Ca^{2+} (calcium), K^+ (potassium), Mg^{2+} (magnesium), Na^+ (sodium), Fe^{2+} or Fe^{3+} (iron), NH_4^+ (ammonium), and H^+ (hydrogen)—and negatively charged **anions**—Cl^- (chloride), SO_4^{2-} (sulfate), HCO_3^- (bicarbonate), OH^- (hydroxide), and NO_3^- (nitrate).

Soil temperature exerts an important control over both its chemical and biological processes. Below 0°C (32°F) there is essentially no biological activity, and chemical

processes are virtually inoperative; between 0°C and 5°C (41°F), most root growth and seed germination is impossible, but water can move through the soil, and some chemical reactions can occur. Biological activity increases at higher temperatures, although the seeds of many low-latitude plants do not germinate until the soil reaches a temperature of over 24°C (75°F). Temperatures vary both through diurnal and annual cycles and as a function of depth beneath the surface. They lead to the recognition of various **soil-temperature regimes** described by the mean annual soil temperature and average seasonal fluctuations from that mean. Water also plays a key role in soil chemistry and biochemistry, and the amount of water generally available in the soil also leads to the recognition of **soil-water regimes.** Both soil-temperature regime and soil-water regime are important factors when overall soil classification is considered.

Chemical processes in soils are particularly influenced by the clay minerals present. These minerals have crystal structures in which the atoms form layers (Figure 12.4), and the forces bonding the individual layers together are much weaker than those bonding the materials within a single layer. This enables water molecules and various other ions dissolved in the water to penetrate between layers and become loosely bonded into the structure. Ions may also attach in a similar fashion to the surface of the clay particles. Ions and molecules bound to clay particles in this way may be replaced by other ions and molecules in a process of **exchange.** Most commonly, this involves **cation exchange.** Common cations selectively replace specific others in a sequence: aluminum (Al^{3+}) replaces calcium (Ca^{2+}), which replaces magnesium (Mg^{2+}), which replaces potassium (K^+), which finally replaces sodium (Na^+). The capacity of a soil to hold and exchange cations in this way is known as its cation exchange capacity. Clay minerals formed in the early stages of

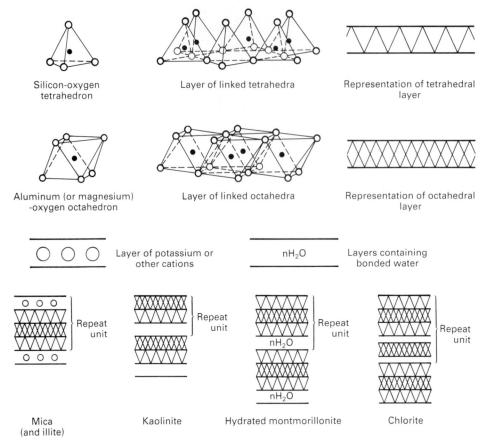

FIGURE 12.4. Crystal structures of some common clay minerals. The basic building blocks are sheets of silica tetrahedra and alumina, or magnesia, octahedra between which layers of potassium, sodium, or other cations or bonded water may lie. Different layer sequences occur in the different clay minerals.

weathering or by less intense weathering, such as **montmorillonite** and **vermiculite,** generally have high cation **exchange capacities,** whereas those of clays formed in advanced stages by intense weathering (e.g., kaolinite) are much lower. Soils with high cation exchange capacities can usually function well in storing plant nutrients and are generally more fertile than those with low exchange capacities.

Another important factor in soil fertility is the acidity or alkalinity of the soil, measured in terms of the pH, the concentration of hydrogen ions (H^+), of the soil. Certain cations in addition to H^+, especially Al^{3+} and $Al(OH)^2$, promote acidic conditions in soil and are considered to be acid-generating; others promote alkalinity, such as the base cations of Ca^{2+}, Mg^{2+}, K^+, and Na^+. Both types of cations must be present in the soil water or sufficiently loosely held in the clays to readily enter the soil water; otherwise, they will have no effect on soil chemistry. Certain crops require near-neutral (pH 7) values, but other plants may show considerable preference for either acidic or alkaline soils, a factor that strongly influences the distribution of plant types. Soils with

a pH less than 6 require the addition of **lime** (calcium oxide or calcium carbonate) to bring the pH closer to neutral if most farm crops are to be successfully cultivated. Acidic soils are also commonly deficient in other nutrients and may require the addition of fertilizers as well as limestone to raise the pH.

Soil Characteristics

Before considering the differences among soil types, it is useful to emphasize some of the most important properties and characteristics of soils that might form the basis for a classification scheme.

Color is an obvious property that can be described using quantitative scales. Sometimes, it arises directly from the parent matter that weathers to form the soil, but commonly it arises during the soil-forming process. For example, black color comes from organic matter, and red color comes from iron oxide.

Texture is used to classify soils by following a U.S. Department of Agriculture scheme of defining the percentages of sand, silt, and clay present in the soil. The three components are defined in terms of particle size.

Sand—2.0–0.05 mm diameter

Silt—0.05–0.002 mm diameter

Clay—less than 0.002 mm diameter

The boundaries are drawn somewhat differently than those used by geologists. It is also important to note that the term *clay* is used purely to describe particle size and not mineralogy (Figure 12.5). A mixture in which all three of these materials occur in substantial amounts is called **loam.** Soil texture is important because it largely determines the extent to which water is retained or passed. Pure clay holds the most water, and pure sand holds the least. Hence, sandy soils require more frequent watering. Clay-rich soils take water very slowly, so there is a danger of losing surface runoff if irrigation is used.

Consistency is a property that relates to the stickiness of wet soil or the plasticity of moist soil. Some soil horizons become cemented through the accumulation of minerals such as silica, iron oxides, or calcium carbonate.

Soil Structure refers to the presence and nature of lumps made from clusters of individual soil particles. Such a natural lump is called a **ped,** different from a **clod** that is produced during plowing. Soil structure is described in terms of the shape, size, and durability of the peds, and it is a property of considerable importance in agriculture, affecting the ease of cultivation, susceptibility to erosion, and ease of water penetration into the dry soil. There are four basic types of soil structure: platy, prismatic, blocky, and spheroidal (Figure 12.6).

Soil Horizons are the distinctive horizontal layers (exposed in a vertical **soil profile**) that differ in chemical composition and structure (Figure 12.7). The two major classes of soil horizons are *horizons of organic matter* and *mineral horizons of differing compositions.* The former (labeled with a letter O) is made of plant and animal debris; it commonly has an upper horizon (O1) of recognizable plant material underlain by the decomposed material (humus) of the O2 horizon. Mineral horizons consist of detrital particles of sand- and silt-size mineral fragments and of clay minerals and other similar weathering products. The A horizon overlies the B horizon and typically contains more organic matter; the B horizon contains more mineral matter and is generally less friable. Underlying the B horizon may be a C horizon of weathered parent material and the bedrock labeled the R horizon (Figure 12.7). In detail, the variations found in soil profiles are extensive, and the system of labeling them is suitably complex.

Soil Classification

Older systems of soil classification emphasized factors such as climate, relief, and parent material as controlling soil formation. A widely used scheme of this type was developed by

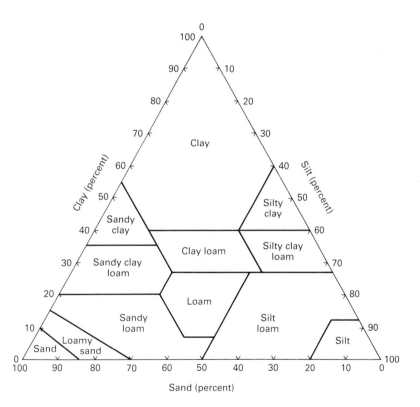

FIGURE 12.5. A triangular diagram illustrating the textural classification of soils. Note that, in this classification, the terms *clay* and *sand* refer only to the sizes of particles and not their compositions.

(a)

(c)

(b)

(d)

FIGURE 12.6. An illustration of the four basic soil structures: (a) blocky (angular) soil from a B horizon in western New York, (b) granular (spheroidal) soil from an A horizon in southwestern Kansas, (c) platy soil from an A horizon in central Iowa, and (d) prismatic soil from a B horizon in central South Dakota. The scales are all in inches. (Photographs courtesy of Roy W. Simonson, Soil Conservation Service, U.S. Department of Agriculture.)

the U.S. Department of Agriculture in 1938 to recognize three orders of soils: **zonal soils,** formed under conditions of good drainage with marked involvement of climate and vegetation; **intrazonal soils,** formed under conditions of poor drainage (e.g., bogs); and **azonal soils,** formed under conditions nonconducive to the development of any real soil profile (e.g., on steep slopes and in certain deserts). Further division into a number of suborders was followed in this classification by the recognition of great soil groups. The names of some of these groups reflect the important influence of Russian scientists in this field (e.g., podzol and chernozem), and others reflect American contributions (e.g., prairie soils and chestnut soils). However, by the latter half of the twentieth century, it became increasingly clear to soil scientists that classification schemes of this type were inadequate. They were both insufficiently comprehensive and based on unsup-

ported and often untestable assumptions about the mode of soil formation. New approaches were adopted that led to the presentation of a **Comprehensive Soil Classification System** (CSCS) at the Seventh International Congress of Soil Science in 1960; as apparent from its name, the system is sometimes known as the "Seventh Approximation." The system relies on the characteristics of the soils (morphology and composition) with every attempt being made to quantitatively define these characteristics and to use readily observable features. The CSCS is based on a hierarchy with six levels: orders (10), suborders (47), great groups (185), subgroups (more than 1000), families (more than 5000), and series (more than 10,000). The smallest distinctive division of the soil of a given geographical area is termed the **polypedon,** and every polypedon falls within only one of the ten **soil orders.** A variety of criteria are used to uniquely define each

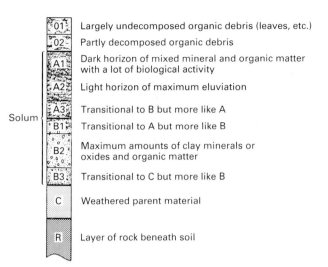

FIGURE 12.7. The designation of horizons for a hypothetical soil profile that could represent a forest soil in a cool, moist climate.

of the orders, and these may include gross composition (e.g., percent clay, percent organic matter); degree of development of soil horizons and presence or absence of certain diagnostic horizons; and the degree of weathering of the soil minerals (possibly expressed by cation exchange capacity).

Soil Distribution

The processes of formation and problems of classification of soils are topics that naturally lead to the distribution of soils (Figures 12.8 and 12.9). Figure 12.8 is a cross section from the southwest to the northeast of North America and shows the differences in soil type and thickness. The map in Figure 12.9 is oversimplified, but it does show the correlations to be expected between soil types and climate. For example, it shows the aridisols being located in the world's great deserts and the oxisols in the great tropical zones. This overall pattern of soil distribution must be kept in mind when considering the utilization, management, and conservation of soils.

SOIL TYPE AND LAND USE

The soil classification systems provide the basis for discussing soil use in agriculture on a global or regional scale. The potential use of a soil depends on its particular properties. However, suitable soils are not the only factors governing successful utilization of agriculture land—there are other factors, of which the most important is the water supply. The practical exploitation of soils through agriculture may be one of several forms of utilization of the land in a particular area. Conflicts result from problems of land management and may involve individual landowners, communities, companies, or local and national governments.

Soils and Agriculture

Soils that can grow crops are usually referred to as fertile. This means that the soil is rich enough in the nutrients needed for the sustained growth of plants and trees useful to people. The actual capacity of the soil to support such growth is called its productivity, and this depends on whether the soil is fertile and has a structure and consistency that makes it easy to till. Tilling aerates the soil, allows the passage of water, and promotes the spreading of plant roots. Despite adequate rainfall, some soil is unproductive because it drains too quickly; it is too **permeable.** Other soils may be barren because they are **impermeable** to moisture.

Productive soils belong only to certain categories named in the CSCS classification. In general terms, soils of mountainous areas and deserts (entisols and aridisols) are nonproductive, whereas the most productive soils include the mollisols, alfisols, and spodosols of temperate and more humid areas. Oxisols and many ultisols of subtropical and tropical areas are also chiefly unsuited to agricultural use because many essential nutrients have been removed, leaving an infertile soil that may be hard and brick-like, such as many laterites and bauxites. The inceptisols of the tundra will not support agriculture because the ground is often frozen; the organic-rich histosols of many bog land areas are often too acidic for utilization.

FIGURE 12.8. Idealized soil profile from the southwest to the northeast of the North American continent. Note that the thickest and richest soils occur in the Midwest. Soils in the desert Southwest, where it is arid, and in the subarctic Northeast, where it is cool, are much thinner.

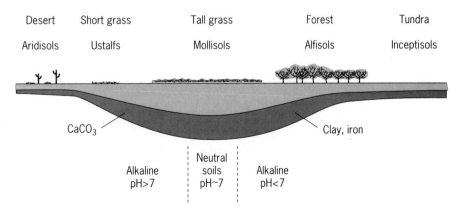

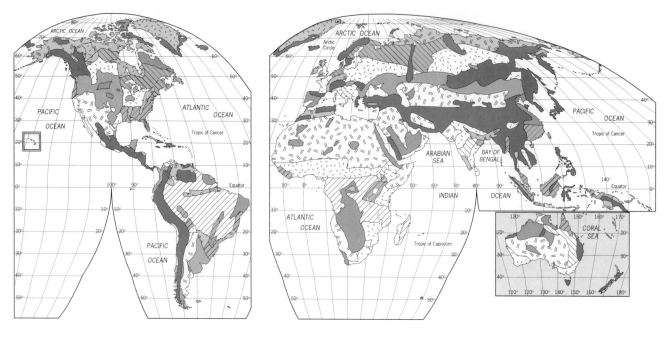

FIGURE 12.9. A generalized map showing world distribution of soils. (Modified from Soil Conservation Service, U.S. Department of Agriculture.)

Productive soils, like many other types of resources, are very unevenly distributed over the surface of Earth (Figure 12.9). On average, only about 10 percent of Earth's land surface (3 percent of the total surface) is productive cropland. This cropland, despite the importance of the seas and oceans as sources of food, is estimated to produce 97 percent of the world's food. The percentage of cropland varies markedly from country to country, being very high in flat-lying, well-watered regions such as the Netherlands and much less in mountainous countries such as Switzerland or in arid countries such as Saudi Arabia. Whereas desert soils are estimated to cover about 17 percent of Earth's land surface, the continent of Australia is about 44 percent desert, Africa is about 37 percent desert, but Eurasia is only 15 percent desert. However, do all these desert areas need to be unproductive? In theory, the answer is no. Deserts include some potentially fertile and productive areas; the main factor preventing their utilization is a lack of water. The ques-

tion then becomes one of cost because water is precisely the resource that is least available in desert areas. It would be required in enormous volumes to counter the losses through evaporation. In areas where the irrigation of the desert takes place on a large scale, nature has generally provided a water supply in the form of a great river or underground aquifer. Perhaps the most outstanding example of this is the Nile River in Egypt, around which formed one of the world's first agriculturally based societies.

Unproductive land areas due to factors other than lack of water supply may, in theory, be made productive. Problems concerning the permeability of the ground or the absence of essential nutrients may be remedied by farming methods and the use of chemicals and fertilizers (see Chapter 10). Seven chemical elements are needed for plant growth: hydrogen, oxygen, nitrogen, carbon (all four originally from the air and water), phosphorus, potassium, and calcium (all three originally from minerals in the soil). Another nine elements are

THE DUST BOWL

"Now the wind grew strong and hard and it worked at the rain crust in the corn fields. Little by little the sky darkened by the mixing dust, and the wind felt over the earth, loosened the dust, and carried it away. The wind grew stronger. The rain crust broke and the dust lifted up out of the fields and drove gray plumes into the air like sluggish smoke. . . . All day the dust sifted down from the sky, and . . . it settled on the corn, piled up on the tops of the fence posts, piled up on the wires; it settled on roofs, blanketed the weeds and trees."
John Steinbeck, *The Grapes of Wrath*

The *Dust Bowl* is a term first applied in the 1930s to an area of approximately 20 million hectares (50 million acres) in the west central United States (Texas, Oklahoma, New Mexico, Kansas, and Nebraska) (Figure 12.10). The area expanded episodically, extending as far north as the Dakotas, as far west as Arizona, and as far east as the Mississippi River. Throughout that decade, vast dust storms stripped soil from fields and devastated farmlands, forcing many families to abandon their homes (as shown in the opening photograph for this chapter). These areas of the high plains had been natural grasslands that experienced episodic rainfall and occasional periods of prolonged drought. Although subjected to high winds, large temperature fluctuations, and violent rainstorms, the grasses usually served as anchors in the soils, preventing excessive wind or water erosion.

The first homesteaders moved into the Dust Bowl area after the Civil War; they were successful during wet years, but they struggled through droughts. By the 1920s, the farms mostly cultivated wheat, a grain that was in demand but did not resist wind erosion as well as the natural grasses. Consequently soils began to drift. Drought followed in the 1930s, and erosion rapidly accelerated. In 1934, high curtains of dust developed in the strong winds and were carried out to the Gulf of Mexico and as far east as the Atlantic Coast. The dust storms were blinding and created numerous respiratory problems. Buildings, vehicles, and even livestock were sometimes buried beneath migrating sand dunes constantly creeping in response to the driving winds. The devastating effects on families, many of which were forced to leave the area, were chronicled by John Steinbeck in his novel *The Grapes of Wrath*. Rainfall returned to normal in the 1940s and ended the worst period of the Dust Bowl, but drought conditions in the 1950s and 1960s resulted in local problems similar to those of the 1930s.

Erosional conditions experienced in the Dust Bowl are a combined consequence of weather variations and imprudent human activities. Drought is an episodic occurrence in many areas and will weaken vegetation, hence allowing some increase in wind and water erosion. Arable farming, in which all vegetation is first stripped by plowing and then only selectively replaced by planting crops in rows, exposes the land surface to rapid erosion by wind or rain during storms. The use of deep furrows to break up wind action at the ground surface, the use of crops that better anchor the soil, and the introduction of extensive irrigation systems that ensure early crop growth have reduced the effects of the wind and rain that devastated so many areas in the Dust Bowl. In addition, farmers are increasingly turning to *no-till* agriculture, in which the seeds (especially corn) are drilled into the ground, thereby not loosening soil; erosion then does not become a severe problem.

Unfortunately, the rapidly increasing populations in many regions today are forcing people to attempt farming on marginal and semiarid lands. In several parts of Africa, the combination of prolonged drought and inappropriate farming practices are causing Dust Bowl conditions to recur.

needed in minor or trace amounts: magnesium, sulfur, boron, copper, iron, manganese, zinc, molybdenum, and chlorine. Nitrogen, phosphorus, and potassium are generally added as fertilizers in substantial amounts. Nitrogen deficiency is commonly corrected by adding ammonia compounds (such as NH_4NO_3 or $(NH_4)_2SO_4$) or various nitrates (NO_3^-). In the

eastern and central United States, the nitrogen content of the soil to a depth of 100 centimeters (40 inches) is estimated to be 5000–17,000 kilograms per hectare (approximately 11,000–37,000 pounds per acre), making up about 0.2 percent of the soil by weight. Phosphorus makes up roughly 0.025–0.075 percent of the plowed layer of farmed land in the

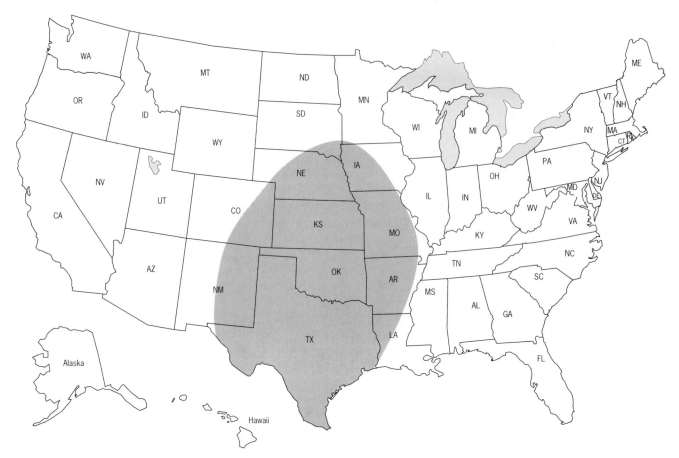

FIGURE 12.10. Map showing the *Dust Bowl* region of the United States in the 1930s.

United States, and its deficiency is remedied by the addition of phosphate fertilizers. Potassium is commonly present in the surface layers of the soil in much greater amounts than nitrogen or phosphorus (averaging perhaps 2 percent in productive soils), although much of this may be held in mineral structures and be unavailable for immediate uptake by plants. Deficiency in readily available potassium can be countered by adding potassium chloride (KCl). The elements needed in only minor trace amounts can be readily supplied by spraying with appropriate additive compounds or by adding to the major fertilizers. It has been noted already that extreme acidity or alkalinity of soils has very adverse effects on fertility; nutrients may be destroyed or removed under such conditions. Acidic ground is, of course, treated with lime in order to increase the pH to nearer neutral values.

Previously unproductive land may therefore be converted to productive agricultural land; the limiting factors are the cost of the process, the return on an investment of this kind, and the alternative uses of the land. These are all concerns of land management.

Land Management

Ever since the dawn of agriculture, it has been apparent that not all of the land surface contains sufficiently fertile soils or lies in climatic zones suitable for raising crops. It is also ob-

vious that the amount and percentage of cropland varies markedly from one country to another. Thus, very mountainous countries such as Switzerland or very arid countries such as Saudi Arabia have little land suitable to agriculture. Flatter, well-watered land such as Belgium and France have much greater agricultural potential. On a worldwide average, only about 10 percent of the world's land surface is considered cropland. In a sense, then, only a small portion of the land resource is actually a reserve; it is this that must be used and preserved to provide the agricultural foodstuff for the world's growing population. The vast oceans provide a large amount of food, but recent estimates suggest that the land provides 97 percent.

Land is an unusual resource because it can be put to a range of different uses, many of which are mutually exclusive. Land prices, tax laws, and lifestyles, ranging from the nomadic tribespeople of Africa and Asia to the traditional village communities of old Europe and the urban sprawl of some U.S. cities, all influence the ways in which land is managed. For example, the total land area of the United States is approximately 930×10^6 hectares (2300×10^6 acres); slightly more than half of this (57 percent) is devoted to raising crops and livestock, and the remainder goes to a variety of other uses, including forestry (23 percent), urban and transport systems (3 percent), and mining (0.3 percent) (Figure 12.11).

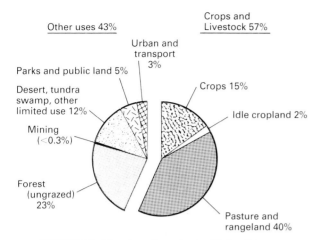

FIGURE 12.11.   Land use in the United States.

velopment, and a staggering 770,000 hectares (1,900,000 acres) were lost to make way for road, airport, flood control, or recreational projects. Balanced against these figures, roughly 890,000 hectares (2,200,000 acres) of land were transformed to crop-producing areas each year through irrigation and fertilization. These processes may have cost $2500 or more for every new hectare added ($1000 per acre). Much of this new cropland has also been added at the expense of former pasture or range land. The pattern of United States population growth and cropland development from 1800 to 1900 is not surprising (Figure 12.12). The steadily rising population cleared more forest and range land to meet its agricultural needs. Since about 1920, although the population continued to increase, the total amount of cropland has remained more or less constant. Improved yields were achieved by using more intensive agricultural methods, greater amounts of fertilizer, better hybrid seeds, and much more intensive irrigation.

There are also cases where new agricultural land has been created by reclamation from the sea. The most famous example is the extensive network of dikes in the Netherlands, a system commenced over 300 years ago enabling the Dutch to reclaim 20 percent of the land area of their country from

The overall pattern of land use is constantly changing. The total land area used for raising crops in the United States is approximately 190,000,000 hectares (470,000,000 acres). In an average year during the last decade, roughly 142,000 hectares (350,000 acres) were lost to make way for urban de-

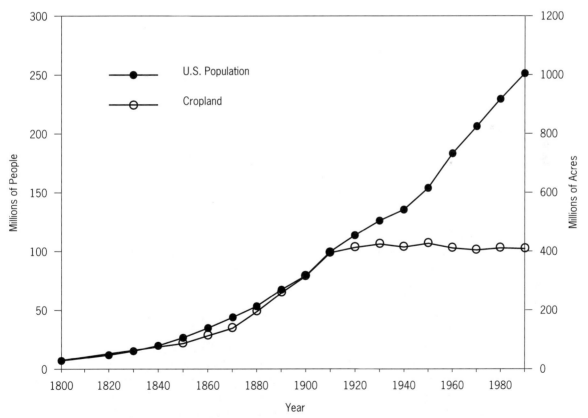

FIGURE 12.12.   The United States' population and cropland each increased approximately 14 times from 1800 until 1900. Since the 1920s, the amount of cropland has remained nearly constant as productivity has increased through the use of improved farming practices, new hybrid crops, irrigation, and more intense use of fertilizers. (From D.W. MacCleery, *American Forests*, FS542, U.S. Forest Service, Department of Agriculture, 1992, p. 22.)

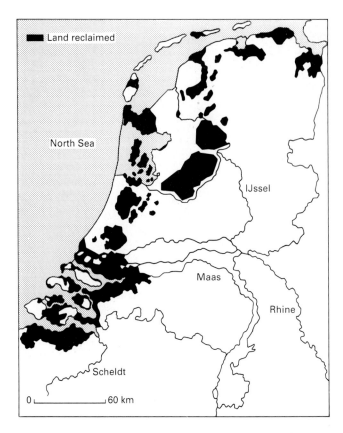

FIGURE 12.13. The areas shown in dark represent more than 20 percent of the land area of the Netherlands that has been reclaimed from the sea by the construction of dikes and the pumping away of water. Dikes were built as early as 1000 A.D., and windmills were used to pump water from the reclaimed areas in the early 1400s. (Courtesy of Royal Netherlands Embassy.)

coastal submergence (Figure 12.13). However, in 1953, 1800 people were drowned and 47,000 buildings were lost due to storm damage and flooding. This has now been averted by closing large estuaries with vast dams (Figure 12.14) to put the dikes out of reach of storm tides.

The utilization of soil as an agricultural resource must inevitably come into conflict with the alternative uses to which a particular area of land could be put. A good illustration of this problem involves the large areas of the central United States. Many areas that have underlying coal at shal-

FIGURE 12.14. More than half of the area of the Netherlands lies at or below sea level. The 30-kilometer long Barrier Dam, constructed in the 1930s to hold back the sea, has transformed Zuyderzee from a seawater estuary into a freshwater lake known as IJssellmeer. It has also allowed the draining of more than 165,000 hectares of land areas for use in farming and housing. (Courtesy of Royal Netherlands Embassy.)

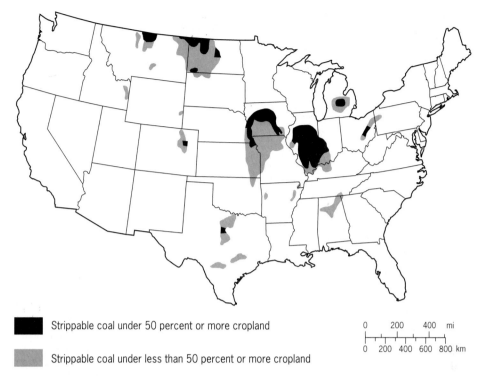

Strippable coal under 50 percent or more cropland

Strippable coal under less than 50 percent or more cropland

FIGURE 12.15. A map of the United States showing cropland areas overlying coal suitable for strip mining. (Based on U.S.D.A. Economic Research Service Publication No. 480, 1971.)

low depth that could be removed by strip mining are the croplands responsible for much of the United States' wheat and corn production (Figure 12.15).

The encroachment of alternative forms of land utilization, whether urban development, road construction, or mining operation, poses an obvious threat to the soil resource and food production chain dependent upon it. However, another more serious threat is that posed by the degradation and deterioration of soils by natural agencies, human intervention, or both.

EROSION AND DETERIORATION OF SOILS

Soil Erosion

Without the binding and stabilizing effect of organic matter and vegetation, which combine with the mineral fragments to make up the soil, the earth would soon be swept away by wind and rain into rivers and the sea. In fact, such erosion is the ultimate fate of nearly all soils and part of the continuous process of recycling natural materials. However, the rate at which this process is taking place, the extent to which human intervention is affecting that rate, and whether or not the soil resource is being depleted by erosion more rapidly than it is being regenerated by chemical weathering are all concerns.

The rate of natural erosion varies from one area to another and depends on local geology, climate, and topography. For example, the Amazon River drainage basin is lowering at a rate of 4.7 centimeters per 1000 years, removing 780 million metric tons of material a year from the area; the Congo River basin's figures are estimated to be 2.0 centimeters per 1000 years and 133 million metric tons of material. Neither of these basins has been significantly affected by human activities, but they are none-the-less changed. Before humans appeared, according to geologic evidence, the rivers of the world carried approximately 9.3×10^9 metric tons of material into the oceans annually. After people intervened with extensive cultivation, this figure rose to 24×10^9 metric tons, roughly two and a half times the original rate. More recent studies of worldwide erosion rates reported in 1995 that rivers are removing 75×10^9 metric tons of soil from the continents every year, most of which comes from agricultural land. Subsequent degrading of the land is estimated to have damaged or destroyed one-third of the world's arable land and will soon be evidenced in declines in world agricultural production. A detailed study of one area near Washington, D.C., illustrates the effects of different human activities on erosion rates. The area was originally forest (before the year 1800), and erosion was estimated to be reducing the ground level by 0.2 centimeters per 1000 years. Throughout the nineteenth century, forests were cleared and the land was

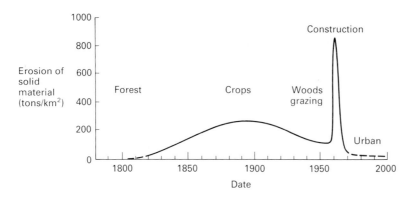

FIGURE 12.16. Variation in rate of soil erosion as a function of land usage in an area near Washington, DC, since 1800. (From Judson, "The Erosion of the Land," *American Scientist*, 56 (1968) p. 356. Reprinted by permission.)

developed for farming. During that time, the erosion rate rose to 10 centimeters per 1000 years. A partial return to forest and grazing land in the early to middle 1900s reduced the rate to about 5 centimeters per 1000 years. A period of massive construction in the 1960s then caused a very rapid erosion rate of 1000 centimeters per 1000 years. Consequent urbanization has now brought the rate back to about 1 centimeter per 1000 years (Figure 12.16). This study illustrates the pronounced effect that human activities can have on the destruction of soil by erosion.

Soil Depletion, Deterioration, and Poisoning

In areas of natural vegetation where there is no intervention by humans in the chemical and biological cycles involving the soil, organic and inorganic nutrients are returned to the soil when plants shed their leaves or die. There is no loss of such nutrients unless, for climatic reasons, excess leaching occurs. However, most crops are totally removed from the ground, leaving nothing to replenish the soil. If action is not taken to counteract this depletion, yields will fall and crops will become dwarfed, deformed, or diseased; ultimately, the soil will become barren.

Soils may also be unable to support most or all plant growth because of the presence of relatively large amounts of certain toxic substances. An excessive amount of a substance necessary for plant growth may also prove toxic. For example, flowering plants and trees will not grow where soil water contains more than a small amount of sodium chloride. Toxic substances may be naturally present in the soils but may also be introduced by humans as a by-product of various extraction and production industries (see Chapter 4). For example, vegetation destruction has occurred in the vicinity of many mining areas due to sulfurous fumes from smelting operations. The heavily eroded wastelands that have resulted are a stark reminder of the consequences of such abuse of the environment (Figure 12.17).

Desertification and Deforestation

Desertification is a term used in recent years to describe the transformation of once productive agricultural land into a desert or other form of wasteland. Although prolonged drought may appear the obvious cause of desertification, recent studies have shown that people are the chief culprits. Desertification may be caused by overgrazing, excessive

FIGURE 12.17. Severe erosion in the Ducktown, Tennessee, mining district resulted initially from the cutting of trees to provide wood to roast copper ores. The open roasting of the sulfide ores released large amounts of sulfur oxides, much of which were converted into sulfuric acid that killed the remaining vegetation. By the 1960s and 1970s, the entire Copper Basin, shown here beyond the old Burra Burra Mine open cut, was denuded, and erosion had removed nearly all of the upper soil horizons. (Photograph by J.R. Craig.)

SELENIUM POISONING IN THE SAN JOAQUIN VALLEY

Selenium is a naturally occurring, nonmetallic element believed to be essential to human and animal nutrition in trace quantities, but it is toxic when present in higher concentrations. The EPA set safe drinking water standards at a maximum of only 0.01 mg of selenium per liter and classified any solutions with more than 1 mg/liter as hazardous wastes. Consequently the U.S. Fish and Wildlife Service, alerted by deformities and a high mortality rate in newborn water fowl, were not surprised to discover that selenium levels in farm drain waters at the Kesterton National Wildlife Refuge in California were as much as 4.2 mg/liter in 1982 and 1983.

This situation is isolated in the San Joaquin Valley of California, but it has broad implications concerning irrigation practices and the problem of salt buildup in arid and semi-arid soils. The San Joaquin Valley (Figure 12.18) contains some of the most productive farmlands in the United States, but the low rainfall in the region necessitates the irrigation of close to 485,000 hectares (1.2 million acres). Agricultural activity began in the valley in the 1870s, but large scale farming and irrigation did not occur until World War I. Increased production required the pumping of nearly 1 million acre-ft (1.2 billion m^3) of deep groundwater per year by about 1950. As a result, the water table of deep aquifers declined as much as 61 m (200 ft), and some parts of the land surface subsided as much as 9 m (28 ft). Groundwater is contained within several aquifers that are separated from one another by thick impermeable clay beds. Consequently, irrigation raised the water level in near-surface beds at the same time it was being withdrawn from the deeper beds.

In 1967, surface water from the Sacramento-San Joaquin River system was imported through the California Aqueduct and began to replace groundwater. The imported waters drained from the sediments on the western side of the San Joaquin Valley; these sediments contain higher than normal amounts of selenium and other salts. Because of the well-known tendency for salt buildup in irrigated fields in arid regions, a system of groundwater drainage pipes was installed in about 17,000 hectares (42,000 acres) of the fields. These perforated pipes allowed excess water to drain off, thus reducing the waterlogging of soils and the buildup of salts as water evaporates from the surface. This system works well, successfully carrying some 8.5 million m^3 (6900 acre ft) annually along drainage canals into the wetlands of the Kesterton Wildlife Refuge. Unfortunately, these waters also carry dissolved salts and selenium (which is very soluble as selenate, SeO_4^{2-}) into the refuge. Constant evaporation of the water has multiplied the concentration of selenium and resulted in its uptake by water-borne plants and animals to levels as high as 3000 ppm. The result has been especially evident in the water fowl where high levels lead to death and birth deformity.

The selenium poisoning in the San Joaquin Valley points out how a natural mineral can become a serious local problem when modified by human intervention. Similar problems have been documented in at least nine sites in eight western states comprising 1.5 million acres of farmland.

wood cutting, land abuse, improper soil and water management, and land disturbance. It may be slight or severe in extent, but it results in reduced productivity of the land and environmental degradation, which is catastrophic for the local people in extreme cases.

This is not a new problem. The Greek philosopher, Plato, wrote 2000 years ago that Grecian Attica was "a mere relic of the original country. . . . All of the rich soft soil has moulted away leaving a country of skin and bones." The deplorable conditions in Attica were the result of tree cutting, overgrazing, and subsequent water erosion.

The best known modern examples of desertification occur in the Sahel region of central Africa along the south-ern edge of the Sahara Desert. This region includes parts of Mauritania, Senegal, Gambia, Mali, Burkina Faso, Niger, Chad, Ethiopia, and the Sudan. A severe drought from 1969–1973, which first focused world attention on the plight of the Sahel peoples, put the region's agricultural resources under severe strain. Had resource management been good, little or no permanent damage would have occurred, but this was not the case. Overcultivation and overgrazing, in response to drought conditions and growing populations, led to the depletion and erosion of fertile soils. In turn, atmospheric moisture was reduced because fewer plants transpire less water into the air, drought conditions became more prevalent, populations were forced to rely on

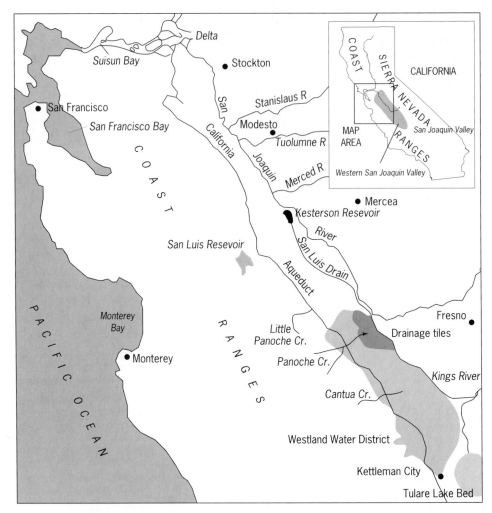

FIGURE 12.18.   Map of the San Joaquin Valley area of California.

smaller land areas for food, and the process of desertification accelerated. At present, desert areas in the Sahel are expanding at rates up to 6 million hectares (14 million acres) per year, and the harrowing sight of thousands of starving people has become all too familiar from news reports from across the world (see also Figure 11.26). Although human suffering caused by desertification is great in Africa, this is not the only area affected; the problem is worldwide (Figure 12.19).

Even in areas of high rainfall, the same human activities that lead to desertification can have other devastating effects. In some of the Caribbean Islands (Figure 12.20), excessive wood cutting, overgrazing by goats, and poor agricultural practices have denuded the eroding hills. These have suffered reduced agricultural productivity (see page 438 and Figure 12.21). The effects of this deforestation are most pronounced in Cherrapunji; here, the wettest place on Earth suffers from water shortages. Cherrapunii, in the mountains of eastern India, receives more than 1270 centimeters (500 inches) of rain yearly, but cutting down trees

now allows all of the water to run off immediately, taking most of the soil with it. In the past, the dense forest held back much of the water, maintaining a high water table and flowing streams. Today, all of the vegetation is gone, and streams are muddy torrents during rains and dry beds when there is none (Figure 12.22).

CONSERVATION—THE KEYWORD FOR SOIL SCIENCE

Soil is a resource upon which the ever-increasing population of the world must rely, but it is an unusual resource because we need to increase the availability of good agricultural soil along with continued use. The problem is one of conservation and soil buildup, and it is a very serious problem. Every continent is losing precious agricultural land because conservation measures are not being taken.

Conservation is concerned with minimizing soil erosion, minimizing the loss of nutrients through leaching, pre-

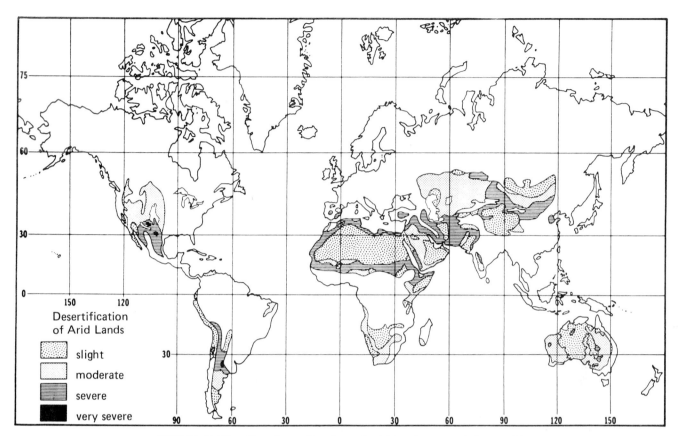

FIGURE 12.19. The desertification of arid lands around the world. The term *very severe* indicates land essentially denuded of vegetation and crop yields reduced by more than 90 percent; *severe* indicates poor range conditions and crop yields reduced by 50–90 percent; *moderate* indicates fair range conditions and crop yields reduced by 10–50 percent; *slight* indicates good range conditions and crop yields reduced by less than 10 percent. (From H. E. Dregne, *Desertification of Arid Lands,* Harwood Academic Publisher, 1983, p. 6. Used with permission.)

FIGURE 12.20. Deforestation of many parts of the islands in the Caribbean has had severe effects on agricultural productivity. Goats in the Fort Charles area of Nevis have been especially effective in destroying the original vegetation, subsequently eroding top soils. (Photograph by B.C.Richardson.)

DEFORESTATION, SOIL EROSION, AND THE DESTRUCTION OF ENVIRONMENTAL ASSETS

Future generations may regard one of the greatest disasters of the late twentieth century to have been the wholesale destruction of natural forest areas in less developed countries. Consider the example of Costa Rica in Central America. Despite a relatively enlightened attitude toward conservation, in which a fifth of the land has been set aside for national parks, 847,000 hectares (2.1 million acres)—28 percent—of Costa Rica's forests have been destroyed between 1966 and 1989 (Figure 12.21). Furthermore, most of the forest was simply burned in order to clear the land for relatively unproductive pastures and hill farms, causing the loss of tropical timber and many plant and animal species. The largest losses were upland in tropical wet forests and tropical moist forests, those that contained the most diverse plant and animal species. Two thirds of the deforestation affected areas in which the forest was the most intensive sustainable use of the land. Only 14 percent of the area cleared was suitable for pasture, despite the livestock industry being a major reason for such deforestation.

Because much of Costa Rica's terrain is steeply sloping and subject to heavy rainfall, therefore making it unsuitable for agriculture, the loss of forest cover led to rapid erosion. Soil erosion rates have been estimated at more than 300 tons per hectare from land used to grow annual crops and nearly 50 tons per hectare from pastures. In fact, between 1970 and 1989, an estimated 2.2 billion tons of soil were washed away; this is enough to bury the Costa Rican capital city of San Jose to a depth of 12 meters.

This destruction of a rich and varied natural environment is undertaken in the name of economic progress. However, the loss of this precious natural asset is rarely discussed when politicians present their analyses of the country's economy. In Costa Rica, for example, 3.2 million cubic meters of commercial timber worth $400 million were destroyed in 1989 (equivalent to $69 per capita), and erosion of soils from farmland and pastures washed away nutrients worth 17 percent of the value of the new annual crops and 14 percent of the value of the new livestock products. Nothing in Costa Rica's national economy reports records these losses in assets. Beyond national economic losses associated with deforestation are possible local and global effects on climate and the atmosphere. Many environmental scientists believe that the cumulative effect of deforestation across the major forest areas of the world could have permanent long term effects on climate, as discussed on page 435.

FIGURE 12.21. Deforestation has greatly reduced the natural forests of Costa Rica. Much of the deforestation here, as in many developing countries, has occurred to provide cropland for rapidly growing human populations.

(a) Natural state

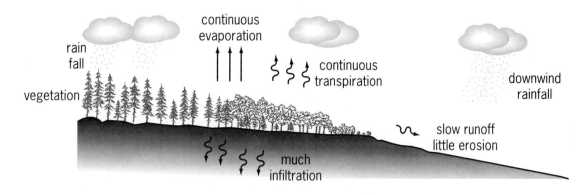

(b) After deforestation

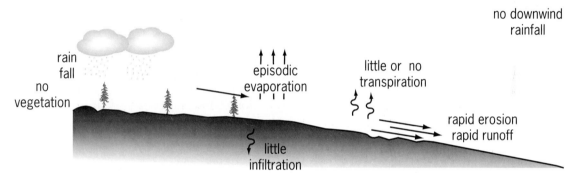

FIGURE 12.22. The effects of deforestation in reducing water retention and infiltration, increasing runoff and erosion, and altering rainfall.

venting the buildup of excess salts or alkalis through drainage control (see Figure 11.36), and restoring nutrients that are removed during cultivation back to the soil through the use of fertilizers. Certain conservation practices are well known, such as crop rotation that involves planting a succession of different crops on the same piece of ground. The principle involved here is that some cultivated crops (e.g., potatoes and turnips) expose the ground to maximum erosion, small grain crops cause less exposure, and grasses protect the ground against erosion very well. Hence, in northeastern United States, a common rotation involves oats, red clover, and potatoes. Another common practice is contour plowing where surface runoff is checked by the furrows (Figure 12.23). Sloping ground can also be terraced to reduce runoff and prevent gullies from forming, and natural channels can be controlled by damming and building ditches. Farmed land can be protected from erosion by planting hedges, wooded areas, and grassy areas; the removal of such protection can prove disastrous, leaving the plowed soil very vulnerable to wind and rain. In many areas, conventional plowing gives way to seed *drilling* in which seeds are buried

at the appropriate depth as a hole is punched or drilled. This procedure reduces the amount of energy consumed because only one pass of a tractor is needed instead of the two or three required with a plow, and it greatly reduces the amount of erosion. One added cost, however, that must be weighed against the benefits is the need for additional herbicides to control the weeds that are normally eliminated by plowing.

Despite the vital importance of soil conservation, the threat to this resource is considerable. The United Nations recently reported that not only is more than one-third of Earth's land surface now desert or semidesert, but another 19 percent of the land surface among 150 countries is threatened. The chief cause of this threat is people—stripping land of trees and other cover, overplanting, overgrazing, ignoring proper land management, and selling good agricultural land for urban development. A special study prepared for the United Nations recently concluded that, "As a result of the unsound use of land, deserts are creeping outward in Africa, Asia, Australia, and the Americas. Worse, the productive capacity of vast dry regions in both rich and poor countries is falling."

FIGURE 12.23. Contour plowing and strip farming in Carrol County, Maryland, are effective ways to minimize the loss of soil by erosion. (Courtesy of Soil Conservation Service, U.S. Department of Agriculture.)

FURTHER READINGS

BOUL, S. W., HOLE, F. D., and McCRACKEN, R. J., *Soil Genesis and Classification,* 2nd ed. Ames, Iowa: The Iowa State University, 1980.

DREGNE, H. E., *Desertification of Arid Lands.* New York: Harwood Academic Publishers, 1983.

DUCHAUFOUR, P., *Ecological Atlas of Soils of the World.* Translated by G.R. Mehury, C.R. Dekimpe, and Y.A. Martel. New York: Masson Publishing Co., 1978.

LAL, R. and STEWART, B. A., *Soil Degradation.* New York: Springer-Verlag, 1990.

LOCKERETZ, W., "The lessons of the Dust Bowl." *American Scientist* 66 (1978) pp. 560–569.

MYERS, N., *Deforestation Rates in Tropical Forests and Their Climatic Implications.* London: Friends of the Earth Report, 1989.

PIMENTEL, D., ed., *World Soil Erosion and Conservation.* Cambridge: Cambridge University Press, 1993.

PIMENTEL, D., HARVEY, C., RESOSUDARMO, P., SINCLAIR, K., KURZ, D., McNAIR, M., CRIST, S., SHPRITZ, L., FITTON, L., SAFFOURI, R., and BLAIR, R., "Environmental and Economic Costs of Soil Erosion and Conservation Benefits." *Science* 267 (1995) pp. 1117–1123.

REVELLE, R., "The World Supply of Agricultural Land." In *The Resourceful Earth,* edited by J. L. Simon and H., Kahn. New York: B. Blackwell Publishers, (1984) pp. 184–201.

SPETH, J. G. *Towards an Effective and Operational International Convention on Desertification.* New York: International Convention on Desertification, United Nations, 1994.

TROEH, F. R., HOBBS, J. A., and DONOHUE, R. L., *Soil and Water Conservation,* 2nd ed. New Jersey: Prentice Hall, Inc., 1991.

TROEH, F. R. and THOMPSON, L. M., *Soils and Soil Fertility,* 5th ed. New York: Oxford University Press, 1993.

13 FUTURE RESOURCES

The search for resources is being carried out under increasingly difficult conditions. Drilling for oil occurs from a synthetic ice island anchored to the floor of the Arctic Ocean off the coast of Alaska. The island was constructed to prevent the drill rig from being damaged by floating ice. (Courtesy of Exxon Corporation.)

You must love the crust of the earth on which you dwell more than the sweet crust of any bread or cake. You must be able to extract nutriment out of a sand heap. You must have so good an appetite as this, else you will live in vain."

Henry David Thoreau, January 25, 1858

FOCAL POINTS

- Population growth, technological advances, economics, and social pressures will determine future resource requirements.
- The exhaustion of the most accessible mineral deposits in the most developed countries will require exploration and exploitation in more remote areas and deeper in Earth's crust.
- The exhaustion of rich deposits will require the exploitation of lower grade deposits.
- The reserves of the abundant metals and materials derived from common rocks are so large that they are effectively inexhaustible.
- Fossil fuels will be exhausted in the relatively near future and will have to be replaced by sustainable energy sources, such as nuclear or solar energy.
- Technological innovation will reduce the demands for some resources used today but will create needs for other new or little used resources.

INTRODUCTION

The uses of both renewable and nonrenewable natural resources are intimately intertwined. The rapidly growing world population, coupled with a rising standard of living, results in the demand for more and more resources. For soil and water, the resource question is quite clear—we must learn to live with what we have. For other resources, and especially metallic ores, the case is not so clear. Our society's use of resources has developed through a combination of technological advances, economic opportunity, and social acceptance. Undoubtedly, changes will occur in the future in response to new technological and economic possibilities or to social pressures. Because we cannot predict these changes, we cannot predict exactly how resource uses will change. Some mineral resources may become very expensive, and others may become abundant and inexpensive. The best that we can do is to look for suggestions in future directions or trends.

FUTURE MINERAL RESOURCES

The first obvious trend concerns geochemically scarce metals, which have productions that go through cycles (see Chapter 3, Figure 3.12). European countries that have been industrialized for several centuries no longer produce most scarce metals. Their mines are either closed or closing because the known ores have been depleted. The pattern observed for Europe can be seen in many parts of the world. Many other countries, such as Australia and Brazil, are still in the period of active exploration for mineral deposits exposed at the surface or buried by only a shallow soil cover; but their resources will soon run out. European countries, and increasingly the United States and Japan, have responded to a shortage of materials from their own mines by importing the balance from countries where ore deposits are still being discovered. This pattern will likely continue for the next 20 years or more because there are still large areas of the continental crust that have not been intensively prospected. The day will come, however, when all of the accessible deposits will have been found and depleted. Where will we turn then?

The challenge will probably be met in several ways, some of which may seem unlikely or even unreasonable by present-day standards. For example, lands previously considered off limits, such as Antarctica, will be tested and eventually mined. Mining is already being carried out in Greenland and in the Arctic islands of Canada north of the Arctic Circle under conditions of extreme difficulty (Figure 13.1). It would be a relatively small step to use similar techniques in Antarctica. Another step will be to intensively explore the ocean floor. Manganese nodules are widely distributed on the deep seafloor, and certain types of metal deposits form along the mid-ocean ridges at water depths in excess of 1500 meters. The known deposits so far are mostly small and mainly of scientific interest. Within the geological record, however, there are other kinds of deposits that seem to have formed through the same submarine processes. This makes it very likely that continued exploration of the seafloor will reveal some of these deposits. Someday, they and the manganese nodules will be mined. In a sense, we can think of the seafloor as another continent to explore for minerals, just like Antarctica. Both the seafloor and Antarctica are very difficult places to work, however, and it is hardly reasonable to think we will turn to such inhospitable places for all our needs—we are likely to seek only the richest and largest ore bodies in such environments.

A more likely place for new ores is the deeper portions of the continents. Excluding digging or drilling an actual test hole, even the most sophisticated techniques used today cannot locate ore deposits beneath 500 meters of barren rock. We believe that more deposits are there to be dis-

Figure 13.1. Mining under difficult conditions. The ore bodies of the Black Angel Mine in Greenland lie beneath a glacier. The mine openings are high up on the cliff of a fjord; all people and materials must be transported by a cable. The only water available for use in the mine is seawater, so special corrosion-resistant equipment had to be designed. (Photograph by F.M. Vokes.)

covered because a few have already been found by accident or brilliant deduction; also, many deposits extend several thousand meters in depth and are only exposed at the surface because random erosion has uncovered them. Unfortunately, that knowledge provides little help in finding deeply buried deposits (Figure 13.2). Here, technological developments might play an important role.

Already, several countries—the former Soviet Union, the United States, Canada, and France among them—have programs aimed at developing a three-dimensional picture of the crust using new seismic techniques (Figure 13.3) and spe-

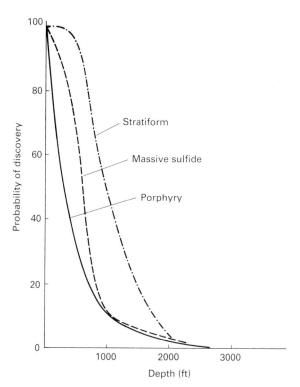

Figure 13.2. The probability that an ore deposit can be found declines with depth. A probability of 100—for ore deposits outcropping at the surface—means certain discovery. A probability of 50 means that half of the deposits can be found. A stratiform deposit, because of its shape, is more likely to be found at low depth than a porphyry copper deposit of the same size.

cial drilling programs. These special programs are only the beginnings of what someday might be full-scale attempts to map details of the Earth's crust down to 10,000 meters or more. When that has been done, a new frontier, larger than the surface of all of Earth's continents, will be opened (Figure 13.4). No one can say when, or if, we will be able to explore and mine the crust at such great depths, but some believe that we might start doing so within the next 20–30 years. The first deep discoveries might be made in Europe, North America, and Australia, where deep mapping is already being carried out.

Eventually, deposits of geochemically scarce metals will all be gone, or they will be so expensive to find and mine that other alternatives will be sought. Low-grade deposits that are not of interest to present-day miners due to high cost are available. One example of large, low-grade deposits is certain black shales that are not only rich in organic matter but have anomalously high contents of metals, such as copper, uranium, cobalt, and zinc. Other examples include certain very large, igneous intrusions, such as the Duluth Gabbro in Minnesota, that contain massive tonnages of very low-grade nickel and copper deposits. The large, low-grade deposits are apparently like most other mineral deposits—small, chemically anomalous volumes of Earth's crust.

Eventually the day will come when a huge population will cause these deposits, too, to be depleted. The world will face the situation discussed in Chapter 8; we will have reached the mineralogical barrier (see Figure 8.55). To transgress that barrier and mine scarce metals hidden in solid solutions will be extremely expensive (Figure 13.5). The pattern shown in Figure 13.5 is conjective, of course, but even if it is wrong in detail, it highlights an important factor—recovery of scarce metals will inevitably be far more difficult and expensive in the future.

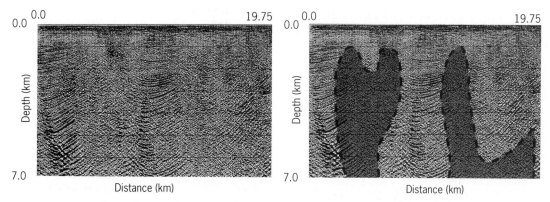

Figure 13.3. Deep 2-D and 3-D seismic imaging techniques will be increasingly used to give information of the structure of Earth's crust and resources lying below the surface. These images show the presence of large salt domes (shaded in the right-hand image) in the Eastern Magdalen basin in the Gulf of St. Lawrence between Newfoundland and Nova Scotia. 3-D imaging permits a view of such salt structures that may have developed hydrocarbon traps. (From L. Lines, *The Leading Edge*, Jan. 1995, p. 47. Used with permission.)

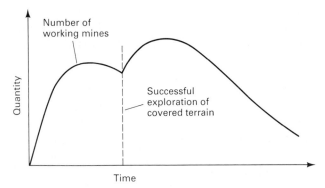

Figure 13.4. A Hewett curve depicting the number of working mines in a country versus time. If a new technological discovery allows deeper, formerly inaccessible terrain to be prospected, a new Hewett curve commences, rising to a new peak as the number of working mines increases. Unless another technological advance is made, the curve will eventually decline to zero when the last mine is depleted.

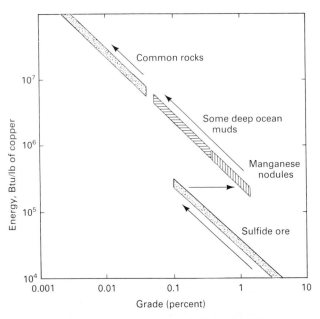

Figure 13.5. A hypothetical depiction of copper production in the centuries ahead. When the rich sulfide ores have been depleted, manganese nodules may be exploited. Some nodules contain more copper than certain sulfide ores, but the cost of recovery is higher for nodules. As nodules are mined, copper-rich deep-sea muds may also be worked; finally, common rocks, such as basalt, may have to be used.

We will, as a society, continue to use the range of metallic resources we use today. What will change is the relative balance of the different metals. The per capita consumption of geochemically scarce metals will, by the year 2100 A.D., probably decline to small fractions of today's values, due partly to their increased costs and partly to their replacement by substitutes (e.g., copper wires can now be replaced by glass fiber optics). In contrast, we can anticipate that the per capita consumption of geochemically abundant metals will remain high and possibly rise on a global basis. The metals of the future will be aluminum, magnesium, titanium, and probably iron, plus a number of nonmetallic substances, like glass and ceramics, made from other abundant materials.

These abundant materials will probably be mined from common rocks in the future. Aluminum will be derived from clays, shales, or other aluminous rocks; iron will come from the astronomically large sedimentary rock units called banded iron formations; magnesium will come from the common rock, dolostone. The materials used for building—crushed stone, ingredients for cement, clays for brick making, glass, and so forth—are all derived from very common rocks. There are no real possibilities of shortages developing for these materials in the future except on a very local basis.

Another group of resources, the critical chemical and fertilizer materials, bears many resemblances to deposits of geochemically scarce metals in that the raw materials are won from special mineral deposits—marine and lake evaporite deposits or marine phosphorite deposits. Deposits of most of these compounds are very large. Furthermore, because most of the desired compounds are soluble to some extent, they are also present in seawater, saline lakes, or saline groundwater. These saline waters will probably be the future sources of a great many nonmetallic chemical resources; even now they are producing compounds in some places (Figure 13.6).

There are some important exceptions to the possibility that future production of non-metallic compounds will be from brines. Some compounds are not very soluble and, hence, are not present in brines. Examples include fluorite (CaF_2), barite ($BaSO_4$), and apatite ($Ca_5(PO_4)_3(F_1OH)$). Of these three, the most important is apatite, the main ingredient of phosphorite and the principal source of phosphatic fertilizers. Phosphates are essential fertilizer ingredients—there are no substitutes (see Chapter 9). The renewable sources of phosphate, such as the bones of animals, the bodies of fish, and the manure from certain animals, are not generated in sufficiently large quantities to meet growing human needs. The only sources of phosphates that we know of beyond today's rich ores are off-shore marine deposits, certain shales, and limestones that contain low concentrations of phosphates. No adequate assessment has been made of the low-grade deposits, but two things seem clear—first, the low-grade deposits are in the same areas as the high-grade ores; second,

Figure 13.6. The large brine recovery plant at the Great Salt Lake. Brine evaporation ponds are visible in the background. (Courtesy of Great Salt Lake Minerals and Chemicals Corporation.)

the magnitude of the low-grade ores seems astronomically large. Hence, nonmetallic mineral resources may present problems in their local distributions, but the total magnitude of these resources does not appear to be a problem. In other words, resources of the future will simply be extensions of today's resources.

ENERGY AND WATER FOR THE FUTURE

Many people perceive a slow change from nonrenewable resources, like oil, gas, and coal, toward a mix of nuclear and renewable sources, such as solar and ocean power (see Chapters 5 and 6). Even though the techniques by which we will convert solar power to electricity are not complete, the sun will likely become our main energy source because it poses few environmental problems. Nuclear power will probably be the second major source with electricity as the way the user receives and uses the energy.

Earth is the water planet; 70 percent of it is covered with ocean. However, we are already experiencing significant problems of insufficient potable water in many parts of the world. The future will certainly see the construction of more major water transport and purification systems to distribute fresh water to population centers and agricultural regions. In addition, the outflow from waste water treatment systems will be more efficiently reused, and the desalinization procedures to convert some of the inexhaustible oceans into potable water will expand and improve. The human race will not run out of water, if for no reason other than the fact that we cannot live without it, but we shall have to expend even more effort and expense in securing the supplies. In 1995, the World Book noted that water would be the most critical resource in the early parts of the twenty-first century.

TECHNOLOGY AND INNOVATION

Eventually, a society will emerge that is not limited or threatened by overall supply constraints. How the global society will reach this point is not precisely known. The world's population will probably exceed 11 billion people during the next 100 years. Somehow, society will have to respond to the needs and aspirations of a population of this size more rapidly than technologies can be invented to solve the problems. In short, the needs will have to be met to a great extent through technologies already developed and through use of resources already identified. To do this, however, will require maximum, efficient, and innovative uses of all Earth's resources. An elegant example of such use is the invention of the charcoal briquette used for barbecues. It resulted from the application of a simple, existing technology to a common, but incompletely used, resource by one of America's most innovative geniuses, Henry Ford.

Before 1920, Ford operated a sawmill in the hardwood forests around Iron Mountain, Michigan, to make wooden parts for his successful Model T. Ford. With distaste, he watched the piles of wood scraps grow, and he sought a way to use them. Most charcoal available up to that time was made in lumps. It was not uniform in size or heat output and was used primarily as an industrial fuel or for wood-burning stoves. Ford's idea was to chip the wood into small pieces and turn it into charcoal. Then, he planned to grind it into a powder, add a binder, and compress the mix into the pillow shape of the common charcoal briquette. He called his friend, inventor Thomas Alva Edison (Figure 13.7), to design the plant. By early 1921, Ford's plant was complete and in full operation, using every wood scrap it generated and even condensing the vapors in the smoke.

Figure 13.7. Henry Ford and his associates who were responsible for producing the first charcoal briquettes. From the left, Harvey Firestone, Henry Ford, Thomas Alva Edison, and E.G. Kingsford, the first manager of the briquetting plant. (Courtesy of the Kingsford Products Company, a subsidiary of the Clorox Company.)

Power came from Ford's dam and hydroelectric facility nearby, and the wood by-products that were drawn off during the charring process were run through a condenser to make ketones for the paints used for Ford's cars and methanol for antifreeze. The briquettes were sold to industry and later to the public through his automobile agencies. E.G. Kingsford, a relative who owned one of Ford's earliest automobile sales agencies, was named manager of the briquette operation. A company town, Kingsford, was built nearby. This is the origin of the Kingsford brand on one of the popular present-day briquettes.

The resources exist; the needed inventive genius is also available. However, the consequences of resource use can sometimes lead to severe disruption of living space. The challenges posed by the needs and aspirations of a population of 11 billion or more people, the uneven distribution of the natural resources required to meet the needs, and the pressures on the environment as the resources are produced and used will all make the next 100 years the most crucial and difficult years the human race has ever faced. Every detail of our societies will have to be examined and reexamined in the process.

FURTHER READINGS

CAMERON, E. N., *At the Crossroads: The Mineral Position of the United States.* New York: John Wiley and Sons, 1986.

KESSLER, S. E., *Minerals, Resources, Economics and the Environment.* New York: MacMillan College Publishing Co, Inc., 1994.

SKINNER, B. J., "A Second Iron Age Ahead." *American Scientist* 64 (1976) pp. 258–270.

WOLFE, J. A., *Mineral Resources.* New York: Chapman and Hall, 1984.

APPENDIX: CALENDAR OF EARTH RESOURCES EVENTS

Events related to the origin, discovery, use, politics, cost, and environmental impact of Earth resources occur every day. Some events are of immediate impact (e.g., the discovery of oil or an embargo) whereas others have a delayed or more subtle impact (e.g., the birth of a great inventor or the passage of an environmental regulation). This calendar offers a cross section of these events and the regularity with which they occur. It can, however, present only the anniversary of one of the many events which have occurred every day.

Jan. 1, 1901   Spindletop oil gusher ushered in the East Texas fields

Jan. 2, 1975   The first day since 1934 that the American public was allowed to hold gold without a permit

Jan. 3, 1961   The only fatalities at an American nuclear plant occurred at a reactor near Idaho Falls, Idaho

Jan. 4, 1995   The Berkshire County Council, U.K., voted to permit the drilling of oil exploration wells on the grounds of Windsor Castle

Jan. 5, 1993   Oil tanker *Braer* ran aground in the channel between Scotland and the Shetland Islands spilling 25 million gallons of oil

Jan. 6, 1974   The U.S. went on daylight savings for two years to conserve electricity—a response to the OPEC oil embargo

Jan. 7, 1913   The modern petroleum cracking process was invented by William M. Burton

Jan. 8, 1986   The U.S. and Canada issued a joint report on acid rain recommending that the U.S. government help industry

Jan. 9, 1970   The market price of gold fell below the official price of $35.00 per troy ounce

Jan. 10, 1976   A gas leak caused an explosion in the basement of a hotel in Fremont, Nebraska, killing 18 and injuring 50

Jan. 11, 1966   Floods caused by the heaviest rainfall in Rio de Janeiro, Brazil, resulted in flooding and landslides, killing 239

Jan. 12, 1909   A coal mine disaster at Switchback, West Virginia, killed 67

Jan. 13, 1971   The U.S. Department of Interior released a study approving construction of the Alaskan pipeline

Jan. 14, 1970   The President of General Motors predicted the production of an essentially pollution free car by 1980

Jan. 15, 1971   The Aswan High Dam on the Nile was formally dedicated by Egyptian President Anwar Sadat

Jan. 16, 1968   ARCO announced the discovery of oil at Prudhoe Bay, Alaska

Jan. 17, 1706   Benjamin Franklin was born in Boston, Massachusetts

Jan. 18, 1980   The price of silver reached an all time high of $50.35 per troy ounce

Jan. 19, 1813   Sir Henry Bessemer, inventor of the Bessemer steel making process, was born in Hertfordshire, England

Jan. 20, 1989   200 gold miners were killed near Nazca, Peru, by an explosion and fire

Jan. 21, 1980   The market price of gold reached an all time high of $850 per troy ounce

Jan. 22, 1993   The U.S. Public Health Service announced studies showing that mercury in dental amalgams is not a health hazard

Jan. 23, 1980   President Carter said that the United States was prepared to go to war to protect the oil supply routes from the Persian Gulf

Jan. 24, 1848   James Marshall found gold in the American River at Sutter's Mill—this led to the California Gold Rush

Jan. 25, 1988   A coal mine explosion and fire near Las Esperanzas, Mexico, trapped 140 miners, 34 of whom perished

Jan. 26, 1975   OPEC ministers met in Algiers to discuss how to meet and bargain with oil consumers regarding energy, raw materials, and the world economy

Jan. 27, 1880   A U.S. Patent was granted to Thomas A. Edison for his electric lamp

Jan. 28, 1991   Iraqi troops set fire to more than 700 oil wells in Kuwait

Jan. 29, 1907   A coal mine disaster at Stuart, West Virginia, killed 84 miners

Jan. 30, 1934   U.S. Gold Reserve Act stopped U.S. minting and circulation of gold coins

Jan. 31, 1934   The official price of gold was raised from $20.67 to $35.00 per troy ounce

Feb. 1, 1995   Flood waters that ravaged Belgium, Germany, France, and the Netherlands began to recede; the 300,000 displaced began to return home

Feb. 2, 1848   Mexico ceded lands of seven western American states to the United States in the treaty of Guadalupe Hidalgo

Feb. 3, 1963   The oil tanker *Marine Sulphur* vanished off the southeast coast of the U.S. with 39 crewmen missing

Feb. 4, 1865   The Nevada legislature passed an act giving 50 years of rights to build and operate tunnels to mine the Comstock silver lode

Feb. 5, 1970   Algeria announced a four-year plan to increase oil exports by 50 percent to raise revenue to develop a more self sufficient economy

Feb. 6, 1964   Cuba cut off water supplies to the U.S. base at Guantanamo Bay

Feb. 7, 1974   Egypt began clearing the Suez Canal closed to the passage of oil tankers and freighters since the Arab-Israeli War of 1967

Feb. 8, 1973   An underground fire in the West Drienfontein gold mine near Johannesburg, South Africa, killed 26

Feb. 9, 1974   As a result of gasoline shortages, several governors and U.S. congressmen call for gasoline rationing in the United States

Feb. 10, 1848   The first production of iron in the Lake Superior District by the Jackson Mining Company

Feb. 11, 1847   Thomas A. Edison was born in Milan, Ohio

Feb. 12, 1983   The coal freighter *Marine Electric* sank off Chincoteague, Virginia, with 33 lost

Feb. 13, 1960   France exploded its first atomic bomb in the Sahara Desert

Feb. 14, 1971   The Persian Gulf oil producing nations and western oil companies signed agreements of prices and marketing

Feb. 15, 1982   *Ocean Ranger,* a semisubmersible oil rig, listed and sank off Newfoundland with the loss of 84 lives

Feb. 16, 1955   General Electric announced their syntheses of diamonds

Feb. 17, 1817   A street in Baltimore became the first to be lighted with natural gas supplied by America's first gas company

Feb. 18, 1965   An avalanche swept down from the Le Duc glacier near Stewart, British Columbia, burying a mining camp and trapping 40

Feb. 19, 1974   The U.S. Senate passed an emergency energy bill addressing energy conservation because of the OPEC oil embargo that started in 1973

Feb. 20, 1975   Flooding of the Nile River was the worst in 20 years, wiping out 21 villages

Feb. 21, 1885   The Washington Monument was dedicated

Feb. 22, 1956   President Eisenhower approved the sale of U-235 for peaceful atomic power production in the free world

Feb. 23, 1886   Charles M. Hall discovered the process of aluminum production

Feb. 24, 1991   United Nations forces attacked Iraqi forces in Kuwait

Feb. 25, 1977   The oil tanker *Hawaiian Patriot* burned, releasing 27 million gallons of oil

Feb. 26, 1919   The U.S. Congress established the Grand Canyon National Park in Arizona

Feb. 27, 1943   The U.S. Mint began producing zinc-coated steel pennies to conserve copper for the war effort

Feb. 28, 1972   British coal miners returned to work, ending a seven week strike that forced large-scale power cuts

Feb. 29, 1936   The Boulder Dam on the Colorado River was completed; the 221-meter high dam forms 185-kilometer long Lake Mead

March 1, 1977   Flooding of an anthracite mine in Pennsylvania swept away timbers, choking tunnels and killing 9 miners.

March 2, 1915   A mine disaster in Layland, West Virginia, killed 112

March 3, 1847   Alexander Graham Bell was born in Edinburgh, Scotland

March 4, 1962   U.S. Atomic Energy Commission announced the operation of the first nuclear power plant in Antarctica at McMurdo Station

March 5, 1970   A nuclear proliferation treaty went into effect as a result of the ratification by 43 nations

March 6, 1626   Peter Minuit bought Manhattan Island for the Dutch from the Man-a-hat-a Indians for trinkets valued at $24

March 7, 1876   U.S. Patent 174,465 was granted to Alexander Graham Bell for the telephone

March 8, 1924   A mine disaster at Castle Gate, Utah, killed 171 miners

March 9, 1957   Earthquake measuring 8.3 on the Richter scale in the Aleutians created a tsunami that caused more than $3 million in damage in Hawaii

March 10, 1959   President Eisenhower announced imposition of quotas on oil imports into the United States

March 11, 1992   Denison Mines placed the lid on the last barrel of U_3O_8, symbolically closing Canada's largest underground uranium mine

March 12, 1984   A British coal miners' strike closed 174 mines in protest of the planned closing of several uneconomical mines

March 13, 1884   An explosion in a Pocohontas, Virginia, coal mine killed 114 and blew houses off their foundations

March 14, 1994   A fiery collision of a tanker and a freighter in the Bosphorus killed 11 and spilled 29 million gallons of oil

March 15, 1848   The first printed report of the discovery of gold at Sutter's Mill appeared in the San Francisco *Californian*

March 16, 1978   The tanker *Amoco Cadiz* grounded near Portsall, France, spilling 62 million gallons of oil

March 17, 1975   The U.S. Supreme Court ruled that the federal government, not states, can control continental shelf oil drilling

March 18, 1991   President Salinas ordered the shutdown of the largest oil refinery in Mexico City to eliminate a source of air pollution

March 19, 1968   President Johnson signed a bill into law eliminating the necessity that 25 percent of U.S. currency be backed by gold reserves

March 20, 1973   The Shah of Iran announced the nationalization of Iran's foreign-operated oil industry

March 21, 1993   Four days of Agung volcano eruptions in the Philippines killed 1600 and destroyed 123,000 acres of cropland

March 22, 1975   A technician using a candle to check air leaks caused $100 million in fire damage at Brown's Ferry Nuclear Plant, Alabama

March 23, 1989   University of Utah chemists announced discovery of "cold fusion," but the experiments have not been confirmed

March 24, 1989   Exxon *Valdez* ran aground in Prince William Sound, Alaska, spilling 11 million gallons of crude oil

March 25, 1947   A coal mine disaster at Centralia, Illinois, killed 111 miners

March 26, 1912   A coal mine disaster at Jed, West Virginia, killed 83 miners

March 27, 1975   The first section of the Trans-Alaska pipeline was laid at the Tonsina River

March 28, 1979   A meltdown occurred at the nuclear reactor at Three Mile Island, Pennsylvania, the worst U.S. nuclear accident ever

March 29, 1982   The El Chichon volcano in Mexico, dormant for centuries, erupted spewing one billion tons of ash and rock, killing 100

March 30, 1983   NYMEX introduced the concept of futures in the crude oil market for the first time

March 31, 1932   The Ford Motor Company introduced the V-8 engine for automobiles

April 1, 1946   400,000 United States' coal miners went on strike, closing most U.S. coal mines

April 2, 1792   The U.S. Mint established the minting of the gold eagle ($10) coin

April 3, 1898   A great snow slide killed 43 miners near Chilkoot Pass on their way to search for Yukon and Klondike gold

April 4, 1974   An airplane crash killed 77 gold miners flying home to Malawi from the mines in South Africa

April 5, 1982   The Mt. Galurggung volcano in Indonesia erupted, killing 200 and destroying much cropland

April 6, 1993   A radioactive waste tank exploded and burned at the Siberian City of Tomsk-7, contaminating 2500 acres of land

April 7, 1869   The Yellow Jacket fire at Comstock Silver Lode in Virginia City, Nevada, killed 37 miners

April 8, 1952   The U.S. government siezed control of the nation's steel mills to avert a strike

April 9, 1968   South Africa announced that it would not sell gold in the official or free markets because prices were too low

April 10, 1973   The USGS announced evidence of oil and gas 30–50 miles off the east coast from Maine to New Jersey

April 11, 1956   President Eisenhower signed a $760 million bill to build four dams on the Upper Colorado River

April 12, 1989   European Parliament voted in favor of U.S. 1983-type automobile emissions controls

April 13, 1979   Personnel began the final processes to permanently shut down the damaged Three Mile Island nuclear reactor

April 14, 1935   Colorado's worst *Dust Bowl* storm left drifts that stopped cars and trains

April 15, 1981   A methane gas explosion at Dutch Creek No. 1 mine in Redstone, Colorado, killed 15 miners

April 16, 1964   A formal announcement appeared in the *Northern Miner* of the discovery hole of the Kidd Creek ore deposit at Timmins, Ontario

April 17, 1492   King Ferdinand signed papers permitting Christopher Columbus to sail

April 18, 1906   San Francisco earthquake measuring 8.3 on the Richter scale caused more than $400 million damage and killed more than 700

April 19, 1955   A gold mine cave-in at Minas Gerais, Brazil, killed 30 miners

April 20, 1980   Iran threatened to cut off oil shipments to Japan unless Japan was willing to pay $35 per barrel—Japan refused

April 21, 1991   A coal dust explosion in a shaft killed all 147 miners in a mine in Shanxi Province, China

April 22, 1970   The first Earth Day was celebrated to emphasize antipollution programs and the preservation of the environment

April 23, 1989   Heavy rains caused the collapse of a gold mine in Burundi, killing more than 100 miners

April 24, 1970   Ships from the U.K. and Iceland rammed and fired live rounds in a dispute over fishing rights and territorial limits in the North Atlantic

April 25, 1942   The world's worst mine disaster killed 1549 miners in Honkeiko coal mine in Manchuria

April 26, 1986   An explosion at Kiev's Chernobyl nuclear plant in the Ukraine

April 27, 1978   A collapsing scaffolding at a power plant cooling tower killed 51 workers at Willis Island, West Virginia

April 28, 1914   A coal mine disaster at Eccles, West Virginia, killed 181 miners

April 29, 1973   Rising flood waters inundated more than 6 million acres of farmland south of St. Louis, Missouri

April 30, 1803   The Louisiana Territory was purchased by the United States from France

May 1, 1486   Christopher Columbus laid before Isabella of Castile his petition requesting support for his voyage

May 2, 1982   Exxon announced it was terminating the Colony Shale Oil Project in Colorado after spending more than $1 billion

May 3, 1881   A fire began in two major mines of the Comstock silver lodes, Silver City, Nevada, and burned for three years

May 4, 1976   The Israeli government signed an agreement with a U.S. oil company to develop a new oil field in the Israeli occupied (but Egypt owned) Sinai Peninsula

May 5, 1964   Water began flowing in the Israeli pipeline from the Sea of Galilee to the southern Negev Desert region for irrigation

May 6, 1937   The airship *Hindenburg,* filled with hydrogen, exploded and burned at Lakehurst, New Jersey

May 7, 1958   The flooding of a coal mine near Nagasaki, Japan, killed 29 miners

May 8, 1979   A U.S. Patent was issued for growth of synthetic cubic zirconia, the most widely used diamond imitation

May 9, 1992   A methane explosion in Westray Coal Mine in Plymouth, Nova Scotia, killed 26 miners

May 10, 1872   President Grant signed the Mining Act of 1872 that governed U.S. mining for more than 120 years

May 11, 1977   A methane gas explosion in a coal mine at Hokkaido, Japan, killed 25

May 12, 1944   935 Allied planes bombed Germany's synthetic fuel factories

May 13, 1607   Captain John Smith and 105 others in three ships landed in Virginia, establishing the first English settlement in the New World

May 14, 1996   The first National Windmill Day was observed in the Netherlands

May 15, 1973   Libya, Iraq, Kuwait, and Algeria briefly halted oil flow to western nations in a symbolic protest of their recognition of Israel

May 16, 1971   An explosion in a coal mine near Quettz, West Pakistan, killed 32

May 17, 1985   A methane gas explosion killed 36 miners at Hokkaido, Japan

May 18, 1980   Mt. St. Helens in Washington exploded, killing 60

May 19, 1848   John Sutter, on whose land gold was found, said of this day "the great rush from San Francisco arrived at the fort"

May 20, 1977   Swiss voters approved construction and operation of a nuclear power plant in Switzerland

May 21, 1964   The world's first nuclear powered lighthouse went into operation in Maryland on the Chesapeake Bay

May 22, 1868   "The Great Train Robbery" occurred in Marshfield, Indiana, in which robbers made off with $96,000 in gold, bonds, and cash

May 23, 1966   The British collier *Kaitawa* ran aground at Pandora Banks, New Zealand, and sank, killing 29

May 24, 1844   Samuel Morse sent the first telegraph message, "What hath God wrought," over lines between Baltimore, Maryland, and Washington, D.C.

May 25, 1985   A tropical cylone flooded the eastern Delta region of Bangladesh, ruining crops and killing thousands of people

May 26, 1908   A giant oil gusher at Masjid-i-Suleima ushered in the oil prominence of Persia (present day Iran)

May 27, 1937   The Golden Gate Bridge opened at San Francisco, California

May 28, 1901   Shah Muzaffar al Din signed a 60-year lease for oil concessions in Persia with William Knox D'Arcy

May 29, 1848   "The rush for gold . . . the whole country resounds with the sordid cry of Gold, Gold!" appeared in the San Francisco *Californian*

May 30, 1975   The U.S. Government announced that it would sell 500,000 troy ounces of gold on the open market on June 30, 1975

May 31, 1889   A 72-foot wall of water swept through Johnstown, Pennsylvania, killing 2200 and destroying the center of the city

June 1, 1965   An explosion in Yamano Coal Mine at Fukuoka, Japan, killed 237 miners

June 2, 1973   The oil tanker *Esso Brussels* was rammed by a large ship while lying at anchor in New York harbor

June 3, 1979   The Ixtoc I oil well failed and spilled more than 100 million gallons of oil into the Gulf of Mexico

June 4, 1973   The *Wall Street Journal* reported that the U.S. would build the world's largest desalinization plant to make Colorado River water usable for Mexico

June 5, 1933   The United States' dollar went off the gold standard

June 6, 1967   Arab oil ministers called for embargo against countries friendly to Israel, one day after beginning of Arab-Israel war

June 7, 1494   The Treaty of Tordesillas was signed by Portugal and Spain dividing the lands of the New World

June 8, 1979   A methane gas explosion in Bell Island Salt Mine near New Iberia, Louisiana, killed five miners

June 9, 1972   15 Caribbean nations announced support for the setting of territorial limits at 12 miles and the establishment of 200-mile seabed natural resource limits

June 10, 1972   Flash floods damaged downtown Rapid City, South Dakota

June 11, 1971   Finland became the first nation to formally sign an agreement to ensure the peaceful use of nuclear materials

June 12, 1897   A Richter 8.7 earthquake at Cherrapunji, India, did extensive damage

June 13, 1968   Hull failure of the tanker *World Glory* off South Africa spilled more than 13 million gallons of crude oil

June 14, 1972   The U.S. EPA banned most uses of DDT

June 15, 1752   Benjamin Franklin proved that lightning is electricity with his kite experiment

June 16, 1872   Prospectors claimed to have found diamonds, sapphires, and rubies in the Colorado Territory (probably true)

June 17, 1914   Winston Churchill introduced a bill so that the British government would acquire 51 percent of the Anglo-Persian Oil Company

June 18, 1971   The Venezuelan Chamber of Deputies passed a bill to eventually nationalize foreign-owned oil operations

June 19, 1978   The U.S. Senate voted to allow clearly justified exemptions to the Endangered Species Act

June 20, 1977   The first oil flowed into the Alaskan Pipeline at Prudhoe Bay

June 21, 1960   A U.S. patent was granted to General Electric Company for the synthesis of diamonds

June 22, 1989   Freeport McMoRan Gold Company poured its two-millionth ounce of gold from its Jerritt Canyon, Nevada, operation

June 23, 1974   Five oil companies agreed to pay $9.5 million for damages in a 1969 oil spill in Santa Barbara Channel off the coast of California

June 24, 1882   The first gold mining company, General Prospecting Co. of Burghers of the ZAR, formed in the Rand area, South Africa

June 25, 1876   George A. Custer and 225 cavalry men, protecting gold interests, were killed by Indians at Little Big Horn, Montana

June 26, 1965   Rain-loosened coal cinder piles and mud buried houses, killing 24 at Kawasaki City, Japan

June 27, 1985   Explosion of gases in a sewage pipe killed 24 in Chongquing, China

June 28, 1983   A 100-ft section of Interstate 95, weakened by water flow, collapsed at Greenwich, Connecticut

June 29, 1767   The British Parliament approved the Townshend Revenue Act, imposing taxes on resources and materials shipped to America

June 30, 1975   The U.S. government sold 500,000 troy ounces of gold at an auction

July 1, 1992   European Community legislation went into effect requiring new cars to have platinum catalytic converters

July 2, 1900   Count Ferdinand von Zeppelin launched his first hydrogen-filled air ship

July 3, 1990   The price of rhodium metal rose about $7000 per troy ounce

July 4, 1977   Canada approved the construction of a pipeline across its territory to transport natural gas from Alaska to the lower 48 states

July 5, 1944   A mine disaster at Belmont, Ohio, killed 66 coal miners

July 6, 1988   The Piper Alpha oil platform in the North Sea exploded, killing 167 workers

July 7, 1961   A natural gas explosion in a coal mine in Dolna Suce, Czechoslovakia, killed 108 miners

July 8, 1896   William Jennings Bryan, a Democratic presidential candidate, delivered his "Cross of Gold" speech, seeking restoration of the bimetal standard for U.S. currency

July 9, 1984   The largest one day drop in the price of gold occurred—$25.50

July 10, 1991   President Bush lifted U.S. economic sanctions against South Africa and allowed the importation of gold Krugerrands

July 11, 1991   ARCO announced the development of a cleaner-burning gasoline for use in California

July 12, 1991   A giant sinkhole, 150 feet across and 60 feet deep, swallowed a house in Florida

July 13, 1969   The United Arab Republic signed an agreement to build an oil pipeline to bypass the Suez Canal, which had been closed in the 1967 war

July 14, 1967   The U.S. treasury halted sales of silver at the nominal value of $1.29 per troy ounce

July 15, 1979   President Carter outlined a 10-year national energy program to reduce U.S. dependence on foreign oil

July 16, 1955   A fire in an underground uranium mine near Aue, East Germany, killed 33 workers

July 17, 1913   Winston Churchill said, "If we cannot get oil . . . we cannot get a thousand and one commodities necessary for the preservation of Great Britain."

July 18, 1993   Massive flooding covered millions of acres in the Upper Mississippi Valley, displacing tens of thousands of people and causing millions of dollars in damages

July 19, 1985   The failure of an earthen dam at Stave, Italy, sent a wall of water and mud down an alpine valley, killing 250

July 20, 1969   The first lunar landing occurred with Neil Armstrong becoming the first human to set foot on the moon

July 21, 1992   A Japanese research institute announced the development of a palladium-catalyst for diesel engines

July 22, 1892   The *Murex*, the first oil tanker, sailed from West Hartlepool, to Batum on the Black Sea

July 23, 1965   The U.S. congress passed the Coinage Act, eliminating the use of silver in coins and authorizing dimes and quarters made with copper and nickel

July 24, 1980   The American Petroleum Institute reported that U.S. oil imports dropped by 14 percent in the first half of 1979

July 25, 1941   The U.S. government froze all Japanese financial assets, preventing Japan from buying oil from the U.S.

July 26, 1956   Egypt nationalized the Suez Canal

July 27, 1866   The first undersea cable between the U.S. and Europe was completed

July 28, 1977   The first oil arrived at the Valdez tanker terminal after passing the entire length of the Alaskan pipeline

July 29, 1588   The English navy defeated the Spanish Armada in the battle of Gravelines

July 30, 1971   The Venezuelan President signed legislation to nationalize the oil industry

July 31, 1976   Twelve inches of rain fell in six hours, generating a 30-foot wall of water that swept down Big Thompson Canyon, Colorado, killing 130 campers

Aug. 1, 1993   The Mississippi River crested at 49.4 feet in St. Louis, Missouri, the all-time high water level

Aug. 2, 1990   Iraq attacked Kuwait, taking control of all of its oil fields

Aug. 3, 1492   Christopher Columbus set sail from Palos, Spain, on his first voyage to the New World

Aug. 4, 1977   President Carter signed a measure establishing the Department of Energy

Aug. 5, 1954   International oil companies signed a 25-year production and marketing agreement with Iran

Aug. 6, 1945   80,000–200,000 people were killed when the first atomic bomb was dropped on Hiroshima, Japan

Aug. 7, 1979   Highly enriched uranium was accidentally released from a top secret nuclear fuel plant at Erwin, Tennessee

Aug. 8, 1956   A fire in the Casier du Bois mine in Marcinelle, Belgium, trapped 276 miners, 262 of whom died

Aug. 9, 1960   Standard Oil of New Jersey announced oil price cuts of up to $0.14 per barrel, which precipitated the formation of OPEC

Aug. 10, 1993   Fifty tons of limestone were dropped by helicopters into Friday Run National Forest in Virginia to counteract acid rain

Aug. 11, 1807   Robert Fulton's first steamboat *Clermont* made a successful trial run

Aug. 12, 1976   An explosion in an oil refinery tower at Chalmette, Louisiana, killed 13

Aug. 13, 1521   Spanish conquistadores conquered the present-day Mexico City area from the Aztecs

Aug. 14, 2126   Swift-Tuttle comet could collide with Earth, causing much disruption of human activities

Aug. 15, 1932   Greensboro, North Carolina, *Daily News* reported the discovery of a 12-lb gold nugget near Charlotte, North Carolina

Aug. 16, 1896   "Skookum Jim" discovered "Bonanza Creek," a rich gold-bearing tributary of the Klondike River in Canada

Aug. 17, 1959   The Hebgen Lake, Montana, earthquake and Madison landslide killed 27 people

Aug. 18, 1965   President Johnson declared Delaware River watershed, including New York City, a drought disaster area

Aug. 19, 1848   The discovery of gold in California was reported in the *New York Herald*—a leading contributor to the Gold Rush

Aug. 20, 1983   President Reagan lifted controls on the exportation of gas pipeline equipment to the Soviet Union

Aug. 21, 1986   1500 people and 7000 cattle were killed by the sudden release of gases from Lake Nyos in a volcanic crater in Cameroon

Aug. 22, 1962   The U.S. nuclear ship *Savannah,* the world's first nuclear-powered cargo ship, completed its maiden voyage

Aug. 23, 1892   The *Murex,* the first oil tanker, sailed through the Suez Canal

Aug. 24, 79 A.D.   The eruption of Mt. Vesuvius buried Pompeii and Herculaneum in Italy

Aug. 25, 1958   25 people died in New Delhi, India, from drinking contaminated water

Aug. 26, 1963   The U.S. Department of Interior proposed a 30-year $4 billion program to develop lower Colorado River water resources

Aug. 27, 1859   The world's first oil well, drilled by Edwin L. Drake in Titusville, Pennsylvania, struck oil

Aug. 28, 1963   An explosion in the main shaft of a large potash mine in Moab, Utah, at the 2700-foot level killed 18 people

Aug. 29, 1974   Norway announced the discovery of a large oil and gas field in the North Sea with 2 billion barrels of recoverable oil and 50 billion cubic meters of gas

Aug. 30, 1994   A methane gas explosion in a coal mine in the southern Philippines killed 71 miners

Aug. 31, 1987   An elevator carrying gold miners dropped to the bottom of a 4600-foot (1400 meter) deep gold mine shaft in South Africa, killing 62

Sept. 1, 1973   Libya announced the nationalization of 51 percent of all foreign oil company operations

Sept. 2, 1977   The U.S. Energy Administration and the Canadian National Energy Board agreed to the exchange of 10,000 barrels of oil daily to help keep U.S. refineries supplied

Sept. 3, 1977   An earth tremor caused the cave-in of two South African gold mines, killing more than 20 miners

Sept. 4, 1888   George Eastman received a patent for his roll-film camera and registered his Kodak trademark

Sept. 5, 1976   Flood waters eroded and broke a 442-foot high earth dam in Pakistan, flooding more than 5000 square miles

Sept 6, 1492   Christopher Columbus sailed west from the Canary Islands in his search for a route to the Far East

Sept. 7, 1970   A methane gas explosion blocked a coal mine entrance and trapped 34 miners at Sorrange, Pakistan

Sept. 8, 1900   More than 6000 people were killed when a large hurricane struck Galveston, Texas, in the worst loss of life in U.S. disaster history

Sept. 9, 1970   The U.S. Treasury Secretary defended the Nixon Administration's proposal to tax lead additives in gasolines as a way to reduce air pollution and raise revenue

Sept. 10, 1969   Oil leases to sites on Alaska's North slope were sold in Anchorage for more than $900 million

Sept. 11, 1936   President Roosevelt dedicated Hoover Dam in Nevada by pressing a key to start the hydroelectric generation of electricity

Sept. 12, 1848   The arrival of a ship carrying $2500 of California gold started a near riot in Valparaiso, Chile

Sept. 13, 1922   The highest shade temperature on Earth's surface, 136.4°F, was recorded at El Azizia, Libya

Sept. 14, 1979   The price of gold reached an unprecedented level of $345.80 per troy ounce

Sept. 15, 1977   President Carter announced a plan to set aside about one-quarter of Alaska as national parks, wilderness areas, and wildlife refuges, thus limiting oil exploration

Sept. 16, 1994   Exxon was ordered to pay $5 billion to commercial fishermen for Exxon *Valdez* damage in Prince William Sound, Alaska

Sept. 17, 1954   Australia's first uranium plant opened at Rum Jungle, Northern Territory

Sept. 18, 1884   Frederick Struben exposed the gold rich Confidence Reef in South Africa

Sept. 19, 1844   A survey party discovered the great iron ores of the Marquette Range on the upper peninsula of Michigan

Sept. 20, 1519,   Ferdinand Magellan set out from Spain in search of a western passage to the Spice Islands of Indonesia

Sept. 21, 1893   The Duryea brothers test drove the first gasoline-powered automobile in Springfield, Massachusetts

Sept. 22, 1898   The discovery of gold at Anvil Creek began the rush to the Nome Mining District of Alaska

Sept. 23, 1970   "Brownouts" occurred along the East Coast of the United States as a prolonged heat wave taxed electrical power reserves

Sept. 24, 1994   A jury awarded $9.7 million to the Alaskan Native Corporations as a result of damages caused by the Exxon *Valdez* oil spill

Sept. 25, 1513   Vasco Nunez de Balboa discovered the Pacific Ocean

Sept. 26, 1940   The U.S. government banned the export of all iron and steel scrap to Japan to try to limit potential war buildup

Sept. 27, 1915   An explosion of a gasoline-filled railroad tank car killed 47 people in Ardmore, Oklahoma

Sept. 28, 1993   An explosion of a natural gas pipeline along a major highway in Venezuela killed 36 people

Sept. 29, 1969   Heavy rains caused extensive flooding across the deserts of Algeria and Tunisia, killing hundreds of people and flooding phosphate mines

Sept. 30, 1954   The world's largest asbestos mill was dedicated at Asbestos, Quebec, by the Johns-Manville Corp.

Oct. 1, 1908   Henry Ford introduced the Model T Ford, the first mass-produced car

Oct. 2, 1979   The Argyle Diamond Pipe was discovered in western Australia

Oct. 3, 1994   The U.S. EPA banned chemical waste dumping in the Gulf of Mexico, about 230 miles south of the Florida panhandle

Oct. 4, 1955   The first solar-powered telephone call was made at Americus, Georgia

Oct. 5, 1966   A sodium cooling system leak at the Enrico Fermi demonstration nuclear reactor near Detroit caused a shutdown

Oct. 6, 1848   The steam ship *California* left New York on its maiden voyage to San Francisco, carrying gold seekers

Oct. 7 1957   A fire at the Windscale plutonium production facility in England spread radiation that led to numerous deaths

Oct. 8, 1942   The U.S. War Production Board Order L-208 went into effect, closing U.S. gold mines (to try to boost copper production)

Oct. 9, 1964   A landslide at Wan-li, Taiwan, engulfed a sulfur mine, entombing 25 miners

Oct. 10, 1913   The waters of the Pacific and Atlantic met for the first time in the Panama Canal when the Gamboa dam was blown up

Oct. 11, 1811   The first steam powered ferryboat, the *Juliana,* was put into service between New York City and Hoboken, New Jersey

Oct. 12, 1973   The chairmen of four major U.S. oil companies told President Nixon that the 100 percent oil price increase asked by OPEC was too much

Oct. 13, 1992   The U.K. government announced the closure of 30 coal mines with 30,000 miner layoffs

Oct. 14, 1913   A fire in the Mid-Glamorgan Coal Mine in Wales killed 439 miners

Oct. 15, 1927   The first commercial oil well in Iraq, Baba Gurgur No. 1, came in as a gusher flowing 95,000 barrels per day

Oct. 16, 1973   OPEC announced an immediate 70 percent increase in the price of oil

Oct. 17, 1956   The world's first full-scale nuclear power plant began generating electricity at Calder Hall on the west coast of England

Oct. 18, 1867   The United States took formal possession of Alaska after paying Russia $7.2 million

Oct. 19, 1973   Libya, an OPEC member, announced a boycott of oil sales to the United States

Oct. 20, 1973   Saudi Arabia, the largest OPEC country, announced a boycott of oil sales to the United States

Oct. 21, 1966   A huge coal waste pile failed and buried a school in Aberfan, Wales, killing 116 children and 26 adults

Oct. 22, 1913   A mine disaster at Dawson in the Northwest Territories killed 263 miners

Oct. 23, 1991   The Fifth U.S. Circuit Court of Appeals overturned EPA regulations that banned most asbestos use in the United States

Oct. 24, 1973   Dense fog and smoke from a burning garbage dump caused a 65 vehicle pile-up on the New Jersey Turnpike, killing 9

Oct. 25, 1973   The Organization for Economic Cooperation and Development met in Paris to discuss the potential of oil sharing if needed as a result of the OPEC embargo

Oct. 26, 1825 The Erie Canal was opened with a barge leaving Buffalo, New York

Oct. 27, 1979 An underground fire at the Unsong Coal Mine, Korea, killed 42 miners

Oct. 28, 1990 Heavy rains flooded the Brewer Gold Mine in South Carolina, causing the release of cyanide solutions that killed more than 10,000 fish

Oct. 29, 1929 "Black Tuesday," the collapse of the New York Stock Exchange that led to the Great Depression

Oct. 30, 1973 The Netherlands imposed a ban on Sunday driving to conserve oil supplies

Oct. 31, 1916 The British War Cabinet said to spare no efforts to destroy the German oil supplies in Romania

Nov. 1, 1755 Lisbon, Portugal, was devestated by an earthquake and the following fire and tsunami, which killed 50,000 people

Nov. 2, 1986 A large chemical spill from a chemical plant at Schweizerhalle, Switzerland, contaminated the Rhine River

Nov. 3, 1975 A gas explosion at a coal mine in Figols, Spain, killed 27 people

Nov. 4, 1922 Howard Carter discovered the doorway to the burial vault of King Tutankhamun, which contained great golden archeological treasures

Nov. 5, 1969 The oil tanker *Keo* suffered a hull fracture and spilled 9 million gallons of oil off the coast of Massachusetts

Nov. 6, 1869 Cornelius Hendrik took a bottle of stones found by his children in the Kimberly area of South Africa to a company store and learned that one was a diamond

Nov. 7, 1805 The Lewis and Clark expedition reached the Pacific Ocean at the mouth of the Columbia River

Nov. 8, 1958 The Hope diamond (45.52 ct), valued at $1.5 million, was donated to the Smithsonian Institution by Harry Winston, a New York jeweler

Nov. 9, 1963 A coal dust explosion in a mine killed 450 Japanese miners

Nov. 10, 1975 An iron ore carrier, with 26,000 tons of iron ore pellets, sank in 20-ft waves and 65-mph winds in Lake Superior, killing 29

Nov. 11, 1991 The first formal note about the discovery of diamonds in the Northwest Territories of Canada was published

Nov. 12, 1970 A typhoon generated 30-ft tidal surges that killed more than 200,000 in Bangladesh, the worst human disaster in the twentieth century

Nov. 13, 1973 British Prime Minister Heath declared a national emergency and reduced England's energy supplies by 10 percent because of the OPEC embargo

Nov. 14, 1969 A mine elevator dropped 3500 feet in Salisbury, Rhodesia, killing 120 miners

Nov. 15, 1533 Francisco Pizarro and his conquistadores rode into the Inca capital of Cuzco in what is now Peru

Nov. 16, 1973 President Nixon signed a bill authorizing the construction of the Trans-Alaska oil pipeline

Nov. 17, 1869 The Suez Canal was opened, allowing ships to sail from the Red Sea into the Mediterranean without rounding the cape of Africa for the first time

Nov. 18, 1755 The Salem, Massachusetts, earthquake happened, one of the largest ever to occur in New England

Nov. 19, 1984 An explosion at a gas storage facility at Tlalnepantla near Mexico City killed 452 people

Nov. 20, 1980 Lake Peigneur drained into a salt mine in the Jefferson Island Salt Dome, Louisiana, when an oil well accidentally drilled into the mine.

Nov. 21, 1978 A coal mine train derailed going into a mine one-half mile deep, killing 7 at Doncaster, United Kingdom

Nov. 22, 1922 A mine disaster at Dolomite, Alabama, killed 90 coal miners

Nov. 23, 1980 4800 were killed in a series of earthquakes that devastated southern Italy

Nov. 24, 1848 A report published in the *New York Herald* stated that "California gold fever broke out in New York"

Nov. 25, 1980 The U.S. EPA issued new air quality standards for National Park and Scenic areas in 36 states

Nov. 26, 1916 The Romanian government blew up its oil fields to prevent them falling into the hands of the German army

Nov. 27, 1992 Ecuador dropped out of OPEC, the first nation to do so since its formation in 1960

Nov. 28, 1973 The U.S. Secretary of the Interior approved a commercial leasing plan for the development of oil shales on Federal Land in Colorado and Wyoming

Nov. 29, 1966 The iron ore carrier *Daniel J. Morrell* sank in 60-mph winds on Lake Huron wih the loss of 28 lives

Nov. 30, 1972 The Soviet Union began operation of the world's first commercial fast-breeder reactor at Sherchenko, northeast of the Caspian Sea

Dec. 1, 1959 Antarctica became an international preserve, free from resource exploitation

Dec. 2, 1942 The first human-directed nuclear chain reaction was carried out at the University of Chicago

Dec. 3, 1992 The Greek tanker *Aegean Sea* ran aground at La Coruna, Spain, spilling 21.5 million gallons of oil

Dec. 4, 1970 President Nixon ordered the Interior Department to take over the states' responsibilities for oil and gas production of offshore federal lands

Dec. 5, 1492 Christopher Columbus landed in Haiti where he stayed for four weeks and found gold

Dec. 6, 1884 U.S. Army Engineers completed construction of the Washington Monument

Dec. 7, 1941 The Japanese struck Pearl Harbor in Hawaii and precipitated the United States' entry into World War II

Dec. 8, 1992 An avalanche of rain-soaked mud buried a gold mining camp at Llipi, Bolivia, killing 75 miners

Dec. 9, 1911 A coal mine disaster at Briceville, Tennessee, killed 84

Dec. 10, 1993 The Princeton University fusion reactor produced 5.6 million watts of power, the greatest yield to date

Dec. 11, 1992 90-mph winds from a severe winter storm flooded New York

Dec. 12, 1992 A Richter 6.8 earthquake centered near Maumere, Indonesia, destroyed 80 percent of the town and generated a 25-meter high tsunami

Dec. 13, 1978 The U.S. mint began stamping Susan B. Anthony $1 coins

Dec. 14, 1970 U.S. Secretary of State Kissinger met with King Faisal of Saudi Arabia to discuss how to get the OPEC oil embargo lifted

Dec. 15, 1917 French Prime Minister Clemenceau said gasoline was "as vital as blood in the coming battles" of World War I

Dec. 16, 1954 H.T. Hall first synthesized diamonds at General Electric using high-pressure techniques

Dec. 17, 1903 Orville and Wilbur Wright completed the first powered flight on level ground at Kitty Hawk, North Carolina

Dec. 18, 1942 The U.S. government approved an act to produce steel cents in order to conserve copper for the war effort.

Dec. 19, 1972 The tanker *Sea Star* released 32 million gallons of oil into the Gulf of Oman

Dec. 20, 1987 More than 3000 people died when a passenger ship and an oil tanker collided in the Philippines

Dec. 21, 1990 The European Community Environmental ministers agreed to exhaust emissions limits for all new cars produced in their countries

Dec. 22, 1973 The Japanese Cabinet adopted a declaration ordering a 20 percent reduction in oil and electrical usage because of the OPEC oil embargo

Dec. 23, 1958 A gasoline tank exploded in Brownsville, Texas, killing 4 and injuring 200

Dec. 24, 1980 The U.S. EPA proposed curbs on the air emissions from diesel trucks and buses

Dec. 25, 1973 The Arab petroleum producers announced that they would ease the oil embargo of western countries except for the United States and the Netherlands

Dec. 26, 1967 Oil was struck at Prudhoe Bay on the North Slope of Alaska

Dec. 27, 1975 372 miners died in a coal mine at Dhahbad, India, when explosions drained millions of gallons of water into the mine

Dec. 28, 1899 The Royal Dutch Shell Oil Company struck oil in Indonesia

Dec. 29, 1973 Egypt and four oil-producing Middle Eastern nations signed a contract to construct a pipeline from the Red Sea to the Mediterranean Sea

Dec. 30, 1853 The United States bought the 45,000 square miles of the Gadsden Purchase from Mexico

Dec. 31, 1879 Thomas A. Edison publically demonstrated his incandescent electric lightbulb for the first time

Glossary

abundant metals: Metals with an earth crustal geochemical abundance of at least 0.1 percent.

acid mine drainage: Waters issuing from an active or abandoned mine that are made strongly acidic by the decomposition of sulfide minerals, usually pyrite, FeS_2.

acid rain: Rainfall that is abnormally acidic; generally attributed to the presence of nitrous and sulfur oxide pollutants in the atmosphere.

acre foot: The volume of water required to cover one acre to a depth of one foot; 325,900 gallons; 1,233,500 liters.

activated charcoal: Highly absorbent charcoal produced by heating granulated charcoal; used to absorb gases or dissolved substances, especially gold.

adit: A horizontal tunnel serving as an entrance into a mine.

age-sex pyramids: Diagrams that display the distribution of population in terms of age and sex.

aggregate: Any hard, inert construction material (e.g., sand, gravel, crushed stone) used in the preparation of concrete or as a roadbed.

alchemy: The medieval science of chemistry, one objective of which was to transform base metals into gold; another was to discover a universal cure for disease and a means of indefinitely prolonging life.

algoma-type: A type of banded iron formation whose formation can be attributed to submarine volcanic exhalation.

alkali feldspars: A series of silicate minerals involving solid solution from $KAlSi_3O_8$ (potash feldspar, orthoclase) to $NaAlSi_3O_8$ (albite).

alkalinization: The buildup of salts of calcium, sodium, and potassium in soils due to evaporation.

alloy: A substance composed of two or more metals or a metal and a nonmetal.

alluvial fan: A low, gently sloping conelike accumulation of sediment that has been deposited where a stream issues from a mountain valley onto a plain.

alluvium: Unconsolidated sediments deposited by running water.

Alpha particle: A subatomic particle, having an atomic weight of 4 and a +2 charge (equivalent to a helium nucleus), released during radioactive disintegration.

alumina: An oxide of aluminum, Al_2O_3, which has numerous uses in the chemical industry and as an abrasive.

amalgamation: The formation of alloys of precious metals, generally gold, with mercury; usually done as a means of capturing small grains of the precious metal.

amorphous: A material without a regular crystal structure.

anaerobic digestion: The breakdown of organic material by microorganisms in the absence of oxygen.

andalusite: A mineral, composition Al_2SiO_5; widely used in the manufacture of ceramics and glasses.

anhydrite: A mineral, composition $CaSO_4$; an evaporite mineral.

anion: A negatively charged atom.

annealing: The process of holding materials at high temperatures, but below their melting points, in order to change physical properties such as brittleness and machinability by causing changes in the sizes and shapes of individual grains.

anorthosite: An igneous rock composed almost entirely of the mineral plagioclase feldspar.

anthracite: Coal of the highest rank, usually with a carbon content of 92–98 percent.

apatite: A mineral with the general formation of $Ca_5(PO_4)_3$ (F, OH, Cl) that constitutes a major source of phosphorous.

aplite: A light-colored, fine-grained igneous rock consisting largely of quartz and potassium feldspar.

aqueduct: A conduit or channel built to convey water from one place to another.

aqueous: Of, or pertaining to, water.

aquifer: A rock formation that is water bearing.

artesian well: A well in which the water level rises above the level of the water table because it is under pressure in a confined aquifer.

asbestos: A general term applied to any of a group of fibrous silicate minerals that are widely used for industrial purposes because they are incombustible, nonconducting, and chemically resistant.

asbestosis: Chronic lung inflammation caused by prolonged inhalation of asbestos particles.

asphaltene: A solid, noncrystalline black hydrocarbon residual of crude oils or other bitumen.

assay: The test of the composition of an ore or mineral, usually for gold or silver.

atmosphere: The mixture of gases that surround Earth; composed approximately of 78 percent nitrogen, 21 percent oxygen, 1 percent argon, 0.03 percent carbon dioxide, and variable amounts of water vapor.

atmospheric inversion: The abnormal condition in which a layer of warmer air overlies a layer of cooler air.

atomic substitution: The substitution of one element for another on the lattice sites in a crystalline solid.

attapulgite: (palygorskite) A clay mineral of composition $(Mg,Al)_2Si_4O_{10}OH \cdot 4H_2O$.

azonal soil: In U.S. classification systems, one of the three soil orders; lacks well-developed horizons and resembles the parent materials.

backfill: Rock debris, usually derived from mining or mineral processing, that is placed in mined-out areas of a mine.

ball clay: A light-colored, organic-containing highly plastic refractory clay used in making ceramics; so named because of the early English practice of rolling the clay into balls approximately 35 centimeters in diameter for storage and shipping.

banded iron formations: The largest iron deposits; sedimentary rocks consisting of alternating bands of iron oxide minerals, iron silicates, and silica; also called banded jaspilite and itabirite.

banded jaspilite: A synonym for banded iron formations.

barite: A mineral, composition $BaSO_4$; a heavy, soft mineral widely used in oil drilling muds and as a filler in paints, papers, and textiles.

basalt: A dark, fine-grained igneous rock composed chiefly of plagioclase, feldspar, pyroxene, and olivine.

base cation: Cations such as Ca^{2+}, Mg^{2+}, K^+, Na^+.

base metal: Generally any nonprecious metal, but used today to refer to metals such as copper, lead, zinc, mercury, and tin that are neither precious nor used as ferroalloy metals.

batholith: A large intruded mass of igneous rock generally with a surface exposure of greater than 100 square kilometers and usually composed of medium- to coarse-grained rocks.

bauxite: The principal ore of aluminum; a mixture of amorphous and crystalline hydrous aluminum oxides and hydroxides.

benches: Level, shelflike, areas in open-pit mines where ore and waste rocks are extracted.

beneficiation: The process of producing a concentrate of valuable ore minerals through the removal of valueless gangue minerals.

bentonite: A soft, plastic, porous, light-colored rock consisting of colloidal silica and clay; has the possibility of absorbing large quantities of water; forms as a result of the weathering of volcanic ash.

Beta particle: A high-energy electron released during radioactive decay.

biochemical oxygen demand (BOD): The amount of oxygen required by microorganisms in natural waters of a river, stream, or lake.

biogenic gas: Gas formed as a result of bacterial action on organic matter.

biomass: The total amount of living organisms in a particular area, expressed in terms of weight or volume.

biosphere: The living sphere around Earth; encompasses all living species from the highest points on mountains to deepest parts of the ocean.

biotite: Dark mica of composition $K(Mg,Fe)_3[(Al,Fe)Si_3O_{10}](OH,F)_2$.

bittern: A solution, such as seawater, that has been concentrated by evaporation until salt, sodium chloride, has begun to crystallize; bitterns typically contain high magnesium contents.

bitumen: A general term applied to dark-colored liquid to plastic hydrocarbons such as petroleum and asphalts.

bituminous coal: High rank black coal containing 75–92 percent carbon; commonly contains several percent volatile gases.

black smoker: A seafloor vent issuing hot fluids, which on mixing with seawater, precipitate very fine grained sulfide minerals that look like black smoke.

blast furnace: A furnace in which the combustion of the fuel is intensified by a blast of air; usually used to smelt iron.

block caving: A mining method in which a large mass (block) of ore is undermined and then fractured by blasting and allowed to collapse under its own weight. The ore is removed in a series of tunnels cut beneath the ore zone.

blowout: An oil or gas well in which very high pressures encountered during drilling are sufficient to force the drill out the top of the drill hole; this usually results in the fountaining of oil, gas, and water as a gusher.

bog iron deposits: Accumulations of soft, spongy hydrous iron oxides that form in bogs, swamps, shallow lakes, and soil zones.

boghead coal: A coal composed primarily of algal debris.

borax: A mineral, composition $Na_2B_4O_7 \cdot 10H_2O$; a light-colored compound formed during the evaporation of alkaline lakes; widely used in the preparation of soaps, glasses, ceramics, and other materials.

brass: An alloy of copper with zinc.

breccia: A coarse-grained clastic sedimentary rock composed of angular rock fragments set in a finer grained matrix; also said of any type of rock that has been highly fractured by igneous or tectonic processes.

breeder reactor: A nuclear reactor that produces more fissionable material than it consumes.

brimstone: A common and commercial name for sulfur.

brine: Seawater that, due to evaporation or freezing, contains more than the usual 3.5 percent dissolved salts.

British thermal unit: *See* BTU.

Bronze Age: The period in the development of a people or region when bronze replaced stone as the material for making tools and weapons.

bronze: An alloy of copper with tin.

brown ores: Brown colored iron ores consisting of a mixture of amorphous and crystalline iron hydroxides.

BTU: British thermal unit, the energy required to raise 1 lb of water 1°F.

building stone: A general term applied to any massive, dense rock suitable for use in construction.

by-product: Something produced in the making of something else.

cable-tool drill: A method of drilling in which the cutting bit is attached to a long steel cable; cutting is accomplished by the bit being raised and dropped again and again.

calcining: The roasting of limestone to drive off CO_2 to make lime, CaO.

calcite: $CaCO_3$; a common mineral; the principal constituent of limestone.

caliche: A layer of calcite that forms in soils in arid and semiarid regions as a result of the evaporation of calcium-bearing groundwaters.

calorie: A unit of energy defined as the energy required to raise the temperature of 1 gram of water 1°C.

cannel coal: A compact sapropelic coal consisting primarily of spores accumulated in stagnant water.

caprock: An impervious body of anhydrite and gypsum with minor sulfur and calcite that overlies a salt dome.

carat: A common term with two meanings: (1) a standard unit, 200 milligrams, for weighing precious stones; and (2) a term used to define the purity or fineness of gold and meaning one twenty-fourth (pure gold is 24 carat).

carbon cycle: The cyclical movement of carbon compounds between the biosphere, lithosphere, atmosphere, and hydrosphere.

carbonation: A chemical weathering process in which carbon dioxide dissolved in water converts oxides of calcium, magnesium, and iron into carbonates.

carbonatite: A carbonate rock of apparent magmatic origin; commonly a host for rare-earth elements.

cartel: A combination of independent business organizations formed to regulate production, pricing, and marketing of goods by the members.

cassiterite: A mineral, composition SnO_2; the most important ore of tin.

catagenesis: Physical and chemical changes intermediate between near-surface diagenesis and deep burial metagenesis; used especially in reference to organic matter.

catalysis: Acceleration of a chemical reaction by an element or compound that is not incorporated into the reaction products.

catalyst: A substance that accelerates a chemical reaction without remaining in the reaction products.

catalytic cracking: The use of catalysts to break heavier hydrocarbons into lighter ones.

cation exchange: The exchange of one cation for another, especially by clay minerals.

cation: A positively charged atom.

cement rock: A limestone with a sufficient clay content that it becomes cement upon calcining.

cement: A binding material; *see* Portland cement.

chain reaction: Where one reaction leads to further reactions, a controlled chain reaction (see Figure 6.3) occurs in a nuclear reactor, an uncontrolled chain reaction occurs in a nuclear weapon.

chalcopyrite: Mineral, $CuFeS_2$; a major ore of copper.

channelization: The straightening, and sometimes deepening and lining, of a stream or river channel so that the water flows more rapidly; commonly used to alleviate flooding.

chelation: The retention of a metallic ion by two atoms of a single organic molecule.

chemical flooding: The injection of chemicals into an oil well to promote the release of oil trapped in the rocks.

chemical weathering: The process of weathering by which chemical reactions convert the original minerals into new mineral phases.

china clay: A commercial term for kaolin used in the manufacture of chinaware.

chlorofluoromethane: Compounds such as $CFCl_3$, used as propellants in aerosol cans; can damage the ozone layer in Earth's upper atmosphere.

chromite: A mineral, composition $FeCr_2O_4$; the principal ore mineral of chromium.

clastic: An adjective describing rocks or sediments composed of fragments derived from pre-existing rocks.

clay: A term with two common meanings: (1) a natural rock fragment smaller in diameter than 1/256 millimeter; and (2) any of a group of hydrous sheet structure silicate minerals.

cleavage: The general tendency of a mineral or rock to split along natural directions of weakness.

Clinton type: A fossiliferous sedimentary iron ore rich in hematite and goethite of the Clinton or correlative formations in the Silurian sandstones of the eastern United States.

clod: A lump of soil produced by artificial breakage such as plowing. *See* ped.

coal: A combustible rock containing more than 50 percent by weight and more than 70 percent by volume of carbonaceous matter derived from accumulated plant remains.

coalification: The process by which plant material is converted into coal.

coke: A combustible material consisting of the fused ash and carbon of bituminous coal, produced by driving off volatile matter by heating in the absence of oxygen.

col: An old British term for coal.

cold-working: Shaping of metals at room temperature by hammering or rolling; a process that hardens and strengthens the metal.

comminution: The process of crushing and grinding ores to break ore minerals loose from the valueless gangue minerals.

concentrate: Ground and beneficiated product that consists of one or more ore minerals that have been selectively removed from the original mixture of ore and gangue minerals.

concrete: A construction material consisting of pebbles, sand, or other fragments in a cement matrix.

conduction (of heat): The process by which heat is transferred by molecular impact without transfer of matter itself; the principal manner by which heat is transmitted through solids.

cone-of-depression: The depression in the water table that develops around a well from which water is being pumped.

confined aquifer: An aquifer bounded above and below by impermeable beds.

conglomerate: A coarse-grained clastic rock comprised of coarse rounded fragments set in a finer matrix.

consumption (of water): The use of water such that it is not returned to the groundwater or surface water source from which it was drawn.

contact metamorphism: The thermal, and sometimes introduced chemical, effects occurring in a rock resulting from the intrusion of an adjacent igneous body.

continental shelf: That portion of the continental margin that lies between the shoreline and the continental slope.

convection: The movement of material, gaseous or liquid, wherein the hotter portion rises and cooler portions descend as a consequence of differences in density.

convert (metallurgical): The process of passing oxygen through a molten mass of sulfides in order to convert iron sulfides into iron oxides so that the iron may be more readily separated into the slag.

corundum: A mineral, composition Al_2O_3; the second hardest mineral after diamond. In clear, colored crystals it is known as sapphire or ruby if blue or red, respectively.

cracking: The process by which heavier hydrocarbons are broken into lighter ones.

critical mass (in a nuclear reaction): The amount of uranium required to maintain a chain reaction in a nuclear reactor.

critical(ity) (in a nuclear reactor): The condition at which a nuclear reactor is maintained in order to sustain a chain reaction.

crosscut: Passageway of a mine that is cut perpendicular to the long dimension of the deposit.

crushed rock: Any rock material that has been crushed for use as fill, for road beds, or for construction aggregate.

crushing (of rock): The process of breaking rock into smaller fragments to facilitate the separation of the ore minerals from the gangue.

cupellation: The process of freeing silver or gold from base metals by using a small bone ash cup, called a cupel, and lead.

dam: A barrier built across a river or stream to hold back water.

decay (radioactive): Spontaneous, radioactive transformation of one nuclide to another.

deoxyribonucleic acid: DNA, the substance within the chromosomes of living cells that carries hereditary instructions and directs the production of proteins.

depletion allowance: A tax deduction on mineral resources initiated as an incentive for the producers to explore for new deposits to replace the present materials being depleted.

desertification: The expansion of desertlike conditions as a result of natural climatic changes or human-induced activities such as overgrazing or farming.

deuterium: An isotope of hydrogen containing one proton and one neutron in its nucleus.

diagenesis: Physical and chemical changes that occur in a sediment after deposition and during and after lithification but not including weathering or metamorphism.

diamond: A cubic form of carbon; the hardest mineral, widely used in jewelry and as an industrial abrasive.

diaspore: A mineral, composition AlO(OH); a light-colored compound that occurs in bauxite.

diatomite: A rock or unconsolidated earthy material composed of accumulated siliceous tests of diatoms; single-celled marine or freshwater plants.

dimension stone: Building stone that is quarried and shaped into blocks according to specifications.

diorite: Igneous rocks generally composed of amphibole, plagioclase, pyroxene, and sometimes minor amounts of quartz.

direct shipping ore: Ore of sufficiently high grade that it can be profitably shipped to a smelter without first requiring beneficiation.

distillation (or fractionation): The process of separating crude oil into various liquids and gases of different chemical and physical properties.

dolomite: A mineral, composition $CaMg(CO_2)_2$; a common sedimentary carbonate mineral; also commonly, but incorrectly, used to refer to a rock composed of dolomite.

dolostone: A rock composed of dolomite.

doping: The process of introducing trace amounts of an element into another element or compound to produce desirable electrical or other properties.

doré bar: The mass of gold and silver bullion recovered from the refining of ores.

dredging: The excavation of ore-bearing or waste materials by floating barge or raft equipped to bring up and process, or transport, the materials.

drifts: The passageways of a mine that are cut parallel to the long dimension of a deposit.

dry steam: Natural geothermal systems dominated by water vapor (steam) with little or no liquid in the system.

dunite: A rock composed almost entirely of olivine.

emery: A granular mixture of corundum and varying amounts of iron oxides (magnetite or hematite); used as an abrasive.

energy: The capacity to do work.

equivalent rainfall: The amount of water, including rainfall and runoff, to which an area of land is subjected.

eutrophication: The process by which waters become deficient in oxygen due to an increased abundance of dissolved nutrients and decaying plant matter.

evaporation: The process by which water is converted from a liquid to a vapor.

evaporite: Sedimentary rock that forms as a result of the evaporation of saline solutions.

evapotranspiration: The transfer of water in the ground to water vapor in the atmosphere through the combined processes of evaporation and transpiration.

exchange: The process by which a mineral, especially a clay, gives up one cation bound to its lattice for another cation in solution.

exchange capacity: The quantitative ability of a mineral to exchange ions with a solution.

exfoliation: The process by which thin concentric shells or flat layers of rock or mineral are successively broken from the outer surface of a larger.

face: The wall in a mine where ore is being extracted. To remove the ore, holes are drilled into the face and filled with explosives; the explosives are detonated to break the rock so that it can be removed.

fast breeder reactor: A nuclear reactor in which fuel is made or "bred" in a blanket of ^{238}U wrapped around the core.

fault: A surface or zone of rock fracture along which there has been displacement.

feldspar: A group of fairly abundant rock-forming minerals of the general formula $MAl(Al,Si)_3O_8$ where M is K, Na, Ca, Ba, Rb, Sr.

feldspathoid: A group of uncommon aluminosilicate minerals of sodium, potassium, or calcium and having too little silica to form feldspar.

ferric: Referring to the oxidized form of iron, Fe^{3+}.

ferro-alloy metal: Any metal that can be alloyed with iron to produce a metal with special properties.

ferromagnesian mineral: Iron- and magnesium-containing minerals.

ferromanganese: An alloy of iron and manganese used in iron smelting.

ferro-manganese nodules: Rounded, concentrically laminated masses of iron and manganese oxides and hydroxides that form on the floors of oceans and some lakes.

ferrosilicon: A synthetic phase FeSi used in the steel industry as a means of removing oxygen from iron and steel during smelting.

ferrous: Referring to the reduced form of iron, Fe^{2+}.

fertilizer: Natural or synthetic substances used to promote plant growth.

filler: A mineral substance added to a product to increase the bulk or weight, to dilute expensive materials, or to improve the product.

fire clay: A siliceous clay rich in hydrous aluminum silicates, capable of withstanding high temperatures without deforming; hence used in the manufacture of refractory cements.

fission (nuclear): The process by which a heavy nuclide is split into two or more lighter nuclides by the addition of a neutron to the nucleus.

fissure: A surface or fracture in rock along which there has been distinct separation.

flint: A dense, fine-grained form of silica, SiO_2, that was commonly used in the making of stone tools and weapons.

fluid inclusion: Small droplet of fluid trapped within a crystal during initial growth or during recrystallization.

fluorite: A mineral, composition CaF_2; a common and variably colored substance widely used in the preparation of glasses, the manufacture of hydrofluoric acid, and the smelting of aluminum.

fluorspar: An alternate name for fluorite.

flux: Any substance that serves to promote a chemical reaction; also, the number of radioactive particles in a given volume of space multiplied by their mean velocity.

fly ash: Fine particulates that are formed during the burning of fossil fuels, especially coal.

forsterite: A mineral, composition Mg_2SiO_4; a member of the olivine series of minerals.

fossil fuel: A general term for any hydrocarbon deposit that may be used for fuel—petroleum, natural gas, coal, tar, or oil shale.

fractionation: *See* distillation.

Frasch process: A method of sulfur mining in which superheated water is forced down a well to melt sulfur that is then pumped to the surface for recovery.

fuel element (or fuel rod): The long rodlike assemblies that contain the U_3O_8 pellets used as fuel in a nuclear fission reactor.

fuller's earth: A fine-grained earthy substance (usually a clay) possessing a high absorptive capacity; originally used in fulling woolen fabrics, the shrinking and thickening by application of moisture.

fusion (nuclear): The combination of two light nuclei to form a heavier nucleus; a reaction accompanied by the release of large amounts of energy.

gabbro: A dark-colored, coarse-grained igneous rock composed primarily of plagioclase feldspar, pyroxene, and olivine.

galena: A mineral, PbS, that serves as the major source of lead.

galvanizing: The coating of zinc on iron or steel to prevent rusting.

gangue: A general term for the nonuseful minerals and rocks intermixed with valuable ore minerals.

garnet: A group of minerals of general formula $A_3B_2(SiO_4)_3$ where A = Ca, Mg, Fe^{2+}, and Mn^{2+} and B = Al, Fe^{3+}, Mn^{3+}, and Cr.

gasohol: A mixture of gasoline and alcohol used as a fuel for automobiles.

geochemical balance: The distribution of chemical elements and chemical compounds among various types of rocks, waters, and the atmosphere.

geochemical cycling: The cyclical movement of chemical elements through Earth's lithosphere, hydrosphere, and atmosphere.

geopressured zone: A rock unit in which the fluid pressure is greater than that of normal hydrostatic pressure.

geothermal energy: Useful heat energy that can be extracted from naturally occurring steam or from hot rocks or waters.

geothermal field: An area where there is the development, or potential development, of geothermal energy.

geothermal gradient: The rate of increase in temperature in Earth as a function of depth; the average is 25°C per kilometer.

geyser: A natural hot spring that intermittently ejects water or steam.

Global 2000 Report to the President: A report on the status of the world's resources, population, and environment from 1975 to 2000 A.D. prepared for President Carter in 1980.

gneiss: A coarse-grained, layered, metamorphic rock.

goethite: The hydrated ferric oxide mineral, $FeO \cdot OH$.

gossan: The mass of iron oxides and hydroxides that forms when iron sulfides are exposed to weathering at or near Earth's surface.

grade: The content of a metal or a mineral in a rock; usually expressed as a percentage by weight for most ores.

granite: A coarse-grained igneous rock consisting mainly of quartz and potassium feldspar, usually accompanied by mica, either muscovite or biotite.

granodiorite: A coarse-grained igneous rock consisting mainly of quartz, potassium feldspar, plagioclase, and biotite.

graphite: A mineral, composition C; a soft, black compound with a pronounced cleavage, widely used as a lubricant.

gravel: A general term for both naturally occurring and artificially ground rock particles in the size range 2–20 millimeters in diameter.

greenhouse effect: Increase of the content of CO_2 and other gases that absorb radiation from the earth; the warming of Earth's atmosphere brought about by an increase in the CO_2 content.

guano: Accumulated bird or bat excrement; mined locally as a source of fertilizer.

gusher: An oil or gas well in which the high pressures encountered during drilling are sufficient to cause fountaining of the oil, gas, and accompanying water at the surface.

gypsum: A mineral, composition $CaSO_4 \cdot 2H_2O$; formed by evaporation of seawater and used to make plaster of Paris.

Haber-Bosch process: A process perfected in Germany in the early 1900s by which nitrogen from Earth's atmosphere is fixed into ammonia so that it can be used in fertilizers and chemicals.

half-life (of an isotope): The time required for half of the quantity of a naturally radioactive isotope to decay to a daughter product.

halite: A mineral, NaCl; the most abundant material dissolved in seawater.

heap leaching: A process by which a solvent, such as a cyanide solution or an acid, is allowed to percolate through a pile (or heap) of crushed rock to dissolve out a valuable mineral resource (such as gold or copper).

heliostat: An assemblage of mirrors that is programmed to automatically track the sun to constantly focus the sun's rays on a central receiver.

hematite: A mineral, composition Fe_2O_3; an important ore mineral used as a source of iron, as a polishing powder, and as a cosmetic (rouge).

homogeneous reactor: A nuclear reactor in which the fuel and moderator are intimately mixed.

horsepower: A unit for measuring power; originally derived from the pulling power of a horse. The rate at which energy must be expended in order to raise 55 lbs at a rate of one foot per second.

humic coals: Coal derived from peat by the breakdown of plant matter by organic acids.

humus: The generally dark, more or less stable part of the organic matter of the soil; it is so well decomposed that the original sources cannot be identified.

hydration: The process by which water is chemically bound in a chemical compound.

hydraulic mining: The use of high-pressure jets of water to dislodge unconsolidated rock or sediment so that it can be processed.

hydro-mulching: The application of a soil covering by means of a high-pressure hose; used to prevent evaporation and erosion.

hydroelectricity: Electricity generated by water-driven turbines.

hydrogenation: A chemical process in which hydrogen is added to complex hydrocarbons to yield less complex molecules that have higher H to C ratios.

hydrograph: A diagram recording the relationship between time and the quantity of water leaving a drainage basin.

hydrolysis: A chemical process by which a compound incorporates water into its structure.

hydro-seeding: The application of seed to barren soil surfaces by means of a high-pressure hose.

hydrosphere: The waters of Earth.

hydrothermal alteration: Mineralogic changes in rocks resulting from interactions with hydrothermal solutions.

hydrothermal solutions: Hot, aqueous solutions, some of which transport and deposit ore minerals.

igneous: A term applied to a rock that has solidified from magma.

ilmenite: A mineral, composition $FeTiO_3$; a principal ore mineral of titanium.

impermeable: Referring to a rock, sediment, or soil that does not permit the passage of fluids.

in situ leaching: The extraction of metals or salts by passing solutions through rocks that have been fractured but not excavated.

inclines (in mines): Drifts or shafts in mines that are at an angle to the horizontal.

industrial mineral: Any rock, mineral, or other naturally occurring substance of economic value, exclusive of metallic ores, mineral fuels, and gemstones.

inertial confinement: A means of confining the plasma in a fusion nuclear reactor.

ingot: A mass of cast metal as it comes from a mold or a crucible.

intrazonal soil: One of the soil orders; all soils with more or less well-developed soil characteristics reflecting the dominant influence of relief, parent rock, or age over that of climate.

ion: Any charged atom.

ion exchange: The reversible replacement of certain ions by others, without the change in the crystal structure.

Iron Age: The period that began about 1100 B.C. with the widespread use of iron for tools and weapons. It followed the Bronze Age and, in a sense, continues today.

ironstones: Sedimentary rocks of large lateral extent that contain significant amounts of iron oxides, hydroxides, and silicates as coatings on, and replacements of, sedimentary mineral fragments and fossils.

irrigation: Process of supplying water to the land to promote the growth of crops.

isotopes: Species of the same chemical element having the same number of protons but differing numbers of neutrons in the nucleus.

itabirite: A metamorphosed banded iron formation consisting of thin bands of hematite and silica.

joule: A unit of energy equal to 0.24 calorie; the flow of one ampere of electrical energy for one second at a potential of one volt.

kaolinite: A mineral, composition $Al_2Si_2O_5(OH)_4$; a common, light-colored clay mineral.

kerogen: Fossilized, insoluble organic material found in sedimentary rocks; can be converted by distillation to petroleum products.

kiln: An oven used to harden, burn, or dry substances; especially to convert clay products into ceramics.

kilowatt hour: A unit of electrical power consumption indicating the total energy developed by a power of one kilowatt acting for one hour.

kilowatt hour: A unit of energy equivalent to one thousand watthours.

kimberlite: The rock type in which diamonds occur; a porphyritic alkalic peridotite containing olivine, mica, and chromium-garnet.

kyanite: A mineral, composition $Al_2Si_2O_5$; a compound found in certain metamorphic rocks and used in the manufacture of ceramics and glass.

lag-time diagram: A diagram that illustrates the relationship between rainfall and surface runoff of a drainage basin in terms of time.

laterite: A highly leached soil zone in tropical regions that is rich in iron oxides.

leach pad: The impermeable layer of material placed beneath a heap leach pile to allow for the collection of metal-bearing fluids.

leachate: A watery solution that has drained out of a landfill or a heap leach pile.

leucoxene: A general term for fine-grained alteration products of ilmenite, $FeTiO_3$.

level (in a mine): A main underground passageway leading out from a shaft that provides access to mine working.

liberation (of minerals): The freeing of valuable mineral particles from valueless gangue.

lightweight aggregate: Aggregate of appreciably lower specific gravity than normal rock or aggregate; prepared by using very lightweight clays or porous materials.

lime: The compound CaO; usually prepared by calcining limestone.

limestone: A bedded sedimentary rock comprised largely of the mineral calcite, $CaCO_3$.

limonite: A general term for amorphous brown, naturally occurring hydrous ferric oxides with a general composition of approximately $2Fe_2O_3 \cdot 3H_2O$.

lipids: Fats or fatty oils.

liquid immiscibility: The inability of two liquids to mix and form a single, homogeneous liquid. Oil and water are immiscible.

lithosphere: The rocks forming the surface of Earth to a depth of about 60 kilometers and which behave as rigid plates.

loam: A rich, permeable soil composed of a friable mixture of organic matter and roughly equal proportions of clay, silt, and sand.

macadam road: A road made by the addition of successive layers of finer and finer pulverized rock; named for the developer of the process, John McAdam of Scotland.

macerals: The organic components of coal. Macerals are to coal what minerals are to a rock.

mafic: A term applied to igneous rocks composed primarily of one or more ferromagnesian minerals (most mafic rocks are also basic, i.e., having SiO_2 contents less than 54 percent).

magmatic differentiation: The changes that occur in the composition of a magma during processes of crystallization.

magnesia: The compound MgO widely used in refractories. The rare mineral periclase has this composition.

magnesite: A mineral, composition $MgCO_3$; an ore mineral of magnesium and of the raw material used to produce MgO.

magnetite: A mineral, composition Fe_3O_4; an important ore of iron.

malleability: The property of a metal that allows it to be plastically deformed under compressive stress, such as hammering.

manganese nodules: *See* ferro-manganese nodules.

mantle: The zone of Earth that lies below the crust and above the core (from approximately 10–30 kilometers to 3480 kilometers).

marble: A coarse-grained rock composed of calcite; usually formed by metamorphism of a limestone.

marginal reserve: That part of the reserve base of a mineral resource that borders on being economically producible.

marsh gas: *See* swamp gas.

matte: A mixture of metal sulfides and oxides produced by melting ore mineral concentrates.

metagenesis: Physical and chemical changes that occur in response to the high temperatures and pressures of deep burial; used especially in reference to organic material.

metal: An element or alloy possessing high electrical and/or thermal conductivity that is malleable and ductile.

metamorphic: Pertaining to rocks in which the minerals have undergone chemical and structural changes due to changes in temperature and pressure.

metamorphism: The mineralogical and structural changes of solid rocks in response to the changes in temperature and pressure resulting from burial or adjacent igneous intrusion.

metasomatism: Change in the character of a rock, as in metamorphism, when chemical constituents are added or removed in the process.

methane: A colorless, odorless, flammable gas, CH_4; the principal constituent of natural gas.

mica: A group of sheet silicate minerals with a general formula of $(K,Na,Ca)(Mg,Fe,Li,Al)_{2-3}(Al,Si)_4O_{10}(OH,F)_2$.

milling: The crushing and grinding of ores so that the useful material may be separated from gangue materials.

mineral resource: The sum of a group of valuable minerals in a given volume of crust.

Minette type: A variety of sedimentary iron ore; the European equivalent of the North American Clinton type ores.

mining: The process of extracting mineral substances from the earth, usually by digging holes or shafts.

Mississippi Valley type: A term applied to a class of mineral deposits that is widespread in the drainage basin of the Mississippi River; zinc and/or lead sulfide ores that occur in carbonate rocks.

moderator (in a nuclear reactor): The medium, such as graphite, that moderates the flux of neutrons produced during radioactive decay.

Moh's scale: A standard of 10 minerals by which the relative hardness of a mineral may be rated. From softest to hardest, they are talc, gypsum, calcite, fluorite, apatite, orthoclase, quartz, topaz, corundum, and diamond.

monazite: A rare-earth phosphate mineral, $(Ce,La,Nd,Th)(PO_4)$.

montmorillonite: A common clay mineral with the general formula, $R_{0.33}Al_2Si_4O_{10}(OH)_2 \cdot nH_2O$ where R is Na^+, $K^\cdot$, Mg^{2+}, Ca^{2+}.

mullite: $Al_6Si_2O_{13}$; a rare mineral but a common synthetic material in ceramic products.

muscovite mica: White mica of composition $KAl_2[AlSi_3O_{10}](OH)_2$.

muskeg: A bog with deep accumulations of organic material forming in poorly drained areas in northern temperate or arctic regions.

natural gas: A mixture of hydrocarbon gases, principally methane.

nepheline syenite: An igneous rock composed essentially of plagioclase feldspar and the feldspathoid mineral nepheline, $(Na,K)AlSiO_4$.

niter: Naturally occurring potassium nitrate; saltpeter.

nitrogen: Chemical element number 7; 78 percent of Earth's atmosphere and one of the most important fertilizer elements.

noble metal: A metal with marked resistance to chemical reaction; a term often applied to gold, silver, mercury, and the platinum metal group; synonymous with precious metal.

non-ferrous metal: A general term referring to metals that are not normally alloyed with iron.

nonmetallic minerals: A broadly used term for minerals that are extracted other than for use of the metals they contain or for use as fuel.

non-point sources: Sources of pollution that are dispersed such as farm fields, road surfaces, etc.

nonrenewable resources: Resources that are fixed in total quantity in Earth's crust.

norite: A coarse-grained igneous rock composed of plagioclase and an orthopyroxene.

nuclear fission: The breakdown of a large nucleus (e.g., of uranium) to smaller nuclei with the emission of large amounts of energy.

nuclear fusion: The joining together of the nuclei of very light elements (hydrogen, lithium) to form heavier elements with the release of large amounts of energy.

nuclear reactor: The vessel in which nuclear fuels are reacted to generate heat, in turn used to raise steam and drive turbines.

nugget: A small solid lump, especially of gold.

obsidian: Volcanic glass; usually black but also red, green, or brown.

oil: *See* petroleum.

oil mining: The process of mining oil-bearing rock so that it can be processed to extract the oil.

oil shale: A fine-grained sedimentary rock containing much bituminous organic matter incorporated when the sediment was deposited.

oil window: The set of temperature and pressure conditions, developed during burial of a sediment, that lead to the conversion of organic water into petroleum.

olivine: A mineral, composition $(Fe,Mg)SiO_4$; an igneous mineral used in making refractories.

open-pit mining: Mining from open excavations.

ophiolite complex: A sequence of mafic and ultramafic igneous rocks including metamorphic rocks, whose origin is associated with the early phases of ocean floor rifting.

ore: Resources of metals that can now be economically and legally extracted.

ore deposit: Equals "reserve" when referring to metal-bearing concentrations.

ore mineral: Broadly used to include any mineral from which metals can be extracted.

osmotic pressure: The pressure resulting from the movement of molecules or ions in a fluid through a semipermeable membrane as they seek to establish the same concentrations on both sides of the membrane.

overburden: The valueless rock that must be removed above a near-surface ore deposit to permit open-pit mining.

oxidant: A compound or element that brings about oxidation.

oxidation: Combination with oxygen; more generally, any reaction in which there is an increase in valence resulting from a loss of electrons.

ozone: O_3, a form of oxygen produced by lightning and by solar radiation interacting with the upper atmosphere; important in reducing the penetration of UV radiation through Earth's atmosphere.

palygorskite: A mineral, composition $(Mg,Al)_2Si_4O_{10}OH \cdot 4H_2O$; a variety of clay that is sometimes fibrous and used as asbestos.

parabolic reflector: A concave reflector so shaped that the impinging sun's rays are focused by reflection onto a central tube that becomes heated; the tube contains a fluid that transports the heat for use elsewhere.

peat: An unconsolidated deposit of semicarbonized plant remains accumulated in a water-saturated environment such as a swamp or bog. The early stage of coal formation.

ped: A naturally formed granule, block, crumb, or aggregate of a soil. *See* clod.

pegmatite: An exceptionally coarse-grained igneous rock; sometimes contains rich accumulations of rare elements such as lithium, boron, fluorine, niobium, tantalum, uranium, and rare earths.

pellets: Small, solid particles of material, especially those formed of iron oxide grains and used as a feed stock to smelt iron.

per capita: Per unit of population; for each person.

per capita use: The amount of something used by each person during a standard time period, generally per day or per year.

peridotite: A coarse-grained igneous rock composed chiefly of olivine and pyroxene.

perlite: A volcanic glass with a rhyolitic composition, a high water content, and a characteristic cracked pattern.

permeable: A rock, sediment, or soil with the capacity of transmitting a fluid.

petroleum: A naturally occurring complex liquid hydrocarbon that after distillation yields a range of combustible fuels, petrochemicals, and lubricants.

phosphate(s): Compounds, including some minerals, containing phosphorus in the form of the phosphate (PO_4) anion.

phosphorus: Chemical element number 15; one of the most important fertilizer elements.

photocell: A layered chemical cell that produces electricity directly from light energy.

photochemical conversion: A chemical conversion that proceeds by the addition of energy in the form of electromagnetic radiation.

photochemical reaction: A chemical reaction promoted by the presence of electromagnetic radiation.

photoelectrochemical conversion: The chemical process active in a photogalvanic cell.

photogalvanic: A term used for a chemical reaction in which solar energy is converted directly into electrical energy.

photosynthesis: The process by which green plants use the radiant energy from the sun to create hydrocarbons and release oxygen.

photovoltaic cell: *See* photocell.

pH: A measure of acidity expressed numerically from 0 to 14; neutral is 7, with lower values representing more acid conditions. Specifically, the negative logarithm of the H^+ concentration.

pickling (of metals): The use of an acid bath to cleanse the surface of metal castings, sheet metal, etc.

pig iron: The raw iron produced during the smelting of iron ore.

pigment: A coloring agent.

pitchblende: A massive, brown to black, fine-grained variety of uraninite, UO_2; a term commonly applied to any black uranium ore.

placer: A surficial mineral deposit formed by mechanical concentration of mineral particles from weathered debris.

plagioclase feldspars: A series of silicate minerals involving a solid solution from $CaAl_2Si_2O_8$ (anorthite) to $NaAlSi_3O_8$ (albite).

plasma: A fourth state of matter (solid, liquid, gas, plasma) capable of conducting magnetic force, usually generated by application of extremely high temperatures.

plaster of Paris: Partially dehydrated gypsum, $CaSO_4 \cdot \frac{1}{2}H_2O$.

podiform: Referring to ore bodies with an elongate lenticular shape; especially some chromite ores.

point source: A single point, such as a smoke stack or pipe, from which pollution emanates.

pollution: The presence of abnormal substances or abnormally high concentrations of normal substances in the natural environment.

polymorph: One form of a mineral that is known to exist in more than one crystallographic form. Graphite and diamond are polymorphs of carbon.

polypedon: A three-dimensional body of soil consisting of more than one recognizable soil type.

porosity: The property of containing many holes.

porphyry: An igneous rock that contains large crystals embedded in a fine-grained groundmass.

portland cement: A calcium alumino silicate produced by calcining limestone and clay; this finely ground product will recrystallize and set when water is added.

potable water: Water that is safe for human use.

potash: A term locally used for potassium oxide or potassium hydroxide or to define the potassium oxide content of minerals.

potassium: Chemical element number 19; one of the most important fertilizer elements.

power: The measure of energy produced or used as a function of time. *See* horsepower.

pozzolan cement: A cement formed by grinding together hydrated lime and a pozzolana, a natural volcanic glass capable of reacting with the lime at ordinary temperatures to form cement compounds.

precious metals: The scarce metals that have high value—traditionally, gold, silver, and the platinum group metals.

primary mineral: A mineral formed at the same time as the rock enclosing it by igneous or hydrothermal processes.

primary recovery: Petroleum production that occurs as a result of natural flow or pumping.

prior appropriation (of water): The law that permits the buying and selling of specified amounts of water from a stream for beneficial use. The appropriations are honored in order of the oldest first.

pumice: A light-colored, vesicular, glassy rock formed by the eruption of gas-rich lava from a volcano.

pumped-water storage system: Hydroelectric power systems in which excess electricity as low demand times is used to pump water into a storage area so that it can be used subsequently to generate electricity.

pyrite: A mineral, FeS_2; fools gold.

pyrolysis: Chemical decomposition by the action of heat.

pyrometallurgy: The metallurgical process involved in separating and refining metals where heat is used, as in roasting and smelting.

pyroxene: A group of silicate minerals of general formula $WSiO_3$ (or $XYSi_2O_6$) where W = Mg, Fe; XY = Mg, Ca, Fe, Na, Li, etc.

pyroxenite: A rock composed primarily of pyroxene.

pyrrhotite: A mineral, composition $Fe_{1-x}S$; a common iron sulfide compound.

quarry: An open surface working usually dug for the extraction of building stone.

quartz: A mineral, composition SiO_2; a very common compound that is hard, lacks cleavage, and does not weather rapidly.

quartzite: A metamorphic rock derived from sandstone and composed primarily of quartz.

quick silver: A term for mercury, Hg.

radioactivity: *See* decay (radioactive).

raise (in a mine): A vertical opening connecting two levels of a mine.

rank: A coal classification based upon physical, chemical, and thermal properties.

rare-earth elements: The 15 elements from atomic number 57 to 71, including, for example, lanthanum (La), cerium (Ce), neodymium (Nd), and europium (Eu).

recycling: The reuse of metals or other materials.

refining: Metallurgically—the process of extracting pure metals from their mineralogical forms; petroleum—the process of distilling and cracking crude oil to produce a wide variety of separate hydrocarbon liquids and gases.

refractory: A term used for unreactive materials with high melting points used to line the furnaces in which metals are smelted.

regolith: A general term for the surface layer of loose material that forms as a result of the weathering of rock.

renewable resources: Resources that are naturally replenished by processes active in or on Earth's crust.

reserve (of minerals): Mineral resources that can now be economically and legally extracted.

reserve base: That part of an identified resource that meets certain minimum physical and chemical criteria to present economic potential and that has a reasonable potential for becoming economic within planning horizons.

reservoir rock: Any rock with adequate porosity and that contains liquid or gaseous hydrocarbons.

resource: Naturally occurring concentrations of liquids, gases, or solids in or on Earth's crust in such form and amount that economic extraction of a commodity is currently or potentially feasible.

retort: A furnacelike chamber used to distill volatile materials or to carry out the destructive distillation of coal or oil shale. Heat is usually applied externally, and the decomposition products are collected by cooling the gases so that different compounds condense at different temperatures.

return flow: Water that reaches a groundwater or surface source after release from the point of use and thus becomes available for further use.

rhyolite: A fine-grained extrusive igneous rock consisting largely of quartz and potassium feldspar.

ribonucleic acid: RNA, a substance similar to DNA; it carries out DNA's instructions for making proteins.

Richter Scale: A scale used in the quantitative evaluation of the energy released by earthquakes.

riparian: Pertaining to the shoreline areas of a body of water. Riparian law allows landowners to draw from a lake or stream adjacent to their property if their use does not harm other users.

roasting: Heating of an ore to bring about some change, usually oxidation, of the sulfide or other minerals.

rock salt: Coarsely crystalline halite, naturally occurring or synthetically prepared.

room and pillar mining: A mining method in which rock, coal, or ore is removed from a series of openings with a series of intervening columns (pillars) left to support the overlying rocks.

rotary drilling: The commonest method of drilling. A hydraulic process in which a hard-toothed drill bit is attached to a rotating drill pipe. As the pipe turns, the bit grinds into the rock; the loose pieces are carried to the surface by fluid circulated down the center of the pipe.

rutile: A mineral, composition TiO_2; the principal ore of titanium; used as a white paint pigment.

saline water: Water that contains 1000 or more milligrams of dissolved solids per liter, especially NaCl.

salinization: The buildup of salts, usually NaCl, in soils as a result of evaporation.

salt dome: Dome or pinnaclelike structure of rock salt, halite, which has risen through sediments above a bed of salt due to differences in densities.

saltpeter: Naturally occurring potassium nitrate; niter.

saltwater intrusion: The movement of salt water into an aquifer, usually as a result of excessive extraction of fresh water near coastal areas.

sand: Detrital rock fragments $\frac{1}{16}$ to 2 millimeters in diameter; natural sands are composed almost entirely of quartz.

sandstone: A medium-grained, clastic sedimentary rock composed of sand-sized particles (usually quartz).

saponite: A mineral, composition $(Ca/2,Na)_{0.33}(Mg,Fe)_3(Si_{3.67},Al_{0.33}O_{10}(OH)_2 \cdot 4H_2O$; a soft, soapy, light-colored clay.

sapropelic coal: Coal derived from organic residues (finely divided plant debris, spores, and algae) in stagnant or standing bodies of water.

scarce metals: Metals whose average crustal abundance is less than 0.1 percent.

secondary mineral: A mineral formed later than the rock enclosing it and usually at the expense of earlier formed primary minerals.

secondary recovery: Oil production resulting from procedures, such as the injection of water, steam, or chemical compounds into a reservoir in order to increase oil production beyond primary production.

sedimentary: Pertaining to rocks formed from the accumulation of fragments weathered from preexisting rocks or by precipitation of materials in solution in lake or seawater.

seismograph: An instrument that records vibrations of the earth, especially those from earthquakes.

sepiolite: A mineral, composition $Mg_4(Si_2O_5)_3(OH)_2 \cdot 6H_2O$; a common clay that is widely used for ornamental carvings; also known as meerschaum.

serpentine: A group of minerals, general composition $(Mg,Fe)_3Si_2O_5(OH)_4$; widely formed in metamorphism with varieties including gems (jade) and asbestos (chrysotile).

serpentinite: A rock composed primarily of serpentine group minerals and formed through the alteration of preexisting ferromagnesian minerals such as olivine and pyroxene.

shaft (of a mine): A vertical entrance into a mine.

shale: A fine-grained, indurated, detrital sedimentary rock formed by the compaction of clay, silt, or mud and with a partially developed rock cleavage.

silicon chip: A chip of silicon metal to which trace amounts of other elements have been added in order to affect the electronic properties.

sillimanite: A mineral, composition $Al_2Si_2O_5$; a compound found in metamorphic rocks and used in the manufacture of ceramics and glass.

skarn: An assemblage of lime-bearing silicates derived from limestones and dolomites by the introduction of silicon, iron, and magnesium, usually adjacent to an igneous intrusion.

slag: The nonmetallic top layer that separates during the smelting of ores; it is usually rich in silica, alumina, lime, and any other materials used to flux the smelting.

slate: A compact, fine-grained metamorphic rock formed from shale; it possesses the property of rock cleavage whereby it can be readily parted along parallel planes.

smectite: A term applied to the montmorillonite group of clay minerals.

smelting: The chemical reduction of a metal from its ore usually by melting to separate the metal from a slag; the process of melting ore minerals to separate the metals from the nonvaluable phases.

smog: Fog that has become mixed and polluted with smoke.

soda ash: Sodium carbonate.

soil: The unconsolidated earthy material that overlies bedrock and that is a complex mixture of inorganic and organic compounds; the natural medium to support the growth of plants.

soil order: One of ten major subdivisions in the "Comprehensive Soil Classification System."

soil profile: A vertical section through a soil that reveals the different physical and chemical zones that are present.

soil temperature regime: The changes in temperature experienced by a soil in a normal annual cycle.

soil water regime: The changes in the amounts of water present in a soil during a normal annual cycle.

solar energy: The total energy in the sun's radiation.

solid solution: A solid crystalline phase in which the composition may vary by one or more elements replacing others, e.g., Fe replacing Mg in the olivine minerals Mg_2SiO_4-Fe_2SiO_4.

solution mining: The extraction of resources by solutions instead of conventional mining procedures. *See* in-situ mining.

soot: A black substance consisting mainly of carbon from the smoke of wood or coal.

sour gas: Hydrogen sulfide, H_2S, that commonly occurs in minor quantities with petroleum or natural gas.

source rocks: Sedimentary rocks containing the organic matter that under heat, pressure, and time is transformed into liquid or gaseous hydrocarbons.

special metal: Metals such as tantalum and beryllium that are used increasingly because of unusual properties important to industry.

sphalerite: A mineral, ZnS, that serves as the principal ore of zinc.

spinel: A mineral, composition $MgAl_2O_4$; a common accessory mineral in many rocks; also refers to a crystal structure, common to some ore minerals, in which the external shape of an octahedron is often seen.

spot market: The buying and selling of commodities for immediate delivery at a price agreed upon at the time of sale.

stainless steel: An iron-based alloy containing enough chromium to confer a superior corrosion resistance.

stannite: A mineral, composition Cu_2FeSnS_4; an ore of tin.

steam flooding: The injection of superheated steam down an oil well in order to promote the release of oil trapped in the rocks.

steel: An iron-based alloy; other metals or substances are alloyed with the iron to impart specific properties such has hardness or strength.

Stone Age: The period in human culture when stone was used for the making of tools; it began with the first humans and ended at various times in different places (e.g., about 3000 B.C. in Egypt and Mesopotamia) when bronze was used to make tools.

stope: The roomlike area in a mine where ores are extracted.

stratification: The layerlike nature of a sedimentary rock.

stratiform: Referring to an ore deposit that is layered and parallel to the enclosing strata.

stratigraphic traps: Sedimentary units such as sandstone lenses into which oil migrates and is prevented from further movement by surrounding impermeable layers.

strip mining: The removal of coal or other commodity by surface mining methods in which extraction is carried out in successive strips of land.

structural traps: Folded or faulted rocks into which oil migrates and from which farther migration is prevented.

subduction: The process in which one crustal plate descends beneath another.

subeconomic resource: That part of identified resources that does not meet the economic criteria of reserves or marginal reserves.

subsidence: The natural or artificially induced dropping of the land surface resulting from the removal of the underlying rocks either by mining or groundwater solution.

superphosphate: A soluble mixture of calcium phosphates produced by reaction of phosphate rock with sulfuric acid; used as fertilizer.

surface runoff: The water that flows directly off the land surface and the water that, after infiltrating into the ground, is discharged onto the surface.

swamp gas: Methane, CH_4, produced during the decay of organic matter in stagnant water.

syenite: An igneous rock comprised largely of potassium feldspar, any of the feldspathoid minerals, and an amphibole. Quartz is rare or absent.

taconite: A term used in the Lake Superior district for laminated iron ores consisting of iron oxides and silica or iron silicates.

tactite: An alternate name for skarn.

tailings: The valueless materials discarded from mining operations.

talc: A mineral, composition $Mg_3Si_4O_{10}(OH)_2$; it is extremely soft, making it a valuable lubricant and cosmetic ingredient.

tar: A dark, oily, viscous mass of hydrocarbons.

tar sand: Sand deposits in which the interstices of the grains are filled with viscous hydrocarbons.

thermal cracking: The application of heat to break heavier hydrocarbons into lighter ones.

thermal maturation: The progressive change in organic matter in sedimentary rocks resulting from increasing temperature as the depth of burial increases.

thermal pollution: Abnormal heating of the environment, usually rivers, caused by the combustion of fossil fuels, by nuclear power generation, or industrial processing.

thermogenic gas: Gas formed as a result of the thermal breakdown of organic matter.

tidal energy: Energy derived from the movement of water during the rise and fall of the tides.

transpiration: The release of water vapor by plants during their normal respiration.

traps: Rock structures or beds in which oil accumulates and is prevented from further migration.

tritium: A synthetic isotope of hydrogen containing one proton and two neutrons in its nucleus; its half-life is 12.5 years.

tuff: A compacted deposit of volcanic ash.

ultramafic: Said of igneous rocks composed chiefly of one ferromagnesian mineral (most ultramafic rocks are also ultrabasic, i.e., having SiO_2 contents less than about 44 percent).

vadose: Referring to water in the uppermost soil, the zone in which most intergranular interstices are air filled.

vein: A sheetlike infilling of a fracture by hydrothermally deposited minerals often containing ore minerals.

vermiculite: A group of clay minerals that are characterized by the tendency to undergo extreme expansion when heated above 150°C; widely used as an insulator and as a component in lightweight construction materials.

vesicles: Cavities in a lava formed by the evolution of gas during the rapid cooling of a molten lava.

vitrification: The formation of a glassy or noncrystalline substance.

water flooding: The injection of water into an oil well to promote the release of oil trapped in the rock.

water rights: The right to draw and use (and sometimes sell) water drawn from a lake, river, or underground source.

water table: The surface in a soil or rock below which all the voids are water filled.

watt: A unit of power equal to work done at a rate of one joule per second; approximately equal to 1/746 horsepower.

weatherability: The rate at which weathering affects the physical and chemical nature of a rock or mineral.

weathering: The progressive breakdown of rocks, physically and chemically, in response to exposure at or near Earth's surface.

wet steam: Natural geothermal systems dominated by hot waters with associated steam.

winze: A vertical opening connecting two levels of a mine; the same as a raise.

withdrawal: The extraction of water from a surface water or groundwater source.

work: Usually the result of applied force, defined as the product of the force and the displacement; usually expressed in foot-pounds, joules, or kilowatt-hours.

yellowcake: A general term for yellow oxidized uranium oxide arising from concentration in the mining and processing of uranium ore.

zeolite: A group of hydrous aluminosilicate minerals characterized by their easy exchange of water and cations; used as catalysts in oil refining.

zircon: A mineral, composition $ZrSiO_4$; a common accessory mineral in many rocks; the main source of zirconium.

zonal soil: One of the soil orders that have well-developed characteristics; reflect the agents of soil genesis, especially climate and the action of organisms.

INDEX

Earth Statistics

Earth Dimensions and Mass

Earth radius—equatorial	6378 km	3963 mi
—polar	6357 km	3950 mi
—average sphere	6371 km	3959 mi
Crustal thickness—continents	25–30 km	16–9 mi
—oceans	10–15 km	6–9 mi
Mantle thickness	2900 km	1802 mi
Outer core thickness	2420 km	1504 mi
Inner core thickness	1050 km	652 mi
Mass of Earth	5.98×10^{21} metric tons	
Mass of ice	$25\text{–}30 \times 10^{15}$ metric tons	
Mass of oceans	1.4×10^{18} metric tons	
Mass of crust	2.5×10^{19} metric tons	
Mass of mantle	4.05×10^{21} metric tons	
Mass of core	1.9×10^{21} metric tons	

Areas of the Major Continents and Oceans

Continents

Asia	$44{,}120{,}650 \text{ km}^2$	$17{,}035{,}000 \text{ mi}^2$
Africa	$30{,}134{,}650 \text{ km}^2$	$11{,}635{,}000 \text{ mi}^2$
North America	$24{,}436{,}650 \text{ km}^2$	$9{,}435{,}000 \text{ mi}^2$
South America	$17{,}767{,}400 \text{ km}^2$	$6{,}860{,}000 \text{ mi}^2$
Antarctica	$13{,}209{,}000 \text{ km}^2$	$5{,}100{,}000 \text{ mi}^2$
Europe	$9{,}971{,}500 \text{ km}^2$	$3{,}850{,}000 \text{ mi}^2$
Australia	$7{,}705{,}300 \text{ km}^2$	$2{,}975{,}000 \text{ mi}^2$
Greenland	$2{,}175{,}600 \text{ km}^2$	$840{,}000 \text{ mi}^2$
Total major continents	$149{,}520{,}700 \text{ km}^2$	$57{,}730{,}000 \text{ mi}^2$

Some Selected Countries

former Soviet Union	$22{,}403{,}500 \text{ km}^2$	$8{,}650{,}000 \text{ mi}^2$
Canada	$9{,}976{,}700 \text{ km}^2$	$3{,}852{,}000 \text{ mi}^2$
United States	$9{,}520{,}800 \text{ km}^2$	$3{,}676{,}000 \text{ mi}^2$
South Africa	$1{,}224{,}000 \text{ km}^2$	$472{,}600 \text{ mi}^2$
United Kingdom	$244{,}000 \text{ km}^2$	$94{,}200 \text{ mi}^2$

Major Oceans and Seas

Pacific Ocean	$165{,}721{,}000 \text{ km}^2$	$63{,}985{,}000 \text{ mi}^2$
Atlantic Ocean	$81{,}660{,}000 \text{ km}^2$	$31{,}529{,}000 \text{ mi}^2$
Indian Ocean	$73{,}445{,}000 \text{ km}^2$	$28{,}357{,}000 \text{ mi}^2$
Arctic Ocean	$14{,}351{,}000 \text{ km}^2$	$5{,}541{,}000 \text{ mi}^2$
Mediterranean Sea	$2{,}966{,}000 \text{ km}^2$	$1{,}145{,}000 \text{ mi}^2$
South China Sea	$2{,}318{,}000 \text{ km}^2$	$895{,}000 \text{ mi}^2$
Bering Sea	$2{,}274{,}000 \text{ km}^2$	$878{,}000 \text{ mi}^2$
Caribbean Sea	$1{,}943{,}000 \text{ km}^2$	$750{,}000 \text{ mi}^2$
Gulf of Mexico	$1{,}813{,}000 \text{ km}^2$	$700{,}000 \text{ mi}^2$